SELECTED LETTERS OF
ROBERT FROST

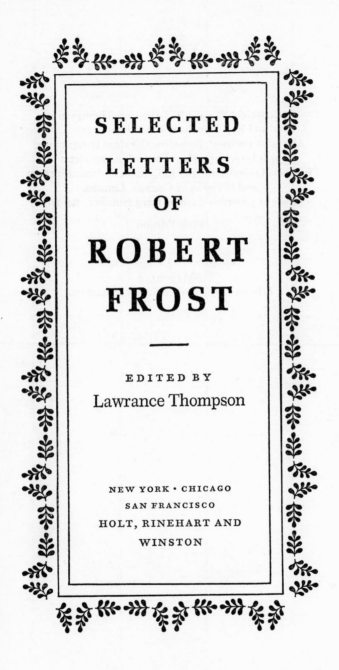

SELECTED
LETTERS
OF
ROBERT
FROST

EDITED BY

Lawrance Thompson

NEW YORK · CHICAGO
SAN FRANCISCO
HOLT, RINEHART AND
WINSTON

First Edition

Designer: P. J. Conkwright
88427–0114
Printed in the United States of America

CONTENTS

❦

CONTENTS

INTRODUCTION

᭤᭤᭤

ROBERT FROST as personality and poet enchanted the American people, and won a deservedly special place in their hearts. His charm was heightened by his manner of seeming to be so natural, direct, and confiding in all forms of communication; but he was never as natural as he seemed. Even as the majority of his admirers misunderstood the apparently simple artistry of his poems, so they failed to recognize the dramatic masks he wore. He had his reasons, not the least of them being a need to protect his excruciating sensitivities.

His intimate friends and relatives understood the masks and tried to fathom the complexities concealed behind them. At least a few of his friends even foresaw that after the poet's death important adjustments would have to occur in the public response to the man and his work. The various processes of unmasking would include sympathetic explanations of the difference between the myth and the man; but the task would be delicate.

Now that the time has come for making these adjustments, perhaps the best immediate procedure is to continue and extend the process already begun with the publication of Frost's letters to Louis Untermeyer and to John T. Bartlett; the process of permitting the poet to unmask himself, at least partially, through the utterances he made in his private correspondence. Such revelations are limited, however, because the same instinctive reticences which inspired him to employ dramatic and stylistic masks in his poems and in his platform appearances often drove him to related forms of epistolary subterfuge. He knew that, and he even acknowledged it: "I have written to keep the over curious out of the secret places of my mind both in my verse and in my letters . . ." Nevertheless, there is no other first-hand source of revelation which takes us so intimately behind the various masks as that provided by Frost's letters. Turning different sides of his personality to different recipients of his letters, he thus created a fascinating self-portrait which was colored and enriched by meaningful inconsistencies, self-contradictions, and partial concealments.

vii

Because one can make so many different uses of Robert Frost's correspondence, no single criterion was employed in selecting the present group from a total of more than fifteen hundred letters examined. Choices were made with an eye to providing the most complete portrait possible of the man, his work, and his life: facts, events, friendships, enmities, circumstances, obsessions, commitments, family crises, habits, ideas, beliefs, prejudices, theories, and practices. Further enrichment was sought and obtained by interweaving chronologically nearly one hundred letters written to or about the poet. In this arrangement, continuities have been suggested by dividing the whole into ten sections or life-chapters.

If, then, we may read the letters as an autobiographical and dramatic narrative, we should also be aware that they provide valuable raw materials for biography. When considered merely as autobiography, they reveal Frost's tendency to explain and defend whatever he understood of his own acts and motives; but when approached as the raw materials for biography, they enable us to challenge some of the poet's explanations and to draw our own independent conclusions.

One purpose of the editor is to invite any thoughtful and imaginative reader to "roll his own" biography of Robert Frost from these "makings" prior to the appearance of any formal biographies of the poet, including one in preparation by the editor. The advantages thus gained are many, and the risks are few; a considerable number of revelations made in these letters create biographical problems which are not likely to be resolved in adequate fashion until placed in contexts larger than those given here. But the editorial handling of these letters is calculated to make this volume serve many immediate and practical uses, even in matters of quick reference. Hence the supplementary inclusion of an extensive "Chronology" of biographical facts, a selective "Genealogy," and a carefully derived "Index."

If these letters are used initially to clarify discrepancies between the mythic and actual Robert Frost, as is hoped, certain warnings are in order lest the general public jump from one false extreme of assumption to another. Those who knew the poet largely from his poetry and his public appearances — and who take pleasure in remembering the evidence of his affirmations, encouragements, cherishings, tenderness, humor, wit, playfulness, and joviality — may not be prepared to see how often his private correspondence reveals periods of gloom, jealousies, obsessive resentments, sulking, displays of temper, nervous rages, and vindictive retaliations. Partly because he lacked confidence in himself, he suspected the presence of enemies everywhere, and he frequently indulged his passion for hurting even those he loved. "I'm a mere selfish artist most of the time," he admitted to one correspondent.

All of his self-deprecations complicate rather than simplify the problem of understanding Robert Frost. They suggest, through a mingling of frankness and guilt, his own constant awareness of the tension between his commitments as an artist and as a human being. If the artist in him demanded priority, as it almost always did, he never forgot that he had made two different kinds of promises and that he wanted to keep them both.

The predicament of the man-and-artist is an old theme on which Frost plays new variations. Permit any excruciatingly sensitive young man to develop all the ambitions and drives of an incipient artist. Let early failures make him self-protectively proud and scornful of scorners. Add extra measures of physical illness, often inseparable from emotional and mental anxieties. Enable him to succeed at nothing he thinks important through years of more intensely ambitious effort than he would ever be willing to acknowledge afterward. Give him enemies enough; and even give his enemies reasons to mock him for his pride, arrogance, and failure, until he is nearly forty years old. Then suddenly grant him unexpected attention and fame — abroad. Let him come home to the vicissitudes of criticism and praise, but let him keep trying, striving, driving until he has earned a steadily increasing recognition and adulation. Under these circumstances anyone might become unbearably vain. Robert Frost did not; but his later letters indicate an unquenchable thirst for honor and glory, as though the ultimate balm of innumerable tributes could never quite heal the wounds he suffered in those agonizingly long years of failure and neglect.

There are other reasons why the letters — with their revelations of unsuspected foibles, weaknesses, inconsistencies, and faults — should not seriously diminish our admiration of Frost's gifts, strengths, and attainments. He was the first to acknowledge his limitations as human being and as artist. More than that, under all the self-encouraging and self-protective pride, even under the arrogance and boastfulness which his closest friends saw and understood, there remained recurrent self-doubt and intermittent lack of confidence. It expressed itself nowhere more touchingly than in his genuinely wistful hope that he might lodge at least a few poems where they would "stick like burrs" and prove hard to get rid of. His private evaluation placed him lower on the scale of poets than the position he actually won.

Perhaps the letters which disclose the inseparability of his troubled search for his own artistic idiom and his desperate quest for valid ways to meet the difficulties of his daily life may lead the reader to a deeper sympathy and understanding. How to express one's self and how to defend one's self became two inseparable themes for him. Early in his struggle to answer those questions he went to suicidal depths of discouragement, and he returned with only a partial understanding of his own psychological situation. But by the time he began teaching a course in psychology at Plymouth Normal School, in 1911, he felt that his first-hand experiences had qualified him adequately for making practical applications of his own answers. One of his central insights was that every individual should try to confront, recognize, and accept the circular relationship between constructive and destructive forces of personality; relationships which might make intelligible (even if not always controllable) "the good of evil born" and the evil born of good. He was fascinated by any human capacities for integrating such ambivalent forces, no matter how faultily and provisionally.

Whenever Frost learned of anyone's complete collapse, and understood it as stemming from failure to keep under control the inner destructive forces, he was saddened without being surprised; his first-hand knowledge of such dangers heightened his understanding. Since boyhood he had been troubled by his own unbalancing emotional storms, and he had grown up with a younger sister, Jeanie, who frightened him with her defensive recoils into illusion. The impact of Jeanie's story on her brother's personal drama is so important that several of her letters are included here. Some of his own letters reveal that for years he dreaded the eventual and incurable nervous breakdown which overtook Jeanie, and he foresaw the pathetic result: her death, years later, in a mental hospital. There were times when his ever-active guilt made him blame himself for having hurt her in ways which might have contributed to her plight. But there were other times when he had all he could do to cope with his own destructive and recurrently suicidal tendencies, particularly when crises drove him to violent outbursts of rage.

Another kind of guilt, closely related, may be found in the letters: a recurrent suspicion that his own struggle for artistic fulfillment had encroached harmfully on his responsibilities as husband and father. His expressions of anxiety over the ailments of his wife and children may serve to counterbalance his often-repeated confession that he was merely a selfish artist and a bad man. If he had been only that, he would not have suffered so much over the many illnesses and deaths which beset his immediate family; he would never have remained so intensely conscience-stricken to the very end of his life.

How did Frost ever bear up under the devastating griefs and heartbreaks caused by all those untimely deaths? A good answer was given by a clergyman who, knowing the poet well, called him "a Job in our time." Many of the later letters give new pertinence to that analogy. Like Job, our puritanical poet seemed to find his most bitter sorrows and doubts made bearable by his capacity to accept loss and pain as mysterious trials administered by an inscrutable and yet benevolent deity. Even the most secular of Frost's friends felt that to differ with him concerning this assumption which gave him consolation desperately needed, would have been an act of cruelty. A deep religious faith had been nurtured in Frost by his mother during his childhood, and although he subjected different aspects of this faith to severe challenge, mockery, and skepticism, he never rejected it for long. Partly from shyness and partly from a desire to express his non-conformist religious independence by uttering heresies, he often encouraged misunderstandings; and strangers cited his apparent blasphemies as evidences that Frost was an atheist. He never was. But his curiously Greek-Roman-Scotch-Yankee temperament responded with sympathetic vigor to the Aeschylean proverb that God helps those who help themselves — particularly in the task of discovering how to survive and how to go on living in this world after each new loss might temporarily injure the desire to survive.

This modern Job found some of his most genuine comforters in words and in his own capacity for manipulating them afresh to discover his own insights. Although he might be thought too Victorian to acknowledge any theraputic value in the act of ordering words, he more than once formulated his belief that there is a close relationship between three different kinds of creative work: the divine act of creation, the human artist's pleasure in ordering, and every man's daily obligation to control and order as best he can the potential chaos of his energies. Frost said this obliquely in letter 322, written to *The Amherst Student* in response to birthday congratulations. Beginning pleasantly with word-play on "age" and "the ages," he went on to make an ironic criticism of anyone claiming to live in the worst of all possible ages: "It is immodest of a man to think of himself as going down before the worst forces ever mobilized by God." Then, as a possible remedy for pessimistic boastfulness, he added the following suggestions:

"When in doubt there is always form for us to go on with. Anyone who has achieved the least form to be sure of it, is lost to the larger excruciations. I think it must stroke faith the right way. The artist, the poet, might be expected to be the most aware of such assurance, but it is really everybody's sanity to feel it and live by it. . . ."

Robert Frost would not have minded our viewing his most cherished beliefs concerning how and why he wrote some of his best poems — or even some of his best letters — as extensions of these ideas. His creative acts continuously provided for him "a momentary stay against confusion." He granted that such a "stay" was "not necessarily a great clarification, such as sects and cults are founded on" — and herein lay his Emersonian heresy. He bluntly rejected all the conventional stays which dogmatists call permanent; all the metaphors of doctrine which, according to Frost, too soon freeze into literalism and lose their poetry. Furthermore, he said, the metaphors of the church provide the wrong kinds of "stay," because they deny the need for continuous thrusts of heart, mind, spirit, in the quest for new ways to refresh sight and insight. For him, the metaphors of his own poetry served as oblique affirmations of faith. "Belief, Belief. You've got to augment my belief in life or people mightily or cross it uglily," he advised a young writer. "I'm awfully sure of this tonight." He was sure of this on any night, particularly when the way was dark; and some of his best thoughts were night thoughts. Creative writing re-enforced his belief, and his sanity. If anyone tried to tell him that the art of writing didn't require the augmentation of belief, he was quick to take exception.

For Frost, form and ordering were so integral with subject matter that he often talked about the fusion between what a poem tried to say and how the poet tried to make the poem say it. Moreover, some of his best letters were constructed with such artistry that the full meaning is missed if not seen through the ordering. A glance at a few passages may illustrate this point and may simultaneously show certain analogies between his poetic and his letter-writing art.

A good starting place is provided by Frost's definition of style, as given in letter 244. Apparently dissatisfied with Buffon's famous assertion that "the style is the man himself," and perhaps hoping to improve on his beloved Emerson's claim that "a man's style is his mind's voice," Frost worked out this attractive twist: ". . . style in prose or verse is that which indicates how the writer takes himself and what he is saying. . . . His style is the way he carries himself toward his ideas and deeds."

Suppose, however, that the writer is Frost and that he carries himself primarily as a lyric poet. Then from lyric to lyric, and even at times from letter to letter, the mercurial changes in mood find reflection in changes of style and tone, so that the reader must make tentative responses lest a passing mood be mistaken for a fixed attitude, conviction, or belief. For example, in letter 146 written to Louis Untermeyer in 1916, a mood of bitter discouragement is reflected in form and subject matter: ". . . The poet in me died nearly ten years ago. Fortunately he had run through several phases . . . before he went. The calf I was in the nineties I merely take to market. I am become my own salesman."

Are we to interpret those flat declarations as facts? Or as lies? No. But rather as elements in a postured hyperbole, written while Frost must have been suffering through a particularly dark period of discouragement. The poet in him had not died, and he knew that; he also knew his friend would understand the posture of this letter as an implicit call for reassurance. Back came the reassurance, promptly, but it was no longer needed; the poet's mood had already changed. Nevertheless, the fusion of style and subject matter in letter 146 may serve as a valuable illustration of the Frostian definition in-

volving "how the writer takes himself and what he is saying."
Some further definitions which occur in letter 244 may help
to clarify related problems:

"Many sensitive natures have plainly shown by their style
that they took themselves lightly in self-defense. They are the
ironists. . . . I own any form of humor shows fear and inferiority. Irony is simply a kind of guardedness. So is a twinkle.
It keeps the reader from criticism. . . . Humor is the most
engaging cowardice. With it myself I have been able to hold
some of my enemy in play far out of gunshot."

According to Frost, then, different elements of style may
be used not only as masks but also as weapons of defense —
or offense. In his letter-writing and in his poems, he sometimes
carried himself lightly, ironically, humorously, for purposes of
mere self-defense; but at other times he used the same stance
for purposes of attack. Until we understand and become familiar with his different uses of irony, we are in danger of misunderstanding important elements in his poems and in his letters.

For example, Frost once fashioned a dramatic mask out
of an ironically assumed posture — and employed it too subtly
— in a now famous poem originally used as a gently teasing
letter: "The Road Not Taken." The inspiration for it came from
Frost's amusement over a familiar mannerism of his closest
friend in England, Edward Thomas. While living in Gloucestershire in 1914, Frost frequently took long walks with Thomas
through the countryside. Repeatedly Thomas would choose a
route which might enable him to show his American friend a
rare plant or a special vista; but it often happened that before
the end of such a walk Thomas would regret the choice he had
made and would sigh over what he might have shown Frost if
they had taken a "better" direction. More than once, on such
occasions, the New Englander had teased his Welsh-English
friend for those wasted regrets. Disciplined by the austere
biblical notion that a man, having put his hand to the plow,
should not look back, Frost found something quaintly romantic
in sighing over what might have been. Such a course of action
was a road never taken by Frost, a road he had been taught to
avoid. In a reminiscent mood, not very long after his return to
America as a successful, newly discovered poet, Frost pretended to "carry himself" in the manner of Edward Thomas
just long enough to write "The Road Not Taken." Immediately,

he sent a manuscript copy of the poem to Thomas, without comment, and yet with the expectation that his friend would notice how (the poem pivots ironically on the un-Frostian phrase, "I shall be telling this with a sigh." As it turned out Frost's expectations were disappointed. Thomas missed the gentle jest because the irony had been handled too slyly, too subtly.

A short time later, when "The Road Not Taken" was published in the *Atlantic Monthly* for August 1915, Frost hoped that some of his American readers would recognize the pivotal irony of the poem; but again he was disappointed. Self-defensively he began to drop hints as he read "The Road Not Taken" before public audiences. On one occasion he told of receiving a letter from a grammar-school girl who asked a good question of him: "Why the sigh?" That letter and that question, he said, had prompted an answer. End of the hint. On another occasion, after another public reading of "The Road Not Taken," he gave more pointed warnings: "You have to be careful of that one; it's a tricky poem — very tricky." Never did he admit that he had carried himself and his ironies too subtly in that poem, but the circumstances are worth remembering here as an illustration that Frost repeatedly liked to "carry himself" dramatically, in a poem or letter, by assuming a posture not his own, simply for purposes of mockery — sometimes gentle and at other times malicious.

Consider an example of malice where the initial posture is so blindingly obvious that the ulterior use made of it may be misunderstood. ("I should like to be so subtle at this game," Frost confided to one of his correspondents, "as to seem to the casual person altogether obvious.") Letter 178 was inspired by the poet's receiving from his friend Untermeyer a new issue of the socialistic-communistic periodical, *The Liberator*. The acknowledgment clearly indicates that Frost must have been completely disgusted by everything he found in the issue. But he begins by pretending to a reversal of roles; he writes as though he were Untermeyer anticipating Frost's reaction, and he uses Untermeyer's familiar salutation, "Dear Robt." Thus the ground rules of the game are established, making it possible for Frost to give the initial advantage to Untermeyer. He places in the mouth of his opponent a cluster of verbal attacks against Frost's acknowledged conservatism and prudery. But the stylistic posture thus assumed amounts to a pleasant bit of Indian wrestling which is calculated to throw the opponent off-balance. Midway in the letter, Frost shifts his weight gradually, through a process of distorting Untermeyer's values until they are made to appear ridiculous. Thus the game which had begun as an obvious joke is ended with subtly resentful and satiric malice. In addition, the whole is sweetened with a fused element of retaliation. Untermeyer had previously published a group of poetic parodies which had included Frost, who had not been amused. Now the tables are turned, because the stylistic mode of letter 178 is parody-with-a-vengeance.

Some interesting variations on that stylistic mask, that dramatic posture, may be found in Frost's editorial poems. At the start of the scornful pair of quatrains, "Not All There," the poet seems to speak from an atheistic viewpoint; but the assumed posture merely sets up the abhorred stance, initially, for purposes of knocking it down in the end. The "punch line" of the second quatrain undercuts and ridicules the atheistic way of looking. In retrospect the title itself may be understood as re-enforcing the scornful tone and meaning of the whole poem. Another variant of this poetic and stylistic masking-unmasking occurs in the equally bitter and sarcastic poem, "Provide, Provide."

Far more equivocal and tantalizing postures of masking may be found in many of Frost's letters to his younger friend, Sidney Cox, where the tone of malicious teasing is often hidden beneath rhetorical questions and answers. Sometimes the prevailing view of the entire letter will finally point up the implicit Socratic ironies scattered through it. But at other times the reader who experiences moments of doubt, confusion, and dizziness may come with relief to the overt warning given Cox in letter 334:

"Look out I don't spoof you. About five years ago I resolved to spoil my correspondence with you by throwing it into confusion the way God threw the speech of the builders of the tower of Babel into confusion. My reason is too long to go into tonight . . ."

His "reason" may be conjectured quite accurately from the representative Frost-to-Cox selections in this volume, but the warning is useful here in a broader sense. It suggests the protean quality in the stylistic maskings employed by Robert Frost. As further evidence of the protean, consider only one

more example, this time an exchange of letters with Professor
G. R. Elliott of Amherst. In letter 351-b, after Elliott makes a
half-serious and half-joking protest that Frost has unfairly
and maliciously accused him of "indoctrinating" students with
missionary utterances, Elliott exonerates himself by quoting a
letter from a former student. Having settled this point to his
own satisfaction, and at Frost's expense, Elliott jokes on, also
at Frost's expense. The tactical error thus made and com-
pounded can best be explained by reference to a few humorous remarks Frost made in another connection: "I hate so to be
crossed I have come to think not being crossed is the one
thing that matters in life. I can think of no blissfuller state
than being treated as if I was always right." In that pleasant
self-deprecation is wrapped a kernel of serious fact, and most
of the poet's friends made careful allowances for his hating to
be crossed. Elliott's allowances, this time, were merely insuffi-
cient, and they brought down on his head a typically Frostian
punishment.

Frost's answer, in letter 352, begins disarmingly with a
posture of praise, which is calculated to throw his opponent
off-guard. Later in the letter only a hint of ultimate direction
appears when Frost casually corrects Elliott on a detail of fact:
the student who was Frost's source for the initial accusation
had not said his professor preached humanism in his classes.
On the contrary, he had implied that Elliott was "wracking the
devil in him with your Christianity." This light hint, foreshad-
owing heavier and heretical pressure on Elliott's missionary
spirit, is given more weight when Frost adds that the student
"is a sadly sinful young man such as for the sake of whom I
could conceive of your saying to a class, as you said to me once,
one can no more be religious, outside of the church than one
can be patriotic without belonging to a country. (You should
have said, without belonging to the army.)" If, for the moment, the tension between opposing viewpoints is clearly ex-
posed, Frost immediately seems to give ground by pretending
once more to side sympathetically with Elliott: "I don't believe
it is even in bad taste for you to talk in that missionary way."
The same tone is maintained, but with equivocation, when
Frost adds, "I just wanted to be sure if you were going to use
poetry for the salvation of souls you had counted the cost to
poetry. But you deny in your letter that you ever had used poetry for the salvation of souls. Really it would be all right with

me if you had." So far, the ambiguities dominate the central meanings, and the reader is left in doubt. But the resolution begins with the use of two analogies which are not flattering to Elliott's position, and a few sentences later the cat is let out of the bag when Frost employs profanity: "Use poetry or friendship or anything else you please to corner me for my soul's salvation. We are all each other's keepers. Look at Japan in China, England in India. . . . Jesus Christ! let's be Christians." End of the game — and rough.

It would be a mistake to conclude from this evidence that the letter-writing art of Robert Frost is always deceptively subtle. He varied his style to meet inner and outer needs, so that some of his letters are straightforward, even as some of his poems are. But a careful reading of these letters will serve to unmask many facets of the man, his life, and his works. The point to keep in mind is that Frost was often so foxy that at many different times and in many different places he deliberately set out to deceive his public and his private "readers." In all its different forms of confiding, his art was intermittently "tricky" enough to justify our cautious remembrance of his warning to Sidney Cox: "Look out I don't spoof you."

NOTES ON THE EDITING

꙰

ROBERT FROST'S LETTERS to both Louis Untermeyer and
John T. Bartlett are already in print,* but some of the poet's best
letters to these two men are also included in these "selected
letters." Besides representing an important correspondence
and a reflection of Frost's life and thought, these particular letters become enriched when placed in the larger framework of
this volume. Since Louis Untermeyer and Mrs. Margaret Bartlett Anderson graciously made their letters available to the
editor many years ago, the original sources and their locations
are given.

Frost prided himself so much on his ability to arrange
words meaningfully that he felt he could omit some of the conventional uses of punctuation. A more serious problem has
been created in these letters by his acknowledged weakness as
a speller. At times, and only to avoid confusion on the part of
the reader, bracketed punctuation marks or corrected spell-
ings have been added.

The place, date, valediction, and signature have been
simplified, the full data being used only when new and additional information is supplied to the reader. Wherever un-
dated letters are included, a bracketed and approximated
date, derived from a postmark or other circumstantial source,
has been supplied by the editor.

Since neither Frost nor any other correspondent used
ellipses they are always added by the editor, as follows: three
dots wherever a part of a sentence is omitted, four dots wherever a full sentence or more is omitted, three bracketed dots
wherever a full paragraph or more is omitted.

The "Table of Letters" gives an entry number for each
letter included, the recipient of the letter, the date, an abbreviated reference to the form of the original letter — or of
the copy from which the transcript was made for this volume

* *The Letters of Robert Frost to Louis Untermeyer* with a commentary
by Louis Untermeyer. New York: Holt, Rinehart and Winston, 1963.
Robert Frost and John Bartlett: The Record of a Friendship by Margaret
Bartlett Anderson. New York: Holt, Rinehart and Winston, 1963.

— and an abbreviated reference to the location of the original letter or the copy.

The "Acknowledgments" give the source for letters, listed by entry number, in alphabetical order by source.

The "Chronology" supplies data which may be used by the reader not only to clarify some references in the letters but also to serve as a quick guide to such high points in the poet's life as the awarding of degrees and honors. This material is divided into the same periods as the ten parts or chapters.

The "Genealogy" in the appendix illustrates the relationships within the Frost family, and includes Robert Frost's great-grandchildren who were born during his lifetime.

The "Index" is enriched with topical headings which are grouped under "FROST, ROBERT LEE," so that they may suggest complexities by talking back and forth to each other. Under some of them, a sufficient number of Frost's aphoristic phrases and sentences have been quoted to give at least the flavor of a concordance. Here again, however, the primary goal is to facilitate quick and accurate reference, thus to heighten the value and usefulness of the letters themselves.

TABLE OF LETTERS

❧❧

THE SHORT TITLES which are used to indicate locations of letters in the following table are fully explained in the subsequent list of "Acknowledgments."

Abbreviations used to indicate the physical form and state of each letter which served as the source for the transcription made by the editor are explained below:

AL-FD	autograph letter, first draft
AL-FD-R	autograph letter, first draft, with revisions
ALS	autograph letter, signed
ALS-C	autograph letter, signed (a copy made by the author)
P	printed version of the letter, original not available
TEL	telegram
TEL-C	copy of the telegram sent or received
TEL-FD	telegram, first draft
TEL-FD-R	telegram, first draft, with revisions
TL-C	typewritten letter, copy or carbon of the original
TL-FD	typewritten letter, first draft
TL-FD-R	typewritten letter, first draft, with revisions
TLS	typewritten letter, signed
TL-U	typewritten letter, sent unsigned

I · LEWISTOWN, COLUMBUS, AND
SAN FRANCISCO · 1873-1885

[1873]

I. W. P. Frost, Jr., to I. Moodie   ALS Virginia   c. 1 Feb.
II. W. P. Frost, Jr., to I. M. Frost   ALS Virginia   13 July

[1874]

III. W. P. Frost, Jr., to M. B. Frost   ALS Virginia   25 Oct.

[1876]

IV. I. M. Frost to W. P. Frost, Jr.   ALS Virginia   1 Nov.

[1883]

V. I. M. Frost to S. Newton   ALS Dartmouth   17 June

[1906]

20.	To William Hayes Ward	ALS Huntington	24 Feb.
21.	To Susan Hayes Ward	ALS Huntington	17 July
22.	To Susan Hayes Ward	ALS Huntington	29 Oct.
23.	To Susan Hayes Ward	ALS Huntington	26 Dec.

[1907]

24.	To Susan Hayes Ward	ALS Huntington	12 Jan.
25.	To Susan Hayes Ward	ALS Huntington	c. 1 July
26.	To Susan Hayes Ward	ALS Huntington	6 Aug.
27.	To Susan Hayes Ward	ALS Huntington	8 Sept.
28.	To Susan Hayes Ward	ALS Huntington	4 Nov.

[1908]

29.	To Susan Hayes Ward	ALS Huntington	c. Jan.

[1911]

30.	To Susan Hayes Ward	ALS Huntington	19 Dec.
31.	To Susan Hayes Ward	ALS Huntington	28 Dec.

[1912]

32.	To Susan Hayes Ward	ALS Huntington	15 Jan.
33.	To Susan Hayes Ward	ALS Huntington	10 Feb.
34.	To Thomas B. Mosher	ALS Virginia	19 Feb.
35.	To Thomas B. Mosher	ALS Virginia	4 Mar.
36.	To Wilbur E. Rowell	ALS Princeton	25 June
37.	To Wilbur E. Rowell	ALS Princeton	16 July

IV · LONDON, BEACONSFIELD, AND GLOUCESTERSHIRE · 1912-1915

38.	To Susan Hayes Ward	ALS Huntington	15 Sept.
38-a.	E. M. Frost to M. Lynch	ALS Dartmouth	25 Oct.
38-b.	Mrs. M. L. Nutt to RF	ALS Dartmouth	26 Oct.
39.	To Thomas B. Mosher	TLS Dartmouth	19 Nov.
40.	To John T. Bartlett	ALS Virginia	25 Dec.
41.	To Ernest L. Silver	ALS Dartmouth	25 Dec.
42.	To Sidney Cox	ALS Dartmouth	26 Dec.

[1913]

43.	To Harold Brown	ALS Middlebury	7 Jan.
44.	To John T. Bartlett	ALS Virginia	26 Feb.
45.	To John T. Bartlett	ALS Virginia	c. 18 Mar.
45-a.	E. M. Frost to M. Bartlett	ALS Virginia	18 Mar.
46.	To John T. Bartlett	ALS Virginia	c. 4 Apr.

VII · AMHERST, COLORADO, CALIFORNIA, TEXAS, AND FLORIDA · 1926-1938

VIII · BOSTON, HARVARD, MIAMI, AND RIPTON · 1938-1943

[1939]

[1940]

[1941]

[1942]

IX · CAMBRIDGE, DARTMOUTH, MIAMI, AND RIPTON · 1943-1949

TABLE OF LETTERS

[1960]

[1961]

[1962]

[1963]

ACKNOWLEDGMENTS

THE PLEASURABLE TASK of locating, transcribing, and assembling copies of letters written by or about Robert Frost has been carried out by the editor slowly for a period of more than twenty-five years. It is a continuing task, for many known and unknown letters of Frost remain to be found and collected. For the present, however, the editor is eager to acknowledge his debts and appreciation to the many individuals who assisted him during the phase of work now brought to provisional completion. He has tried to name all such individuals at the conclusion of these Acknowledgments and regrets any possible omissions. But there are some names which deserve special and immediate expressions of gratitude.

Mrs. Kathleen Morrison, secretary to Robert Frost during the last twenty-five years of his life, has helped the editor immeasurably during all of those years and has co-operated with him to the fullest extent since the poet's death. To her, as thoughtful and considerate friend and also as immediate heir of the Frost manuscripts and letter files, in accordance with the terms of Robert Frost's will, the editor makes foremost acknowledgment of appreciation and gratitude.

Mr. Alfred C. Edwards, President of Holt, Rinehart and Winston, Inc., and executor of the estate of Robert Frost, has done so much more for the editor than grant formal permission to publish the Robert Frost letters, which are the literary property of the estate. He has provided access to past and present correspondence in the files of Holt, Rinehart and Winston; he has added letters from his own private files; and he has helped to overcome difficulties in securing important letters which could not otherwise have been included. These and many other forms of assistance, rendered by Mr. Edwards, are acknowledged with profound gratitude.

Mr. Charles R. Green, Librarian Emeritus of The Jones Library of Amherst, Massachusetts, labored lovingly to give that library the first major collection of Frost first editions, letters, manuscripts, and a wealth of supporting reference works. He has continued to make The Jones Library one of the most valuable centers for Frost research. In addition, he acted as co-compiler, with Mr. W. B. Shubrick Clymer, of *Robert Frost: A Bibliography,* which was published by The Jones Library in 1937. But even prior to that time this editor turned to Mr. Green and to The Jones Library for information, and has gratefully returned many times over the years for assistance always generously given.

To Mr. Edward Connery Lathem, Associate Librarian of Dartmouth College, the editor wishes to express a distinctive debt. For several years Mr. Lathem has provided information about Frost letters at Dartmouth. During the past few years he has demonstrated an ingenious capacity for gathering more and more of the poet's correspondence to Dartmouth College Library, and has kept this editor informed of his latest acquisitions. Because of Mr. Lathem's intimate and scholarly knowledge of matters relating to Robert Frost, and also because of his own first-hand experience as an editor of letters, he was asked at an early stage of the preparation of the manuscript to act as first reader. The care with which Mr. Lathem combed it, and the tact with which he made many excellent suggestions for editorial improvements, are causes for exceptional indebtedness, now acknowledged with very deep gratitude.

I am especially pleased to acknowledge the quality and the quantity of assistance very generously given me by Mr. Clifton Waller Barrett, whose magnificent collection of Robert Frost books, manuscripts, and letters is in many ways second to none. Before, during, and after the time when that collection was given to the University of Virginia as part of the Clifton Waller Barrett Library of American Literature, it was made available to me through each phase of its phenomenal development. The loyalty and thoughtfulness with which Mr. Barrett expressed his consideration for my research combined scholarship with friendship.

To the Research Assistance Fund of Princeton University I am particularly grateful for aid, in this project, and to Princeton University for grants of leave.

While the manuscript of this book was being prepared for the printer and while the proofs were being corrected, the editor has been helped in many different ways by many members of the firm of Holt, Rinehart and Winston, Inc., in particular Mr. Stanley Burnshaw; but in meticulous ways by the editor, Mrs. Louise Waller. Her suggestions for improving the structural arrangement of the parts, and even for improving the style of the notes, have been so valuable that in a special sense she has become a collaborator. For all of her help, but particularly for her painstaking concern for important details, the editor is happy to express his appreciation and indebtedness.

Formal acknowledgement to libraries, publishers, and individuals for giving me access to letters and then extending permission to print or reprint each of them is made below, using the entry numbers employed in the "Table of Letters." Abbreviations of location, as used in the "Table," dictate the alphabetical arrangement:

Abercrombie: Mrs. Lascelles Abercrombie and Mr. Ralph Abercrombie, The Park, Highgate, London N6, England. (104, 140)

Academy: The American Academy of Arts and Letters, 633 West 155 Street, New York, New York. (327)

Agnes Scott: Agnes Scott College Library, Decatur, Georgia. (323-a, 324)

Amherst: Amherst College Library, Amherst, Massachusetts. (179, 192, 196, 201, 204, 217, 218, 251, 258, 260, 313, 317, 326, 333, 351-b, 352, 362, 394, 410, 466)

Armstrong: Mrs. A. J. Armstrong, The Browning Library, Baylor University, Waco, Texas. (398)

Atlantic: Editorial Office, Atlantic Monthly, 8 Arlington Street, Boston, Massachusetts. (113-a, 119-a)

Bacon: Mrs. Leonard Bacon, Peace Dale, Rhode Island. (337) (337)

Best: This Is My Best: Anthology of 93 of America's Greatest Living Authors edited by Whit Burnett. New York, Random House, 1942, p. 43. (390)

Bradford: The Letters of Gamaliel Bradford, 1918-1931 edited by Van Wyck Brooks. Boston, Houghton Mifflin, 1934, p. 171. (243-a)

Buffalo: Lockwood Memorial Library, Buffalo, New York. (364, 368)

Camarillo: St. John's Seminary Library, Camarillo, California. (84)

ACKNOWLEDGMENTS

Chicago: University of Chicago Library, Chicago, Illinois. (77, 145, 150, 151, 152, 155, 171, 175, 182, 184, 199, 208, 219, 228)

Clymer: Mr. W. B. Shubrick Clymer, Mayfair Farm, Harrisville, New Hampshire. (8-a, 128)

Coffin: Mr. R. P. T. Coffin, Jr., St. Paul's School, Concord, New Hampshire. (353, 356)

Cohn: Mrs. Louis H. Cohn, 360 East 55 Street, New York, New York. (421, 423, 424, 425, 429)

Colby: Colby College Library, Waterville, Maine. (386)

Collamore: Mr. H. Bacon Collamore, 53 Mountain Brook Road, West Hartford, Connecticut. (62, 82, 94, 95, 100, 137, 329)

Colorado: University of Colorado, President's Files, Boulder, Colorado. (370)

Congress: Library of Congress, Washington, D.C. (106, 133, 143, 146, 157, 170, 172, 178, 183, 193, 195, 197, 203, 212, 214, 223, 226, 233, 234, 244, 246, 250, 256, 272, 285, 292, 294, 296, 300, 301, 308, 310, 312, 314, 315, 323, 345, 357, 374, 381, 387)

Cook: Mr. Reginald L. Cook, Pulp Mill Bridge Road, Weybridge, Vermont. (206, 243, 265)

Cooley: Miss Mary E. Cooley, 703 South Forest Avenue, Ann Arbor, Michigan. (264)

Dartmouth: Dartmouth College Library, Hanover, New Hampshire. (V, 38-a, 38-b, 39, 41, 42, 47, 54, 54-a, 55, 57, 60-a, 61, 63, 65, 66, 68, 69-a, 69-b, 70, 74, 75, 78, 79, 80-b, 86, 87, 88, 90, 91, 92, 93, 96, 97, 99, 101, 102, 103, 107, 112, 117, 118, 124, 142, 154, 154-a, 160, 166, 176, 186, 215, 216, 249-b, 252, 252-a, 253-a, 255, 261-a, 262-a, 262-b, 263, 263-a, 263-b, 270, 271, 278, 289, 290-a, 293, 293-a, 294-a, 294-b, 299, 300-a, 303-a, 303-b, 315-a, 316, 316-a, 318, 319-a, 321, 327-a, 329-a, 332, 334, 336, 341, 343, 344, 346, 348-a, 377, 382, 391, 396, 400, 416, 422, 427, 433, 433-a, 433-b, 434, 435, 435-a, 436, 436-a, 436-b, 436-c, 437, 440, 440-a, 440-b, 441, 441-a, 441-b, 442, 443, 443-a, 443-b, 444, 445, 446, 446-a, 447, 448, 449, 449-a, 451, 451-a, 451-b, 452, 453, 454, 458, 459, 460, 461, 462-a, 463, 464, 465)

Door: *Through Heaven's Back Door: A Biography of A. Joseph Armstrong* by Lois Smith Douglas. Waco, Baylor University Press, 1951, pp. 137-138. (229)

ACKNOWLEDGMENTS

Farm-Poultry: The Farm-Poultry Semi-Monthly (Boston, Massachusetts), Vol. 15, No. 5 (15 Feb. 1904), p. 106; Vol. 15, No. 6 (1 Mar. 1904), p. 116. (18, 19)

Fraser: Mr. Willard E. Fraser, 118 South 38 Street, Billings, Montana. (296-a, 297, 298, 311, 351-a, 358, 363, 384, 393, 415)

Frost: Mr. William Prescott Frost, 4760 Briars Lane, Eugene, Oregon. (302, 304, 359, 367, 403)

Gilbert: Mr. Edgar Gilbert, Gilbert Laboratories, Morristown, New Jersey. (261)

Goodwin: Mr. Jonathan Goodwin, 750 Main Street, Hartford, Connecticut. (426)

Guide: New Hampshire: A Guide to the Granite State by Workers of the Federal Writers' Project. Boston, Houghton Mifflin, 1938, p. 103. (349)

Haines: Mr. John W. Haines, Midhurst, Hucclecote, Gloucestershire, England. (81, 114, 126, 149, 162, 200, 209, 253)

Harvard: Harvard University Library, Cambridge, Massachusetts. (16, 108, 119, 129, 147, 159, 169, 174, 177, 180, 225, 232, 237, 249-a, 249-c, 249-d, 325, 456, 456-a, 457, 460)

Holt: Holt, Rinehart and Winston, Inc., 383 Madison Avenue, New York, New York. (For current files only. Older files, including those of Henry Holt and Company, have been deposited in the Princeton University Library and letters drawn from those files are here acknowledged under "Princeton.") (417)

Hopkins: Johns Hopkins University Library, Baltimore, Maryland. (242, 286, 369)

Howes: Mr. Martin K. Howes, Swift River, Massachusetts. (268, 277, 279, 284)

Huntington: Henry E. Huntington Library, San Marino, California. (5, 6, 7, 8, 9, 10, 11, 12, 13, 14, 15, 17, 20, 21, 23, 24, 25, 26, 27, 28, 29, 30, 31, 32, 33, 38, 49, 121, 274, 274-a)

Jones: The Jones [public] Library, Amherst, Massachusetts. (1, 2, 3, 4, 57-a, 85, 110, 115, 155-a, 205, 220, 227, 230, 231, 235, 238, 239, 240, 245, 257, 263-c, 274-b, 275, 280, 305, 307)

Kohn: Mr. John S. Van E. Kohn, 10 Soundview Circle, White Plains, New York. (51, 365, 371, 373)

ACKNOWLEDGMENTS

Melcher: Mr. Daniel Melcher, 45 Dodd Street, Montclair, New
Jersey. (189, 241, 247, 249, 273, 281, 282, 287, 319)

Michigan: Archives of the University of Michigan, Michigan
Historical Collections, Ann Arbor, Michigan. (212-a, 213,
216-a)

Middlebury: Abernethy Library of American Literature, Middlebury College, Middlebury, Vermont. (43, 105, 130,
131, 144, 168, 181, 185, 188, 207)

New York: New York Public Library, New York, New York.
(123, 134, 286)

Pittsburgh: University of Pittsburgh Library, Pittsburgh,
Pennsylvania. (283, 358-a, 360, 378, 378-a, 379)

Poetry: Poetry: A Magazine of Verse (Chicago), Vol. 92, No.
6 (Sept., 1958), p. 398. (450)

Princeton: Princeton University Library, Princeton, New Jersey. (36, 37, 50, 56, 72, 75-a, 76, 80, 87-a, 87-b, 87-c,
96-a, 132, 132-a, 153, 161, 187, 188-a, 193-a, 194, 202,
210, 224, 225-a, 253-b, 253-c, 288, 295, 330, 347, 351,
354, 375, 376-a, 380, 385, 388, 389, 392, 395-a, 399, 401,
406, 413, 419, 419-a, 420, 428, 431, 438, 439, 455, 462)

Schmitt: Mr. Howard G. Schmitt, 43 Rosedale Avenue, Hamburg, New York. (98, 111, 127, 156, 163, 432)

Snow: Mr. Wilbert Snow, Weathersfield Avenue, Middletown,
Connecticut (303)

So. Cal.: University of Southern California Library, Los Angeles, California. (211)

Stanford: The Papers of Bernard DeVoto, Stanford University Library, Stanford, California. (331, 335, 338, 339,
340, 348, 350, 355, 361, 372, 395-b)

Stockhausen: Mr. William Stockhausen, Satterlee, Warfield
and Stephens, 460 Park Avenue, New York, New York.
(221)

Student: The Amherst Student, Amherst College, Amherst,
Massachusetts, 25 March 1935, pp. 1-2. (322)

Texas: University of Texas Library, Austin, Texas. (122, 164,
248, 266, 290, 302-a, 321-a, 328, 331-a)

Tufts: Tufts University Library, Medford, Massachusetts.
(342)

Untermeyer: [Files have been deposited in the Library of Congress and letters drawn from them are acknowledged under "Congress."]

Vermont: University of Vermont Library, Burlington, Vermont. (262)

Virginia: The Clifton Waller Barrett Library of the University of Virginia Library, Charlottesville, Virginia. (I, II, III, IV, 16-a, 34, 35, 40, 44, 45, 45-a, 46, 48, 52, 52-a, 53, 58, 59, 60, 64, 67, 69, 71, 73, 80-a, 83, 89, 113, 116, 120, 120-a, 125, 135, 136, 138, 141, 148, 158, 167, 222, 254, 259, 267, 269, 276, 291, 306, 339-a, 366, 376, 383, 395, 397, 402, 404, 405, 407, 408, 409, 411, 412, 414, 418)

Wellesley: Wellesley College Library, Wellesley, Massachusetts. (109, 139, 165, 190)

Wyoming: Department of English, University of Wyoming, Laramie, Wyoming. (368-a, 374-a)

World: The New York World [newspaper], 24 June 1923, "Editorial Section," p. 1. (191)

Yale: Yale Collection of American Literature, Yale University Library, New Haven, Connecticut. (173, 180-a, 198, 236, 309, 320, 337)

The editor wishes to make public expression of his deep and continuing gratitude to the following individuals who were of special assistance to him in the task of locating and obtaining copies of letters during the past twenty-five years: Mr. Charles D. Abbott, Mrs. Lascelles Abercrombie, Mr. Ralph Abercrombie, Mr. Sherman Adams, Mrs. Ann Allen, Mr. Hervey Allen, Mr. Wallace M. Alston, Mrs. Margaret Bartlett Anderson, Mrs. A. J. Armstrong, Mrs. Leonard Bacon, Mr. Carlos Baker, Mrs. Lesley Frost Ballantine, Mr. Julian P. Barclay, Mr. Clifton Waller Barrett, Mr. Earle J. Bernheimer, Mrs. Gamaliel Bradford, Mr. Stanley Burnshaw, Mrs. Edna Hanley Byers, Mr. Alexander Clark, Miss Sylvia Clark, Mr. W. B. Shubrick Clymer, Mr. R. P. T. Coffin, Mr. Louis Henry Cohn, Mrs. Marguerite Cohn, Mr. H. Bacon Collamore, Mr. Reginald L. Cook, Mrs. Avis DeVoto, Mr. William S. Dix, Miss Lois Smith Douglas, Mr. Alfred C. Edwards, Mr. Dwight D. Eisenhower, Mr. T. S. Eliot, Mr. G. Roy Elliott, Mr. Daniel A. Fineman, Mrs. Edith Hazard Fobes, Mr. Joseph Fobes, Mr. Frederic Fox, Mr. Willard E. Fraser, Miss Anne Freudenberg, Mrs. Lillian LaBatt Frost, Mrs. Phyllis Gordon Frost, Mr. Robert Frost, Mr. William Prescott Frost, Mr. Edgar Gilbert, Miss Mary Goodwillie, Mr. Charles R. Green, Mr. John W. Haines, Mr. Willis E. Herbert, Mr. Edward R. Hindley, Mrs. Katherine

ACKNOWLEDGMENTS

Hindley, Mr. Raymond Holden, Mr. Parkman D. Howe, Mr. Harold E. Howland, Mr. William A. Jackson, Miss Caroline Jakeman, Mrs. Matthew Josephson, Mr. John F. Kennedy, Mr. John S. Van E. Kohn, Mr. Edward C. Lathem, Miss Helen Browning Lawrie, Mr. William Rowell Locke, Mr. Clifford P. Lyons, Mr. Archibald MacLeish, Mr. Charles Madison, Mr. Newton F. McKeon, Mr. Lincoln MacVeagh, Mr. Daniel Melcher, Mr. Frederic G. Melcher, Mr. H. L. Mencken, Mr. Richard W. Morin, Mrs. Kathleen Morrison, Mr. Theodore Morrison, Mr. Ray Nash, Miss Haida Newton Parker, Mr. John Edwin Pomfret, Mr. Victor E. Reichert, Mr. Wilbur E. Rowell, Mr. Howard G. Schmitt, Mrs. Ernest L. Silver, Mr. William M. Sloane III, Mr. Wilbert Snow, Mr. Roger E. Thompson, Mr. Lionel Trilling, Mrs. Emma Smith Turner, Mr. Louis Untermeyer, Mr. Wade Van Dore, Mr. Herbert Faulkner West, Miss Viola C. White, Mrs. Sabra Peabody Woodbury, and Mr. John Cook Wyllie.

CHRONOLOGY

⋙⋘·

DETAILS OF EVENTS, names, dates, and places which are mentioned obliquely or obscurely in the letters may be found in the following chronology. Confusions concerning the correct year of RF's birth are noted at pertinent points. The poet eventually admitted that during most of his life he had often felt uncertain whether he was born in 1874 or 1875. He was aware, he said, that sometimes he had given the date as 1874, and sometimes as 1875, finally settling upon 1875 — erroneously. Although the San Francisco earthquake and fire destroyed the pertinent official records, at least three extant documents help to establish 1874 as the correct date:

(1) A letter written by RF's father from San Francisco, dated 25 October 1874 (quoted as letter III), in which "little Bob" is referred to as a "baby now seven months old."

(2) A paraphrase (in the *Second Report of the Secretary of the Harvard Class of 1872*, published June 1875) of a letter written by RF's father from San Francisco, summarizing biographical data and giving the birth date of RF as 26 March 1874.

(3) Records in the office of the Clerk of the City of Lawrence, Massachusetts, which show that when RF obtained his marriage license in December of 1895 he gave his birth date as 26 March 1874.

The inconsistency of RF on this matter may be illustrated by citing a pair of statements he made in 1916 — the year when he seems to have made the erroneous shift. He gave 26 March 1874 as his birth date, in a letter which was paraphrased in the *Harvard College Class of 1901 Secretary's Fourth Report* (Cambridge, 1916); but he gave the date as 26 March 1875 to *Who's Who* (Volume 9, 1916-1917). Throughout the next forty years, *Who's Who* continued to carry that incorrect date without any objection from RF.

Two examples of consequent confusion may be mentioned. A so-called "Fiftieth Birthday Dinner" was given in honor of RF in New York City on what was in fact his fifty-first birthday, 26 March 1925. The U. S. Senate sent "Seventy-fifth

Birthday" felicitations to him on 24 March 1950, just two days prior to his seventy-sixth birthday.

Long after the poet began to make consistent use of 1875 as the year of his birth many occasions must have reminded him of earlier uncertainties. At his insistence the subject came up for discussion between RF and the editor on 6 April 1949, when the following ironic exchange occurred:

"When was I born?"

"One year earlier than you say you were."

"I thought so."

Even then, he seemed indifferent to the error, and made no immediate attempts to correct it. The first published statement about it was based on information given by the editor to a researcher for *Time* magazine, and it appeared in a "cover story" (*Time*, 9 October 1950, p. 76) as a footnote.

I · LEWISTOWN, COLUMBUS, AND
SAN FRANCISCO · 1873-1885

[1844]

2 Oct.   RF's mother's date of birth: Isabelle Moodie, born at Leith, seaport of Edinburgh, Scotland, of Scottish parentage.

[1850]

27 Dec.   RF's father's date of birth: William Prescott Frost, Jr., born at Kingston, New Hampshire.

[c. 1853]

When nine years old Isabelle Moodie sailed from Scotland to America with her widowed grandmother; they landed in Philadelphia en route to Columbus, Ohio, and took up residence with relatives there.

[c. 1861]

Isabelle Moodie completed secondary school education in Columbus, Ohio, and became a teacher in the public schools there.

[1868]

June William Prescott Frost, Jr., completed secondary school education in Lawrence, Massachusetts.

[1872]

June William Prescott Frost, Jr., was graduated from Harvard College with honors, Phi Beta Kappa.

Sept. William Prescott Frost, Jr., began serving as headmaster of Lewistown Academy in Lewistown, Pennsylvania; and Isabelle Moodie began teaching at Lewistown Academy.

[1873]

18 Mar. William Prescott Frost, Jr., and Isabelle Moodie were married, in Lewistown, Pennsylvania.

9 July William Prescott Frost, Jr., reached San Francisco, seeking work as a journalist.

Nov. Isabelle Moodie Frost reached San Francisco.

[1874]

26 Mar. Robert Lee Frost born in San Francisco.

[1876]

25 June RF's sister, Jeanie Florence Frost, born in Lawrence, Massachusetts.

[1885]

5 May RF's father died of tuberculosis in San Francisco and his widow and children accompanied the body across the country for burial in Lawrence, Massachusetts, as he had requested.

II · SALEM AND LAWRENCE · 1885-1900

[1885]

Sept. RF's mother moved with her two children from Lawrence, Massachusetts, to Salem, New Hampshire, and began teaching in a public school there.

[1888]

Sept.   RF began his four-year course of study in the Lawrence (Massachusetts) High School.

[1890]

Spring   RF wrote first poem, a ballad inspired by his reading W. H. Prescott's account, in *The Conquest of Mexico*, of the temporary Indian victory over Cortez in Mexico City. The poem, entitled "La Noche Triste," was published in the (Lawrence) *High School Bulletin*, May 1890. Three other poems by RF appeared in the *Bulletin:* "Song of the Wave" (May 1890), "A Dream of Julius Caesar" (April 1891), and "Class Hymn" (June 1892).

[1892]

June   "The Traitor," a poem by RF, published anonymously in the Phillips Andover *Mirror*.
RF was graduated from Lawrence High School, sharing valedictorian honors with Elinor Miriam White; also Class Poet. Won the Hood Prize for Scholastic Excellence.

Sept.   Began attending Dartmouth College; remained in attendance less than one semester.

[1893]

Spring   RF taught an eighth-grade class in Methuen, Massachusetts.

Summer Worked as light-trimmer in the Arlington Mill, Lawrence, Massachusetts.

[1894]

Winter   RF worked as gate-tender, Arlington Mill, Lawrence, Massachusetts.

Spring   Taught for a term in a district school, Salem, New Hampshire.

Mar.   RF's poem, "My Butterfly: An Elegy," was bought by *The* (New York) *Independent*. To celebrate the event, he privately printed a first book of poems, *Twilight,* in an edition of two copies, and presented one copy to Elinor Miriam White. *Twilight* contains: "Twilight," "My Butterfly," "Summering," "The Falls," "An Unhistoric Spot."

Fall   Made runaway excursion to New York City, to Virginia, and to the Dismal Swamp. Destroyed his copy of *Twilight*.

1

8 Nov.   "My Butterfly: An Elegy" published in *The Independent.*

Dec.   Began work as newspaper reporter for the Lawrence (weekly) *Sentinel.*

[1895]

Winter   RF left the *Sentinel* and worked briefly as a newspaper reporter for the Lawrence *Daily American.*

Spring   RF taught, with his mother and sister, in a private school owned and managed by his mother.

19 Dec.   Was married to Elinor Miriam White in Lawrence, Massachusetts.

[1896]

20 Aug.   RF published a second poem in *The Independent:* "The Birds Do Thus."

25 Sept. First child born to RF and his wife, a son named Elliott.

[1897]

13 Jan.   RF published a third poem in *The Independent:* "Caesar's Lost Transport Ships."

30 April Published a poem entitled "Greece" in the Boston *Evening Transcript.*

Sept.   Began attending Harvard College as a special student.

9 Sept.   Published a poem entitled "Warning" in *The Independent.*

[1899]

31 Mar.   RF formally withdrew from Harvard College; returned to Lawrence, Massachusetts, to live.

28 April Second child born, a daughter named Lesley.

[1900]

8 July   First child, Elliott, died of *cholera infantum;* was buried in Lawrence, Massachusetts.

III · DERRY AND PLYMOUTH · 1900-1912

[1900]

Oct.   RF moved with his family to Derry, New Hampshire, and settled on a farm purchased there for his use by his grandfather, William Prescott Frost.

2 Nov.   Mother died of cancer, in the Alexander Sanatorium, Penacook, New Hampshire; was buried in Lawrence, Massachusetts.

[1901]

27 June   RF published a poem, "The Quest of the Orchis," in *The Independent*.

10 July   Paternal grandfather died, willing to RF the Derry farm and a relatively substantial annuity.

[1902]

27 May   Third child born, a son named Carol.

[1903]

Feb.   RF published a prose sketch or short story entitled "Trap Nests" in a monthly periodical, *The Eastern Poultryman;* the first of eleven prose pieces published during a three-year period in two regional poultry periodicals.

Mar.   Went to New York City with his family, rented a furnished apartment there, and stayed for a month.

27 June   Fourth child born, a daughter named Irma.

[1905]

29 Mar.   Fifth child born, a daughter named Marjorie.

Aug.   RF went alone to Bethlehem, New Hampshire, seeking relief from acute hay fever.

[1906]

9 Mar.   RF published a poem, "The Tuft of Flowers," in the Derry *Enterprise*.

16 Mar.   Published a poem, "Ghost Houses," in *Youth's Companion*.

Spring   Began teaching part time at Pinkerton Academy.

Aug.   Went with his family to Bethlehem, New Hampshire, for the hay-fever season; rented rooms in the home of an Irish farmer, John Lynch.

Sept.   Began teaching full time at Pinkerton Academy.

11 Oct.   Published a poem, "The Trial by Existence," in *The Independent*.

[1907]

27 Feb. RF contributed "The Later Minstrel," a poetic tribute to Longfellow, for use in Pinkerton chapel
exercise celebrating the centennial of Longfellow's
birth; the poem was printed as a broadside.

Mar. Published "The Later Minstrel" in the Pinkerton
Critic.

1 Mar. Published a poem, "The Lost Faith," in the Derry
News.

Mar. Stricken with pneumonia; ill for several weeks.

18 June Sixth child born, a daughter named Elinor Bettina, who died within two days after her birth.

Aug. For a second time took his family to Bethlehem,
New Hampshire.

Oct. Published a poem, "A Line-storm Song," in *New
England Magazine*.

Dec. Took his family to New York City during his
Christmas vacation from Pinkerton Academy.

[1908]

26 Mar. RF published a poem, "Across the Atlantic," in
The Independent.

Aug. For a third time took his family to Bethlehem,
New Hampshire.

[1909]

May RF published a poem, "Into Mine Own," in *New
England Magazine*.

20 May Published a poem, "The Flower-boat," in *Youth's
Companion*.

Aug. Spent part of the hay-fever season with his family
at Lake Willoughby, Vermont, botanizing and
camping in tents.

Sept. Left the Derry farm; moved with his family to a
second-floor apartment which he rented in Derry
Village.

Oct. Published a poem, "A Late Walk," in the Pinkerton
Critic.

[1911]

June RF ended his teaching duties at Pinkerton.

Aug. For a fourth time took his family to Bethlehem,
New Hampshire.

Sept. Moved with his family to Plymouth, New Hampshire, and taught at the New Hampshire State

Normal School in Plymouth for one academic year: 1911-1912.

16 Nov. Sold the Derry farm.

Dec. During Christmas vacation, made trip alone by train to New York City for literary purposes.

IV · LONDON, BEACONSFIELD, AND

GLOUCESTERSHIRE · 1912-1915

[1912]

Sept. RF sailed with his family aboard SS *Parisian* from Boston to Glasgow; went by train to London; lived for one week in a London hotel before renting a house in Beaconsfield, Buckinghamshire.

3 Oct. Published a poem, "October," in *Youth's Companion.*

26 Oct. MS of *A Boy's Will* accepted for publication by David Nutt and Company, London.

Nov. Published a poem, "My November Guest," in *The Forum.*

7 Nov. Published a poem, "Reluctance," in *Youth's Companion.*

[1913]

April *A Boy's Will* published in London, around the first of the month.

Aug. Went by boat with his family from London to Leith, Scotland; spent two weeks in the coastal village of Kingsbarns, Fifeshire, on the Firth of Tay.

[1914]

April RF moved with his family from Beaconsfield to London; briefly took rooms above Harold Monro's Poetry Bookshop at 35 Devonshire Street.

May Moved with his family from London to Gloucestershire; remained in the country there for nine months until his departure for the United States.

15 May *North of Boston* published in London.

[1915]

13 Feb. RF sailed with his family from Liverpool aboard SS *St. Paul.*

V · FRANCONIA AND AMHERST · 1915-1920

[1915]

20 Feb. *North of Boston* published in New York City by Henry Holt and Company.

22 Feb. RF landed in New York City; sent family to the home of John Lynch in Bethlehem, New Hampshire; visited briefly in New York, Boston, Lawrence before joining his family.

April *A Boy's Will* published by Henry Holt and Company. Made arrangements to purchase farm in Franconia, New Hampshire.

7 May Phi Beta Kappa Poet, Tufts College.

[1916]

19 June Phi Beta Kappa Poet, Harvard College.

Nov. *Mountain Interval* published.

16 Nov. RF elected to membership in the National Institute of Arts and Letters.

[1917]

Jan. RF began teaching at Amherst College; continued teaching there until May 1920.

Nov. Dramatic narrative poem entitled "Snow" awarded cash prize of $100 by *Poetry: A Magazine of Verse.*

[1918]

2 May Honorary M. A., Amherst College.

[1920]

May RF resigned from Amherst College; returned to Franconia.

VI · SOUTH SHAFTSBURY, MICHIGAN, AND

AMHERST · 1920-1926

[1920]

Oct. RF moved with his family from Franconia, New Hampshire, to South Shaftsbury, Vermont.

[1921]

19 July Made his first appearance at Bread Loaf School of English in Ripton, Vermont.

Sept. Moved with his family to Ann Arbor, Michigan, to begin his duties as "Poet in Residence" at the University of Michigan, a one-year appointment.

[1922]

19 June Honorary M. A., University of Michigan.

Sept. Returned to the University of Michigan as a "Fellow in Creative Arts," a one-year appointment.

[1923]

15 Mar. *Selected Poems* published.

18 June Honorary L. H. D., University of Vermont.

3 Nov. RF's son Carol Frost married to Lillian LaBatt.

15 Nov. *New Hampshire* published.

Nov. Returned to Amherst College with the title "Professor of English"; stayed until 1925.

[1924]

11 May Pulitzer Prize for *New Hampshire.*

16 June Honorary Litt. D., Middlebury College.

18 June Honorary Litt. D., Yale University.

15 Oct. First grandchild born: William Prescott Frost, son of Carol and Lillian LaBatt Frost.

[1925]

26 Mar. RF honored at a so-called "Fiftieth Birthday Dinner" in New York City.

4 May Participated in Bowdoin Institute of Modern Literature celebrating the centennial of Longfellow's graduation from Bowdoin.

Sept. Returned to the University of Michigan as a Fellow in Letters, a permanent appointment from which RF resigned after one academic year.

[1926]

14 June Honorary Litt. D., Bowdoin College.

VII · AMHERST, COLORADO, CALIFORNIA, TEXAS, AND FLORIDA · 1926-1938

[1926]

Sept.   Returned to Amherst College as Professor of English; remained, under various arrangements, until 1938.

[1928]

Aug.   Revisited England with his wife and daughter Marjorie; went alone to Ireland; returned to United States in November.

19 Nov. *West-running Brook* published.

[1929]

7 Sept. RF's sister, Jeanie Florence Frost, died.

[1930]

16 June Honorary Litt. D., University of New Hampshire.
1 Nov. *Collected Poems* published.
13 Nov. Elected to membership in the American Academy of Arts and Letters.

[1931]

2 June Pulitzer Prize for *Collected Poems*.
Aug. Lecturer, Writers Conference, University of Colorado.
Sept. With his wife, traveled from Colorado to California to visit Carol and Lillian Frost.
12 Oct. Honorary L. H. D., Wesleyan University.
24 Nov. Purchased home on Sunset Avenue, Amherst, Massachusetts.
11 Dec. Received Russell Loines Poetry Prize of $1,000 from the National Institute of Arts and Letters.

[1932]

24 May Phi Beta Kappa Poet, Columbia University.
1 June Honorary Litt. D., Columbia University.
20 June Honorary L. H. D., Williams College.
23 June Started west again with his wife to visit their children in Colorado and California.

Nov.   Elected Honorary Member, St. Botolph Club, Boston, Massachusetts.

[1933]

April   With his wife, made trip to Texas; gave ten public readings in eleven days.

3 June   His daughter Marjorie Frost married to Willard E. Fraser in Billings, Montana.

20 June Honorary Litt. D., Dartmouth College.
         Elected Associate Fellow, Pierson College, Yale University.

[1934]

April   With his wife, made emergency trip to Billings, Montana, to visit daughter Marjorie suffering from child-bed fever; followed her to the Mayo Clinic, Rochester, Minnesota, where she died on 2 May 1934.

10 Dec. Obeying doctor's orders, RF and his wife left Amherst for Key West; their first visit to Florida.

[1935]

1 March RF gave a reading at the Winter Institute of Literature, University of Miami, Florida.

July   Lecturer, Writers Conference, University of Colorado.

[1936]

Jan.   RF returned with his wife to Florida; gave three lectures at the Winter Institute, Miami.

Spring   Charles Eliot Norton Professor of Poetry, Harvard University.

20 May   A *Further Range* published; Book-of-the-Month Club selection.

8 June   Honorary L. H. D., St. Lawrence University.

10 June Honorary L. H. D., University of Pennsylvania.

16 June Honorary L. H. D., Bates College.

18 Dec. RF and his wife arrived in San Antonio, Texas, to spend the winter.

[1937]

1 April RF and his wife returned to Amherst after staying fourteen weeks in San Antonio.

23 April RF elected to membership in the American Philosophical Society.

3 May   Pulitzer Prize for *A Further Range*.
24 June Honorary Litt. D., Harvard University.
3 Oct.   Mrs. Frost underwent operation for cancer.
8 Dec.   RF and his wife arrived in Gainesville, Florida, planning to stay until April.

[1938]

21 Mar. Mrs. Frost died in Gainesville of heart attack; was cremated in Jacksonville, Florida.

VIII · BOSTON, HARVARD, MIAMI, AND
RIPTON · 1938-1943

[1938]

20 April Memorial service for Mrs. Frost in Johnson Chapel, Amherst College.
June   RF resigned from Amherst College, sold his home there; returned to South Shaftsbury.
23 June   Elected to Board of Overseers, Harvard College.
24 Aug.   Participated in Bread Loaf Writers' Conference, Ripton, Vermont; remained there for the entire session.
Sept.   RF moved to Boston; lived briefly at St. Botolph Club; moved into an apartment at 88 Mt. Vernon Street.

[1939]

18 Jan.   RF awarded Gold Medal for Poetry, National Institute of Arts and Letters.
16 Feb.   *Collected Poems* (enlarged edition) published.
April   Made an extended reading tour: Iowa, Wyoming, Utah, Kansas, Indiana, Michigan.
24 April Honorary L. H. D., University of Colorado.
10 May   RF appointed Ralph Waldo Emerson Fellow in Poetry, Harvard University.
Summer   Purchased the Homer Noble Farm in Ripton, Vermont; spent the summer there.
Nov.   Appointed an Associate of Adams House, Harvard University.

[1940]

8 Jan.   RF sold only exiting copy of *Twilight* to E. J. Bernheimer for $4,000.

10 Jan.	Underwent operation at Massachusetts General Hospital.
Feb.	Went to Key West, Florida, for postoperative recuperation; visited with Hervey Allen in Coconut Grove, Florida, on way home.
May	Purchased five acres of undeveloped land near home of Hervey Allen in South Miami, Florida, for the erection of a winter home.
22 May	Phi Beta Kappa Poet, Tufts College.
9 Oct.	RF's son, Carol, committed suicide in South Shaftsbury, Vermont.

[1941]

31 Jan.	RF awarded Gold Medal, Poetry Society of America.
Feb.	Spent a month in Florida, Gainesville and Coconut Grove.
Spring	Purchased home at 35 Brewster Street, Cambridge, Massachusetts, and moved into it from his apartment at 88 Mt. Vernon Street, Boston.
17 June	Honorary Litt. D., Princeton University.
19 June	Phi Beta Kappa Poet, Harvard University.
5 Dec.	Phi Beta Kappa Poet, College of William and Mary.

[1942]

Feb.	RF went to Florida as guest of Hervey Allen; supervised the assembling and completion of a prefabricated winter home, "Pencil Pines," on Davis Road, South Miami; a second unit added later.
23 April	*A Witness Tree* published.

[1943]

3 May	Pulitzer Prize for *A Witness Tree*.

IX · CAMBRIDGE, DARTMOUTH, MIAMI, AND

RIPTON · 1943-1949

[1943]

Fall	RF severed connections with Harvard; became George Ticknor Fellow in the Humanities at Dartmouth College; continued the Dartmouth affiliation until 1949.

28 Dec. Hospitalized with pneumonia in Hanover, New Hampshire.

[1944]

Feb. Recuperated at "Pencil Pines" in Florida.

[1945]

26 Mar. *A Masque of Reason* published.
20 Oct. Honorary Litt. D., Kenyon College.

[1946]

May *The Pocket Book of Robert Frost's Poems* was published.

[1947]

Jan. *The Poems of Robert Frost* published in Modern Library edition.
22 Mar. Honorary LL. D., University of California.
28 May *Steeple Bush* published.
16 Sept. *A Masque of Mercy* published.

[1948]

22 Feb. RF elected Honorary Member, Massachusetts Chapter of the Society of the Cincinnati.
7 June Honorary Litt. D., Duke University.
20 June Honorary Litt. D., Amherst College.

[1949]

April *Complete Poems 1949* published.

X · CAMBRIDGE, AMHERST, WASHINGTON, MIAMI,
AND RIPTON · 1949-1963

Oct. Life appointment, Simpson Lecturer in Literature, Amherst College.
16 Nov. Gold Medal awarded by the Limited Editions Club to RF as "that American author who is considered to have written the book most closely approaching the stature of a classic."
8 Dec. Award from "Author Meets the Critics" for *Complete Poems 1949*.

[1950]

24 Mar. U. S. Senate adopted resolution extending felicitations to RF on his so-called seventy-fifth birthday.
12 June Honorary Litt. D., Colgate College.
20 June Honorary Litt. D., Marlboro College.
Sept.   *Complete Poems* reissued in two volumes by the
Limited Editions Club.
6-8 Oct. RF attended "The Poet and Reality: A Conference
in Honor of Robert Frost" at Kenyon College.

[1951]

3 June Honorary Litt. D., *in absentia,* University of Durham, England.
3 June Honorary Litt. D., University of Massachusetts.

[1953]

3 Mar. Received an award from the Academy of American Poets.
8 June Honorary Litt. D., University of North Carolina.

[1954]

25 Mar. Eightieth Birthday Dinner in New York City;
Aforesaid distributed to guests as a memento of
the occasion by the host, Henry Holt and Com-
pany.
26 Mar. Eightieth Birthday Dinner in Amherst given by
Amherst College.
13 June Received "First Annual Poetry Award," Boston
Arts Festival.
4-19   In South America; sent by U. S. Department of
Aug.   State as a delegate to the World Congress of
Writers, São Paulo, Brazil.
14 Oct. Received Citation for Distinguished Service to
Education from the New Hampshire Education
Association.
27 Oct. Received Medal for Distinguished Service in the
Field of American Literature from the Theodore
Roosevelt Society.
15 Nov. Honorary LL. D., University of Cincinnati.

[1955]

May   "Robert Frost Mountain" so designated in Ripton,
Vermont, by act of the Legislature of the State of
Vermont.
12 June Honorary LL. D., Dartmouth College.

8 Dec. Honorary Litt. D., University of Rhode Island.

[1956]

23 Mar. Medal of Honor, New York University.
11 June Honorary LL. D., Colby College.

[1957]

21 May RF left New York by plane for London to make a "good will mission" under the auspices of the U. S. Department of State.
4 June Honorary Litt. D., Oxford University.
13 June Honorary Litt. D., Cambridge University.
19 June Honorary Litt. D., National University, Ireland.
30 Aug. Honorary L. H. D., Ohio State University.
16 Nov. Awarded Gold Medal by the Holland Society of New York.

[1958]

16 Jan. Gold Medal for Distinguished Service (the Alexander Droutzhay Memorial Award) presented by the Poetry Society of America.
22 Mar. Medal for Achievements in the Arts awarded by the Signet Society, Harvard College.
21 May Appointed Consultant in Poetry in the Library of Congress; term from October 1958, to May 1959.
8 Oct. Emerson-Thoreau Medal, American Academy of Arts and Sciences.
17 Nov. Huntington Hartford Foundation Award.

[1959]

26 Mar. Eighty-fifth Birthday Dinner, Waldorf Astoria Hotel, New York City; host, Henry Holt and Company.
10 April Honorary L. H. D., Miami University.
21 April Honorary Litt. D., Syracuse University.
7 May Awarded $1,000 from Dickinson College "in recognition of distinguished achievement in the arts."
7 June Honorary Litt. D., Tufts University.

[1960]

30 Jan. Honorary LL. D., University of Florida.
2 April Honorary L. H. D., Hebrew Union College (Jewish Institute of Religion).
12 Sept. President Dwight D. Eisenhower signed bill of

Congress authorizing a Congressional Gold Medal
for RF.

[1961]

20 Jan. RF participated in the inauguration ceremonies
for President John F. Kennedy; read "The Gift
Outright."

31 Jan. Honorary LL. D., University of Miami.

9-27   Abroad in Israel; spoke and read as Samuel Paley
Mar.   Foundation Lecturer at the Hebrew University,
Jerusalem; spoke and read in Athens, Greece;
stopped in London, given a birthday luncheon by
the U. S. Ambassador, David K. E. Bruce.

3 June   Honorary Litt., D., Windham College.

4 June   Honorary Litt. D., Boston University.

21 July Named "Poet Laureate of Vermont" by action of
the Vermont State Legislature.

[1962]

7 Jan.   RF attended dedication of "Robert Lee Frost Elementary School" in Lawrence, Massachusetts.

4 Feb.   Hospitalized by pneumonia in Miami, Florida.

26 Mar. In Washington, D. C., President Kennedy presented him with Congressional Medal at White
House; attended gala birthday dinner where he
was honored by two hundred notables; host, Holt,
Rinehart and Winston, Inc.

26 Mar. *In the Clearing* published.

16 June Honorary LL. D., University of Michigan.

29 Aug.- RF made "good-will mission" to U.S.S.R. under
9 Sept. auspices of the U. S. Department of State.

22-24   Participated in National Poetry Festival, Library
Oct.   of Congress, Washington, D.C.

8 Nov.   Awarded Edward MacDowell Medal, New York
City.

13 Nov. Honorary L. H. D., University of Detroit.

3 Dec.   Entered Peter Bent Brigham Hospital, Boston, for
observation and tests.

10 Dec. Prostate operation.

[1963]

5 Jan.   RF awarded Bollingen Prize in Poetry of $2,500.

29 Jan. Died in Peter Bent Brigham Hospital; cremated.

16 June Ashes interred, cemetery of First Congregational
Church, Old Bennington, Vermont.

SELECTED LETTERS OF
ROBERT FROST

LEWISTOWN, COLUMBUS, AND
SAN FRANCISCO · 1873-1885

HERE GIVEN as preliminaries are five letters written by the parents of Robert Frost during their courtship and the early years of their marriage.

William Prescott Frost, Jr., was born in Kingston, New Hampshire, on 27 December 1850. He received his secondary school education in Lawrence, Massachusetts, attended Harvard College, and was graduated with honors, Phi Beta Kappa, in the Class of 1872. For one year, 1872-1873, he served as headmaster of Lewistown Academy, a private school in Lewistown, Pennsylvania. There he met, courted, and married Miss Isabelle Moodie, who was teaching English at the same school.

Born near Edinburgh, Scotland, on 2 October 1844, and orphaned early in her life, Isabelle Moodie was reared by her paternal grandparents in Edinburgh. Her widowed grandmother brought her to the United States when Isabelle Moodie was nine years old. She was taken at once to Columbus, Ohio, where she lived with an uncle. Later she taught for several years in Columbus before going to Lewistown Academy in the fall of 1872. She and William Prescott Frost, Jr., were married in Lewistown on 18 March 1873.

At the end of the school year, in June 1873, the bride and groom went to Columbus, and visited briefly with her relatives before he set out for California to look for work and establish a home. He arrived on 9 July 1873 in San Francisco and at once sought employment as a journalist. Isabelle Moodie Frost stayed with an uncle in Columbus until November 1873 and then made the journey to California with friends. Their first child was born in San Francisco on 26 March 1874. Because of his New England father's Copperhead sympathies, he was named Robert Lee Frost.

3

After three years of marriage, Robert Frost's parents became estranged. Isabelle left her husband in the spring of 1876 and crossed the continent with her two-year-old son to visit with her husband's parents in Lawrence. There she gave birth on 25 June 1876 to her second child, Jeanie Florence. The three of them joined Miss Sarah Newton, Isabelle's close friend of school-teaching days, at her home in Greenfield, Massachusetts, and spent most of the summer there. Letter V makes oblique reference to that visit although it was written nearly seven years later to convey condolences to Sarah Newton on the death of her father.

In the early autumn of 1876, Isabelle and her two children went from New England to Columbus and stayed for some time with relatives. By means of continued correspondence, she and her husband managed to overcome their estrangement; their reconciliation must have occurred prior to the writing of Letter IV. Late in the autumn of 1876, Isabelle returned to San Francisco with her children, accompanied by a friend of her Columbus school days, Miss Blanche Rankin. During the next six years Blanche Rankin lived with the Frosts in San Francisco and came to be known to the children as Aunt Blanche.

A few months prior to his wife's return, William Prescott Frost, Jr., made a bet that he could win a six-day walking race against a professional walker. He lost the race. Even worse, the exertion caused a physical collapse, and within months he contracted tuberculosis.

Although he was never very successful in any of his journalistic or political enterprises, he still drove himself strenuously. Nine years later he died of tuberculosis in San Francisco at the age of thirty-four on 5 May 1885. His dying request was to have his body returned to Lawrence for burial, but his father had to send funds before the request could be carried out.

Isabelle and her children accompanied the coffin across the country for the interment in Lawrence. Because she could neither afford a ticket back to San Francisco nor bear to ask her affluent relatives in Columbus for help, Isabelle remained among strangers in New England, where she sought employment as a teacher. After various discouragements and difficulties, she obtained a position in the autumn of 1885 as a teacher of several grammar-school grades, in a one-room schoolhouse in the village of Salem, New Hampshire.

I · WILLIAM P. FROST, JR., TO ISABELLE MOODIE

Miss Moodie   [*c.* 1 February 1873]   [Lewistown, Pa.]

"He either fears his fate too much,
"Or his deserts are small,
"Who puts it not unto the touch
"To win or lose it all." *

As I take my pen to make the avowal which I purpose in this note, the above quotation very well reflects my feelings. I am taking a step in the dark, — never a step before in which I have had so little to indicate to me whether the issue was to be a happy one or the reverse. May the darkness quickly give way to a light than which none could bring to me more of happiness. Whether what I am to write will come to you as a surprise, — whether anything in my conduct has led you to surmise a sentiment stronger than warm friendship, — of this, too, I know nothing. At the risk of being tedious I will attempt to tell you, as far as feeble words will permit me, what are my real sentiments towards you, as also the course of their growth.

It is now five months since I shook hands with you on your arrival here. To say that I liked you at the very outset of our acquaintance would be superfluous, — for who could do otherwise? Yes, I liked you. That was all. I have always thought that that was the only feeling I could have towards any woman. And I little dreamed that this sentiment, — if sentiment it can be called, — was to be supplanted by a passion whose hold upon me, oh! how dear a hold! has now for some time been stronger than any other tie that connects me with the world, and which makes my heart beat faster, faster, faster, as I write these lines. But I am anticipating. As I became better acquainted with you, I saw in you a nearer approach to my ideal of a true woman, joined with the native cultivation and refinement of a lady, than I had ever chanced upon among any of my lady friends. I admired you, I respected you, I felt for you the warmest friendship, but — I did not love you. No such sentiment was in my heart, no thought of it in my head. But ere long your voice went not

* A relatively accurate version of the second stanza in the poem entitled "My Dear and Only Love" by James Graham, First Marquis of Montrose (1612-1650).

5

only to my ears, but straight to my heart. It awoke a thrill there such as I had never known before. As I sat here at my table and heard you singing in your room, my heart beat in unison with every line. To know that you were there even when I could not hear you was a pleasure to me. When I heard your footsteps retreating along the hall, my heart seemed to shrink within me. And when you returned I was as happy as at the recovery of a long-lost treasure.

But enough of this: pardon my dwelling upon it; it may seem nonsense to you, but to me it is everything.

I asked myself, is this love? And I answered myself, no. For a long time, — it seems to me as I look back upon it to be a long time, — I obstinately refused to acknowledge to myself that I loved you. As well might I have disputed my very existence. And when once I did acknowledge it, my love pervaded my whole being. It has ennobled me, it has given me higher aspirations; it has almost seemed to me that when we have been talking together on religious questions, my love for you drew me so close to you in spirit that I could believe with you in Christianity, in the love of God, in the divinity of Christ, — things which are to you precious truths, to me enigmas.

You have called me phlegmatic, and I quite agree with you that my temperament partakes of that character. But, Belle Moodie, darling Belle, my love is as opposite to that as are the antipodes to us. If any one can love you more passionately, more devotedly, than I do, then may you possess the love of that one, and not mine. Little have you thought what pleasure I have experienced when you have sat with me to study. There can be to me only one happiness greater than that of loving you and being in your company, and that is to know that my love is returned. Several times within the past few weeks I have been on the point of making an avowal to you, so potent is your presence over me, but I preferred this method of doing it, thinking that I could more fully express myself than in speech.

And now, do you ask me whether I do not see obstacles in the way of my love? I answer, yes, and I have weighed them, so far as it lay in my power to do, carefully. In the first place there is the disparity in our ages. The world commonly looks upon that as a barrier. But how often is it overstepped. And I never have known of people living the less happily for so doing. To me it seems that the heart is the first thing to be consulted, then the character, the tastes, the pursuits, and lastly, such considerations as station in life, and age; and if, as in this case, the difference in age is not very remarkable, that those other considerations may utterly outweigh it. We ought by this time to understand one another's character and tastes very well. I ask no farther acquaintance to learn what these are in you, and I believe that they will be found more congenial in few married people than in us. Secondly, you are a Christian — I am not. How far that is an obstacle in your eyes, I know not. In mine it is none at all. I am always for allowing the widest liberty of opinion. And my unbelief has not a grain of obstinacy in it, so far as I am aware. It is rather lack of belief, than unbelief. This point, then, is one for you, and not me, to consider. Thirdly and lastly, you have said to me that you thought you "should never marry." Oh, how many, many times have I turned those words over in my mind, and hoped in my inmost heart that they were not the expression of a fixed resolve. Your secrets, I ought not, and I desire not, to pry into. I know nothing of your past life, your disappointments, your troubles. I have inferred from what you have said to me that they were not few. But has all this anything to do with the present? Is not the real question this? do you see in me that which you can love? that which you can rely upon as a support in the rugged ways of life? If you do, I ask you now for that wealth of affection which it is yours to bestow on me, and I offer you in return a love than which, if more worthy, I am sure you can at least find none more devoted.

I feel that you have in a large measure my destiny in life under your control. Your answer to this will mark a turning-point in my life. A person of my character cannot transfer his love at will. What is yours now is yours for life. You cannot reject it. You can only refuse to reciprocate it. Whatever your answer may be, you can lose nothing, but I — I — *every-thing*, I know; then, you will think well before you reply.

Yours, dear Belle

Devotedly and ever   Wm. P. Frost, Jr.

II · WILLIAM P. FROST, JR., TO ISABELLE MOODIE FROST

My Darling Wife

13 July 1873
San Francisco, California

Am I selfish, darling, in my intense longing to have you come to me, and does my selfishness blind my better judgment? If this is true, I am very, very sorry, and if you think it is, I ask you simply to substitute your feelings and your judgment for mine in deciding, and do as you think best. But I — I am a perfect baby. I have always heretofore ridiculed homesickness, having been an utter stranger to it myself. But a year has worked a wonderful change in me. And it is the influence of my Belle, my darling Belle, that has done it. My love for you, — a love such that I never could have dreamed it could possess me, — has made me a very child in my feelings towards what we call "home." Home is now to me the sweetest thing in life and home is anywhere in the wide world where you are. Where you are not, everything is bleak and desolate. Never has my heart been so terribly heavy as since Wednesday last when I came to realize that I had at length reached the looked-for scene of my efforts, and that my Belle is three thousand miles away. I sit down to write a newspaper article — my heart is not in the work — my thoughts cannot be kept on the subject in hand — and I complete the task with the feeling that I have not done justice to myself. I have no real acquaintance with a soul here, — nor have I any wish to make any while you are from me, — and I sit in my nice room, which is a dismal prison to me, or walk out on the street, feeling as if I was divorced from all that can make me happy. I lie awake half the nights long, and my troubled sleep is crowded with all sorts of phantasms in which you figure chiefly. My thoughts of how we are to get a living are nearly all fled, I have no fears on that score now, and my whole feeling is centered in this, this cruel separation, I cannot, cannot bear it. I cannot believe that it is right for me to sit here, laying aside the longing of a loving husband for the presence of his darling wife, and coolly count the chances of our not starving to death if you come to me. Why, Belle, if there were no tangible ground whatever to argue from, I *know* that two persons of our education, ability to do one thing or another, and knowledge of the world, need not come to actual want so long as they are willing to work. Therefore my heart and my judgment cry aloud to you, *come, come, come.* I *entreat* you to *come. Come,* and trust Providence for the result. Let us, as we pledged to do not yet four months ago, share in love and devotion our fortunes together. On my side I am willing to do *anything* that is honorable, to endure *anything,* if I can but have my darling with me. *Oh, do come now.*

And now what are the prospects? I wrote for the Bulletin yesterday on the Retirement of Bismarck, and it came out as a *leader* last evening. I wrote for the Chronicle last evening on the Packing of Juries. It was accepted, but did not appear this morning, — probably crowded out. Now is there not every encouragement for me thus far? I am writing, mind you, on trial and with a tacit understanding that if my efforts are satisfactory an engagement will be made with me. Now the fact that every one of my contributions thus far has been accepted as editorial, — and I have made six, — is certainly indicative that they are not *un*satisfactory, and I have strong hopes that before this week is ended I shall make some kind of an engagement with one or the other of these papers. Nor can I think that the two chief papers of San Francisco will offer anything *less* than $25. a week for the services of a person whose work they so readily accept. Then as to your getting work to do, I saw Marsh again yesterday, and he said his business is so fluctuating that he could not assure you of anything like permanent employment, but he has no doubt he can give you more or less to do, and he thinks some might be got of other phonographers. The pay is 20 cts. a page, and they call 30 pages a good day's work for an excellent transcriber.

Now, if you come, as I can't help thinking you will, I want to give you some minute travelling directions which I think you would do well to observe carefully. And first let me repeat my suggestion that you borrow money right at home if you can, so as to save this insupportable delay. On further reflection I think you had better have $175. in your pocket when you start, as it is possible that they will charge you extra for your trunk over the Pacific R. R., if it is much above regulation weight. Be sure to take a lunch basket or box with you, enough to make ten or a dozen meals from, and if you put cans in, take something with you for opening them, which the porter of the sleeping car will do for you, if you ask him. Have $5. dollars in silver to use this side of Colfax, Cal., the last point where currency is received. . . .

But I forgot to say that you say that you had better provide yourself at the start with a "Pacific R. R. folder," such as you saw me have, to tell you the stations and points of interest on the road. You change cars at Ogden [Utah]. As soon as you stop there, go to the Pullman office and get your berth for San Francisco. Don't offer silver for anything you buy anywhere unless it is demanded. On the afternoon of your last day's journey a man will come through the cars who will take your checks, giving you a receipt for them, and deliver your baggage at 737 *Pine Street*. Pay him 75 cts. if he asks for it. Beware of strangers on the journey, but if you meet some gentleman whom you are sure you could trust, he might give you some advice or assistance, perhaps. I don't think, however, if you follow my directions carefully, you need have any trouble. I am sure I hope so, darling. I will keep watch in the papers for your coming (give your full name and address to the man who will call for it the day before you reach here) and will meet you at Oakland, either on the wharf, or on the ferry-boat. If by any chance I should miss you at either of these places, wait at the wharf at S. F. a few minutes before taking conveyance for 737 Pine St. Your lunch basket the porter on the cars will take care of for you, handing it to you whenever you want it. There, that is all.

And now, my Belle, you don't know how happy your first letter, which I received yesterday morning, made me for a time. Its loving words were very, very sweet to me, but they only revived my drooping spirits for a short time, for . . . [letter incomplete]

III · WILLIAM P. FROST, JR., TO MARY BLUNT FROST

My Dear Grandmother   25 October 1874   San Francisco

Perhaps a few lines from your faraway grandson would not be without interest to you in your lonesome hours. Let me see; it is nearly two years now since I saw you last, and almost as long since I left home. These two years have brought many changes to me. They have changed me from a country schoolmaster to a city editor. They have brought me a wife and a baby now seven months old. They have sent me away across the continent 3500 miles from home. And what will the next two years do for me? Well, we shall see. So much may happen to us in this busy world that it is the heart of prudence not to count too certainly on the future. My present expectation is that California will continue to be my home for some time to come. The climate, I think, agrees with me excellently. It is a healthy place in which to raise children, and so I may stay here until I can take home to their grandparents a whole car-load of young Frosts. We are all well, particularly the little boy, who, in fact, has never seen a really sick day in his short life. Belle says she is going to have his pictures taken this week, and then you shall have a chance to see how much like his fa-ther and grandfather he is. I know you will say he could not be mistaken for anybody but his papa's own boy. I was so sorry when I heard that Prescott and Teenie had lost their little one. It would be hard for us to lose little Bob now, but it would be much harder if he should be carried off after reaching the age that Pres.'s little girl did. I suppose, grandmother, you hope that you never will have to change your residence again during the rest of your days. Your years are too heavy upon you now for you to be changing your home. Father's letters tell me that you are getting feebler year by year. Long since you passed the boundary of three score and ten. I know you are ready when you are called. But I hope the call will not come for a good while yet. Aunt Sarah, I believe, has suffered much from rheu-matism of late. I was glad to read in a recent letter from home that she was somewhat better. I wonder how uncle Messer likes his new home. Little Mabel must have grown to quite a big girl now. Give my love to her, to Pres. and his wife, and to aunt and uncle. Belle desires to be remembered to you . . . [letter incomplete]

IV · ISABELLE MOODIE FROST TO WILLIAM PRESCOTT FROST, JR.

1 November [1876]
Columbus, Ohio

My Darling Husband,

Yours of October 23rd reached me on Monday last. You seemed well and happy, enthusiastically so over politics. I sin-cerely hope that such severe labor will not make you sick. It

scarcely seems wise for you with so many duties pressing on
every side to do so much. I know how deeply interested you are
in the present campaign, but you should not entirely forget
that excellent proverb suited to all kinds of warfare,

"Discretion is the better part of valor."

I hope for your sake that the Democrats will win. As for myself
I would like a change just to satisfy my curiosity. I wish to see
if the Democratic party can get public affairs out of their
present mess.

But, Darling, do please take good care of yourself. I do
want you to be well and strong so that you may be spared to
your dear ones a long time. It is such a blessed thing for people happily married to grow old together and to live to take
care and love their little ones. Robbie keeps pretty well at
present. Of the baby I can only write ditto to what I have already written — healthy, pretty, and good. I am sure she will
be good with her papa if he will not tease her.

About naming her I am again undecided and will not
entirely make up my mind until I see you. The folks in the
house are all so devoted to her and take care of her so much
that I feel quite like naming her for some one of them. Florence seems to worship her, and since her return from Cincinnati I take her only to dress and nurse.

Columbus in spite of hard times is just as gay as ever;
visiting and visitors are the order of the day. This morning
Cornie Doherty's sister took Robert and me for a drive. The
weather being charming we enjoyed it extremely. I observed
as many changes in the city as I see in the people. It has
grown wonderfully, now claiming 50,000 inhabitants.

This afternoon callers. This evening callers. Bob is just as
queer as ever about some things. Scarcely looks at lady visitors
but is most happy to climb upon gents knees. A young gentleman called this evening one of my old pupils and it was quite
amusing to see the devotion of the little fellow. In saying "God
bless dear papa" before going to bed he insisted on saying also
God bless Mr Jamieson.

I fear you will not enjoy my letter very much for my head
is tired with company which makes thinking anything but
easy.

I shall leave about the last of Nov or the 1st of Dec and
shall prefer to come overland. The week before starting I will

write the exact day. There are two lady friends here who are expecting to go about the same time therefore I will lay my plans to leave when they do. A Mrs Noble and Mrs Doherty. The latter had an invitation to return in M. Latham's private car but does not wish to go as soon as he intends.

They are expecting me to make a visit in Cincinnati. I will probably go about the 16th of this month remaining there until I leave for home. When you send the money for the trip, put it in Alexander Proctor's name Cincinnati Ohio. Care James Gamble 26 Clark St. If my funds get low before I leave for C I will borrow a little from Effie and pay her when you send me. It is so dirty here and we are so continually on the go that I need lots of clean clothes. There is no time for anything but company. Tonight Florence, "little sister," Robbie and I go out to Bartlett's to tea. They send their carriage for us and will send us home. Poor Mrs B is very much changed, taking her husband's death so hard.

I am enjoying myself ever so much. The constant excitement of company is so new that I get a little fatigued by evening. It is quite enjoyable for a season but I must say I would not like it all the time.

This letter has been laid down and picked up many times since the date was written. I shall look anxiously, almost, for your letters until I leave for home for I am afraid you are overworking yourself. Kisses from the children to darling papa.

With deep love, I remain ever your devoted wife

Belle

All my friends make inquiries about you and those who met you speak of the childrens resemblance to you, particularly Bob's.

V · ISABELLE MOODIE FROST TO SARAH NEWTON

17 June 1883
My dear Sarah   San Francisco, California

And so your dear, good father has been called home. We will not weep that he has gone even though he was dear to us and we love to go back and think of all that was so kind, so true, so genial in him. How well I remember that afternoon sitting under the maples his noble face and head, the pleasant

13

smile and most of all his words of truth. I can even now recall his words. They had the true ring and although the sound had lost some of its accustomed harmony it was only because the earthly part was worn and ready to return to dust, but his soul was never out of tune and it has only sought a sphere where it may be attuned to higher and holier harmonies.

I love to think of such a man in the other world. So soon he will have lost the old and worn look and could you be with him he would appear as you knew him in the vigor of manhood, enhanced of course with a heavenly beauty.

The newspaper notice of him and of your family was very pleasant and in a measure comforting. For while you knew how good and useful his life had been it is a pleasure to know that others appreciate the fact.

Your dear mother will feel the change more than any of the rest. So many years they have gone in and out together, now that she must walk the path without him will make her feel lonely indeed.

Give her my loving sympathy. May the dear Savior be with her to comfort her in her trouble.

Do you hear anything from Henry. I should think this news would have some good influence upon him.

Have I written in answer to your last? I do not remember.

I rejoice that you are so successful in your life work. If we are only faithful in what lies before us when it is all over and we are passing from this scene the thought will make things look brighter. My life is very busy with plain and even homely duties but my hopes are so sweet that I often enjoy what naturally I do not like.

My husband meets with little success that helps us although in his bus[i]ness he gives satisfaction but I have much to be thankful for and most of all that my mind is settled in the matter of religion for you know my nature is religious.

Give my love to Belle and Lucy — Annie I mean — and with loving sympathy for your dear self I am ever your true friend

Belle M. Frost

SALEM AND LAWRENCE · 1885-1900

IN THE AUTUMN of 1885, Robert and Jeanie Frost were en-
rolled as students in the multi-grade schoolroom where their
mother was teaching. Until then "Robbie" had never completed a full year of formal schooling because of childhood ailments which seemed largely traceable to his excruciating
sensitivities. His mother had tutored him at home during the
San Francisco years.

His closest friend at Salem was a lively daredevil classmate, Charlie Peabody, who taught the California boy how to
bend a birch which grew at the edge of the school yard. But in
less than a year Charlie's tomboy sister, Sabra, made such a
strong appeal to "Robbie" that he fell in love with her and even
found the courage to tell her so. Four of the notes he wrote
her, apparently during school hours in the autumn of 1886,
fortuitously survived, forgotten for years in the secret compartment of a wooden pencil box which belonged to Sabra Peabody.
They are the earliest Frost "letters" which have been found to
date.

Frost completed three years of schooling in Salem and
then began to commute to the Lawrence, Massachusetts, high
school. The Peabody children did not continue their formal
education, and the Frost children lost touch with them in
1889, when Mrs. Frost took a better teaching position in Methuen, Massachusetts, and moved her family there. Frost continued at the Lawrence high school.

During his four years of study there, "Robbie" did such
distinguished work that he was graduated as co-valedictorian
in the Class of 1892, sharing honors with Elinor Miriam White.
The co-valedictorians fell in love and became secretly engaged
during that summer. In the fall he was sent to Dartmouth College by his paternal grandfather, who hoped the boy might become a lawyer. But Frost had already grown impatient with
formal schooling and he remained at Dartmouth less than a

15

semester. He left to teach an eighth-grade class in the Methuen public school in the spring of 1893. During the next two years he drifted casually from one odd job to another while pleading with his sweetheart in letter after letter that she should leave college to marry him.

Elinor Miriam White, the daughter of a Universalist minister in Lawrence who had turned cabinet-maker after renouncing his faith, was at St. Lawrence University in Canton, New York. She was determined to earn her degree before she married, even though her very firm resistance was the cause of intermittent estrangements which marred the courtship. She also insisted that her future husband establish himself in a career or at least have steady and remunerative employment before the wedding.

Prospects seemed to brighten for Frost when he sold his first poem, "My Butterfly: An Elegy," to a celebrated New York periodical, *The Independent*. The Wards, a brother and sister then working on the editorial staff of *The Independent*, soon came to meet Frost, and their acquaintance with him gradually grew into a friendship. In 1894, soon after the Wards had praised the literary qualities of "My Butterfly," Frost took five of his poems to a Lawrence printer and had them made up into a very thin book which he called *Twilight*. The entire edition consisted of two leather-bound copies, one for Elinor White, the other for himself. But when his fiancée seemed insufficiently impressed by the gift, and also seemed to be showing interest in several suitors at St. Lawrence University, Frost despondently destroyed his own copy of the book. Immediately thereafter he struck an even more dramatic posture of despondency when he tried to throw his life away in unconvincing fashion by making a mysterious trip to and through the Dismal Swamp of Virginia.

In the spring of 1895, Frost began to work for his mother in a private school she had opened in Lawrence. Elinor joined the small teaching staff in the fall, having completed her four-year college course in three years. With the obstacles thus removed, the couple was married on 19 December 1895. They continued to work as teachers until almost the time when their first child was born, a son they named Elliott.

Even before that, Frost's very limited success as a poet and his growing interest in teaching made him decide to study Greek and Latin with a view to becoming a teacher of both subjects in a high school. Enrolling as a special student at Harvard College in the autumn of 1897, he stayed there for nearly two full academic years, at the same time continuing to work in his mother's private school. Near the end of March 1899, he formally withdrew from Harvard to give more help to his mother.

Doctor's orders and the threat of tuberculosis turned Frost from school-teaching to farming. At first he rented a house in the country outside Methuen and set himself up in the poultry business. It was hard work, and neither he nor his wife had the strength for it. The death of their first child on 8 July 1900 of *cholera infantum* came as an almost unbearable shock to both parents. Late in the fall of 1900 they moved to a small farm in Derry, New Hampshire, purchased for them by Frost's paternal grandfather. A friend of high-school days, Carl Burrell, stayed with them long enough to teach Frost the rudiments of farming. Soon after they had settled in Derry, Frost's mother died of cancer at the age of fifty-six. She was buried beside her husband in Lawrence, in the same cemetery plot where young Elliott Frost had been interred.

Thus the second phase of Frost's life came to a close, burdening him with griefs and discouragements.

1 · To Sabra Peabody

Age 12

Dear Sabe,   [September 1886]   [Salem, N. H.]

I read your letter with great pleasure and will try and answer it in a very few lines. I liked those leavs you gave me and put them in my speller to press. I have got [to] read a composition after recess and I hate to offaly.

I have got to stop now so as to learn my Geography.

From your loving   Rob.

2 · To Sabra Peabody

love   Don't show this

Dear Sabe,

I enjoyed reading your letter very much. You need not excuse yourself about writing for mine is as bad. Those nuts I gave you were not as good as I expected but I am glad you liked them. As usual I cant think of much to write. I wish you were at the supper last night but we did not have much fun because their were not enough there. I suppose Eva [Peabody] hasnt gotten back yet. Are you going to the Hall to-morrow night. I must stop now and remember and write soon.

From your loving   Rob

3 · To Sabra Peabody

Dear Sabe,-

I read your loving letter with great pleasure as I always do. As you could not think of much to say neither can I. I hope you will have a good time tonight and I guess you will and I would like to go if I didnt have to go some where else.

Ever your faithful lover.   Rob

4 · To Sabra Peabody

Dear Sabe,

I will answer your letter to let you know that I am well and hope you are the same. About me liking Lida [Storer] better than you you are all wrong because I like you twice as much as I do her and always have thought more of you than any other girl I know of. I thought you were going to the entertainment the other night but I didn't see you there. I saw Eva Hattie and your mother there. There is no fun in getting mad every so [often so] lets see if we cant keep friends Im sure I am willing. I know I have not treated you as I ought to sometimes and sometimes I don't know wheather you are mad or not and we have gotten mad and then we would get friends again ever since Westons party when I first came here. There are not many girls I like but when I like them I fall dead in love with them and there are not many I like just because I can have some fun with them like I can Lida but I like you because I cant help myself and when I get mad at you I feel mad at myself to.   From your loveing   Rob

5 · To William Hayes Ward

HOPEFULLY RF began to send manuscripts of his early poems to publishers of periodicals even while he was a student at the Lawrence High School. He thus became familiar with rejection slips long before the day in March 1894 when he received his first acceptance: a letter from William Hayes Ward, the editor of the celebrated New York periodical, *The Independent*. With the letter was a check for fifteen dollars sent in return for the manuscript of "My Butterfly: An Elegy." RF's elation was reflected in the following reply.

Editor of the Independant,

age 20

Dear Sir:-   28 March [1894]   Lawrence, Mass.
          The memory of your note will be a fresh pleasure to me when I awaken for a good many mornings to come; which may as well confirm you in the belief that I am still young. I am. The poem you have is the first of mine that any publication has accepted. At about the same time however that I sent you this, I disposed of three others in a similar way in other quarters. As yet they are not returned. As for submitting more of my work, you may imagine I shall be only too glad to avail myself of your kindly interest. Nevertheless since I have but recently discovered my powers, I have, of course, no great amount of verses in store and furthermore, being still inexperienced of myself, I cannot easily tell when I will have. But I shall not forget my obligations.
          If you mean what might be called the legitimate education I have received when you speak of "training" and "line of study," I hope that the quality of my poem would seem to account for far more of this than I have really had. I am only graduated of a public high school. Besides this, a while ago, I was at Dartmouth College for a few months until recalled by necessity. But this inflexible ambition trains us best, and to love poetry is to study it. Specifically speaking, the few rules I know in this art are my own afterthoughts, or else directly formulated from the masterpieces I reread.
          I sincerely hope I have done nothing to make you overestimate me. It cannot be, though, for rather than equal what I have written and be satisfied, I will idle away an age accumulating a greater inspiration.
          There is no objection to using my name with the poem.
                    Yours   Robert Lee Frost.
                    Tremont St., Lawrence, Mass.

6 · TO SUSAN HAYES WARD

IN THE OFFICE of the New York *Independent*, the literary editor was Miss Susan Hayes Ward, sister of the editor in chief. Beginning in

April of 1894, and continuing for many years, Miss Ward wrote sympathetic and encouraging letters to RF. Here follows the first of his many letters to her during their long friendship.

Dear Miss Ward,   22 April 1894   Lawrence

It is just such a letter as you wrote me that I have been awaiting for two years. Hitherto all the praise I have received has been ill-advised and unintelligent; all the criticism, this general one upon the rueful fact that I, once the friend of so and so, should have at last turned poetaster. So that something definite and discriminating is very welcome. My thanks unlimited! Yet the consideration is hardly due me. Take my word for it that poem ["My Butterfly"] exaggerates my ability. You must spare my feelings when you come to read these others, for I haven't the courage to be a disappointment to anyone. Do not think this artifice or excess of modesty, though, for to betray myself utterly, such an one am I that even in my failures I find all the promise I require to justify the astonishing magnitude of my ambition.

You ask to know more of me. This is certainly very tempting. It might well throw one into a talking trance which nothing could dispell but a reversal of the charm. I am inclined to think, too, that I have several attributes akin to those of that Franco-Russian introspectionist (whose name I dare not attempt in writing.) But whatever the inducements to the contrary I must promise to content myself with but a slight sketch.

When I am well I read a great deal and like a nearsighted person follow the text closely. I read novels in the hope of strengthening my executive faculties. The Polish triology "With Fire and Sword," "The Deluge" and "Pan Michael" are engaging me at present. Thomas Hardy has taught me the good use of a few words and, refering still to me, "struck the simple solemn." And as opposed to this man, Scott and Stevenson inspire me, by their prose, with the thought that we Scotchmen are bound to be romanticists — poets. Then as for poems my favorites are and have been these: Keats' "Hyperion," Shelley's "Prometheus," Tenneson's "Morte D'Arthur," and Browning's "Saul" — all of them about the giants. Besides these I am fond of the whole collection of Palgrave's. So far everything looks auspicious. But it is necessary to admit that I teach "orthography" in a district school: and that in the fitness of things, the association of Eugene Aram with children in this capacity seems no more incongruous than my own. In fact so wholly uncongenial is the work that it has become for me a mere test of physical endurance. For several weeks now when not teaching I have spent my time lying around either consciously sleeping or unconsciously waking and in both cases irresponsibly iratable to the last degree. It is due to my nerves — they are susceptible to sound. Consequently the prospect is not bright — for the immediate future at least. When in this condition I can neither read nor write: nevertheless I find a few hours for study and, as I say, always entertain great hopes.

I have never read Lanier's poetry nor the volume of his you mention. I have read no technical works. The extent of my studying now is a little Greek and, for relaxation, French. Of course I have a great desire to master the former for reasons that would be commonly given. Homer is very difficult for me as yet, though, and I am often entirely discouraged. But I assure you, some time, money or no money, I shall prove myself able to do everything but spell.

I have not succeeded in revising the poem ["My Butterfly"] as you requested. That Aztec consonant syllable of mine, "l", spoils a word I am very sorry to dispense with. The only one I think of to substitute for it is "eddying" which of course weakens the impression — although I am not sure but that it merely changes it. The would-be cadence howe'er may be incorrect also, but I did not suspect it at the time. It is used in the same sense as "at any rate" would be in that case. But I cannot sustain the usage by any example I have in mind: and when once I doubt an idiom my ear hesitates to vouch for it thereafter. The line, "These were the unlearned things," is wretched. It refers directly to the two lines preceeding and indirectly to the answer inevitable to that question "And did you think etc." which answer would be, God did nevertheless! Yet the line is manifestly redundant as well as retruse and I must invent one to supplant it. I shall prefer to hear from you again, if it is not asking too much, before I return the copy, not only so that I may gain time but also that I may have the benefit of your further advice.

Yours by right of discovery   R. L. Frost.

Two of these are the returned poems and the other is no better.

7 · To Susan Hayes Ward

Dear Miss Ward,-   10 June 1894   Lawrence

It is clear this letter must be in the nature of a defence. Since last I wrote I hope I have aged enough not to seem so callow and distasteful as I used: at any rate I have been thoroughly overhauled in search of affectations.

Yet even as I am, my inclination would be to give thanks immoderately for that volume of Lanier's poems. As you expected I have been very much interested in the memorial; and I have been enthused over what I conceive to be Lanier's theories of art. I wish I had the Elizabethan knack of expressing gratitude.

Will you allow me to correct several wrong impressions I seem to have given you? My pride sees nothing degrading in teaching. We provincials affect Bohemianism — experience, give us experience! I have sold newspapers "on the streets of" San Francisco and worked in the mills and on the farms of New England. My pride is peculiar.

And my friends! how have I betrayed my friends! True, they have not encouraged me much as a poet: but if I were so accomplished as to be able to improvise a few heroic metres for them by the camp-fire next summer, be sure they would appreciate me. Written poetry is rather ineffectual after all, unless artists are the readers of it.

It has been painful for me trying to induce a passion like the one that is the spirit of my poem. I am afraid I can not revise the thing. I am greatly dissatisfied with it now. Do you not think it would be well to suppress it. If I am not overworked this summer I promise to write you something better by far. Nevertheless I have cancelled one line, altered two, and now the whole is at your disposal.

Explain my cancelled line this way. I close the idea, Jealous of immortality. (tentative period) Then there is an afterthought. In a way everything is immortal that outlives me. Things I don't care for will do this. You have not — you were fair. (Then repeat) Jealous of immortality — (And add) In one so fair at any rate.   Really   Robert L. Frost.

8 · To Susan Hayes Ward

22 August 1894

Dear Miss Ward:- 35 Cambridge St. Boston

Surely you have not received my last letter. I shall be sorry if it is too late to arrange to meet you. Write to me at least.

For I percieve that my childishness in regard to poem (said poem) may have become wearisome. It is very trying to be noticed, you know. But give me another chance: I may have disqualified myself for a political career by one foolish act but I cannot have for a literary one:- all the cannonized afford me consolation.

I am learning to spell.
I am writing better poetry.

It is only a matter of time now when I shall throw off the mask and declare for literateur mean it poverty or riches.

You are amid real poetry, I presume; and I can imagine that a conventional verse or stanza and the familiar see-saw of phrases in antithesis, would distemper you.

Sincerely   Robert L. Frost.

8-a · Maurice Thompson to William Hayes Ward

10 November 1894

Dear Dr Ward   Crawfordsville, Indiana

You asked me to look at the poem, *My Butterfly,* in this week's paper, by Mr. Frost.

I am a trifle dizzy over the election, feel as if a hogshead of salt had rolled over me; but I am not stupid enough yet to fail to see the extreme beauty of that little ode. It gives me a pang to know that its author is poor. To be a poet and be poor is a terrible lot. What hope is there? I have felt the gag in my teeth whenever I wanted to sing — and I'm not much of a poet — a gag that can speak and say to me: "No! go grind for bread! Let the rich men like Tennyson and Swinburne and Lowell and Browning and Holmes do the singing; what right has a poor man to waste his time and breath with song?" But all the same were I a rich man that young Frost should not leave school "for financial reasons." Going back to the poem

My Butterfly, it has some secret of genius between the lines, an appeal to sympathy lying deep in one's sources of tenderness; and moreover its art is singular and biting, even where the faulty places are almost obtruded. My wife read it aloud to me the other evening when my eyes ached after too hard a day's work; and it made me ashamed that I could feel discouraged when I thought of the probable disappointment in store for young Frost all his life long. If I had a chance to say my say to him I should tell him to forget that he ever read a poem and to never pen another rhyme. I told my brother that years ago and now he is a great lawyer instead of a disappointed poet with a gag in his mouth! I was a better lawyer than he when I was lured away by the Muses. If Frost has good health tell him to learn a trade or profession and carry a sling-shot in his pocket for [the Muse] Aoede.

Always sincerely yours   Maurice Thompson

9 · To Susan Hayes Ward

Dear Miss Ward,-   4 December 1894   Lawrence

Now that you have ceased expecting to is the time you hear from me. The occasion is, or was, the appearance in print under your supervision of my first poem. I am going to thank you. Four weeks ago and until Friday last I was in Virginia, North Carolina, and Maryland, very liberally and without address, so that I have not been aware of my own doings as expressed in the phrase I "published a poem." That is the point of points:- I thank you tardily because I for my part have been out of time a little while, and thank you because you and not I published a poem, a work that certainly requires qualities I lack. And the poem does look well — don't you think it does?

Before proceeding further I percieve I must assume an attitude, or else endanger the coherency of my remarks, — for my natural attitude is one of enthusiasm verging on egotism and thus I always confuse myself trying to be modest. It is my rule to be despondent to be dignified (or coherent) and I might be cynical for the same purpose, but really unless it be enthusiastically I am at a loss to know how to comport myself on the present occasion. You see I am just returned from experiences so desperately absorbing that I am nothing morbid now and can enjoy the poem as freshly as if it were but lately written and I had not since wasted eight months in ineffectual aspiration.

Yes, I think sound is an element of poetry, one but for which imagination would become reason. I justify the use of dialect in this way: it contributes to the illusion (perhaps) and gives the artist the courage of his imaginings. Kipling says nearly all he says under the influence of sound. I am so fond of sound that I was wishing the other day he would write some more poetry. Listen to that! — when we generally read poetry because we are in the business and it is written.

I have one or two poems to send you when I find time to revise them. Sincerely Robert L. Frost.

10 · To Susan Hayes Ward

THE SECOND PARAGRAPH of this letter quite clearly implies that RF sent two poems with his letter for Miss Ward's consideration. But all of the poems which RF enclosed with his letters to the Wards were separated from them before the files of *The Independent* were acquired by the Henry E. Huntington Library. It is therefore impossible to determine which poems were sent in which letters.

Dear Miss Ward,- 28 December 1894 Lawrence

It is no use: I must let you know now. All the thought of visiting you, so many things to talk with you about filled my mind, seeming to urge as necessary my visiting you, that I was long in realizing the unaltered, patient fact that I could not. I want to find some good friend of mine whom I can satisfactorily authorize to admit for them the incapacity of my enemies. I will not repeat what they say. But did not *you* say the line Its two banks etc. [in "My Butterfly"] was intelligible? O I had many things to talk about, and I am very very sorry that, as you express it, it will be unwise for me to reach New York.

There is no need to introduce these verses. I have reason to hope that you will discover their purpose unaided. But do not be too hard on the untitled American one, because I like it and it is not American.

With thanks, regrets, and best wishes,
Rob't L. Frost.

11 · To Susan Hayes Ward

Dear Miss Ward,-   30 January 1895   Lawrence

You are not to pardon my remissness: but it is the truth that you have wished me well to such good purpose that I have been busy night and day for two weeks. I am a reporter on a local newspaper!

You will guess what I have been thinking about all this time — especially just after waking. There are those they can harm with impunity, but in my case they will make me a martyr. I am endorsed now by a professional critic.

If it is seriously I must speak, I undertake a future. I cannot believe that poem was merely a chance. I will surpass it. Maurice Thompson will not hope to discourage me by praising me surely? I would tell him that he is not so inscrutable as he might be when he does so inconsistently.

I needed your good words and as you see they have not been in vain. You give me a new courage: at last I feel as if I could afford to be modest.

My newspaper work requires a brave effort. They assure me I have much to learn particularly in the way of writing; but what care I: I have done the best I can with what I know: and if I know everything I have reached my limit. Let them teach me.

I am saving you one or two unpretentious poems — concerning which I have my doubts.

Yours sincerely   Robert L. Frost.

12 · To Susan Hayes Ward

25 January 1896
Dear Miss Ward,   Central Building   Lawrence

Perhaps you had better not waite any longer. I have done my level best, in the time that has elapsed since last you heard from me, to make good my promise as a poet. But I fear I am not a poet, or but a very incomprehensible one.

The enclosed are an excuse for writing to you, nothing more. You will not find what you want in them, although it is not for me to say anything against them, who have learned to be thankful for little things.

Do not think but what I would have been glad to hear from you any time these six months, but of course I could not expect to. Possibly I may now when you come to understand the good and sufficient reasons for my long silence.

Robert Lee Frost.

13 · To Susan Hayes Ward

Dear Miss Ward,   8 July 1896   Lawrence

You are to hear from me now only because school is closed and I am quite rested having slept more or less soundly for a whole week night and day. Well I did what I tried to do so that the future is not so uncertain though it is not with success as it is with failure which is final, while success to a coward is only suspense, the most awful of tortures.

You sent me a poem by John Bennett. You didn't say what you thought of it but if you will kindly do so to Mrs Smith, for *me*. There could hardly be two opinions in regard to it. Tell Mrs Smith, Very nice. O say! — Yes I am right. Upon inquiry I find that it is a John Bennett who designed the cover of the current Chap-Book. It must be the same. Why he's somebody already.

I fear me my idiom is greatly confused tonight and I shall not write very much. O these Yorkshiremen. One would do well to avoid them when he can and as for walking abroad with them all day and seeing things through their eyes, it is unpardonable. I verily believe there is such a thing as not knowing whether you have opened your lips or not. Speech is a strange thing and however little thought preceeds it, it is still distinct from thought and the proof is that the one may be utterly at variance with the other and the thought be no less definite.

But to the point. If it is not too late I am anxious to avail myself of your kindness and publish one more poem before I die. It is ten to one however that you are off on a vacation and this will not come to your notice for some time. Whatever happens is for the best. You are not obliged to change your plans out of consideration for me. I know you wouldn't. I offer you my suggestion for the closing line of the poem nevertheless in case you are still at liberty to use it.

And overhead the petrel, wafted wide.*

* The line quoted above "for the closing line of the poem" is the closing line of "Caesar's Lost Transport Ships," the first draft of which had been written around 1892. The poem was printed in *The Independent*, 14 January 1897.

27

This is tedious and I know it and I would fain curb myself but cannot. There is one thing I can do. I can make an end: which I hereby do, with rememberences for all in particular.   R. L. Frost.

14 · To Susan Hayes Ward

Dear Miss Ward,   15 August 1896   Lawrence
You were very considerate in the matter of the title. I presume the other poem as emended was not satisfactory. Will you let me know?

There are other things I would like to know. Write me if you are not too busy.

We are about to move down town again to open school. I am becoming dangerously interested in that concern, to the exclusion I fear of things more lofty. [Don't believe him.] *

Miss Ward has been enjoying the warm weather? *Now* what has my friend to say about life in the city. There is much to be done for the poor isn't there if Bryan were only the man to do it.

But I must hear from you directly before I continue. I have lost touch with mankind and must approach the individual circumspectly.

Remember me to Miss Hetta please. Tell her that I am botanizing will I nill I. You make the laws and an enthusiast here is found to enforce them. I am overwhelmed with books on the subject. Mrs. W. S. Dana [*How to Know the Wild Flowers*] and I don't know who all!

Be sure to write.   R. L. Frost.

15 · To Susan Hayes Ward

Dear Miss Ward:-   27 December 1896   Lawrence
Don't think because I haven't written I haven't once thought of you all this time. I have thought of you often and as often tried to write to you but in vain. It is just possible you do not understand this: all I can say is *I* do, though to no purpose. I wish I were reporting again and writing so much a day under compulsion. Then you would get the letters!

---

* RF's bracketed insertion; the first of two which occur in the letters selected. The other occurs in letter 28.

The last I heard of you you were on your way to Bath Me., *not* to see Mr Sewell. You were opening the campaign so to speak in the Republican interest. Since then how many calamitous things have not happened to the disappointment of how many people, particularly in the state of Colorado.

As nothing that happens matters much and as most of my thoughts are about myself I am always at a loss for likely subject matter. I am the father of a son if that is anything. What would William Canton say under such circumstances. My soul what wouldn't he say!

It has dawned upon me that those were proofs you sent me and should have been corrected and returned. They were all right as they were. Many thanks.

And a Happy New Year! May you discover an immortal genius and enter into your earthly reward. If ever I improve beyond recognition I will let you discover me over in part payment for all you have done. You think I couldn't disguise my handwriting?*   Sincerely yours,   Robert L. Frost

16 · To LeBaron Russell Briggs

Dear Sir: 11 September 1897   Lawrence

You are the one it seems for me to submit my case to if you will be so kind as to consider it. You will discover the propriety as I proceed.

I desire to enter Harvard this fall if possible as a candidate for a degree from the outset. It came to me as a surprise only the other day that I might reasonably hope to do so consequently I find myself somewhat unprepared for examination. This is the great difficulty. I graduated from the Lawrence High School as many as five years ago (having in 1891 passed examinations for admission to Harvard occupying seven hours for which I hold a certificate.) It is true that since that time I have been teaching school and tutoring more or less in Latin Algebra and Geometry. Still my studies are all at loose ends. In particular I have neglected my Greek. If proficiency in English were any consideration, I make no doubt I could pass an examination in that. You will find verses of my inditing in the current number of the Independent and others better in back numbers. I might possibly pass in French also and in

* The valediction and signature of this letter are in the handwriting of Elinor M. Frost.

Physics and Astronomy for that matter but in Greek I fear not. You'll say it doesn't sound very encouraging.

Another embarrassing circumstance is the fact that once upon a time I left Dartmouth without having applied to the proper authorities of that paternalism for an honerable dismissal. I stood not upon the order of my going but went incontinently — for reasons I am free to explain. I assure you the matter will bear looking into.

This is the whole case not very clearly or succinctly stated. The question is what will you advise me to do. Let me say that if I enter college it must be this year or never. It will be hard if a fellow of my age and general intelligence (!) must be debarred from an education for want of technical knowledge representing less than two months work. All I ask is to be admitted. I don't care how many conditions you encumber me with. I will take the examinations if you say so, or I will enter as a special. I am anxious to hear from you soon. Rev. John Hayes of Salem or Rev. W. Wolcott of this city will answer questions with regard to me.

Respectfully   Robert L Frost

16-a · LeBaron Russell Briggs to Robert Frost

Harvard College,

My dear Mr. Frost: Cambridge, March 31st, 1899

I am glad to testify that your dismissal from College is honorable; that you have had excellent rank here, winning a Detur as a result of your first year's work; and that I am sorry for the loss of so good a student. I shall gladly have you refer to me for your College record.

Sincerely yours,   L. B. R. Briggs,

Mr. R. L. Frost.   Dean

DERRY AND PLYMOUTH · 1900-1912

IF ANY ONE PERIOD could be counted as most important in the life of Robert Frost, for both the man and the poet, it would be the nine years at the farm in Derry, New Hampshire, from the fall of 1900 to the fall of 1909. The period began in a mood of complete discouragement, even despondency. Driven into the country by his doctor's warnings, Frost feared that he might be suffering from the same disease that had killed his father at an early age. But his half-serious and half-casual pleasure in playing farmer and poultryman had a good effect on his general health. At first very shy and diffident in the new community, he soon began to study, admire, and imitate the peculiarities of his farmer neighbors. In their lives, and in his own farm chores, he found new subject matter for poetry and a new attitude toward the mingled pain and pleasure of cherishing. During those nine years he wrote almost all the poems of *A Boy's Will,* several of the dramatic narratives of *North of Boston,* many of the pieces of *Mountain Interval,* and enough other poems to permit the appearance of at least one "Derry poem" in each new collection he was to publish.

Compared with his neighbors, who eked out marginal livings from their farms, Frost was relatively wealthy. His paternal grandfather gave him financial support, while still retaining legal possession of the farm property. When he died on 10 July 1901, William Prescott Frost left a will stating that his grandson was to have "free use and occupancy" of the farm during the next ten years, after which time the farm would legally become his grandson's property. It also specified that in the ten-year period Frost would receive an annual sum of five hundred dollars from a trust fund that was a part of the estate; that thereafter he would receive eight hundred dollars annually, and his sister, Jeanie, would receive a smaller annual payment, until both interest and principal were exhausted. Any neighboring farmer would have considered the initial annuity of five hundred dollars more than enough to make ends meet.

Unlike his neighbors, Frost refused to be bound by farming. On two important occasions his literary interests took him with his growing family to New York City. Another excuse for vacationing and travel was provided by his annual attacks of hay fever, which became increasingly troublesome. In the summer of 1905, and for several years after that, he spent at least part of the hay-fever season in the White Mountains at Bethlehem. Further neglecting his farm, he started to teach full time at Pinkerton Academy in the fall of 1906. Three years later he gave up the farm entirely and settled his family in Derry Village, a move prompted partly by the educational needs of his children and partly by his desire to be nearer to Pinkerton.

As a teacher Frost employed so many unconventional classroom procedures that his originality attracted the attention of Henry Clinton Morrison, then State Superintendent of Public Instruction. Much to his own surprise and discomfort, Frost let himself be drafted to talk before teachers' conventions on how to interest students in reading and writing. In the fall of 1911, when Ernest L. Silver gave up his duties as Principal of Pinkerton Academy to become the head of the New Hampshire State Normal School at Plymouth, Morrison arranged to have Frost go there with Silver.

But the poet grew tired of teaching as he had earlier grown tired of farming, and he led his family into daydream discussions of possible travels in foreign countries. Any distant hideaway would do for Frost if only he could isolate himself, as a stranger, and get more writing done. Suddenly and impulsively, out of all that dreaming, a choice was made. As Elinor Frost later phrased it (see letter 38-a), ". . . we decided to come to England and find a little house in one of the suburbs of London, and two weeks from the day of our decision, we were on our way out of Boston Harbor."

The financial means for that exciting venture were obtained from the sale of the Derry farm in November 1911 and the increased annuity payment from his grandfather's estate in the same year.

17 · To Susan Hayes Ward

FARMING and writing contended throughout RF's years on the Derry farm; one indication of the struggle is in the following letter, written only a few months after the Frosts moved to Derry. The complete heading of this letter is recorded because it indicates a discrepancy worth noting. RF got his mail in the West Derry post office; but his farm was actually three miles south of Derry Village. For purposes of editorial clarification, the heading given after this is simply Derry rather than the post office address of West Derry.

15 January 1901

Dear Miss Ward   Lock Box 140   West Derry, N. H.

Perhaps you will care to know how authorship progresses. I send you this selection from the poems I have been writing with a view to a volume some day. If you can use it I shall be glad to have you.   Sincerely   R. L. Frost

18 · To the Editor of *Farm-Poultry*

IN 1903, while RF was engaged primarily with poultry farming in Derry, he turned to the writing of fiction and published a total of eleven sketches in two magazines: *The Eastern Poultryman* and *The Farm-Poultry Semi-Monthly*. (For bibliographical details and for the texts of these eleven sketches, see *Robert Frost, Farm-Poultryman* edited by Edward Connery Lathem and Lawrance Thompson.)

One of the sketches, published by RF in *Farm-Poultry* for 15 December 1903, was a straight piece of factual reporting entitled "Three Phases of the Poultry Industry," and devoted to descriptions of three picturesque farms near Derry. Unfortunately, that article mingled fiction with fact on just one point, and thus betrayed Frost's attempts to pose as an expert. He made the mistake of claiming that his friend and neighbor, John A. Hall, owned some extraordinary geese: "Mr. Hall's geese roost in the trees even in winter." Dryly challenging that statement in a letter to the editor, a Massachusetts farmer named H. R. White concluded with mock-serious Yankee wit, "Now I am 45 years old and have been among geese all my life time, and I can never remember seeing a goose in a tree. I thought if I could get a breed of that kind I could dispense with coops."

Commenting on Mr. White's letter, the editor of *Farm-Poultry* wrote, "Mr. Frost will have to explain." And so he did, in two letters; but he made another factual error in the first of them. It appeared in *Farm Poultry* for 15 February 1904, as follows:

Editor FARM-POULTRY :-

In reply to Mr. White's (and yours) of recent date in regard to the error in the article on Mr. Hall's place, there is this to say:-

Geese would sleep out, or float out, let us say, where hens would roost in the trees. To be sure. But what more natural, in speaking of geese in close connection with hens, than to speak of them as if they *were* hens? "Roost in the trees," has here simply suffered what the grammarians would call attraction from the subject with which it should be in agreement to the one uppermost in the mind. That is all. But the idea will have to stand, viz., that Mr. Hall's geese winter out, — and that is the essential thing. Mr. White is not after geese that roost in the trees, but geese that don't need coops. Well, Mr. Hall has them that prefer not to use coops, whether they need them or not. My impression is that he has them in several varieties, and I'll risk my impression. But Mr. Hall is a good fellow and will be glad to tell Mr. White about his geese himself — doubtless, also, to do business with him.   R. L. F.

19 · To the Editor of *Farm-Poultry*

THE EDITOR of *Farm-Poultry* began his comment on letter 18: "Mr. Frost seems not to be aware of the fact that geese generally remain out of doors by choice practically all the time. The same thing may be said of ducks. My Indian Runner ducks (now deceased) would stay out in a snow storm from daylight to dark rather than go into a comfortable shed where they were well sheltered and amply provided with bedding. . . ."

Before that editorial corrective had time to appear in print, RF tried to extricate himself further by writing again in his own defense, this time a letter for the signature of the relatively illiterate John Hall. Obviously anticlimactic, the letter thus forged was published in the issue of *Farm-Poultry* for 1 March 1904 under the caption, "Geese Don't Roost, but Some Ducks Do." (For RF's retrospectively humorous comment on this delicate literary episode, and his acknowledgment of authorship of this letter, see letter 45.)

Editor FARM-POULTRY :-

I noticed Mr. H. R. White's letter in your paper asking about the kind of geese I keep that sleep out in the winter. They are Toulouse, Embden, and Buff. They don't roost in trees. I don't know how Mr. Frost made that mistake, for of course he knows better.

We have often talked about the way they take to the water

at night, a favorite place for them to hang up being on a stone just under water. A good many nights in winter, as well as in summer, I have no idea where they are; and I think they are better every way out doors as long as there is any water not frozen over. But speaking of geese in trees, I don't suppose Mr. White has ever seen a duck in a tree. I have. And I once had a duck that laid her eggs in a tree high enough to be out of reach from the ground, and brought off twenty-two ducklings. These were Brazilians, and I don't know what they won't do.

It has always seemed strange to me how people succeed in keeping geese shut up. If I shut mine up they begin to be restless right away, and go off in looks, especially plumage. Mr. White needn't think because I let my geese run wild I think any less of them than other folks. They are good ones, — as they ought to be with the advantages I give them. They win, too, where they are shown.

The records in your paper ought to show what they did in Lawrence this year; but I notice they don't. So Mr. Frost was pretty near right about my geese; and if Mr. White wants some good ones that a little rather than not sleep out, I've got them.

JOHN A. HALL

20 · To William Hayes Ward

ONLY SEVEN of RF's poems were accepted for publication by Dr. William Hayes Ward while the latter served as editor of *The Independent*, but RF continued to submit to him. It is probable that "The Trial by Existence" was one of the poems sent with the following letter, the original of which bears a note written apparently by Ward: "The poems sent were uncommonly good." "The Trial by Existence" appeared in *The Independent* 11 October 1906 (see letter 23).

Dear Dr Ward: 24 February 1906   Derry

I trust I do not presume too much on former kindness in addressing these verses to you personally. Sending MS to the Independent can never be quite like sending it anywhere else for me.

I often think of you and your sister in my work. I believe Miss Ward left the staff of the Independent some years ago to write books. Please remember me to her either formally or by showing her any of my verses — whether you can use them or not.   Sincerely yours   Robert Frost

21 · To Susan Hayes Ward

My dear Miss Ward,-   17 July 1906   Derry

My wife will be visiting at Pocantico Hills [New York] next week, and that is so near you I thought I should like to have her call on you, if you happened not to have gone away for your summer vacation. Would there be any afternoon of the week after July Twenty-fourth when it would be convenient for you to see her? Very truly yours   Robert Frost

22 · To Susan Hayes Ward

My Dear Miss Ward,-   29 October 1906   Derry

I suspect from the fact that I saw no proof [galley of "The Trial by Existence"] that I was rushed into print perhaps a little ahead of my turn by favor. Well I am not the one to complain of that, even though as a result I am made to look as if I intended to rhyme life with life and lived in Derby (where the ram lived.) The great thing is to get out where one can be read. That I was read this time I have tangible evidence in a letter from the Vice-Something of a pencil company who liked my idea well enough to want to see it restated in honest prose. The Vice-Something, mind you. His motives for so much flattery would have been less liable to misconstruction had his letterhead and envelope been freer from advertisement of his own goods.

Ever since Elinor came back from New York breathing inspiration, I have been ambitious to get some of my larger thoughts into shape for you; but it seems they won't be driven — not at least by a sick man. There's one about the Demiurge's Laugh (good title?) which if I can take it by surprise some day ought to be made to mean something. Meanwhile there are these. Believe me, it is not from anything like neglect that I have not sent them sooner. Since the ragweed dusted, I have done nothing and written nothing — except my own epitaph provisionally like this:

> There was a poor mortal believer
> Who gave way to a thought of hay fever:
>   He coughed like a cold
>   Till over he rolled
> And went into the hands of a receiver.

A very false gallop of verses which I achieved in despite of my invention and which I insert here with some hesitation, it having met with no especial success in the family. But to my poems. My fear is that you will feel overwhelmed by the number. You need read of them only so long as your patience holds out. Too bad that they are still a little timid. Daring is with me a plant of slow growth — or say health is. But I shall get the right tone yet, give me time.

Last week's Independent came with its only poem a reprint of one that appeared in the Oct. 27th issue. It does seem too bad to waste good space in that way. These things were not thus in the old days when I read your editorial accompanying Hovey's Elegy on the Death of Parsons, and then and there gave you my allegiance whether you had need of it or not. I call it your editorial — I think likely you wrote it. It was in the fall of 1892 and I was at Dartmouth then with C. F. Richardson neglecting my studies for Palgrave, which I had just got hold of. (Halcyon days!) I remember your generosity to Hovey very well: you likened the exaltation of his close to Milton's sunken daystar that yet anon repairs his drooping head. It seems to me like yesterday. And only last spring the Independent took a whole page to declare itself the immemorial friend of poets. But if it expects the slighted poets to believe its protestations, it must not get into the habit of stopping a gap twice with the same poem. Now must it?

Elinor joins me in sending love and wishing you joy of the Winter Town.   Sincerely   Robert Frost

23 · To Susan Hayes Ward

My dear Miss Ward,   26 December 1906   Derry

If the hero as poet has been saying something to give offense, won't you vouchsafe a line to say whether it is about poetry and the Independent, and won't you forgive it if satisfactorily explained? Really there was provocation that you could know nothing about. I had just begun teaching at Pinkerton Academy when my poem about the heretofore ["The Trial by Existence"] turned up in the school library. Its effect was startling. From the moment of its appearance, all the teachers abruptly broke off all but the most diplomatic relations with me. Put to it for a reason, I thought at first that my poem had

37

led them to question my orthodoxy (if not my sanity.) Then I thought that a flock of teachers would be more apt to loathe me for misspelling Derry than for grafting Schopenhauer upon Christianity. Mr Merriam says that I was twice wrong. I had made myself unpopular by the simple act of neglecting to give Pinkerton the credit for harboring the poet that wrote the poem. It was too funny. But while it lasted and I was still guessing, I was rather miserable. Then it was I wrote the letter which I ask you to forgive, but which I know you can't. It seems as if I took these things more seriously than I used to before I was twenty. You must remember, too, that life doesn't look the same away off here as it does in N.Y.

Sincerely   Robert Frost

24 · To Susan Hayes Ward

My dear Miss Ward,   12 January 1907   Derry

So I was not to be pacified until I had gotten a sick friend propped up on pillows to write me a reassuring letter. I am duly ashamed now that I have read the reassuring letter. I might have known that it would be because you were busy or ill if you were silent. But don't for a moment believe that it was anxiety about my poems that made me so blindly inconsiderate.

We have all been miserably sick with grippe, too, so that we know how to sympathise with you on that score — if we are not quite so clear in our provincialism as to what it might mean to miss an oratorio. We humbly trust that you may be able to make it up to yourself for missing that by attending (when you are well and around again) a few selected operas at one house or the other.   Sincerely   Robert Frost

The poems enclosed are not for review.

25 · To Susan Hayes Ward

THE FOLLOWING fragment of a letter, apparently written to Miss Susan Hayes Ward concerning a poem submitted to *The Independent* but not accepted for publication can be dated circumstantially from the reference to the Frosts as "the merest convalescents." During the winter and spring of 1907, RF came close to death from a severe case of pneumonia, and recovered very slowly. On 18 June 1907 Elinor Frost gave birth to her sixth child, a daughter, Elinor Bettina Frost, who lived only two days.

The elliptical Scotch aphorism in the postscript of this letter must have been remembered by RF from Robert Burns's poem, "To a Mouse." It serves RF in this letter as an oblique plea to the editors of *The Independent* to publish a poem he had submitted earlier. By only slight extension, the aphorism means: "To ask for an occasional ear of corn, out of a large harvest, is an appeal so modest that it should be granted."

[*c.* 1 July 1907] [Derry]

[. . .] poem, though I say it who am not an editor and was not intended to be. I am half afraid they do not appreciate its unusual blend of humor with vague beauty over on Fulton St. or it could not have gathered dust as long as it has. However I forgive them, and only wish my muse were as much to their high purpose as they once found that of the author of The Cry of the Children.

Yes we are both the merest convalescents for the present (Mrs. Frost will write and tell you all about it sometime), barely equal to wishing you one good wish of health and happiness between us.   Sincerely   Robert Frost

A daimen icker in a thrave's a sma' request.

26 · To Susan Hayes Ward

NOT ALL of the poems RF submitted to Miss Ward were sent as enclosures; some of them were written on the same sheet as the letter. This letter appeared on only one side of a folded sheet, and the first inside page contained a poem called "Choice of Society." It was an early version of "The Vantage Point," published later in *A Boy's Will*. The second inside page contained the following postscript at the bottom: "Another infliction on the next page." On the last page there was an early version of "A Dream Pang"; before it was published under the same title in *A Boy's Will*, RF revised it somewhat.

Dear Miss Ward:-   6 August 1907   Derry

I must add my word to urge the visit Mrs Frost proposes in her letter. It would be so very pleasant to see you again and there would be so many things to talk about, that here we are accustomed to keep locked in the bosom of the family from one year's end to another. I sent the inoffensive poem to the unoffending editor and soon, I expect, I shall be enough richer to buy a few more books — Meredith, Dobell, Yeats, and one or two others I shall have to think up. (Have you anything to suggest?) So that you would find us right in the middle of five or six new enthusiasms. That would not bore you too much, I hope. But of course if you are going to plead poverty and stay at home, I have nothing to say. We too have tasted poverty (and all but death) — at the hands of the general practitioner if not of the specialist. It *is* too bad that we are not where we could see you more easily. Sometime we intend to be nearer New York than we are, if it can come about in the right way. But that is one of the dreams. Poetry, I am afraid, will be less likely to bring us there than prose.

Sincerely   Robert Frost

27 · To Susan Hayes Ward

8 September 1907

My dear Miss Ward,-   c/o John Lynch   Bethlehem, N. H.

I have carried a wrong impression from your last letter. As that left it, I thought we were to expect you at such a time in mid-September as you should later fix, and nothing remained for us but to wait to hear from you again. Our plans remain unchanged except that we must leave here a few days earlier than we intended — on the twenty-fourth of this month instead of the first of next — which I trust will make no material difference to you. It would be the greatest disappointment not to have you come so you must not fail us. You are really not very far from us over across the mountains as the light flies in the morning. People here go down to the surf at Old Orchard [Maine] and return the same day like Freedom rejoicing in each of the two mighty voices, one of the Sea, one of the Mountains.

Rather strangely I have a letter from your brother dated identically with yours Sept 4. In it he accuses me of false grammar — justly, justly, if we are to look at it in the right way instead of in the way I tried hard to look at it to eke out a triple rhyme. As a teacher I am behind both my hands with mortification.

You will write again then and tell me what train you take from Portland so I will know when to meet you at Bethlehem. There will be a drive for you at this end of the journey, but not of fifteen miles — only three. We are higher up in the world than Bethlehem even. I am glad to think you will enjoy the mountain air.   Sincerely yours   Robert Frost

40

28 · To Susan Hayes Ward

My dear Miss Ward,-   4 November 1907   Derry

We have been at home [from Bethlehem] for some time, but this is the first opportunity I have had to say so in so many words. I know you will forgive my not writing sooner when I tell you that my little capacities have been taxed to the utmost in getting our English department to rights at school. On top of everything else I have been asked to prepare a historical article on the Academy — in prose. Naturally I consume some part of every day merely dreading to undertake that. But written it will have to be, if I am to save my reputation as a poet (upon which everything hangs.) I am beginning to commence to *think* about *casting* about for my material. Elinor has been wanting to write to you, but I have claimed precedence, and she, too, has been unco busy.

I am moved to melancholy reflexion by the news that comes to us that you have been buying potatoes in Bethlehem. When you were an editor, do I think for a moment that you ever went that far out of your way for a poem? Did you ever send to Derry for a poem? No, the poetry sought you, not you the poetry — else you got along famously on prose. And what are potatoes, pray? Starch. You may ask the man who writes the advertisements for Grape-nuts [sic(k)]* I cannot help but think. One of my appletrees, standing stock still and rooted, earns more money in a year than I can earn with all my locomotion and artistic detachment. The moral seems to be that I must write more and better poetry if I hope to compete in the market with things to eat.

How long ago and far away Bethlehem is already. Our summer was one of the pleasantest we have had for years. But it is almost hard for me to believe in the reality of it now. I have been that way from boyhood. The feeling of time and space is perennially strange to me. I used to lie awake at night imagining the places I had traversed in the day and doubting in simple wonderment that I who was here could possibly have been there and there. I can't look at my little slope of field here with leaves in the half dead grass, or at the bare trees the birds have left us with, and fully believe there were ever such things as the snug downhill churning room with the view over five ranges of mountains, our talks under the hang-

* RF's bracketed insertion, see footnote letter 14.

ing lamp and over the fat blue book, the tea-inspired Mrs.
Lynch, baseball, and the blue black Lafayette [Mountain].
There is a pang there that makes poetry. I rather like to gloat
over it.   Sincerely yours   Robert Frost.

29 · To Susan Hayes Ward

DURING RF's Christmas vacation from his teaching duties at Pinkerton Academy, in 1907, the Frost family made an excursion to New
York City. The following fragment of a letter seems to have been
written soon after the Frosts had returned to Derry.

[c. January 1908]   [Derry]

[. . .] he hadn't. We resolved then and there not to lie about
where we had been for fear of being doubted whether we lied
or not. We went right to work to make our observations on the
sun moon and Orion just as scientific and non-committal as
possible. So you can rely on everything I have said in this letter.

You say you are coming to live over back here in So. Berwick [Maine]. Why then we'll be neighbors. You'll be less than
a stone's throw from us. Indeed we regularly play football with
a team that regularly plays with the So. Berwick boys. I have
been half way to S. Berwick on foot. We Frosts claim the
whole region thereabouts by right of having settled it and
fought Indians in it. So I'd really be more at home in it than
you will be. I must send you sometime some Whitmanism of
mine on my bad ancestor the Indian Killer [Charles Frost]
who sleeps under a bowlder in Eliot Me.* But that won't be till
you lend me the poems by the Sweet Singer of Mich.† which
you promised me once. Meanwhile we are all from Margery
up and from me down   Very truly yours,   Robert Frost

30 · To Susan Hayes Ward

A SPECIAL Christmas present, made by RF and sent to Miss Ward
with the following letter, was a manuscript booklet containing
seventeen of his unpublished poems and inscribed: "Susan Hayes

* The reference is to a sixty-three-line blank verse poem entitled "Genea-
logical," which RF never published. See appendix.
† The quaint versifier, Julia A. Moore (1847-1920), admired by Mark
Twain and, later, by Ogden Nash.

Ward from Robert Frost, Christmas 1911." The folded sheets were carefully stitched into a blue heavy-paper wrapper. This was perhaps the first of many booklets similarly made and presented to friends by RF on special occasions.

Dear Miss Ward:-   19 December 1911   Plymouth
    I don't know where you are, nor how you are, nor how you are at present disposed toward minor poets. And I have been such a laggard in letter writing that I don't believe I deserve to know. Well then take this book of manuscript verse as a peace offering. I thought it might be nearer right in the circumstances than anything I could buy in the book mart. It represents, needless to tell *you,* not the long deferred forward movement you are living in wait for, but only the grim stand it was necessary for me to make until I should gather myself together. The forward movement is to begin next year. Luckily I am not George B. McClellan to have to fear being removed from command by the politicians just on the eve of accomplishment. So it is still manâna, you see. But don't think to laugh with impunity at my boast as you may have laughed at the boasts of so many others before. In my case you would find yourself mistaken. Elinor will tell you so. I should so very much like to see you for a talk on such vanities that I should so very much be inclined to run down to New York for a two day's visit toward the end of next week (or some other time) if you asked me. You are to think of me now as a dweller in Plymouth in the White Mountains where I teach psychology in the State Normal School. I am sending along as collateral that authentic bit of family history ["Genealogical"] I once promised you. I sha'n't apologize for the Whitmanesque. To these things let me add Christmas greetings for the season, but more especially friendly greetings for all the year round.

                         Sincerely yours   Robert Frost

31 · To Susan Hayes Ward

Dear Miss Ward: 28 December 1911   Plymouth
    I so burned four or five of my fingers on merry Christmas morning that I have been afraid I ought to give up the idea of visiting you this week. It was not so much the pain, which I

walked off in a few hours, as the disfigurement that troubled me. I was almost sure I shouldn't be fit to be seen for a while. But two days have made a great improvement in me and at this writing I haven't very much left to show for my meddling with the hot steam-pipes and by tomorrow should have less. And though getting along in years like other folks, I still find myself young enough to hate and abhor giving up what I have once really set my heart on. So I am coming to have a spoken word with you, if no more than a word. And this as of obligation; for how are we going to continue to read each other's letters satisfactorily unless we renew in memory from time to time the image of the living voice that informs the sentences. I shall start from here Friday and should reach you early Saturday. I can have till Monday afternoon with you, I think, provided I can get leave to omit a lecture or two on Tuesday morning. Till I see you then.

Sincerely yours,   Robert Frost

32 · To Susan Hayes Ward

Dear Miss Ward:-   15 January 1912   Plymouth

It wasn't to be expected that I would get back to business the minute my train arrived; and I didn't. And that was not because I can't move as fast as a train when I am on a train, but because it is so much further from the literary to the psychological than it is from little New York to Plymouth. I have been a constant sufferer since my visit with you from that Where-was-I-when-I-left-off or What-did-I-say-last feeling as I should have made complaint before if I had felt constrained to write you before I got safely and thoroughly home. I must tell you that one day — I couldn't for the life of me say how afterwards — I actually turned a recitation in the History of Education into a recitation of irrelevant verse. But there's no harm done, perhaps even some good. At any rate Elinor and I think so. It will never be counted against you with us that you have encouraged my poor Muse with interest when you couldn't with praise.

If this doesn't look like a very long letter to be writing to a friend and benefactor (by actual count of words it will prove longer than it looks), please remember who it was that Luther thought the proper target to throw ink at by the bottleful. Not the friend and benefactor of anyone in particular was it?

Sincerely yours   Robert Frost

Sonnet on the next page for my "Moth and Butterfly" book.*

33 · To Susan Hayes Ward

Dear Miss Ward:-   10 February 1912   Plymouth

You should receive almost simultaneously with this your long-lost Sweet Singer. I ought to say that I don't think I laughed at her as much as I should have if I had been a hearty normal person, and not something of a sweet singer myself. She is only a little more self-deceived than I am. That she was not altogether self-deceived I conclude from the lines in which she declares it her delight to compose on a sentimental subject when it comes into her mind just right. There speaks something authentic anyway.

Two lonely cross-roads that themselves cross each other I have walked several times this winter without meeting or overtaking so much as a single person on foot or on runners. The practically unbroken condition of both for several days after a snow or a blow proves that neither is much travelled. Judge then how surprised I was the other evening as I came down one to see a man, who to my own unfamiliar eyes and in the dusk looked for all the world like myself, coming down the other, his approach to the point where our paths must intersect being so timed that unless one of us pulled up we must inevitably collide. I felt as if I was going to meet my own image in a slanting mirror. Or say I felt as we slowly converged on the same point with the same noiseless yet laborious strides as if we were two images about to float together with the uncrossing of someone's eyes. I verily expected to take up or absorb this other self and feel the stronger by the addition for the three-mile journey home. But I didn't go forward to the touch. I stood still in wonderment and let him pass by; and that, too, with the fatal omission of not trying to find out by a comparison of lives and immediate and remote interests what could have brought us by crossing paths to the same point in

* The "Sonnet on the next page" was "In White," an early draft of "design," first published in *American Poetry, 1922, A Miscellany.*

the wilderness at the same moment of nightfall. Some purpose I doubt not, if we could but have made it out. I like a coincidence almost as well as an incongruity. Enclosed is another in print. The Marion C. Smith you were talking of when I was with you I was very certain I had heard of somewhere, but I didn't know where. It must have [been] here. Heard of her? Yes it is almost as if I had met her in the pages of the [Youth's] Companion.

Nonsensically yours   Robert Frost

34 · To Thomas B. Mosher

A PICTURESQUE gourmet, dilettante, and book collector, with a taste for blue-china poetry, fine printing, and pornography, Thomas Bird Mosher (1852-1923) began in 1891 to publish and pirate attractive little reprints of good works not well known in the United States. Supplementing the series of "Mosher Books," he also published a vest-pocket-sized monthly anthology entitled *The Bibelot* (1895-1915), each issue containing reprints of short pieces of prose and poetry selected from obscure but significant works.

The correspondence between RF and Mosher began after the publisher somehow saw in manuscript RF's then unpublished poem, "Reluctance," and wrote requesting permission to purchase it for use in one of his publications. The following letter brings the relationship to completion. Belatedly, "Reluctance" appeared in a somewhat compromised position as a prelude to a small book-sized "Catalogue" of Mosher imprints (1913). (See letter 63.) But prior to that publication, "Reluctance" appeared in *The Youth's Companion* for 7 November 1912, and also in *A Boy's Will*.

My dear Mr Mosher: 19 February 1912   Plymouth

I was just saying of my poetry that it didnt seem to make head as fast as I could wish with the public, when the letter came in which you said almost the identical thing of your Bibelot. But you could add of your own motion that you were getting, you supposed, all that was coming to you. Not to be outdone by you in philosophy (which is my subject of instruction) I made myself say it after you for a discipline: I suppose I am getting all that is coming to me. (These are harder words for me to pronounce than they could ever be for you — for reasons.) And then see how soon I had my reward. The very next day what should my poetry bring me but a check for twenty-five dollars, which is more than it ever brought before at one time. Some part of this belongs to you in simple poetic justice. Five dollars, say. You wouldn't tempt me to spend forty dollars on the Bibelot or anything else if you knew the ambitious schemes I have at heart, imposing habits of the strictest economy for the next ten years. But I can, and herewith do, send five dollars for books; and without impropriety, I trust, to satisfy my sense of the fitness of things, I copy on the inside of this sheet the poem by which I earned it, glad of the chance to show poem of mine to one whose life is so conspicuously devoted to the cause of poetry.

Very truly yours,   Robert Frost

35 · To Thomas B. Mosher

My dear Mr. Mosher: 4 March 1912   Plymouth

You must have my whole story of the poem Reluctance. It was The Atlantic that had returned it and left me in that dejection your letter lifted me out of. I am not for the High Seas (or should I say the High C's) yet it seems; and you must not think it of me. The Companion took the poem. Following hard upon that piece of good luck The Forum took another poem which I call My November Guest. I suppose both poems were accepted with Reluctance as I was assured by The Atlantic that the first was rejected with Reluctance, more than the usual Reluctance. I do not say that either of them heralds a new force in literature. Indeed I think I have others still under cover that more nearly represent what I am going to be. They are a beginning — that is all, and in print, with the chance of making friends, should encourage me to make more.

If it is anything for you to know it, both your letters have been a help in the work I have set my hand to. What that work is I know full well and what it entails. I expect nothing. Even the small mercies you speak of I have schooled myself to think of as too large for me. My great difficulty is going to be to get a hearing with the crowd-deafened editors. And there are other difficulties. I think I have considered them all and for the most part face them with serenity. Only there are impatient moments when I need the good word of a sympathizer to recall me to a sense of my philosophy.

Sincerely yours   Robert Frost

36 · To Wilbur E. Rowell

WILBUR E. ROWELL, a lawyer in Lawrence, Massachusetts, had been appointed executor of the estate of RF's grandfather, William Prescott Frost, who died on 10 July 1901. Rowell carried out the legal arrangements with sympathetic care and shrewd skill. Beginning on 10 July 1902, he made annual payments to RF until the total amount reached $12,903.15. The final payment was made on 10 July 1923.

Dear Mr. Rowell: 25 June 1912   Plymouth

I must be letting you know that I shall be here (and no longer at Derry) when the time comes round to make the annual award. I felt almost sorry to be so far from Lawrence when the syndecalist strike was on. How much Lawrence has and has not changed since I left the town twelve years ago! The Letts and the Portuguese and the Greeks and the Syrians are all quite new. But at the same time they appear not to have altogether displaced the older population. I never heard of the Syrian dentist who was for dying a martyr to the cause at the hands of the militia. But I was going to say I knew all the other people the papers mentioned from Clark Cart to John Breen. I went to one college with Danny Murphy, to another with Louis Cox. I went to the Hampshire St. school with John Breen. I am proudest to have known John — as you may suppose.

Very truly yours,   Robert Frost

37 · To Wilbur E. Rowell

ON 10 July 1912 Rowell wrote to RF: "I send you herewith a check for $800 for the annuity due you from the estate of your grandfather," and continued by saying that in settling the estate of the late Elihu Colcord, RF's uncle, an executor named Abbot had found "some books, photographs and other things that may be of use." Then he asked how to dispose of them.

Dear Mr. Rowell: 16 July 1912   [Plymouth]

I don't know just what to say about the things Mr Abbott has in keeping. It is kind and thoughtful for you to have troubled yourself with them at all, and I am unwilling to trouble you further. Perhaps if you could give me Mr Abbott's address, I could write to him for some idea of what there is and so make up my mind whether the case calls for a trip to Lawrence. I should suppose not. No books my uncle collected are likely to be of any value. Possibly there may be photographs I should like to keep in the family; but those it might not be too much to ask Mr. Abbott to have bundled and sent to me.

Thank you for the check.   Very truly yours   Robert Frost

IV

LONDON, BEACONSFIELD, AND
GLOUCESTERSHIRE · 1912-1915

IF THE Derry years had enabled Robert Frost to discover what was native to the grain of his talent, the years in England brought public recognition after he had almost despaired of attaining it. He was willing to assume that because he had reached the age of thirty-eight without attracting very much attention as a poet his chances for future success were slight. Arriving in England without any letters of introduction and knowing not a single soul there, he was also aware that the responsibilities presented by his family would not leave him much time for writing. But in spite of all his later protests that he did not go to England to seek a publisher, not two months had passed before he took the completed manuscript of *A Boy's Will* down to London, from Beaconsfield, and left it with the firm of David Nutt and Company. It was soon accepted for publication.

He had inherited some of his father's gambling instincts, and he took additional risks on his talent as a poet. Instead of waiting in Beaconsfield to see how his little book might make out with reviewers, he began a public-relations campaign to attract the attention of authors in London who might help to promote the book. He arranged to attend the opening of Harold Monro's Poetry Bookshop, and there made the acquaintance of F. S. Flint, a prominent figure in the early stages of the Imagist movement. It was Flint who told Ezra Pound about Frost, but it was Frost who went to call on Pound as soon as he had the opportunity.

By the time *A Boy's Will* was published, Frost had met and cultivated friendships with several important poets and critics who helped him greatly by reviewing and praising his book. In America the first review to appear was Ezra Pound's, in *Poetry* magazine for May 1913, and much of the biographi-

50

cal information it gave concerning the newly discovered poet of New England had been acquired directly from Frost. But the esthetic and temperamental differences of the two men quickly resulted in estrangement.

More congenial to Frost were the acquaintances he developed with the "Georgian" poets, Wilfrid W. Gibson and Lascelles Abercrombie. They persuaded him to move with his family from Buckinghamshire to Gloucestershire, so that he might become their neighbor. By the time *North of Boston* was published, in May of 1914, he had become so skillfully enterprising as his own promoter that some of the best reviews reflected his careful coaching. He acknowledged one such case, critically, in letter 81.

The outbreak of the First World War in August 1914 severely limited Frost's prospects in England. As a result, he was soon making plans to return to the United States, knowing that arrangements had been made for the publication of his books there, but fearing his possible neglect by American reviewers. Once again, and well in advance, he marshalled the assistance of friends who might help him. John T. Bartlett and Sidney Cox responded eagerly by giving him printed notice; but, as it turned out, he did not need their aid.

Of all the friends that Frost made in England the most important to him was Edward Thomas. Born of Welsh parents and inclined to darkly introspective brooding, Thomas was a thwarted and discouraged prose writer at the time he and Frost met. A dedicated naturalist, an Oxford scholar, a graceful stylist, and an excellent critic, he derived from Frost a stimulus so powerful that it gave new direction to his talents. Frost insisted that Thomas had so far neglected his true calling, that if he would cast his literary observations of nature and human nature into verse form he would discover himself. It was good advice and Thomas later expressed his indebtedness by dedicating his first and only volume of poems to Frost. Thomas was killed in action at Arras, France, on Easter Monday, 1917, before that volume was published. The shock and grief caused by that loss found expression in many of Frost's letters and in one poetic tribute, "To E. T."

38 · To Susan Hayes Ward

15 September 1912   The Bungalow
Dear Miss Ward: Beaconsfield   Buckinghamshire

Perhaps I ought not to conceal from you, as one of the very few mortals I feel in any sense answerable to, that I am in the mood called aberrant. Psychology holds me no longer. What have I taught for, anyway, but to confute my well-wishers who believed I was not enough of the earth earthy to be above a fool? And now that I have proved myself as a teacher in two departments of learning without benefit of college, my soul inclines to go apart by itself again and devise poetry. Heaven send that I go not too late in life for the emotions I expect to work in. But in any case I should not stay, if only for scorn of scorn — scorn of the scorn that leaves me still unnoticed among the least of the versifiers that stop a gap in the magazines. The Forum gives me space for one poem this year; the Companion for two. The Independent, longest my friend, has held one of my poems unprinted now these three years. So slight is my consideration. I may be too old to write the song that once I dreamed about ("The tender touching thing") — at least I can achieve something solid enough to sandbag editors with.

Here we are between high hedges of laurel and red-osier dogwood, within a mile or two of where Milton finished Paradise Lost on the one hand and a mile or two of where Grey lies buried on the other and within as many rods as furlongs of the house where Chesterton tries truth to see if it won't prove as true upside down as it does right side up. To London town what is it but a run? Indeed when I leave writing this and go into the front yard for a last look at earth and sky before I go to sleep, I shall be able to see the not very distinct lights of London flaring like a dreary dawn. If there is any virtue in Location — but don't think I think there is. I know where the poetry must come from if it comes.

Sincerely yours always   Robert Frost

38-a · Elinor M. Frost to Margaret Lynch

THE LYNCH FARM, where the Frosts had spent summer months from 1906 through 1911, was on the "South Road" from Bethlehem to

Franconia. The four Lynch children, two boys and two girls, were older than the Frost children. The oldest Lynch daughter had married a local farmer, William A. Green, and their children are mentioned in this letter. For earlier references to the Lynch family see letters 27 and 28.

Dear Mrs. Lynch:-   25 October 1912   Beaconsfield

I know you have wondered many times what has become of the Frost family, and I am sure you will be very, very much surprised to learn that we are way across the ocean, in England.

You see, last summer we spent several weeks trying our very best to decide where we wanted to go, and gradually we came to feel that it would be pleasant to travel about the world a little. And finally we decided to come to England and find a little house in one of the suburbs of London, and two weeks from the day of our decision, we were on our way out of Boston Harbor. We stored our furniture, and brought only bedclothes, two floor rugs, books, and some pictures. We sailed from Boston to Glasgow, and enjoyed the ocean trip on the whole, though Mr. Frost, Lesley and I were quite seasick for a few days. The younger children escaped with only a few hours discomfort. The last day of the voyage we skirted along the north coast of Ireland, and thought the dark, wild looking headlands and blue mountains very beautiful. We landed at Glasgow in the morning, and travelled all day across Scotland and England, arriving at London about seven oclock. From the station, we telephoned for rooms at the Premier Hotel, and after securing them, drove in a cab to the hotel, feeling greatly excited, you may imagine, at being all alone, without a single friend, in the biggest city in the world. We stayed in the hotel a week, while Mr. Frost was busy looking for a house in the towns about. I took the children about the city as much as I was able during the day, and nearly every evening Mr. Frost and I went to the theatre. London was splendid. The absence of elevated railways and trolley cars make it a much more beautiful city than New York, I think. They use the motor bus, which finds its way as it pleases among the other vehicles in the street, and also the "tubes," which are underground electric railways.

After a tiresome search, Robert found this little cottage we are in now. We have been here just six weeks. It is in the town of Beaconsfield, twenty miles out of London. The rent is higher than we expected it would be, for we were told rents were very cheap here, but it is a dear little cottage of five rooms. It is a low cottage, built of stucco, with vines growing over it, and we have plenty of land with it — a large grassy space in front, and a pretty garden behind, with pear trees, strawberry beds and lots of flowers. We bought enough furniture to get along with for about $125, and shall sell it again when we leave. Our plan is to stay here for a year, and then go over to France for a year, if our courage holds out.

The children are having a very good time, but they are homesick sometimes. Of course it is quite an education for them to see another land and another people. We can go into London occasionally. I find the housework easy, for one can buy a great variety of well-baked, wholesome bread and cake at the bakeries. I find the price of food and clothing just about the same as at home, though there is a great deal of talk everywhere, you know, about things being cheaper over here.

Mr. Frost is busy doing some writing which he has had in mind to do for a long time. We have all taken some very pleasant walks out into the country.

I hope you and Mr. Lynch are well, and all the Greens. I should like to see you all very much indeed. Do write soon and tell me all the news. By the time we see you again the Green children will be quite grown up — all except little William. I suppose he is a great pet.

With love and best wishes to all of you.

Sincerely your friend   Elinor M. Frost

38-b · Mrs. M. L. Nutt to Robert Frost

RF reached London with his family on or about 14 September 1912. He settled his family in Beaconsfield, Buckinghamshire, on or about 21 September 1912. Approximately one month later he took his manuscript, *A Boy's Will*, to the firm of David Nutt and Company in London. All his dealings there were with Mrs. M. L. Nutt, whom RF mistakenly assumed to be the widow of David Nutt. She was actually the widow of Alfred T. Nutt, son of the deceased David Nutt. This minor point was first cleared up, along with many other more important points, by Edward Connery Lathem in *Robert Frost: His "American Send-off"* — *1915*, published in 1963.

Mrs. M. L. Nutt was a native of France, which may account for her seeming to have difficulty with the English idiom, "cut and dried," in the following letter of acceptance.

26 October 1912

Dear Mr. Frost   6 Bloomsbury Street   London

I have looked through your MS and I am personally interested in the treatment of your theme. I am therefore disposed to bring out your poems if the proposal I can put before you and which would be on the principle of a royalty payment will suit you. I cannot put a dry and cut proposal before you as yet, as I want to think a little about the most suitable form to give to the book but I hope to be in a position to do so very soon.   Faithfully yours   M. L. Nutt
                        David Nutt [and Company]

39 · To Thomas B. Mosher

Dear Mr. Mosher: 19 November 1912   Beaconsfield

One has some bad luck, but one has some good luck, too. The Amphora [a Mosher anthology] is beautiful luck, not unqualified, I must confess, by the intelligence that my poem ["Reluctance"] just missed a place in it. Your offer to print a volume of mine is the same kind of mixed pleasure. The Dea knows I should like nothing better than to see my first book, "A Boy's Will," in your Lyric Garland Series. It even crossed my mind to submit it to you. But under the circumstances I couldn't, lest you should think I was going to come on you as the poor old man comes on the town. I brought it to England in the bottom of my trunk, more afraid of it, probably, than the Macnamara of what he carried in his. I came here to write rather than to publish. I have three other books of verse somewhere near completion, "Melanism," "Villagers," and "The Sense of Wrong," and I wanted to be alone with them for a while. If I ever published anything, I fully expected it would be through some American publisher. But see how little I knew myself. Wholly on impulse one day I took my MS. of A Boy's Will to London and left it with the publisher whose imprint was the first I had noticed in a volume of minor verse on arriving in England, viz., David Nutt. I suppose I did it to see what would happen, as once on a time I short-circuited a dynamo with a two-foot length of wire held between the brushes. What happened pleased me at first — in the case of the MS., I mean. I am not so sure how I feel about it now. David Nutt made me a proposal on a royalty basis. I have signed no contract as yet, but after what has passed, I suppose I am bound to sign, if pressed, almost anything that doesn't seem too one-sided. I expect the publisher will drive a hard bargain with me: who am I that he shouldn't have a right to? One thing that disconcerts me, however, is the eleventh-hour claim he makes on my next three or four books, verse or prose. I wish I knew what you would say to that. I suppose I ought to be proud to be so much in demand: the embarrassment is so novel in my experience. But wont it seem traitorously un-American to have all my first work come out over here? And how about you in whose hands I should feel so much happier and safer. And then there is Richard Badger [a "vanity publisher"] of Boston who has asked to see material for a book. Why couldn't you have spoken two weeks sooner and saved me all this perplexity? It seems to me you owe me something in the way of helpful advice for not speaking. Perhaps I can stave off that contract till I can get an answer from you. Have I made a serious mistake in going to David Nutt? Do you know anything about him (or her, if I may drop the business fiction)? Am I too far committed to draw back? I am nearly the worst person in the world in a muddle like this.

Once again let me say how much I think of the book — the books — I have had time to look at but one yet. I am going to have you send two or three books to a young friend in Vancouver, but I leave the order for another letter, when I shall have had leisure to pick and choose.

Very truly yours,   Robert Frost

You will notice my corrected address.

40 · To John T. Bartlett

JOHN T. BARTLETT was one of RF's favorite students at Pinkerton Academy. After his graduation from Pinkerton in the Class of 1910, and after his brief period of study at Middlebury College, he married a Pinkerton classmate, Margaret Abbott. They moved to Canada and settled temporarily in Vancouver, where he became a newspaper reporter. The following letter reflects RF's interest in Bartlett's activities there. For extensive background information, see *Robert Frost and John Bartlett: The Record of a Friendship* by Margaret Bartlett Anderson.

25 Dec. 1912

Dear John:-   The Bung. Hole   Beaconsfield

I worry about you when I don't get one letter from you in a month. You never say anything about Alec any more. The new press must be in: has it made no difference in your arrangement with him? It is such matters as that that I am interested in. Is there nothing in the wind? I suppose I am lead to expect kaleidoscopic changes in your fortunes from the way things went when you first struck pay dirt. Not that I want to see you earning any more money — or even as much. I hoped that you would settle down, domesticate, so to speak, on one or other of your two papers and be satisfied with one salary. I infer that you are working at all hours. That may do for a short time. It can't last forever. No matter if it isnt hurting you — and I should like assurance on that head — it is leaving you small leisure for self-improvement (to put it in that ugly utilitarian way). It leaves you small leisure for the good old reading — that's the way I like better to say it. I don't say you must get on. I won't say it. But I do say you must invite your soul. Write something for me, something for someone better than your Vancouver reading public. I venture a hat that you wouldn't have to try very long if you set your John-T. wits to it, to make a place for some of your stuff in some of the weeklies here like T. P.'s or the new Everyman's. Shape it short. Give it a touch of the color of the far west where the Frazer goes out. Emphasize the social values. Give it a pain, a laugh, a thrill. And there you are. I am at you again as I was in the beginning. I haven't forgotten your Hindu boy. Nothing ever came of him. A pity. But there's better fish you know — The question is who's characters out there? Whom do you run across that you could give a Londoner the feeling of? To the devil with this kind of preaching though unless you are going to take some stock in it. I have half a mind to go to writing up Vancouver myself.

It is altogether painful to me not to hear from you. The long letter Mrs Frost had from Margaret was some consolation. But we must hear more and more definitely about your health and your satisfaction in your work. Gifts of God is it? Well don't let that scare you into redoubling your efforts to make money when you are working double shifts as it is. Take care of yourself. I'm fond of you in my blundering way. I'm glad your mother doesnt know how fond I am or she might make it a ground for disliking me. One advantage of being so far off is the freedom it confers of saying things in writing I couldn't say to your face. I never had more than one real row with you and that was about Pamir. I was reminded of that today when I was browsing over Asia with Carol. You were the best pupil I ever had and Margaret was the next best. So dont you do a single thing that I don't want you to. I am not expected to say much about the Gifts of God I hope. All I say is dont let them influence you or divert you from your chosen way. Dont let them reduce you to the ranks. Only then will they live and grow up to thank you. Don't you fall into any error about the value of more than enough money at this stage of the game.

I should defy even Sarah Couch* (wasn't that her name?) to make anything out of what I have written if she should open my letter for reasons of state or motives of curiosity.

Sahrahh's distant relative Quiller-Couch (I can recall the assumed modesty of the squint and curtsy with which she claimed him through the bars of the P. O. window) is very great shucks in these parts. Great on anthologies.   R. F.

41 · To Ernest L. Silver

AS PRINCIPAL of Plymouth Normal School, Ernest L. Silver had looked with suspicion on RF's plan to go abroad for purposes of devoting his full time to writing and had argued that he should continue teaching at Plymouth. The correspondence between the two men, during RF's absence in England, reveals the strain placed on their relationship by Silver's doubts.

Dear Mr. Silver:-   25 December 1912   Beaconsfield

The way you keep calling for a literary letter, just as if I hadn't given you one in that laconic monograph on the Neanderthal hoe. I might follow it up with another on the Boadicean chariot with the scythes left off the axles in which the milkmen deliver their milk. But if the first was too archaeological to be literary, possibly the second would be too historical or military. . . .

In a last mad attempt to be literary (before I actually am literary) let me ask you to reread Lorna Doone from start to finish and see if you don't say it gives the impression that we have real winters here. By we I mean me and the king and Lord Burnham and the rest of the English. Recess of five

* Sarah Couch was the postmistress in West Derry, New Hampshire, during the years when RF called at that post office for his mail. She was deeply interested in genealogy, and was the first to inform RF of his Frost ancestry in Eliot and Kittery, Maine. See Appendix.

minutes during which you comply with my request. All right, you have reread Lorna. What do you say? We have real winters? Well, we haven't. Yon book is the damndest piece of unrealism. I saw it praised the other day for moderation. But — what don't we get praised for! To date I personally haven't seen a flake of snow. There are three feet of mud on the level — I mean I speak on the level. A douce farmer-man backs up his dump-cart to his mangel wurtzel pile to get a load. He has previously cut the ground up a good deal and to-day he incontinently goes in to the hubs of his wheels and the knees of his horse. He loses his temper and goes home to dinner without his horse. Maybe he comes back in the afternoon with a shovel to rescue the poor beast and maybe he doesn't come back till next week after he has heard the Sunday sermon on the immanence of the spirit. He knows the horse is perfectly safe all the time. No one can steal it without taking more trouble than it is worth. It can sink in just so far and then something, an old Roman pavement I venture to say, will stop it. And meanwhile the horse patiently stands through several rains the very type and image of the English lower class taught to know and accept its place. We have had ice (a few times) on the rain barrel if that constitutes winter. And one morning early in December the papers were out with scare heads like this:

ENGLAND IN THE GRIP OF FROST

I accept the omen, says I, I accept the omen. Better so than that Frost should be in the grip of England. And yet when all is said the season is far from balmy. There's a slant of wind we get that's daggers in the pulmonary lung. And when you scrape your face the stubble on your razor blade looks greyer than before you came down with seasickness, but it's owing to mould, nothing but mould. I set out to be literary and only succeed in being meteorological and pathological, you see.

Between you and me, though, I know what would be literary and highly literary. To talk about myself. I have been keeping this back for effect. You have doubtless heard through my friend Concubar [Mrs. Frost] that I am publishing the first book and that is the good news you refer to in your Christmas postal. I signed articles a week or two ago [16 December 1912] for my first five books prose or verse (should I ever live to write so many). I'm not likely to live, what with this climate and the way I am burning the candle at both ends. Intemperance is my curse. There is nothing I do or don't do that I don't overdo. Last summer it was tennis [in Plymouth, New Hampshire] till the family trembled for my reason. Since I reached Beaconsfield it has been verse "like a pawing horse let go" (I was almost forgetting to ring in quotations). When I ask myself in the words of the song, "Oh why left I my home, Why did I cross the deep," I have to confess it was to write prose and earn an honest living. Poetry is not a living. It is not even a reputation to-day. It is at best a reputation next year or the year after. And yet I always feel as if I was justified in writing poetry when the fit is on me — as it was last January. Very little of what I have done lately goes to swell the first book, just one or two things to round out the idea. You may look for a slender thing with a slender psychological interest to eke out the lyrical. Call it a study in a certain kind of waywardness. My publisher is David Nutt of London and Paris, a friend as it turns out of Bergson's.

I got some of the news from The Prospect* but not enough. I am homesick at times.

Sincerely yours   Robert Frost

42 · To Sidney Cox

WHEN RF was just beginning to teach at the Normal School in Plymouth, New Hampshire, he accidentally met Sidney Cox, then a young man teaching in the Plymouth High School. The development of their lifelong friendship is described in Sidney Cox, *A Swinger of Birches: A Portrait of Robert Frost* (New York, 1957), for which RF wrote an introduction.

Dear Sydney Cox: 26 December 1912   Beaconsfield

I fully intended to write you some word that should reach you somewhere near Christmas time. You might need it to help you over the vacation and you might not. I knew you wouldn't be going down East this year. At any rate you would have time to read it if you didn't have time to answer it. But you have no idea of the way I mismanage myself since I broke loose and ceased to keep hours. It seems as if I did nothing but write and write and everything else I planned to do went where the Scotchman's sixpence went when *he* went to London. If you don't know that story you can ask me about it next time you see me.

---

* *The Prospect* was the Plymouth Normal School newspaper, forwarded by Silver.

You will accept I suppose a note that shall be no more than promissory of more to come. I write chiefly to assure you of our pleasure in your good letter as I should have written the minute I received the characteristic postal that came posting on its heels. It needed no apology. You were enthusiastic about your studies, matter-of-fact about your menial duties, a happy combination that strikes me as peculiarly American. What more could anyone ask in one off-hand letter? But if the letter was good enough for us, the postal was better. That rises to heights almost universal in that it voices the complaint of everyone who writes anything, viz., that nothing he writes quite represents his thought or his feeling. It is as hard to fill a vacuum with nothing as it is to fill a poem (for instance) with something. The best one can hope for is an approximation. Wilfred Meynell calls his latest volume of poetry Verses and Reverses and owns in a preface that they are mostly reverses. There you have it. The veteran learns to value what he writes as little for graces of style as for spelling. What counts is the amount of the original intention that isnt turned back in execution. Symonds [Arthur Symons] says Dowson (the sad sinner) for once says everything in Cynara. I wonder what Dowson would say if he were alive as he might have been with a little less liquor and a little more of the water one sees so seldom over here — never a drop of it in lunch rooms, railroad stations, or streets.

There that's all I can give you now.

Of course Miss Howard must make us a visit if she is coming to England. Tell us more about her plans when you write next time. Mrs. Frost says she will join me in my next letter. R. F.

43 · To Harold Brown

DURING the early months of his stay in England RF doubted the success of his venture. Fearing that he might need to teach again when he went home, he continued to keep in touch with educators in New England. Harold Brown was an assistant to Henry Clinton Morrison, State Superintendent of Public Instructions in New Hampshire from 1904 to 1917. Morrison had played an important part in helping RF climb from a teaching post at Pinkerton Academy to the faculty of the New Hampshire Normal School in Plymouth. This letter seems to carry out the first part of a request made by Harold Brown.

Dear Mr. Brown:-   7 January 1913   Beaconsfield

I have sent for your departmental ditty on the Colebrook [New Hampshire] High — more for the sake of having it than anything else. I am in no immediate need of rereading it. I was on the point of asking for half a dozen copies to distribute among the educational acquaintances I am likely to make once I set seriously about visiting schools. I am glad the bulletin was so generally noticed. It was a good stroke for you, Mr. Morrison, and the State.

Thus far I have visited but one English school. My reception was cordial enough after the ice was broken. But the fact that there was any ice to break showed a difference between schools here and in America. I made up my mind that I shouldn't really go visiting schools till I got around to ask Mr Morrison or some of you fellows for an introduction to the honorable board of education whose headquarters are in London. Time enough for that when I get my first book off my hands and two or three more off my mind.

(This pen works like respiration.)

My book wont be much larger than yours — fifty or sixty pages I figure it. It should be out some time in February. Its safe mediocrity is attested by the good luck it has had to start with. I had to show it to but one publisher, and he takes it entirely at his own risk, a thing they tell me, that doesn't happen to anybody's first book over here. It never happened to any of George Meredith's books (of verse) as long as he lived. It must have happened to mine because, as I say, it was so very ordinary and because I didn't know enough to be afraid it wouldn't happen. So far, so good.

I seem to forget just what event I had brought myself down to in my last letter. I think I had reached England, if you mean by reaching England — well, what do you mean by reaching England? What do I mean? I have been asking myself. Did I reach England when I went on board ship? Of course the ship was English — all ships are — and I could have been arrested there by English officers for any crime done in England (such as writing a bad poem). Legally I was on English ground. Or did I reach it when I got outside the three mile limit on the American coast and onto the high seas? It is well known that England owns the oceans now-a-days, and those that dig canals between them only dig for her. Or did I reach it when I first saw the coast of Galway which, peaceful though it looked through the haze, is where the wild and fascinating Irishman still snipes the deputies of the absentee landlord? Or did I reach it when I nearly got myself thrown overboard by a Scotchman for innocently calling the fleet I saw off the Mull of Cantire English instead of British? (I was finding out that if Ireland loves England in one way Scotland loves her in another.) Or did I reach it when I set foot in "Glasgie mud and dirt"? Or when we picniced, the six of us by ourselves, in the snug compartment of the toy train for eight hours on end straight across the counties to Euston station in London? Or when I paid thrippence thruppence or six cents for my first London Times sometimes called in New York The Thunderer for the Jovian majesty of its pronouncements? Or when I heard G. B. Shaw tease the Suffragettes at one of their own meetings till they didn't know whether he had come to help (as advertised) or hinder them? Or when I got my card of admission to the library of the British Museum? Or when I came here to Beaconsfield to live behind a fifteen-foot hedge of American laurel more flourishing than any I ever saw in America? Or, being a teacher, wasn't it until I entered my first English school?

A word or two about that school. It was a rambling brick structure nowhere more than a storey high and covering a good deal of ground. I walked right into it from the earth of the yard to the tile floor of the room of the highest grade. There was no step up or down. There was a large open fireplace more for ventilation than warmth. The desks were for all the world like what you may see in one or two of the oldest halls at Harvard, one long backless bench of three inch stuff for the haunches, one long ditto a little higher for the elbows, books, and papers. The lighting was generous. I saw two or three battered old Broadwood pianos about and heard them too. The lads in broad white collars sang "Odds, bobs, hammers and tongs" for me. That was all good. Text books were scarce and I will not say antiquated, for that is a fault we Americans are too apt to find, but unpedagogical. Beaconsfield is a fairish-sized town fifteen miles from the largest city in the world. It has no library for child or man. So much the more need for a working library in the school. What I was shown interested me. I heard its history. Lord Burnham, the school patron, keeps it up by occasional gifts of books that come to his newspaper

63

office for review. It is what Lord Burnham didn't want and what none of his office assistants wanted — leavings. There are perhaps 200 volumes in all, absolutely non-literary and non-educational, as dead wood as so many volumes of eighteenth century sermons. So much for equipment.

I saw too little of the teaching to judge it justly, I liked the teachers and I liked their looks. Two of the seven or eight I met were men. I should have said that the school takes care of all the poor children of the town for as many years as any of them go to school, say five or six at most. The teachers have classes of about forty apiece. The two men made two rooms of one by drawing a green baize curtain between them. I had some talk with the principal and have meant to see him again. He is a gentle body, well read in a different way from most of our men. He knows the literary names better than the educational — He had not heard of Montessori. Neither for that matter had his teacher of the kindergarten. I did not allow myself to be surprised. Some people save themselves a lot of trouble by not hearing of new things too soon. You can see how. I counted it more to Mr. Baker's discredit that he was proud of his school library than that he hadn't heard of Montessori. He had the common skepticism about the value of psychology to teachers. He put it to me straight if I thought the stuff was worth very much. "It's deep, I know" he wound up by way of voluntary concession.

I have said a good deal already or I should like to tell you about the children. They were well enough when one considers what they were. One would have to go to the slums of the city for their like in face and form in America. I did not see the sprinkling of bright eyes I should look for in the New England villages you and I grew up in. They were clean enough — the school sees to that. But some of them were pitiful little kids. Mr Baker stood them on their seats for me to inspect like slaves in the market — cases of malformation and malnutrition. Too many of these in proportion, I thought. But you have to remember that no one here sends his children to the government schools if he can possibly send them elsewhere.

We heard from Miss Murphy about the result at Durham. And afterward Mr Silver wrote about it in accents so sincerely sorry that I am left in doubt whether I did the man an injustice or not last summer. I wish I knew.

I want you to keep that road broken through the Notch. Regards from all of us to both of you.

Lesley is going to make out for you a schedule of studies such as obtains in the kind of dame's school she is attending.

It is now two o'clock in the morning in Beaconsfield and eleven o'clock at night in Colebrook — time to go to bed in either place.　　　　　　Sincerely yours　　Robert Frost

44 · To John T. Bartlett

Dear John:-　　　　　　26 February 1913　The Bung. Hole

About now you are in receipt of my coverless book.* Now you are reading it upside down in your excitement. What's the matter? You look pale. I see it all as true to life as in a melodrama. Your wife gathers around the table. The dog gets stepped on — the Indian Runner Dog. And Ruksh the dog utters a fearful cry. No canine cry is that, etc. It curdles the Annie Frazier River. A chair goes over.

"Wait," you say.

"Wait a minute!"

"Hold on!"

"Give me time!"

"I tell you I can understand this if you give me time and dont hurry me!"

"In fact it isnt that I cant understand it."

"I can understand it all right."

"But I cant believe it."

"It is what I may call the startlingness of the intelligence."

"Suppose I were to telegraph you from Raymond [the New Hampshire birthplace of John Bartlett] or some other center where things happen and news is manufactured that Sir Peg a Ramsey had demonstrated on the zylophone that there was more radium than neon and helium than yes than in no."

"You would be excited, wouldn't you?"

"Come own up. Of course you'd be."

"It would make all the difference in the world."

"You'd feature it — you'd call attention to it in a leader."

"Well it's like that — only — what shall I say?"

* This "coverless book" is no longer in the Bartlett papers. It may have been a dummy paste-up of galleys or page proofs of *A Boy's Will*.

"Only more serious, more momentous."

"So unlike poetry — except Masefield's."

"If a man has anything he wants to break to us let him use prose — prose is his vehicle."

"Listen to this — it comes with too great a shock in verse."

"Get ready:"

"eurt saw thguoht I lla fo erus erom ylnO"

"It is too, too much."

And so you run on till Mrs. Margaret interposes with a woman's good sense:

"Perhaps if you read it right side up it wouldn't mean so much."

"It might not mean anything."

Still I think you will treat the book kindly for my sake. It comes pretty near being the story of five years of my life. In the first poem I went away from people (and college); in the one called A Tuft of Flowers I came back to them actually as well as verbally for I wrote that poem to get my job in Pinkerton as little Tommy Tucker sang for his supper, and Brer Merriam read it for me at a Men's League Banquet in Derry Village because I was too timid to read it myself.

Elinor will be writing to Margaret soon. She has been prevented from doing anything extra by various cares and anxieties of late. Lesley has resprained an ankle she sprained in Derry once and it makes a very bad case. She may be two months off her feet. The specialist in London was grave about it. That is hard on a mother. Lesley had a chance to see her own bones in the x-rays. R. F.

45 · To John T. Bartlett

My dear dear John:-   [c. 18 March 1913]   [Beaconsfield]

Your last letter rather piles on the agony. But we are not going to let it worry us too much. You will be writing in a day or two that Margaret is better or has gone through the operation [for appendicitis] all right and that Gerry has ceased to press you for further copy on the critturs of your imagination.

But you are terribly overwrought. I see you in a vision as you appeared the day Doe hit you in the eye. If you don't look as wild as that, you feel enough worse to more than make up for it. And yes, I repent that I didn't get out there where I could perhaps do or say or be a little something to help you over a bad place.

You mustn't fake articles any more. Not even in details. Them's orders. I'll tell you why. It's taking an unfair advantage. Of whom? Of the public? Little I care for them. They would deceive themselves were there no one else to deceive them. Of your fellow journalists then? I suspect that they can hold up their end. No it is taking an unfair advantage of the gentlemen who profess fiction. I used to think of it when I faked in a small way for another paper named the Sun which was published in Lawrence Mass. All I had to do was to claim for my yarns the virtue of fact and I had story writers of twice my art and invention skun a mile. I thought of it again when partly for the fun and partly for the lucre I tried my hand at poultry journalism. I wrote up one or two poultrymen as you did Biblical Smith, filling in the gaps in my knowledge with dream material. I think I managed fairly well except for the time I spoke of John Hall's geese roosting in the trees. I should have let geese severely alone. It took an artistic letter from John Hall himself (I wrote it for the douce man) to save me from the scandal that started. I had a little right on my side. As a matter of fact John Hall had among others a few Brazilians that sometimes roosted on a pollared willow and even on the chimney and he could honestly say so (if some one would write the letter for him, for he was without clerkly learning). But I was uncomfortable all the time until I settled back to write out-and-out stories. It had occurred to me previously that some fiction not purporting to be true otherwise than as fiction is true, true to the life of the farm and especially the poultry farm, wouldn't derogate from the serious not to say solemn interest of a poultry journal. I succeeded in creating a limited demand for it and was making a very little money when I decided I could make more in Pinkerton. I tell you all this to show you. A little faking in our salad days is none so sinful — a novice naturally takes it as a lark — he can't feel that he has tasted the full flavor of the world the flesh and his grown-up-man's job if he hasn't tried it. But you will soon sicken of it, if you havent sickened already. Give us a rest about the money you need. I don't want you to get rich too fast.

I speak lightly enough. All the same I shall feel mightily relieved when you write that the danger of your being found out in the Manuel-and-His-Little-Shell game (Conchita must mean shell) is safely past. What I fear is that someone on the Sea Island will rise up to question your authenticity — or the Spanish Consul if there is such a thing on the coast. I should be scared blue if I were in your predicament. No harm in my saying as much at this distance since by the time you hear me you will either have come through safely or have been ridden on a rail out of the Sun office. We will laugh at all these worries some day when we are collaborating on a brisk novel of Vancouver in the days of the land speculation.

Our love to Margaret. Both of you are young and brave and fine and the best stuff ever. Write 'em as short as you please but write oftener. And we like to see the paper once in a while. R. F.

45-a · Elinor M. Frost to Margaret Bartlett

Dear Margaret:- 18 March 1913 [Beaconsfield]

We have all felt very badly to know how ill you have been. It is terrible that you should have appendicitis at such a time, and it must have been so hard for John to see you suffering. I think it is much better for you to have the operation now, as soon as you are strong enough for it — perhaps it has already taken place. We seem such a fearful distance apart at such a time as this — two weeks is such a long time to wait for news. I wish very much that I had been there through your trouble. I am not much to lean on, but still my presence might have been a little help, and I am sure that Robert would be a great comfort to John during the time you are in the hospital. I hope with all my heart that you will be much stronger after the operation is over.

Lesley's ankle is getting better, but the doctor thinks she ought not to step on it for two weeks yet. She is very nervous, of course, and it is difficult to make her days pass pleasantly. On pleasant days she sits out in the sunshine for an hour or two. For the last week or two the larks have been back from the South, and quite a flock of them stay in the field that lies over the hedge on one side of our house. I can understand now why the lark is the subject of so much English poetry. Every few minutes one will rise from the ground, as if overcome by emotion, and soar straight up in the air until one can scarcely see him, singing all the while such a sweet, rapturous song, and then let himself straight down again, singing until he reaches the ground. I never heard such a lovely bird song. A great many kinds of flowers are blooming here now. As the weather is much improved, I think we shall have some nice walks when the injured ankle is well again. [. . .]

> With a great deal of love and sympathy from your friend
>
> Elinor M. F.

46 · To John T. Bartlett

Dear John,-   [c. 4 April 1913]   [Beaconsfield]

I have nothing to write about except our anxieties for you and Margaret and my anxieties for the success of my book which are two so incommensurable things that they ought not of right to be brought together in one letter. However one must write something, for you will be wanting to hear. A letter now and then even if it seems an answer to nothing in particular can't come amiss. I know I could bear to get one from you oftener than I do. I have no regular correspondent on the other side either in Derry or in Plymouth. I cut myself off from the Derry crowd in disgust when John C gave the Academy to that Roman-Anglican-Catholic Congregationalist son of the man that did such things at the Plymouth Normal School. I rather deliberately queered myself with Silver and the Plymouth crowd by laying it on pretty thick though with studied modesty, about my little achievements here in answer to their clamor for something literary from the neighborhood of Westminster Abbey. You see I could talk about myself on that for a joke and call it highly literary. Instead of lingering over the tombs and busts in the Abbey (where I have never been) I talked in simple truth about my book. I had it in for them. Silver asked three times for something literary. Then he got it. He hasn't yipped since. The Lord do so to me and more also if I could help it. And I was artful enough to leave something untold that I could send around and make sure of his getting as if by accident by way of Mrs Frost and some of the ladies. He's an awfully mild master, is Silver, when he has you where he can pay what he wants to. But he's jealous to a fault. I know where he lives. The story when pieced together amounted to just this — I don't know whether I have bothered you with it before. I found a publisher for my book in the first office I walked into. The firm pays all expenses of publication which is a very unusual thing in the case of a first book. I am under contract to let the same firm have my next four books if I ever write any more. I had hardly signed this contract when I had requests for a book from two American publishers, one a most flattering thing from Mosher of Portland, whose letter-press is considered perhaps the most beautiful in the States. I seem to have found a friend in Mosher. Some time when you are happy and feeling flush I wish you would send him a dollar for a year of his little magazine of reprints called The Bibelot. His address is Portland, Maine. You will like the magazine.

I have got off the track a little bit. But I think I have told you about the whole story as Silver had it. Where the anxieties come in? Bless you, all that hit my Plymouth friends so hard is just the beginning of a book's career. I am in mortal fear now lest the reviewers should fail to take any notice of it. Such a work isn't sold in the bookstores but through the notices in the papers entirely. It is going the rounds now and it remains to be seen whether it will fall flat or not. Something however it has already done for me in ways too mysterious to go into. It has brought me several interesting friendships which I can tell you about without exciting any jealousy in your breast because you know that I care more for you and your opinion of me (formed when I was fifteenth in command at Pinkerton) than for the opinion of all the rest of them put together. Yeats has asked me to make one of his circle at his Monday Nights when he is in London (and not in Dublin). And he told my dazzling friend Ezra Pound that my book was the best thing that has come out of America for some time. Of course we needn't believe that. I spent the evening with Yeats in his dark-curtained candlelit room last week. We talked about The Land of Heart's Desire among other things. He is the big man here in poetry of course, though his activity is largely dramatic in late years. I have met Maurice Hewlett within a day or two. Hewlett not very intimately. You know him for his novels. He himself cares only for his poetry. And then there is May Sinclair the author of The Divine Fire etc. etc. I took tea with her yesterday and expect to go there again shortly. She professes to see something unusual in my book. I like that of course because she is known as an expert in new poetry. She is the lady who made the reputation of Vaughn Moody, Torrence and

Edwin Arnold [Arlington] Robinson by naming them as the principal poets in the States. And Ezra Pound, the stormy petrel, I must tell you more about him when I have more time. He has found me and sent a fierce article to Chicago denouncing a country that neglects fellows like me. I am afraid he over did it and it may be a mercy all round if it isn't printed. It is likely to be though as he always seems to have his way with the magazine it has gone to [*Poetry*]. All this ought to be enough to satisfy me for the time being you will think. But dear dear. The boom is not started yet. And then there is the money question. I am going to run short and have to go to the American Consulate for assisted passage home. There is little money ahead. Hewlett was boasting that he had three pounds, his first royalty on a book of poems published four years ago. Gosh.

I hope this letter will pass two or three coming the other way and bringing good news of Margaret and of you.

Affectionately   R. F.

47 · To Sidney Cox

2 May 1913

Dear Sydney Cox:-   The Bung Hole   Beaconsfield

It grows a long time since we heard from you and I begin to wonder whether or not you can have gone over to the enemy. There is the other possibility that you have been addressing letters as above and that the Eng. postman has failed to see the Am. joke. This, you must bear in mind is The Bungalow. It is only The Bung for short and Hole by discourtesy. You are not on terms to be calling it that. We who love it call it anything we please like the affectionate father in H G Wells' story who called his favorite daughter Maggots. We are all pretty much at home here by now. You ought to see us, theoretically up to our eyes in the flowers of an English spring. I could say actually if we were as our neighbors amateurs of gardening. I like that about the English — they all have time to dig in the ground for the unutilitarian flower. I mean the men. It marks the great difference between them and our men. I like flowers you know but I like em wild, and I am rather the exception than the rule in an American village. Far as I have walked in pursuit of the Cypripedium, I have never met another in the woods on the same quest. Americans will dig for peas and beans and such like utilities but not if they know it for posies. I knew a man who was a byword in five townships for the flowers he tended with his own hand. Neighbors kept hens and let them run loose just to annoy him. I feel as if my education in useless things had been neglected when I see the way the front yards blossom down this road. But never mind; I have certain useless accomplishments to my credit. No one will charge me with having an eye single to the main chance. So I can afford perhaps to yield a little to others for one spring in the cultivation of one form of the beautiful. Next year I go in for daffodils.

I think I understood Yeats to say the other night that Tagore whose poetry is the latest big thing here, has been visiting your college at Urbana. I meant to ask Yeats more about it. I wonder if you met Tagore. Very likely I shall run across him before he goes back to Bengal. I was to have met him at Ernest Rhys', Sunday but decided in the end to take some other day for my call when I could have Rhys more to myself. Tagore comes to Yeats here as the greatest English poet. How slowly but surely Yeats has eclipsed Kipling. I have seen it all happen with my own eyes. You would expect to see Tagore seeking Kipling for his Indian sympathies and interests. But no, he is drawn to Maeterlin[c]k on the continent and to Yeats on these islands. Sincerely yours   Robert Frost

48 · To John T. Bartlett

Dear John: [c. 10 May 1913]   Beaconsfield

I have to be chary of my favors to get anything out of you. The book [A Boy's Will] goes with this as per your kick of recent date. You are now supposed to order of your own motion and without undue pressure from me not less than fifteen nor more than twenty copies at forty cents (inclusive of post) the copy. You must do this of the publisher and not of me so as to make it look as if I had taken hold in the far west (why, God only knows). Then you must get me a notice in the most literary of the Vancouver dailies or weeklies. Make it personal if you like, a sort of news item. Like this: Jaunty Bart., the popular and ever censorious fakeer of the Sun staff is in receipt of etc etc. till you get to "allow me to sell you a couple" (quoting from Alice). You know the sort of thing. Be sure to say, This is

hot stuff. A few choice copies left. Call it a farm product without fear of contradiction. It is inevitable (that's the word) as
inevitable as a cabbage or a cucumber (if the cut worms don't
get it.) Funny how you and I both go in for farming. I am
looked on as someone who has got the poetry of the farm. Can't
you ring me into one of your columns in the Montreal Star? In
a word do your dambdest and hang the consequences. I am
mes enfants

> Living in you more than you can imagine.   R. F.

49 · To Susan Hayes Ward

Dear Miss Ward:-   13 May 1913   Beaconsfield

I must have displeased you with my last letter [see 38]
else I should have heard from you in reply before this. I am trying to think what I said that was so bad. I remember that I
was tragical (and that is an offense against taste) but it was in
a vein that wasn't meant to be taken *too* seriously. I must have
been tragical with you before in similar circumstances. It
seems to be my "awful way of doing business." Still it is just
possible the reason I haven't heard from you is because you
felt you had nothing to say until you saw how my rash adventure was going to turn out. To date it has turned out the book
[*A Boy's Will*] I am sending, which is a good book in spots. I
don't need to tell you. The beauty of such things as Into My
Own, My November Guest, A Dream Pang, Mowing, and Reluctance is that they are not just post-graduate work, nor post-
post-graduate work, but the unforced expression of a life I
was forced to live. That seemed not to matter to anyone at
home. Already it has attracted the attention of Yeats, Newbolt,
Rhys, Pound and Miss Sinclair over here. Maybe I was hasty in
coming away before showing my verse to any American publisher in book form. I don't feel sure. As it turned out Mosher
of Portland would have taken it. He wrote of his own motion to
ask for a book for his Lyric Garland Series when it was too late
and I had made an arrangement with David Nutt. I showed
my manuscript to the one firm. It was as simple as that. I had
nothing to pay. I shall have royalties. And I am under some
sort of contract to let David Nutt have my next book and the
next after. I seem in a fair way to become an Englishman.

And yet we are very very homesick in this English mud.
We can't hope to be happy long out of New England. I never

knew how much of a Yankee I was till I had been out of New Hampshire a few months. I suppose the life in such towns as Plymouth and Derry and South Berwick is the best on earth.

Elinor and I pool our regards.

Sincerely yours   Robert Frost

50 · To Wilbur E. Rowell

6 June 1913   The Bungalow,
Dear Mr. Rowell:-   Reynolds Road, Beaconsfield

Would it be possible for you to send me the money in some sort of cashier's check, made in duplicate, on some London bank? The ordinary check would have to go back to the States before I could get it cashed and I haven't the time to lose waiting for it. Indeed I almost feel like asking you to mail the check a few days earlier than usual if it would not be too irregular a proceeding. It would be ten days on the way, so that if it isn't sent till July 12 I shall have to wait for it till well toward the end of the month and my wish was to get away to France with friends by July 15. It would be harder for me to handle it in France than here where I am known. I have published a book here and expect to publish another before Christmas. Will you kindly drop me a line to let me know what to expect?   Sincerely yours,   Robert Frost*

51 · To Thomas B. Mosher

Dear Mr Mosher: 15 June 1913   Beaconsfield

I am sending you the book in question [A Boy's Will]. You will be glad to hear that it has done things for me over here. Since about the time I won your recognition everything seemed to be going right with me. Perhaps you have seen some of the reviews. Ezra Pound acclaimed me publicly. Yeats has said in private that the book is the best thing American for some time. May Sinclair has been showing it to people. Dont ask me how they ever found it in the confusion of all sorts of stuff that comes from the press. It must be my good luck. A little of the success I have waited for so long wont hurt me. I

---

* At the bottom of this letter, Wilbur Rowell wrote, "July 1, 1913 pen letter not copied, remitting $750 . . ."

rather think I deserve it. And I dont want you to think I dont deserve it. And I dont want you to think that I have had so much of it that I wont thank you for anything you will do to help me in the States — and elsewhere.

Sincerely yours   Robert Frost

52 · To John T. Bartlett

Dear John: [c. 16 June 1913]   Bucks

What do you say if we cook up something to bother the enemies we left behind in Derry? It won't take much cooking, but what it does will come on you. You have two of my reviews now. If you haven't I will see that you have others to take their place. One is good for one reason; the other for another. Pound's [*Poetry: A Magazine of Verse*, May, 1913] is a little too personal. I don't mind his calling me raw. He is reckoned raw himself and at the same time perhaps the most prominent of the younger poets here. I object chiefly to what he says about the great American editors. Not that I have any love for the two or three he has in mind. But they are better ignored — at any rate they are better not offended. We may want to use them some time. The other I value chiefly for its source, The English Review, the magazine that found Masefield and Conrad. The editor himself [Norman Douglas] wrote that particular notice.

I am sending you one more review which you can hold on to for a while. One more still and we shall have the ingredients of our Bouillabais[s]e (sp.) assembled. If nothing slips up we will get that in the August number of The Bookman (English). The editor has asked me for my photograph and a personal note to accompany the review. I suppose everything depends on whether I look young enough in my photograph to grace the ballet. Why did you wear me out teaching you things you knew already?

Well then in August, say, as soon as you get The Bookman you can begin a little article for Morse-back of The News and Enterprise like this:

Former pupils of R. F. at Pink may be interested to learn of the success of his first book published in London. A recent number of The Bookman (Eng.) contains etc. — You are not to get the least bit enthusiastic — I know you my child. Keep

75

strictly to the manner of the disinterested reporter. Make the article out of the reviews almost entirely. In mentioning The English Review you might mention the fact that it is a leading literary monthly here.

All this is if you have time and inclination. It will necessitate some typewriting. I would copy Ezra Pound's article so as to get rid of the break about the editors. Leave in any derogatory remarks. We like those. I fancy I should leave out the quotation from "My November Guest" which mangles a poem that needs to be taken as a whole and they quote it as a whole in the Poetry and Drama review I am enclosing. You see the scheme is to make The Bookman affair the occasion for your article and then drag the rest in by the ears. Say simply "The following is taken from —" Or if you see some other way to go about it, all right. You might do it in the form of a letter to the News, beginning, "I thought former pupils of R F at Pink etc" and sign yourself J. T. B. Anything to make Mrs Superior Sheppard and Lil' Art' Reynolds unhappy. (You put these people into my head.) But I suppose I care less about teasing my out-and-out enemies than my half friends like John C. Chase. I told you how I charged John C. forty dollars for the catalogue and when he winced told him that I didn't get it often but when I did I got about that much for my poetry. He never quite got over that. He clipped a cheap joke on poets one day and sent it to me by Miss Bartley so that she would share in my discomfiture. I only stood it tolerably well. I didn't mind it at first as much. I got tired of it.

Affectionately, mes enfants   R. F.

From Poetry and Drama 2s. 6d. (Quarterly) June 1913 London Devonshire St, Theobalds Road.

"x x x x Be it said, however, that Mr. Frost has escaped from America and his first book has found an English publisher. So much information extrinsic to the poems is necessary. Their intrinsic merits are great, despite faults of diction here and there, occasional inversions, and lapses where he has not been strong enough to bear his own simplicity of utterance. It is this simplicity which is the great charm of the book and it is simplicity that proceeds from a candid heart:

My November Guest
(Quoted in full)

Other poems almost or quite as perfect as the one above are: A Late Walk, To the Thawing Wind, Mowing, Going for Water, Reluctance. Each poem is the complete expression of one mood, one emotion, one idea. I have tried to find in these poems what is most characteristic of Mr. Frost's poetry; and I think it is this: direct observation of the object and immediate correlation with the emotion — spontaneity, subtlety evocation of moods, humor, an ear for silences. But, behind in the all is the heart and life of a man x x x x"

The first and last sentences are too personal for my taste. I am not bothered so much by the faultfinding. A little of that won't hurt me.

There was a favorable but unimportant review in T. P.'s Weekly a month or so ago. I have lost track of it. I think it quoted the first poem in the book and mentioned In a Vale. Maybe you have seen it.

You might say that A Late Walk was published in The Pinkerton Critic [October 1910].

I have become acquainted with the author of this [F. S. Flint].

52-a · Elinor M. Frost to Margaret Bartlett

Dear Margaret,   [c. 3 July 1913]   [Beaconsfield]

It does seem so good to get a letter from you again, and to know that you are all right. Of course I have reasoned that if anything were at all serious John would let us know about it, but at the same time I have felt certain misgivings about your health, and feared that you might be terribly weak after all your suffering. How fortunate it was that the fine spring weather came to tempt you out of doors. I know exactly how you felt, for the seasons here are much the same as with you, I imagine, and the many weeks of rain and cloudy skies were very depressing. At first, when the pleasant days began to be frequent, I did not have much faith in their going on and on but really we have had as many as six weeks of perfect weather, and England is certainly a charming place in summer. Lots of birds and flowers entirely new to us, you know, and quantities of roses in our own garden. We didn't plant anything. Rob didn't feel in the mood to bother with it, and I haven't had any time, what with teaching and sewing and

77

housework. But there are so many fruit trees in the back garden that it is a pleasant spot anyway. The currants and raspberries are just getting ripe. We have had a number of pleasant picnics. We pack a lunch into several different bags, so that we can share the load and tramp off two or three miles through the lanes and paths.

We are all feeling ever so well except Lesley. Her ankle is well again, but there is a tendency to flat-foot after the severe strain, and her general health is not very satisfactory. She is growing very fast this year, and somehow she hasn't much strength for anything except growing.

I hope, my dear, that you do not try to do too much housework. I think it is *very necessary* for you to take good care of yourself for several years to come, and you must learn the art of "letting things go" just as I had to learn it long, long ago. How could I ever have lived through those years when the children were little tots if I had been at all fussy about my housework? Do not try to cook much — wash dishes only *once* a day and use no rooms except kitchen, bedroom and sitting-room, and hire someone to come in and sweep up once in two weeks. That is often enough where there are only two of you. I hope, indeed, that you won't have any more appendicitis, and I almost wish that the old appendix could have been taken out, so that there would be no more danger of it. You and John will have to be very careful, won't you, that you do not become pregnant again for a while. Without doubt, the doctor has cautioned you. You are very young yet. There is plenty of time for a family when you are older and stronger.

I am very glad you and John like Robert's book. Of course I love it very much, and have been somewhat disappointed that the reviewers have not been more enthousiastic. How can they help seeing how exquisitely beautiful some of the poems are, and what an original music there is in most of them? Rob has been altogether discouraged at times, but I suppose we ought to be satisfied for the present to get the book published and a little notice taken of it. Yeats has said to a friend, who repeated the remark to Robert, that it is the best poetry written in America for a long time. If only he would say so publicly, but he won't, he is too taken up with his own greatness.

Robert has made some pleasant acquaintances among the younger writers in London, and several of them have been out to see us. We have become very well acquainted with the family of one of the professors at London University — Professor Gardner. His wife is author of a Greek grammar and is very kind-hearted, clever and impulsive. There are three children, a daughter, 22 years old, who is an artist, and two younger children, Lesley and Carol's ages. We like them all very much, and they have been very nice to us, but they live on the other side of London, in Surrey, and we cannot see much of them. [. . .]

I thought it so sweet of John to begin his letter "Dear Rob." When we all meet once more, you two must call us by our first names, if it wouldn't seem too strange to you, for, while we are really about twice as old as you are, we don't *feel* at all old. [. . .]

A great deal of love for you both from your friend

Elinor M. Frost.

53 · To John T. Bartlett

Dear John:-　　　　　　Fourth of July [1913]　　Beaconsfield

Those initials you quote from T. P.'s belong to a fellow named Buckley and the explanation of Buckley is this that he has recently issued a book with David Nutt, but at his own expense, whereas in my case David Nutt assumed the risks. *And* those other people Buckley reviewed are his personal friends or friends of his friends or if not that simply examples of the kind of wrong horse most fools put their money on. You will be sorry to hear me say so but they are not even craftsmen. Of course there are two ways of using that word the good and the bad one. To be on the safe side it is best to call such dubs mechanics. To be perfectly frank with you I am one of the most notable craftsmen of my time. That will transpire presently. I am possibly the only person going who works on any but a worn out theory (principle I had better say) of versification. You see the great successes in recent poetry have been made on the assumption that the music of words was a matter of harmonised vowels and consonants. Both Swinburne and Tennyson arrived largely at effects in assonation. But they were on the wrong track or at any rate on a short track. They went the length of it. Any one else who goes that way must go after them. And that's where most are going. I alone of English writers have consciously set myself to make music out of what I may call the sound of sense. Now it is possible to have sense

without the sound of sense (as in much prose that is supposed
to pass muster but makes very dull reading) and the sound
of sense without sense (as in Alice in Wonderland which
makes anything but dull reading). The best place to get the
abstract sound of sense is from voices behind a door that cuts
off the words. Ask yourself how these sentences would sound
without the words in which they are embodied:

You mean to tell me you can't read?
I said no such thing.
Well read then.
You're not my teacher.

———

He says it's too late.
Oh, say!
Damn an Ingersoll watch anyway.

———

One-two-three—go!
No good! Come back—come back.
Haslam go down there and make those kids get out of the
track.

———

Those sounds are summoned by the audile [audial] imagination and they must be positive, strong, and definitely
and unmistakeably indicated by the context. The reader must
be at no loss to give his voice the posture proper to the sentence. The simple declarative sentence used in making a plain
statement is one sound. But Lord love ye it mustn't be worked
to death. It is against the law of nature that whole poems
should be written in it. If they are written they won't be read.
The sound of sense, then. You get that. It is the abstract vitality of our speech. It is pure sound — pure form. One who
concerns himself with it more than the subject is an artist.
But remember we are still talking merely of the raw material
of poetry. An ear and an appetite for these sounds of sense is
the first qualification of a writer, be it of prose or verse. But if
one is to be a poet he must learn to get cadences by skillfully
breaking the sounds of sense with all their irregularity of accent across the regular beat of the metre. Verse in which there
is nothing but the beat of the metre furnished by the accents

of the pollysyllabic words we call doggerel. Verse is not that. Neither is it the sound of sense alone. It is a resultant from those two. There are only two or three metres that are worth anything. We depend for variety on the infinite play of accents in the sound of sense. The high possibility of emotional expression all lets in this mingling of sense-sound and word-accent. A curious thing. And all this has its bearing on your prose me boy. Never if you can help it write down a sentence in which the voice will not know how to posture *specially*.

That letter head shows how far we have come since we left Pink. Editorial correspondent of the Montreal Star sounds to me. Gad, we get little mail from you.

Affectionately R. F.

Maybe you'll keep this discourse on the sound of sense till I can say more on it.

54 · To SIDNEY COX

Dear Cox:-   10 July 1913   Beaconsfield

I get your story and I am sorry for you. The only thing I don't understand is the philosophical not to say meek way in which you take your luck. You attribute it to your lack of self confidence. What would that mean I wonder. Are you any less sure of yourself than are others of your age? And is it in religion or in business or in politics or in society or in love? One thing I know: you will not be any more sure for a while after an experience like this. I don't like it for you.

If you want my opinion, I think it all comes of your overhauling your character too much in the hearing of others. You give your case away as Tennyson did his when he confessed that wherever he wrote King Arthur he had in mind Prince Albert. He spoiled the Idyl[l]s for the present generation (I mean our own) and perhaps for all generations to come. And yet the poems are neither better nor worse for the confession. You *must not* disillusion your admirers with the tale of your sources and processes. That is the gospel according to me. Not that I bother much to live up to it.

And if you want my opinion, there is one other thing that enhances your effect of extreme youth. You are too much given to being edified — benefited, improved by everybody

81

that comes along, including me. You must learn to take other people less uncritically and yourself more uncritically. You are all eaten up by the inroads of your own conscience.

To get back to your trouble. I can't account for the calm you preserve except on the assumption that you hope there is still hope. Be frank about that. If it is anything to you, or can result in anything, for us to meet Miss Howard, Mrs Frost and I will be glad to have her out to see us in August. But if the affair is closed I am afraid I should only be awkward in meeting her. What should I say. I am not good at talking about everything but what is in the back of my mind. But you shall decide. Do you have something like a real wish that we should talk with her — for some secret reason that you may not want to own to even to yourself? Let me know soon. I will scold you more in my next letter.   Sincerely yours   Robert Frost.

54-a · ELINOR M. FROST TO SIDNEY COX

Dear Mr. Cox:-   [10 July 1913]   [Beaconsfield]

I think it's very sociable for you to wish to hear from me, also, and I am very glad to write. I should have done so before, but I have been very busy, as usual. Over here, I have a smaller house to take care of than in Plymouth, and in other ways my housework is easier but I am teaching the children myself, and of course that takes time. We cannot afford to send them to good private schools, and it is quite out of the question to send them to the free County Council schools, for it would be too awful to take them home speaking Cockney English, wouldn't it? Either kind of school would be bad for our children, for one kind would influence them to look down on a certain part of humanity, and the other to look up to the other part of humanity. I think our American school system very much superior to anything there is in England.

The children are all very well now and are growing so fast that I begin to feel very small myself. I think they will all be taller than I am. They do not like England as well as America, though London seems a wonderful and fascinating place to them. Sometimes I have wished that we had taken lodgings in the city itself instead of a house so far out, as the life there would have been more exciting for us all, but of course it is much better for the children's health out here. London is a foggy, smoky place. Beaconsfield is a pretty town, and there are delightful walks in all directions, across smooth fields separated by hedge-rows, and through stretches of beautiful old beech woods. All through May and June we have had charming weather, and the country has seemed very lovely after the many weeks of gloomy skies during the winter. The birds which we have never seen before, the skylark, the cuckoo, and the English blackbird, have been very entertaining to us.

I am glad that you have enjoyed your work at college so much. . . . The English have such a wrong idea of America, but you couldn't expect anything else from the sort of American news that gets printed in the papers here; anything vulgar and sensational about us is welcomed, and only confirms what they had already thought of us.

And so Miss Howard is coming abroad this summer — I felt very sorry to hear the news in your last letter, for I saw plainly last year how happy you were in your affection for her. I do not count self-confidence as one of the endearing qualities of our natures, and perhaps she will come to feel differently about it after a time.

I am sorry you are not near enough to us to come and see us this summer. We seem so far away from home and friends.

With all good wishes, I am Sincerely your friend,

            Elinor M. Frost

55 · To Thomas B. Mosher

Dear Mr. Mosher:-   17 July 1913 Beaconsfield

I like the decision with which you speak and am content to let you prefer Reluctance to any thing else I have written. Nevertheless the book contains a dozen poems that are at least good in the same kind and for the same reason. In Mowing, for instance, I come so near what I long to get that I almost despair of coming nearer.

I am made too self-conscious by the comment on my first book to think of showing another like it for some time. If I write more lyrics it must be with no thought of publication. What I *can* do next is bring out a volume of blank verse that I have already well in hand and won't have to feel I am writing to order. I had some character strokes I had to get in somewhere and I chose a sort of eclogue form for them. Rather I dropped into that form. And I dropped to an everyday level of diction that even Wordsworth kept above. I trust I don't terrify you. I think I have made poetry. The language is appropriate to the virtues I celebrate. At least I am sure I can count on you to give me credit for knowing what I am about. You are not going to make the mistake that Pound makes of assuming that my simplicity is that of the untutored child. I am not undesigning.

You will be amused to hear that Pound has taken to bullying me on the strength of what he did for me by his review in Poetry. The fact that he discovered me gives him the right to see that I live up to his good opinion of me. He says I must write something much more like *vers libre* or he will let me perish of neglect. He really threatens. I suppose I am under obligations to him and I try to be grateful. But as for the review in Poetry (Chicago, May), if any but a great man had written it, I should have called it vulgar. It is much less to my taste than the shorter reviews in Poetry & Drama and in The English Review. The more I think of it the less I like the connection he sees between me and the Irishman who could sit on a kitchen-midden and dream stars. It is so stupidly wide of the mark. And then his inaccuracies about my family affairs! Still I think he has meant to be generous.

I wish sometime if you know Robinson you could put me in the way of knowing him too — *sometime,* if it comes right. Not a month ago I was asking Miss Sinclair if she shouldn't have put him ahead of Moody and Torrence in her article of a few years back in the Atlantic. She said that Robinson was the only one of the three she still cared for.

You *know* I want you to use my poem in your catalogue.

Sincerely yours　Robert Frost

About my book in America. I shall do nothing for the present. Seymour of Chicago was out here from London to talk about it. Mrs. Nutt is going to have to be very much consulted in the matter. These are things I don't know very much about.

R. F.

56 · To Wilbur E. Rowell

Dear Mr. Rowell:-　　　　　　　17 July 1913　Beaconsfield

The money is here in good season and thank you very much. You can send the remainder later when I get back. I shall not be away from England more than two or three weeks. We are getting most out of things we see and the people we meet right here in London. The book has done rather well. At any rate it has done this much: it has introduced me to other people who write. I shall be glad to send a copy, though I am not too sure that you will care for my sort of stuff — so very personal in this first book. You might call it a farm product, written as practically all of it was five years ago on the farm in Derry. The next book, if it comes off, should be more objective and so perhaps more generally interesting.

Sincerely yours   Robert Frost

57 · To Ezra Pound

IN HIS LETTER to Mosher dated 17 July 1913, RF had complained that Ezra Pound had been "bullying" him with threats of neglect because RF refused to "write something much more like *vers libre*." The tension between the two poets increased until it reached a crisis, which caused RF to write the following revised-first-draft free-verse parody which he considered sending to Pound as an implicit declaration of independence. But after he had thus unburdened himself of some of his bitterness, RF sent a draft of the parody to F. S. Flint, apparently with a willingness to be advised. Flint's answer (letter 57-a) soothed RF to the point of keeping the document from Pound. Nevertheless, Frost kept his draft, and eventually gave it to the Dartmouth College Library with the understanding that it should not be shown or published during his lifetime.

[c. 20 July 1913]   [Beaconsfield]

I am a Mede and Persian
In my acceptance of harsh laws laid down for me
When you said I could not read
When you said I looked old
When you said I was slow of wit
I knew that you only meant
That you could read
That you looked young
That you were nimble of wit
But I took your words at their face value
I accepted your words like an encyclical letter
It did not matter
At worst they were good medicine
I made my stand elsewhere

I did not ask you to unsay them.
I was willing to take anything you said from you
If I might be permitted to hug the illusion
That you liked my poetry
And liked it for the right reason.

You reviewed me,
And I was not sure —
I was afraid it was not artis[ti]cally done.
I decided I couldnt use it to impress my friends
Much less my enemies.
But in as much [as] it was praise I was grateful
For praise I do love.

I suspected though that in praising me
You were not concerned so much with my desert
As with your power
That you praised me arbitrarily
And took credit to yourself
In demonstrating that you could thrust anything
      upon the world
Were it never so humble
And bid your will avouch it

And here we come close to what I demanded of you
    I did not want the money that you were disbursing
    among your favorites
    for two American editors.
                   Not that.
All I asked was that you should hold to one thing
That you considered me a poet.
That was [why] I clung to you
    As one clings to a group of insincere friends
      For fear they shall turn their thoughts against him
        the moment he is out of hearing.
The truth is I was afraid of you

57-a · FRANK S. FLINT TO ROBERT FROST

MOST OF the letters from RF to Flint are now held in escrow by the
Library of the University of Texas. When made available, they may
reveal the extent of RF's indebtedness to Flint, who introduced him
to so many poets in London in 1913. The following letter suggests

how Flint managed to stay on good terms with Harold Monro's Poetry Bookshop coterie while working closely with such proponents of the Imagist Movement as Ezra Pound, T. E. Hulme, and Amy Lowell, who was visting in England. Flint's primary purpose in this letter is to mollify RF's resentments against Pound and to dissuade him from sending to Pound the parody-declaration (letter 57).

It would seem that RF's letter to Flint must have complained of Flint's relationship to Pound, as revealed by Flint's review of *Ripostes,* published in Monro's *Poetry and Drama* for March 1913 (Vol. 1, No. 1), and showing evidence of Pound's collaboration. Defending himself from the charge of partisanship with Pound, Flint cites the unfair treatment given Pound by the mouthpiece of the conservative English Poetry Society, *The Poetry Review,* a mouthpiece as hostile to Monro as to Pound, who in turn were enemies.

Dear R. F., [26 July 1913] [London]

We mustn't be too hard on E. P. I *asked* him to help me write that review (1) because I didn't know what to say about the book and (2) because I thought he had been treated badly by the *Poetry Review* and that this might be some measure of reparation!

Your "poem" is very amusing! I think it might annoy him! We were together with Hulme at 67 Frith St. on Tuesday evening. He was very talkative! You know I think his bark is much worse than his bite; and that much that seems offensive to us externally is merely external and a kind of outer defense — a mask. His letter to Monro, for instance, is not by any means in the same spirit as his reception of Monro's letter. That was only childish play for your benefit, I dare say. At any rate, he refuses M's gold, and says there must be other contributors who want it more; will not contribute — for very good reasons, I think; and so on. All the same he irritates; and we mustn't allow ourselves to be irritated, don't you think? Don't you feel it as a weakness?

I am seeing T. E. Hulme tomorrow, and I will ask him when he could meet us both, as you suggest. I deny that I am a metrical expert: Hulme is always interested in ideas, and always gives something in return.

Has my poem floored you?

I have left your letter at home; so forget whether there are any other points in it. A vous de coeur. F. S. F.

I spoke to Monro about printing your new work. He was responsive.

58 · To John T. Bartlett

Dear John:-   6 August [1913]   Beaconsfield

I have had no word out of you to encourage me to go on with the material for the article you were going [to do] to please John G. and Henry's Mother with. You should have three reviews in hand, the one from Poetry, the one from The English Review and the one from Poetry and Drama. I am sending the personal notice from the August English Bookman. You may use them or not in the way I suggested; I shan't care too much if you don't. I know you must be very busy. Consult your own inclination.

No one of the articles but should be used with some judgement. This Bookman piece for instance makes me out as able to earn a living on a farm with both hands in my Norfolk-jacket pocket. Rats. I should rather you would eliminate that. The word "stark" in it will do well enough, though it is wide enough of the mark. As things go here in criticism it passes for a term of praise. "Bizarre" is a way off for A Hundred Collars. But never mind it was kindly meant. And the editor only knew the poem by hear say. On the whole I think the Bookman article needs manipulation as little as any. It is fairly discrete.

Be sure to get rid of the slam at America in the English Review article; also in the "Poetry" and "Poetry and Drama" articles. The remark about the Great American Editors is not quite fair either to the editors or to me. For the rest I leave it to you.

Don't let the paragraph in T. P.'s worry you. This getting reviewed for poetry over here is all sorts of a game. The explanation of the T. P.'s reviewer is this. He is my rival for the affections of David Nutt (publisher) and his own little volume of verse hasn't been reviewed at all.

I dont know whether I am a craftsman or not in your sense of the word. Some day I will take time to explain to you in what sense of the word I am one of the few artists writing. I am one of the few who have a theory of their own upon which all their work down to the least accent is done. I expect to do something to the present state of literature in America. That is why I dont want any slaps at my friends at home.

Now don't you do a thing you aren't moved to. Perhaps for some reason you think poorly of the Derry News plan. Would it be better to do it for the Manchester Union?

I am very busy myself for a person whose temperament is so self-obstructive. The next book begins to look large. Though I cant be sure that I will be ready with it this fall. I should like to sell some of it to the magazines first. A few hundred dollars earned that way might save my neck.

No use saying that we wish we heard from both of you more often.   Affectionately   R.

59 · To John T. Bartlett

Dear John: [7 August 1913]   Beaconsfield
   [. . .] I always feel perfectly right for a whole day after I have had a letter from you. You and your tale of Aggy-papers! And do you remember little Dicky Potter, Ben Bolt? You despised him for a farmer once and now look at your writing rabbity poultry articles for a farm journal. We never know. You were studying Greek then; Potter is doubtless teaching it now. Turn, fortune, turn thy wheel and lower the proud.

   One of the curious fatalities in our lives is that without collusion we have simultaneously turned our minds to run on rusticity. You will gather from the Bookman article (which I sent yesterday) what my next book is to be like. I ought to send you some of it. I may decide to call it New England Eclogues. Which do you think from the following list of titles you would prefer to read? The Death of the Hired Man, The House-keeper (or Slack Ties), The Wrong, A Servant to Servants, The Code (of Farm Service), Swinging Birches, Blueberries, The Mountain, A Hundred Collars, The Cellar Hole, The Black Cottage. All are stories between one hundred and two hundred lines long. I have written one today that I may call The Lantern if Mrs. Frost doesn't dissuade me: she doesn't think it a fit. None of the lot is a love affair except the Cellar Hole and I am not sure that that isn't least successful of all.   R.

60 · To John T. Bartlett

THIS LETTER nicely illustrates a tendency which grew in RF as the years passed: the expression of obsessive resentments, through letter-writing, as a way of "blowing off steam." In letter 52-a, Mrs. Frost made clear the kindnesses of the family of the distinguished archaeologist, Ernest Arthur Gardner, to the Frost family. A graduate of Cambridge University, Gardner served as Director of the British School of Archaeology at Athens from 1887 to 1895, became Professor of Archaeology at University College, London, and published many volumes on his subject. Notice the inconsistency with which RF spells the Gardner family name.

30 August 1913

Dear John: Kingsbarns, Fifeshire

To relieve my feelings just a word from Scotland on the funny holiday we are having with the Professor Gardiners. They are a family I got entangled with at the opening of the Poetry Shop in High Holborn last winter. It was not my fault at all. I want you to know one thing: I have thrust myself and book on no one here. I have made my way partly on my merits, mostly on my luck, but I have never forced my way one inch. These Gardiners are the kind that hunt lions and they picked me up cheap as a sort of bargain before I was as yet made. I ought not to draw them too unsympathetically, for they have meant to be kind and I count it to their credit that they have embraced the whole family in their attentions. But, but! There is a string to it all, I find. They are a one-hoss poet and artist themselves and at the present moment they are particularly keen on lions as creatures who may be put under obligations to review them in the papers. Sic ad astra itur in London town. It would make you weep. The Missus Gardiner is the worst. Nothing would satisfy her but we must all pack up and come to Scotland (Firth of Tay) to be near them for two weeks. So we let ourselves be dragged. Now the question is what do we think of their book. Well, I haul off and start to say what I don't think with appropriate sops to my conscience. But such integrity as I have is all literary. I make a poor liar where the worth of books is concerned. I flounder and am lost. Thus much in the historical present. The Gardners don't like me any more. They despise my judgement and resent my tactlessness. But here I am on their hands. They are a gentleman and must carry it off with manners. Himself being an archaeologist (London University) he proposes to entertain us of an afternoon by conducting us to a cave near St Andrews for a look at an elephant a horse and an ass done by paleolithic man on the walls. These are the first drawings (or cuttings) of cavemen discovered in the British Isles and as Gardner discovered them and the discovery is going to make a stir when it is announced presently naturally we were expected to feel the honour of being taken into what is as yet a profound secret. But, but! Same old hoodoo of my too critical mind. I wanted to see the animals and I saw them. There were many marks on the cave wall, some wavy grooves due to water, some sharp-edged depressions due to the flaking off of the sandstone strata. It would have been strange if some of the marks hadn't accidentally looked like something. The sandstone was so soft and moist that a little rubbing easily made them look more like something. Animals are always the better for rubbing. And think of it — tracery like that and in such a substance assumed to have lasted for ten — twenty thousand years. Why I'd be willing to leave it to the cave men as to whether they had anything to do with the elephant the horse or the ass. I'll bet the layer of sandstone they are on hasn't been uncovered five hundred years if it has been a hundred. I begin to think I must be some archaeologist myself, I doubted the authenticity of this prehistoric menagerie so easily. The beasts left me cold. I tried to rise to the moment, but the cave was clammy and there were other things, principally the literary literature. Still I have no doubt a rumpus will be raised over Gardner's discovery. Sic ad astra itur in highbrow circles. Let's see didnt you dig up a Neanderthal man in the Vancouver city dump?

Not a word to your city editor about all this. I am betraying a confidence in consigning it to paper. But damn —

St Andrews is old enough anyway without the cave drawings. We stood in the town under a tower that has figured in history since the sixth century — St Regulus' Tower. All round us were the ruins of the great cathedral that John Knox preached his followers into setting on fire during the Reformation. I haven't given you much of this sort of thing. Sounds very travelly.

Dont write to me here. We are only Fifing for a couple of weeks. Pretty little village Kingsbarns — where the king used to store his grain when his capital was Dunfermline town and his Piraeus at Aberdour (read again the ballade of Sir Patrick Spens.) Right foreninst us is the Bell Rock Lighthouse which was the Inchcape Bell of Southey's poem. The children like it. I suppose it wont hurt my New Hampshire impressions as I have always been afraid learning a new language might hurt my English style.   Affectionately   R. F.

60-a · Ralph Hodgson to Robert Frost

AS THIS LETTER makes clear, it was the poet Wilfrid W. Gibson through whom RF met the poet Ralph Hodgson. It was Hodgson, in turn, who introduced RF to Edward Thomas. See letter 69-a.

RF's poem here mentioned was probably "The Death of the Hired Man," which was circulated in manuscript form among friends of Gibson.

14 September 1913

Dear Frost,   The Red House   Buntingford, Herts.

Forgive me for keeping your poem a day or two longer than I ought to have done. I very much like it, and imagine it must be unique in American poetry; it is like nothing I have seen from your country, and I forsee a welcome for it in ours. It was a great pleasure to me to meet you the other day, I owe Gibson a good turn for that. I am down here for a few days but hope to renew our acquaintance directly I get back if you are about town.   With best wishes

Sincerely yours   Ralph Hodgson

61 · To Sidney Cox

Dear Cox: [c. 15 September 1913]   Beaconsfield

Suppose I put off scolding you the rest [letter 54] till another time and allow myself the freedom in pencil of saying anything that comes into my head. I wonder if there is anything in particular you would like to know about how life goes over here and I wonder if I am mind-reader enough to guess what it would be.

There is Yates you spoke of as being rated by the departmental professor considerably below that good boy from Oxford, the sing-songing (as distinguished from the song-singing) Alfie No-yes. Do you want to hear what I think of him? If you are where you can lay hands on the Oxford Book of Victorian Verse I can talk to you from that. It gives Noyes plenty of space to show his paces. "When spring comes back to England" is pleasant enough lilt — the children like it — very likely it is the best thing Noyes has done. But no one would say that it was stirring. The second poem with the tiresome "mon bel ami" refrain expects you to be moved at the thought that Venus has settled down to suckle John Bull's baby by an English hearth. The thought is not stirring: the note is not deep enough to be stirring. Swinging is not stirring, you know. Neither is swelling necessarily stirring. The poem in which he gets Francis Thompson "purpureally enwound" swells, but who cares a pin. I wish I knew what you thought he had written that got below the surface of things. I believe he has preached a little — is preaching now on the subject of peace. I recall a poem beginning, Beyond beyond and yet again beyond! What went ye forth to seek oh foolish fond." That strikes a note. ("Foolish fond" is rather awful.) I doubt if there is very much to him however. He is nothing for the American people to rage over. His attractive manners and his press agents have given you an exaggerated idea of his importance.

Yates' lines

> "For the good are always the merry
> Save by an evil chance"

are worth all of Noyes put together.

"Who dreamed that beauty passes like a dream?" That line fairly weeps defiance to the un-ideal, if you will understand what I mean by that. The Rose of the World, The Fiddler of Dooney, The Lake Isle of Innisfree, Down by the Sally Gardens, The Song of the Wandering Aengus, the Song of the Sad Shepherd — those are all poems. One is sure of them. They make the sense of beauty ache.

> "Then nowise worship dusty deeds."

Such an untameable spirit of poetry speaks there. You must really read Yates. He is not always good. Not many of his longer things are more than interesting. But the Land of Heart[']s Desire is lovely and so is On Shadowy Waters in poetry and Cathleen Ni Hoolihan in prose.

Some one the the other day was deriving all the Masefield and Gibson sort of thing from one line of Yates' Land of Heart[']s Desire:

> "The butter's at your elbow, Father Hart."

Oh Yates has undoubtedly been the man of the last twenty years in English poetry. I won't say that he is quite great judged either by the way he takes himself as an artist or by the work he has done. I am afraid he has come just short of being. The thing you mention has been against him. I shouldn't care so much — I shouldn't care at all, if it hadn't touched and tainted his poetry. Let him be as affected as he pleases if he will only write well. But you can't be affected and write entirely well.

You'll be thinking this is an essay on something. Lets be personal for a change.

I had a chance to see and hear the other night how perilously near Yates comes to believing in fairies. He told with the strangest accent of wistful half belief of the leppercaun (spell it) two old folks he visited had had in a cage on the wall. The little fellow was fine and sleek when they trapped him, but he pined in captivity until they had to let him go. All the time they had him another leppercaun hung about the house mourning (in silence) for him. And when the old folks out of pity let him go the two fairies hurried off hand in hand down the glen. Yates I could see, was in a state of mind to resent being asked point blank what he thought of such a story. And it wouldn't have been best for anyone to go on the assumption that he told it to be amusing. My Catholic friend Liebich tells me he for his part didn't know but that everybody had some sort of belief in fairies. He said it was something like the belief in the communion of saints.

There's a good story I had pretty directly from Mrs. Sharp about how she was out with her husband (Fiona Macleod) walking somewhat ahead of him in an English lane one day when she saw something childlike with a goat's legs scuttle into the woods. She stood still with astonishment. Her husband came up. "William, what do you think? — a faun! I saw him."

"It's nothing," said William without coming to a standstill, "such creatures are all about this part of the country."

We are just back from a two week's journey in Scotland. We went up the coast to Dundee by boat and from there by train to Kingsbarns a little old town close to St. Andrews. We saw some sights inevitably though we were not out sightseeing. The best of the adventure was the time in Kingsbarns where tourists and summer boarders never come. The common people in the south of England I don't like to have around me. They don't know how to meet you man to man. The people in the north are more like Americans. I wonder whether they made Burns' poems or Burns' poems made them. And there are stone walls (dry stone dykes) in the north: I liked those. My mother was from Edinburgh. I used to hear her speak of the Castle and Arthur's Seat, more when I was young than in later years. I had some interest in seeing those places. The children saw the Black Watch march into the Castle with a band of bagpipes.

The trouble with this sort of composition is that one could go on with it forever. I have told you enough to show you what we are doing with ourselves. If I haven't — well today we walked to Jordans and stood between Penn's grave and the graves of his five little children. It is not far to go. We have done the walk before. We mean to get down to church there some day. The meeting house is much as it was in Penn's day. Only the money-changers have got a foothold in it — I mean the sellers of picture postalcards to the fugitive American. I don't know who is to blame for this, the Englishman or the American. People here blame the latter. Etc etc etc etc

You may do anything you can to give the boys of Poland [New York] a better chance for all I care, I am not always a doubter. Have me in mind five or six years from now when results begin to show. You must work off your enthusiasm in any way you can.

Tell us about the new job. You will soon be drowning your cares in unlimited theme-correcting. Mortify the flesh, old man. Suffer. My soul, how you like it.

Sincerely yours   Robert Frost.

62 · To Harold Monro

Dear Monro: 12 October [1913]   Beaconsfield

I regretted not being able to join you in Frith St. I was away on a long tramp when your card came yesterday and did not get in till late. Perhaps next meeting — if you have decided to have another meeting. Thanks for thinking of me.

Of course I very much want you to print something of mine. At the same time I doubt if the poem you have chosen is as representative as the Hundred Collars. You may say that it will bear printing alone better than the Hundred Collars; and that, to be sure, is a consideration. I have felt from the first that it was too much to ask you to use two poems at once.

You can tell me more about it when I am with you to consider your exceptions to The Fear.

Sincerely yours   Robert Frost

63 · To Thomas B. Mosher

Dear Mr Mosher: 24 October 1913 Beaconsfield

I had your letter and the two copies of your catalogue with my poem ["Reluctance"] where I am pleased to see it. There is but one thing more you could do for me at present and possibly there are too great difficulties in the way of that. The most insuperable would be your not wanting to do it. Then there is Mrs. Nutt. Still I am very jealous of Bottomley,* whom I expect to know shortly through Travelyan [Robert Calverley Trevelyan]. Perhaps I shouldnt equal myself to Bottomley, and I won't: but I give you fair warning I am going to have my moderate success in these islands. The signs are not wanting. The review you speak of is one of them. The kind of people the book is interesting is another. [Laurence] Binyon had me to lunch the other day with [Robert] Bridges. When I can get rid of this house I am to go to Gloucester to live, to be with Wilfrid Gibson and Abercrombie. I am out with Pound pretty much altogether and so I don't see his friend Yeats as I did. I count myself well out however. Pound is an incredible ass and he hurts more than he helps the person he praises.

These Englishmen are very charming. I begin to think I shall stay with them till I'm deported. If I weren't so poor I should plan to stay five years anyway.

Don't take me as urging my book on you too seriously. I have made no move to urge it on anyone over there and am like to make none until people have had time to hear of it a little. I suppose that sort of thing will keep. I am an almost fatally patient person as a tale I could tell would show. At anyrate I have no strength to batter out against the indifference of those who will meet me with a "Who are you?" or "Go get a reputation."

Parts of my next book should begin to appear here and there soon. Monro told me he would use A Hundred Collars and perhaps one other eclogue (or what you will) in the Dec. Poetry and Drama. Poetry (Chicago) has announced something — I don't know what — very likely The Black Cottage. The book will not be named as Mrs Nutt had it but more likely "New Englanders" or "New England Hill Folk." † The name is

---

* Mosher had already published the poems of Gordon Bottomley in an American edition.
† The catalogue of David Nutt and Company, issued in 1913, advertised the title of the new RF book as *Farm Servants and Other People*.

about the only part not ready to go to press. The poems are rather too long for most magazines. I think I may offer one or two to [Mitchell] Kennerley but I have little hope of his seeing them in the ruck. I think of him as more than usually overwhelmed with manuscript. Of course I should like any money I can get from the magazines. One has to live and eat.

Well well. This letter has run into lengths.

Sincerely yours   Robert Frost.

64 · To John T. Bartlett

[*c.* 5 November 1913]

Dear John   The Bung Hole, Still

Never you let that silly business of remembering me to my Derry friends put any strain on your feeling for me. I keep not hearing from you; and I begin to be afraid I have asked you to do more than you could do or wanted to do. Very likely you didn't like the idea of stirring 'em up in our old haunts. I don't know that I blame you. It was just my impulse. You are quite free to beg off in the matter. I trust it is no worse than that. It occurs to me as possible that you may have tried to deliver the article on Birch Street and got a snub for your pains. It would have been through no fault of yours, but you may have been uncomfortable about it all this time. The whole thing is of no importance — utterly. I ought not to give way to thoughts of revenge in the first place. Still there were a few people in Derry who vexed me and one or two who did more than that and I am human enough to want to make them squirm a little before I forgive them.

You are about all I saved from the years I spent in Derry, you and Margaret, and the three children born to us on the farm, and the first book that was mostly written on the farm before I attended school at Pinkerton. I really care not a fig either way for or against any one else I fell in with in my teaching days. I don't want you to grow cold in letter writing. You are to act always on the assumption that we are going to get together again across the meridians. Of course we are. I always think if you would take measures to strike up a correspondence for one of these London papers you would sooner or later land here among the literary people, and with better prospects of staying than I have because you know how to make

97

money. Think it over. I am reminded of you every time I see a special article from British Columbia.

You mus[t]n't take me too seriously if I now proceed to brag a bit about my exploits as a poet. There is one qualifying fact always to bear in mind: there is a kind of success called "of esteem" and it butters no parsnips. It means a success with the critical few who are supposed to know. But really to arrive where I can stand on my legs as a poet and nothing else I must get outside that circle to the general reader who buys books in their thousands. I may not be able to do that. I believe in doing it — dont you doubt me there. I want to be a poet for all sorts and kinds. I could never make a merit of being caviare to the crowd the way my quasi-friend Pound does. I want to reach out, and would if it were a thing I could do by taking thought. So much by way of depreciation before I begin. Now for it, a little of it.

I suppose I arrived in a sense the other day when Laurence Binyon asked me to lunch with Robert Bridges the Laureat[e]. It meant this much: Binyon had decided that my book was one of the few and he was good enough to want me to have my chance with the Chief. So I took it. That is the best sounding thing I have to tell. I don't know that it pleased me any more than to find [R.C.] Trevelyan, a man who is known as a patron of art, with my book in his pocket. He had bought it on the recommendation of somebody who is supposed to know all about poetry. I am sure that it pleased me less than the friendly attentions I have had from Wilfrid Gibson and Lascelles Abercrombie. These fellows you can know if you can get hold of either Q's Oxford Book of Victorian Verse or The Georgian Anthology. They are something more than my casual acquaintances. If or when we can get rid of this house I am going down into Gloucester to live near them. The second book is what has drawn them to me. Some of the manuscript has been passed around and they have seen it.

I think that's all except that Mrs. Nutt in her devotion to my cause has already announced the second book without waiting for me to say the word. So the anxiety of finding a publisher is off my mind. As the boys say here, It is success enough if your first book does well enough to get you a publisher for the second. The book should be out in February. You shall have some of it before then if you write me a decent letter and give me your new address. Gone out of the rabbit business, hey?

Ain't working the land? Easier to write about it? Think I don't understand?

You and Margaret ought to see how few pieces of furniture we keep house with. It is cosy enough, but it would be a lesson to you in plain living. I would give anything if you could drop in on us. Affectionately Rob

65 · To Sidney Cox

[c. 8 November 1913]
Dear Cox The bung-hole still

You must send me these two reviews back if you will. Not that I want them to treasure; I am not given to laying up for myself treasures of that kind. But I may want them to impress one more person with before I get through. On second thought, I will consent to spare the one from *The Academy* on condition that you send it to the professor who found my quality so indefinable. (Don't get mad! it has never entered my head but that he meant to be nice: thank you for showing him the book.)

We have just had Guy Fawkes Gun Powder Plot Day which for squibs or firecrackers is to our Fourth-of-July as water is to wine or as poor damp pop-corn is to good pop-corn. I saw nobody hanged in effigy — not even L[l]oyd George, though he must have been hanged many times over.

Yours R. F.

Have I sent you David Nutt's Catalogue?

66 · To Sidney Cox

Dear Cox: [c. 26 November 1913] Beaconsfield

The next thing to do is to get married and, as the hero of one of the eclogues in "North of Boston" says, "forget considerations." Go out of yourself some fine morning and by way of celebration lick something if it is no more formidable than the Peace Movement. You do right to damn grammar: you might be excused if you damned rhetoric and in fact everything else in and out of books but the spirit, which is good because it is the only good that we can't talk or write or even think about. No don't damn the spirit.

99

You will be all right (Do the theme-children — Charles Lamb had dream-children — do the theme-children still want to spell it alright?) You ought to be a tremendous force for something when the right touch releases you. A belief in fairies may be just the thing. What are they but the Irresponsibilities, and a precious source of inspiration midway between heaven and hell. We haven't always to be either good or bad you know. Or rather you don't know, but a lady has been sent to tell you. There are whole days when the fairies and a belief in them will justify you in being gay, nothing but gay.

I preach. But this is the last time. You will not need to be preached to any more. Not even by your own conscience! Give yourself a chance. The world is ourn.

Let's hear a little more about it at your leisure. I feel sort of half introduced to someone. Take your time. As it comes natural.

Mrs. Frost and I were at a play on Saturday in which we were asked point blank to profess our faith not only in fairies, but in devils and black art as well. So I suppose I shall have to. Do I, then? I do, as they say in the marriage ceremony. Only I shall have to be allowed to define in what sense. But that is another story and a lifelong one.

I'm glad for you. So also is Mrs Frost. She wants me to tell you that specially from her. It is not the first time we have had to be glad for a friend in need lately. First there was John [Bartlett] of Vancouver. Then it was Wilfrid Gibson and now it is you. Well well. Be young, mes enfants.

Ever yours   Robert Frost.

67 · To John T. Bartlett

Dear John: 8 December 1913   Beaconsfield

[. . .] In the same mail with Margaret's letter came a copy of *The Plymouth Normal School Prospect* with a reproduction of the whole of what you did for me in The [Derry] News. You exercised the proper discretion. If I have a fault to find it is with the rosy picture you painted of our life in the pretty London suburb inextricably involved in the literary society of the great. But the exaggeration does your heart credit and it wont hurt me as much as it will some people in Derry. (Christ forgive me the sin of vengefulness: from this hour forth I will have no more of it. Perhaps I only say so because for the moment I am sated.) We *could* go among the great (in our humble way — we are far from important yet) but at the same time we can't. Our means forbid. Wander not from the point I keep making that we are playing a rather desperate game with our little wealth. The poets here are of three kinds — the poor rats in one room and a suit of clothes with no family to take care of and much too cunning to be caught in that trap, the gentlemanly minors with a graceful weakness for verse and by common consent quite rich enough to indulge it and the few like Masefield who arrive at one jump. I am like none of these. I must make my way very slowly: such is my doom I am afraid. There will be little money return directly from my poetry — at least for the present. Indirectly if I am clever enough and strong enough I may get some part of a living out of it by following it up with commercial prose. Mrs. Nutt looks for that. The paralyzing thought is that I was always a poor hand to do what I had to do: I write bad stuff under pressure. So you see I am no stranger to worry. All is not beer and skittles that wears the look at six thousand miles.

I think Silver may have written the few words of introduction to your article in *The Prospect*. He spoke of you as a "distinguished journalist of Vancouver" and formerly a pupil of mine, at Derry. Very nice of him all round. I didn't know how he would relish my glorification. I never know how to take him, as friend or enemy. I used to notice he believed what I said about people. I stood in with him that much. I never said you were even better than you showed in school without seeing sooner or later its effect on him. Now it is working the other way. I helped establish your reputation with him and now you are increasing mine with him. We must both walk up and simultaneously ask a big favor of him when he gets to be king of New Hampshire.

I don't know how much of the new book to send at once. It will be more fun to throw it to you in pieces. Here are four or five to start with. *Poetry and Drama* for this month will have two more: *Poetry* at an early date one and perhaps two. I'll see that you get those. *Poetry and Drama,* a quarterly, costs so much it will have to be my Christmas present to you this year. I am literally and disgustingly busted. The book will be called "North of Boston."

The loveliest stroke you did for me was telling Hamilton

Mabie about the other book. I am only afraid he may have too much trouble in getting hold of it. I haven't gone looking for a publisher in America yet. Mrs Nutt sent out two copies over there for review. We got a rise out of one of them, The Dial, Chicago.

I'll be writing again soon; and Elinor will be writing to Margaret. Both write as often as you can: you have no idea how much we look for your letters.

Affectionately   Rob

In "North of Boston" you are to see me performing in a language absolutely unliterary. What I would like is to get so I would never use a word or combination of words that I hadn't *heard* used in running speech. I bar words and expressions I have merely seen. You do it on your ear. Of course I allow expressions I make myself. War on clichés.

68 · To ERNEST L. SILVER

Dear Mr Silver   8 December 1913   Beaconsfield

I suppose I am to take that complementary copy of The Prospect, complementary in more ways than one, as a letter from you. The handwriting on the envelope would seem to be yours, and anyway the advertising I am given in the magazine is your work. So thank you. I can stand it. I have about come to the conclusion that a man can stand being overpraised better than underpraised. Strange, ain't it? If John lays it on a little thick anywhere, you have to remember John was a favorite pupil and never disliked anything I said or did. The only trouble is that he must make it sound to an American ear as if my poetry had made my fortune. Of course any royalties on a forty-cent book have done no such thing. At most poetry can pave the way for prose and prose may or may not make money. I have still the battle all before me and with not much stomach for the money-making part of it. I am less inclined to prose than I thought I was when I looked into the future out of a normal school window in Plymouth. I was always that way: Two or three days on end I would write prose, first having resolved it was the thing for a man with a family to do. But just when I thought I bade fair to produce a novel, right in the middle of chapter three or four I would bring up in another inconsequential poem. Sort of incorrigible I am. Once I actually did write some half dozen short stories I sold to Farm Poultry (Boston) for ten dollars apiece. That was about as far as I ever got.

No it remains to be seen whether I shall take hold and earn a living as a writer. I find writing hard work. I have been a harder boss on myself than ever you were on me. I am clean shucked out by this last book — (North of Boston, I have decided to call it). There's some hope that I may die again. If I were sure, I'd try to take out some more insurance. This is the side of the picture John didn't give you — the funny side.

[. . .] You bet we'll be glad to see some one from home. Of course no amount of success can keep us here more than another year after this. My dream would be to get the thing started in London and then do the rest of it from a farm in New England where I could live cheap and get Yankier and Yankier. We may decide to go home this year. I wish I knew how you were fixed at the cottage — on account of the furniture. Is the state going to build you a parsonage? Or shall you live on where you are or were?

[. . .] Homesickness makes us news-hungry. Every time the postman bangs the letter-slot-door our mouths go open and our eyes shut like birds' in a nest and we can't move for a moment. *The Prospect* mentions some names we know — none too many. That was good as far as it went. I seem to live more in Plymouth than in Derry.

Remember me to everybody.

Sincerely yours   Robert Frost

69 · To John T. Bartlett

RF's promise (letter 67) to send John Bartlett a copy of *Poetry and Drama* (December, 1913) as a Christmas present was generously fulfilled. The gift was spiced with marginal comments, which amounted to a long letter. In this transcription the bracketed editorial notes give the page of each comment together with the title and author of the contribution. Contextual references indicate that these comments were written on or about 15 December 1913.

[Page 395, opposite the poem "Flycatchers" by Robert Bridges] I heard this great man in a brave theory of rhythm at lunch at the Vienna Cafe not long since. He holds that our syllables are to be treated in verse as having quantities of many shades. That is to say they are quarter, third and fifth notes as the case may be. Who knows not that, nor acts upon it, is no poet. Well here we have him acting upon it, we are to presume. Poor old man. He is past seventy. It is the fashion to play up to him. He still seems capable of the emotion of disgust. Mind you he has done good things.

[Page 395, opposite the poem "My Spirit Will Not Haunt the Mound" by Thomas Hardy] Hardy is almost never seen in a public place. When seen he is not heard. They say he looks like a little old stone-mason. He is an excellent poet and the greatest living novelist here. Elinor and I saw a terrible little curtain raiser (hair-raiser would be better) called the Three Travellers that he made. One traveller after another came in out of a storm to a feast in a cottage. The first is a convicted sheep stealer escaped from jail where he was to have been hanged next morning. The second is the hangman on his way to the jail to hang him. He sits with the convict on the same high bench and sings him a hanging song. He gets his rope out of a bag — But I believe it is all in a short story somewhere. You may have read it.

[Page 396, opposite the poem "The Enchanted Hill" by Walter de la Mare] This seems ineffectual. But the author is the one man we are all agreed to praise here. His "The Listeners" is the best poem since the century came in. He is hardly of the fashion, which makes it the stranger that he is so much honored. Earns his living by reading manuscripts for a publisher.

[Page 402, opposite the poem "The Funeral of Youth: Threnody" by Rupert Brooke] This boy I have met once. He is near you now, in Calif. He effects a metaphysical sarcasm and would be a later John Donne.

[Page 404, opposite the poem "He Wonders Whether to Praise or to Blame Her" by Rupert Brooke] We know this hardly treated girl [Phyllis Gardner] oh very well. Her beauty is her red hair. Her cleverness is in painting. She has a picture in the New English Exhibition. Her mother has written a volume of verse in which he [Rupert Brooke] gets his. Very funny. No one will die.

[Page 405, opposite "The Way that Lovers Use" by Rupert Brooke] Wow!

[Pages 406-415, first printings of RF's "The Fear" and "A Hundred Collars"; no marginal comments]

[Page 416, opposite the poem "Revolt: An Ode" by John Alford] This boy has taken a dislike to me on account of a review in which he suffered in comparison with me. Here we get down to someone who just can't write poetry.

[Page 421, opposite the poem "The Bird of Paradise" by W. H. Davies] Davies is lovely; tramped America till he lost a leg under a freight car. Came home and sold his own ballads on penny sheets till they gave him a pension to take him off the streets. Has done some good things in unconscious art. Said he to me, "I remember you were there the other night. I spoke to you didn't I? But I was awful. After you went I went out of the restaurant a minute for one more drink and I never found my way back."

[Page 428, after specific lines in a poem entitled "The Old Witch in the Copse" by Frances Cornford, RF comments in praise of them as illustrating his own theories concerning "the sound of sense"]

[Page 429, opposite "Children of Love" by Harold Monro] The gloomy spirit that edits this. No one can laugh when he is looking. His taste in literature is first for the theological and after that for anything that has the bite of sin. He got up a penny sheet of Blake to sell in the slums and you ought to have seen the risky selections he made. But dear me everybody is writing with one foot in the red-light district.

[Starting on page 485, John Alford reviews sixteen volumes of American poetry, including separate works by William Ellery Leonard, Cale Young Rice, William Rose Benét, Horace Holley, Isabelle Howe Fiske, Clinton Scollard, Herman Hagedorn, Amy Lowell, and Ezra Pound. Alford's second paragraph begins, "Now it is just as well to state at the beginning that I can find no support to a belief that there is any such thing as American poetry; just as an examination of the Metropolitan Museum of New York finally destroyed my idea that there was any such thing as American art."] This is what makes it impossible that I should live long under a criss-cross flag. Me for the three colors the bluebird wears. This cub doesn't know how to find his way around among American writers. No one he mentions is thought anything of on the other side — no one of recent date. Emerson is so American, so original, especially in form. I'll bet you five he couldn't read him if he tried. Whitman and Poe ad stomachache.

[Page 486, after Alford's harsh comments on Cale Young Rice, Clinton Scollard and Charlton M. Lewis] Not that I weep for these.

[Page 487, opposite Alford's observation, "Mr. Pound is a unique phenomenon, for he has succeeded in being an American, a man of culture and a poet, all at the same time."] The magazine has had a row with Ezra. This is olive branch. Monro needs him in his business.

69-a · EDWARD THOMAS TO ROBERT FROST

THERE IS evidence that RF and Edward Thomas first met at a favorite restaurant for literary men of the day, St. George's, in St. Martin's Lane in London on 5 October 1913. It is possible that the following letter indicates the time of their second meeting. Their most meaningful period of friendship occurred in August of 1914, when they lived next door to each other in Gloucestershire.

Among the many Thomas letters that RF kept, this is the earliest.

17 December 1913

Dear Frost (if you don't mind) [London]

I should be glad to see you again & Flint for the first time on Monday next at St. George's at 4. You remember the place in St. Martin's Lane where we first met. Top floor. I think Davies and Hodgson will be there.

Yours sincerely   E. Thomas

69-b · SUSAN HAYES WARD TO ROBERT FROST

[c. 25 December 1913

My dear Robert Frost   North Berwick, Maine]

I congratulate you on the recognition you are receiving, but far more on pluck and ability. I remember with what delight I carried your "Butterfly" down to Washington and read it to Bliss Carman and Charles Roberts and asked if that wasn't the real thing. I was sure you had it in you then. Possibly you may not remember but you told me that you wrote that poem when you first began to realize that poetry ought to "sound well."

But this card is to wish you joy and pleasure and happiness and that "higher than happiness," blessedness, and may you be kindly led into all truth.

Yours faithfully   Susan Hayes Ward

Give the bairns my love and blessing.

70 · To SIDNEY COX

Dear Cox   19 January 1914   Beaconsfield

Absolve me of trying to make you think of me as hobnobbing with the great over here and I am ready to begin my *very* short talks based on Quiller-Couch. I'm far from important enough for the likes of the Poet Laureate to have sought me out. I'm simply going to tell you about him because I happen to have eaten at the same table with him by an accident. I was visiting Lawrence Binyon (see anthology) when Bridges turned up. I have a right to tell you how the king looked to the cat that looked at him.

He's a fine old boy with the highest opinion — of his poetry you thought I was going to say — perhaps of his poetry, but much more particularly of his opinions. He rides two hobbies tandem, his theory that syllables in English have fixed quantity that cannot be disregarded in reading verse, and his theory that with forty or fifty or sixty characters he can capture and hold for all time the sounds of speech. One theory is as bad as the other and I think owing to much the same fallacy. The living part of a poem is the intonation entangled somehow in the syntax idiom and meaning of a sentence. It is only there for those who have heard it previously in conversation. It is not for us in any Greek or Latin poem because our ears have not been filled with the tones of Greek and Roman talk. It is the most volatile and at the same time important part of poetry. It goes and the language becomes a dead language, the poetry dead poetry. With it go the accents the stresses the delays that are not the property of vowels and syllables but that are shifted at will with the sense. Vowels have length there is no denying. But the accent of sense supercedes all other accent overrides and sweeps it away. I will find you the word "come" variously used in various passages as a whole, half, third, fourth, fifth, and sixth note. It is as long as the sense makes it. When men no longer know the intonation on which we string our words they will fall back on what I may call the absolute length of our syllables which is the length we would give them in passages that meant nothing. The psychologist can actually measure this with a what-do-you-call-it. English poetry would then be read as Latin poetry is now read and as of course Latin poetry was never read by Romans. Bridges would like it read so now for the sake of scientific exactness. Because our poetry must sometime be as dead as our language must, Bridges would like it treated as if it were dead already.

I say you cant read a single good sentence with the salt in it unless you have previously heard it spoken. Neither can you with the help of all the characters and diacritical marks pronounce a single word unless you have previously heard it actually pronounced. Words exist in the mouth not in books. You can't fix them and you dont want to fix them. You want them to adapt their sounds to persons and places and times. You want them to change and be different. I shall be sorry when everybody is so public-schooled that nobody will dare to say Haow for What. It pleases me to contemplate the word Sosieti that the reformers sport on their door plate in a street in London. The two i's are bad enough. But the o is what I love. Which o is that if we must be exact.

Bridges wants to fix the vocables here and now because he sees signs of their deteriorating. He thinks they exist in print for people. He thinks they are of the eye. Foolish old man is all I say. How much better that he should write good poetry if he hasn't passed his time. He has been a real poet, though you never would judge it from a thing in the Dec[ember] Poetry and Drama in which he takes the unsentimental view of teachers that they cram us with dead dry stuff like the dead flies on the window sill.

You will have to import your own books I'm afraid, unless Sherman French & Co of Boston would get them for you. Books and postage in the awful quantity you mention would cost you four American dollars. You mustn't get one book more than you honestly feel that you can dispose of. No silly promises are binding.   Yours   R Frost

Make you a present of all the words I have misspelled in this letter. They'll do you good if they correct a little your tendency to think as a teacher that everything must be correct.

71 · To Thomas B. Mosher

Dear Mr. Mosher: 20 January 1914 Beaconsfield

All that Richard [Badger] says and more also. It seems to me you must lead the pleasantest life north of Boston.

North of Boston, by the way, is the name of my *forthcoming* book which at your suggestion I am offering to Sherman-French. Here again I have to thank you and Bill Reedy* too — whether anything comes of it all or not. Do you think I ought to send Reedy a copy of my book — first book? I have hardly been noticed in America. Mrs Nutt sent but two copies over for review, one to the Dial and one to some newspaper. The whole continent remains virgin soil to me.

You spoke once on a time of giving up the Bibelot after a volume or two more. You must think twice before you do it. I sometimes dream you may use it yet to foster something very American in literature. It isn't always the subsidized ventures that accomplish things. "Poetry" (Chicago) hasn't done anything but foster Pound and a few free-verse friends. I wonder if you noticed the comparison [Ford Madox] Hueffer instituted in it between De La Mare and F. S. Flint. And I wonder what you thought of it. Do you know De La Mare's "Listeners"? Beautiful book. I have a copy of Flint's "In the Net of the Stars" if you haven't seen it. Flint belongs to Pound's clique. Hueffer patronizes it en bloc.

Sincerely yours Robert Frost.

Later. I met Mrs. Nutt in London to-day and got politely rebuked for having entered into correspondence with Sherman-French about my book. I was told that I must write at once and refer Sherman-French to David Nutt; also that I must not think I had the right to publish so much as a poem in a magazine during the term of my contract with David Nutt. Dearie me! I feel quite upset, the more so as I have already sold to magazines some five of the sixteen poems in "North of Boston," rather I should say in honesty the more so as I haven't sold more than five of the sixteen poems. This must be a "good crowner's quest law." R. F.

* William Marion Reedy had reprinted RF's "Reluctance" in the recently metamorphosed and already famous *Reedy's Mirror* (St. Louis) soon after Mosher had printed it in his "Catalogue."

72 · To Wilbur E. Rowell

Dear Mr. Rowell   15 February 1914 Beaconsfield

There is a matter of fifty dollars still due me which you haven't forgotten, but are probably holding till I tell you where and when I want it sent. Will you kindly send it here as soon as convenient. I shall be two or three months longer in Beaconsfield, after which I go to Hereford to be with Wilfrid Gibson the English poet for a year — two or three more books before I go home — One is going through the press now and another is ready when the publisher is ready.

Very truly yours Robert Frost

73 · To John T. Bartlett

Dear John: 22 February 1914 Beaconsfield

[. . .] I set a good deal of store by the magazine work you are doing or going to do. That is your way out of bondage. You can — must write better for a magazine than there is any inducement to do for a daily.

My notion is that your work is coming on. Your style tightens up. What you will have to guard against is the lingo of the newspaper, words that nobody but a journalist uses, and worse still, phrases. John Cournos who learned his trade on the Philadelphia Record, where he went by the nickname of Gorky, has come over here to write short stories. He is thirty. His worst enemy is going to be his habit of saying cuticle for skin.

I really liked what you wrote about me. Your sentences go their distance, straight and sure and they relay each other well. You always had ideas and apprehended ideas. You mustnt lose that merit. You must find some way to show people that you have initiative and judgement. You must "get up" new things as new even as a brand new department for some paper.

[. . .] I want to write down here two or three cardinal principles that I wish you would think over and turn over now and again till we *can* protract talk.

I give you a new definition of a sentence:

A sentence is a sound in itself on which other sounds called words may be strung.

110

You may string words together without a sentence-sound to string them on just as you may tie clothes together by the sleeves and stretch them without a clothes line between two trees, but — it is bad for the clothes.

The number of words you may string on one sentence-sound is not fixed but there is always danger of over loading.

The sentence-sounds are very definite entities. (This is no literary mysticism I am preaching.) They are as definite as words. It is not impossible that they could be collected in a book though I don't at present see on what system they would be catalogued.

They are apprehended by the ear. They are gathered by the ear from the vernacular and brought into books. Many of them are already familiar to us in books. I think no writer invents them. The most original writer only catches them fresh from talk, where they grow spontaneously.

A man is all a writer if *all* his words are strung on definite recognizable sentence sounds. The voice of the imagination, the speaking voice must know certainly how to behave how to posture in every sentence he offers.

A man is a marked writer if his words are largely strung on the more striking sentence sounds.

A word about recognition: In literature it is our business to give people the thing that will make them say, "Oh yes I know what you mean." It is never to tell them something they dont know, but something they know and hadnt thought of saying. It must be something they recognize.

A Patch of Old Snow

In the corner of the wall where the bushes haven't been trimmed, there is a patch of old snow like a blow-away newspaper that has come to rest there. And it is dirty as with the print and news of a day I have forgotten, if I ever read it.

Now that is no good except for what I may call certain points of recognition in it: patch of old snow in a corner of the wall, — you know what that is. You know what a blow-away newspaper is. You know the curious dirt on old snow and last of all you know how easily you forget what you read in papers.

Now for the sentence sounds. We will look for the marked ones because they are easiest to discuss. The first sentence sound will do but it is merely ordinary and bookish: it is entirely subordinate in interest to the meaning of the words strung on it. But half the effectiveness of the second sentence is in the very special tone with which you must say — news of a day I have forgotten — if I ever read it. You must be able to say Oh yes one knows how that goes. (There is some adjective to describe the intonation or cadence, but I won't hunt for it.)

One of the least successful of the poems in my book is almost saved by a final striking sentence-sound (Asking for Roses.)

Not caring so very much *what* she supposes.

Take My November Guest. Did you know at once how we say such sentences as these when we talk?

She thinks I have no eye for these.

———

Not yesterday I learned etc.

———

But it were vain to tell her so

———

Get away from the sing-song. You must hear and recognize in the last line the sentence sound that supports, No use in telling him so.

Let's have some examples pell-mell in prose and verse because I don't want you to think I am setting up as an authority on verse alone.

My father used to say —

You're a liar!

If a hen and a half lay an egg and a half etc.

A long long time ago —

Put it there, old man! (Offering your hand)

I aint a going [to] hurt you, so you needn't be scared.

Suppose Henry Horne says something offensive to a young lady named Rita when her brother Charles is by to protect her. Can you hear the two different tones in which she says their respective names. "Henry Horne! Charles!" I can hear it better than I can say it. And by oral practice I get further and further away from it.

Never you say a thing like that to a man!

And such they are and such they will be found.

Well I swan!

Unless I'm greatly mistaken ——

112

Hence with denial vain and coy excuse
A soldier and afraid (afeared)
Come, child, come home.

The thing for me to do is to get right out of here while I am able.

No fool like an old fool.

It is so and not otherwise that we get the variety that makes it fun to write and read. *The ear does it.* The ear is the only true writer and the only true reader. I have known people who could read without hearing the sentence sounds and they were the fastest readers. Eye readers we call them. They can get the meaning by glances. But they are bad readers because they miss the best part of what a good writer puts into his work.

Remember that the sentence sound often says more than the words. It may even as in irony convey a meaning opposite to the words.

I wouldn't be writing all this if I didn't think it the most important thing I know. I write it partly for my own benefit, to clarify my ideas for an essay or two I am going to write some fine day (not far distant.)

To judge a poem or piece of prose you go the same way to work — apply the one test — greatest test. You listen for the sentence sounds. If you find some of those not bookish, caught fresh from the mouths of people, some of them striking, all of them definite and recognizable, so recognizable that with a little trouble you can place them and even name them, you know you have found a writer.

Before I ring off you may want to hear the facts in the case of us.

We are still in Beaconsfield but trying hard to get rid of our house six months before our lease is out in order to get away into Gloucester with Wilfrid Gibson and Lascelles Abercrombie (see Victorian anthology for both of them).

Book II, North of Boston, should be out now. The publisher is dilatory. I shall have another book done (out and out plays this time) before she gets Book II out. This is rough on me because I feel that now is the time to strike while there is a certain interest in me for what I have done.

I expect to be roasted more for Book III than for Book II — if for no other reason, because the fact is out that I am an American. That nasty review by Alford in the magazine I sent shows you how they feel toward us here. He begins by saying he can't get hold of enough books to find out whether we have any literature or not and then he proceeds to say we have none. I am sure he will lay for me somewhere. And there are others who have me marked.

J. C. Smith (editor of an edition of Shakespeare and several other classics for the Oxford library) will give an evening to a new American poet named Me before an Edinburgh literary society in March.

Poetry (Chicago) printed in Feb the thing I call The Code. Did I send it to you? If I didnt, you may want to look it up. It may be in the library.

No money comes in of course yet. I won't make much from poetry — I suppose you know that. I talk about prose but as long as I can put off writing pot boilers I shall. It seems to me as I look at it now I had much rather farm than write for money.

We plan to go home in September of 1915. I dont know where I shall settle. You may be coming back to New England some time. Somehow we must plan to be together.

The children all keep well but as they have found the schools impossible here they come pretty heavily on Elinor. She has not been at all well this year. I may have to give up my wilder schemes and turn to money making for the family. Not that I am ever asked to. On the contrary.

I wonder if there is anything more you are as anxious to hear as I am anxious to hear more about you.

Our love to you both. And may God amend my spelling.

Affectionately   Rob

74 · To ERNEST L. SILVER

Dear Mr. Silver: 23 February 1914   Beaconsfield

I may lose the last part of your letter, or sell it for the autograph, or give it away, but the exordium with its generous tribute to my modesty I shall keep as long as I am liable to want a job and have use for a testimonial.

I'm really more modest than I look sometimes when resenting imaginary affronts to my dignity. But I'm not as modest as I ought to be — a thing I dont intend to worry over any more because it doesn't matter whether I am modest or not if I can get enough modest men to say I am modest.

I am grateful for your good opinion but you mustn't try to spur me on to do great deeds with the names of Brown [letter 43] and Mariman. It is too cruel. Suppose I should excel in the way I have always wanted to and should make one or two honestly good but unprofitable short poems, do you think Brown would estimate the achievement as anything above a badly written bulletin for Washington? No, I can't stack up against Brown. I have neither strength nor expectation of life.

What funny things I am talking about. Here I am ready to think the worst of Brown's conceit because he hasn't taken the trouble to write to me. If you'll testify to his modesty as you do to mine, it will be all off — I shall harbor nothing against him. I leave it to you to say whether his new job has struck him out like a pouter pigeon and thrawn his neck about.

I have really made the acquaintance of but one school-man and of him entirely through my writing. He is a Scot in Edinburgh named J. C. Smith who earns his living I believe as inspector of the five or six so-called teacher's training colleges in Scotland. With all the work he must have to do, he still finds time to edit Shakespeare for the Oxford press and run after everything new in English literature. Like all of them over here he reads in half a dozen languages and like all the educated ones I have met over here he is so utterly unassuming that you might look and not see him. He is in the civil service which may partly explain his comfortable unaggressive assurance. He doesnt have to think of holding his own against anyone. He doesn't have to think of getting on. Oxford too partly explains him. The saying is that a man who has been to the English universities always appears to know less than he knows; a man who has been to the Scotch appears to know more than he knows. I don't mean that Smith's knowledge doesn't show when and where it should. The last time I saw him I don't know how many poems by all sorts of great poets he recited whole. He would say to me "How does that lyric of Shelley's go? 'Life of life thy lips enkindle —' You know it. Help me." And when I didn't help him, he would proceed to reconstruct the poem himself. Somewhat different from being a brow-beating school boss with nothing on the brain but statistics. Mind you I don't mean to imply that we haven't plenty of good men at home. Smith is no more than human. I wouldnt paint him so. I only mean you would like him. When you come over whether I am still here or not, he will be one person I shall want you to meet. — I suppose Whitcher is a fine sort. What he talks about represents so much genuine enthusiasm and not just desire to impress.

While I am on the subject of people let me tell you about the Welshman Davies. It has been a strange life over here more on account of the people I have seen than the places. I have hardly been sight-seeing at all. I will send you a magazine for your own particular self with something by Davies and something of my own in it. I'm not afraid that what I write will hurt anyone, but what Davies sometimes writes the growing girl would as well not read. Davies is the kind of poet you read about. He has a pension from the British Govt. on his merits, so we wont question him as a poet. As a personality he is lovely. He said to me the other day, "Didn't I see you at Monro's supper at Picorini's? I thought so. I was in pretty bad." I assured him I really hadnt noticed it until he began to talk about revisiting Baltimore for an oyster sandwich. "Well," he said, "it was worse after you went. I left the room to go to the lavatory and I got lost. I can't remember whether I went out for another drink. But I never got back." He ought to have been more ashamed than he was. He was late at supper anyway and those that stayed after I went did so out of respect for him.

Later I heard him talking in simple wonder at himself for never having been moved in the flesh by his landladies, two old maids who made his bed and fed him on the British plan of ordering the provisions and sending the bills to him to foot. "You know how I am," he said to Hodgson, another frank poet who follows the prize ring. Then he wound up by denouncing them as thieves for living on the provisions they handled for him.

Dont blush if I tell you a little more like this. Hulme is a hulking English squire of thirty who holds forth on philosophy. He is just home from Germany with the intelligence that people there are genuinely lamenting the decay of British coarseness. He tells it triumphantly as something he had noticed and set himself to arrest. He has a Tuesday evening at which he talks to mixed society about anything that comes into his head. Not long ago one evening it was how he was out here in Bucks somewhere at a Russian actress' country house and heard two very minor poets just down from Oxford ad-

dressing her in erotic verse of their own. Passion and emula-
tion had sent both of them up tall trees. Alford (author of the
stupid roast on American literature in the magazine I am sending) would shout to the wind "Come lie with me!" or words to
that effect. Are they not written in a book by Alford recently
published at his own expense? He spoke of her marmoreal
legs. (His in the book.) All of which made Hulme laugh so
that the Russian actress had to rebuke him for not knowing
how to take a thing as it was meant. But the best was: The
shouts of the arboreal poets had attracted a small crowd outside the paling that no one noticed till a boy cried, "Say, Mister,
are you nesting?" Alford was not nesting as it turned out. The
other fellow won the lady's favor or favors and is now her
housemate outside the law.

You'll be afraid I am losing my innocence. Anyway you
will realize how far it is possible to get from Plymouth and
Derry for seventy-five dollars.

It is necessary to make some distinctions in all the above.
Hulme is not immoral in thought or action. Plain-speaking is
part of the conservatism he affects and preaches. Davies may
be bad enough, but he is what you would call naturally rough.
He has a good heart and he is something of a marvel when
you consider that he has come up from tramping and selling
shoestrings on the street. Alford I rather loathe and Russian
actresses.

There, I ought to have restricted myself to the weather
and set myself to correct the bad impression I gave you of
this climate last winter. It has not been half bad this winter.
We have seen the sun for whole days and often several days in
succession. All told we may have had three weeks of frost and
two snow storms. Maximum thickness of ice less than two
inches.

[. . .] The poor, I have made up my mind, have a hard
hard time here, with no houses to live in and no wages to buy
common food with. I heard a great man say that the English
shilling would buy as much as the American dollar. He should
have known better. In this town eggs have been sixty cents a
dozen all winter. . . .

And there are thousands of people here, men I mean,
who earn from 20 shillings down to 10 a week. I have seen and
talked with people who have brought up families on less than
20. There are kinds of food they simply never taste. The chil-

dren go to work the minute the law allows and help out with sixpence a day. The old mothers whose usefulness is more or less past instead of puttering about the house and minding the baby go into the field to work picking up stones at a shilling a day. I saw three of them at it in the rain. They gathered the flints (size of a fist or two) and carried them clear off the field in their aprons without the help of horse or cart.

But the worst of it is not this. These people are allowed to call only a small part of their soul their own. I mustn't go into that. It will keep till I get home.

1915 will see us back in America, and in many ways glad to get back. The fortunate monopolize too much here. The fortunate are very delightful people to meet, they afford so many of the virtues and graces. But one can't help seeing the unfortunate who may afford a virtue or two but not one grace, I am afraid. I should want my children to grow up in America. Sincerely yours Robert Frost

75 · To Sidney Cox

Dear Cox 3 March 1914 Beaconsfield

Would you or would you not lend me a matter of twenty-five or fifty dollars (if fifty is too much, twenty five) to help me out of a tight place? I am making a change which will cost a little and for various reasons it has to come just when I am out of money. I might have to keep you waiting till I get my allowance in July and then again if returns from certain things come in I may be able to repay you at once. I have several things out which will appear in magazines if they can be got in before my book appears. If not I lose on them. Mrs Nutt is against me in the matter of my selling to the magazines. She seems jealous of my getting cold cash for anything that in book form is so unprofitable. She seems to, I say. I don't know quite what to make of her. She is friendly enough except when we are on the subject of magazines and American publishers. She acts as if she thought I was up to something. Last time I saw her she told me frankly she thought I had no right under my contract to traffic in my poetry before I'd brought it to her. This is embarrassing.

Don't hesitate to refuse me the loan if you must: I had

rather ask a favor like this of you and John [Bartlett] than anyone else. I ought to be able to go to the trustees of my grandfather's estate, but they have always been chiefly trustees of his hostility to my poetry.

You will be amused to hear that the Edinburgh English Society will give a whole evening to a new American poet named Me, this month. Too bad my book isnt out to take advantage of the local interest that may stir up.

Now you be perfectly honest.

Yours ever and whether or no,

Robert Frost.

75-a · JEANIE FLORENCE FROST TO WILBUR E. ROWELL

Mr. Wilbur Rowell, Lawrence, Mass.,

Dear Mr. Rowell,-   8 March 1914   Atco, New Jersey

My brother is, I am afraid, embarrassed for money this spring, (I am afraid he would be very much displeased if he knew that I was writing to you.)

He was promised $125 for two of his poems by "Poetry" (Chicago). But now they've had them nearly six months, and if they hold them much longer the book, "North of Boston," will be out, and they can't use them.

Mosher, of Portland, gave him a good offer to bring out this book, which I supposed he would accept. Instead he is letting Nutt a London publisher bring out this second book. I would think that there would be more money in publishing in this country.

An Edinburgh literary society will give an evening to him as a new American poet. He has been asked down to read his poems. Mosher copied one of his poems into his catalogue and Bill Reedy copied it into the "Mirror" in St. Louis. He's had very fine reviews . . . and several things published lately in English magazines.

I have reason to know that he needs $75 at least. Of course he hasn't the slightest idea that I am writing to you. I am in hopes that he will realize rather more from his new book "North of Boston" than from his first book of poems. . . .

What he has published was written in his early youth, when he lived on the farm in Derry and did not teach at Pinkerton Academy, and lately since he left off teaching.

I am going to tell my brother that I am writing you, as I do not think it would be right to keep it from him.

I am worried about him and I would be very glad if you felt willing to send him $75. His address is The Bungalow, Beaconsfield, Buckingham, England.

Very truly   Jeanie Frost

76 · To Wilbur E. Rowell

Dear Mr. Rowell: 26 March 1914   Beaconsfield

Thank you for the fifty dollars and for the hundred so close upon its heels. Thank you too for your friendly letters. Jean was quite right: I find the money very convenient at this moment to help me make the move to Gloucester, where, as I think I told you, I am going to be with my friends Gibson and Abercrombie, the English poets.

My address there will be Iddens, Leadington, Ledbury. I shall be very nearly on the line between Gloucestershire and Herefordshire.   With our best wishes.

Sincerely yours   Robert Frost

77 · To Harriet Monroe

Dear Miss Monroe   26 March 1914   Beaconsfield

I have carelessly let this cheque lie only to discover, now when I could use it, that it is unsigned. So I shall have to trouble you with it.

While I am writing may I ask if you could publish my "Black Cottage" in May or June? I should be very grateful. It will have to come soon to be ahead of my next book, North of Boston.   Sincerely yours   Robert Frost

Before your answer can reach me I shall be at Iddens, Ledington, Ledbury, England.

78 · To Sidney Cox

26 March 1914 Beaconsfield
Dear Sidney   (This being my birthday.)

(I think it should be first names between us by this
when it is already first names between me and my later-found
friends in England.)

I have no friend here like Wilfrid Gibson whom I am going
to join in Gloucestershire next week. We bid a long farewell to
London to be near him and Lascelles Abercrombie. The cottage
is already found for us. Iddens it is called — in Ledington
Ledbury. You must address us there from now on. I don't know
but I suppose we shall sleep under thatch. Those other poets
do.

I was worried about the money to make the move, but we
shall pull through all right. You shall have your suit of clothes
and know at the same time that we are not in straights.

We shall make a week of it in London before we drink silence and hide ourselves in cloud. I sold some poetry to Poetry
and Drama and I propose to take it out in room rent in the
upper floors of the Poetry Shop in Devonshire St Theobalds
Road London W. C. if you know where that is. I may have told
you about it. It sells nothing but poetry. The fellow that runs it
and edits the quarterly I speak of is a poet and all about him
are the poets my friends and enemies. Gibson had a room there
for a year before he married the proprietor's secretary. Epstein, the futurist sculptor, the New York Polish Jew, whose
mind runs strangely on the subject of generation, whose work
is such a stumbling block to the staid and Victorianly but who
in spite of all is reckoned one of the greatest living geniuses,
will be across the hall from us. All the poets will be in and out
there. It will be something that Lesley of the children will be
sure to remember.

We mean to do the city for the youngsters as much as I
am capable of doing a city or anything else. There must be a
great deal to see in London if one will look for it. There is the
Tower and — well there simply must be something else. I
must get a guide book.

I really do take an interest in the historical places. I
didn't fail to notice that I passed the scenes of two battles —
Eversham and Worcester — when I was travelling the other
day. But I dont know what I would have done if I had been

121

set down in either of them. It thrilled me enough merely to see the names on the stations. I got as much out of seeing Dunfermline town from the train as from straggling around Edinburgh Castle for a day. The best thing in Edinburgh Castle was the Black Watch on parade. Places are more to me in thought than in reality. People are the other way about. (Probably not so — I am just talking.)

I ought not to be talking. I have really too much else to do till we get away. I meant this to be but a short letter to make you easy on my score. I shall write you more at length when we are nearer the Severn Sea (see in Anthology the really good poem by Davidson. Poor Davidson.)   Yours ever   R. F.

79 · To Sidney Cox

18 May 1914   Little Iddens
Dear Cox: Ledington   Ledbury

I have taken particular pains to write the address legibly and do you take notice. We are actually in Gloucestershire but near the line and our postoffice is at Ledbury in Herefordshire. This is a great change from Beaconsfield which was merely suburban. We are now in the country, the cider country, where we have to keep a barrel of cider for our visitors and our hired help or we will have no visitors nor hired help. So we are in the way of adding drink to cigarette smoking in the record of our sins. Even Elinor gets drawn in since the only kind of ladies we know over here are all smokers. I think the only house I visited where the cigarettes weren't passed around was Ernest Rhys'. I never thought of that till this moment. I don't know why it was, probably because Rhys himself isn't a smoker. His son is though.

Let's see — you say be personal. I wish I knew what you meant by personal. I thought I was egotistically so in telling you of my encounter with the greatest poet (titular) in England. I believe I told you what I told Bridges about the science of verse, matter that is of the highest importance and not yet to be found in book form on earth. The novelty if you didn't miss it was the definition of a sentence which is calculated to revolutionize the teaching of literary composition in the next twenty years.

My late encounter with the man who considers himself

the second greatest poet in England and heir apparent to the Laureateship was of another description. He is the Davies (W. H.) of the Victorian Anthol. I saw something of him in London — once, as I think I told you, at a dinner in Soho where he made an exhibition of himself. He is the unsophisticated nature poet of the day — absolutely uncritical untechnical untheoretical. He has the honor of having a pension from the British government. Society runs after him. He sells upward of 100£ worth of small poems in a year. His success seems to have hurt him a little and its not strange that it has when you consider his origin. Six years he tramped in America till he fell under a freight car and lost a leg. Then he came home and stumped about selling shoe strings and penny rhyme sheets. Then my friend Adcock discovered him and the rest has followed — recognition from Shaw Conrad and everyone else that counts. The poems in the Anthol are a fair sample of what he can do. No one at the present time can get those flashes in a line as he can. His note is Elizabethan. No one doubts that he is a very considerable poet, in spite of several faults and flaws everywhere. But his conceit is enough to make you misjudge him — simply assinine. We have had a good deal of him at the house for the last week and the things he has said for us to remember him by! He entirely disgusted the Gibsons with whom he was visiting. His is the kind of egotism another man's egotism can't put up with. He was going from here to be with Conrad. He said that would be pleasant because Conrad knew his work *thoroughly*. After waiting long enough to obscure the point we asked him if he knew Conrad's work *thoroughly*. Oh no — was it good? We told him yes. He was glad we liked it.

He set about encouraging Lesley to write about nature. It would be good practice for a child. He admitted that he had used it up as copy. Lesley is old enough to have to struggle to keep a straight face in such circumstances. There now, he said, see that little bird, that little green one, I wonder what kind he is. Says Lesley It's a sparrow and it isn't green, is it? And Davies stumped into the house. He doesn't really know nature at all. He has lately been telling the British public that the American Robin isn't red breasted and it has no note that he ever heard.

I suppose he is the most naively wicked person that walks, or should I say limps? He always makes me think of Fergu-

123

son's Scorney Bull (in The Vengence of the Welshmen of Ti-rawley.) — he's that lewd and lame. His private life is public property, so he makes no bones of speaking in any company of the women he spends his money on. They are cheaper than in America and I don't suppose his tastes are up to the most expensive ones here: the one of his fortnight before coming down to the country cost him thirty shillings. The strange thing is he is humanly fond of his creatures and takes their side against the respectable kind. I believe he has written a simple-hearted book about them in which they are rather finely discriminated — the golden girls he has met. He's a little weathered man with none of the personal charm of the lady-killer remember. Yet Bernard Shaw considers that he has made himself an authority on the ladies (daughters of Lilith) our society builds on, but prefers to know nothing about. I have no doubt he knows much more about them than about birds cows and flowers. He really cares little for nature except as most other people do in books. He asked me confidentially before he left why I had been so foolish as to get so far from London.

If this isn't being personal, let me try what I can say in a few words about where we are. The important thing to us is that we are near Gibson; we are far from any town. We are on a lane where no automobiles come. We can go almost anywhere we wish on wavering footpaths through the fields. The fields are so small and the trees so numerous along the hedges that, as my friend Thomas says in the loveliest book on spring in England, you may think from a little distance that the country was solid woods.

You mustnt mind if I write and never look back. I write few such long letters to anyone as I write to you. I have to save myself for other things. Elinor and the children wish to be remembered. Lesley will hardly be one of the children much longer. She is as tall as her mother and reads a decent paragraph of Caesar off without looking up more than a couple of words. Sometimes too she does a paragraph of English writing I admire.

Here's hoping the best for you next year. Did you get the raise you asked for?   Yours ever   R. F.

Later.   My book seems to be out, though I haven't seen it yet. I have had these slips from the publisher. Perhaps you could send them where they would so some good. . . .

80 · To Wilbur E. Rowell

IN THE preceding letter to Cox, RF wrote, "My book seems to be out," and in this letter to Rowell he adds, "We go to the reviewers with the second book this week." *North of Boston* was published in London on 15 May 1914, and for some time thereafter RF's letters contain many references to reviews, the most important of which were:

First, and favorable, an unsigned article in the London *Times Literary Supplement*, 28 May 1914.

Lascelles Abercrombie wrote a long and sympathetic review entitled "A New Voice" which appeared in *The Nation* (London), 13 June 1914. Excerpts from this review were quoted in "The Listener" column of the Boston *Evening Transcript*, 8 July 1914.

Ford Maddox Hueffer published a long review, "Mr. Robert Frost and *North of Boston*," in *The Outlook* (London), 27 June 1914.

W. W. Gibson did a one-column review, "Simplicity and Sophistication," *The Bookman* (London), July 1914.

The London *Times Literary Supplement* printed further favorable comments in "Some Recent Verse," 2 July 1914.

A full-page article devoted to *North of Boston* appeared in *The English Review*, August 1914.

Harold Monro's review appeared in *Poetry and Drama*, September 1914.

The first long review in America was Ezra Pound's "Modern Georgics," which appeared in *Poetry*, December 1914.

Dear Mr. Rowell   20 May 1914   Little Iddens

Will you let me take advantage of your offer to the extent of another twenty pounds? Or ten pounds would do — just which you find convenient. I shall greatly appreciate the favor.

We go to the reviewers with the second book this week. We are excited as you could expect us to be in this quiet corner of a quiet country.   Sincerely yours   Robert Frost

80-a · Elinor M. Frost to Leona White Harvey

TO UNDERSTAND certain references in this letter some background is needed concerning EMF's two older sisters, Leona and Ada. Leona married Nathaniel Harvey, a farmer in Epping, New Hampshire, and they had three children: Vera, Hilda, and Alan. During the Derry years, 1900 to 1911, the Frosts occasionally visited the Harveys in Epping. Ada, as a young woman, had seemed to be a hopelessly bedridden invalid, but she had been cured by Christian Science. She moved from Lawrence, Massachusetts, to Washington, D. C., where she became a Christian Science practitioner, and married.

Dear Leona   [*c*. 20 June 1914]   Little Iddens

I was ever so pleased to get your letter the other day and to know that you are getting on fairly well. I haven't been feeling at all well for three or four weeks and am really not strong enough to write you a very long letter, but I will write what I can. Rob wrapped up copies of his two books for you yesterday, and I will send them with this. The second book has been out five or six weeks and I will send you also a good review of it in last week's Nation, which is about the best of the English Weeklies. . . . There have been other good reviews, but I haven't any extra copies of them.

We are enjoying a beautiful summer. The weather has been almost perfect since the middle of April, though we have had too many rainy days this last week. I wish I could make you feel what a lovely country this is. When we first came, the meadows were covered with yellow daffodils and the cuckoo had just begun to sing. For nearly 2 months it sang all day long, but it has already stopped singing. The pastures here are so rich that they are just as green as the mowing and wheat fields, and they are separated by dark green hedges and bordered by huge elms. Great flocks of sheep and herds of cows are everywhere. From a hill about four miles away, one can see the Severn river winding along, and the mountains of Wales in the distance. The cottage we are living in is very old — about 350 years old, and all the floors downstairs are brick tiled and the beams show above. We have five rooms and the rent is only $50 a year.

Wilfrid Gibson and his wife live about a mile from us and Abercrombie with his wife and two children are three miles away. We see them all often. We have had quite a little company since we came, and some friends from near London have been down and taken lodgings near us. Edward Thomas, who is a very well known critic and prose writer has been here with his two children and he is going to bring his whole family to lodge near us through August. Rob and I think everything of him. He is quite the most admirable and lovable man we have ever known.

I don't know whether we shall stay here through next winter or not. It will be a little dreary here in winter, I am afraid. At least it will seem so after such a glorious summer as this.

I have been feeling quite worn out. The household and teaching and the excitement of meeting so many people constantly, has been almost too much for me. Three weeks ago I felt that I was on the edge of complete nervous prostration, but I pulled out of it and am feeling considerably better now. I fear that I am not really able to write the letter to the Washington doctor that you spoke of, but I will keep it in my mind and some day when I feel in the mood for it, I will try it. In your next letter, give me his exact address. About Alan, my advice would be not to go to law. You could not change his feeling toward you in that way and it would certainly upset you and Nat and the children completely. It would be a dreadful experience. I have not heard from mama since Alan went to Washington. I wrote to her in such a way that she knew I disapproved of what she had done. I don't see how Alan could be so bad as to turn against his father and mother in that way. It must be that he thought as Ada had plenty of money, he could have an easier time with them and be able to buy whatever he wanted. I can't account for it in any other way, for I remember the last time I saw him he used to ridicule Christian Science and seemed altogether opposed to Ada's influence. Well, he may not like it so well after a while, and it would be better, I think, to let him come to his senses gradually. . . .

With much love,   Elinor

81 · To John W. Haines

A GLOUCESTER POET, botanist, barrister, John W. Haines was related by marriage to Lascelles Abercrombie. Soon after the Frost family moved to Gloucestershire, RF met Haines and began a friendship that continued warmly through many years. During both his subsequent visits to England, in 1928 and in 1957, RF visited Haines in Gloucestershire.

Dear Haines   [*c.* 1 July 1914]   Little Iddens

Thank you for the [*Nation*] review — Abercrombie's work as your wife thought. I liked it very well. The discussion of my technique wouldn't have been what it was if Abercrombie had had nothing to go on but the book. He took advantage of certain conversations in which I gave him the key to my method and most of his catchwords. "Method" is the wrong way to call it: I simply use certain principles on which I accept or reject my own work. It was a generous review to consider me in all ways so seriously and as I say I liked it.

I don't believe I had one uneasy moment with you the

other day from the moment I saw you throw the [train] car door open. I should think you were the kind of person I could ask over here to sprawl — not call. I object to callers more and more in my old age. In my wife's present state of health I have to do some of the meals (so to call them), but you won't mind that will you? And you will overlook some other things if we can laze and talk for a day. You must come on the early train and go on the late. Thomas has been with us after being with Bottomley in the north. We had a day on your mountain [May Hill]. You are to meet him when he is here for the month of August — and a mighty fine fellow you'll say he is. When are you going to ask me to Gloucester to meet your wife?

Sincerely yours   Frost

82 · To John Cournos

A RUSSIAN JEW with an extraordinary gift for failure, John Cournos had reached London from Philadelphia shortly before RF met him through Harold Monro. Cournos had hopes of becoming a novelist. He earned money by hack work of various kinds, and offered to send articles on RF back to the United States. RF assisted and encouraged him. (See letters 84 and 85.)

Dear Cournos: 8 July 1914   Little Iddens

Thanks for your good news. I have just read Hueffer's article and I like every word of it. What more could anyone ask for a while.

My versification seems to bother people more than I should have expected — I suppose because I have been so long accustomed to thinking of it in my own private way. It is as simple as this: there are the very regular preestablished accent and measure of blank verse; and there are the very irregular accent and measure of speaking intonation. I am never more pleased than when I can get these into strained relation. I like to drag and break the intonation across the meter as waves first comb and then break stumbling on the shingle. That's all but it's no mere figure of speech though one can make figures enough about it.

I am down here farming on my own for economy this summer, where I should be glad to see you if you ever range so far. I shall be in London from the 20th on for a few days and will look you up then if I may.

You mustn't say such things about New York to a poor cuss who may have to go back there to live some time.

Sincerely yours   Robert Frost

83 · To Thomas B. Mosher

Dear Mosher   27 July 1914   Little Iddens

I have thought of you in connection with my new book several times since its appearance. It has done so well here that I should almost venture to send you a copy in spite of your well-known predilection for the manner of the nineties. There have been long and remarkably favorable reviews from all quarters from some of which you may have gathered what I am about. The two and a half columns in The Nation put the case very well and so did the shorter article in The Times. Hueffer's three columns in The Outlook rather bungled the technical question but on the whole I could not quarrel with it. All these you are likely to have seen. I am sending one or two others you would probably miss. Please tell me if on considera-tion you have reason to think you would care for the book and I shall be only too happy to see that you have one from my hand. You were one of the first to see me coming — you are nearly the only one thus far in America — and I should like to know that I had not lost favor with you at the same time that I was gaining it with really a good many important people over here.   Sincerely yours,   Robert Frost.

84 · To John Cournos

Dear Cournos: 27 July 1914   Little Iddens

Back to the woods again — or rather the fields. There are no trees but hedgerow elms for ten miles around here.

I have got you the book [probably *North of Boston*] and I meant to have before this copies of the Bookman and Pell Mell reviews. I will send them along as soon as they come. You have The Outlook. If not, say so, and I will send it. Here are The Times and Nation reviews with passages marked as of inter-est to me.

One thing to notice is that but one poem in the book will

intone and that is "After Apple Picking." The rest talk. I spoke of a particular line I like in "The Fear:"

"She pushed past him and got it for herself"

I also think well of those four "don'ts" in Home Burial. They would be good in prose and they gain something from the way they are placed in the verse. Then there is the threatening

"If — you — do!" (Last of Home Burial)

It is that particular kind of imagination that I cultivate rather than the kind that merely sees things, the hearing imagination rather than the seeing imagination though I should not want to be without the latter.

I am not bothered by the question whether anyone will be able to hear or say those three words ("If — you — do!") as I mean them to be said or heard. I should say that they were sufficiently self expressive. Some doubt that such tones can long survive on paper. They'll probably last as long as the finer meanings of words. And if they don't last more than a few hundred years that will be long enough for me — much longer than I can hope to be read.

I have ordered the picture from High Wycombe.

I shall be glad to see your story when it is ready, and see you too if you can come down. We may be nearer London before winter. This is a good country but —

Sincerely yours   Robert Frost.

84-a · MRS. HENRY HOLT TO ROBERT FROST

RF's long association with the publishing firm of Henry Holt and Company came about when Mrs. Henry Holt somehow found and admired an English edition of *North of Boston* before any copies of it had been imported for distribution in the United States. Her note of appreciation, which follows, was the first which RF received from a stranger in America concerning *North of Boston*. (See letters 87-a, b, and c.)

7 August 1914
Dear Sir: Four Winds Farm   Stowe, Vermont

Your book "North of Boston" interests me very much. Do you live in Vermont? If so, you may know my brother's book "Stowe Notes." If you don't know it, & would care to, as your book makes me think you would, and will let me know of your address, I will send the book to you. My mother knows the people about here better than I do, & she finds many similar to them in your verses: certainly you have New England in them!

I hope I am not taking too much of a liberty in writing this note, but probably you will not be displeased to know of our interest.　　　　　Sincerely yours,　Florence I. Holt

85 · To John Cournos

Dear Cournos:　　　　　　[c. 15 August 1914]　Little Iddens

I've been think of you in these hot times. I don't suppose you are going to run away to America. I'm not. I am too much committed. But it's going to be poor picking for some of us before it's over. We ought to pull through better in the country than you in the city. I hope you see your way clear.

I find that there are no more Bookmans of July to be had. The news agent has just sent me several copies of the Aug number in hopes I may make those do instead. It doesn't much matter unless you think Gibson's review might have special weight in America and especially with the Transcript which has been his chief boomer on the other side. I will make one more effort to get a copy or two. Perhaps Adcock will find them for me.

I have just seen the notice in the August Eng. Review — almost the best I have had, I should think. And I have just heard that The Transcript has been talking about my send-off in The Nation. Let me hear how things are with you.

　　　　　　　Sincerely yours　Robert Frost

86 · To Sidney Cox

Dear Cox　　　　　　20 August 1914　Little Iddens

You must think I have been and gone to war for the country that has made me a poet. My obligation is not quite as deep as that. If I were younger now and not the father of four — well all I say is, American or no American, I might decide that I ought to fight the Germans simply because I know I should be afraid to.

The war is an ill wind to me. It ends for the time being the thought of publishing any more books. Our game is up. There

131

will really be genuine suffering among the younger writers. My friends have all been notified by the editors they live on that there will be no more space for special articles and reviews till the war is over. De la Mare (greatest of living poets) has just lost twelve or fifteen hundred a year by being dropped by the publisher he reads MS for.

So we may be coming home if we can find the fare or a job to pay the fare after we get there.

I don't mean to complain. I like the war and the idea of abolishing Prussia, if there is any such thing.

The book was lucky in one respect. It may not have had time to sell much; at least it had made its mark with the reviewers. I give you a list of the chief articles about it in case you should care to look them up. No book of verse has had as much space given it for a good while.

Eng Nation	June 13	3 Cols
Outlook	June 27	3 Cols
Pell Mell Gazette	June 20	
Egoist	July 1	Col
Times	July 2	
Bookman	July	Col
News & Leader	July 22	Col
Eng Review	Aug	Page
New Weekly	Aug 8	Col

They have all been ridiculously favorable [letter 80, editor's note]. The Times has talked of the book three times. I understand that there has been an article in the Boston Transcript based on the Nation article. *And* the Plymouth (N. H.) Public Library has bought me. And I have had a letter from [Mrs. Henry Holt in] Stowe Vermont which showed that the book had penetrated to that village behind a mountain.

I will send you a book as soon as ever I can afford to and with it one or two of the reviews you might not be able to see easily. Will you be good enough to send them along to some professor of literary inclination?

We are here or in this neighborhood till we sail for home. Probably that means for some time. We are going to share house with the Abercrombies for the winter to cut down expenses for both families. Abercrombie is a poet too. See your Anthology. Our address there will be (you can write to me there in answer to this): The Gallows, Ryton, Dymock, Gloucestershire.

I have talked enough about myself for your purposes and mine. Let's hear about you.   Yours ever   Frost

87 · To Sidney Cox

THE FOLLOWING LETTER seems to indicate that RF sent some copies of a small, thin-paper four-page folder issued by David Nutt and Company as a flyer for *North of Boston*. It quoted some of the most favorable English reviews, and was printed not earlier than mid-August.

Dear Cox,   [*c.* 25 August 1914]   [Little Iddens]

I should take it kindly if you would pass these along. Anything you can do for me just at this time will be a double service. My only hope is that some interest will be taken in the book in America: here none can be from now on: people are too deeply concerned about the war. Did I ask you if you would try to find an article about this Nation article in The Boston Transcript. It must have appeared in late June or early July. I should like to see a copy of it very much.

Luck to you in every way   R. F.

87-a · Henry Holt and Co. to David Nutt and Co.

THE FOLLOWING excerpts (letters 87-a, b, and c) from letters exchanged by representatives of Holt and Nutt mark the beginning of arrangements for an American publisher for RF.

2 September 1914   [New York City]

. . . Mrs. Henry Holt, who is very enthusiastic over Robert Frost's NORTH OF BOSTON, has very kindly loaned us her copy. The two readers we had look at these poems found them uncommonly interesting and, while we cannot see a paying market here for this particular volume, still we are so interested in this author's work that if you have some later book of his for which you would care to offer us the American rights, we would be most happy to consider it. . . .

87-b · DAVID NUTT AND CO. TO HENRY HOLT AND CO.

12 September 1914   London

. . . We are in receipt of your letter concerning "North of Boston." We think that if you recognize the value of Mr. Frost's work you must also see that his books will make their way steadily. We could not offer you rights of his new book if you do not push the present volume to some extent. . . .

We consider that under present political circumstances American publishers ought to show some willingness to help English publishers who have had sufficient daring and intelligence to recognize the talent of one of their countrymen. . . .

87-c · HENRY HOLT AND CO. TO DAVID NUTT AND CO.

12 September 1914   [New York City]

. . . Following our letter of September 2nd in regard to Frost's "North of Boston" we are inclined on further consideration to take a small edition of this book, say 150 copies in sheets, if it has not already been placed in the American market, and if you can supply them at a reasonable price.

Of course, while we admire this book, it would not, we fear, be worth our while to take it up unless you could assure us that we can have the refusal of the American market on the author's next book. . . .

88 · TO SIDNEY COX

[17 September 1914]

Dear Cox   Ryton   Dymock   Gloucestershire

You wont catch me complaining of any war — much less of a great war like this that we wage on both sides like mystics for a reason beyond reason. Some philosopher has spoken for the Germans: "The hour of obedience has come" — the hour of the triumph of German obedience, religious and secular, the hour for the rest of the world to learn to obey. Just so we thought the Germans thought. Therefore we go out to kill them. I wish we might lose none of our own in the struggle but Norman Angell, David Starr Jordan, Andrew Carnegie, Alfred Noyes and the Peace-editor of The Independent. No I love this war regardless of what it does to me personally. That, I fear, is going to be a good deal, though nothing of course in comparison with what it will do to thousands of Englishmen. It ends my little literary game — that's all. No more books from anybody for the present. And the fact seems to be that it needed just one more book to clinch my business. As it is I am caught betwixt and between. No need to go into it. Enough to say that if I spend money here another year I spend it for nothing. I shall just have to try to get home and live to write another day. I have two fervent hopes. One is that the Germans may not sow the Western Ocean with mines before I cross with the family and the other is that I may find something to do to make up for lost money when I get across.

I havent read Lockhart and I dont think I should much care for him from what you say. Not that I ask for analysis. I am in love with the kind of books that get along without it. But I have little interest in Scott — the Scott at least that Lockhart seems to have seen, the gentleman the goodfellow the entertainer the knight (was it) of Abbottsford (I once lived for a year in a barn of a hotel of that name in San Francisco.)

There are many answers to old Bridges. I dont know the one I had in mind when I wrote to you. I can always find something to say against anything my nature rises up against. And what my nature doesnt object to I dont try to find anything to say against. That is my rule. I never entertain arguments pro and con, or rather I do, but not on the same subject. I am not a lawyer. I may have all the arguments in favor of what I favor but it doesnt even worry me because I dont know one argument on the other side. I am not a German: a German you know may be defined as a person who doesnt dare not to be thorough. Really arguments don't matter. The only thing that counts is what you cant help feeling.

Who wants to fix the present sounds of words? Who by any diacritic device could fix them on paper if he wanted to? No one in God's world can pronounce a word that he hasn't heard. No one can pronounce a word unless he can pronounce the whole language to which it belongs.

The fellow I'm living with at present is the last poet in your Victorian Anthology. If you want to see him to better advantage you must look him up in the Georgian Anthology where he shows well in a long poem called "The Sale of St Thomas." Or if I can find it I will send you some time the copy of New Numbers containing his "End of the World" a play

135

about to be produced in several places — Birmingham next week, Bristol soon, and Chicago some time this winter. He is one of the four treated in an article in the Nineteenth Century lately — Gibson, Masefield, Davies and Abercrombie. I've told you about Davies. Did I tell you he was down here with us and one night the Gibsons limped him over on his wooden leg three miles in the rain from their house to Abercrombies? They hurried poor Davies till the sweat broke out all over him. It was partly out of spite. They had been having a bad time together as rivals in poetry. To make it full and running over for Davies they told him he ought to be proud because he was going to see the greatest poet in England. "Huh," says Davies, when he arrives in the dooryard dead beat, "good thing it's the greatest poet in England." He said it bitterly, but the Gibsons taking him at his word hurried in to tell Abercrombie that by consent of Davies he was the greatest poet in England. But that's what Davies thinks he is himself. And that is what Gibson, or Gibson's wife, thinks Gibson is. (Gibson and Davies both make more out of their poetry than Abercrombie. Davies sells well here and Gibson in America.)

Abercrombie has written a good deal of prose for a living. You ought to be able to find something of his in your library — his "Thomas Hardy" his "Epic" or his "Speculative Dialogues."

We are in another old house, this time under a very ancient thatch: the bottom layer of straw is rye — perhaps put on two or three hundred years ago. We are away in the country where you wouldn't think we would have any part in the excitement of war. But we haven't escaped being taken for spies. As writers we are a little mysterious to the peasant kind. They have had the police busy about us — about Abercrombie, too, in spite of the fact that he is well connected in the "country." They confused me in some way with a Dutchman we had with us, a Van Doorn with an accent and a long black beard. They suspected Abercrombie because a year ago he entertained a strange artist lady who goes about the country on her hands and knees because she's paralyzed or thinks she is. Sometimes she rides in a pony cart. She has to be lifted in and out of that. She gets anybody to pick her up off the ground. She is all wasted to nothing. But as the country folk remember her she might well have been a German officer in disguise.

This is supplementary to that other letter with the reviews. I shall write again soon and send you if you will let me some of David Nutts folders advertising my book.

> Elinor joins me in sending regards — best.
>
> Yours ever   R. F.

89 · To Thomas B. Mosher

Dear Mr. Mosher: October 1914   The Gallows

I am content to leave it that way. Anything you care to give — It is not for me to make terms with you. All I have in mind is to reach through you an American public. So long as you get me read I shall ask no questions about royalties. Mrs. Nutt however is another matter. She would say that as one of her indentured poets I have no right to be corresponding with an American publisher even in friendship. In fact she has just forbidden me to have anything to do with American publishers. I must refer them all to her. She will be the difficulty. Lately her mood has been especially bitter. You have heard perhaps of her attack on the Mirror because it quoted two verses from Henleys England. She demanded five guineas for the breech of copyright. To my knowledge she has been asking St John Adcock fifty guineas for six of Henley's poems he wanted for an anthology. She is a well-meaning but far from reasonable lady of business.

We are very quiet in spite of the war. An occasional hob-nailed boot on the metalled lane is all that disturbs us — that and a certain fear we dont know what of. It wont be of Zeppelins at this distance from big towns and it wont be of invading armies — yet. I doubt if we are going to be invaded at all.

I hope the war may not make as much difference in your business as you feared.   Sincerely yours   Robert Frost

90 · To Sidney Cox

Dear Cox   October 1914   The Gallows

It warms me cockles to see you so enthusiastic over my book. Three or four more such friends and I should be a made man. You have done so much more than you ought already that you wont object to doing a good deal more for me. So I send you with the book certain circulars to scatter. To be most effective they should go to people who care especially for you or for me or for poetry. But if you like you may give them to some boy to distribute on the street corner when the mills are emptying at night. Or flutter them yourself from the tail end of an electric. Don't count on doing too much execution with them. Not everyone will find them persuasive and not everyone will like the book as well as you would like to have him. A good many simple souls, educated and uneducated, will miss the "poeticisms" by which they are accustomed to know poetry when they see it.

Sometime we *must* discuss that minister [in "The Black Cottage"] and his creed. I make it a rule not to take any "character's" side in anything I write. So I am not bound to defend the minister you understand.

We grow more and more concerned for our future. The prose I sometimes talk of writing for bread and butter would simply bring me nothing now if I wrote it. I may have to go home soon. The difficulty there is that the expense of getting home would leave me under the necessity of getting a job for a while till I got on my feet again. I should awfully like a quiet job in a small college where I should be allowed to teach something a little new on the technique of writing and where I should have some honor* for what I suppose myself to have done in poetry. Well, but I mustnt dream.

Sincerely yours   Robert Frost

*Just a little little bit.

91 · To Sidney Cox

Dear Cox   [c. 1 November 1914]   The Gallows

This is only to say that Henry Holt will supply the book in America. Will you write that on any circulars you have still to send out?

They say the germans have made the whole Atlantic unsafe. This raises questions for me.

1) Do I dare to go home now?
2) Won't it be more dangerous to go every day we delay?

3) Won't it be impossible to get money across to live on pretty soon?

4) Do I dare to stay?

Perhaps you think I am joking. I am never so serious as when I am.

If you never hear from me again, write Henry Holt and Co Publishers New York, on the circulars and let it go at that.

Yours ever   Robert Frost

You got the book I sent?

92 · To Thomas B. Mosher

Dear Mr Mosher   November 1914   [The Gallows]

It is lucky I warned you, if you mind trouble. Mrs Nutt bears you no good will as I found out when I tried to get her to look at some of your book work. Some people are best not stirred up.

You would have been too late for my book anyway. Someone else took it some time ago, I am informed. I want to thank you for your interest just the same.

I see you have begun reading De la Mare. And you find him not a "free verster." Some careless reviewer had let you in wrong as to his classification. I knew you would like him when you gave him a fair trial. The nineties produced no single poem to put beside his "Listeners." Really the nineties had very little on these degenerate days when you consider. Yeats, Jonson [Lionel Johnson] and Dowson they had, and that is about all. De la Mare and Davies are the equal of any of them in lyric and Abercrombie (whom I mustn't praise too much for he is in the house with me) leaves them all behind in the sublime imaginative sort of thing. I wonder you haven't discovered Davies. He seems in your line.

This war mars all for the like of us, but it does so much worse for a million others that I don't feel justified in worrying let alone complaining.

Let me congratulate you on the completion of your Twenty Years' Bibelot. I wish you sales.

Sincerely yours   Robert Frost

93 · To SIDNEY COX

Dear Cox   December 1914   [The Gallows]

I am glad you are going into it with me and one or two others. [Edward] Thomas thinks he will write a book on what my definition of the sentence means for literary criticism. If I didn't drop into poetry every time I sat down to write I should be tempted to do a book on what it means for education. It may take some time to make people see — they are so accustomed to look at the sentence as a grammatical cluster of words. The question is where to begin the assault on their prejudice. For my part I have about decided to begin by demonstrating by examples that the sentence as a sound in itself apart from the word sounds is no mere figure of speech. I shall show the sentence sound saying all that the sentence conveys with little or no help from the meaning of the words. I shall show the sentence sound opposing the sense of the words as in irony. And so till I establish the distinction between the grammatical sentence and the vital sentence. The grammatical sentence is merely accessory to the other and chiefly valuable as furnishing a clue to the other. You recognize the sentence sound in this: *You,* you —! It is so strong that if you hear it as I do you have to pronounce the two you's differently. Just so many sentence sounds belong to man as just so many vocal runs belong to one kind of bird. We come into the world with them and create none of them. What we feel as creation is only selection and grouping. We summon them from Heaven knows where under excitement with the audile [audial] imagination. And unless we are in an imaginative mood it is no use trying to make them, they will not rise. We can only write the dreary kind of grammatical prose known as professorial. Because that is to be seen at its worst in translations especially from the classics, Thomas thinks he will take up the theme apropos of somebody's scholarly translation of Horace or Catullus some day when such a book comes his way for review.

I throw all this out as it comes to me to show you where we are at present. Use anything you please. I am only too glad of your help. We will shake the old unity-emphasis-and-coherence Rhetoric to its foundations.

A word more. We value the seeing eye already. Time we said something about the hearing ear — the ear that calls up vivid sentence forms.

We write of things we see and we write in accents we hear. Thus we gather both our material and our technique with the imagination from life; and our technique becomes as much material as material itself.

All sorts of things must occur to you. Blaze away at them. But expect to have to be patient. There are a lot of completely educated people in the world and of course they will resent being asked to learn anything new.

You aren't influenced by that Beauty is Truth claptrap. In poetry and under emotion every word used is "moved" a little or much — moved from its old place, heightened, made, made new. See what Keats did to the word "alien" in the ode. But as he made it special in that place he made it his — and his only in that place. He could never have used it again with just that turn. It takes the little one horse poets to do that. I am probably the only Am poet who haven't used it after him. No if I want to deal with the word I must sink back to its common usage at Castle Garden. I want the unmade words to work with, not the familiar made ones that everybody exclaims Poetry! at. Of course the great fight of any poet is against the people who want him to write in a special language that has gradually separated from spoken language by this "making" process. His pleasure must always be to make his own words as he goes and never to depend for effect on words already made even if they be his own.

Enough of that. I dont blame your good friend. Nor do I blame the poor educated girl who thought the little book was difficult. The "contents" notes were a piece of fooling on my part. They were not necessary and not very good.

I'd like to thank specially the fellow who picked out Mowing. I guess there is no doubt that is the best poem in Book I. We all think so over here. Thank Hatch for me too. Don't forget.

And thank yourself for all you are doing for me. I need it in this game.

I should like a good talk or three with you. On the war if you choose. On anything. You are going to do a lot all round I know. Your opinions are worth listening to because you mean to put them into action — if for no other reason. But there is no other reason as important. What a man will put into effect at any cost of time money life or lives is sacred and what counts. As I get older I dont want to hear about much else.

I have nearly written myself tired for tonight.

Write often and keep my courage up.

Yours ever   R. F.

Get rid of that Mr. on my name next letter or take the consequences.

94 · To HAROLD MONRO

Dear Monro   December 1914   [The Gallows]

I have been enjoying the book you sent [*Children of Love*]. I find I like something in most of the poems though I like you best when you are least theological as in London Interior and Great City. In neither of these do you make me tremble for my peace of mind or my growing children or whatever it is you make me tremble for elsewhere. You turn life rather too terrible by the use of such words over a cat drinking milk as "creeping lust," "transfigured with love," "dim ecstasy," "her world is an infinite shapeless white," "holy drop," and "lies defeated." I suppose I ought not to shrink from seeing resemblances to our humanity on the lower side, but I feel as if they pulled me down or dizzied me — I don't know what. But I am writing nonsense. I quite go with you the length of "Children of Love." That wisdom is lovely and not dark. Of course it is sad that the two lovers should have some time met and not hit it off together.

Think of me as engaged in a little war on my own down here with a bad game keeper who attacked me for going where he allowed the Gibsons to go as gentry. Me he called a "damned cottager." *Now* who will have the better claim to the title of the People's Poet? Thomas says it is the best testimonial I have had and I must get my publisher to use the game keeper in advertising me — that is, if I survive my war with the brute — and even if I don't —

Some times I wish I were in London.

Yours Ever   Robert Frost

My wife's choice is "Overheard in a Salt Marsh." I like that, too. But the two I have named, London Interior and Great City are best. They are altogether fine.   R. F.

95 · To Harold Monro

IN THE ISSUE of *Poetry and Drama* for December 1913, Harold Monro had published two of RF's blank verse dramatic narratives: "The Fear" and "A Hundred Collars." In this letter, passing reference is made to Monro's having published in *Poetry and Drama* for December 1914, four of RF's shorter poems: "The Sound of Trees," "The Cow in Apple Time," "Putting in the Seed," and "The Smile."

Dear Monro   December 1914   [The Gallows]

I can't believe I was the least bit sarcastic but if I seem so it was just as bad and you deserve as much credit for forgiving me and placing me so well in such a good number of P & D [*Poetry and Drama*] and offering me your spare room when I should come to London. I wish I could get in to see you and I may try to soon — before the rain of bombs begins. Meanwhile I am sending a friend of mine, J. W. Haines, a Gloucester lawyer, to call. I should like to ask you to say a friendly word to him if he turns up at the shop when you happen to be in. He reads and buys more poetry than anybody in the West Countree. He's a good judge of the stuff. I know he would be flattered to have the chance to tell you he likes your book and to expostulate with you for not going straight on with P & D.

Don't put your inclination to preach off on the parson in you. Everybody has it. I know I have, and in me sea and land meet (as they do at the shore): I am a son of sailors (pure) on one side and farmers (pure) on the other. And as Alfred tells Amy Lowell well, it is written in P & D.

You take what I say about the cat drinking milk too seriously. The phrases I picked out were merely a dotted outline of an anthology or kind of anthology that scares me. Some time I will tell you a story about "resemblances to our humanity on the lower side" — a British Museum story — in verse. It will have to be when nobody is with me because I'm not supposed to touch any but rural themes.

I understand that the Gibsons were pleased with your handling of their twins.   Yours ever   Robert Frost

96 · To Ernest L. Silver

Dear Silver,   23 December 1914   [The Gallows]

I ought not to have begun stirring up my friends so impulsively. The fact is the war took me by surprise and for a time I thought I had lost by it pretty much all I played for. I have lost some money, undoubtedly, but perhaps not so much that I can't hope still to go to a farm when I go home, as I originally intended. It may be necessary for me to teach a year or so somewhere to catch up and it may not. At any rate I shant sign on with Pease till I know my own mind better.

No one quite knows what the war has done to him yet. We may be dead, the whole crowd of us, and not able to realize the fact. It is as hard to know how the war has affected us individually as it is to tell off hand what the war is all about, or to understand a modern battle.

I suspect a modern battle hasnt got to be and wont continue to be the futile thing it is. It remains a stand-off to date because no man big enough has had time enough to seize the tactical use of all the weapons science has dumped down on us since the last great war. No one is sure where so simple a thing as the Maxim should come in. So both sides are fighting just not to lose. It was like that in naval warfare when Rodney and Nelson came on the scene. It always takes time for the Nelsons to emerge from the brass-bound peace generals and win victories. The peace-trained men are good enough to hold the other peace-trained men. Both do it by the book. Each knows what the other knows. There can be no secrecy and no surprise. But all that is changed the minute a man appears with one fresh idea (big idea) of his own. No spy will find that out and no military critic either perhaps until years after. They say Napoleon didn't know his own big idea to state it to the day of his death, and only acted on it when in top form and perfect health. It is in all the books now. I haven't the least doubt there are twenty decisive victories in succession for the right man in the telling use of rapid fire guns alone. I wonder which side will be the first to find the right man.

As for what it is all about: I heard an old cottage woman say this to the proposition that England was fighting for Belgium: "In a way we are — the same as we would fight for a wall we had put between ourselves and danger." No sentimental rot there.

In spite of all you may hear to the contrary from interested parties, Germans and English conscriptionists with an ax to grind, enlistment goes forward perfectly. There are soldiers swarming over everything. I have seen them by thousands in all stages of development — some of them veterans, already wounded, recovered and on their way to the front again. These last are the ones to pity. I knew personally of one who had been wounded and temporarily blinded by a bursting shell. He was getting well enough to go back but his nerve was gone and he was crying every day at the prospect. A Colonel Gordon home with a paralyzed arm, showed a photograph of the officers of his regiment taken before the war and he said every one of them was wounded, dead, or in the madhouse.

English people assume that they have the sympathy of Americans, at least of New Englanders, and I suppose they are not wrong.

I may look in on you before many weeks for my furniture. Nothing is certain except that poetry is a drug here now and that I feel as if I ought to get the children out of any danger there is, however slight. We are always homesick. So that if I can see my way I may take passage in February or March.

> With our regards
> Sincerely yours   Robert Frost

96-a · JEANIE FLORENCE FROST TO WILBER E. ROWELL

24 December 1914   South Fork,
Dear Mr. Rowell,-   Penna.   Care of C. D. Costlow

I feel very anxious about my brother and his family, who, I feel, are making a mistake in remaining in England.

My brother, I know, is now very anxious to bring his family back to this country but he has written me in his last letter that the Admiralty has warned them that the Germans have been sowing mines between England and America. . . .

Henry Holt is publishing my brother's book, "North of Boston" in America. It is, I think, not yet available, but will be in a week or so. As conditions are, in England, not a great number of copies have been sold, I suppose.

My brother is, I know, short of money. I don't know exactly how much he has or whether he has sufficient with which to bring his family across.

I am afraid that they might be obliged to flee and not have enough.

Don't you think it would be safer for you to advance him $200 on his annuity if you feel that you can do so. . . .

My brother can teach when he gets here. Mr. Morrison, State Supt. of Education in New Hampshire said that he was the best teacher of English in that state. So I know that my brother could easily get a position to teach English. . . .

Very truly,   Jeanie Frost

97 · To SIDNEY COX

Dear Cox   2 January 1915   [The Gallows]

Be sure to send your article as soon as you have it. I see you really doing something in the next few years to break into the worst system of teaching that ever endangered a nations literature. You speak of Columbia. That reminds me of the article on American literature by a Columbian, George Wood-bury [Woodberry], in the Encyclopaedia Britannica. I wish you would read it or the last part of it just to see that we are not alone in thinking that nothing literary can come from the present ways of the professionally literary in American universities. It is much the same in the Scottish. Everything is research for the sake of erudition. No one is taught to value himself for nice perception and cultivated taste. Knowledge knowledge. Why literature is the next thing to religion in which as you know or believe an ounce of faith is worth all the theology ever written. Sight and insight, give us those. I like the good old English way of muddling along in these things that we cant reduce to a science anyway such as literature love religion and friendship. People make their great strides in understanding literature at most unexpected times. I never caught another man's emotion in it more than when someone drew his finger over some seven lines of blank verse — beginning carefully and ending carefully — and saying simply "From there to — there." He knew and I knew. We said no more. I don't see how you are going to teach the stuff except with some such light touch. And you cant afford to treat it all alike, I mean with equal German thoroughness and reverence if thoroughness is reverence. It is only a moment here and a moment there that the greatest writer has. Some cognizance of the fact must be taken in your teaching.

Well I didnt intend to be running on like this so soon again but somehow you set me off. I have my work to think of too — though I dont get on with it to speak of in these unsettled times. The war has been a terrible detriment to pleasant thinking in spite of all I can do to approve of it philosophically. I don't know whether I like it or not. I don't think I have any right to like it when I am not called on to die in it. At the same time it seems almost cowardly not to approve of it on general principles simply because it is not my funeral. It seems little minded. There we will leave it. I hate it for those whose hearts are not in it and I fear they must be many, though perhaps not so many as it is the fashion to make them out, nor so many as they were in Nelson's navy for example where more than half the sailors, some say, were "pressed" that is to say, kidnapped. One of the most earthly wise of our time thinks the common soldiers do actually know what they are fighting for and he has said so in the only good war poem I have seen. (Thomas Hardy's my man.) There are many possibilities. The soldier may know. He may not know as in Southey's After Blenheim. He may be at fault for not knowing, deficient in national imagination. He may be the larger for not knowing: he may have been a fool always when he thought he knew, playing into the hands of captains and kings. It may be as the Syndicalists hold that his interest is no longer in nations (never was in fact) but in the federation of industrial groups without masters. This must be a slippery piece of paper — I run to length so easily on it.

There are about half a dozen things I wanted to say to you before ringing off — business things.

The first is that you mustnt take me so seriously. You may be just as friendly as you like. I shall need your good opinion of my books in the fight that is ahead for them in my own country.

That brings me to my second. I fear I am going to suffer a good deal at home by the support of Pound. This is a generous person who is doing his best to put me in the wrong light by his reviews of me: You will see the blow he has dealt me in Poetry (Chicago) for December, and yet it is with such good intention I suppose I shall have to thank him for it. I don't know about that — I may when I get round to it. The harm he does lies in this: he made up his mind in the short time I was friends with him (we quarreled in six weeks) to add me to his party of American literary refugees in London. Nothing could be more unfair, nothing better calculated to make me an exile for life. Another such review as the one in Poetry and I shan't be admitted at Ellis Island. This is no joke. Since the article was published I have been insulted and snubbed by two American editors I counted on as good friends. I dont repine and I am willing to wait for justice. But I do want someone to know that I am not a refugee and I am not in any way disloyal. My publishing a book in England was as it happened. Several editors in America had treated me very well, particularly those of The Companion, The Forum and The Independent. It was not in anger that I came to England and there was no shaking of dust off my feet. Pound is trying to drag me into his ridiculous row with everybody over there. I feel sorry for him for by this time he has nearly every man's hand against him on both continents and I wouldn't want to hurt him. But I feel sorry for myself too. You can imagine the hot patriot I will have become by the time I get home. And then to be shut out! I dont see that it is possible to do anything publicly to dissociate myself from Pound but do you think it would be a discreet thing for you to say a word to [Stuart P.] Sherman or perhaps (what do you think?) even write a short letter to the Sun or The Times or both saying that you have reason to know that I would have no pleasure in that part of Pound's article in Poetry that represented me as an American literary refugee in London with a grievance against Amer[ican] editors. The article was very generous. Pound was a generous person who had gone out of his way to do me several favors, for which you supposed me grateful. But you knew I had favors to thank American editors for, too. A good deal of my first book (in fact one third) had been published in American magazines — the three I have named (you could name them.) My publishing over here was as it happened. I had come across to write rather than to publish. And it was too bad to use a tolerably good book in honest verse forms to grind axes on. Books have enough to contend against anyway.

You could say something like that to Sherman if you thought he would be likely to have been offended by the article in Poetry. Many have seen it and been offended. Do as you please. I leave the Sun and Times to your discretion. Sometimes it is better not to take arms against such misfortunes.

I am not quite heart broken over the way it has gone in this matter. I have done what I have done and I believe I have made place enough for myself to be sure of a hearing for anything else I do. I ask no more. I should like now to go to a small college with the chance of teaching a few ideas or barring that I shall get me a farm where between milking one cow and another I shall write Books III IV & V and perhaps draw a few people about me in time in a sort of summer literary camp. We will talk of this some day.

Do you suppose it might be worth my while to sing myself to [Henry Noble] M[a]cCracken? I am half inclined to try.

Write when you aren't too busy. I haven't heard what proportion of good boys you have had to work with where you are.   Yours ever   R. F.

P. S. We won't stir the Pound matter up I think. You can take what I have written as so much entertainment. If ever anyone gives you the chance in public or otherwise — well you have the facts and you can use them. Pound sought me in every instance. He *asked* for the poem he speaks of ["The Death of the Hired Man"] and then failed to sell it. It was even worse than that. I had demanded the poem back when I learned the name of the magazine [*Smart Set*] he was offering it to but he went ahead in spite of me. And there began our quarrel. I thought never to see him again. But when Book II came out he asked me for "copies" (plural) for review in such a way that I couldn't refuse to meet what looked like generosity half way. It wouldn't do to go into this, but what I have written in the body of the letter you could use should I be attacked when Holt sends out copies for review. Of course it is quite possible that I exaggerate the importance of Pound's article. Let's hope so.

We think of home all the time.

98 · To Edward Thomas

BY THE TIME RF began to make plans for taking his family back to the United States from England, his friendship with Edward Thomas had developed to the point where the two men had seriously discussed the possibility that Thomas might go to America with the Frosts for a visit and that he might later bring his family along. Although these plans were spoiled by the war, Thomas's fifteen-year-old son, Mervyn, did go back with the Frosts and lived briefly with Russell Scott, a relative of Thomas' in Alstead, New Hampshire. This letter refers to developments of the plans for Mervyn.

Dear Thomas   [c. 1 February 1915]   [The Gallows]
Nothing but business this time. It's what I'm full of.

I wish you would ask one or two kinds of people before I

see you if they think the American Liners much to be preferred for safety to any other in this crisis. My own idea is that there would be no special danger in sailing by a White Star-Dominion Liner. We should save money and get put down nearer where we wanted to. I'd not give the matter two thoughts if it wasnt for the children. Just throw out a feeler where you happen to.

Did I say that our day would be somewhere near the twentieth of February? If you wrote Tuesday you should certainly have an answer by that time but with not many days to spare. As I understand it your best way will be to let me speak for a berth for Merfyn [Mervyn] now. You will have to put down a holding fee of two pounds and be prepared to lose it if Scott goes back on you. Authorise me to do it for you when I am in Gloucester seeing about our berths.

I have just stumbled onto a difficulty which, however, I think can be got over. If Merfyn were going with one of his parents he could be as young as he saw any object in being. Since he is sailing without either of them he should appear as sixteen years old in the manifest. So I am told. I dont know what there is in it. I will enquire further. You might see what you can find out by writing to the American Consulate in London. Say you are sending a son to — Scott in America to be educated. Say who you are and who I am that he is going with. Ask if he would better have a passport. Say he may be staying a matter of a year or two and leave it to the consul to mention ages if he likes to. Hurry this up.

Can you hold off your visit till Saturday? We are not sure to be at Ledington till Friday late. Elinor is tired to begin with so I don't suppose we can hope to do our packing in less than several days. Let me know what train.

Great to see you again. There's a lot to say.

We had long talks with Miss [Eleanor] Farjeon. Seldom I have such a chance to expand. I should like to think I hadnt bored her with First Principles. — Oh and by the way let her know that Wilfrid has been here fondling me, but saying cruel things about Viola Meynell for having used my poem where it doesnt fit.* He happens to have her book for review. He will slate her. He spoke with peculiar animus that I had no right to understand yet thought I did understand. Bless it all.

* See postscript to letter 99.

Oh and one more thing. I figure it this way.
From Liverpool to Portland or Boston
    (second class)   11 £
From London to Liverpool   —
From Portland or Boston to Keene (direct)   12 s
Inci- and accidentals   ! £

Yours ever   R. F.

99 · To SIDNEY COX

Dear Cox   2 February 1915   [Little Iddens]

No more letters here please. We sail for home by the St Paul from Liverpool Feb 13. If you want to be first to welcome us you can drop us a line on that c/o the American Line New York. I should think it might reach us. Be sure to name the boat and her date of sailing. I shall enquire for a letter.

You and I wont believe that Gibsons is a better kind of poetry than mine. Solway Ford is one of his best. It is a good poem. But it is oh terribly made up. You know very well that at most all he had to go on was some tale he had heard of a man who had gone mad from fear and another of a man who had been pinned and overtaken by the tide in Solway. I am even inclined to think he invented the latter. It hardly sounds plausible. The details of what he asks you to believe his hallucinations were are poetical but not very convincing. And then look at the way the sentences run on. They are not sentences at all in my sense of the word. The sentence is everything — the sentence well imagined. See the beautiful sentences in a thing like Wordsworth's To Sleep or Herrick's To Daffodils.

Remember, a certain fixed number of sentences (sentence sounds) belong to the human throat just as a certain fixed number of vocal runs belong to the throat of a given kind of bird. These are fixed I say. Imagination can not create them. It can only call them up. It can only call them up for those who write with their ear on the speaking voice. We will prove it out of the Golden Treasury some day.

Current Opinion was kind. I have to thank you for *so* much notice in America. There was a grudging note that I suppose didn't escape you. Never mind. The book is epoch making. I dont ask anyone to say so. All I ask now is to be allowed to live.

151

You have been splendid. Poetry needs just the kind of help you are giving me.

I wish you and your friend could be in places near me next summer.

I do this in a hurry. Don't expect to hear again till I send you a card from the boat.

Bluffers are the curse. I sometimes have my doubts of all the High Schools together. Your German friend is probably a sceptic as regards the higher education of the masses. I am not really with him: at the same time —   Yours ever   Frost

Words are only valuable in writing as they serve to indicate particular sentence sounds. I must say some things over and over. I must be a little extravagant too.

For goodbye The Nation named N. O. B. among the four best books of verse for 1914 and Viola Meynell used the Pasture poem to introduce her latest novel Columbine. I wish Sheffauer [Robert Haven Schauffler] might have seen N. O. B. It seems more in his line than Book I.

100 · To Harold Monro

Dear Monro   [c. 13 February 1915]   [Liverpool]

This with my best goodbyes. Thanks for everything. I had intended to see you before leaving but at the last moment we go rather precipitously; so that I am scanting duties. Anyway I don't want too much made of my going or I should feel as if I were never coming back. I shall be back just as soon as I have earned a little more living. England has become half my native land — England the victorious. Good friends I have had here and hope to keep.   Yours ever   Robert Frost

101 · To F. S. Flint

                                              [c. 13 February 1915]
Dear Flint   U. S. M. S. "St Paul"   [Liverpool]

I ought to know by the length of your silence that you dont want to write to me any more — cor silicis. And if you don't I ought to have pride enough not to ask you to. But no matter: I must at least say goodbye to the man who opened England to me. You are good.   Sincerely yours   Frost

FRANCONIA AND AMHERST · 1915-1920

ROBERT FROST and his family sailed from Liverpool on the night of 13 February 1915 and landed in New York City on the 22nd. Resigned to the possibility that he might have to return to teaching to earn a living, Frost nevertheless hoped that royalties from his American publisher would allow him to play at farming again in New Hampshire. He favored the Franconia region of the White Mountains because he had become attracted to it during his flights from Derry in the hay-fever seasons. Temporarily he could count on the hospitality of John Lynch, the Irish farmer in Bethlehem with whom he and his family had stayed in former years. Frost sent his wife and children ahead to the Lynches while he tarried in New York to enlarge his small American literary reputation.

At the office of Henry Holt and Company he was encouraged by Alfred Harcourt, then head of the trade book department. Harcourt enthusiastically reported that an initial 150 copies of *North of Boston*, imported from England in sheets and bound with a tipped-in title page bearing the Holt imprint, had been largely bought up by dealers in the Boston area prior to the publication date of 20 February; that 200 additional sets of sheets had already been ordered from England; that a favorable review of *North of Boston* had been written by the influential Amy Lowell and had appeared in the *New Republic* on publication day; that plans were already completed for printing American editions of *North of Boston* and *A Boy's Will*. Harcourt urged Frost to spend a few days in New York, particularly to join him at a lunch with the editors of the *New Republic* and to attend a dinner meeting of the Poetry Society of America. Frost agreed to attend both functions, where he was warmly welcomed as America's newest poetic discovery.

Even greater satisfaction awaited him in Boston. Harcourt had arranged for him to be met there by two locally prominent literary figures, Nathan Haskell Dole and Sylvester Baxter, who served as cordial publicists for him. On his own he telephoned Amy Lowell to thank her for her review, and was invited to Brookline for dinner. He also dropped in on William Stanley Braithwaite, editor of an important poetry column in the pages of the Boston *Evening Transcript,* and made a friend of Braithwaite. He visited Ellery Sedgwick, editor of the *Atlantic Monthly,* and was taken to Sedgwick's home that evening for dinner, where he met the William Ernest Hockings. The next day he lunched at Cambridge with the Hockings and was persuaded to spend two nights with them. Sylvester Baxter also entertained Frost, as did Nathan Haskell Dole.

A side trip from Boston to Lawrence gave Frost an opportunity to see old friends there and to ease the financial pinch by calling on Wilbur E. Rowell, executor of his grandfather's estate. By the time Frost joined his family at the Lynch farm, he had completed a very impressive stage of his initial promotion campaign in America.

From Bethlehem he continued to cultivate by mail the friendships of those editors and critics and poets who might be of help. For the first time in his life, he began to read his poems at public gatherings for twenty-five or fifty dollars a reading. All the fright he felt on a platform was expelled as nervous energy in this new phase of his determination to swell his literary reputation.

During the first year after his return from England, Frost devoted so much time to such non-creative activities that he over-committed himself in many ways. When his publisher begged hard for a third volume of poetry, he hurriedly and somewhat resentfully assembled *Mountain Interval,* which was published in November of 1916. At almost the same time he accepted an invitation to join the faculty of Amherst College, hoping that his presence there might resolve his precarious financial position.

Straining this way and that, the poet fell prey to anxieties, as his letters of this period make clear. At Amherst he quickly became irritated by President Alexander Meiklejohn's liberal experiments in education and took a strong dislike to several of his colleagues. When vacation let him escape from distasteful academic duties, he retreated to Franconia, only to find other annoyances caused by "summer people" who called uninvited at his newly purchased farm. What bothered him most was that in winning some fame he had lost his valued leisure and independence. The quantity of his writing steadily fell off, and after the publication of *Mountain Interval* his maturing reputation temporarily declined. Only three new poems of his appeared in periodicals during 1917; only one in 1918; none in 1919.

By the spring of 1920, Frost began to take corrective measures. In a burst of resentment, he resigned from Amherst; in a moment of rage, he decided to move his family away from all the unpleasantness in Franconia. Temporarily, he convinced himself that he wanted to live within commuting distance of his publisher in New York; and he even went so far as to consider buying property in southern Connecticut. But new friendships around Arlington, Vermont, resulting from a reading he gave there, pulled him in that direction. In the summer of 1920 he sold his Franconia farm, bought an ancient stone farmhouse with four hundred acres of land in South Shaftsbury, and in October went there to live.

Yet for some time he could not recover his equilibrium. Physically and emotionally exhausted, he felt that this phase of his literary career, which had begun with so much promise, had ended in failure. But the mood of depression did not last long, and it was followed by a strong resurgence of creative power.

102 · To Sidney Cox

NOTICE the mailing instructions in this letter: "I am on the way to Bethlehem New Hampshire. Write to me there in care of John Lynch." Thereafter, in his many letters from the Lynch farm, RF used the place heading, "Littleton, New Hampshire," because mail was delivered by rural free delivery from the Littleton post office, not from Bethlehem. For purposes of editorial clarification, the headings on letters written from the Lynch farm, beginning with letter 103, have been simplified to [Bethlehem].

Dear Cox   [c. 2 March 1915]   [Lawrence, Massachusetts]

Your letter was the first thing I read in America. In fact I read it before I was in America that's to say before I passed quarantine. You are always encouraging.

I wish I could afford to visit you at Sc[h]enectady and see you first and then anyone else you cared to bring along.

I ran spank on to your S[c]hauffler (pronounced Shoffler) in New York and made him a friend. I think we can like each other despite the irreconcilability of what we write. You must meet him.

You know that the Holts have my book out. Pretty cover. But the best of the Holts is that they are going to be a father to me.

Did you see what Amy Lowell had to say in The New Republic for Feb. 20. She will pervert me a little to her theory, but never mind.

I am on the way to Bethlehem New Hampshire. Write to me there in care of John Lynch. I wish we might be near you in the summer somehow. More of my plans when I know more of them myself.   Allers yours   R. F.

103 · To Sidney Cox

Dear Cox   13 March 1915   [Bethlehem]

Write to me as soon as you can to say you got my letter from New York and understood my reasons for not going to Schenectady. I was aching to see you and almost hoped you would propose coming to us. You have a salary and can go and come as you please. When I got to Lawrence where I could ask for money (and might or might not get it) I had less than fifty cents left in my pocket. You can read Browning's "Up at the Villa" for a proper statement of why a man of my means might live in the country. As a matter of fact I like the country and might live there all the time of choice. At the present moment however I must live there of necessity. I am not rich enough to live even for a few weeks in the style you suggested in Schenectady.

I didn't get through New York and Boston without more attention than you may think I deserve from my fellow countrymen. The Holts are splendid. If you want to see what happened in Boston, look me up in the Boston Herald for Tuesday March 9 under the heading Talk of the Town. A number of my old editorial enemies actually asked me for poems. Let us weep before it is too late.   Yours ever   R. F.

104 · To Lascelles Abercrombie

Dear Abercrombie   15 March [1915]   [Bethlehem]

That was a good shove you gave us in going and it lasted us till we ran bang into an inspector at the gangway in Liverpool who was for keeping us in England till our greatness ripened a little more. Very well says I, maybe you know more about what's good for me than I do myself. I like England and I'm willing to stay if some one else will take the responsibility. But I give you fair warning: if I dont go now I wont go at all. I shall become a British subject and "run for" the Laureateship. That seemed to make him think. He let us go on board — muttering.

We withheld our speed and didnt sail till dark; and we had when we did sail two battleships with us all down the Irish Sea — to pick us up I suppose if we got into the water for any reason. But we didn't get undermined and we didnt get torpedoed — else you would have heard of it before this. We got kicked about a deal for nine whole days and seasickened and discouraged from ever crossing again.

Then we came to New York and were hailed by one or two intelligent people as a poet and family. In the excitement of the moment I made two or three promises that I cant fulfill unless you send me two or three copies of the New Number containing The End of the World because I can't afford to buy them and I'm no longer living at The Gallows where I can steal them.

If I forget England! My thanks for all you did to make her what she is to me. Now go ahead and win the war.

My love to you all and especially to the little boy I taught while he was young and there was yet time, a way to make a big splash with a small object and a small splash with a large object. Ask him if he remembers.

Let me know how your plans for coming over are coming on.   Yours ever   Robert Frost

105 · To William Stanley Braithwaite

THE FLATTERING attentions paid to the Negro poet-critic-anthologist, William Stanley Braithwaite, by RF helped to keep this critic in RF's corner. Like RF's other critical acquaintance, Louis Untermeyer, Braithwaite had acquired influence as a critic and reviewer just prior to RF's return from England. Starting in 1913, Braithwaite supplemented his writing of a weekly column on poetry for the Boston *Evening Transcript* by editing and issuing a somewhat indiscriminate annual, *Anthology of Magazine Verse and Year Book of American Poetry*. RF wasted no time in courting favors from Braithwaite; he called on him immediately after his arrival in Boston on his very first visit.

RF used the same epistolary tactics on Braithwaite, here, which he had employed earlier to gain the assistance of Cox and Bartlett; the same tactics he used later on Untermeyer. The essential procedure was to fill a letter with tendentious confidences, facts, ideas, and theories which had the makings of good "copy" for explanatory articles on RF, the poet and man. Braithwaite responded satisfactorily. His first *Transcript* article on RF was "A Poet of New England: Robert Frost a New Exponent of Life" (28 April 1915); his next was "Robert Frost, New American Poet" (8 May 1915).

Dear Mr Braithwaite: 22 March [1915] [Bethlehem]

I've got as far as finding you the copy of Book I [*A Boy's Will*], I promised you. Perhaps as a busy man you wont resent my telling you what to read in it if you are going to read at all. It is the list I always give to friends I wish the minimum of suffering: pages 1, 2, 4, 7, 9, 14, 20, 22, 23, 25, 26, 34, 41, 42 (once printed in the Transcript) 45, 46 (8-18 line — first poetry I ever wrote that I could call my own — year 1892) and 49. Don't read those unless you have to, but don't read the others on any account.

The book is an expression of my life for the ten years from eighteen on when I thought I greatly preferred stocks and stones to people. The poems were written as I lived the life quite at the mercy of myself and not always happy. The arrangement in a book came much later when I could look back on the past with something like understanding.

I kept farm, so to speak, for nearly ten years, but less as a farmer than as a fugitive from the world that seemed to me to "disallow" me. It was all instinctive, but I can see now that I went away to save myself and fix myself before I measured my strength against all creation. I was never really out of the world for good and all. I liked people even when I believed I detested them.

It would seem absurd to say it (and you mustn't quote me as saying it) but I suppose the fact is that my conscious interest in people was at first no more than an almost technical interest in their speech — in what I used to call their sentence sounds — the sound of sense. Whatever these sounds are or aren't (they are certainly not of the vowels and consonants of words nor even of the words themselves but something the words are chiefly a kind of notation for indicating and fastening to the printed page) whatever they are, I say, I began to hang on them very young. I was under twenty when I deliberately put it to myself one night after good conversation that there are moments when we actually touch in talk what the best writing can only come near. The curse of our book language is not so much that it keeps forever to the same set phrases (though Heaven knows those are bad enough) but that it sounds forever with the same reading tones. We must go out into the vernacular for tones that havent been brought to book. We must write with the ear on the speaking voice. We must imagine the speaking voice.

I say all this biographically to lead up to Book II (North of Boston). There came a day about ten years ago when I made the discovery that though sequestered I wasnt living without reference to other people. Right on top of that I made the discovery in doing The Death of the Hired Man that I was interested in neighbors for more than merely their tones of speech — and always had been. I remember about when I began to suspect myself of liking their gossip for its own sake. I justified myself by the example of Napoleon as recently I have had to justify myself in seasickness by the example of Nelson.

I like the actuality of gossip, the intimacy of it. Say what you will effects of actuality and intimacy are the greatest aim an artist can have. The sense of intimacy gives the thrill of sincerity. A story must always release a meaning more readily to those who read than life itself as it goes ever releases meaning. Meaning is a great consideration. But a story must never seem to be told primarily for meaning. Anything, an inspired irrelevancy even to make it sound as if told the way it is chiefly because it happened that way.

I have run on unpardonably. I couldn't write a whole biography; so I just had to plunge into the middle of things. I have pretty well jumbled the story of how I see my own development and some of my theories of art. You are not going to use anything directly, I take it. You will be sure to veil what is too personal. This isn't quite the same as an interview. I have met you and now we are getting further in getting acquainted.

Ask me for anything I don't think to supply for your newspaper article. Probably you want a few dates and data.

I was born in San Francisco forty years ago. My father was an editor out there. He died when I was young.

I went to the public schools in Lawrence Mass. I was married there.

My farm was in Derry, New Hampshire.

I taught literature at Pinkerton Academy, Derry, and psychology at the Normal School, Plymouth for the five years before I went to England.

In England I saw a good deal of two or three literary circles in London for a year or two and then went down into Gloucestershire and Herefordshire for another year. I never saw *New* England as clearly as when I was in Old England.

Just to show you that the interest in my work over there was partly on the technical side or where the material shades off into the technical I enclose a circular my English publisher got out. The quotation from The Nation was used by The Listener in the Transcript (July 8).

No more of this.

May I hope really to see something of you when I am in Boston again? I'd like to have a talk about poetry by ourselves alone.   Sincerely yours   Robert Frost

106 · To Louis Untermeyer

HAVING established himself prominently, both as poet and critic, before RF returned from England, Louis Untermeyer wrote some of the earliest, the most enthusiastic, and the most influential articles and reviews of Frost's poetry. Built on that foundation, their mutual admiration society survived many vicissitudes. Their long correspondence may be found in *The Letters of Robert Frost to Louis Untermeyer* (Holt, Rinehart and Winston, New York, 1963), but representative letters of RF to Untermeyer are included here whenever pertinent to the larger context.

Dear Mr. Untermeyer: 22 March 1915   [Bethlehem]

What must you think of a silence as long as this to a letter as good as that? But let me tell you by way of what places the letter has just reached me: the office of The New Republic; the office of Henry Holt; South Fork, Penna; Wildwood N. J., and Philadelphia. Such is the fact, though I can't prove it by the envelope which has been travelling some of the time in other envelopes.

Your cordiality is especially warming. There's not a person in New York I should have had more pleasure in meeting than Louis Untermeyer. For I was already feeling a good deal acquainted with you from having heard your name so often mentioned under a certain thatch roof in Ryton Dymock Gloucestershire England.

You make me wonder if I hadn't better get back to New York in a month or two. I can just see and hear myself having a good time with you somewhere where there's not too much noise of the city. I could tell you a lot about Abercrombie.

You are all too good about "North of Boston."

Sincerely yours,   Robert Frost

You weren't thinking of coming to Boston in May, were you? I believe I am expected there somewhere round the fifth.   R. F.

107 · To SIDNEY COX

Dear Cox   22 March 1915   [Bethlehem]

Of course you wouldn't be anything so petty as miffed. But you might be honestly hurt or disappointed if you weren't given thoroughly to understand.

Dont worry too much about my money difficulties. Some time I will tell you exactly how it is I can be down to my last shilling and yet in no immediate danger of coming on the town. I am always more or less in trouble but it wont be for five years or so that I'll be in jail or the poorhouse. My only hope in those days will be my children or such of them as think well of me — don't judge me too hardly for having written poetry. There's Marj — she told Mrs Lynch, I'm told, that I was a good one to write poetry and to bring up children. She's very likely wrong, but as long as she believes what she says —

And a word more to you my son. You are to dispense with further talk of disparity between us. I have never had such thoughts and I dislike having them thrust upon me.

Thus shamelessly I send you the Herald scrap [clipping of the column "Talk of the Town" by Sylvester Baxter from the

161

Boston *Herald* for 9 March 1915]. If the fellow who wrote it seems to know more of my goings and comings than he could without complicity of mine, the reason is because he is a lovely old boy and quite took possession of me while I was in Boston. When he wasn't actually with me like Mary's lamb he was keeping track of me by telephone. I believe he is doing for me on principle. He's got me on his conscience. The Ellery Sedgwick of the piece is mine ancient enemy the editor of The Atlantic.

Yours ever   Robert Frost.

108 · To Nathan Haskell Dole

Dear Dole   26 March 1915   [Bethlehem]

Do it some more in red ink. You write well in any ink or in pencil for anything I know to the contrary: but if this letter is a fair sample and if I am any judge you are at your best and truthfullest in red ink.

I am slow to recover from the awful dazing you gave me in Boston. I was afraid my special pertness was never coming back. I sat on the edge of the bed for days together rubbing my eyes and (yawning I was going to say but no) crying at intervals like Balaam mourning for her children, "The cuss is all gone out of me!"

Possibly it is. I shall know better when I have made up the rest of my lost sleep. At my age a fellow forgets kindness and shakes off obligations with the greatest difficulty. Still it can't be I am going to let myself sink under benefactions at the age of forty. I shall yet manage to do something I owe it to my friends and relatives not to do.

Perhaps reading to the Phi Beta Kappa is the thing. That should get me into sufficient trouble to make me feel at home. You know I can't read. Why would you put temptation in my way? For I suppose you did it.

Another experience I cant seem to get over is Ellis Island. I dreamed last night that I had to pass a written examination in order to pass the inspection there. There were two questions set me.

1. Who in Hell do you think you are?
2. How much do one and one make?

Note. Candidates are advised to use influence in passing inspection. They are warned that if they think they are Christ or

Napoleon or a poet they will do well not to say so if they dont want to be deported as of unsound unsounded and unfathomable mind. They are warned also against any levity in their answer to the second question. It will count heavily against them in the highest official circles if they try to get round the difficulty by answering that one and one if they are of opposite and conflicting sex may produce a dozen.

When I dream at all, I always dream good sense.

Some time I will read your Rose of the Kennebec and glad of the chance.

We have these mountains pretty much to ourselves at this time of year.

In May I shall probably be seeing you again.

My wife is sure I will forget to thank you for the good coffee.

My best to all your household.

Yours ever   Robert Frost

This is my birthday.

109 · To George Herbert Palmer

WHEN RF was a special student at Harvard, from 1887 to 1889, George Herbert Palmer was a professor of philosophy with a strong secondary interest in Greek, English, and American literature. He and his distinguished wife, Alice Freeman Palmer, were frequently at home to selected groups of Harvard students, and thus RF came to know them.

My dear Prof. Palmer: 2 April 1915   [Bethlehem]

This from you is great happiness. Any time these twenty years if I had been asked to name my own judges to judge me when I was ready I should have chosen you for one. You may wonder where I have come near you to have learned such respect for your judgement. It is not altogether in your writing; for I have sat with you in the room walled all on one side with poetry and heard you talk of Old Walt and of the farmer's wives in Boxford (I think) who liked to hear you read "The Ring and the Book." So that when I call on you, as I shall hope to soon, it will not be for the first time in my life.

Thank you for your kindness.

Sincerely yours,   Robert Frost

110 · To WILLIAM STANLEY BRAITHWAITE

Dear Mr Braithwaite   4 April 1915   [Bethlehem]

I trust you got the small book [*A Boy's Will*]. I want to be sure to have that right. You bought the other in my presence with such a friendly little flourish.

Sincerely yours   Robert Frost

111 · To EDWARD THOMAS

REFERENCE has been made to the way in which RF, in England, helped to change and revitalize the direction of Edward Thomas' literary career. Many of Thomas' letters to RF contained newly written poems, and this answering letter begins with RF's comment on one such poem, "Lob." RF later waged an intensive and successful campaign to have Thomas' poems published in America, first in periodicals and then in book form (see letters 152, 155, 156).

When Thomas' son, Mervyn, reached America with the Frosts, the immigration officials temporarily barred his entrance and held him for one night at Ellis Island. RF phoned Mervyn's guardian, Russell Scott, in Alstead, New Hampshire, to ask for advice, and was told to get in touch with Scott's brother, Arthur, or his wife, Mrs. Mildred Minturn Scott, then living in New York City. Thus RF got to know the Arthur Scotts, who were influential in clearing young Thomas' immigration papers. This letter refers to the Arthur Scotts and also to Taber Minturn, a brother of Mrs. Scott.

Dear Edward   17 April 1915   [Bethlehem]

The goodness is in Lob. You are a poet or you are nothing. But you are not psychologist enough to know that no one not come at in just the right way will ever recognize you. *You* can't go to [Edward] Garnett for yourself; *you* can't go to De la Mare. I told you and I keep telling you. But as long as your courage holds out you may as well go right ahead making a fool of yourself. All brave men are fools.

I like the first half of Lob best: it offers something more like action with the different people coming in and giving the tones of speech. But the long paragraph is a feat. I never saw anything like you for English.

What you say of Taber I shan't fail to pass along to his sister. I am going to Stowe [Vermont] tomorrow at her invitation to see if I can find a farm there.

We are still unsettled. Hopes grow in every way but one.

I should say we seem to have hopes of everything except more money. If some of these editors who profess to love me now had only loved me in time to buy my poems when they were in MS. It's not in me to take hold and write them anything to catch them in the mood.

I shall have Merfyn [Mervyn] come to see us as soon as ever we know where we are. Scott bores me too, though I never got nearer him than talking on the telephone at 400 miles distance. I don't so much mind his messalliance as I do all his muddle headed compromises to avoid the single compromise of making it a marriage. I had to laugh when his sister-in-law told me he was ready to make it a common-law marriage if she would come into the game to save Merfyn. She was the lovely one — with a twinkle in her mind. But she wasnt messing up with Scott's troubles. And I couldn't blame her when I had seen and heard. Mind you, she's fond of Scott.

You must be wrong about your Christian Science Transcript. There is a C. S. Monitor and there is a Boston Transcript. I should like to see that review. I have thought (but I wouldnt say anything to you about it) that you might pick up some work over here as you come along up to us through Boston and New York. By all the signs there should be a few people in both places I could introduce you to. Thats more than I could have said three months ago.

Jolly to think of you at the Duke of Marlborough. She that standeth in the shoes of the first Duchess is an American and if you pleased her might be able to introduce you to more people over here than I can.

Will you have to visit the battlefields of Oudenarde Blenheim and Malplaquet?

I have just had two letters from you at once. The mails continue to come safely through. I wonder when we shall get the first letter sunk.

Poor [Jack] Haines will be sorry you couldnt get down to see him.

You ought not to be left out of this: I have had one note from Wilfrid in which he says Ellery Sedgwick writes that he had a pleasant talk with me on English traits peculiarities idiocyncracies etc. Wilfrid wishes he could have heard that talk! I wish he could. It was all about Wilfrid's nice feeling for country society *and* the Albrights. Amy Lowell says I have no sense of humor, but sometimes I manage to be funny without that gift of the few. Not often, you know. Ellery Sedgwick (ed of the Atlantic) wanted to let it all out, but didn't quite dare.

Did I tell you Sedgwick said Wilfrid rather invited himself over here — asked Sedgwick outright if he couldn't arrange him a tour. That is not as I had it from Wilfrid. He was under the delusion that he had been urged to come over and save the country.

Looked at a little farm yesterday right forninst Lafayette.

We are with the Lynches. Old Lynch hates England but entertains no nonsense as to what would happen if Germany won. Every Yankee in America (practically) wants England to win — England and France. They all think you will win, but perhaps not this year. But few consider the war any affair of ours. No one goes into a war on general grounds of humanity. We extend sympathy on general grounds of humanity. We fight only when our material interests are touched. Yours were when Belgium was invaded; ours weren't. Damn the Germans. Did I tell you of my friend Alice Brown the novelist who hung up a picture of the Kaiser in her barn and drove nails into the face like a damsel in Malory doing despite to a knights shield?

Well I have run on. Let short and frequent letters be the rule.

Let me keep the poems. I suppose you want the woodsy letter from the parson. I believe I'll hold it over a while though to show to Ellery Sedgwick. I would not have him run off with the idea that because I poked a little fun at Wilfrid I am no lover of the English — when they right.

Yours ever   R. F.

112 · To Harold G. Rugg

Dear Sir   20 April 1915   [Bethlehem]

You are correctly informed: I was some part of a year at Hanover with the Class of 1896. I lived in Wentworth (top floor, rear, side next to Dartmouth) in a room with a door that had the advantage of opening outward and so of being hard for marauding sophomores to force from the outside. I had to force it once myself from the inside when I was nailed and screwed in. My very dear friend was Preston Shirley (who was so individual that his memory should be still green with you) and he had a door opening inward that was forced so often that it became what you might call *facile* and opened if you looked at it. The only way to secure it against violation was to brace it from behind with the door off the coal closet. I made common cause with Shirley and sometimes helped him hold the fort in his room till we fell out over a wooden washtub bathtub that we owned in partnership but that I was inclined to keep for myself more than my share of the time. I may say that we made up afterward over kerosene. One of us ran out of oil after the stores were closed at night and so far sacrificed his pride as to ask to borrow of the other.

I'm afraid I wasn't much of a college man in your sense of the word. I was getting past the point where I could show any great interest in any task not self-imposed. Much of what I enjoyed at Dartmouth was acting like an Indian in a college founded for Indians. I mean I liked the rushes a good deal, especially the one in which our class got the salting and afterwards fought it out with the sophomores across pews and everything (it was in the Old Chapel) with old cushions and even footstools for weapons — or rather fought it to a standstill with the dust of ages we raised.

For the rest I wrote a good deal and was off in such places as the Vale of Tempe and on the walk east of the town that I called the Five Mile Round. I wrote one of the poems I still care for at about that time. It is preserved in my first book, "A Boy's Will." I wrote while the ashes accumulated on the floor in front of my stove door and would have gone on accumulating to the room door if my mother hadn't sent a friend a hundred miles to shovel up and clean house for me.

You are the third person I have found common interest with in Willoughby. There are never many people at the lake at any one time and yet there seem a good many who have been there. I too expect to get back there some summer — probably not this. Isn't Pisgah (otherwise Willoughby) your mountain for the ferns? I have found some things on the Hor side (chiefly Braun's Holly and an orchid whose name I should know again if I saw it) but more on the other along the great cliff. Don't put me down for a botanist. I wonder if you ever met a farmer named Emerson who lives just above the dam on the Barton road. He's a product of the flowers of the region. I think of him as the Calypso man.

I am just this minute off for Stowe in your state. I believe I can see from this "sidehill" in the White Mts the tip of

Camel's Hump in the Green Mts. I shall be somewhere in that neighborhood this evening.

Probably Holt would send you copies of my books if you will let me ask him to.   Very truly yours   Robert Frost

113 · To John T. Bartlett

FOR FAMILY REASONS the Bartletts had returned from Vancouver by the time the Frosts came back from England. Living once again in Raymond, New Hampshire, they were occasionally able to exchange visits with the Frosts. Reference to a possible meeting between RF and Bartlett occurs in the last paragraph of this letter.

Dear John,   [c. 20 April 1915]   [Bethlehem]

There seems nothing to talk about on my side but the winning subject of the fortunes of my book. Some day there will be an end of that. You can't wonder that it is a good deal on my mind with a review appearing every few days and letters coming in from all quarters. I wish I could describe the state I have been thrown into. I suppose you could call it one of pleasurable scorn when it is not one of scornful scorn. The thought that gets me is that at magazine rates there is about a thousand dollars worth of poetry in N. O. B. that I might have had last winter if the people who love me now had loved me then. Never you doubt that I gave them the chance to love me. What, you ask, has come over them to change their opinion of me? And the answer is What? — Doubtless you saw my countenance displayed in The [Boston] Herald one day. The Transcript will [do] me next. The literary editor [Llewelyn Jones] of The Chicago Post writes to say that I may look for two columns of loving kindness in The Post in a day or two. It is not just naught — say what you will. One likes best to write poetry and one knew that he did that before one got even one reputation. Still one can't pretend not to like to win the game. One can't help thinking a little of Number One.

I couldn't or wouldn't go into all this with anyone else as I am inclined to go into it with you. I feel as if it couldn't hurt you, (you are no fool) and may even do you some good. I want you to see young what a thing it is. Not that I'm on exhibition as a very terrible example — more as an amusing and edifying example. I don't say that any one should actually be warned to avoid my mistakes. But there they are for anyone to avoid who likes to and knows how to.

You alone of my American friends haven't wished me a pot of money out of my poetry. Is it because you are too wise or because you have too good taste or because you are too unworldly to have thought of it. And yet I need money as I suspect you may yourself.

Are you saving your talk of plans for when I am South again in a week or two? Say any thing you choose that comes into your head without fear of actual hurt to me. Write it, John. It will give me something to think of.

Affectionately   Rob

113-a · EDWARD GARNETT TO ELLERY SEDGWICK

RF liked to tell the story of the banter and teasing between himself and Ellery Sedgwick when he first sold poems to *The Atlantic Monthly*. That story has been documented and extended in Edward Connery Lathem's *Robert Frost: His "American Send-off" — 1915*. As Sedgwick seemed to be debating whether to publish any or all of three poems RF had thrust upon him ("Birches," "The Road Not Taken," and "The Sound of Trees"), Garnett's unsolicited offer to the *Atlantic* of an essay in praise of RF must have had some effect on Sedgwick. Two letters (113-a and 119-a) help to explain elements in RF's letter of thanks to Garnett (letter 122) for the essay, "A New American Poet," printed in the issue of the *Atlantic* for August 1915 as an accompaniment to RF's three poems.

Dear Mr. Sedgwick,   24 April 1915   [London]

Owing to the typist's delay I could not send you last week my critical paper "A New American Poet," which I mail herewith. Since writing you last I have learnt that an American edition of "North of Boston" has been issued by Holt & that it has received some attention on your side, but I take it that Mr. Frost's poetic quality is too original to penetrate quickly to any but a select audience. Therefore I hope my paper may not only interest your readers, but may receive attention & comment in the wider circle of the Press.

Of Mr. Frost I know nothing personally, but a few particulars given me by Mr. Edward Thomas who sent me "North of Boston." Possibly you know more than I do — which is simply that he hails from a New England farm, has paid a long visit to England, & has returned only a few weeks ago to the States. Mr. Frost as a poet, however, *is a very considerable figure in-*

deed, not to be classed in any way with Mr. Undermeyer & his associates, who I see are vociferously advertizing the claims of "The New Poetry," or with the class of poetic dilettanti who contribute to Miss Harriet Monro[e]'s magazine "Poetry."

From what Mr. Thomas told me I fancy these fellow poets, or poetlings, are not particularly anxious to herald Mr. Frost's achievement; the former, if I may judge from my examination of "their" work in "Poetry," are *negli[gi]ble,* whereas Mr. Frost is really *representative,* carrying on those literary traditions of New England, which are associated with talents as diverse as Hawthorne, Thoreau & Sarah Orne Jewett. If anything I have erred in *understanding* Mr. Frost's claims to the attention of American readers; but I prefer that my verdict should be cool & unbiassed. Although I rely entirely on my own judgment in this matter, I understand from Mr. Thomas that the few notices "North of Boston" received on this side, though short, owing to the War, practically confirm my belief that since Whitman's death, no American poet has appeared, of so *unique a quality,* as Mr. Frost.

It is possible that by the time my article reaches you that your own critic of poetry may have written something for "The Atlantic Monthly" on Mr. Frost's claims. If so you will no doubt append a footnote to my paper, saying it has interest as coming from an independent, English critic. . . .

114 · To John W. Haines

Dear Haines,   25 April 1915   [Bethlehem]

I feel angry but it is an Englishman's anger that after all the talk of what Ki[t]chener's army was going to do in the spring you should have let the Germans be beforehand with you in opening the spring campaign. Some part of me that doesn't fit too tight inside actually gets right up and starts to go somewhere to do something about it. Rotten news. I'm sick of it. And SO ARE MY CHILDREN. We threaten to have our paper stopped.

Every day I have said "Tomorrow the advance on Berlin will begin." Damned lucky if it isn't the advance on Paris.

What I long for is certainties where I have fixed my heart. I am not permitted to be certain of anything. It is the same with my own personal affairs as with the war. From over there I thought I saw what must be easy when I got home. I have been looking for a farm for three months and no nearer settled down now, than I was on board the St. Paul. The year will be lost as far as farming is concerned if I don't find what I want at a possible price before many days.

I am not altogether to blame for having failed thus far of my object in coming home. There have been distractions on distractions. If I was a man dazed by the reviews that happened to me last summer and the friendliness of the English, what am I now? These people once my enemies in the editorial offices are trying to be my generous friends. Some of them are making hard work of it. Some are makng very hard work. They can't help trying to explain away my success with the English critics. It must be due to my lack of polish. And I sit so scornful of the pack and yet so willing to get all the glory going and see my books sell that you would think I was in some dream. It has a curious effect on me. Twenty years I gave some of these people a chance. I wish I were rich and independent enough to tell them to go to Hell. You ought to have seen the lovely recollections I did (by request) of my life at Dartmouth College. I ought to have kept a copy for you. You know me well enough to have read under the surface of it. Elinor said I simply mustn't gratify anybody by doing the usual thing about all I owed to my alma mater. And I didn't. I wasn't hypocrite enough for that. I had a little fun.

I weep inwardly over it all.

Remember there are good people against whom I harbour no resentment. There's Alice Brown and Sylvester Baxter and Louis Untermeyer and Llewellyn Jones and Amy Lowell and nearly the whole staff of The New Republic and Albert Shaw. I'm glad of such friends in a country where I had not one three years ago.

While this excitement lasts you will see that it would be affectation for me to pretend not to be interested in it. It means nothing or next to nothing to my future poetry; it may even hurt that; but there is me personally to send you a good review now and then just as if I was as vain as you think I am. The one by Louis Untermeyer you might pass along to Abercrombie. Untermeyer is a friend of his I have heard. All others keep to yourself.

I'll write you out a little poem about the brook on my old farm. It always dried up in summer. The Hyla is a small frog that shouts like jingling bells in the marshes in spring.

Won't flirt with your cousins.

Get me credit with your wife for having said that.

Yours ever,   R. F.

Send along your review.

115 · To Louis Untermeyer

THE FOLLOWING LETTER refers to Untermeyer's review of *North of Boston*, which had appeared in "The Friday Literary Review" section of the Chicago *Evening Post* for 23 April 1915, page 11. On that same page, Llewellyn Jones, the Literary Editor of the *Post,* devoted an editorial to RF. Jones began his editorial, "With the American publication of 'A Boy's Will' as well as of 'North of Boston' another American poet of the first importance is before the American public. Whether it is the American public's own fault that Mr. Frost's work was not accessible to it sooner, we cannot say, but if we remember correctly, Ezra Pound wrote in *Poetry* a year ago to the effect that Mr. Frost had been refused a hearing by American publishers . . ."

Dear Untermeyer: 30 April 1915   [Bethlehem]

There are a dozen things in your article that I should like to thank you for in detail, but I must stop for just one of them now. You make the point that there must be many poetical moods that haven't been reduced to poetry. Thanks most of all for seeing that, and saying it in a review of book by me.

You see so well the necessity of our being generous to each other as fellow artists. I probably don't deserve all your praise, but you'll never be the poorer for having uttered it, and trust my enemies to discount it where it needs discounting.

I am in your book [*Challenge*] almost as I write and full of the large spirit of it. You are the same in your letters, in your reviewing, and in your poetry. Really I knew you in England [see 107]. I admire and envy you for knowing what you want to urge in prose and verse. I shall love your book.

All this is in haste. My chief object in writing is to get you word in time that I am to be at Sylvester Baxter's, 42 Murray Hill Road Malden Mass on April 4. On April 5 I shall be at Tufts College. On April 6 and on for several days at Baxter's again.* Will you look me up there? — or call me up? Baxter

* In haste, apparently, RF wrote "April" in each case where he meant to write "May." As planned, he did go to Baxter's, to Tufts College, and again to Baxter's, on May 4th, 5th, and 6th, respectively. See "Chronology."

would be glad to have you come to see us both. I did think, though, that I should like it if we could steal away somewhere by ourselves.*

Yours ever   Robert Frost

I must thank Jones.

116 · To John T. Bartlett

8 May 1915

Dear John: 42 Murray Hill Road   Malden Mass
      I got through my Phi Beta Kappa and my speech before the Authors Club but what does it matter about me? I'm sick this morning with hate of England and America because they have let this [sinking of SS *Lusitania*] happen and will do nothing to punish the Germans. They can do nothing. I have no faith in any of them. Germany will somehow come out of this war if not completely victorious at least still formidable and needing only time to get wind for another round. Dammit.
      I cant get away till some day next week.

Rob

What a world it is

117 · To Sidney Cox

Dear Cox   16 May 1915   [Bethlehem]
      Jessie B. [Rittenhouse] was all right. I ask no more than temperate praise from any of them. Temperate praise in the long run will help me most. And do you remember that when you get your chance to write of me as you know me. Don't let your admiration run away with you. Consider appearances in public. Make the most of the advantage of having known me personally to correct any lies about me that may be current. But don't overdo the praise.
      The only nastiness in Jessie B's article is the first part where she speaks of the English reviews as fulsome. There she speaks dishonestly out of complete ignorance — out of

---

* See letter 105, to the poet-critic-anthologist, William Stanley Braithwaite, for a similar ending: "I'd like to have a talk about poetry by ourselves alone."

some sort of malice or envy I should infer. Her anthology with the silly name made a very bad miss in England.

She has no right to imply of course that I desired or sought a British-made reputation. You know that it simply came to me after I had nearly given up any reputation at all. That you may have a chance to tell 'em some day.

Jessie B. has a right to think what she pleases of Book I. I know pretty well what she thinks and why she thinks it.

You mustnt judge of how things are going with me by the limited number of papers you see. Already I have had in America more notice than any American poet in many years. I mean public notice. Privately I have been overwhelmed with the friendship of Howells, George Palmer, Mrs Marks, Alice Brown, Basil King, E. A. Robinson, Mrs T. B. Aldrich and any number of others you might or might not know. I tell you this to set your mind at rest. I don't like to see you so troubled about me when I am the envied of all my fellow craftsmen.

One of my best friends is young Louis Untermeyer. [Robert Havens] S[c]hauffler didnt pan out very well. He showed jealousy of my British made reputation. I suspect you didn't tell me all he said in his letter to you. I found him a treacherous second-rate mind.

So rest easy. Take life easy as the leaves grow on the tree. When you see your chance do what you can for me. There are several false impressions at large that I should like to see nailed.

Since you are not going to college next year perhaps you will feel that you can afford a visit to us in the summer. We hope to be settled on a farm of our own before long. We have found what we want in Franconia.

The summer-camp scheme will have to wait a while.

Be good. R. F.

118 · To Harold G. Rugg

Dear Mr Rugg   16 May 1915 [Bethlehem]

A complimentary (very complimentary) copy of The Third Rail* has just arrived with your name in a corner of the wrapper to remind me that when I ran away to Boston two weeks ago I left a friendly letter of yours unanswered. I fully meant to do something about it before I got home but you may

* *The Third Rail,* a Dartmouth undergraduate periodical.

imagine how it was: what with lecturing and reading and seeing and being seen (to put it thus shamelessly) in all the two
weeks I found not a quiet moment that I could call my own.

But that is past now and I am myself again or shall be in a
few days. And before long I hope to be settled on a farm of my
own in Franconia, where I shall want you to visit me for a
good talk when you will. Perhaps you will lead me to some flowers I havent met before and I can get some information out of
you without effort and without price. The farm is already fixed
upon. But there is a difficulty about moneys. The owner is going up on what he first asked when he thought I was a farmer
and before he saw me depicted in the papers as a poet.

Will you thank Mr Griffith for his good article if you are
in the way of seeing him? Something he says in it puts it into
my head that I could give you an interesting talk over there on
"Technique and the Imagination." I should be glad of any
chance you can get me to earn a little by lecturing or reading.
I am booked for a lecture at Wellesley soon and at several other
places next winter. I have several ideas on the bare art of writing that I must promulgate in self-defense. Braithwaite has
been doing what he could with them in the last two Saturday
Transcripts. Sincerely yours Robert Frost

119 · To Amy Lowell

21 May 1915   [Bethlehem]
Hail first President of the
Poetry Society of New England! (*bis*)
If I liked your poetry before
You may imagine how much more
I shall like it after this.

Note rhyme and believe me

Seriously yours   Robert Frost

119-a · Ellery Sedgwick to Edward Garnett

Dear Mr. Garnett:— 26 May 1915   [Boston]
It is true, I was a bit apprehensive at first of a separate
paper on Frost, as I had asked an American reviewer to in-

clude his book prominently in a general survey of contemporary poetry shortly to be written for The Atlantic. In the sequel, however, I have seen that review and am not satisfied with it, although, on account of various complications, it may well appear in The Atlantic. Thus, it happens that I am more obliged to you than I thought for your own paper which I gladly accept. Thank you especially for making it so short. A half-length paper on the subject lends itself most conveniently to our use.

I feel a genuine obligation to print an appreciation of Frost. A few weeks before you wrote, he happened to come into my office. I found him quite delightful — as unspoiled as when he left his Vermont plough for his quite extraordinary adventures in poetical England. I took him home with me to dine and we had much talk about his theories of poetry which seem to me intelligent and genuinely distinctive. They concern themselves especially with his attempts to reproduce in his lines the very tones of the voice. The magnificent rotundities which have created our English tradition of poetry have, he thinks, served their great purpose. He does not, like the futurists, with whom he is little in sympathy, attack the parent stock of poetry, but holds with justice that the piping modern voices we have so long heard about us are simply thin echoes of sounds once great. In place of all this copying, he would substitute a new attempt to interpret human nature by the slight inflections of the voice which in our common speech mean so much. The word, *oh,* for instance, interprets a whole series of moods according to its inflection.

By an odd accident, your enthusiastic letter concerning Frost had just reached my desk and I was in the very act of opening it, when Frost, who had once again returned from his farm, came in to see me. I bade him sit down and then read judicious extracts from your note. His blue eyes opened very wide, and, of course, he is enormously keen to have me print your appreciation — which I shall be glad to do. . . .

[unsigned]

120 · To John T. Bartlett

Dear John: [c. 2 June 1915]   Franconia N. H.

We expect to be in this place from now on for a while. It will have to do.

I think the war may end in five years in favor of the Germans. In that case Canada will join us to save herself, and all the British will steal away over here to live. North America will become the larger island of the English-speakers of the world. Maybe you don't see it as I do. But the prophecy stands. I wish I had been able to do it in ink, so that it would be more permanently of record, but I am off here by the Gale river with nothing but water to dip into if I had a pen, and all I have is a pencil.

It was good to see you all. Take care of yourself or I shall transfer to the baby all the ambitions I have had for you.

Love to you all.   R.

I had best leave to Elinor to urge you to come up soon and for long. She feels sure she can prevail on Margaret.

120-a · ELINOR M. FROST TO MARGARET BARTLETT

My dear Margaret   [c. June 1915]   [Bethlehem]

I have been thinking every day since Rob got home that the farm business would be settled, and that I would write to you as soon as it was settled, to see if you couldn't come immediately for a visit. But the owner of the farm has given us a lot of trouble. . . . Every two or three days we have thought that it was all up, and that we would have to begin to hunt elsewhere, and it has kept us very nervous. Now, however, we are really on the point of moving. The man comes for the trunks tomorrow. The farm is only three miles from here, you know. The furniture hasn't come up from Plymouth yet, but it will probably come the last of the week, and the people who are moving out can leave enough beds for us to manage with until then. We are all eager to get there, and it has been very hard waiting.

Now can't you and John and the baby come for a long visit, a month at least. . . .

[. . .] I think we shall enjoy our new home very much. I wish the house was just a little larger, but its such a cheerful, cosy place that I am willing to endure some inconveniences. The view is very fine, and the village of Franconia is exceptionally attractive. All I ask is that the children will like the school there and will find a few nice children for companions.

They have been out of school for so long that it will be a bit difficult for them to fit in, I fear, and I tremble at the possibility of their disliking the whole place, and if they *should* — well, it would be still harder to sell the farm than it has been to buy it, I am afraid. [. . .] We all send much love.

Affectionately yours,   Elinor

121 · To Susan Hayes Ward

Dear Miss Ward   8 June 1915   Franconia

You must have got hold of a very old paper if it was published before I read at Tufts. I was there on May 5 — then and thereabouts. I thought of you, but with all I had on hand, getting to you at South Berwick was out of the question. There were forty eleven things prearranged for me and by the time I had got two-thirds through with them I was shucked out and had to come home.

Home is here in the mountains now and probably will be for some time. We have drawn off to think over what we have done. I shall probably get south for lectures a few times in the winter and sometime soon when I am down I mean to see you. Elinor and I would both like to make a special trip to see you, but we can't afford it. I wish you would visit us here as you did years ago.   Yours always   Robert Frost

122 · To Edward Garnett

Dear Mr Garnett: 12 June 1915   Franconia

I have tried two or three times to answer your letter but everything I started to say ran off into the unpatriotic. You see I was still fighting American editors — I hadnt heard that peace had been declared and I had quite believed Sedgwick when he told me he didn't see how he could use your article because he had already handed me over for review to some single-bed she professor with a known preference for the beautiful in poetry. I knew I should never have such another piece of good luck as your help at this moment and I was discouraged. Sedgwick was teasing me: he meant all the time to publish the article; and I should have known as much, but it has been a long fight with editors, my rage has gathered considerable headway and it's hard to leave off believing the worst of them.

Sedgwick has just written me a beautiful letter and sent me fifty-five beautiful dollars for poetry. He says he will be good to me. He says you give me "great praise, perhaps too great," but never mind, he will risk it on me as being too old to be spoiled by flattery. I have to thank you for these signs of grace in Mr Ellery Sedgwick.*

What you say for me is bound to have a tremendous effect. I can see the impression you made by the way you came to judgement last winter on the novelists. We are all prepared to envy anyone you think well of.

Most of the reviewers have made hard work of me over here. That is partly because they use up their space groping for the reason of my success in England. (I was rather successful though not with the editor of The English Review — as you observe.) What you are good enough to call my method they haven't noticed. I am not supposed to have a method. I am a naive person. They get some fun out of calling me a realist, and a realist I may be if by that they mean one who before all else wants the story to sound as if it were told the way it is because it happened that way. Of course the story must release an idea, but that is a matter of touch and emphasis, the almost incredible freedom of the soul enslaved to the hard facts of experience. I hate the story that takes its rise idea-end foremost, as it were in a formula such as It's little we know what the poor think and feel — if they think and feel at all. I could name you an English poet the editor of the English Review admires, all of whose stories are made on just that formula. The more or less fishy incidents and characters are gathered to the idea in some sort of logical arrangement, made up and patched up and clothed on.

This is not all apropos of myself. I'll tell you a poet with a method that is a method: [D. H.] Lawrence. I came across a poem of his in a new Imagiste Anthology just published here, and it was such a poem that I wanted to go right to the man that wrote it and say something.

* RF added a postscript in the margin to indicate his further indebtedness to Garnett: "You seem to have made a friend for me in W. D. Howells. There is the best American, if you want to know the truth. RF." (See editor's note to letter 211 for a summary of RF's brief but very cordial relations with Howells.)

You must know that I am grateful to you — and to Thomas — but I was that to Thomas before.

But it's hard in these times not to think nationally and owe my gratitude to England instead of to any man or men of England. We sailed from Liverpool on February 13 but we left our hearts on the other side at least for the duration of the war. We have tried to wish the States into the war. But we cant talk to our neighbors. They are too indifferent to please us. Here on the edge of it all the fight shades off into a sort of political argument no more rancorous than we are used to at election times. The Yankee will go his joking way till something hits him harder than the loss of the lives on the Lusitania. That's not to say that a very large majority of us are not on your side. I think I can explain our state of mind. We are just near enough to the Civil War to remember that we fought it and just far enough from it to have cooled off and forgotten our reasons for fighting it. We have come to doubt if we ever had any reasons. We doubt if any nation ever had any reasons for any war. So passionate reasons always evaporate. But — there is this: in passion they can be renewed. Give us time to warm up. There is no hurry. The war won't be over for some years yet.   Sincerely yours   Robert Frost

123 · To Edwin Arlington Robinson

Dear Robinson: 13 June 1915   Franconia

Don't think I have been all this time trying to decide what your play [The Porcupine] is if it isnt a comedy. I have read it twice over but in no perplexity. It is good writing, or better than that, good speaking caught alive — every sentence of it. The speaking tones are all there on the printed page, nothing is left for the actor but to recognize and give them. And the action is in the speech where it should be, and not along beside it in antics for the body to perform. I wonder if you agree with me that the best sentences are those that convey their own tone — that haven't to be described in italics. "With feline demureness" for instance is well imagined as it is, but do you suppose it wouldnt have been possible to make the sentence to follow indicate in itself the vocal posture you had in mind. I don't say. I see a danger, of course, not unlike the danger of trying to make the dialogue describe the dress and personal appearance and give the past history of the characters. This in no spirit of fault-finding. I merely propose a question that interests me a good deal of late.

I have had to tell a number of people in my day what I thought of their writing. You are one of the few I have wanted to tell — one of the very few. Now I have my chance to tell you. I have had some sort of real satisfaction in everything of yours I have read. I hope I make that sweeping enough.

I owe Braithwaite a great deal for our meeting that day.

Always yours   Robert Frost

124 · To SIDNEY COX

Dear Cox: 24 June 1915   Franconia

Thanks for your article. It's the right stuff. I wonder how far you would dare to go in describing your direter method in teaching English. . . .

I'm blessed if I dont believe sometimes that the whole subject of English was better neglected and left outside the curriculum. School is for boning and not for luxuriating. We dont want much school even when we are young, that is to say, we want a great deal more of life than of school. And there is no use in this attempt to make school an image of life. It should be thought of as a thing that belongs to the alphabet and notation. It came into life with these. Life must be kept up at a great rate in order to absorb any considerable amount of either one or the other. Both are nonsense unless they mix well with experience. They are the past and the future and the distant, and the problem is to bring them to bear a little on the present and the near, to make them make some difference even the slightest. Too much time spent on them is either an injury to the infant or a waste of time on the infant that refuses to be injured. Literature — I dont know where literature comes in, if it comes in at all. It is ever so much more of life anyway than of school. It is almost too emotional for school handling, almost too insubordinate and unconventional. . . .

Yours ever   Robert Frost

Have you any way of finding out for me the correct spelling of the name of some professor of English in the University of Penn. who seems to sign himself Cornelius Weygant. Print it out for me.

125 · To Walter Prichard Eaton

This letter is representative of the many acquaintances, friendships, and correspondences, which grew out of meetings between the Frosts and the "summer people" who came from distant regions to spend their vacations in the White Mountains. Walter Prichard Eaton — dramatic critic for New York newspapers, essayist of the New England countryside, and later an associate professor in the Yale School of Drama — spent summers near RF in Franconia. Their mutual friend here mentioned, was probably Sidney Snow, a Unitarian minister from Chicago who spent his summers at Sugar Hill. Other summer residents whose names appear significantly in subsequent letters include Rev. and Mrs. J. Warner Fobes, Miss Mary Goodwillie, Raymond Holden, Ernest Poole, and Judge Robert von Moschzisker.

My dear Mr Eaton   15 July 1915   Franconia

Will you mind if I write to thank you for a thing I have just had from Snow? I mean your Barn Doors and Byways. You make it perfectly clear to me why you are provoked with yourself for having let the editors put you off your poetry. I never read such books without wondering how they came to be in prose. And before this I have expostulated with their authors for doing them in prose. My British friend Edward Thomas whose work yours reminds me of in some ways has had to listen to me. Sometimes I get him to write a poem. I have had one in the post from him lately.

I think poetry itself is to blame. It seems to want to exclude too much. And if left to its own tendencies, I believe in time it would exclude everything but love and the moon. That's why it's none the worse for a little rough handling once in a while. Do it a violence, I say, if you have to to make it aware of what's going on around it.

Far be it from me though to regret that all the poetry isn't in verse. I'm sure Im glad of all the unversified poetry of Walden — and not merely nature-descriptive, but narrative as in the chapter on the play with the loon on the lake, and character-descriptive as in the beautiful passage about the French-Canadian woodchopper. That last alone with some things in Turgenieff must have had a good deal to do with the making of me.

Yours is a lovely book — full of things I wish I had thought of first — so we are quits there. It is a poem just to mention driving into a strange barn to bide the passing of a thunder storm.

You were somewhere near my old haunts when you were at your grandfather's at Reading. I have been right through Reading in my walks from Lawrence to Boston and I believe I considered that at Reading I had done half my distance.

And somewhere near my present haunts you say you are going to be this summer. I dont just make out where you see Moosilauke from. It cant be far from here; for we see it looking southward down or rather up the valley of the Ham Branch. You wont fail to make us some sign, will you? I have looked forward to meeting you.   Sincerely yours   Robert Frost

126 · To John W. Haines

Dear Haines,   17 July 1915   Franconia

There's a heartache that attends remembering hopelessly distant places and it is as definite as if it were due to strains put upon actual tentacles by which the heart makes fast to all the places it ever staid overnight in. The thought of Gloucester with me not there is a melancholy. That's why it is so natural to write of haunts we aren't haunting. Next thing you know I shall be reversing my machinery and writing of England from America. What would my friends all say to that? Shall I be allowed to write of anything but New England the rest of my life? And May Hill without me for evermore is as sad as the world should be without me the day after I die. You could be there, but I, though I am as free to think May Hill as you, I cannot come near it.

Thomas did me a nice little picture of you out with your flower canister just as on the day when I first met you the better part of the way up from the Greenway to Little Iddens. These things are a pleasant pain. . . .

Some day the war will end one way or the other (decisively I trust) and then you will come to see us. I wonder what you will say to our cheerful self-sufficiency as a nation. You'd think

> Europe might sink and the wave of her sinking sweep
> And spend itself on our shores and we should not weep;
> Our cities would not even turn in their sleep.*

We don't really care what happens over there. It doesn't touch us nearly enough. At least we can't see that it does. We stand

* These three lines are all that survive from a much longer poem by RF.

lost in sentimental contemplation. Not one nation in the whole fight is out for anything but its own interest. We tell ourselves that the one thing we would not go to war for is self-interest. The fact of course is that that is the only thing we would go to war for. We are only able to hold the high opinions of ourselves we do because our interests are not touched. You can't make it our war any way you look at it. *We* can't by trying. If we look uncommonly foolish at the present moment, it is from trying overhard to enter into the spirit of a row we weren't prepared for and don't understand. I believe the Germans have written of *us* as having done our part to drive them to desperate measures by the step we took outward into world politics when we went to the East Indies. But we are blissfully unconscious of having done anything to make an enemy by a simple act of business expediency. We may have heard of the Germans' view, but we suspect them of being too philosophical and of looking for the bottom of things that haven't got a bottom or a bottom worth looking for.

I tell you these things for the fun of it. Be careful to distinguish between what I say as speaking for the country and as speaking for myself. You know the views I hold. I like the Germans, but they must excuse me if I want to see them exterminated. Abercrombie's poem won't do — the small one you sent me I mean. Too Bryanesque.   Love to you all.

Always yours   R. F.

127 · To Edward Thomas

Dear Edward: 31 July 1915   Franconia

I am within a hair of being precisely as sorry and as glad as you are.

You are doing it for the self-same reason I shall hope to do it for if my time ever comes and I am brave enough, namely, because there seems nothing else for a man to do.

You have let me follow your thought in almost every twist and turn toward this conclusion. I know pretty well how far down you have gone and how far off sideways. And I think the better of you for it all. Only the very bravest could come to the sacrifice in this way. Davies is only human but he is a robber who cant forget stealing while his neighbor has anything left to steal.

I have never seen anything more exquisite than the pain

you have made of it. You are a terror and I admire you. For what has a man locomotion if it isnt to take him into things he is between barely and not quite standing.

I should have liked you anyway — no friend ever has to strive for my approval — but you may be sure I am not going to like you less for this.

All belief is one. And this proves you are a believer.

I cant think what you would ask my forgiveness for unless it were saying my poetry is better than it is. You are forgiven as I hope to be forgiven for the same fault. I have had to over sate myself in the fight to get up. Some day I hope I can afford to lean back and deprecate as excessive the somewhat general praise I may have won for what I may have done.

Your last poem Aspens seems the loveliest of all. You must have a volume of poetry ready for when you come marching home.

I wonder if they are going to let you write to me as often as ever.   Affectionately   R. F.

128 · To Harold Monro

Dear Monro: 7 August 1915   Franconia

The trouble has been altogether with the she who calls herself David Nutt. She has steadily refused me permission to let you have the poems for the chapbook. You may know what she is to everybody. She is trying to be particularly nasty to me as being of a nation not represented on the firing line in this war. So she puts it and it sounds patriotic. But I havent failed to discover that her real grievance against me is that I wont write war letters to the papers to get my name before the public and help her sell books.

She carries her not quite disinterested disapprobation so far that she refuses to give me an accounting. I am told that my contract with her is very bad: still it does seem to call for an annual accounting and for royalties of 12% on both my books. This is the only hope I see, namely that she may have let me out of her clutches by violating the contract. Of course I dont know, but I am going to enquire. Abercrombie very generously offers to have it out with her for me.

I had set my heart on the chapbook. And I never thought of such a thing as her standing in the way. I was within an ace

185

of letting you go ahead with it without asking her permission, on the assumption that it was not strictly a book and so not subject to the terms of the contract. A chapbook seems more like a magazine than a book. Luckily I decided to be on the safe side — or I might have got you into trouble.

I wonder what would happen if *you* asked her for the poems. She might listen to you. I suppose she would say she was afraid of losing the American copyright. You could promise to take care of that: I will take care of it for you.

I am glad poetry goes on in spite of the war — or is it because of the war? I shouldn't like war if it were incompatible with poetry as some seem to think it is incompatible with Christianity.

Yes what you people began for me has gone merrily on over here. But I am less grateful to you than homesick for you. I often long to look in on you in your Holborn slum. Will there be beds for me if I turn up there with a few more children some day?   Yours ever   Robert Frost

129 · To Amy Lowell

My dear Miss Lowell: 13 August 1915   Franconia

There is an ominous note in your letter that seems to tell me you are getting ready to throw me over as a poet of the elect ostensibly on the ground that I am become a Best-seller when really it will be because I haven't convinced you that I like your book. What's the use of my trying to say anything now when I am in a corner? You will be sure to ascribe my prettiest compliments to fear. But I leave it to [Joseph Warren] Beach if I didn't tell him I liked the book when I was a free agent. You know my little weakness for dramatic tones. I go so far as to say that there is no poetry of any kind that is not made of dramatic tones. Your poetry always speaks. I wish sometimes you would leave to Browning some of the broader intonations he preempted. The accent-on-the-you sort of thing. But that's a small matter (or not so large as it might be): the great thing is that you and some of the rest of us have landed with both feet on all the little chipping poetry of awhile ago. We have busted 'em up as with cavalry. We have, we have we have. Yes I like your book and all I lay up against you is that you will not allow me a sense of humor. Occurs to me a simple way to make you: I could make up my mind to stand outside your Poetry Society until you did.

Sincerely yours,   Robert Frost

130 · To WILLIAM STANLEY BRAITHWAITE

Dear Braithwaite: 14 August 1915   Franconia

Would you come up about now? — and fetch along the book you gave me? I cant say that we are quite settled yet, but we are not likely to be this year and what's that to keep us from seeing our friends if they are such as will make allowances for us without being asked to? Don't you think we could kill a week walking and talking? I am bursting with sounds I want to utter about the sound of poetry. Be careful how you refuse me. If you dont come I shall be sure it is because you are too nice to have anything to do with the author of a Best-seller (non-fiction) which is what I am told I have become. Isn't it — well hard to know how to take?

Sincerely yours   Robert Frost

131 · To WILLIAM STANLEY BRAITHWAITE

IN THIS LETTER RF refers to Ezra Pound's attack, recently published in the Boston *Evening Transcript,* on Braithwaite. In part it read as follows:

"I notice in *Current Opinion* for June a quotation from your paper to the effect that my friend Robert Frost has done what no other American poet has done in this generation 'and that is, un-heralded, unintroduced, untrumpeted, he won the acceptance of an English publisher on his own terms' etc. Now seriously, what about me? . . . No, sir, Frost was a bloated capitalist when he struck this island, in comparison to yours truly, and you can put that in your editorial pipe though I don't give a damn whether you print the fact. You might note *en passant* that I've done as much to boom Frost as the next man. He came to my room before his first book *A Boy's Will* was published. I reviewed that book in two places and drew it [to] other reviewers' attention by personal letters. I hammered his stuff into *Poetry* . . ."

Dear Braithwaite: 24 August 1915   Franconia

Go right ahead with your " 'anthology' " and come up here in October when you are free. Nothing can beat October in these mountains. You wait till you see. But you must stay for more than a couple of days.

Thanks for all the good words of your letter. You contrive to be inspiring — you and Robinson.

I shall be honored if you will use the poems in your book, honored enough if you will use two, honored beyond dreams if you will use three.*

No I haven't seen Pound's letter. What new terms of abuse has he found for your review? Why would you review him? He needs letting alone. The English have ceased to give him space in their papers.

Any time, then, in September or October. Take your choice. We'll have good talks.

Sincerely yours   Robert Frost

132 · To Alfred Harcourt

Dear Harcourt: 30 August 1915   [Franconia]

[. . .] I mustn't go into harrowing details, but really I have reached a pass where I must earn a little or perish. I trust you see no reasons legal moral or ethical why I should not accept that part in the success of my books that you wanted me to have. Let me speak frankly: at this moment when I have so much to be glad of in the general approval of my book, I am actually nearer worrying about money than I have had to be for a number of years.

It will be a help to see you for a good talk.

Yours ever   Robert Frost

132-a · Alfred Harcourt to Robert Frost

Dear Frost: [c. 5 September 1915]   [New York]

Here's a check for $200. We are going to take our chances with Mrs. Nutt, and pay you what would amount to a royalty of 10% on our sales of *North of Boston* and *A Boy's Will* in our own reprint. We expect to continue the honorarium unless we should be stopped. . . . We shall give you a report of sales on the 25th of each October and April.

* Braithwaite included "Birches" and "The Road Not Taken" in his *Anthology of Magazine Verse for 1915;* they had previously appeared in *The Atlantic Monthly* for August, 1915.

Don't worry. You're going to be able to publish poetry and get your just dues. We'll go into all that when you come down. Of your troubles that I've heard, hay-fever is the worst.

Ever yours,   Alfred Harcourt

133 · To Louis Untermeyer

Dear Louis   9 Sept. 1915   Franconia

Let me call you that in the hope of softening a little the light with which you burn too bright for these old eyes. You mustn't be so intellectual with me. I shan't be at ease till we are on emotional terms where there is no more controversy neither is there any danger of crediting one or the other with more or less than we mean. Then we shall know when we are fooling because we shall be always fooling like a pair gay with love. We shan't mean anything too profoundly much except perhaps that we are friends and that nothing else matters between friends. That is the only sincerity: all else is an approximation. It sounds like the loss of something, and it is — of competition, of the sharpening of wits and of the criticisms that makes us look to ourselves. But friendship is like that: it may not be as strengthening as enmity, and then again it may. At any rate it is different. The beauty of enmity is in insecurity; the beauty of friendship is in security.

Even here I am only fooling my way along as I was in the poems in The Atlantic (particularly in The Road Not Taken) as I was in what I said about Spoon River. I trust my meaning is not too hidden in any of these places. I can't help my way of coming at things.

. . . [Edgar Lee] Masters . . . was too romantic for my taste, and by romantic I'm afraid I mean among other things false-realistic. Such are my limitations. But don't scold me. It is a small matter. It's but a qualification moreover of a real liking for the book. I like it better for what it is than for what a lot of people take it for. . . .

And you are naught with all that nonsense about being in W. S. B.'s [Braithwaite's] anthology so that you can review it in The Post. Your fault is that you are too active-minded. You may be as nimble as you please when you move; but most of the time you must plan to lie still. Otherwise you will think of something that is nothing. Only those thoughts are worth anything that we have in despite of our indolence. You mustn't larrup your faculties under penalty of being unreal. You mustn't intend to have an idea strike you any more than to have an automobile. Then if the auto strikes you —

And as for your parodies — why, you are a child if you think I mind them. They are not my kind of fooling; but they are a constituted kind and of course much better than mine. The best of your parody of me was that it left me in no doubt as to where I was hit. I'll bet not half a dozen people can tell who was hit and where he was hit by my Road Not Taken.

. . . I may have to take a run in [to New York] on business with the Holts on or about the twenty fifth. I should wish to avoid the many, but if it came right you might give me a glimpse of your Clement Wood and your James Oppenheim. . . .

With the devout Tennysonian wish that that which I have written here may He within Himself make pure (I refuse to look back at it) I am, my dear Poet,

Sinceriously yours   Robert Frost

134 · To Edwin Arlington Robinson

Dear Robinson: 15 September 1915   Franconia

Both your speculations interest me, particularly the first one as to whether or not I care what you think of me. It may not pain you to hear that as long ago as May Sinclair's paper in The Atlantic I marked you down as one of the few people I intended some day to know. Miss Sinclair didn't succeed in interesting me in Moody or Torrence. What has kept me from seeking your friendship all these years is the fear you might be troubled to find anything to like in my work. I knew I liked yours: that much was right. But I should never actually seek a fellow author's friendship unless everything was right, unless he saw something in me as I saw something in him and there was little or nothing to cover up and lie about in our opinions of each other.

Your second speculation was as to whether or not I was satisfied with myself. I am in a way. I'm rather pleased to have attained to a position where I dont have to admire my work as much as I had to when no one else admired it. It's a relief not to have [to] say more for it than I mean any more.

I am afraid I can't be in Boston in time to catch you unless you are staying over into October. But I am to be in New York on the quiet soon (seeing Harcourt of Holts about my royalties), and if I could look you up there. You say you go to New York about the first of the month. Will you tell me if that is definitely decided and where I will find you by yourself in New York, if it is?   Yours ever   Robert Frost.

135 · To WALTER PRICHARD EATON

My dear Eaton: 18 September 1915   Franconia
      . . . It was nice of Howells to do what you say [article on RF in *Harper's* for September 1915] wasnt it? Long long ago my mother was a little schoolma'am in Columbus Ohio when he was there and I have heard her speak of meeting him once or twice in society when Columbus society was gay in the sixties. He has always stood for something to me away off and high up. So that I felt that I had rounded some sort of a circle when he did what you say.
      You don't mention my having had a whole article to myself in The Atlantic as among my signal honors: from which I infer that you don't like the article. I wonder why. Others seem to ignore it on purpose. I wonder what's the matter.
      I was grateful to both Howells and Garnett for making so little difficulty of my blank verse. I have nothing in common with the free-verse people. There is no more distressing mistake than to assume that I have. (Some of the western reviewers have been assuming it) I am really not so very novel — take it from me. I am only interesting to myself for having ventured to try to make poetry out of tones that if you can judge from the practice of other poets are not usually regarded as poetical. You can get enough of those sentence tones that suggest grandeur and sweetness everywhere in poetry. What bothers people in my blank verse is that I have tried to see what I could do with boasting tones and quizzical tones and shrugging tones (for there are such) and forty eleven other tones. All I care a cent for is to catch sentence tones that haven't been brought to book. I dont say to make them, mind you, but to catch them. No one makes them or adds to them. They are always there — living in the cave of the mouth. They are real cave things: they were before words were. And they are as definitely things as any image of sight. The most creative imag-

ination is only their summoner. But summoning them is not all. They are only lovely when thrown and drawn and displayed across spaces of the footed line. Everyone knows that except a free-verster. It is the conventional thing. It may not be in the text-books but everyone knows it though he may have lost sight of it in an age of mere diction and word-hunting. Now Tennyson ——

I bore you stiff. . . .   Always yours   Robert Frost

136 · To Lascelles Abercrombie

Dear Abercrombie   21 September 1915   Franconia

I must hurry and write you a letter before anything goes click in your mind against me and shuts me out forever.

If thoughts were letters I should have been all right: you would have had a plenty of me since we drank plum wine together out of a lime juice bottle at Leddington, and if they were visits — but they are not visits, so what's the use of iffing. All I was going to say was that if they were visits how often I should have looked in on you to see how you were bearing up under all the trouble you were having.

Catherine would take a long time recovering from such a terrible thing. Wonderful to escape at all. Your news was only partly news to us. Still we did not know the worst, though we had been told there was something seriously the matter. Everyone seems to leave it to someone else to tell us what is going on over there, so that between one friend and another we learn next to nothing.

You will be sorry to hear that Elinor is altogether out of health and we are in for our share of trouble too. It is the old story: what she has been through so many times [pregnancy]. But we are not as young as we once were. I'm sure I don't know how it will be with her. The doctor frightens me about her heart. But this is something you mustnt mention in your letters.

It comes particularly hard on us just at this moment when our fortunes begin to look up a little — when people seem to want to put money in our way and make of us, if we will go ahead and let them. Not that we haven't enjoyed life before. I dont mean anything so disloyal to the past or so unlucky to say as that. We have taken our pleasure as we went. But there have been one or two things we have had to wait for till we found help in England and one of them has been success (limited). It is something I suppose we could have done without. Nevertheless — Anyway I confess I like it so well myself that I should have been sorry if the rest of the family had had to go entirely without it.

When I say people want to give us money I dont mean Mrs Nutt and her office boy alone. Nononono! I dont mean them two at all. I have never had one penny or one word of accounting from Mrs Nutt and I should like nothing better than just to cry Havoc and let you work on her. I wish you could settle her for me by yourself the way you settled the gamekeeper. But I suppose there ought to be some sort of concert. I am seeing my American publisher's lawyer in New York this week to find out what can be done to save me from the fool's contract I signed. What do you say if when we are ready on this side and I say the word, you strike from that? I don't know what you think of doing but anything you please will suit me.

I shall be only too happy to be brothers with you in your next enterprise if you will have me. I cling more than I can tell you to your friendship in poetry. Yours was the first praise over there and there will never be any other just like it. We must try to manage. But if I cant join you I cant. I have told you, I think, that Mrs. Nutt forbade me to let Monro have anything for a chapbook. She even holds that I have no right to sell poetry to magazines. She will oppose us. You mustn't have too much trouble on my account. And then there's the question of time. How much time have we? Tell me more. I will be prompter in answering again.

Now I should like to go out into the yard and shake hands with your big cold pump till his iron tank was as full of water as my heart is of Ryton memories.

Our best to you all.   Affectionately   Robert Frost

I forgot to mention the war in this letter. And I ought to mention it, if only to remark that I think it has made some sort of new man and a poet out of Edward Thomas.   R. F.

————

Sept. 30, 1915

I decided not to go to post with this till I knew more definitely what my predicament was with Mrs Nutt. I now know all the law in the matter. I am bound by the contract unless she refuses to render an account on my two books within the sixty days I have given her. The contract calls for two more books which if I have to give them I intend to write in prose. I shall make very short work of them, padding them with quotation. I have long contemplated the possibility of having to do this dirty trick and my lawyer agrees that it may be necessary. My minister agrees that it may be justifiable. There seems to be nothing you can do at present except countenance my practices. I should welcome any suggestion from you as to what I should write the two books on. I shall write them on the same subject from different points of view. For my own protection I intend to sink a cryptogram in the text that will say to the public when I furnish the key in the newspapers: Mrs. or Madam mistook her Man. Dont think too badly of me.   R. F.

137 · To Harold Monro

Dear Monro: 9 October 1915   Franconia

So help me, it is exactly as I tell you and not at all as you suspect. I was pleased when you asked me for stuff for a chapbook and I went right to work on Madam Nutt to get her permission to give it. I have been at her off and on ever since about this time last year. It has all been in the matter of just one thing. You must not doubt my friendship for a moment. So far as I am concerned I am not afraid to let you publish the poems. Suppose it were in violation of my contract with the Madam. It wouldn't be on me but on you she would descend for damages. I don't know very much about these things, but as I see it there is just the chance that she might have a case against you. All would depend of course on whether a chapbook could be made to appear a book in a court of law. I don't believe it is a book. You don't believe it is? The question is how much would you be willing to risk on your opinion. The risk would be all yours. You can have the poems if you want them. Only I want you to understand the situation. I don't want to get you into trouble. I ought to warn you that Madam Nutt will make trouble if she can. I haven't improved her disposition by a year's nagging and I don't suppose the success of my books in pirated editions on this side has improved it any either.

I have this suggestion to make: perhaps you will prefer

to wait for the chapbook till we see what can be done to extricate me from the lady's clutches. We are considering there is a little hope for me in the fact that I am quite capable of fulfilling the rest of the contract in books of very bad prose. It wouldn't take much more to make me write her two (that's all are called for I think) books on Boston Baked Beans between now and Christmas. I am about out of love with her. Too bad to miss a chance to quote Arnold, "For I am passing weary of her love." When I heard that bombs had been blowing holes in Bloomsbury it was with half a hope that perhaps a small one had hit her in the office safe at No 6 Bloomsbury St and blown my contract into little bits of white paper the size of a moth. You see how Christian I was. I wished her no harm personally. And you see the reward of my Christianity. I wished modestly and got nothing. Instead of coming near her the Germans seem to have come within an ace of you. You must be careful to keep from under them.

I have written you this nice long letter with no other object than to keep on the good side of you so that you won't give up the idea of the chapbook but will bear it in mind till my affairs are straightened out and I am free to do what I please with what I write. Therefore don't mistake me.

Yours ever   Robert Frost

138 · To John T. Bartlett

Dear John: circa 21 October 1915   Franconia

Be good to him! And that doesn't mean simply not to write poetry for a living. For his sake you are bound to shun *every* folly, ginseng, Belgian hares, squabs, wonderberries, mushrooms, Orpingtons, alfalfa, Angora goats, Mexican rubber stock for the small investor and the Honduras Lottery. Those are the things as well as poetry you have to have in mind when you pray saying "Lead us not into temptation but deliver us from evil." For now you are a father twice over and must give up childish ways in favor of your children. I'd like to be your wife for about five minutes some day till I could knock the whole duty of the responsible head of a family into your head. I'd have no more of this romancing in agriculture. I speak partly from concern for your own future. Suppose your sons grow up to be sensible men. How will you feel when you begin to realize that they were judging you. They will be earning fifty seventy-five a hundred dollars a week. About that time you will have got round to skunks and will be starting a skunk farm — chuck full of your subject, all the lore of deodorizing skunk skins so as not to make the hair come out and of picking up a skunk by the tail without consequences — full of figures too such as these: Assuming that a skunk will produce twenty five polekittens in an off year it ought to do say one fourth as well as a rabbit and we all know what a rabbit will do — but assuming to be on the safe side that it will produce no more than twenty-five and that except for a considerable loss in overalls which you have had to bury without benefit of clergy, the twenty-five have cost you nothing to rear and the market price of a pelt — why it ought to be two dollars if its a scent oughtn't it and so on. How will you feel, I say, if when you talk like that you catch your two solid and citizenly sons winking at each other on the sly? You will feel like as if it was a tragedy if I may speak like another Reynolds. You will feel as if you had vainly wasted your life in vain. The moral is that the least little thing starts me moralizing these days and this is not a little thing.

Bless the whole lot of you.

The score now stands 4 to 2 in favor of us. But the game is young yet, or at least you are.   Affectionately   R.

139 · To Katharine Lee Bates

BEST KNOWN for her poem, "America the Beautiful," Katharine Lee Bates taught English literature at Wellesley College from 1885 to 1925, and frequently brought RF to Wellesley to give talks and readings. She was also active in the New England Poetry Society, and served more than once with RF at Mt. Holyoke College in judging poetry contests held for undergraduate writers of verse (see letter 190).

My dear Miss Bates: 21 October 1915   Franconia

I base my faith on Rossetti that what two friends ask for for me I must sooner or later get. If you *will* remember me for a lecture and reading at Wellesley when it can be thought of as being my turn. It's the colleges I look to for the chance to say certain things on the sound of poetry that are going to trouble me as long as they remain unsaid. Not everybody would be interested in my ideas. I'm not sure that many would be out-side the circles where books are made and studied. They have value I should say chiefly in education and criticism. Call them theories, if you will be careful to distinguish them from specu-lative theories. These are descriptive. I make them sound for-midable here because I am under restraint not to go into them, but really I can be quite off-hand with them fetching them edgewise between poems as I read. All this is for when my turn comes — if it ever does come.

Meanwhile I should be most happy to earn fifty dollars in the way you suggest. I could leave the time to you to fix. Either Thursday you name would suit me.

I am afraid I have been betrayed by the friendliness of your letter into saying a good deal for myself. Will you forgive me? Thank you for your good words.

Sincerely yours   Robert Frost

140 · To Lascelles Abercrombie

Dear Lascelles: 1 December 1915   Franconia

Just a word to you and Catherine to let you know that we are out of those woods — though perhaps not yet far enough to feel safe in crowing. We are still six in the family, no more and, thank God, no less.

And we hope you are all well and confident.

Yours ever   Rob Frost

141 · To John T. Bartlett

Dear Johnah: 2 December 1915   Franconia

We are suddenly out of our misery and nothing to show for it. It has been so much worse than we remembered it from times past that we had begun to suspect that something must be wrong. It turns out that nothing has been right for three months. Elinor has been unspeakably sick. But I think we are safely out of the woods now. I will write in a better frame of mind when I write again.   Affectionately   R.

142 · To Harold G. Rugg

Dear Mr. Rugg: 2 December 1915   Franconia

Mrs. Frost has been very ill for some days and is still in a serious condition. You will forgive my having put off writing to you.

January 22 will suit me.

I should like not to get very far from the subject of sound in my talk. How would "Imagination and the Voice" do? — or "New Sounds in Poetry"? I could give you "New Hampshire Gold" which would be a homily on the exceptional in life and poetry. My own preference would be for "New Sounds in Poetry." Something would depend of course on the character of the audience you have in mind for me. I gave this or virtually this, five times last week. It was most successful with the new poetry society in the Harvard Graduate School and with a group of Cambridge people, professors and their wives.

I should like seventy-five dollars for my pains. . . .

Sincerely yours   Robert Frost

143 · To Louis Untermeyer

Dear Louis: [1 January 1916]   [Franconia]

[. . .] Mind you I haven't read Fannie [Stearns Davis] and I haven't read Braithwaite's g. d. book — I got one of the children to read it for me and tell me about it. All that saved the fat obstacle from the worst fate that overtakes paper was your name and mine on the flyleaf.

No, I didn't read the book. I'll tell you what I did do, though. I took the Midnight Horror out of Littleton not long ago, and on the train with me I had about as many good-looking boys and girls as there are great poets in the book. They were of the Lisbon High School which had just beaten at basket-ball for a second time the Littleton High School. And they were yelling glad. And this is what they kept saying all together and out loud: it came somewhere near expressing my feelings, though at the same time it shocked me: since as you know I am not a swearing man: I couldn't help liking the liberty taken in the rhyme: all the old rhyme pairs are so worn out that I'm ready to permit anything for the sake of a fresh combination: this was a new one to me — it may not be to you: well here goes: I mustn't put you off any longer: this is what the good looking children said:

> Lisbon *once* — Lisbon *twice!*
> *Holy jumping Jesus Christ!*

Maybe you don't like me to talk this way. I can see that I am going to make enemies if I keep on. Still that won't be anything new or strange. I had nothing but enemies three years ago this Christmas.

Why go into details? Granted that there are a few good poems in the book — I read yours and liked it because it *says* something, first felt and then unfolded in thought as the poem wrote itself. That's what makes a poem. A poem is never a put-up job so to speak. It begins as a lump in the throat, a sense of wrong, a homesickness, a lovesickness. It is never a thought to begin with. It is at its best when it is a tantalizing vagueness. It finds its thought and succeeds, or doesn't find it and comes to nothing. It finds its thought or makes its thought. I suppose it finds it lying around with others not so much to its purpose in a more or less full mind. That's why it oftener comes to nothing in youth before experience has filled the mind with thoughts. It may be a big big emotion then and yet finds nothing it can embody in. It finds the thought and the thought finds the words. Let's say again: A poem particularly must not begin thought first.

Say! When I get started! What?

Thanks for your defense in The Call. You and I have got inside of each others breast works. I shall be glad when you can like anything I do. But don't feel obliged to like it (I know you won't — you are an honest man). I mean to hang on to you as a friend whatever you have to say of my poetry.

I shall come to see you if I stop more than three hours in New York. That dinner comes just wrong. I have engagements for a little money on the day before it and the day after — and, by rights, just on it.

I'm glad for your wife she has found a backer in Amy Lowell. I'm hoping to be more and more her backer when I see more of her work. There's an opening there she's making for herself — I don't mean with any person or persons — I mean in a realm.

You mustn't mind me. Some days you would think I knew it all, to see me on paper. In reality I am only a poor man on

199

ration. Its a hard winter and I'm hard up and sometimes I harden my heart against nearly everything.

You came into our Christmas to make us a good deal happier. . . .

If there were no God — but there is one, that's just the point — he's come back at the smell of blood on his altars — and he hasn't come back in pieces (two or more) like Biela's comet the last time it turned up — He is still One. [. . .]

R. F.

144 · To WILLIAM STANLEY BRAITHWAITE

Dear Braithwaite: 21 March 1916 Franconia

You shall have the poem on Shakespeare if I can write it — and nothing said of pay. You rather scare me by asking for anything I haven't written. My faculties scattered like a brood of young partri[d]ges the minute you spoke. I'm ashamed of myself for being like this. Don't lay it up too much against me. I may be able to come to [in] time. Other redoutable fellows will any way from Maine to Indiana; so that Shakespeare shan't lack for praise nor you for material to fill your space.

I heard good words of you at Mount Holyoke. These are piping times and surely you are one of the pipers.

Remember: if I possibly can!

Sincerely yours Robert Frost

145 · To HARRIET MONROE

My dear Miss Monroe: 22 March 1916 Franconia

Greedy, I must seem. I don't want to be that even for the sake of variety. It would take too long to tell you in self-defense how I figured it out that I ought to have two hundred for my "Snow." It was probably partly on the basis of what you paid me for something else aforetime. But I am always open to conviction. Have us talk the matter over, as the Germans would say to Wilson.

You aren't going to be in Philadelphia by any chance when you are in New York are you? Because if you are you could easily run across us there by a little contriving. I shall be with Cornelius Weygandt of the University of Penn. from the first to the third and possibly fourth of April. I should like very much to see you if a way could be found. Let's see if we can't manage it. I write principally to say this, and not to haggle over the price of poetry.   Sincerely yours   Robert Frost

146 · To Louis Untermeyer

Dear Old Louis   [4 May 1916]   [Franconia]

When I have borne in memory what has tamed Great Poets, hey? Am I to be blamed etc? No you ain't. Or as Browning (masc.) has it

> That was I that died last night
> When there shone no moon at all
> Nor to pierce the strained and tight
> Tent of heaven one planet small.
> Might was dead and so was Right.

Not to be any more obvious than I have to be to set at rest your brotherly fears for my future which I have no doubt you assume to be somehow or other wrapped up in me, I am going to tell you something I never but once let out of the bag before and that was just after I reached London and before I had begun to value myself for what I was worth. (Toop.) It is a very damaging secret and you may not thank me for taking you into it when I tell you that I have often wished I could be sure that the other sharer of it had perished in the war. It is this: The poet in me died nearly ten years ago. Fortunately he had run through several phases, four to be exact, all well-defined, before he went. The calf I was in the nineties I merely take to market. I am become my own salesman. Two of my phases you have seen so what shall I say . . . Take care that you don't get your mouth set to declare the other two (as I release them) a falling off of power, for that is what they can't be whatever else they may be, since they were almost inextricably mixed with the first two in the writing and only my sagacity has separated or sorted them in the afterthought for putting on the market. Did you ever hear of quite such a case of Scotch-Yankee calculation? You should have seen the look on the face of the Englishman I first confessed this to! I won't name him lest it should bring you two together. While he has never actually betrayed me, he has made himself an enemy of me and all my works. He regards me as a little heinous. As you

201

look back don't you see how a lot of things I have said begin to take meaning from this? Well.

But anyway you are freed from anxiety about my running all to philosophy. It makes no difference what I run to now. I needn't be the least bit tender of myself. Of course I'm glad it's all up with Masters, my hated rival. He wasn't foresighted enough, I'll bet, to provide against the evil day that is come to him. He failed to take warning from the example of Shelley who philosophized and died young. But me, the day I did The Trial by Existence (*Boy's Will*) says I to myself, this is the way of all flesh. I was not much over twenty, but I was wise for my years. I knew then that it was a race between me the poet and that in me that would be flirting with the entelechies or the coming on of that in me. I must get as much done as possible before thirty. I tell you, Louis, it's all over at thirty. People expect us to keep right on and it is as well to have something to show for our time on earth. Anyway that was the way I thought I might feel. And I took measures accordingly. And now my time is my own. I have myself all in a strong box where I can unfold as a personality at discretion. Someone asks with a teasing eye, "Have you done that Phi Beta Kappa poem yet?" "No, I don't know that I have, as you may say." "You seem not to be particularly uneasy about it." "Oh, that's because I know where it's coming from, don't you know." Great effect of strength and mastery!

Now you know more about me than anyone else knows except that Londoner we won't count because he may be dead of a lachrymous.

And don't think mention of the war is anything to go by. I could give you proof that twenty years ago in a small book I did on Boeme and the Technique of Sincerity I was saying "The heroic emotions, like all the rest of the emotions, never know when they ought to be felt after the first time. Either they will be felt too soon or too late from fear of being felt too soon.

Ever thine   R. F.

I must give you a sample from the fourth book, "Pitch-blende." As a matter of fact and to be perfectly honest with you there is a fifth unnamed as yet, the only one unnamed (the third has been long known as "Mountain Interval") and I think the most surprising of the lot (circa 1903). But none of that now. [. . .]

147 · To Amy Lowell

Dear Miss Lowell: 14 May 1916   Franconia

Your "without hesitation" is good supreme court stuff. I wish I could tell one poem from another with that assurance. The best I can do is to tell what some poems mean sometimes better than anybody seems to be able to tell what my recent poems in The Yale Review mean.* I consented to act as judge in two contests of poetry lately and I confess before I had done I couldnt tell an indifferent poem from a bad one, I had so worked myself into a state of overconsciousness. Very important in our business to know an indifferent poem from a bad one.

I am sorry but I cant really afford to make the trip to Boston for your meeting this week. Ask me in June or if not then, in January or February of 1917 when I expect to be down along on purpose for just such things for a while. I hate to seem to stand outside of anything — I am always grieved when asked if I belong to the Masons or the Rebeccas to have to say No — and if I could be persuaded that I could do the [New England] Poetry Society any good or it could do me any harm I don't know but that I'd begin to save up money etc etc making the most of the want of money in my apology in forma pauperis all the way.

But seriousness aside (I guess you'd think it was serious if all you had to keep an establishment on was an occasional ten dollars for a poem you only wrote for fun anyway), I shall hope to see you sometime a good deal sooner than I can promise to be at the Poetry Society to be reduced to the ranks.

I've been trying to tell Louis of New York, but I haven't got around to write it out yet, that I was asked to read poetry at the movies the other night to give the people time to get into their seats before the main part of the show began. I was advertised on the bills like this: Prayer by the Rev. Soandso. Poems by R. F. Pictures, Life of Christ, 5,000 feet. I was advertised first and invited afterwards. I wasn't there.

You may not believe that and if you don't you won't believe this: a neighbor got into the house on the pretext of wanting to sell me seeds. He began on me the minute we sat down with "How are the books coming on, Mr. Frost?" Next he said "Poetry exclusively I believe it is with you?" Next very re-

* Sequence of poems, "The Hill Wife," in The Yale Review, April 1916.

spectfully, "What do you ask apiece for them?" And when I answered "Seventy-five cents and one dollar and twentyfive cents," he told me "Poole gets one dollar and fifty." [Ernest] Poole of "The Harbor" summers further up the mountain. All I ask is your sympathy.

Shall you be where I can find you in the middle of June?

Always sincerely yours   Robert Frost

148 · To John T. Bartlett

Dear John   [30] May 1916   Franconia

A letter once in a while can do no harm to him that sends or him that receives, though damn letters as a rule. There are a few people I might enjoy writing to if there weren't so many I had to write to. I remember the time when I looked forward to an evening of writing to you. I'd rather see you now than write to you. Strange, aint it?

Of course there's a whole lot about the art of writing that none of us ever masters. We all remain duffers and properly dissatisfied with ourselves. I'm not speaking of the art of letter writing but of the longer art of writing for the Country Gentleman. It is touch and go with any of us. Now we get it for a little run of sentences and now we don't.

There are tones of voice that mean more than words. Sentences may be so shaped as definitely to indicate these tones. Only when we are making sentences so shaped are we really writing. And that is flat. A sentence *must* convey a meaning by tone of voice and it must be the particular meaning the writer intended. The reader must have no choice in the matter. The tone of voice and its meaning must be in black and white on the page.

I will take a look around for you up here. I had counted on the Lynches. But from what I hear they may be too crowded to take any one in this summer. A son has come home with his family to stay with them for a while. I'll see them however as soon as I get back from this trip. I'll find somebody to take you in.

I wish I could see you this time. But I can't honestly. I'm longer away than I ought to be every time as it is. I'll leave here on the 2 P.M. tomorrow — leave the house at 1 P.M. — get to Boston at 9 P.M., take the midnight for New York, reach

New York at 7 A.M. Thursday, take the 8 A.M. for Philadelphia, reach Philadelphia at 10 AM, read, get away on the midnight for New York, take 7 AM train Friday for Providence, read, sleep, take early morning train for Boston for a little business and then scoot for home. You see the kinds of jaunts I take. The Harvard one on [June] the 19th will be the last. (You must get down to Boston for that to please me.) Some time in July the family will move down to Plymouth for a week while I talk to the summer school seven or eight times. But that is another thing. None of us will suffer by that particularly.

Well old man *stay* on the map. Elinor will write and tell Margaret what to do. But you stay on the map.

As always   R.

149 · To John W. Haines

Dear Jack,   4 July 1916   Franconia

I have said that I would start praying for you just the minute there was a good forward movement for my prayers to join forces with. And I believe the forward movement has come. They are off, and my heart's with them with all the love I bear England for the time I met you or we met you first between the Greenway and Leddington with your canister for tall flowers, for May Hill, for the fern we groped on the little cliff for by the light of a match in your English winter twilight and for the evenings by your books of all the poets (those I can stand and those I can't stand), just you and I and your wife together. Old man, I shouldn't have seen you at all if I wasn't going to see more of you. I shouldn't have seen England if I wasn't going to see more of her. You both become an increasing pain as you are. I can't say much of my affection for you because I seem not in a position to do anything to prove it. Probably I am saying more now than the Censor will pass if he opens this. He will say talk is cheap: why don't I come over and fight for England if I love her so? But its not like that. A Censor couldn't be expected to understand. My politics are wholly American. I follow my country in regions where the best of us walk blind. I suppose I care for my country in all the elemental ways in which I care for myself. My love of country is my self-love. My love of England is my love of friends. That may be the higher kind of love, but it is not the kind to make me

205

quite dangerous. Which is the point. But I want you to win —
now! — on this drive — come on! — and be done with your
troubles, so that you and I can sit down and talk again in peace
of mind either here on a White Mountain or there on a Malvern
among old fortifications where your race long ago perhaps extended itself in every faculty as desperately as they are straining today. Carol says "In Berlin tomorrow!" All backward to
the German Rhine! How is it the German song goes?

Affectionately, Robert Frost

150 · To Harriet Monroe

Dear Miss Monroe: 13 July 1916   Franconia

I was on the point of suggesting that it might be well to
hold "Snow" over till as late as early next year. Timeliness is no
particular object with you I suppose; just the same when a
thing is so obviously of January February or March I dont see
how it can lose anything in coming out in one of those
months. What do you say if I have the manuscript for a
while again to look over and touch up when I happen to light
on it lying around? Have no anxiety about the money. Where
we are now we can live on our debts. I wouldn't play into your
hands by admitting so much if I were writing to you merely as
an editor. It is between poets I say it and I make no bones of it.

Sincerely yours   Robert Frost

151 · To Harriet Monroe

Dear Miss Monroe: 17 August 1916   Franconia

I was born to be an awful bother. It now looks as if I were
not going to get out of giving Harcourt another book this fall.
And I shall need every poem I have written in the last three
years to swell it to book-like proportions. That as good as takes
"Snow" away from you, doesn't it? It makes me sorry. I had set
my heart on having another poem in "Poetry" before I turned to
play- and novel-writing. What can you say to relieve me? I suppose you couldn't think of lugging me in prematurely in October? *

* "Snow" appeared in *Poetry,* November 1916; *Mountain Interval* was
also published in November 1916.

I should be glad to go to Chicago for $150 and take my chances on picking up a little more. The money would be much — we won't say it wouldn't — but the great thing would be to see you and Vachel Lindsay. . . .

Sincerely yours   Robert Frost

152 · To Harriet Monroe

Dear Miss Monroe: 4 September 1916   Franconia

Harcourt writes me that you've got snow in Chicago already. Sounds wintry.

After you've got me off your mind, I wish you could find time to look at a few little poems an English friend of mine [Edward Thomas] has been writing since he turned soldier. He is known for prose rather than for verse. If you care at all for what I enclose I shall be tempted to tell you who he is. He has a quality.

I have had a frivolous summer. Too many pleasant people in the neighborhood. It will be different when — to quote from a poem you may never have seen ["Christmas Trees"]

> The city has withdrawn into itself
> And left at last the country to the country.

Sincerely yours   Robert Frost

153 · To Alfred Harcourt

Dear Harcourt,   December 1916   Franconia

Better. Bad cold — that was all, but too close on the heels of the other one. I was in bed a week. . . .

Here's that damned Hell-I-Can [Edward J. H. O'Brien] turned up again with the base insinuation that people like what I write because of the reputation you have made for me. I don't like the business but I don't want to antagonize anyone whose friendship won't hurt us. Am I too hard on O'Brien. Do you approve of that pair (him and Braithwaite)? I get to railing and I can rail myself into damning my best friends to Hell. Sometimes I think I need holding in.

A case in point. You remember how I flew off the handle because I suspected a certain poet [Stark Young] got me to read my poetry at his college [Amherst] in order to get me to find him a publisher for his poetry. Well I didn't find him a publisher did I? And here he comes with an invitation to me to give two half courses at his college from January on for $2,000. I'm humiliated. And it ain't the first time in forty years. I seem to go plum crazy.

This about the college must be a secret. I haven't decided yet.

Tell me about de la Mare. It comes to me round the ring that you are to have another book of his. Is that right? I mustn't be too hard on de la Mare either. I have little enough to go on with regard to him. Tell me.

More when I am more scrumptious.

Love to all   Always yours
Robert Frost

154 · To SIDNEY COX

Dear Cox: [c. 7 December 1916] [Franconia]

It gives me real pleasure to hear of your pleasure and your friend's pleasure in the book. Why mar it by raising the specter of your poor past professor, to argue with? It can do me no good to be reminded of him. It's uncomfortable to be at a feast with a fellow who suddenly pushes back his chair and gets up to gesticulate with his napkin at somebody nobody else can see.

I know you do it from conscientiousness — not to hide from me anything that may be bothering you. You needn't be so scrupulous with me. I shall forgive you if you keep some unimportant doubts from me.

You do awfully well with the book. I could ask no more generous reviewer than you would be. But you mustn't be misled by anything that may have been laid down to you in school into exaggerating the importance of a little sententious tag to a not over important poem. The large things in the book — well I won't name them — you know better than to think the Oven Bird is of them. Probably the best thing in the book is The Old Man's Winter Night. That seems to be the consensus of opinion among the professors I get letters from — if we are going to leave it to professors.

I like different people to like different things. I shouldn't mind your exalting the Oven Bird so much if your reasons were better. Let's not strain, let's not worry. Have a good time most of the time.

I shall be off professoring a little on my own pretty soon and if I have a chance I shall try to find you in New York. The trouble with New York is it thinks people ought to be glad to read to it for nothing. That's why I keep away from it.

Always yours   Robert Frost

154-a · ALEXANDER MEIKLEJOHN TO ROBERT FROST

AMHERST COLLEGE
AMHERST, MASSACHUSETTS
OFFICE OF THE PRESIDENT

December 16, 1916

Mr. Robert Frost,
Franconia, N. H.

Dear Mr. Frost:

This morning at the chapel service I read "The Road Not Taken" and then told the boys about your coming. They applauded vigorously and were evidently much delighted at the prospect. I can assure you of an eager and hearty welcome by the community. I hope you did not get too tired when you were with us and that the cold is altogether gone. I beg of you to let us know if there is anything that anyone here can do to help in the plans which Mrs. Frost and you are making for coming and getting settled.

I am writing to the Treasurer asking him to send you on January first a check for $350 and on each first of the month succeeding for six months a check for $275. If this arrangement is not satisfactory I hope you will let me know.

With kindest regards to both of you and with very eager anticipation of your coming, I am

Sincerely yours,   Alexander Meiklejohn

155 · TO HARRIET MONROE

Dear Miss Monroe: [c. 7 January 1917]   [Franconia]

Here I sit admiring these beautiful poems [of Edward Thomas; pen name of "Edward Eastaway"] but not daring to urge them on anyone else for fear I shall be suspected of ad-

209

miring them for love of their author. If Edward Eastaway gets killed before the war is over (he is with the artillery) there will be plenty found to like them and then where will my credit be for having liked them first. After all is it any worse for me to like them because I know their author (but I *don't* like them for that reason) than for others to like them because they know he is dead.

I'm afraid all these I send are coming out in an Annual the Georgian group will publish in February. I wish you could think you could crowd just one of them into your February Poetry so as to be ahead of the Annual — the Annual wouldn't get over here perhaps before March and it might not then. "Old Man" is the flower of the lot, isn't it?

You may not have heard that I am just off to profess poetry at Amherst for six months. So when you write again think of me as in Amherst Mass.

Sincerely yours   Robert Frost

155-a · EDWARD ARLINGTON ROBINSON TO ROBERT FROST

2 February 1917

Dear Frost   66 West 83 Street   New York, N. Y.

Let me thank you for your book [*Mountain Interval*] which came to me the other day by way of the Macmillans. I don't know how long they have had it, but I do know that they are remiss in such matters.

In "Snow," "In the Home Stretch," "Birches," "The Hill Wife" and "The Road Not Taken" you seem undoubtedly to have added something permanent to the world, and I must congratulate you. I like everything else in the book, but those poems seem to me to stand out from the rest; and I fancy somehow that you will not wholly disagree with me. Please give my best regards to Mr. [Stark] Young, and believe me

Yours always sincerely
E. A. Robinson

156 · To Helen Thomas

My dear Helen: 6 February 1917   Amherst

I am writing this to you because I think it may be the quickest way to reach Edward with questions I must have an answer to as soon as possible.

I have found a publisher for his poems in America. But there are several things to be cleared up before we can go ahead.

Has Edward sold the 'world' rights to his English publisher or only the English rights? That is to say is he free to deal directly with an American publisher?

Dont you think he ought to throw off the pen-name [Edward Eastaway] and use his real name under the circumstances? Shall we make him? Tell him I insist.

Would he object very much if I took it into my head at the publishers suggestion to write a little preface to the book to take the place of the dedication?

I am not going to ask permission to take up with the offer of ten percent royalty. Any royalty is all right. The thing is to get the poems out where they may be read.

My hope is that Edward hasn't lost the right to let us set the book up over here.

I have just sold two or three of the poems to Harriet Monroe of Poetry, Chicago. The money will have to come to me and so to you unless we decide at once to use real names.

Isn't this rather pleasant news for the soldier? — damn his eyes.

I am a teacher again for the moment and we are all here at Amherst, Mass, the town of my college.

I wonder if it would be too much trouble for Merfyn to write a pretty little note to Frederick Howe, Commissioner of Immigration, Ellis Island New York to thank him for the glimpse he gave him of these United States and to tell him that he is safely back in his own country and promised as a soldier when his country shall want him? I have meant to ask Merfyn myself. I had a nice letter from him awhile ago.

I doubt if his country is going to need him. I suspect that all that is happening is some ingenuity of the Germans to bring the war to an early close without having to seem beaten. I don't know just what they are up to. I think, though, they are

211

looking for a way to let go of the Lion's tail. I begin to think we shall be seeing you all again before long.

Always yours   Robert

157 · To Louis Untermeyer

Dear Louis: 8 February 1917   Amherst

The Girl with All Those Names [Blanche Shoemaker Wagstaff] got hers — and poetic justice is done — the eternal verities are verified. Now she can kiss anything she pleases.

You don't tell me, though! — I won't believe she writes poetry about kissing dead Adonis anywhere. Anywhere in America!

Me art hakes Anna numness panes me cents.

Go in and kill them all off with my love.

The latest thing in the schools is to know that you have nothing to say in the days of thy youth, but that those days may well be put in learning how to say something 'gainst when the evil days draw near when thou shalt have something to say. Damn these separations of the form from the substance. I don't know how long I could stand them.

No Chicago this trip. The dates were too sprawling. At most three or four days were all I had a right to steal from the college.

[. . .] I ain't so sanguine about the war as you are. I'm getting ready to use it to advertise my last book. Goodbye —

R.F.

158 · To John T. Bartlett

IN THIS letter the primary subject is how to cope with physical and nervous illnesses. With a somewhat puritanical austerity, RF repeatedly maintained that crises could be forestalled if an individual took corrective measures soon enough. The "one person lost" could be a reference either to his father or his sister, Jeanie; but the "person saved" is almost certainly a reference to himself. He frequently claimed that Jeanie should have taken corrective measures.

John Bartlett, recipient of this letter, made the following pertinent note from a conversation with RF much later, on 9 April 1934: "We all have our souls — and minds — to save, and it seems a miracle that we do it; not once, but several times. He could look back and see his hanging by a thread. His sister wasn't able to save hers. She built the protecting illusion around herself and went

212

the road of dementia praecox." (Typescript notes, University of Virginia Library.)

Dear John: 13 February 1917   Amherst

You will have heard I am teaching again. I have to do something for the country once in so often even when it isn't at war.

And speaking of war, what kind of a trouble have you children got yourselves into? Didn't I tell you you would have to stick at nothing to get over these hard times? You have still your reserves — things you wont give up. But you'll have to give up everything for a little while. Those boys ought to go on a visit to one of their grandmothers. You can do a lot for them. But if you're the least like me, not enough to take them entirely off Margaret's mind. She's got to be relieved of them to get well. That's sure. She can't afford to be foolish for a moment, and neither can you. I have seen right in my own family one person lost by not taking instant and out-and-out measures and another person saved by taking them. The business can go either way you want it to, but I'm afraid generally as most of us are entangled in life and obligations, it inclines to go the wrong way. Cut and run away from every care: that is the rule. Nothing else will do. No faltering. I saw the way my father fed his hopes on one concession after another. It was my first tragedy.

Some time when you are near a bank will you cash this check and use it for any little thing for Margaret? You can pay it back to me when I am old and neglected, with interest at one tenth of one per cent — or as much more as you like if I am very much neglected. I mean to get up to see you [in Raymond, New Hampshire], but I can hardly make it now. I am expected to stay on the job most of the time.

Tell me a lot about things.

Affectionately   Rob

159 · To Amy Lowell

Dear Miss Lowell: [c. 20 February 1917]   Amherst

[. . .] I want you to know that I was elected a horficer of the [New England] Poetry Society without my knowledge or consent. I think it best not to do anything to undo what has been done. Best let things slide. My being elected in such an irregular way does not make me of the party of those who elected me that I can see.

I am sorry Mrs [Josephine Preston Peabody] Marks has gone to war with you. What is the matter with her? She ought not to let herself be made unhappy by another person's success. Let's not be too hard on her. I understand she is seriously an invalid.

[. . .] Your distinguished brother* sent some hot shot into our quasi-pacifism here yesterday when he spoke of some differences between countries that can only be cut through with the sword and when he told us that the League to Enforce Peace printed the word Enforce in red letters. I have had a course of upwards of five lectures under him this year (that is to say since last June). I should think that many ought to count as a course, shouldn't you? — especially since I liked them a whole lot.

Well I am   Sincerely yours   Robert Frost

160 · To Sidney Cox

Dear Sidney Cox: 3 March 1917   Amherst

Dont you want to come out here and talk over some week end. I've meant to look you up in New York but I been on nothing but the fly and the jump every time I've been through New York this winter. I'd write you a letter but that I've soured on letter writing for good and all.

Keep a stiff upper lip and maybe the Germans won't hurt you.

Where shall we lock Block? † — I mean if we start interning. Things begin to look pretty internal for the stray Hun.

Laugh and the world laughs with you.

I'm now a third rate authority on the Four PP, Gammer Gurton and such.   Allers yourn   Robert Frost

161 · To Alfred Harcourt

Dear Alfred: 20 April 1917   Amherst

Thank you for letting me know where you have gone to with all my money. I am counting on that money to keep me

---

* Abbott Lawrence Lowell, then President of Harvard University.
† Alexander Bloch, a school-teaching friend of Sidney Cox's.

while I write another poem. I dont know why I should want to write another poem except that I have always planned to and there seems to be a demand for such a thing especially if [it] could turn out a war poem.

So dont let me lose track of you till I have got the poem written anyway.

Sounds sad — sounds like the last of me, doesn't it? Well it's about the last of all of us — the way things are going. This college is melting away under us (let 'er melt): you say your business is pickéd; and there's certainly something nightmarish in the elasticity of a modern battle line by which you can push into it as far as you like almost anywhere but you cant push through it or pinch ahold of it.

The great question is what shall the poem be about, since there is only to be one more. But we can talk that over the last time I come to see you in a few weeks. We may as well have it about something elementary or do I mean elemental or what do I mean? Suppose we call it Vale and then enlist either in the Potato Army or in the Ship Building Army like these blooded young heroes of the College and leave it to vainglorious hot-heads to throw themselves away in battle. It seems so immodest to set up to be a hero.

Franconia beckons to us. We have had enough of Stark Young's stark disingenuousness. Welcome the wilderness where no one comes or has come except in an expensive touring car. Sun-treaders (as Browning says). There are a lot of good things I believe in, but for the life of me I cant always enumerate them at a moments notice.

The best of misunderstanding any one is that it sort of disposes of him and clears your mind of him and so leaves you with one less detail in life to be bothered with. Of course it is the same with understanding. Of what use is either understanding or misunderstanding unless it simplifies by taking away from the sum and burden of what you have to consider. There are a hundred off poets in a new anthology for example; I get rid of one half of them by understanding, of the other half by misunderstanding, and the danger of my mind's being overcrowded with poets or my brain's being congested with 'em is passed. What a thing misunderstanding is. I sing misunderstanding.   Always yours   Robert Frost

162 · To John W. Haines

Dear Jack   27 April 1917 Amherst

  I haven't written for a long time because there was nothing to write except that I was sick at heart. There is nothing to write now except that Edward Thomas was killed at Arras on Easter Monday which is no more than you already knew. But what are we going to do about it? I wish I could see you.

                  Robert

163 · To Helen Thomas

Dear Helen: 27 April 1917 Amherst

  People have been praised for self-possession in danger. I have heard Edward doubt if he was as brave as the bravest. But who was ever so completely himself right up to the verge of destruction, so sure of his thought, so sure of his word? He was the bravest and best and dearest man you and I have ever known. I knew from the moment when I first met him at his unhappiest that he would some day clear his mind and save his life. I have had four wonderful years with him. I know he has done this all for you: he is all yours. But you must let me cry my cry for him as if he were *almost* all mine too.

  Of the three ways out of here, by death where there is no choice, by death where there is a noble choice, and by death where there is a choice not so noble, he found the greatest way. There is no regret — nothing that I will call regret. Only I can't help wishing he could have saved his life without so wholly losing it and come back from France not too much hurt to enjoy our pride in him. I want to see him to tell him something. I want to tell him, what I think he liked to hear from me, that he was a poet. I want to tell him that I love those he loved and hate those he hated. (But the hating will wait: there will be a time for hate.) I had meant to talk endlessly with him still, either here in our mountains as we had said or, as I found my longing was more and more, there at Leddington where we first talked of war.

  It was beautiful as he did it. And I don't suppose there is anything for us to do to show our admiration but to love him forever.   Robert

  Other things for other letters.

164 · To EDWARD GARNETT

Dear Mr Garnett: 29 April 1917   Amherst

Edward Thomas was the only brother I ever had. I fail to see how we can have been so much to each other, he an Englishman and I an American and our first meeting put off till we were both in middle life. I hadn't a plan for the future that didn't include him.

You must like his poetry as well as I do and do everything you can for it. His last word to me, his "pen ultimate word," as he called it, was that what he cared most for was the name of poet. His poetry is so very brave — so unconsciously brave. He didn't think of it for a moment as war poetry, though that is what it is. It ought to be called Roads to France. "Now all roads lead to France, and heavy is the tread of the living, but the dead, returning, lightly dance," he says. He was so impurturbably the poet through everything to the end. If there is any merit in self possession, I can say I never saw anyone less put off himself by unaccustomed danger, less put off his game. His concern to the last was what it had always been, to touch earthly things and come as near them in words as words would come.

Do what you can for him and never mind me for the present. I sent you a copy of Mountain Interval, but perhaps it is as well you didnt get it for your review if you were not going to be pleased with it. I can hear Edward Thomas saying in defense of In the Home Stretch that it would cut just as it is into a dozen or more of your Chinese impressionistic poems and perhaps gain something by the cutting for the reader whose taste had been formed on the kiln-dried tabule poetry of your Pounds and Masterses. I look on theirs as synthetical chemical products put together after a formula. It's too long a story to go into with anyone I'm not sure it wouldn't bore. There's something in the living sentence (in the shape of it) that is more important than any phrasing or chosen word. And it's something you can only achieve when going free. The Hill Wife ought to be some sort of answer to you. It is just as much one poem as the other but more articulated so to speak. It shows its parts and it shows that they may be taken by themselves as poems of fashionable length. . . .   Sincerely yours   Robert Frost

165 · To Katharine Lee Bates

Dear Miss Bates   13 June 1917 Amherst

 I have just learned by accident that the meeting of the Poetry Society was last Saturday! And I had thought all the time it was to be next Saturday. How did I make such a mistake and how will you ever forgive me unless I make you realize how sick we have all been and how confused in mind we have had good reason for being. Five out of six of us have been sick in bed. Can I make amends by offering to come and talk to one of your classes next year or will that only be making a bad matter worse? Yours abjectly Robert Frost

166 · To Sidney Cox

Dear Sidney: 12 August 1917 Franconia

 I am going to be very sorry not to be at your war-wedding . . . on the forenoon of August 16th. I can't be more. My own marriage keeps me from your marriage so to speak. That is to say things that follow in the train of marriage keep me — babies and the fear of babies. Since some time before you were with us we haven't known just what we were in for. We don't know now. It seemed like a last putting forth. At times we have been afraid it was something more serious if not more solemn. At any rate I dont think I ought to be away from Elinor as she is. . . . Always yours Robert Frost

167 · To John T. Bartlett

Dear John: [13 August 1917] [Franconia]

 I dont see how I am to get down to see you — I really don't. Elinor has been sick for a long time. We dont know what is the matter with her unless it is something that may come to an end abruptly at any moment. I ought not to be far from her — at any rate till we know more certainly how it is with her. We are all going back to Amherst next month. But you have determined to get away before then. I very much want a talk with you. Would you come here for a day and night if I would foot the bill? This in haste on impulse. Rob.

168 · To William Stanley Braithwaite

My dear Braithwaite: 2 September 1917   Franconia

I'm not dead but sleeping. This is the first letter I have written in I don't know how long.

Of course anything you please of mine for this year's anthology and the obligation all mine. Also for five years' anthology.

I'll tell you presently where I'll have you send a copy or two of those older anthologies you have on hand.

I've heard of you indirectly at the Peterboro Camp* where I suppose you all write a whole lot of poetry and have a high old time reading it to each other. Some time you will be doing a book on the Camp.   Sincerely yours   Robert Frost

169 · To Amy Lowell

Dear Miss Lowell   [22 October 1917]   [Amherst]

I could have fared even badly at your hands and still have had to confess that I liked your book [*Tendencies in Modern American Poetry*]. But I didnt fare badly. What are your few doubts (groundless doubts) of my humor, my ability to go farther or my wisdom in not using dialect as weighed against all you say in my favor. Your generosity from the first has had so much to do with making me that if from now on you reversed yourself and tried to unmake me, I should never be brought to believe you were anything but my friend.

Considering all you found to say of me, it seems to me you have fallen into very few errors of fact, and I may be to blame for those. Please spell it *Elinor* Frost in the two places where you name my wife. The word should be "shock" instead of "shook" in the quotation from A Hundred Collars. Little Iddens was a house in Leddington near Ledbury, Herefordshire, where I lived neighborly with Gibson and Abercrombie from April 1914 to September 1914, about five months. Even if you don't care to bother with the correction in your next edition, I wish you would make a marginal note of the fact that I didn't meet Gibson till I was putting the last touches on North of Boston and I didn't meet Abercrombie till after the MS was in David Nutt's hands. It was the book that got me invited down

* The MacDowell Colony, Peterborough, New Hampshire.

to live with those fellows in the country. I had begun writing it in 1905. I wrote the bulk of it in 1913. One month after the war broke out we left Little Iddens to live with the Abercrombies at their house called The Gallows at Ryton near Dymock, Gloucestershire — three miles away. You see if any of my work was in danger of Gibsonian or Abercrombian influence it was what I wrote of Mountain Interval in 1914: Birches and The Hill Wife and Putting in the Seed and The Sound of Trees. None of this greatly matters, but since you seem bent on accuracy, you might make a marginal note of it, as I say, in script in your copy of your own book.

And for the fun of it you might record in the margin of your book that RF makes no merit of not having used dialect in North of Boston. He says he doesn't put dialect into the mouths of his people because not one of them, not one, spoke dialect.

I don't know that I ever told you, but the closest I ever came in friendship to anyone in England or anywhere else in the world I think was with Edward Thomas who was killed at Vimy last spring. He more than anyone else was accessory to what I had done and was doing. We were together to the exclusion of every other person and interest all through 1914 — 1914 was our year. I never had, I never shall have another such year of friendship.

Would it amuse you to learn that Range Finding belongs to a set of war poems I wrote in time of profound peace (circa 1902)? Most of them have gone the way of waste paper. Range Finding was only saved from going the same way by Edward Thomas who liked it and asked about it now and then and very particularly once in a letter last Spring — he thought it so good a description of No Man's Land. So you see my poems about this war narrow down to The Bonfire and that is more of New England than of what is going on over yonder.

My address is Amherst Mass, though really we are living in the abandoned town of Pelham so close to the woods that if the woods burn our house must go too.

Thanks for everything. But thanks specially for giving An Old Man's Winter Night its due.

Always yours sincerely   Robert Frost

170 · To Louis Untermeyer

Dear Louis: 27 October 1917   Amherst

Under separate cover I have told you why I ain't got no sympathy for your total loss of all the arts [demise of *The Seven Arts* magazine]. You tried to have too many at the present price of certified milk. Why would you be a pig instead of something like a horse or a cow that only has one in a litter, albeit with six legs sometimes, for I have seen such in my old mad glad circus-going days. But that's all put behind me since I discovered that do or say my dambdest I can't be other than orthodox in politics love and religion: I can't escape salvation: I can't burn if I was born into this world to shine without heat. And I try not to think of it as often as I can lest in the general deliquescence I should find myself a party to the literature of irresponsible, boy-again, freedom. No, I can promise you that whatever else I write or may have been writing for the last twenty-five years to disprove Amy's theory that I never got anything except out of the soil of New England, there's one thing I shan't write in the past, present, or future, and that is glad mad stuff or mad glad stuff. The conviction closes in on me that I was cast for gloom as the sparks fly upward, I was about to say: I am of deep shadow all compact like onion within onion and the savor of me is oil of tears. I have heard laughter by daylight when I thought it was my own because at that moment when it broke I had parted my lips to take food. Just so I have been afraid of myself and caught at my throat when I thought I was making some terrible din of a mill whistle that happened to come on the same instant with the opening of my mouth to yawn. But I have not laughed. No man can tell you the sound or the way of my laughter. I have neighed at night in the woods behind a house like vampires. But there are no vampires, there are no ghouls, there are no demons, there is nothing but me. And I have all the dead New England things held back by one hand as by a dam in the long deep wooded valley of Whippoorwill, where, many as they are, though, they do not flow together by their own weight more than so many piled-up chairs — (and, by the way, your two chairs have come). I hold them easily — too easily for assurance that they will go with a rush when I let them go. I may have to extricate them one by one and throw them. If so I shall throw them with what imaginative excess I am capable of, already past the height of my powers (see Amy the next time you are in Boston).

I suppose it's a safe bet that the form your pacificism, your Protean pacificism, takes at this moment is "Down with Mitchel." Next it will be — you say! Do you see these transmogrifications more than one or two ahead? Aw say, be a nationalist. By the love you bear Teddy [Roosevelt]!

Yours while you're still bad enough to need me,

Robert Frost

171 · To Harriet Monroe

HARRIET MONROE sent RF a telegram telling him that *Poetry* magazine had awarded "Snow" a cash prize of $100. He replied with the following telegram.

2 NOVEMBER 1917   AMHERST

DEAR MISS MONROE, MY CONGRATULATIONS TO YOU AND YOUR FELLOW EDITORS OF POETRY ON WHAT IS BOUND TO PROVE A VERY POPULAR AWARD IN THIS FAMILY. I WAS FEELING BLUE WHEN LIKE A BOLT FROM THE BLUE CAME SO MUCH WEALTH AND GLORY. I AM THE MORE SENSIBLE OF IT ALL THAT IT IS MY FIRST REAL PRIZE IN A LONG LIFE. HITHERTO MY UTMOST HAS BEEN A FEW DOLLARS FOR RUNNING AT A CALEDONIA CLUB PICNIC, A PART INTEREST IN A PAIR OF EAR-RINGS, AND A PART INTEREST IN A GOLD-HEADED CANE FOR IMPERSONATIONS AT A MASQUERADE, A GOLD MEDAL FOR SHEER GOODNESS IN A HIGH SCHOOL AND A DETUR FOR SCHOLARSHIP AT HARVARD. ALWAYS SINCERELY YOURS   ROBERT FROST

172 · To Louis Untermeyer

Dear Louis: 7 November 1917   Amherst

Do you want to be the repository of one or two facts that Amy [*Tendencies in Modern American Poetry*] leaves out of account?

For twenty-five out of the first forty years of my life I lived in San Francisco, Lawrence, Mass., Boston, Cambridge, Mass., New York, and Beaconsfield, a suburb of London.

For seven I lived in the villages of Salem, Derry, and Plymouth, New Hampshire.

For eight I lived on a farm at Derry though part of that time I was teaching in the Academy there.

I began to read to myself at thirteen. Before that time I had been a poor scholar and had staid out of school all I could. At about that time I began to take first place in my classes.

I read my first poem at 15, wrote my first poem at 16, wrote My Butterfly at eighteen. That was my first poem published.

With Elinor I shared the valedictory honor when I graduated from the High School at Lawrence, Mass.

I was among the first men at Amy's brother's old college during my two years there, winning a Detur and a considerable scholarship. In those days I used to suspect I was looked on as more or less of a grind — though as a matter of fact I was always rather athletic. I ran well. I played on town school ball teams and on the High School football team. I had my share of fights, the last a rather public one in Lawrence in 1896 that cost me the humiliation of going into court and a ten dollar fine.

It is not fair to farmers to make me out a very good or laborious farmer. I have known hard times, but no special shovel-slavery. I dreamed my way through all sorts of fortunes without any realizing sense of what I was enduring. You should have seen me, I wish I could have seen myself, when I was working in the Arlington Mills at Lawrence, working in the shoe shop in Salem N. H., tramping and beating my way on trains down South, reporting on a Lawrence paper, promoting for a Shakespearean reader (whom I abandoned because, after trying him on a distinguished audience I got him in Boston, I decided he wasn't *truly great!*) Nothing seemed to come within a row of apple trees of where I really lived. I was so far from being discouraged by my failure to get anywhere that I only dimly realized that anyone else was discouraged by it. This is where the countryman came in: I would work at almost anything rather well for a while, but every once in so often I had to run off for a walk in the woods or for a term's teaching in a lonely district school or a summer's work haying or picking fruit on a farm or cutting heels in a shed by the woods in Salem. Gee Whiz, I should say I was just the most everyday sort of person except for the way I didn't mind looking unambitious as much as you would mind, for example. Of course it's no credit to me. I knew what I was about well enough and was pretty sure where I would come out.

Amy is welcome to make me out anything she pleases. I have decided I like her and, since she likes me, anything she says will do so long as it is entertaining. She has been trying to lay at my door all the little slips she has made in the paper on me. She gets it all wrong about me and Gibson and Abercrombie for example. I knew neither of those fellows till North of Boston was all written. All I wrote in the neighborhood of those two was part of Mountain Interval. I doubt if she is right in making me so grim, not to say morbid. I may not be funny enough for Life or Punch, but I have sense of humor enough, I must believe, to laugh when the joke is on me as it is in some of this book of Amy's.

I really like least her mistake about Elinor. That's an unpardonable attempt to do her as the conventional helpmeet of genius. Elinor has never been of any earthly use to me. She hasn't cared whether I went to school or worked or earned anything. She has resisted every inch of the way my efforts to get money. She is not too sure that she cares about my reputation. She wouldn't lift a hand or have me lift a hand to increase my reputation or even save it. And this isn't all from devotion to my art at its highest. She seems to have the same weakness I have for a life that goes rather poetically; only I should say she is worse than I. It isn't what might be expected to come from such a life — poetry that she is after. And it isn't that she doesn't think I am a good poet either. She always knew I was a good poet, but that was between her and me, and there I think she would have liked it if it had remained at least until we were dead. I don't know that I can make you understand the kind of person. Catch her getting any satisfaction out of what her housekeeping may have done to feed a poet! Rats! She hates housekeeping. She has worked because the work has piled on top of her. But she hasn't pretended to like house-work even for my sake. If she has liked anything it has been what I may call living it on the high. She's especially wary of honors that derogate from the poetic life she fancies us living. What a cheap common unindividualized picture Amy makes of her. But, as I say, never mind. Amy means well and perhaps you will come to our rescue without coming in conflict with Amy or contradicting her to her face.

THIS CONCLUDING PAGE of a letter from Robert Frost to Sabra Peabody, written in the fall of 1886 when he was twelve years old, represents one of the earliest known examples of his literary effort—and handwriting. For the complete text, see letter 4, page 18; for the circumstances under which four notes to Sabra Peabody were written and preserved, see page 15.

R. L. Frost, Tremont St, Lawrence, Mass.   1

My Butterfly.
An Elegy.
By R. L. Frost.

Thine emulous fond flowers are dead too,
And the daft sun assaulter, he
That frighted thee so oft, is fled or dead:
    Save only me
    Nor is it sad to thee
    Save only me,
There is no one to mourn thee in the fields.

    The grey grass is scarce dappled with the snow;
Its two banks have not shut upon the river,
    But it is long ago,
    It seems forever,
Since first I saw thee glance
With all the dazzling other ones,
    In airy dalliance,
    Precipitate in love,
Tossed up, tossed up and tangling above,
Like a limp rose wreath in a fairy dance.

Courtesy of Henry E. Huntington Library

THE FIRST PAGE of the manuscript, "My Butterfly," sent to *The Independent* by Robert Frost in March 1894. The peculiar penmanship is like that of letter 5, pages 18-19.

Boston Mass. Aug 22, '94

Dear Miss Ward:—
                Surely you have not
recieved my last letter. I shall be sorry
if it is too late to arrange to meet you.
Write to me at least.

          For I perceive that my childish-
ness in regard to poem (said poem)
may have become wearisome. It is very
trying to be noticed, you know. But
give me another chance: I may have
disqualified myself for a political
career by one foolish act but I cannot have
for a literary one:—all the can conjeed
afford me consolation.
          I am learning to spell.
          I am writing better poetry.

SIGNIFICANT CHANGES are apparent in the contrast between the
style of writing in the manuscript of "My Butterfly" and on this
first page of a letter written about six months later. See letter 8,
page 23, for the full text.

Lawrence Mass Aug 15 '96

Dear Miss Ward,

You were very considerate in the matter of the title. I presume the other poem as emended was not satisfactory. Will you let me know?

There are other things I would like to know. Write me if you are not too busy.

We are about to move down town again to open school. I am becoming dangerously interested in that concern, to the exclusion I fear of things more lofty. [Don't believe him]

Miss Ward has been enjoying the warm weather? Now what has my friend to say about life in the city. There is much to be done for the poor isn't there if Bryan were only the man to do it.

But I must hear from you directly before I continue. I have lost touch with

Courtesy of Henry E. Huntington Library

THIS FIRST PAGE of a letter dated 15 August 1896 (see letter 14, page 28) represents further developments in Robert Frost's handwriting. The characters are more heavily shaded and more consciously controlled, but they are still crudely formed.

Me. not to see Mr. Sewell. You were opening the campaign so to speak in the Republican interest. Since then how many ~~calami~~ calamitous things have not happened to the disappointment of how many people particularly in the state of Colorado.

As nothing that happens matters much and as most of my thoughts are about myself & I am always at a loss for likely subjectmatter. I am the father of ~~the~~ a son if that is anything. What would William Cowla say under such circumstances. My soul what wouldn't he say!

And a Happy New Year! May you discover an immortal genius and enter into your earthly reward. If ever I improve beyond recognition I will let you discover me over in part payment for all you have done. You think I couldn't disguise my handwriting?

Sincerely yours,

Robert L. Frost.

WRITTEN about two months after the previous letter, this dated 27 December 1896 (see letter 15, pages 28-29) indicates a careful Frostian adaptation of the old Copperplate style. The valediction and signature, foreshadowed by the last sentence in the letter, are in the handwriting of Elinor M. Frost and may have some connection with an unsolved problem which is discussed in the headnote to letter 274-a, page 355.

West Derry N.H. Jan 15 '01

Dear Miss Ward

Perhaps you will care to know how authorship progresses. I send you this selection from the poems I have been writing with a view to a volume some day. If you can use it I shall be glad to have you.

Sincerely

R.L. Frost

L. Box 140

REGRESSION in the handwriting style of this letter may have been caused by many factors, including haste and discouragement. The fortunes and prospects of Robert Frost were at a particularly low ebb in January of 1901. See page 31 and letter 17, page 33.

The poems sent were uncommonly good

West Derry N.H. Feb. 24, '01

Dear Dr Ward:

I trust I do not presume too much on former kindness in addressing these verses to you personally. Sending MS to the Independent can never be quite like sending it anywhere else for me.

I often think of you and your sister in my work. I believe Miss Ward left the staff of the Independent some years ago to write books. Please remember me to her either formally or by showing her any of my verses — whether you can use them or not.

Sincerely yours,
Robert Frost

AGAIN DISCIPLINED and more rigorous than in the letter dated 15 January 1901, the handwriting here (letter 20, page 35) is nevertheless consciously modified from that of any earlier letter. It is more casual and relaxed; most of the shading has disappeared.

The Bungalow
Beaconsfield
Buckingham
England

Dear Miss Ward:

Perhaps I ought not
to conceal from you, as one of the very
few mortals I feel in any sense answerable to, that I am in the mood called
aberrant. Psychology holds me no
longer. What have I taught for, anyway,
but to confute my wellwishers who
believed I was not enough of the earth
earthy to be above a fool? And now that
I have proved myself as a teacher in
two departments of learning without
benefit of college, my soul inclines to
go apart by itself again and devise poetry.
Heaven send that I go not too late in life
for the emotions I expect to work in. But
in any case I should not stay, if only for
scorn of scorn — scorn of the scorn that
leaves me still unnoticed among the
least of the versifiers that stop a gap
in the magazines. The Forum gives me
space for one poem this year; the Companion
for two. The Independent, longest my
friend, has held one of my poems
unprinted now these three years. So

Courtesy of Henry E. Huntington Library

PRIDE AND DIGNITY—and discipline—are reflected in the handwriting of this letter written from England on 15 September
1912 (see letter 38, page 52). The crisp margin, the straight
lines of the text, and the blunt representations of characters,
which now slant back, suggest a new boldness and confidence.

I wish for a joke I could do myself, shifting the trees entirely from the Yankee realist to the Scotch symbolist.

Burn this if you think you ought for my protection.

Always yours   R.

173 · To Wilbur L. Cross

AS EDITOR of *The Yale Review,* Wilbur L. Cross had been second only to Ellery Sedgwick of *The Atlantic Monthly* in printing RF's poems after his return from England. The five poems in the sequence, "The Hill Wife" had appeared in *The Yale Review* for April 1916. Under discussion in this letter is the war poem, "Not to Keep," which was first published in *The Yale Review,* January 1917, and was then reprinted in *A Treasury of War Poetry* edited by George H. Clarke and published by Houghton Mifflin in 1917.

Dear Mr. Cross: 22 November 1917   Amherst

Have I done wrong in letting Houghton Mifflin Company take "Not to Keep" without referring them to you for permission? Come to think of it, I cant remember their saying anything about you or about crediting you. I shall be disgusted if I have helped them circumvent you, because I owe the firm nothing and something less than nothing. I didn't actually know that they had taken the poem. They have never made me any acknowledgement in the shape either of thanks or of a complimentary copy of their blessed book and the only advertisement of the book I have seen named every poet in the world as contributing except me.

I'm so bad at letters that I have been hoping against hope that I should be down along some day and could look in on you for a talk that would save me from having to write this.

I have wanted to say a word to you to explain my failure to do anything about Edward Thomas. I find he was too near me. Some time I shall write about him. Perhaps it will come to me to write in verse. As yet I feel too much the loss of the best friend I ever had. And by that I don't mean I am overwhelmed with grief. Something in me refuses to take the risk — angrily refuses to take the risk — of seeming to use grief for literary purposes. When I care less, I can do more.

Always sincerely yours,   Robert Frost

174 · To AMY LOWELL

[Printed letterhead]

AMHERST COLLEGE
AMHERST, MASSACHUSETTS
DEPARTMENT OF ENGLISH

Dear Miss Lowell: December 2 1917

A good way to show forgiveness if you are capable of such an emotion would be to have my young daughter [Lesley] over from Wellesley some day to see you where you sit enthroned. It would mean a lot to her for a long long time afterward not only to have seen you but to have heard you and yes to have been heard a little by you.

I must see you myself before long if only to put it to you while the business is still before the house why I am not by your own showing the least provincial, the most national of American poets — why I ought not to be, anyway. Doesn't the wonder grow that I have never written anything or as you say never published anything except about New England farms when you consider the jumble I am? Mother, Scotch immigrant. Father oldest New England stock unmixed. Ten years in West. Thirty years in East. Three years in England. Not less than six months in any of these: San Francisco, New York, Boston, Cambridge, Lawrence, London. Lived in Maine, N. H., Vt., Mass. Twenty five years in cities, nine in villages, nine on farms. Saw the South on foot. Dartmouth, Harvard two years. Shoe-worker, mill-hand, farm-hand, editor, reporter, insurance agent, agent for Shakespearean reader, reader myself, teacher in every kind of school public and private including psychological normal school and college. Prize for running at Caledonia Club picnic; prizes for assumed parts at masquerade balls; medal for goodness in high school; detur for scholarship at Harvard; money for verse. Knew Henry George well and saw much at one time (by way of contrast) of a noted boss ["Blind" Chris Buckley in San Francisco]. Presbyterian, Unitarian, Swedenborgian, Nothing. All the vices but disloyalty and chewing gum or tobacco.

I liked what you wrote about Robinson as well as he liked what you wrote about me. So he and I are quits there. I liked some of the things you put your finger on in the Masters paper. Not the least of your merits in handling us is your eye for the quotable in our work. You put the best front on all of us by your quotations. I know you must have surprised some prejudiced people with what you were able to find in good old Sandburg.　　　　　Always yours sincerely　Robert Frost

175 · To Harriet Moody

HARRIET MOODY, widow of the poet William Vaughn Moody, made her luxurious Chicago home a rendezvous for visiting poets. She first played hostess to RF there in March 1917 when Harriet Monroe arranged several readings for him in the Chicago area.

Dear Mrs Moody:　　　　　25 December 1917　Amherst

We get a sense from your pranks of your being all around us but at the same time invisible like a deus ex machina. (Do you know that I never noticed before that "the duce" by which we swear is no more than the deus with the "eu" pronounced as in Zeus?) We meet someone who has met someone who has but just now seen you and heard you speak right here in Amherst, we hear you speak ourselves out of the empty air, we are fed by you with candy in a tin box like a bolt from the blue, we get your promise in writing that if we are good and have faith our eyes shall some day (some day this winter) see a better land than this, namely Chicago —

"Where never wind blows loudly, but it lies etc."

You know the rest — all that boastful Sandburgian, or should I say burgundian "with beaded bubbles winking at the brim." I suspect he was paid to do it by the Consolidated Real Estate Agencies to boom Chicago farms. And that was why he was winking. And you can tell him I said so.

But it is hard to have faith in these days when you can actually hear it preached from the pulpit that if those who have only one talent don't know enough to bury it themselves a committee of eugenists should bury it for them, and I owe to a growing doubt whether you exist as a person at all, whether you may not never have been anything more than a principle of good or evil whose promises aren't worth the paper they are written on. Nevertheless I am, I Profess,

Yours as faith-full as circumstances permit

Professor F.

176 · To Régis Michaud

SOME INSCRIPTIONS written on flyleaves of first editions by RF amounted to letters, as for example the following inscription in a first edition of *North of Boston,* which he presented to Régis Michaud (1880-1939). The two men had met in Amherst, Massachusetts, while Michaud served as an Associate Professor of French at Smith College (1917-1919). A common ground of interest was Emerson; Michaud later published two book-length studies of Emerson.

[*c.* January 1918]   [Amherst]

Some twenty-two lines in "Monadnoc" beginning "Now in sordid weeds they sleep" (I dont need to copy them out for such an Emersonian as you, Michaud) meant almost more to me than anything else on the art of writing when I was a youngster; and that not just on the art of writing colloquial verse but on the art of writing any kind of verse or prose. I suffer from the way people abuse the word colloquial. All writing, I dont care how exalted, how lyrical, or how seemingly far removed from the dramatic, must be as colloquial as this passage from "Monadnoc" comes to. I am as sure that the colloquial is the root of every good poem as I am that the national is the root of all thought and art. It may shoot up as high as you please and flourish as widely abroad in the air, if only the roots are what and where they should be. One half of individuality is locality: and I was about venturing to say the other half was colloquiality. The beauty of the high thinking in Emerson's Uriel and Give All to Love is that it is well within the colloquial as I use the word. And so also is all the lyric in Palgrave's Treasury for that matter, no matter at what level of sentiment it is pitched. Consider Herrick's To Daffodils. But sometime more of this when we can sit down together.   Robert Frost

177 · To Josephine Preston Peabody Marks

Dear Mrs Marks: 15 April 1918   Amherst

May I accept your invitation now and wait till I get back from the West late next week to talk definitely about a day for the meeting of the [New England] Poetry Society? I do want to see the Poetry Society before I get much older and both of us, Elinor and I, want to see more of you soon than we were able to see when we were with you in the crowd at Padriac Colum's

to-do. I can't say that I think a great many new poets have occurred since last we met, but enough has happened in poetry
for some talk before we catch up with it.

I am dedicating the swag of my journey this time to
Liberty Bonds. Please remember that when you are tempted to
think ill of me and my works. Remember too that I never think
ill of you and your work, won't you?

Sincerely yours   Robert Frost

178 · To Louis Untermeyer

IN THE following letter RF strikes the posture of writing from, and
thus of parodying, Untermeyer's point of view (see "Introduction,"
pp. xv-xvi).

Date to suit   [6 June 1918]

Dear Robt [Franconia]

Sorry you found nothing in The Liberator you inordinately
liked but my attack on Masters. I can see how you must like
that for personal reasons; and as a matter of fact it was a
pretty piece of writing, especially the first part of it, which I
rather liked myself. But on the whole the merits of the magazine as an aphrodisiac were thrown away on you. To the pure
all things are poor.

I can just know how the very naughty love story of Philip
Dru [by Col. E. M. House] will put you off the main interest
of the book which is poetical and right in your line. Yes my dear
Robt you were disposed from that early San Francisco training
to a life of intrigue and machination. Love is a kickshaw and
dalliance naught, but give you a field like poetry that calls to
the pulling of wires and the manipulation of ropes, to the
climbing of every black reviewer's back stairs for preferment,
and you are there with a suit case in both hands "like an old
stone savage armed." (I know you don't mind my quoting from
your published works.) . . .

But whatever you make of Philip's relations with women
(and I have pretty well covered them in the foregoing) for
your own sake don't let them blind you to the beauty of such
poetry as that of Col. House's chapter on reforming our burial
practices. You can plainly hear the voice of Col. House saying
to his good friend the President after the war is over and the

captains and the kings are licked: And now, Woodrow, what do you say to our doing away with this awful habit of letting dead people down into a hole in the ground and throwing earth into their coffin lid when it would seem so much pleasanter to gather as friends and relatives and see them shoved into a fiery oven and cooked to ashes. Next after the social revolution (I am sorry it had to be so bloody — over a million killed wounded and missing — I can't help wondering where the missing went) next after the social revolution nothing is so dear to me as cremation. And I think chewing is a good thing too. Don't you think something could be done about that. Couldn't the noon hour of the laboring classes be lengthened say ten minutes with the express understanding that unless the actual time consumed in consumption — but I leave to you the formulation of the statute. I never thought when I was half the age I am now that I would ever have a chance to put a notion into practice just because I found I couldn't put it into words. And say, Woodrow, what's the matter with making a law that if anyone dreams a dream often enough to indicate that there's something he wants that he can't have and don't dare to ask for but if he submits his dream in writing to the department of Labor and Parturition and it be found that what he says is true and he really has the dream and often enough to be called habitual and nothing else will take the place of what is lacking in his life, such as more furniture or a different wife or a reputation as a novelist or a kind of food that will agree with him. Well then what do you say, Woodrow, if some other department that shall hereinafter be provided for and gotten up and authorized by Congress shall do everything in its power to make that man happy. Do you feel with me in these aspirations?"

Please legitimatize by signing on this line

————————

179 · To George F. Whicher

When RF made his first appearance at Amherst College in 1916, George F. Whicher had just recently been appointed an associate professor of English. He had previously been an instructor at the University of Illinois after taking his doctorate in English at Columbia University. As an undergraduate he had majored in classical literature. With his father, George Meason Whicher, he had published a volume of poems, largely translations from Latin,

On the Tibur Road (1911). Whicher very quickly became a devoted admirer of RF, and their friendship continued for nearly forty years. This is the first of at least twenty-eight letters written to Whicher by RF.

Dear Whicher:　　　　　　　　21 June 1918　Franconia

　　Two weeks' farming has made me think better of teaching than I did when I left it at Commencement in the first stages of asthma but the last of agoraphobia. When you come right down to it such ills of teaching as man's ingratitude and benefits forgot are as nothing compared with the freezing of one bitter sky in mid-June. Our thermometer dropped to 25 night before last and thirty last night losing us all our seed and a month's growth where months are more precious than they are in your region. That worst night the large farmers fought the cold with fire and water; the small farmers wrapped their gardens up in their own clothes and bed clothes and went without themselves. A lot of good it did. My favorite tomato froze right in my heavy winter overcoat. Our local Budd[h]ist blames it all on the eclipse in conjunction with the new star in Aquila. She was educated at the New Hampshire State Normal School (where I taught) and belongs to the Baptist Church, but she professes Budd[h]ism at the evening meetings, practices transmigration and derives the present more from the future than from the past. For this latitude she insists that cucumbers and watermelons shall be planted before sunrise on the Sunday before the first rain in June — if at all.

　　Oh yes, my novel. I want that to take rank with the epic I accounted for my time with to my friends in England. Just keep that in mind — that I am known to be at work on a novel and you will be a valuable witness to call when I am taken under the law to 'press loafers.

　　Write a lot. Enjoy the war. I've made up my mind to do the second anyway. I dont see why the fact that I can't be in a fight should keep me from liking the fight.

　　Our best to you all.　　　Always yours　Robert Frost

180 · To Amy Lowell

Dear Miss Lowell:　　　　　　November 1918　Amherst

　　(So to call you formally to your face, whatever liberties your greatness as a poet and as a friend may tempt us to take with you behind your back):

I didn't think that was the bad book you may have been lead to suppose from the length of time it has taken me to acknowledge it [*Can Grande's Castle*]. I thought it was a very splendid book both when I read it aloud and when I didn't read it aloud. I delight to see you plank it down to them so-fashion. It's the very next thing this precocious young republic is going to be able to live on. We come on. The war has helped, I'm sure, and besides one thing leads to another. Americans are something at last to go up against. We no longer have to think so much of coaxing 'em along into objective existence. We've got 'em where we can jab it to 'em stiff without fear of having them all to create over again. They can stand art. And by the ton you've given it to 'em!

After all which 'ems I might be excused for signing off Sincerely yours, Emmer, but I prefer to sign myself as of old and always   Your admiring friend   Robert Frost

And by the way when you feel that you can afford it wont you send me an autographed Dome of Many Colored Glass for completeness. Then if none of my boys here steals any of the books you have given me I shall be all right. . . .

180-a · ELINOR M. FROST TO WILBUR L. CROSS

My dear Mr. Cross,-   13 December 1918   Amherst

Here is the essay [by George F. Whicher] which Mr. Frost promised you. He would write to you himself about it, but he is just beginning to regain strength after a very severe attack of influenza.

He wants me to say to you that he has hoped to have a poem of his own to send with it, but certain lines in the poem are unsatisfactory and seem to him likely to remain so. But as he is greatly pleased with this essay, he hopes you will print it now, and not let his friend's [Edward Thomas] memory suffer for want of the poem. This is the time for people to see it, while there is still some interest in Thomas' little volume of poems, and while there is so much interest in soldier poets in general.

Mr. Frost wants me to say, also, that now that the war is over, he will soon be writing poetry for you again.

I hope you will like the essay as much as I myself do. I think it has something of Thomas' own exquisiteness.

We are both charmed with the little book you sent, and thank you for it.

Mr. Frost has not been at all well, this fall. He has been sick in bed twice, and this time has been very ill indeed. We are planning to go South in February for the spring months, and are hoping to see poetry begin again.

Faithfully yours   Elinor M. Frost

181 · TO MARGUERITE WILKINSON

Dear Mrs Wilkinson: 19 February 1919   Amherst

My serious fault not to have written you sooner. I meant the best. Lesley was to have found you with a message from me long ago and we ourselves were to have been in New York where we expected to see you before this.

I am glad you decided for An Old Man's Winter Night and The Gum Gatherer. I didnt want to be the one to direct you to the Gum Gatherer; but it is a favorite of mine if for no other reason than because it is the only poem I know of that has found a way to speak poetically of chewing gum. The Code can very well be passed by for once. It has been reprinted rather more than its share.

Will you see to it for me that the word "fill" is changed to "keep" in the line "One aged man — one man — can't etc." I dont know how it ever got printed "fill." I only noticed it lately. I think I must always have read it aloud "keep." That's the way I first wrote it.

I gather from what you let fall in your letters that you have found a fresh way to make a book about poetry. It [*New Voices*] sounds to me as if it is bound to do well. I shall look forward to seeing it.

I wanted Lesley to meet you. If you have time for youngsters, won't you ask her round some afternoon? She is at Fernald Hall, Barnard College. She will tell you of my adventures with my wicked English publisher who has never paid me a cent for my books or even rendered an account. Us sufferin' authors! With greetings to Mr Wilkinson,

Always yours friendly   Robert Frost

182 · To Harriet Moody

Dear Mrs. Moody   19 March 1919   Amherst

(Still to keep to a mode of address that no one else of equal pretensions to your friendship seems to use):

Though I'm not as well as I ought to be and there are other obstacles in the way of our getting to Chicago to see you this spring, I am resolved to try to make it if only for a very short visit. You'll have to squeeze both the lectures into the one week, April 14-19 and leave me Tuesday the 15th free for a little talk I may do for some of the free verse gentry.

We'll talk over the summer school plans when I get there. It may be I had rather put off the summer school till a year from now. I could keep it (if it would keep) for some thing ahead to prolong life a moment if I should burst my bonds here as teacher and run wild again. I strain at those bonds all the time and of course they only cut deeper the more I strain. It might be a good thing if you mustered against our coming your religion such as it is to help me endure what I ought to endure for my sins and my family. You can tell me your idea of duty and I'll counter with why I think nobody that talks round poetry all the time or likes to hear talk round poetry can ever write poetry or ever properly read it for that matter. I suppose simply that it is the nature of God to have it so. It is not that generalizations from poetry are so wholly bad if they make themselves as it were spontaneously and after the fact. God has only made them fatal when they are used school fashion as the approach to poetry. The general notion having been laid down by the professor it then becomes possible to enjoy the particular poem as an illustration of it or as a case under it and as nothing else.

But don't mistake my getting mad about it in your presence for getting mad at you. You may be as much to blame as you please for this or anything else it will make no difference to me: I shall remain   Always your devoted friend

                                                Robert Frost

183 · To Lila Cabot Perry

Dear Mrs. Perry,   3 April 1919   Franconia

So I'm to be President of the [New England] Poetry Society because I wasn't at your last meeting to say I wouldn't be

President, just as I seem to be expected at Wellesley on the eleventh for the simple reason that I haven't said I wouldn't be there on the eleventh. Neither have I said that I wouldn't be there on the twelfth or the thirteenth or the fourteenth or any other day you have a mind to name. . . . I must protest at this reverse way of being taken. Must I be assumed guilty till I am proved innocent but more than that must I be assumed guilty of every particular deed and thought that I haven't specifically declared myself innocent of? (As for instance Maria Halpin's baby.)

But seriously now do you think it was friendly of you all to make me an official when you must have seen how superstitious I am about holding office. I thought I saw a way out of it for us both in not accepting the Presidency you had imposed on me. I thought by silence I could sort of keep from myself what I was in for and in fact privately take the view that I was not a President while at the same time leaving you free to think that I *was* a President. Ingenious you see — and significant: it shows how anxious I am to please you as friends and fellow poets if not as member of any society. But it wouldn't do: you had to spoil it all and make the issue acute between us by proposing to lunch me formally on my job just as you would launch a ship. I may be nervous but I can't help seeing in it a conspiracy to shear me of any wild strength I may have left after two years of teaching in college. As Vachel would say "Let Samson be comin' into your mind."

With protestations of the warmest regard etc.

Robert Frost*

184 · To Harriet Moody

HARRIET MOODY, generous friend of poets, spent most of her time in Chicago. But she also maintained an apartment at 107 Waverly Place in New York City, which she shared with various friends, including Mr. and Mrs. Ridgely Torrence. That arrangement led to the meeting and subsequent friendship between RF and Torrence.

* The following note was appended by RF: "Louis, I wanted you to have a picture of me struggling to climb out of what I have got into out onto the thin ice around me. The letter is a copy of one I am sending to Mrs. Perry . . . Bids fair to rival the famous case of [George Sylvester] Vierick versus the Poetry Society of America only mine illustrates the difficulty of staying out while his illustrates the difficulty of staying in. RF."

Writing to Miss Moody from the Waverly Place address on 4 March 1919, Torrence described his first important meeting with RF as follows:

"Robert Frost came here to dinner last night. He called us up on Sunday and asked whether you were here and he was so disappointed to hear how narrowly he had missed you. He is certainly one of your most loyal appreciators. He agreed to come to dinner yesterday evening and we had a grand evening. We invited the Colums but Molly had just been discharged from the hospital and they couldn't come to dinner. Padraic came later in the evening and added to the general liveliness. We had never had a real heart to heart with Frost before and we were quite carried away by him. He is surely one of the finest things that this country has produced. He is a man, a noble character in addition to being a noble poet. . . ."

RF makes reference to that evening, in the following letter, which is primarily devoted to scolding Harriet Moody for liking British poets too much.

Dear Harriet Moody: 21 April 1919   Franconia

You know I wear your collar (or rather collars: there are two or three of them and they are not worn out yet) and you can do what you please with me. But of course you wouldn't do such a thing as this comes to. Enter distinguished Englishman, exit extinguished American. Padraic may think my sympathy with his Ireland is just Blarney I give him. It's not that I love Ireland more for loving England less and less. But I do love a country that loves itself. I love a country that insists on its own nationality which is the same thing as a person's insisting on his own personality. Isn't an idea any better for its being my own out of my own life and experience? Isn't it? Isn't a literature any more to us for being our own? It is, whether you think so or not. No danger about or not insisting on our own nationality in business and diplomacy. But that is only on the material plane. My concern is that some day we shall go in to back ourselves on the intellectual and spiritual plane. Won't we seem poor stuff the way we whoop it up for anything imported in the arts? Other things being unequal, the visitor having all the advantage in other things, I should still make him feel if I were an American that, just because he was imported, he couldn't expect any more adulation than our own home-grown poet. But of course I'm not an American. Let's go back on America together.

Wretched that we should be away off up here when you are to be in Cummington. When do we meet again?

I had the good evening at your house in New York with the great-faced noble Ridgely.

Always faithfully yours   Robert

185 · To MARGUERITE WILKINSON

My dear Mrs. Wilkinson: 21 April 1919   Franconia

I didn't telegraph because I saw nothing to object to in what you said about my processes. As nearly as I can tell that's the way I work. I meant to make no particular merit of it however. I worked for twenty years as I had to by force of circumstances and I work now as I have to from force of habit formed then. I have never been good at revising. I always thought I made things worse by recasting and retouching. I never knew what was meant by choice of words. It was one word or none. When I saw more than one possible way of saying a thing I knew I was fumbling and turned from writing. If I ever fussed a poem into shape I hated and distrusted it afterward. The great and pleasant memories are of poems that were single strokes (one stroke to the poem) carried through. I won't say I haven't learned with the years something of the tinker's art. I'm surprised to find sometimes how I have just missed the word. It wasn't that I was groping for my meaning. I had that clear enough and I had thought I had said the word for it. But I hadn't said within a row of apple trees of it. That's the way it was I suppose with that word "fill" in the Winter Night poem. I had the perfectest conviction of having said "keep" there and I believe I had read it aloud as "keep" for some time before I saw that I had written "fill." "Fill" is awful!

I sometimes I often live to dislike a poem I have dashed off like lightning out of a clear sky, but first or last I never like a poem I have written any other way. I make them in haste and repent of them at leisure. I dont know that I would have taken the leisure I took if the editors and such hadn't forced it on me. They took care that I should take time to judge my own work. Not that I like to judge it or that I have attained to security in my judgments. I'm still fearfully afraid of committing anything to print — just as you seem to be. A book on publication day is what Sherman said war was. But don't you worry. Your book will be all right. It sounds to me like a good sort of thing to do and I'm absolutely sure we shall enjoy reading it.

Lesley has enjoyed knowing you. We appreciate your kindness to her.   Faithfully yours   Robert Frost

186 · To ALFRED HARCOURT

WHEN Alfred Harcourt left Henry Holt and Company to establish the firm which is now Harcourt, Brace and World he invited several of his friends, including RF, to join the new house. As this letter indicates, RF was willing to accept the invitation. Later, after he learned that Holt refused to release copyrights on his first three books, he decided to remain with Holt.

Dear Alfred: 21 May 1919   Franconia
     There is only one answer possible to your question. I am under obligations to Henry Holt & Co for endless favors. But so far as I am concerned you are Henry Holt & Co. You are all the Henry Holt & Co I have known and dealt with. Where you go I naturally go. I am with you with all my heart. I promise to do all I can to make you a great publisher even as I expect you to do all you can to make me a great author.
                         Always yours   Robert Frost

187 · To WILBUR E. ROWELL

Dear Mr. Rowell: 6 June 1919   Franconia
     I turn to you for help about the enclosed letter [concerning a bill unpaid by his sister]. You will know where Jean is to send it to her if you should decide she ought to act on it. She has instructed me to pay no attention to the writer. But I'm not so sure she can afford to ignore him. I should think he might have means of getting even with her that she hasnt taken into account, such as writing further innocent letters of inquiry to other people. He could easily make her pretty public with the teachers' agencies and school journals.
     It is only right to tell you that Jean may not thank you for your good offices in this matter — and then again she may. I know that she never thanks me for mine in any matter. I give her outright about a hundred dollars a year which she doesn't show any gratitude for because she loftily chooses to regard it as a loan. She is too difficult a person for me. You will know better than I what you can do with or for her.
     I don't know just why she is keeping out of this man's

way unless it is because she is afraid if he finds her he will put the Mill River people on her track. She thinks the Mill Riverites chased her out of town for talking pro-Germanism Bolshevism and internationalism and are still after her to make her salute the American flag. She had a wild time in Mill River, and apparently narrowly escaped violence. No need to go into this with her. I simply tell you so that you may know what there is to go on. You may decide from the premises not to stir her up at all, but to deal with the agency man yourself so as to shield her. The right word from you to him might make it all right till she should have time to earn in peace what she owes him.

Sincerely yours   Robert Frost

188 · To HALLEY PHILLIPS GILCHRIST

MRS. HALLEY GILCHRIST wrote from Arlington, as Vice-president of the Poetry Society of Southern Vermont formally inviting RF to read his poems before the Society early in September of 1919. After a satisfactory date was determined, the Frosts made the visit together, and thus explored for the first time the region which soon attracted them away from New Hampshire. Mrs. Gilchrist had gone to school with Sarah Cleghorn and was intimately acquainted with Dorothy Canfield Fisher. The Frosts purchased the "Peleg Cole place" in South Shaftsbury in July 1920. While they were waiting for renovations to be completed, they lived in Arlington at "the Brick House" owned by Dorothy Canfield Fisher.

Dear Mrs Gilchrist: 29 August [1919] Franconia

I had some idea I would be in friendly country in Arlington. I knew Mrs Fisher and Miss Cleghorn were there and I hoped I might find the Harcourts still there if I came soon enough. But for reasons of health late enough is more important to me than soon enough. I am much more certain to be in reading condition in Arlington on September 13th than on September 6th. By the middle of the month the hay-fever season will be waning and I can begin to think of going almost anywhere with comparative safety. You mustn't take it as any reflection on your Green Mts if as the greatest living authority on where hay-fever is or isn't to be had, I have to tell you there is no refuge in Vermont from it till you come to Stowe and Danville any more than there is in New Hampshire till you come through the Crawford and Franconia Notches.

But as I say the poison flood will be ebbing from the air by the 12th or 13th of the month; it will be fun to let you carry us off on trial; and then if we find breathing good, like Noah's dove we can simply not come back to Franconia but go on to Amherst.

We shall look forward to the ride across states and to seeing you all at Arlington — even a little to reading to you, though I'm not the minstrel I sometimes wish I were and don't pretend to give or experience the pleasure Vachel Lindsay does in public performance.

Glad to hear that the New England hired man persists with you. It was my purpose to immortalize him in death.

Sincerely yours   Robert Frost

188-a · Jeanie Florence Frost to Wilbur E. Rowell

16 September 1919
Dear Mr. Rowell,-   Rockland, Maine

I do not know whether I am going to be able to hold a principalship in any high school in a small town there is such a rough element among some students almost grown men. I was practically unable to hold the school I just took and resigned. The assistant teacher encouraged insubordination among the older boys and made fun of me to my pupils. Otherwise, I might have done better. Finally I suspended a senior ruffian, who then pretended he had walked out and wouldn't return.

The superintendent then, one evening, stepped up to me, *after dark,* (declining to come into the house) as I was going in where I boarded — and began to talk in a discouraging way, making some indirect statements, such as that pupils were leaving the school. Two boys left the first day, and went to another town, because the other boys called them "bears" and "growled" at them, ridiculing them as coming from the backwoods. The superintendent now pretended that these boys left on my account.

I probably could have managed the school had it not been for the assistant teacher, a sister-in-law of the post-master. She made the life of the last teacher none too happy. I had a very pleasant boarding-place with kind people, with a Mrs. Allen who says that on account of the trouble made me she would not board the next teacher. Before I realized how things were going, a son of Mrs. Allen's said "Evelyn, she's a dog." Evelyn was the assistant teacher. But she had a tongue, and a little influence. [. . .]

I am going to look for a rural school until I receive an offer in a graded school, or a position as assistant in a high school, where a man is in charge of the school. But, I have very little money and am staying in Rockland. I am afraid you will be entirely discouraged when I ask you if you can advance me the $33 for next month. I shall take *any sort* of a school within a very short time. . . .   Very truly,   Jeanie Frost

189 · To Frederic G. Melcher

BEFORE he began his long and influential career as co-editor of *Publishers' Weekly,* Frederic G. Melcher had been a bookseller in Indianapolis. A New Englander by birth, he had conducted a wide and successful one-man campaign to stimulate the sale of RF's first two books. The following letter deals with Melcher's first arrangement to have RF talk and read in Montclair, New Jersey, and marks the beginning of their acquaintance. In later years Melcher assisted RF's daughters, Lesley and Marjorie, in various biblipolic activities, including their bookstore in Pittsfield, Massachusetts.

Dear Mr Melcher: 22 September 1919   Amherst
The extenuating circumstances are that I have been all round everywhere lately and not getting my mail most of the time and not attending to it when I get it. And then I'm just a plain bad lot lazy and unbusinesslike. I don't defend myself. I ought not to have made it necessary for you to write me three letters.

To come immediately to what time presses me to tell you — we can leave swapping New Hampshire memories till we sit down together in your New Jersey home: What should you say to some night *early* in December. Will you name one?

I shall intend to read to your audience and perhaps talk to them a little on Vocal Reality.

You will forgive me I hope for such of my sins as are against you.   Sincerely yours,   Robert Frost

241

190 · To Katharine Lee Bates

Dear Miss Bates: 8 October 1919   Amherst

October 31 [at Wellesley College] couldn't be bettered for me.

It seems a long time since last we encountered — was it in the Mt Holyoke poetry contest (as judges)? Do you get excited about all the nonsense that is being said about free rhythms? Free rhythms are as disorderly as nature; meters are as orderly as human nature and take their rise in rhythms just as human nature rises out of nature. I wonder if you dont get impatient with some people who give their sentiment divine against the being of a line between prose and verse. I shall want to hear what you have to say.

Sincerely yours   Robert Frost

191 · To Robert Stanley Breed

EARLIER LETTERS have indicated RF's difficulties with the regime of President Alexander Meiklejohn (1912-1924) at Amherst College. This letter, written to an influential Amherst alumnus and announcing RF's resignation from the Amherst faculty, was quoted in full by Walter Lippmann in "The Fall of President Meiklejohn," which appeared on the first page of the editorial section of the New York *World* for 24 June 1923. It was quoted there as evidence of the conservative spirit at Amherst, which very strongly resisted Meiklejohn's experimental liberalism.

Dear Mr. Breed: 2 February 1920   Amherst

I am forced after all to give up the idea of speaking at the Amherst dinner, and I owe you something more than a telegram in explanation. I have decided to leave teaching and go back to farming and writing. Strangely enough, I was helped to this decision by your invitation. It was in turning over in my mind my subject chosen for the dinner that I came to the conclusion that I was too much out of sympathy with what the present administration seems bent on doing with this old New England college. I suppose I might say that I am too much outraged in the historical sense for loyalty. I can't complain that I haven't enjoyed the "academic freedom" to be entirely myself under Mr. Meiklejohn. While he detests my dangerous rationalistic and anti-intellectualistic philosophy, he thinks he is willing to have it represented here. But probably it will be better represented by someone else who can take it less seriously than I.

There are regrets that I mustn't go into here. The main thing is that I am out of Amherst and it won't be fitting that I should speak for Amherst at the dinner.

Believe me deeply sensible of the friendly treatment I have had from Amherst men and

Most sincerely yours   Robert Frost

192 · To G. R. Elliott

THE LONG and extremely close friendships between members of the Frost and Elliott families had its beginning when G. R. Elliott published an essay entitled "The Neighborliness of Robert Frost" in *The Nation* for 6 December 1919. In RF's first letter to Elliott, which follows, a slight contrast is made between this article and an essay published by Ford Madox Hueffer: "Literary Portraits: Mr. Robert Frost and *North of Boston*," in *The Outlook* (London), 27 June 1914. It would seem that Elliott must have written first to express some twinge of conscience he had about his essay, and that RF begins by reassuring him.

Dear Mr Elliott: 20 March 1920   Franconia

Worse conscience than you need have had! I wasn't liking you because you had liked everything I had written but because you seemed to have read nearly everything I had written. More than anyone else you made your case out of chapter and verse. I had begun to be afraid certain things that had been said about me in the first place (and in praise, mind you) by people who had hardly taken the trouble to read me would have to go on being said forever. You broke the spell. You took a fresh look, and the fun of it is your report, based so evidently on your own observation uninfluenced by anything Ford Hueffer set going, confirms me in some of my better suspicions of myself.

Moreover I think it cant be presuming too much on your criticism to conclude from it that we are more or less sympathetic in our view of things; in other words if in these bad days I propped your mind so also you might be expected to prop mine.

I have asked my daughter at Barnard to send you a copy of one of my less amiable poems in character called Place for a Third. I'm sending herewith several shorter ones I like better

243

myself. The time draws near publishing again. I shall let a few out into the magazines this year and next year book a good many. These enclosed need not be returned. Carol (one of my children) has made the copies for you.

Always yours sincerely   Robert Frost

193 · To Louis Untermeyer

THIS LETTER suggests a conflict in the marriage of RF and Elinor Miriam Frost: the sharp contrast between their religious views. RF regarded his wife's atheistical denials in a defensively light and jocose manner; but they troubled him deeply. He had heard her make such denials repeatedly, starting soon after the death of their first child on 8 July 1900. (See hints in "Home Burial.") In later years, as she experienced other painful losses, she became more skeptical, more intensively bitter.

For a brief time around 1900, RF was inclined to similar notions; the poem "Stars" (published in *A Boy's Will* with the gloss, "There is no oversight of human affairs") was written that year. But he did not maintain that attitude long. Even while his recurrent moods of skepticism and denial gave picturesque colorings to his heretical beliefs, he came to express profound religious affirmations with more and more frequency. A good attempt at stating his peculiar religious position was made in the "Meditation" by the Rt. Rev. Henry Wise Hobson at the Memorial Service for RF, held at Amherst College on 17 February 1963. The "Meditation" was published soon thereafter, in folder form, by Amherst College.

Dear Louis: 21 March 1920   Franconia

[. . .] Elinor has just come out flat-footed against God conceived either as the fourth person seen with Shadrack, Meshack, and Tobedwego in the fiery furnace or without help by the Virgin Mary. How about as a Shelleyan principal or spirit coeternal with the rock part of creation, I ask. Nonsense and you know it's nonsense Rob Frost, only you're afraid you'll have bad luck or lose your standing in the community if you speak your mind. Spring, I say, returneth and the maple sap is heard dripping in the buckets — (allow me to sell you a couple. We can quote you the best white first-run sugar at a dollar a pound unsight and unseen — futures.) Like a woman she says Pshaw. You know how a woman says Pshaw — you with your uncanny knowledge of your own wife. I took out an accident policy limited to death by boiling in a sap pan, swore off on baths, and took up my new life as a farmer today by absent-mindedly boring a hole clear through a two foot maple tree and out onto the other side. "Amatoor!" all the leaves began to murmur. "Book-farmer!" Leaves is of course an anachronism — that well known figure of speech. There weren't any leaves as yet. [. . .]   R. F.

193-a · Wilbur E. Rowell to Robert Frost

Dear Mr. Frost: 29 March 1920   Lawrence

Last Thursday morning the Police Department of Portland, Maine, telephoned to me saying that they had Jeanie Frost in confinement and that she was demented. They wanted me to come there and take her off their hands. This I declined to do. I have neither the authority nor the means to take care of her.

She has been in various places during the fall and winter. When I last heard from her she was in North Yarmouth, Maine. She, with her friend, Miss Merriam, were in Lowell and Haverhill during the winter. They were both ill in Haverhill with influenza but apparently they were not so badly off so that they managed to take care of themselves. I have paid her during the year $300 so that there is little less than nothing available for her now.

I wonder what we ought to do and what we can do for her welfare. If she is really insane and it is necessary for her to be confined in some institution it might be important to know whether she has, anywhere, a legal settlement. Was she born in Lawrence, and were her father and mother residents of Lawrence? I wonder if she has lived long enough in any one place of late to gain a settlement. In most places it takes a fairly long term of residence; I believe it is five years in Massachusetts. . . .   Sincerely yours,   Wilbur E. Rowell

194 · To Wilbur E. Rowell

Dear Mr Rowell: 31 March 1920   Franconia

This is no worse than I have been expecting. The last time we saw Jean she came to us at Amherst a fugitive from a mob that was going to throw her into a mill-pond for refusing to kiss the flag. The war was just ending and she was actually in tears for the abdicated Emperor. Nothing she said or did was natural. I should have had her examined by an alienist then if I had known how to manage it without disturbing her. Looking back I can see that she hasn't been right for years. She has always simply dismayed the children with her wild talk.

As you say the question is What can we do for her. I am made bold by your use of the word "we" to ask if I can come to you for advice before I go to encounter the authorities at Portland. It's a kind word and I appreciate it. It means more trouble for you where you have already had so much.

Jean was born in Lawrence in 1877 [1876] but was never settled to live there except for the ten years from 1890 to 1900. Her mother was settled there from 1890 to 1900. Her father grew up and came of age there, but spent the last years of his life in San Francisco — 1874 [1873] to 1885 to be exact. Might she possibly have a claim on New Hampshire through me? I have had a residence in New Hampshire for twenty years.

If no state will have her and I haven't the means to have her taken care of in a private institution, what happens then? I am too shaken at the moment to know what to propose. It may not be an incurable case. My hope is that what has been pronounced insanity may turn out no more than the strange mixture of hysteria and eccentricity she has shown us so much of. If so, she might be perfectly manageable at large in the company of somebody like Louie Merriam. But I should want them to come to rest somewhere and should feel obliged to contribute a little to make it possible for them to. I wish I knew where to find Louie Merriam.

We are just back from Amherst and in here where letters seem forever in reaching us. Will you wire at my expense if you wish to see me to instruct me as to how I shall approach the Portland police without assuming more responsibility than I am equal to? I may say that there isn't the haste that there would be if my personal attendance could do anything to soothe or comfort Jean. It's a sad business.

Sincerely yours   Robert Frost

195 · To Louis Untermeyer

Dear Louis: 12 April 1920 Franconia

I must have told you I have a sister Jeanie two or three years younger than myself. This is about her. It is not a story to tell everybody; but I want you to hear it if only so that you will understand why I am not as gay as I have been in my recent letters.

The police picked her up in Portland Maine the other day insane as nearly as we can make out on the subject of the war. She took the police for German officers carrying her off for immoral use. She took me for someone else when she saw me. She shouted to me by name to save her from whoever she thought I was in person.

I was prepared for this by what I saw of her a year ago (a year and a half ago) when she came to us at Amherst, a fugitive from a mob in a small town fifty miles away who were going to throw her into a mill pond for refusing to kiss the flag. She got Hell out of the war. She turned everything she could think of to express her abhorrence of it: pro-German, pacifist, internationalist, draft-obstructor, and seditionist.

She has always been antiphysical and a sensibilitist. I must say she was pretty well broken by the coarseness and brutality of the world before the war was thought of. This was partly because she thought she ought to be on principle. She has had very little use for me. I am coarse for having had children and coarse for having wanted to succeed a little. She made a birth in the family the occasion for writing us once of the indelicacy of having children. Indelicacy was the word. Long ago I disqualified myself from helping her through a rough world by my obvious liking for the world's roughness.

But it took the war to put her beside herself, poor girl. Before that came to show her what coarseness and brutality really were, she had been satisfied to take it out in hysterics, though hysterics as time went on of a more and more violent kind. I really think she thought in her heart that nothing would do justice to the war but going insane over it. She was willing to go almost too far to show her feeling about it, the more so that she couldn't find anyone who would go far enough. One half the world seemed unendurably bad and the other half unendurably indifferent. She included me in the unendurably indifferent. A mistake. I belong to the unendurably bad.

And I suppose I am a brute in that my nature refuses to carry sympathy to the point of going crazy just because someone else goes crazy, or of dying just because someone else dies. As I get older I find it easier to lie awake nights over other people's troubles. But that's as far as I go to date. In good time I will join them in death to show our common humanity.*

Always yours   Robert Frost

196 · To G. R. Elliott

My dear Elliott: 27 April 1920   Franconia

I wonder if you have had the poems I sent you long enough to have come round to my way of thinking, that Good-bye and Keep Cold is probably the best of the lot. . . . I sent you three, and the one in blank verse, Place for a Third, made four. Your sepulchral silence on this last is not I hope to be taken as too adverse. You got a copy of an early draught with some roughness on it I had as soon you hadn't seen. I want to crowd it out of your mind with the better version I am enclosing, and then hear what you have to say some time.

I return to the magazines with a group in Harpers in July: Fragmentary Blue, Place for a Third, Good-bye and Keep Cold and For Once Then Something. It is so long since I printed anything I feel as if I were about to begin all over again. For Once Then Something [hendecasyllabics] is calculated to tease the metrists, Fragmentary Blue my personal friends who want to stop my writing lyrics. So be prepared. Perhaps I may as well send you copies of them, if you'll believe that it isnt more than ten times in a life time that I come at any one with manuscript that way. Try not to feel overwhelmed.

Mind you I dont insist on my lyrics — I dont insist on anything I write except as continuing to write it may be regarded as a gentle form of insistance. I find I dont get over liking the few lyrics I ever really liked in my first book. To the Thawing Wind, Reluctance, Mowing, October, My November Guest, Going for Water and one or two others I can't stop to look up the names of. The one I called Storm Fear is interesting as it shades off into the nearly lyrical that you allow me in.

But let's not take trouble to agree on me in particulars.

* See a later expression of these attitudes in RF's poem entitled "The Good Relief."

My chief object in writing this is to say I am to be in Augusta [Maine] Saturday and may call you [at Brunswick] by telephone from there to see if we couldn't meet in Portland somewhere Saturday night. I shall be on my way to Boston for an evening with Copeland's boys Monday.

Sincerely yours   Robert Frost

197 · To Louis Untermeyer

Dear Louis: 14 May 1920   Franc Again

[. . .] I am just back from as far south as New Milford [Conn.] where I had a good talk with Lesley and had half a mind to summon you as per your promise of a recent letter. If I am that far down again next week land-looking as before would it be too much to call you to look at the property I am thinking of buying? Anyway hold yourself ready to be talked to on the telephone. Take a lozenge to clear your throat.

I have three or four houses on the possible list — one at Monson Mass, one at West Springfield Mass, one at Winsted Conn, and one at New Milford. The call of three is pretty much.

I got horribly kicked round for me as I rode. The agents, taking me for I don't know what, descended on me with loud lies to pick my bones. Little they suspected that it was the other way about and I was gluttonously picking theirs for literary purposes. I have an old poem on a real estate agent that only wants a little more material to finish it and make it marketable. I'm not sure that they haven't supplied it.

[. . .] But I'll whisper you something that by and by I mean to say above a whisper: I have about decided to throw off the light mask I wear in public when Amy is the theme of conversation. I don't believe she is anything but a fake, and I refuse longer to let her wealth, social position, and the influence she has been able to purchase and cozen, keep me from honestly bawling her out — that is, when I am called on to speak! I shan't go out of my way to deal with her yet awhile, though before all is done I shouldn't wonder if I tried my hand at exposing her for a fool as well as fraud. Think of saying that as the French have based their free verse on Alexandrines so she has based her polyphonic prose on the rhythms of the periodic sentence of oratory. She couldn't get away with that if she

249

hadn't us all corralled by her wealth and social position. What could "periodic" have to do with it. Periodic sentences have no particular rhythm. Periodic sentences are sentences in which the interest is suspended as in a plot story. Nonsense and charlatanry — that's all that kind of talk amounts to. I'm sure she guessed without looking it up that there must be something recurrent like beat or pulse implied in periodic. She knew ladies were periodic because they recurred monthly. She's loony — and so periodic by the moon herself. Feeling as I do you don't think it would be honester for me to refuse to be bound between the covers of the same book with her, do you?

I wish you could see the mts. now. Lafayette wears one great white mountain birch laid out giantesque in the ravine system on its side like a badge of the north country. I don't know that that is any inducement to you to come up.

Ever yours   Robert Fross

Please let me know to oncet if nearly all this meets with your approval.

198 · To Wilbur L. Cross

Dear Mr Cross: 15 May 1920   Franconia

I should have answered your letter sooner, but I have been busy retiring from education. I discovered what the Amherst Idea was that is so much talked of, and I got amicably out. The Amherst Idea as I had it in so many words from the high custodian is this: "Freedom for taste and intellect." Freedom from what? "Freedom from every prejudice in favor of state home church morality, etc." I am too much a creature of prejudice to stay at listen to such stuff. Not only in favor of morality am I prejudiced, but in favor of an immorality I could name as against other immoralities. I'd no more set out in pursuit of the truth than I would in pursuit of a living unless mounted on my prejudices. There was all the excuse I needed to get back to my farming. [William Ernest] Hocking says if I probed any college to its inmost idea I couldn't teach in it. But by any college Hocking means simply Harvard. The trouble with Hocking is he belongs at Yale where he formed himself in the plastic age. He will never be happy anywhere else. Neither will Mrs. Hocking.

But why these confidences in a letter to one who has never shown the least curiosity in my hearing about Amherst? What I set out to tell you was that, having kicked myself free from care and intellectuality, I ought to find time to polish you off the group of poems I had in mind to offer you — perhaps A Star in a Stone-boat and two or three short poems. Do you think you could stand an unrelated group such as Harpers is about to publish? My plan would be to return to print hurling fistfulls right and left. You may not be willing to fall in with anything so theatrical. I wonder if I know you well enough to ask you to let me wait till some number when the poverty of your material would thrust me automatically into the place of prominence in your make-up. Of course there might never be such a number. I could wait a year to see; and then if there wasn't — You let me know some time when you are not too well off for poetry or prose. No hurry.

Always yours   Robert Frost

199 · To Harriet Moody

My dear Harriet Moody,   6 June 1920   Franconia

I never forget old friends: so you needn't be so reproach-fully silent about it. What keeps me from writing to them is that I forget their street numbers. Why don't you live decently in a small town where you don't need a street number to be found? It goes against me to have to write a letter as I write this without knowing where it's going to and what's to become of it. I only do it to be able to say I have done my duty.

I wonder if you are wondering off there what I have de-cided about the farm at West Cummington. How shall I decide about anything at my age? I *have* kicked myself out of Amherst with some finality. But perhaps you haven't heard what I have been doing. For the moment I have ceased from teaching for-ever or until I shall begin to grow hungry again for food. Manly has asked if I will give a course in prosody some time at [University of] Chicago. That would be, not next year, but the year after, as I understand it, by which time I ought to begin to grow hungry again for food (as distinguished from truth). So I shall probably take him up, though as yet I haven't given him his answer any more than I have you yours about the farm.

To be right the farm at West Cummington would have to give us a summer and winter house of not less than nine rooms and a high school within two miles. I'm afraid it can't be made out or made to do either. And it seems a pity. I'm particularly sorry because I don't see but that it makes it necessary for you to sell there and buy a sugar orchard farm somewhere in New Hampshire or Vermont with us where we can all go into the fancy sugar business.

If this seems to offend against friendship, please remember that I should probably see more of you in one term of lecturing at Chicago than in a cycle of farming at West Cummington. Really now shouldn't I?

And if you are still unplaced, here are a few poems in manuscript enclosed to make a bad matter worse.

Are you coming this way this summer?

Always yours faithfully   Robert Frost

VI

SOUTH SHAFTSBURY, MICHIGAN, AND AMHERST · 1920-1926

"I'VE BEEN SICK, joking aside," Frost had written to Louis Untermeyer on 11 October while still in the process of moving. "The trouble seems to be that I wasn't taken up carefully enough in Franconia nor replanted soon enough in South Shaftsbury." The illness did not last long and the poet soon took root and began to grow vigorously. The most important effect was a period of sustained writing.

During the four years from 1920 through 1923, Frost published thirty-seven poems in periodicals. He collected most of them as "notes and grace-notes" in *New Hampshire,* named after the long and relaxed blank-verse title poem which ended with the now familiar irony, ". . . And restful just to think about New Hampshire. At present I am living in Vermont." That fourth volume sharpened the particularly Frostian combination of playfulness and sadness — it also earned him his first Pulitzer Prize.

But the stimulus of life in Vermont was expressed in several other ways. It led him to join forces with the already established Bread Loaf School of English, that was later complemented by the Bread Loaf Writers' Conference, two projects which interested and involved Frost for the rest of his life. And it led him outside New England to parts of the United States he had never seen before.

When he accepted an invitation in the early summer of 1921 to spend several months of each year at the University of Michigan, first as "Poet in Residence" and then as "Fellow in Creative Arts," he moved into this appointment with great vigor. He helped the students to engage very popular poets — including Amy Lowell, Vachel Lindsay, Carl Sandburg, Witter Bynner, and Louis Untermeyer — to come to Ann Arbor and give public readings. Frost also organized discussion groups, created workshops for students interested in writing, and helped with the undergraduate literary magazine, *Whimsies,* later *The Outlander.*

In that same period he ventured even farther afield. Having previously resisted many attempts by Texans to lure him to their state, to give the "bluebonnets" a chance to see and hear him, the new representative of New England finally agreed to make the long journey by train. During November of 1922 he gave fourteen readings in fourteen days, most of them in Texas, with prologue and epilogue in Louisiana and Missouri.

But nothing could keep him too long from New England, and the tug of war over him that was carried on in the period 1920-1926 by Amherst and Michigan was finally resolved by the poet in favor of Amherst, so that he could be near South Shaftsbury, where his son, Carol, who had married in 1923, was developing a real farm with interest and enthusiasm.

There were additional reasons for his retreat from Michigan to New England. Beset by worries over the increasing illnesses afflicting his wife, his children, and himself, he had become especially anxious over the puzzling physical condition of his youngest daughter, Marjorie. Both her parents realized that Marjorie's nervous symptoms constituted danger signs. Frost even feared that his sister's insanity foreshadowed a fate which might overtake other members of his family. His decision to return to Amherst would, he hoped, give him time to regather his own forces. He went back at the end of this period with comforting assurances from Meiklejohn's successor, President George Daniel Olds, that his teaching duties would be lightened.

200 · To John W. Haines

10 October 1920　　"The Brick House"
My dear Jack,　　　　　　　　　　　　Arlington, Vermont

I have been leaving Franconia, New Hampshire (a German English combination of names) to go and live in South Shaftsbury, Vermont (an English French combination). Our motives for making the change were not political, however, but agricultural. We seek a better place to farm and especially grow apples. Franconia winter-killed apple trees and some years even in July and August frosted gardens. The beautiful

White Mountains were too near for warmth. A hundred miles further South and out of the higher peaks as we shall be, we think we ought to be safer.

You will gather from the address that we are still in a state of transition. We shall be here in Arlington while our furniture is on the way in the train, which in your language is called "goods," but in the language of ourselves "freight." Arlington, Shaftsbury, Rupert, Sunderland, Manchester, Dorset and Rutland, the towns all round us are named after Courtiers of Charles Second. It looks as if some gun powder plot had blown them up at a ball and scattered them over our map. I might wish puritanically they rang a little more Puritanly in my ear. But as you know, I make a point of not being too fastidious about anything, but the main issue.

How could you with[h]old all these years the encouraging things you had written about me? From having the war so much on your mind I suppose — and from modesty. Never mind, they are interposed now just right to lift me out of the blues I have had so many of lately.

Well, the War is over. I don't know that I have said that to you yet. (We'll neither of us ever say it to Edward Thomas). But there are two or three more wars close at hand. There's a good prospect of wars from now on to the end. And the charm of that is that if we are going to have war all the time, it excuses us from thinking and talking of it quite as much as peace all the time excused us from talking about peace. Lets agree never to come nearer the subject of politics, national or international, than I have come in the first sentence of this letter.

Of course, publish anything you like in England. I'm obliged to John Freeman for his interest. He can't be too strong in his prejudices against me for having been held to have influenced Edward a little in his poetry. I wish he and I could meet and be friends. To have poems printed in England will be like, a little like, sitting down of an evening with you in Gloucester. Affectionately, Robert

201 · To G. R. Elliott

Dear Elliott: 23 October 1920 Arlington

I depose that I have moved a good part of the way to a stone cottage on a hill at South Shaftsbury in southern Vermont on the New York side near the historic town of Bennington where if I have any money left after repairing the roof in the spring I mean to plant a new Garden of Eden with a thousand apple trees of some unforbidden variety.

That the health of my family is so-so and I am sorry to hear that you can't quite say the same of yours. Mrs Elliott's ailment [goiter] is something I know little about. Our friend Dorothy Canfield Fisher has had it for some time and so far as I can see seems to be stimulated by it in mind and body. Is it something that comes to nervous high-strung people to make them more nervous and high-strung? — and needn't be serious if it is looked after. You must make Mrs Elliott let up on her interests all she will.

That I am writing my Puritan Poem so to speak and expect to finish it by — and by. Meanwhile look out for my set Snow Dust, The Onset, A Star in a Stone Boat, and Misgiving in The Yale Review; my set Fire and Ice, Wild Grapes, The Valley's Singing Day and The Need of Being Versed in Country Things in Harpers and other sets elsewhere as fast as I can supply the demand.

That I am writing a drama than which — but I spare you.

That I dislike the poetic style of Mr. Harding and that I shall vote for Jimmie Cox if I can persuade myself I dislike his poetic style any less. If I complain of this pair as too much for me on such short notice, you wont think it is from habit of finding fault with what is set before me. I saw the greatness of Cleaveland and Roosevelt and Wilson in time to vote for them. And Wilson *was* a great man. The incalculable hypocracy in all this talk against him for having tried courageously to be a complete leader. Blame him for having failed to be a complete leader but not for having tried to be one. I think he missed being one by just as much as he missed being a complete thinker. The man who could say "nothing permanent is ever achieved by force" was of the class a little too busy to think things out. Of course nothing permanent is ever achieved by anything, though I sometimes half feel as if the end of Carthage was pretty permanently achieved by the Romans. (You won't tell me you see anything so very Punic recrudescent in the world at the moment of writing.) (Or is it with Carthage as with the dinosaur? Force has wiped out the dinosaur, so that he is what is known as extinct. But not so his influence on our course in paleontology: his soul or rather his bones go marching on.)

(There is a difficulty here that I make my excuse for turning from politics as a bad job anyway to say a word about your translation to England. There will be a friend or two I want you to see over there for love's sake if not for art's. Chiefest of these will be Jack Haines of Gloucester. I should think you might like to see something of Walter de la Mare too. I could give you a letter to Masefield. But I only know him by letter, and have no special entree to him that you would not have yourself. You don't know how I wish I were going to see some of those fellows over there. Friendship stirs in me again now that the war is over and off my mind. It is like the spring of the year.

You are going to get a lot of writing done, when you are in England I'm sure. You're not going to spend all your free time looking for signatures of Shakespeare to refute Looney with.

I should have got it in when boasting of the family health that I had had a jaundice in the summer that answered every particular to the diagnosis of jaundice except that it failed to turn me yellow. The doctor was flattering enough to say it would have turned me yellow if there had been any yellow in me to bring to the surface. Little the doctors really know us in our true moral inwardness. If they did they would not make such wild misses in prescribing for us. But seriousness aside I have been too sick or tired or discouraged or something most of the time to stir far from home this summer. I didn't get to Maine again after I saw you last. What awaits me in Augusta takes the strength out of me at the bare thought of going there.

But I must see you soon.

Always yours   Robert Frost

202 · To Ridgely Torrence

Dear Ridgely: 26 October 1920   Arlington

You'll begin to think I don't see the beauty of having a friend on the editorial staff of The New Republic. But I do and I mean to show it by sending you some poems I have on hand just as soon as I can find time and peace of mind to write them all over. I'm moving now (from Franconia, New Hampshire to South Shaftsbury, Vermont), but the day must come when I shall be less moving than I have been, and then I promise you.

You're not going to be where I can run across you in my

first descent on the settlements this week. I must see you, though, when I am down in December if we are going to continue to be anything more to each other than respecters of each other's poetry.   Faithfully yours   Robert Frost

203 · To Louis Untermeyer

[c. 10 November 1920]
Dear Louis: [South Shaftsbury]

I guess you'd better send any letters for me to Bennington, Vermont, R.F.D. No. 1, and leave the rest to the good God we talked all round the other night without liking to name him — such is our modesty in the spirit as compared with our immodesty in the flesh.

And oh but I was sorry we couldn't go with you to Mecca [the Temple, New York City] (since we are on the subject of religion and the flesh). You might have spoken sooner I should think. As it was we didn't see how we could give up the idea of going to see the strike of the chorus and leading lady and the riot of the audience at the Lexington which we had bought tickets for. It was a beauty. We sat a restive hour after starting time and at nine o'clock a solitary man in citizen's clothes came before the curtain to ask us to bear with him five minutes longer: the trunk had been lost but was now found that contained what some lady was going to wear if she wore anything. At ten o'clock the same solitary figure a good deal aged with care reappeared in answer to a fierce and vindictive curtain call to say that it was all off: he had squared the chorus who had started the trouble only to end up in a run-in with the leading lady. He didn't know her name, but we could look it up on the program and remember her in our prayers as responsible for our misspent evening. When he denied his own leading lady in such words, someone behind or in the curtain gave an impetuous treble shriek of "Oh! — you *beast!*" and the curtain was agitated and a great wave ran its length. He had the infuriated audience all on its feet in front of him asking for its money back. He told them not tonight. He couldn't give them their money back because there was none in the box office, but if they would come to Allen and Fabian's the next day something would be done for them. Irma went to recover our eight dollars but all she saw was a fight between two women; she saw the color of no money. He only said what he said to save his life by getting us to go home. He had no money anywhere, poor man. Which just shows you you don't know enough to appreciate how well off you are yourself.

I doubt if we missed much by not hearing anybody sing, though judging from the way she shrieked the leading lady was a soprano — I won't say a good one because I don't know enough to know. We liked the riot and the place full of police. All that was wanting to round off my time in New York was a few bullets flying somewhere. I have to remember we saw a woman stoned in Van Dam St. three nights after election — not because she was a Magdalen but because she was a Democrat. All the little Italians were after her for Fiume and D'annunzio. She fought with them and stood them off facing the stones. She was middle aged. New York, New York! [. . .]

Yours   R. F.

204 · To G. R. Elliott

Dear Elliott: 16 November 1920   South Shaftsbury

It's you, you friend, who have been telling them they want to see something of me at Toronto. Don't think I don't appreciate the chance you gave me with yourself in the first place and have since given me with so many others. Where would I be if it weren't for you and the likes of you?

I'm just going to tell you a matter that may amuse you. You know I left Amherst all so irresponsible. You must have wondered how I could go and come as I pleased on nothing but poetry and yet seem to be taken care of as if I hadn't defied fate. I've wondered myself. The latest interposition in my favor when I had ceased to deserve further clemency is an appointment as *Consulting Editor of Henry Holt and Co.* I owe this under Heaven to Lincoln MacVeagh a younger member of the firm. The pay will be small but large for a poet and the work between you and me will be nothing but seeing MacVeagh once in a while in friendship as I would see you (if you would only come over here.) (Please let me know when you can come.)

I wrote you a considerable letter of late. . . . I said something about having neither heart nor stomach for any of the candidates you had to offer for the Presidency. That was before the mob let out its roar against the life of one poor old broken man. What a roar it was. They say Wilson tries to jest about it. No times are any less brutal than any other times.

Always yours   Robert Frost

205 · To LINCOLN MACVEAGH

WHEN Alfred Harcourt left Henry Holt and Company, Lincoln MacVeagh became the head of the trade department at Holt, and as such, the intermediary between the firm and RF. MacVeagh's very strong interest in classical literature helped to strengthen his friendship with the classics-minded RF. But, as this letter obliquely hints, MacVeagh also arranged a new contract between RF and Holt, which improved RF's financial position. (See letter 204)

Dear MacVeagh: 16 November 1920   South Shaftsbury

Not so much what you did as the way you did it convinces me that I have been right all along in looking for a business relationship into which friendship could enter. I like to see the opposite of cynicism in me rewarded. Of course thanks no end. And thanks to [Herbert] Bristol [President of Holt], too, if you'll convey them. Now we're away for a fresh start and no-body's on our conscience. What's to prevent our achieving something?

Once you asked me for a fair copy of The Onset. I should think it might come in appropriately now.

We're at South Shaftsbury at last. Part of the roof is off for repairs, the furnace is not yet under us and winter is closing in. But we're here. Will you have the address made right on the books so that letters will reach me directly?

The proofs of Mountain Interval [second edition, April 1921] have come in. I guess I won't bother with them. Let's go ahead with the printing. I hope [Araldo] DuChene likes the idea of our using a picture of the head.*

I shall see you somewhere around December 9th when I'm down for my next at Bryn Mawr.

Always yours faithfully   Robert Frost

* During the summer of 1919, the sculptor Araldo Du Chêne had visited his friend Raymond Holden in Franconia, and had modeled a head of RF which was later cast in bronze. A photograph of it was used as the frontispiece for the second edition of Mountain Interval.

206 · To WILFRED DAVISON

Dear Mr Davidson: 19 December 1920   South Shaftsbury

I have been a good deal interested in your new Summer School [Bread Loaf School of English] from afar off. I have been wondering if what is behind it may not be what has been troubling me lately, namely, the suspicion that we aren't getting enough American literature out of our colleges to pay for the hard teaching that goes into them. After getting a little American literature out of myself the one thing I have cared about in life is getting a lot out of our school system. I did what in me lay to incite to literature at Amherst. This school year I shall spend two weeks at each of two colleges talking in seminars on the same principles I talked on there. School days are the creative days and college and even high school under-graduates must be about making something before the evil days come when they will have to admit to themselves their minds are more critical than creative. I might fit into your summer plan with a course on the Responsibilities of Teachers of Composition — to their country to help make what is sure to be the greatest nation in wealth the greatest in art also. I should particularly like to encounter the teachers who refuse to expect of human nature more than a correct business letter. I should have to cram what I did into two or at most three weeks. [. . .]   Sincerely yours,   Robert Frost

207 · To WILFRED DAVISON

Dear Mr. Davison: 27 December 1920   South Shaftsbury

We are agreed on everything but the money. I suppose you offer what you can. But I really couldn't give of my time and strength at that rate — particularly of my strength, which I find I have more and more to consider. It would be stretch-ing a point to offer to come for a week and give five lectures for $150 and my expenses. I am sorry if that seems too much, for I wanted the chance to show my belief in what you have undertaken in literature and teaching.

With all good wishes for it, I am,

Sincerely yours   Robert Frost

208 · To Harriet Moody

Dear Harriet Moody: 20 January 1921   South Shaftsbury

Elinor and I are to be in New York on and about the twentieth of next month. We want to see you for the fun of a good talk before we do or don't decide to take this step into Michigan. Whichever we decide we'll be right. That's why we find it impossible to treat anything as momentous. If you oppose the step too much we shall think you have some reason for not wanting us as near you and Chicago as the steps would bring us. Maybe you think there are enough poets within the first postal zone from Chicago. We shall listen to you with respect and encouraging similes.

One thing as a mere woman of no practical experience you may need to be told: our going to Michigan would not prevent our planting all out doors with pines and apples. We could plant them in New England or in Michigan just the same.

Say (a little abruptly) you haven't seen this beautiful house that captivated us in passing last year. It is the easiest thing in the world for you to visit us here on your way to or from New York. We are on the main line from New York through Albany to Montreal and not more than two hours from Albany. If you can't be in New York in February when we are, will you agree to come here and see how you like this for the apple enterprise? This is important, though I will not have it momentous or even serious. We'll have to act soon.

Thank Theodore Maynard. I should be more pleased with your good opinion if you hadn't told me that time that I might be the best poet in America, but the best in America couldn't hope to come up to the worst in England. Have a little national pride. Don't you know it's provincial to look up to England? So is it to brag about America. What isn't provincial then will be the question before the house at the next meeting.

Always yours   Robert Frost

209 · To John W. Haines

Dear Jack,   20 January 1921   South Shaftsbury

Yes, I saw what you wrote about Edward. You and I cared for him in a different way from the rest of them. We didn't have to wait till he was dead to find out how much we loved him. Others pitied him for his misfortunes and he accepted their pity. I don't know what he looked for from me in his black days when I first met him. All he ever got was admiration for the poet in him before he had written a line of poetry. It is hard to speak of him as I want to yet. You speak of him to my liking as far as you go, and I'm sure that is far enough for the present. I wonder what De la Mare will say in his preface to the poems. Elinor and I once made it a little uncomfortable for De la Mare because he wouldn't come right out in hearty acknowledgment of what Edward Thomas had done for him by timely and untimely praise. I suppose De la Mare had really forgotten. Such we are as we swell up and grow great. I mentioned Edward to Dunsany when I saw him last year, and his memory was not so faulty. Instantly he said, "Did you know him? He saw me first and in the very first review he wrote of me he said everything that has been said by everybody else since." That came unforced.

I remember once hazarding the guess that Edward hadn't been proved wrong so very many times in his first judgment of new poets that came up for judgment. Edward and I were pushing our bicycles up a hill side by side. My "not so very many times" stopped him short to think. He wasn't angry. He was disturbed. What did I know? Did I know of any. He should have said not any. No want of strength and decision there. Two or three times I stopped him short like that with the way I put something. He was great fun. I've often wondered when I began to disappoint such a critical and fastidious person. I remember once thinking I had shocked him irreparably with a terrible parody of one who I believe I have sworn shall be nameless. It was an attempt to be as tragic about the middle classes as the nameless one had been about the lower classes. Edward looked as if he couldn't believe his ears — or wouldn't. I felt that I had gone too far. But no. Later he made me palm it off on Locke Ellis for the actual work of the nameless one. Locke Ellis took it as seriously and denounced so particularly the kind of mind that could conceive anything so repulsive that I never had the courage to un-deceive him as to the authorship.

I think Edward blamed most my laziness. He would have liked me better if I had walked farther with him. He wanted me to want to walk in Wales. And then I turned out a bad letter writer after I came home. That's the worst. I should have written him twice as many letters as I did write. But so should I have written you twice as many as I have. You have to assume that I think of you a thousand times for every once I write to you.

Some day soon we shall see each other and that will be better than many letters. I'm really a person who doesn't want anything in the world but my family and a few friends. And I don't want the friends all dead or in England. I demand sight of them. I could get importunate about it if I let myself. . . .

Affectionately,   Robert Frost

210 · To RIDGELY TORRENCE

My dear Ridgely: 23 January 1921   South Shaftsbury

It is true I am a scout for Henry Holt. How did you penetrate my disguise?

Now what I am particularly out for is left handers with something besides speed on the ball. Now I can't use spitters, the new rule having put them out of business. I can get all the right handers I want out of the college English courses; and straight rather too slow ball artists a little wild on purpose to scare the batter out of the Poetry Society. Get me some good left-handers like yourself and Robinson and I dont care how undeveloped they are: I have a market for them. I will pay you in poems of the realm for every one you bring along. I have heard of a return-ball pitcher in Honolulu. Now this is the rare case of a person with a gift for throwing a ball so that it returns in a circle square triangle or other figure without touching anything (not even the bat of the batter up) to the hand that threw it. Now this obviates the need of a catcher just as some kind of street car obviates the need of a conductor to collect fares and some kinds of poetry obviate the need of a reader. I will give you one epic currency for such a find. Now I am on my way to Honolulu at this moment to look at this bird and if his wing is as per write-up, one wing is all he needs: we can use him. Now there is said to be such a thing as a man on the Nauscopee River who can make one ball look like three at a time coming through the air, two of them of course visionary. Now I should want this visionary if I believed in him. Now I am in a position to make it right with you if you can put me next to anything.

I am enclosing four poems, but you must reject two of them and may reject three or four. . . . I know you won't try too hard to like these poems. That would be not to give them a fair chance.*

Our best to you both.   Always yours   Robert Frost

211 · To Hamlin Garland

ONE OF the tributes paid to William Dean Howells after his death on 11 May 1920 was a memorial service held in the New York Public Library on 1 March 1921. When Hamlin Garland invited RF to participate in that service, the invitation stirred RF's memory of Howells. Shortly after he had returned to America from England in 1915, RF had received a letter from Howells praising *North of Boston* and saying he was eager to meet the man who had become well known for poetry about farm people of a kind which Howells had hoped he was writing in his book, *The Mother and the Father* (1909). As requested, RF called on Howells in New York City. Then Howells devoted part of an "Easy Chair" article in *Harper's* (September 1915) to RF and *North of Boston*. For these reasons and others, RF wanted to attend the memorial service, but because of continuing illness he was unable to be there.

Dear Mr Garland: 4 February 1921   South Shaftsbury

Sick man as I am (I am just up from a week in bed) I am tempted to accept your invitation for the chance it would give me, the only one I may ever have, to discharge in downright prose the great debt I owe Howells.

Howells himself sent me The Mother and the Father after he saw my North of Boston. It is beautiful blank verse, just what I should have known from his prose he would write. My obligation to him however is not for the particular things he did in verse form, but for the perennial poetry of all his writing in all forms. I learned from him a long time ago that the loveliest theme of poetry was the voices of people. No one ever had a more observing ear or clearer imagination for the tones of those voices. No one ever brought them more freshly to book. He recorded them equally with actions, indeed as if they were actions (and I think they are).

I wonder if you think as I do it is a time for consolidating our resources a little against outside influences on our litera-

* As poetry editor of *The New Republic*, Ridgely Torrence published many of RF's poems, the first being "A Brook in the City," which appeared in the issue of 9 March 1921.

ture and particularly against those among us who would like nothing better than to help us lose our identity. I dont mean the consolidation so much in society as in thought. It should be more of a question with us than it is what as Americans we have to go on with and go on from. There can be nothing invidious to new comers, emigrant Russians Italians and the like, in singling out for notice or even praise any trait or quality as specially American. Many of *them* must have it as much as the older stock. It is by what they have of it that they are drawn to what we have of it. We are just one more rough abstraction on some principle we needn't go into here from the mass that other abstractions have been made from before and others still will go on to be made from. Principles are always harder to talk about than men. Our best way to define to ourselves what we are is in terms of men. We are eight or ten men already and one of them is Howells.

The question is do you think I ought to make an engagement I may not be able to keep. I *should* be all right by March 1st. But suppose I weren't.

We must see more of each other for what we hold in common.   Always yours   Robert Frost

212 · To Louis Untermeyer

SHORTLY before RF decided to buy a farm in South Shaftsbury, in 1920, he came close to buying one in Monson, Massachusetts. But his particular feeling about country and city people dissuaded him, as explained in this excerpt from a long letter to Untermeyer: "I keep hearing of [Sinclair] Lewis wanting to better small town people. I'm for bettering or battering them back where they belong. Too many of them get to college."

My dear Louis: 15 April 1921   South Shaftsbury
[. . .] Did I tell you what scared me out of Monson the evening I arrived there to take possession of the farm by the Quarry? It was a bevy of twenty college boys skylarking and swatting each other over the heads with copies of The New Republic in front of the village drug store. It was too early for them to be summer colonists and I had it in the deed of the farm that there were to be no summer colonists in Monson anyway. Says I to myself, says I, and lights out for Boxford Mass, Rochester N. H., Brunswick, Waterford, Norway, Harrison, and Skowhegan Maine. The only hotel in Monson has

bedroom doors that though they may be locked can be seen over and under and I should say crawled over and under from the halls. Those were engaging, so I engaged one door with room, looked at myself credulously in the mirror, and then went out on the street to look for excitement till my family should arrive on the load of furniture that was coming to me. 'Twas graduation at the Academy; everyone was shuffling reverently in white and black to some exercise that I as an outsider couldn't be expected to know the importance of. I didn't want to be an outsider. I was just on the point of mounting the Soldiers Monument and applying in a loud voice to the community at large to be taken in as soon as possible and treated as an insider when I ran bang into my bevy of twenty college boys all obviously out of tune with the village and not the least in the mood of its pitiful little function. They probably thought they were laughing at each other but what they were really laughing at was the notion of their ever having taken the Academy Graduation as an end and aim. At their colleges they had commencements, and there were even things beyond commencements: Rhodes Scholarships if you won them might take you to Oxford where you might hope to acquire a contempt beyond any contempt for small things you could show now. They knew now that there was nothing here that they would not some day be able to scorn. I fled them as I had fled their like thirty years before at Dartmouth. I never could bear the sunsuvbijches belief that they were getting anywhere when they were getting toward their degrees or had got anywhere when they had got them. That's not it exactly; it was more their belief that they were leaving anybody behind who was not getting toward their degrees. I preferred to drop out of their company and be looked on as left behind. Of course all I had to do not to be left behind was to have one solitary idea that I could call my own in four years. That would be one more than they would have. [. . .]

Sufficiently for one letter   Robert Frost

212-a · MARION L. BURTON TO ROBERT FROST

THIS EXCHANGE between RF and Burton, President of the University of Michigan from 1920 to 1925, is an early example of the desire of American colleges to have a working artist on the staff. This tendency may have had its beginning in Ohio as early as 1911, when Western College built a cottage studio on the campus for the composer Edgar Stillman-Kelley. In the same town of Oxford, Ohio, in October 1920, the Trustees of Miami University gave a residence fellowship to the poet-playwright, Percy MacKaye, with a small studio built for him in a grove of trees on the Miami campus. Further impetus to the trend was given by President Raymond M. Hughes of Miami University in November 1920, when he addressed the annual meeting of the National Association of State Universities on the topic "The Most Important University Problem." He proposed that universities and colleges should become patrons of creative artists: ". . . nothing would do more to leaven the increasing materialism of the American university than to have a great creative artist working on the campus."

According to Walter Havighurst (*The Miami Years,* p. 195), RF and Percy MacKaye held the following conversation in New York City during the winter of 1920-1921. "Percy, where are you living now?" "I'm at a college. In Ohio." "What are you doing there?" "Just living, writing. Robert, you ought to get a college to support you." "How can I get one?" "I'll talk to President Hughes. He'll have an idea."

If such a talk occurred, nothing immediately came of it; but an article by Percy MacKaye in *The Forum* magazine for June 1921, "University Fellowships in Creative Arts," had a bearing on future events, when exploratory discussions took place between RF and representatives of the University of Michigan. President Burton was then on leave, and the initial arrangements were made by Acting President M. L. Hughes. On 29 June 1921, President Burton sent RF the following telegram:

AFTER CORRESPONDENCE WITH PRESIDENT HUGHES, I DESIRE HEREBY OFFICIALLY TO OFFER YOU FELLOWSHIP AT UNIVERSITY OF MICHIGAN FOR ACADEMIC YEAR 1921-1922 ON BASIS SOMEWHAT BETTER THAN YOU HAVE INDICATED TO PRESIDENT HUGHES. LETTER FOLLOWS.

My dear Mr. Frost: 29 June 1921   Ann Arbor

I enclose a confirmation of a telegram which I have just sent to you. I am sorry not to have been able to head this matter up sooner but I now have a gift from the Honorable Chase Osborn, former governor of this state, to make possible your coming to Ann Arbor next year.

I am extremely sorry that it is necessary for me to leave Ann Arbor on July 1 to be gone for my summer vacation but I have arranged with our Dean of Students, Joseph A. Bursley, to take active steps to help secure a proper house for you for next year.

I want to be very explicit about this whole matter. I am sure you understand that it is distinctly a one year arrangement. You could not come to Ann Arbor under satisfactory conditions and pay your own house rent on a basis of $3500.

President Hughes telegraphed me that you would accept on that basis. We shall treat you much better. Candidly, for the entire expense of this arrangement for the year we have $5000.

May I suggest that after Dean Bursley and you get in touch with one another by correspondence that you come out here at our expense and look the situation over? It will be well to give Dean Bursley time to see what can be done. Since you are coming for but one year possibly it would be wiser not to move your household goods but for us to rent for you a furnished house if it can be found. Possibly, however, you will have personal preferences for which, of course, we will have only respect. May I assume that you will be with us next year?

Believe me Sir, with high esteem,

Very sincerely yours, M. L. Burton

213 · To M. L. Burton

My dear President Burton: 7 July 1921 South Shaftsbury

You had my telegram accepting your offer. It remains for me to thank you for having chosen me to be a representative of creative literature in this way at Michigan University. We'll waive the question of whether you might not better have chosen someone else for the honor. I should have thanked you almost as much if you had. The important thing is that you should have chosen anyone. I don't know why I am so gratified unless it is because I am somewhat surprised when men of your executive authority (yours and Mr. Osborn's) see it as a part of their duty to the state to encourage the arts; and I don't know why I am surprised unless it is because I base my expectation on what I have observed of our Presidents at Washington. We have had ten or a dozen in the White House in the last fifty years, all good men and all good executives, but only one of the lot [Theodore Roosevelt] of such sight or insight. And we don't think that a large enough proportion for safety, do we?

I can see that the appointment may contemplate the benefit of education a little as well as of poetry and one poet. You would like it to say something to the world for keeping the creative and erudite together in education where they belong. And you would like it to make its demand on the young student. He must be about some achievement in the arts or sciences while yet he is at his most creative period and the college interposes to keep the world off his shoulders. The greatest nonsense of our time has been the solution of the school problem by forsaking knowledge for thought. From learning to thinking — it sounds like a progress. But it is illusory. Thought is good but knowledge is at least no worse and thought is no substitute for knowledge. Knowledge is certainly more material to the imagination than thought. The point is that neither knowledge nor thought is an end and neither is nearer an end than the other. The end they both serve, perhaps equally, is deeds in such accepted and nameable forms as the sonnet, the story, the vase, the portrait, the landscape, the hat, the scythe, the gun, the food, the breed, the house, the home, the factory, the election, the government. We must always be about definite deeds to be growing.

This is a long letter, but you will forgive it to my wish to show my appreciation of what you and Mr. Osborn have done.   Sincerely yours,   Robert Frost

214 · To Louis Untermeyer

Dear Louis: 7 July 1921   South Shaftsbury

No one put it into my head: I thought of it myself: there's that much good in me still, thought that's all there is. I mean there's that much thought for other people. The rest of me is swallowed up in thoughts of myself. All the time you were here I read and read to you from my own works. You were partly to blame. You let me, to try me to see how far I would go in my self-assertion. You were stringing me, so to speak. You gave me all the line you had on the reel. And I took it. But there's this redeeming consideration. It did occur to me of my own motion though not until too late that you also may have had works to read from and were only diffidently waiting to be asked like the decent person you are. I'll be damned. It shows how far we can get along in our egotism without noticing it. I'm a goner — or almost a goner. The terrible example of others I could name I haven't profited by any more than I have by the terrible example of people I have seen die.

> To prayer, to prayer I go — I think I go —
> I go to prayer
> Along a solemn corridor of woe
> And down a stair

In every step of which I am abased;
A cowl I wear,
I wear a halter-rope about the waist,
I bear a candle-end put out with haste.
I go to prayer.*

I shouldn't wonder if my last end would be religious; I weary so of cutting back the asparagus bed of my faults. I wonder what it is about prayer. I have half a mind to try it. I'm going to try to be good, if it isn't too late. Let the columnists mock as they will. Yours RF

215 · To Percy MacKaye

My dear Percy: 16 July 1921 South Shaftsbury

I got a letter off to President Burton as my first duty and then ran for the train to various places. I thought perhaps I might find time to write you my thanks on my travels; but I didn't. I seemed not to be alone for writing at all.

Well your great plan has its start. You have landed me. Who comes next?

I have to thank people in this order or exactly the reverse according to how you look at it: You, President Hughes, President Burton, and Mr Osborn. Of Mr Osborn I can only say, An American statesman and so considerate of the poor poet!

I haven't known exactly what the great plan was and it turns out somewhat different from what I should have expected. But it is all right. I am glad to lend myself to it in almost any shape. It seems the idea is fellowships of just one year in a place. When I said I could accept $3500 a year for myself and family I thought I might be going west for two or perhaps three years. The expense of moving would be distributed over two or three salaries. That amount wouldn't

* This poem was never published by RF; but it appears three times in the letters of RF to Untermeyer with variants. Moreover, the context of each new letter in which it appears gives the poem extensions of meaning. The poem comes a second time in the letter dated 26 September 1921 — less than three months after the first — and it appears after this paragraph:

"I'm in earnest. Just as the only great art is inesthetic so the only morality is completely ascetic. I have been bad and a bad artist. I will retire soon to the place you wot of. Not now but soon. That is my last, my ultimate vileness, that I cannot make up my mind to go now where I must go sooner or later. I am frail."

The third occurrence of this poem may be found in letter 387, dated 15 January 1942.

really have done for one year. President Burton saw that without my having to speak and made it $5000. You can see how a short time in a place will cost much more accordingly. They have rented me a house already for $1250. The house is furnished but they ask me to buy dishes and carpets, or bring these with me which I doubt if I can do. The house is very large, there'll be no hope of running it without one servant. So the money goes. But never mind it's their money in a sense and they want me to live in a style worthy of their own high idea of me. We've made up our minds to be in their hands for a good time and damn the economies. It will be a year-long picnic and we are free minded enough as a family to break off our several affairs and take them up as seriously as ever again after the picnic is over. We're all in for it — all but one [Irma] who will have to be left behind for school. There'll be music and dancing and college yelling. We all like such things. A year of them will do our digestion good and a year out of our selfish pursuits will never be missed in the long run.

People have asked me what I wanted said about my honor in the papers. The question is What you want said to further your plan. Write me a description of it — my particular honor — that will help, will you? I could use it right away in one quarter and another.

Very special. Lesley asks to know how she can get into communication with Arvia [MacKaye's daughter] at Brattleboro.

Our best wishes to all.   Affectionately,   Robert Frost

Where is what you promised me of your recent work?

216 · To Raymond Holden

WHILE the poet Raymond Holden was still a young man, spending his summers at Sugar Hill which was then in the township of Franconia, he made the acquaintance of RF and visited him frequently. After their friendship had developed, RF sold Holden a piece of land from the Franconia farm, and Holden built a summer home on it. Later, when RF moved to South Shaftsbury, Holden bought the remainder of the Franconia farm. The following letter refers to that second transaction.

Dear Raymond   17 July 1921   South Shaftsbury
    In New York last week it came to my knowledge that Madam Nutt's receivers on representation of hers had made a

claim to all the royalties I have ever had from Henry Holt and Co. It is at most a joke or a formality, I think I can say. We are perfectly safe. The law has been covered. Still for fear there should be an attempt made on me for what could be scared out of me I should like it better if the property you bought of me last year stood properly in your name. It would put us all in an awkward position to have them attach it. So please have Mr. Parker make out the deed for me to sign. That's what I sent you the old deed for. (You got it all right, I think you said.)

I am beginning to sniff the air suspiciously on the point of taking flight from these weedy regions. It can't be long before you hear me come crashing through the woods in your direction. Don't shoot till you're sure who it is anyway.

I offended again in New York on Tuesday. I haven't given a good talk in public this year I can safely say. I don't know what's the matter unless it's indifference. I must brace up and try to care a little or else quit the platform for the desk.

Our best to you and Grace and the Du Chênes and may the Lord keep you till we see you again.

Ever yours   Robert Frost

216-a · M. L. Burton to Robert Frost

My dear Mr. Frost: 29 July 1921

Your letter of July 7 was acknowledged by my assistant under date of July 9 and then it was forwarded to me here in the northern woods in Minnesota where I am having a good vacation and rest.

I want you to know that I have read your letter with the keenest interest and satisfaction. You have sensed and expressed so much more adequately than I can just the purposes which we have in mind, that it increases my anticipation of your residence among us next year. You will be interested to know that I have sent copies of your letter to the donor, Mr. Chase M. Osborn, and also to each member of the Board of Regents. . . .

Believe me, with the keenest anticipation of your coming to us next year,

Very sincerely yours,   M. L. Burton

217 · To G. R. ELLIOTT

Dear Elliott: 21 January [1922]   Ann Arbor

You'll begin to think I have made you over to Jack Haines to be friends with you in my place. From what he writes I judge that would suit him. I trust it wouldn't suit you entirely. I'd no more make a friend over to someone else than I would let any one adopt one of my children while I was still alive. No one gets away from me who ever really belonged to me. So you see what you are in for. You may as well make the best of it — unless, of course, you have the heart to find pretext for quarreling with me for the letters I don't write: I suppose I might be insulted into letting you go free. You could try calling me names. You could call me lazy, and see what that would do. If I resent the epithet it is more for its triteness than its fitness. I'm not lazy: I'm just sensible. All the matter with me is that I would rather see a friend once than write him a million letters. Oh much rather. I can't put it too strongly.

This year I am too far away out here to hope to see you. But this is only one year. Next year I shall be in New England again and with a will, where we can touch hands across the mountains. This year to sociability. To the right-thinking no time is ever lost: I don't grudge the time I seem to throw away on my fellow men in banqueting and carousing: you never know what will come of anything. "Out of the good of evil born" Nevertheless I mean not always to flock in crowds — nor long at a time. I must be about my next book or two. I haven't estimated it very closely, but I should think I must have the material on hand for a couple.

I think of you often — you and your family and I'm in a way   Yours too   Robert Frost

218 · To GEORGE F. WHICHER

DURING his first visit to Bread Loaf, in 1921, RF recommended that George F. Whicher be asked to join the staff of the Bread Loaf School of English. The invitation was accepted. In this letter, RF is lobbying on behalf of incorporating an informal course in creative writing in the Bread Loaf School of English. (Preliminary expressions of this pet notion occur in letter 206.) RF's interest in the teaching of creative writing paved the way for the Bread Loaf Writers' Conference in 1926.

Dear George: 8 February 1922   Ann Arbor

It would give you some idea of what you would be in for at Bread Loaf, if I wrote out a few of the things I may have carelessly said up there last summer. I came pretty near going the whole length. I told them they wanted for teacher a writer with writing of his own on hand who would be willing to live for a while on terms of equality almost with a few younger writers. Almost I say. I wouldnt have him go so far as to carry his manuscript to them as they would be free to bring theirs to him. But I would have him stick at nothing short of that. He would assign them work no more than they would assign him work. He would expect to take as well as give in as fair exchange as possible if not ideas of form, then ideas and observations of life. He would stay mainly at the level of the material where he would show to not too much advantage. That is to say he would address himself mainly to the subject matter of the younger writer as in good polite conversation. He would refrain from fault finding except in the large. He would turn from correcting grammar in red ink to matching experience in black ink, experience of life and experience of art. There's the whole back side of every sheet of manuscript for his response. The proof of the writing is in what it elicits from him. He may not need to write it out. He can talk it out before the fire. The writing he has nothing to say to fails with him. The trouble with it is that it hasnt enough to it. Let the next piece have more to it — of Heaven Earth Hell and the young author. The strength of the teacher's position lies in his waiting till he is come after. His society and audience are a privilege — and that is no pose. On the rare occasion when he goes after the pupils it will be to show them up not for what they aren't but for what they are. He will invade them to show them how much more they contain than they can write down; to show them their subject matter is where they came from and what in the last twenty years they have been doing.

I kept repeating No exercises. No writing for exercise. The writer's whole nature must be in every piece he sets his hand to and his whole nature includes his belief in the real value the writing will have when finished. Suppose it is a good bit of family tradition. It must be done once for all. It must be an achievement. And so on. You know how I get going and you know I mean it.

I've been outlining a plan for the reorganization of an

English department with the President of Miami [University] lately. We agreed that it needed three sets of teachers, first a number of policemen with badges and uniforms perhaps but anyway with authority to enter every department in college and mark for the English department separately any and all papers written by students; second, a number of writers creative and critical, and third, a number of lecturers in criticism. There should be absolutely no writing required by an English teacher. The English policemen should do all their hounding in the first year or two and have it over with. The writers and lecturers whould be accessible informally, but at stated times to such youngsters as were pursuing writing on their own account. They would give credit (I mean credits) on application and at discretion. Oh lord look where I've got, and it's 2 A M.

Always yours   Robert Frost

All this plan lacks is someone to carry it out. I wish I had nothing else to do.

219 · To Amy Lowell

Dear Miss Lowell: 22 February 1922   Ann Arbor

Miss Uki Osawa asks me to intercede with you for the young people who have been trying to bring you here to talk and read. These are children. They tell me they began by not offering you enough money. They had nothing to reason from except the hundred dollars they gave Jack Squire, their only poet English or American so far this year and I guess for several years. If a hundred isn't enough ask a little more, but come and read to them. They are your fervent admirers and went after you of their own motion. I know the money is nothing to you except as the measure of how much you are wanted. Let me assure you that in this case you will be thought no less of if you charge no more than to you may seem a merely nominal sum, say, a hundred and twenty five or a hundred and fifty dollars. Make it as low as you will for them. They are taking a good deal on themselves in bringing so many poets at once where so few have ever been before. I suppose they told you they are having Louis, Carl, Vachel, and Witter Bynner too. It will be a great stirring up of poetry here. I'm interested in having you come for the chance it will give me to take it out in talk for all the letters I may intend to write you in the next year or two. Anything to save letter writing. . . .

Good luck to all good enterprise.

Cordially yours   Robert Frost

220 · To Lincoln MacVeagh

Dear MacVeagh: [May 1922]   [Ann Arbor]

[. . .] We've been having a dose of Carl Sandburg. He's another person I find it hard to do justice to. He was possibly hours in town and he spent one of those washing his white hair and toughening his expression for his public performance. His mandolin pleased some people, his poetry a very few and his infantile talk none. His affectations have almost buried him out of sight. He is probably the most artificial and studied ruffian the world has had. Lesley says his two long poems in The New Republic and The Dial are as ridiculous as his carriage and articulation. He has developed rapidly since I saw him two years ago. I heard someone say he was the kind of writer who had everything to gain and nothing to lose by being translated into another language.

Soon home out of this. The children are all already back and at the farming. There shall they see no enemy but foul weather. . . .   Ever yours   Robert Frost

221 · To Wade Van Dore

ONE of RF's most unusual and lasting friendships, which began with the following letter, resulted in a considerable correspondence. While still a very young man working in a Detroit bookstore after having finished junior high school, Wade Van Dore began to read Henry David Thoreau. Inspired particularly by *Walden*, and thus convinced that the mass of men do indeed lead lives of quiet desperation because enslaved by dispensabilities, he embarked on an original life as wanderer and poet, working brieflly as a handyman whenever necessary. A native of the state of Michigan, he became acquainted with the poetry of RF in 1922, and was pleased to find another living writer who seemed to possess so many of Thoreau's qualities. After they had exchanged letters, Van Dore visited New England and met RF at Franconia, during the summer of 1922. For many brief periods during the next thirty years, Van Dore served as

277

hired man on each of three farms owned by RF, but would never bind himself to any work for long. RF became so much interested in the young man's poetry that he helped him find a publisher for his first volume, *Far Lake* (1930). Their friendship, often strained by the peculiarities of each, continued unbroken until RF's death.

Dear Mr Van Dore: 24 June 1922   South Shaftsbury

First about Thoreau: I like him as well as you do. In one book (Walden) he surpasses everything we have had in America. You have found this out for yourself without my having told you; I have found it out for myself without your having told me. Isn't it beautiful that there can be such concert without collusion? That's the kind of "getting together" I can endure.

I'm going to send part of your letter to a farmer in Franconia N. H. where I lived and owned a small property until last year. The farmer is a friend of mine and will listen sympathetically to what I shall say about you. I dont know just what your plan would be. Would it be to camp out for a while on his land and then find a few boards and nails to build a shack of for the winter?

Franconia is my favorite village in the mountains. But it has to be said against it for your purposes that it has no very large library of its own and none nearer of importance to draw on than the State Library at Concord seventy miles away. New England is strewn with libraries as you may have heard, but what little money they have is necessarily spent on books that you and I would have read or wouldn't care to read, that is to say very standard works and harmless insignificant stories for children. I tell you all this so that you may know. I am sure my friend Mr Willis Herbert will be good to you. You will never see such a view as that from his fields. It is a valley view from below the heights. There is no lake in the neighborhood. You have to be content with just Mountains — Lafayette, Cannon, Kinsman, Moosilauke and further off the tip of Washington.

I hope I tell you what you want.

Sincerely yours   Robert Frost

222 · To John T. Bartlett

Dear John   [c. June 1922]   [Ann Arbor]

I've been thinking about you lately and wondering what I could do to get a letter out of you. I suppose I could write a letter to you.

I'm still at Ann Arbor, Mich but the climax of annual improvements is about reached and it wont be many days before we book for home. We are Elinor and I. The children long since went ahead of us to set the hens and watch the apples and pears set themselves. Home is now South Shaftsbury Vermont about seventy miles south of Middlebury. So if I do get a letter out of you let it be addressed to me there.

Lets see you lived once for a little while in Vermont and once for a little while just across from it at Claremont. Where haven't you and I lived for a little while? You've lived a pretty well settled life in Colorado — pretty well.

I guess I lived the longest I ever lived under the same roof on the farm at Derry. I was seven years there. I think of you in many places. Remember the cold day when I put you over the hill on foot toward Littleton N. H.? I cant get over the strangeness of having been in so many places and yet remained one person. I have kept Raymond Derry and a hundred other New England towns alive in my memory not only by passing through them now and then but by thinking of buying a farm in one or another of them. I keep reading of them seriously in Strouts Farm Catalogue. I no sooner get settled in South Shaftsbury than I am at it again for some reason looking for another likely farm that could be bought right. I believe I'll end by buying a number of five hundred dollar farms in all sorts of places and holding them chiefly for the lumber on them but partly for a change of residence when I get restless. I could fix the houses up on them and rent them to medium poor city people who couldnt own their own or didnt want to because it tied them to summer after summer in the same place. What's the matter with that idea? Copyrighted!

Lesley Carol Irma and Margery write that there's all that heart could wish going on on the farm we have. We have a small horse (Morgan) we bought for a saddle horse when very young. We brought it with us at too much expense from Franconia. It has eaten its head off several times over when we have had to board it out in our absence on various errands of mercy and education in the winters. We were just beginning to resent what it had cost us when lo and behold on converting it into a driving horse we find we have a trotter. You may here of Carol or me on the turf next.

Not that I'm losing my interest appreciably in writing as an art. I shall have another book before many years. I've scattered poems enough around in the magazines for two books if I can get up energy enough to gather them together again.

This has been a year to wonder at. I don't know what I havent done this year. I've had no assigned work as you may have heard. I've been supposed to have nothing to do but my writing and the University has been supposed to have nothing to do with me but take credit for my writing. In practice it has turned out humorously. I've been pretty busy dining out and talking informally on all occasions from club meetings to memorial services on the athletic field on Decoration Day. I have felt nonsensical at times. But it's the first year of an experiment. We want to find out if every college couldn't keep one artist or poet and the artist or poet and college be the better for the mutual obligation. There'll be less lionizing when the thing settles down and people get used to the idea. Miami University at Oxford Ohio has undertaken Percy Mackay[e] and Michigan University has undertaken me. That is as far as the idea has got yet. I'm probably coming back next year on a slightly modified plan. I am to be free to be clear away from the place for nine months out of the twelve. I've decided I would have to to get very much done. I'll have a house here but it'll stand empty in memory of me most of the time.

Oh gee I wish I could see you as on the day I left you on the corner in Derry Village and you set off for Vancouver or on the day when I saw you with Margaret sitting on the high bank above the baseball field the year after you graduated or on the night when you turned up at my reading at Exeter [January 1916] or as on the day when you got punched in the eye by one of Kemp's boys from Sanborn (was his name White or Doble or what was it?) or as on the day when you got mad at me about Pamir or something in class or as on the night when you put the candles out on Doc Faustus with your finger ends and generally acted so like the Devil.

There was talk of my ranging west last winter, but I backed out. I'd go if Elinor would go with me next year. I doubt if she will.

Our love to you all   Affectionately   Robert Frost

223 · To Louis Untermeyer

Dear Louis   8 July 1922   South Shaftsbury

I wrote you a letter a week ago which you paid no attention to because I never sent it. It was all about the way the distinguished Greek and Latin Professor's Widow (pronounced Dogie as in The Chisholm Trail) accused me out of a clear sky of having stolen or otherwise nefariously made away with one of the five iron pisspots she would swear she had distributed to the five bedrooms of the house she rented to us in Ann Arbor. She wouldn't claim it was an Etruscan vase. Neither was it Mycenaean or Knossian ware. Nevertheless it represented a loss of fifty cents and she proposed to make a stink about it if not in it. I haven't admitted that I could have stolen a thing I no longer have any use for since I stopped drinking. If I did anything with it, I probably took it out into society to make conversation and lost it. I remember trying hard to break it over Carl Sandburg's head for his new mysticism and madness prepense — but in vain. I may have dented it ten cents worth. I have asked her to let the ton of coal we left her in the cellar go toward that.

I got too bitterly funny about the episode in my other letter. I decided that I didn't mind the bitch as much as I made myself appear. I'm served exactly right for having spent so much of my life tolerating the lower and middle classes. I've been punished often enough in the past for pretending not to see what was wrong with the poor. This is the worst I ever got it for affecting to stand in with the comfortably off. Men[c]ken wins. My democracy has been 99 per cent unrealization. I left the world when I was young for reasons I gradually came to forget. I returned to the world at thirty three (sharp) to see if I couldn't recover my reasons. I have recovered them all right, "and I am ready to depart" again. I believe I will take example of [Emerson's] Uriel and withdraw into a cloud — of whiskers. You may find me pretty brushy when you come by later in the week. It will be for a sign. [. . .]

Pretty much as ever   R.F.

Fail to say much about this in reply. Everybody reads your brilliant letters here; and the girls haven't been let into my shame as yet. Wouldn't it jar you? This is what my year among the teachers comes to. It reads like a fable to express my prejudice against education.

224 · To Wilbur E. Rowell

Dear Mr. Rowell: 27 July 1922   South Shaftsbury

I've been intending all year to tell you something about my sister. But for a guest of the University with no stated duties I was kept pretty busy at Michigan.

Jean is still where she was [State Insane Asylum, Augusta, Maine]. We have been on the point of seeing if some provision couldn't be made for her in the country where she could have a more individual existance not herded in an institution. She has been greatly improved, though not so much so that she isnt to my mind still a problem. Her case has never been clearly diagnosed. Dr Tyson is certain it is not one of dementia praecox. But in spite of the fact that she enjoys longer and longer lucid intervals in which she talks and writes like anyone else, she hasn't a real grip on herself and just when it begins to look as if she could be counted on, goes all to pieces again. I should have very little faith in her trying it in the world again as a free agent. She would be almost sure to neglect herself in the old way and relapse into wretchedness. Understand that I say this not too positively. I might possibly be persuaded to give my vote for putting her on a farm and paying her bills. The worst of it is that would of course necessitate her being thrown with Louie Merriam, who always hovers in the offing. They couldn't be kept apart.

I ought to say that early in the spring when it had been actually arranged for her to leave the hospital and I sent her some money to buy clothes to be in readiness, she had an attack so serious that she resigned herself of her own judgement to stay where she was and handed over my money to the State of Maine to go toward her board. It is all too much for me. Any suggestions you have time to make will be gratefully considered.

With thanks for your friendly interest in these matters, I am   Sincerely yours   Robert Frost

225 · To Gamaliel Bradford

GAMALIEL BRADFORD was an eighth-generation descendant of Governor William Bradford of the Plymouth Colony. A semi-invalid all his life, he became a prolific writer of verse, novels, and plays long before he turned to making the popular biographical studies which he called psychographs. RF met him through Katharine Lee Bates at Wellesley College, admired him greatly, and occasionally visited him in his home at Wellesley Hills. On 31 October 1921, RF wrote to Bradford and asked him to contribute to Louis Untermeyer's annual anthology, *A Miscellany of American Poetry*. Almost concurrently, he recommended the manuscript of Bradford's novel, *Her Own Way*, to Henry Holt and Company. In both of these attempts to help Bradford, he failed; and his consequent embarrassment colors this letter. But the two men remained warm and loyal friends.

Dear Bradford: 31 July 1922   South Shaftsbury
    I had hoped to get down to Boston to see you before you could demand an accounting of me. Perhaps you wouldn't have been as hard on me if you could have had by word of mouth what you now insist on having by letter. My aversion to letter-writing this time is altogether cowardly.
    With the best intention in the world (as I trust you know) I have simply done you a disservice by asking for your poems for Untermeyer's Miscellany. I was assuming too much authority. I had no right to invite you in, and so you aren't in and I am sufficiently rebuked for an officious fool.
    You'll wonder on what grounds I so far mistook myself. Well, no one I ever heard of passed on poems I contributed. I never was consulted about the admission of any one else or the acceptance of anyone else's poems. That seems something to go on.
    I suppose I was complying with every form in telling Untermeyer I meant to ask you for poetry for the Miscellaney and getting his permission to go ahead. I thought that settled it. But not so. All he meant to grant me was permission to submit your poetry to the judgement of the other contributors as a sort of board of consent. Both you and I were only submitting your poetry for approval if we had but known it, and it has been rejected as not up to your mark.
    I'm an unpardonable mess-maker. But forgive me for the admiration I bear your work. Really you *must* forgive me. I'm wretched.
    I don't believe in the buck-passing way the Miscellaney is run and shall get out of it — if I may be considered in.

                    Always yours ineffectually*
                    Robert Frost

*I'm thinking of how my opinion of your novel was overruled in Holt's office. But wait. Give me another chance.

225-a · Wilbur E. Rowell to Robert Frost

Dear Mr. Frost: 1 August 1922   Lawrence

I am sending you herewith a check for $800 for the 1922 payment of the annuity given you in the will of William P. Frost.

I am reserving the annuity payment due your sister. . . .

May I add that the success which attended your literary work and the esteem in which it is held are always a pleasure to me.   Very truly yours,   Wilbur E. Rowell

226 · To Louis Untermeyer

MOUNTAIN-CLIMBING became a favorite activity for RF and his family starting in Bethlehem, New Hampshire, in 1907. After the return from England, and the purchase of a home in Franconia, three of their favorite mountains for climbing were Lafayette, Lincoln, and Liberty. When they moved to Vermont they began to explore the Green Mountains. By far the most ambitious adventure was the plan made by RF, Carol, Lesley, Marjorie, and the latter's high-school friend, Lillian LaBatt, to walk the Long Trail, a distance of 225 miles from Bennington, Vermont, to the Canadian boundary, packing food and blankets and sleeping in mountain shelters. The five of them started on 15 August 1922 from South Shaftsbury, and averaged about twenty miles a day. At Pico Peak, near Rutland, RF needed new footgear. He left the youngsters, promising to go by train from Rutland to Middlebury and thence up past the Bread Loaf Summer School to meet them at the Lake Pleiad shelter on an appointed day. He carried out the promise, met them as planned, and continued with them for several more days until they reached the Mount Mansfield region. At that point RF had to give up. The young people went on without him and completed the 225 miles in seventeen days. RF made his way to Morrisville and then to Wolcott on foot. From there he took the train to St. Johnsbury, Vermont, and on to Littleton, New Hampshire, en route to Franconia to spend the rest of the hay-fever season with his wife in Franconia.

[c. 1 September 1922]
Dear Louis   Wolcott   Vermont   nr Canada

I walked as per prophesy till I had no feet left to write regular verse with (hence this free verse) and that proved to be just one hundred and twenty five miles largely on the trail. Here I am stranded here without Elinor's permission to go on or come home. I slept out on the ground alone last night and the night before and soaked both my feet in a running brook all day. That was my final mistake. My feet melted and disappeared down stream. Good bye.

Gratitudinously yours   R.F.

I should admit that the kids all did two hundred and twenty miles. I let them leave me behind for a poor old father who could once out-walk out-run and out-talk them but can now no more.

227 · To Lincoln MacVeagh

[*c.* 15 September 1922]
Dear MacVeagh: [South Shaftsbury]

The enclosed clipping* will tell you what almost became of me in August and September. I don't feel that it does me personally quite justice. I did some hundred and twenty miles actually on the trail and pretty actually on one leg. In this damned newspaper account I am made to drop out and set off for Franconia on foot. Nothing is said of the privations I underwent after that. Nobody knew or asked what became of me. When I dropped in my tracks from a complication of gangrenous housemaids knee and old man's sore toe I was gone through for what money I had in my pockets that might be useful to the expedition and then left for no good. You'll notice nothing more is said of me. Yet as a matter of fact I survived to walk a hundred and fifty miles further all by myself and sleeping out on the ground all by myself to Franconia up a White Mountain or two and then around Willoughby Lake.

I am sorry to have to admit that the Green Mountain Expedition proper was a success without me. It reached home with just one cent left over in its pockets after having wound up by sleeping one night in the graveyard for want of enough to pay for a nights lodging in the hotel at Johnson. . . .

Ever yours   Robert Frost

228 · To Harriet Monroe

RF's dramatic-narrative poem, "The Witch of Cöos," was first published in the January 1922 issue of *Poetry*. The poem was later

---

* Probably from the Bennington *Banner* for 13 September 1922, which carried the headline LONG TRAIL, 225 MILES, YIELDS TO YOUTH AND VIGOR.

awarded a *"Poetry* Magazine Prize" of $200; this letter is RF's acknowledgment.

Dear Miss Monroe: 4 November 1922   South Shaftsbury

    I don't care what people think of my poetry so long as they award it prizes. You couldn't have pleased me more if you had gone deliberately to work to please me. Some have friends, some have luck, and some have nothing but merit. We'll assume me to have whichever of these will reflect most credit on all concerned.

Yours more than ever   Robert Frost

229 · To A. J. ARMSTRONG

PRIOR to November 1922, RF's public readings had taken him no farther south than Baltimore and no farther west than Milwaukee and Minneapolis. On several different occasions Professor A. J. Armstrong, the Robert Browning devotee at Baylor University in Waco, Texas, had tried to lure him into the southwest. Armstrong finally enlisted the aid of Carl Sandburg, who wrote RF, praised Armstrong as a manager of poets as performers, and added that at Baylor "they not only read a man's books before he arrives but they buy them in record-breaking numbers." Thus encouraged to extend his campaigning, RF permitted Armstrong to make up a schedule. When completed, it called for a total of fourteen readings in fourteen days, starting on 10 November at Sophie Newcomb College, Tulane University, in New Orleans; continuing with appearances in Forth Worth, Dallas, Waco, Temple, San Antonio, and Austin, Texas; and ending on 23 November at Columbus, Missouri. Very bravely and successfully, RF carried out all his assignments. But by the time he reached Ann Arbor, to continue his duties as Poet-in-Residence at the University of Michigan, he was ill. The complete text of the following letter is not available.

[c. 28 November 1922]   [Ann Arbor]

. . . You surely gave me The Great Adventure down there towards Mexico, and I have only myself to blame if it was too fast and furious for my faculties to take in. . . . You are the master manager, and I was ready to say so with my latest breath, which was what I was about down to when I wound up in Missouri. . . . You are the friend indeed of wandering poets (I have no doubt, of poets fixed in their places). Browning is your presiding genius. Under him it is your life to think for poets and to provide for them. I am sure I understand so much from having been in Texas if I understand nothing else.

Sometime on another visit more at leisure "I shall desire more love and knowledge of you. . . ."

230 · To LINCOLN MACVEAGH

28 November 1922
Dear MacVeagh: 1432 Washtenaw Avenue Ann Arbor

I saw before I had gone many miles on the Katy that I wasn't going to last to get to New York . . . If I had been absolutely sure I could have telegraphed "Can't keep appointment. Expect to die November 25th. Sorry." But one doesn't like to make gloomy predictions about one's health. It looks too cowardly. It furnishes the Christian Scientists with too much to go on. One just waits patiently in silence till one's worst fears are realized. Then one can talk or telegraph.

What I suppose I felt coming on was the dengue (pronounced dang you) fever from a mosquito bite I got on my first day at New Orleans (pronounced differently from the way I was accustomed to pronounce it). Or it may simply have been the influenza. I was fighting a bad sore throat when I got to Columbia — fighting it without medicine you understand. And now here I am at Ann Arbor in bed with a temperature. . . .

I had many and various fortunes on the expedition. My best audiences were at New Orleans, Austin, Waco and Temple. These were large and seemed to know what I was joking about. In Fort Worth I was attacked by a Confederate veteran in a front seat. Though named after Robert Lee I dealt with him like Ulysses Grant. The Mexicans in San Antonio failed to attend my lecture. I saw not a single one in my audience and he was a full blooded Astec. . . .

Always yours faithfully   Robert Frost

231 · To LINCOLN MACVEAGH

[c. 18 January 1923]
Dear MacVeagh: [South Shaftsbury]

One after another we went to bed with grippe when we got home until finally Irma went down with pneumonia. It was terrible. We should have all died with her if she had died. But luckily she proved a mild case and is now pronounced out of danger. Yesterday Carol froze an ear and a toe sawing with a cross-cut out in a zero wind. Irma has just given us such a scare however that nothing else will seem very terrible for some time to come.

Except with you folks and with Ridgley Torrence I don't believe I had a very good time in New York. I was trying too hard to do my duty, a thing that never pays.

I'd like to make you a list of the people I met and rather detested. It would be too long. A change of subject is called for. . . .

Thanks for your kindness. You are the only hold (or should I say holt?) the Holts have on me I sometimes think.

My thanks to Mrs MacVeagh too.

Ever yours   Robert Frost

232 · To GAMALIEL BRADFORD

Dear Bradford: 18 January 1923   South Shaftsbury

I've just been reading your Aaron Burr. He's a beauty. On with the job. Don't spare to be a little wicked yourself over these wicked people. Not that I would have you make the judicious grieve, but you can afford to make the judicious guess. Tease us.

The echo of your voice reading has hardly died away in my ears.   Ever yours   Robert Frost

233 · To LOUIS UNTERMEYER

AN ILLUMINATING STORY goes with the following pair of letters. As is hinted by letter 231, RF and his wife went to New York City shortly after Christmas of 1922. They stayed with the MacVeaghs, visited the Torrences, saw the Untermeyers, and attended various gatherings. But for reasons not clear, RF appeared at a house-warming and cocktail party, on 6 January 1923, in the newly opened office of Lawton McCall, then editor of the magazine *Snappy Stories.* Among others at the affair were Burton Rascoe, Carl Van Doren, Harry Kemp, and Christopher Morley. As part of a somewhat impromptu entertainment, Morley read several parodies of T. S. Eliot, whose "The Waste Land" vied for honors with Joyce's *Ulysses* as the literary sensation of the season. In conversation with Rascoe immediately thereafter, RF found fault with Eliot as a poet, and thus offended Rascoe.

Making journalistic use of his conversation with RF, Rascoe first described the *Snappy Stories* party in his next column for the New York *Tribune* ("A Bookman's Day Book," Book Section, 14 January 1923, p. 23), mentioned those he met, and then singled out RF for special comment:

"Robert Frost in voice and demeanor reminds me much of Sherwood Anderson. . . . I admire him very much as a person. I regret that I find almost nothing to interest me in his poems. They are deft, they are competent, they are of the soil; but they are not distinctive. . . . Frost himself has little sympathy for Eliot's work, but then he wouldn't naturally, his own esthetic problem is radically different from that of Eliot's. 'I don't like obscurity in poetry,' he told me, voicing the familiar complaint. . . . 'I have heard that Joyce wrote *Ulysses* as a joke.'"

Using those remarks as a springboard, Rascoe continued at some length in praise of Joyce and Eliot.

It may be that Louis Untermeyer sent RF a clipping of this column; and that RF, always quick to resent criticism of any kind, proposed to retaliate with a letter. But instead of sending the letter (addressed to Rascoe) direct to the columnist, he sent it to Untermeyer as an enclosure with the following note. Untermeyer dissuaded RF from sending the letter (234) to Rascoe. But it deserves a place here as representative of the virulent "punishment" RF could concoct in letter form.

Dear Louis: [20 January 1923]   [South Shaftsbury]

Elinor thinks perhaps I ought not to send a letter like this. You judge for us. If you don't think I'll live to be sorry just put it into another envelope and send it along to Burton.

I came home with grippe. Everybody has had it in the house and Irma has had pneumonia — yes. But it's all right now.

I ought to let one at Burton. If you'd like the fun of seeing me punch him I'll come down and punch.

Ever thine   R.

234 · To Burton Rascoe

THIS LETTER was never sent to the addressee.

You little Rascol: [*c.* January 1923]   [South Shaftsbury]

Save yourself trouble by presenting my side of the argument for me, would you? (My attention has just been called to what you have been doing in the *Tribune*.) Interview me without letting me know I was being interviewed, would you?

I saw you resented not having anything to say for yourself the other day, but it never entered my head that you would run right off and take it out on me in print.

I don't believe you did the right thing in using my merest casual talk to make an article of. I shall have to institute inquiries among my newspaper friends to find out. If you did the right thing, well and good; I shall have no more to say. But if you didn't, I shall have a lot to say.

I'm sure you made a platitudinous mess of my talk — and not just wilfully to be smart. I saw the blood was ringing in your ears and you weren't likely to hear me straight if you heard me at all. I don't blame you for that. You were excited at meeting me for the first time.

You seem to think I talked about obscurity, when, to be exact, I didn't once use the word. I never use it. My mistake with the likes of you was not using it to exclude it. It always helps a schoolboy, I find from old experience, if, in telling him what it is I want him to apprehend, I tell him also what it isn't.

The thing I wanted you to apprehend was obscuration as Sir Thomas Browne hath it. Let me try again with you, proceeding this time by example, as is probably safest.

Suppose I say: Of all the newspaper men I ever met, you most nearly resemble a reporter I once talked with casually on the street just after I had paid ten dollars in court for having punched a mutual friend. I talked to him exactly as I talked to you, without the least suspicion that I was being interviewed. He must have taken sides with the mutual friend, for he ran right off to his office and published everything I had said as nearly as he chose to reproduce it.

There you have what I call obscuration. "I say no harm and I mean no harm," as the poet hath it; but the stupider you are the more meaning you will see where none is intended. The really intelligent will refuse to listen to such old-wives' indirection.

Or again, suppose I say: Just because you have won to a position where you can get even with people is no reason why you shouldn't perform face forward like a skunk, now is it? I only ask for information.

There you have what I call obscuration. "I say no harm and I mean no harm," but the stupider you are the more meaning you will see where none is intended. The really intelligent will refuse to listen to such old-wives' indirection.

Or to "lay off" you personally for the moment, suppose I

say: I learn that someone is bringing out an Anthology of the Best Lines of Modern Poetry. He proposes to run the lines more or less loosely together in a narrative and make them so much his own that anyone using them again will have to enclose them in double quotes, thus:

> " 'What sayest thou, old barrelful of lies?' "
> " 'Not worth a breakfast in the cheapest country un-
>   der the cope.' "
> " 'Shall I go on, or have I said enough?' "

These three lines are from Chaucer, Shakespeare, and Milton respectively. Please verify.

There you have what I call obscuration. "I say no harm and I mean no harm," but the stupider you are the more meaning you will see where none is intended. The really intelligent will refuse to listen to such old-wives' indirection.

Or suppose I say: Good sense is plebeian, but scarcely more plebeian than any sense at all. Both will be spurned in aristocratic circles this summer.

There you have what I call obscuration. "I say no harm and I mean no harm," but the stupider you are the more meaning you will see where none is intended. The really intelligent will refuse to listen to such old-wives' indirection.

I thought you made very poor play with what I said about the obvious. The greatly obvious is that which I see the minute it is pointed out and only wonder I didn't see before it was pointed out. But there is a minor kind of obviousness I find very engaging. You illustrate it, when, after what passed between us, you hasten to say you like me but don't like my books. You will illustrate it again if, after reading this, you come out and say you like neither me nor my books, or you like my books but not me. Disregard that last: I mustn't be too subtle for you. But aren't you a trifle too obvious here for your own purpose? I am told on every hand that you want to be clever. Obviousness of this kind is almost the antithesis of cleverness. You should have defended your hero's work on one Sunday, and saved your attack on mine for another. You take all the sting out of your criticism by being so obvious in the sense of easy to see through. It won't do me the good you sincerely hoped it would.

You are probably right in thinking that much literature has been written to make fun of the reader. This my letter may have been. Do you remember what Webster said or implied about the farmer who hanged himself in a year of plenty because he was denied transportation for his grain? — or what Nemphrekepta said to Anubis?

When my reports are in on your conduct, I may be down to see you again.

I shall be tempted to print this letter some time, I am afraid. I hate to waste it on one reader. Should you decide to print it take no liberties with it. Be sure you print it whole.

Ever yours, Robert Frost

235 · TO LINCOLN MACVEAGH

Dear MacVeagh   [c. 2 June 1923]   [South Shaftsbury]

I've decided to be good and stop writing any more into the . New Hampshire poem. You shall have the manuscript in a week or so now. . . .

Our water system failed us — somewhat mysteriously. There was plenty of water at the spring. The pipes were all new and as they should be. The plumbers were baffled. So it fell to me to see what I could do. First I tasted a drop of the water from the pipes with my head cocked on one side. Then I scratched my head. Then I went directly to a definite place in the system and laying my finger on particular spot said There — if you open the pipes with a stilson there you will find a frog as dead as — Genevera in the water works of Seville. They opened the pipes and it was as I said. But instead of delighting to honor me for the one thing I can do well viz diagnose a difficulty with a mechanism, the most anyone could find to say to me was let it be a lesson to you to keep such a strainer at the spring as will henceforth exclude frogs from the system. So our days pass in pastoral tranquility. So also may yours.   As ever   R. F.

236 · TO WILBUR L. CROSS

Dear Mr Cross: 17 August 1923   South Shaftsbury

Alas and alack as de la Mare's fish said in the pan. Alas one of the poems you wanted is just about to be published in The Century and alack the other has already been published

in The New Republic. But I am the gainer in confidence by
your having wanted them. I accept it as a peace offering.

You strike just the right dubious note in congratulating
me about going back to Amherst. I ought to have been poet
enough to stay away. But I was too much of a philosopher to
resist the temptation to go back and help show the world the
difference between the right kind of liberal college and the
wrong kind. You were on my trail at Ann Arbor. You say you
talked me over with the Lloyds and others there. I know what
you said: that I concerned myself too much for my own good
with what was going on round me. I never could keep out of
things. But I can get out of them. That's my saving virtue. I
will bite the hook if it is baited with an idea, but I never bit one
yet that I couldn't wriggle off before it was too too late.

I was never for detachment, social, moral, or physical. I
like consequences, and I like them objective no less than subjective. They are depth as I understand it. Life's not just touch
and go. You may remember I am not good at short calls. I like
to settle down to something. I went to enquire into a young
philosopher yesterday. I meant to spend the afternoon over
him. If the afternoon had been all, I should have come home as
wise as I went. But fortunately I missed my train and the evening was added to the afternoon and just before midnight and
my next train he all came out: he was a Ph. D. of Harvard
1921 who believed in suicide as the only noble death and in no
God. He said he classified in the census as a monist, but you
could count on there being no moaning of the bar when he
embarked. Now if I hadn't formed the habit of staying round
after everything was supposed to be over, you can see what
I would have missed. And by the way what a detached or de-
tachable young man he made himself seem. [. . .]

Yours faithfully   Robert Frost

237 · To Gamaliel Bradford

My dear Bradford: 24 August 1923   South Shaftsbury

I've just been quoting your Tom Paine and the distinction
you make between his liberalism and that of Thomas Jefferson, the one resting on the minor certainties, the other on the
larger uncertainties. I'm all for the second wherever it shows
itself (and I suppose there have been better examples of it

than Thomas Jefferson). It's the recognition of the littleness of our knowledge in comparison with our ignorance that makes us gentle and considering. You are in the secret. Wish to be a rebel sometimes as I sometimes wish to be a mathematician or a landscape gardener. But don't expect me to let you be anything but what you are. Your melancholy, if not a cure for woes, is at least good relief. I once spent an hour on a park bench with a queer doctor and that was all I could get him to claim for his medicines (simples), that they would give good relief, and often *good* relief. Only reformers, he said, ever effected cures. That wonder happened in Manchester, New Hampshire, if you know where I mean.*

Tom Paine is your second best paper though I doubt if you make him out a really damaged soul. He gets into your classification by courtesy or discourtesy. I'm not quite sure of John Brown's title. Otherwise the assortment is perfect. I love Aaron Burr and P. T. Barnum in the same boat. Burr's was what O'Shaughnessy calls an "exquisite malady of the soul"; Barnum's a deformity for the side show.

Always the friend of all you do.

Robert Frost

238 · To Lincoln MacVeagh

[c. August 1923]   Marr's Camp   Indian Pond
Dear MacVeagh   Tarratine P. O.   Maine

[. . .] What do you suppose? Or don't you suppose anything. It is safest not to suppose anything in this case; because I have to report having found the philosopher I was on the hunt for in myself. On my way home from our talks together I said Why not? And the next day being called on the telephone from Amherst to say what courses I would announce for this year in English, I proposed to give one in philosophy on judgments in History, Literature, and Religion — how they are made and how they stand, and I was taken on by the department like odds of a thousand to one. Well the debacle has begun. Here begins what probably won't end till you see me in the pulpit.

---

* The episode with the "queer doctor" happened in the Derry days, when RF was living near Manchester. It formed the basis for the narrative element near the end of RF's poem "The Good Relief."

This doesn't alter my plan to give some class a lot of reading just off the main line of English literature. I shall want the lists of books you were going to get me and want them badly when I get home out of this toward the middle of next week. . . .   Ever yours   Robert Frost

239 · To LINCOLN MACVEAGH

[c. 20 September 1923]
Dear MacVeagh: South Shaftsbury
    [. . .] The rather terrible discovery has been made that the Amherstians who have read "New Hampshire" are sure I mean Alexander Meiklejohn now of New York by my "New York Alec" and my whole poem as a controversy to the Amherst controversy. I was thunderstruck. Of course the Alec will have to go much as I hate to sacrifice the rhyme.
    The Lankes pictures [woodcuts in *New Hampshire*] are well enough. They haven't the distinction of some of those he gave me however. He's worked in too great haste and not done himself quite justice. I like the grindstone one best, the first in the book probably next best.
    Fifty tried to get into my seminar in Fill [philosophy]. As a first exercise in it I sent them out with lanterns to find the originals in life of the half dozen philosophies we talk and write. Queer doings at Amherst. Plainly our philosophies are but descriptions of a few attitudes toward life already long since taken in living.
    Tell Bunny I said so.   Ever yours   Robert Frost

240 · To LINCOLN MACVEAGH

Dear Lincoln-   19 November 1923   Amherst
    (if it isnt too late to change my name for you). The only move you would have to seek my approval of before you made it would be getting out and leaving me alone with the heirs of Henry Holt. I'll bet that is what you are contemplating: but if I thought at all seriously, I would come right down to New York to talk you out of it. I have had half a mind to come down to New York anyway on general principles. It's not so easy, however, to get away. There seem to be all sorts of demands on

me now down in the contract. I'm very tired and even nervous with it all. Imagine having to give hours every day to boys who aren't satisfied to have you acknowledge and notice their disagreement with you: they insist on your being disturbed by it. I had one in here all yesterday afternoon who simply went wild, *cried*, wept and tore his hair because I stolidly refused to be annoyed by his opinions in art. He called me unfeeling. It's the old story of my frostiness. It makes people weep.

Carol's marriage was only a little of a surprise. He and Lillian had been engaged for some time. They were such children that I didnt want to commit them to each other by taking much notice of the affair or saying much about it. I doubt if I thought it would survive Lillian's first year at college. But it turned out in a way to show that I was no judge of the intensity of children. Lillian's first year at college it was that didn't survive. She quit, homesick, and Carol went right to her mother and got her. It was all done in a week. I may be frosty, but I rather like to look on at such things. And I like children to be terribly in love. They are a nice pair. Lillian is an uncommonly pretty little girl. She is pretty, quiet, and unpractical. She has been a great friend of the girls in the family for some years. All she has done is transfer herself from the girls to the boy. We'll see how completely she deserts the girls.

How much better I like the falling in love than the falling out of love. If it wasn't for the real danger of falling out sooner or later I should like the falling in entirely. My pain of the day today is the news that my friend Chase Osborne of Michigan after forty years of apparently happy married life has just fallen out of love with his wife and she with him. They've been everywhere and into everything together, in the best kind of companionship, a stalwart pair of adventurers and explorers. It is too bad to see them give up beaten by the wear and tear. Something hates us and likes to spoil our fair beginnings. Let me not croak too hoarsely, though I am sick with a cold in the throat. . . .   Ever yours   Robert

241 · To Frederic G. Melcher

Dear Melcher: 24 November 1923   Amherst

What ever I come to Montclair to do, it will be in exchange for your coming here once to talk to my class. That is to say you will speak for the same price I speak for. As long as no money will change hands we may as well be exorbitant and establish high records for ourselves. Suppose we make it Chesterton and Tagore's figure — one thousand dollars. We can decide later whether we will publish it. I'm in doubt whether it mightn't do us more harm than good. It would do something for our dignity to climb into the thousand dollar class: but on the other hand it might merely make us look greedy. . . .*

Always yours   Robert Frost

242 · To Mary Goodwillie

MISS MARY GOODWILLIE, a public-spirited Baltimorean and a distinguished philanthropist, had first met the Frosts at Franconia (see letter 125, editor's note). She brought RF to Baltimore on 1 February 1917 to read before The Contemporary Club. In this letter "the Von Moschziskers" are mutual friends who spent summers at Bethlehem (see 295, editor's note).

Dear Miss Goodwillie   3 December 1923   Amherst

Let me answer your first question of several by saying I remember you so well that I recognized your handwriting on your envelope. And I had just been thinking you were one of those I must try with my new book [New Hampshire] to see if they still preferred the least English poetry to any American poetry. I must send you a copy of New Hampshire with our names written in it if you will let me.

Let me answer your second question by saying that the Von Moschziskers are among the best imaginable.

Your third by saying that I should like to read again for you. Could you have me on February 21, 22, or 23 and do you think I could earn one hundred dollars and my expenses?

Your tenth (unless I am mistaken in my count) by saying that I think I can bring Mrs Frost with me. She is more footloose than she once was now that Lesley is selling books, Marjorie is selling books, Irma is at the Art League and Carroll is married and farming. Lesley and Marjorie expect to have a bookstore of their own presently when the place shall have been pitched on.

With best wishes.   Sincerely yours   Robert Frost

* During the later years of his life, RF frequently did receive a thousand dollars for a single evening of poetry reading.

243 · To WILFRED DAVISON

Dear Mr. Davison: [c. December 1923]   [Amherst]

I don't suppose you would want to come down here for a serious talk with me? I've been thinking I'd like to see either you or Mr. Collins. You've done something with Bread Loaf to make it different from the ordinary American school in more than location, but, as I look at it, not nearly enough. You're missing a lot of your opportunities up there to make a school that shall be at once harder and easier than anything else we have. I'd be interested to tell you more about it if you should come down for a visit overnight; and I'd be interested in coming up for longer than my stay of last summer or the summer before, might even stay a week, if you would excite me with something rather more advanced in educational experiment.

By all means have Powell if a good ordinary academic is all you want That's all he is. He won't set your buildings on fire and he won't start anything you never heard of before. Safety first! But you mustn't expect me to have time for adventures in safety. Just because you are in the woods and mountains is no distinction to talk of. You've got to get into something deeper than woods and mountains. It's to be in the councils of the bold that I have been tempted back to Amherst.

I don't mean to shake you all up. I desist.

Sincerely yours   Robert Frost

243-a · GAMALIEL BRADFORD TO ROBERT FROST

THIS LETTER helps show how RF continued to elaborate and preach his theory of building poetry on "the sound of sense." Bradford challenges part of that theory in a valid way.

Dear Frost:-   5 March 1924   [Wellesley Hills]

[. . .] You left me a lot to think of Sunday. . . . Among other things, I reflected a great deal upon your suggestions as to the fundamental quality of style and the importance of the acted element, that is, of the element of utterance.

When, however, you come to applying all this to the art of the writer, I am not so sure that I quite follow you. It is probable that every writer hears his own composition as well as sees it. But the subtle possibilities of variation in the matter are so wide, that I can hardly feel that you are right in feeling that any one interpretation out of many can possibly be imperatively indicated. Take the *Hamlet* line you instance:

So I have heard, and do in part believe it.

[It is] a line, by the way, constantly quoted in my family. I can imagine half a dozen ways of reading that, and I am not at all sure which would satisfy Hamlet or Shakespeare. . . .

244 · To Louis Untermeyer

Dear Old Louis: 10 March 1924   Amherst

Since last I saw you I have come to the conclusion that style in prose or verse is that which indicates how the writer takes himself and what he is saying. Let the sound of Stevenson go through your mind empty and you will realize that he never took himself other than as an amusement. Do the same with Swinburne and you will see that he took himself as a wonder. Many sensitive natures have plainly shown by their style that they took themselves lightly in self-defense. They are the ironists. Some fair to good writers have no style and so leave us ignorant of how they take themselves. But that is the one important thing to know: because on it depends our likes and dislikes. A novelist seems to be the only kind of writer who can make a name without a style: which is only one more reason for not bothering with the novel. I am not satisfied to let it go with the aphorism that the style is the man. The man's ideas would be some element then of his style. So would his deeds. But I would narrow the definition. His deeds are his deeds; his ideas are his ideas. His style is the way he carries himself toward his ideas and deeds. Mind you if he is downspirited it will be all he can do to have the ideas without the carriage. The style is out of his superfluity. It is the mind skating circles round itself as it moves forward. Emerson had one of the noblest least egotistical of styles. By comparison with it Thoreau's was conceited, Whitman's bumptious. Carlyle's way of taking himself simply infuriates me. Longfellow took himself with the gentlest twinkle. I don't suppose you know his miracle play in The Golden Legend, or Birds of Killingworth, Simon Danz, or Othere.

I own any form of humor shows fear and inferiority. Irony is simply a kind of guardedness. So is a twinkle. It keeps the reader from criticism. Whittier, when he shows any style at all, is probably a greater person than Longfellow as he is lifted priestlike above consideration of the scornful. Belief is better than anything else, and it is best when rapt, above paying its respects to anybody's doubt whatsoever. At bottom the world isn't a joke. We only joke about it to avoid an issue with someone to let someone know that we know he's there with his questions: to disarm him by seeming to have heard and done justice to his side of the standing argument. Humor is the most engaging cowardice. With it myself I have been able to hold some of my enemy in play far out of gunshot.

There are people like John Gould Fletcher I would fain not have let in on myself; if I could have held them off all my life with smiles they could take as they pleased. But John G. pushed through my defenses. Let me tell you what happened. It was amusing. You might like to pass it along to [Ben] Huebsch: you know him so well. You could quote this part of my letter word for word. Three months ago John Gould Fletcher wrote me saying "I learn you have a book out. I wish you would use your influence with Henry Holt & Co. to help me get a book out. I am sending them a manuscript." I spoke to Lincoln MacVeagh in the matter. He said he wouldn't publish John Gould Fletcher's book for two simple reasons: first because it wouldn't sell and second because he hated the kind of thing Fletcher wrote. I said I wouldn't ask him to publish it to get me a good review or save me from a bad one. Obviously he might have published Fletcher's book and charged it up to advertising mine. Maurice Firuski knew about this and made haste to tell me the minute it was out that I had got the bad review in *The Freeman*. No doubt I deserved it on two counts that we needn't go into. But I can't excuse Fletcher his bad taste — worthy of Washington politics or New York business. Have I not written in New Hampshire that it's no wonder poets some times have to *seem* so much more businesslike than businessmen? It is because they are so much less sensitive from having overused their sensibilities. Men who have to feel for a living would unavoidably become altogether unfeeling except professionally. And *The Freeman's* part in it interests me. It just shows how hard it is for an American publication, however lofty its pretensions, to keep from lending itself to blackmail and corruption. [. . .]

You did not err. The story in *The Bookman* was Lesley's. But be more truthful than common. You never recognized it from any family resemblance. You had many clues to help you. The knowledge that Lesley was writing under an assumed name, the personal note on her devotion to stone-breaking in Vermont, and the name Leslie. You mustn't tell her any more that she repeats her father. The charge is dangerous to her further development. She has been held back long enough by our discretion and her own. It's time she let out in prose and verse. The bookstore she has contemplated is going to be a mistake if she is driven to it by our coolness to her in her art. I haven't wanted to do anything to excite her to creation. Anyone of mine who writes prose or verse shall be a self-starter. But neither do I want to hold her from it too much or too long. I know you'll sympathise with me in this as much as in anything I have at heart. I thought her story all poetry. I hadn't seen it before it was in print. [. . .]

Affectionately   Robert

245 · To Lincoln MacVeagh

Dear Lincoln: [c. 24 June 1924]   South Shaftsbury

On the contrary I was thinking that Marianne Moore had been turning you against me. You undoubtedly sent me that little folder today to twit me on her having run into the second edition.* The handwriting was your own personal. Be careful, or you'll make her a household word. Then where would she be? — at once rare and common? Like her for all of me. "All those that change old loves for new, pray gods they change for worse." Speaking of worse, we drew off rather worsted from our year's teaching and lecturing, Elinor worse worsted than I. I would have given anything for a baseball game anytime these three months. But what's a fellow to do that combines so many occupations and arts? . . .

Always yours   Robert Frost

246 · To Louis Untermeyer

Dear Louis: 12 August 1924   [South Shaftsbury]

I haven't reported on Amherst yet. I found that the college does belong as charged to Mr. Dwight Morrow of J. P. Morgan & Co. — your bankers in Paris. But so does Smith College

* With her second book of poems, *Observations*.

belong to Mrs. Dwight Morrow. They might belong to worse.
The Morrows are the kind of rich who take good care of their
playthings. Morrow is certainly intelligent and so liberal, he
tells me, as to have sat in until very recently anyway at the
councils of *The New Republic*. Mrs. Morrow is a member of
the Poetry Society of America. Between them they have just
put David Morton on the Amherst faculty, I am told over the
telephone. The question of David Morton was worrying President Olds when I came away. He could have wished him a poet
he knew more about. I couldn't help him much because I
didn't know much myself. The Morrows pressed for Morton
as the winner of some sort of Poetry Society prize. President
Olds is not young. I have seen him worn out with running to
New York all year for instructions and permissions.

The boys had been made uncommonly interesting to
themselves by Meiklejohn. They fancied themselves as thinkers. At Amherst you *thought*, while at other colleges you
merely *learned*. (Wherefore if you love him, send your only
son and child to Amherst.) I found that by thinking they meant
stocking up with radical ideas, by learning they meant stocking up with conservative ideas — a harmless distinction, bless
their simple hearts. I really liked them. It got so I called them
the young intelligences — without offense. We got on like a
set of cogwheels in a clock. They had picked up the idea somewhere that the time was past for the teacher to teach the
pupil. From now on it was the thing for the pupil to teach himself using, as he saw fit, the teacher as an instrument. The
understanding was that my leg was always on the table for
anyone to seize me by that thought he could swing me as an
instrument to teach himself with. So we had an amusing year. I
should have had my picture taken just as I sat there patiently
waiting, waiting for the youth to take education into their own
hands and start the new world. Sometimes I laughed and
sometimes I cried a little internally. I gave one course in reading and one course in philosophy, but they both came to the
same thing. I was determined to have it out with my young-
ers and betters as to what thinking really was. We reached an
agreement that most of what they had regarded as thinking,
their own and other peoples, was nothing but voting — taking
sides on an issue they had nothing to do with laying down.
But not on that account did we despair. We went bravely to
work to discover, not only if we couldn't have ideas, but if we

hadn't had them, a few of them, at least, without knowing it. Many were ready to give up beaten and own themselves no thinkers in my sense of the word. They never set up to be original. They never pretended to put this and that together for themselves, never had a metaphor, never made an analogy. But they had, I knew. So I put them on the operating table and proceeded to take ideas they didn't know they had out of them as a prestidigitator takes rabbits and pigeons you have declared yourself innocent of out of your pockets trouserlegs and even mouth. Only a few resented being thus shown up and caught with the goods on them.

I went to Middlebury [Bread Loaf] and put the finishing touch on myself and my teaching for the year. I speak literally. I am sick to death almost with having gnothied so many people. It seems to have come hardest on my liver or kidneys this time: whereas in the old days the straight teaching I did, wholly unpsychoanalytic, only ruined my first and second stomachs, particularly the first, the one that I ruminated with. I wasn't happy at Middlebury, the scene of my rather funny failure last year with New Hampshire (the poem, not the book). The Whichers were there, the old man Poetry Societist, George, and the wives, and I was aware that for some reason they were not helping me much. George is his father's son. . . . He catches the germs of the people he's with. I left him a protective wash against Meiklejaundice when I came away. But he got the bug though in attenuated form, as is like him.

Let's talk about something healthier. The farm goes riproaring as no farm ever went with me. Carol has hired almost nothing done this year. He has ploughed and done all the haying himself. Fun to look on at — I always so dreamed of being a real farmer: and seeing him one is almost the same as being one myself. My heart's in it with him. I have to strive not to put my mind in and interfere with advice. Let him go it. We've given him the farm outright, as I may have told you. Lillian is an unspoiled little girl easy to interest in everything in the world. She's hard at it preserving a jar of something for everyone of the 365 days in the year.

Lesley's store is well started. She ought to have some of your books autographed. She'll have to wait for them, I suppose, till you get home. I believe she is at the Williamstown Political Institute today with her truck (called the Knapsack) full of appropriate books to sell. She's almost too enterprising for her health. If you see anything over there such as the little hand-carved figures in wood that might add a touch to the shop, do buy it at my expense. She must have atmosphere. You and Jean [Starr Untermeyer] will like the place when you see it. The address is The Open Book, 124 South St., Pittsfield, Mass.

Don't expect me in the Misc[ellany] this year if you don't want to make me nervous. I'm jaded with the pulls on me that I can't answer to. I've made up my mind that with a few people to abet me I won't do one single thing in verse or out of it or with it till I God damn please for the rest of my natural life. The same for prose. I'm not going to write any more letters of obligation. I'm going to wait till I want to say a particular thing in a particular letter to a particular person if I wait till the Second Coming. What did I get into writing for if it wasn't for fun? This is my first letter under the new ruling. You may be sure it is no letter of obligation!

Ever yours   Robert Frost

247 · To FREDERIC G. MELCHER

Dear Melcher: 10 December 1924   Amherst

The Harvard psychologists have been asking us writers if in our experience the act of creation doesn't just naturally articulate into a state followed by an idea followed by some work. Old Christopher Smart said that what God created had to be determined dared and done. As long as we keep to triplets I don't much care. You take this letter. I determined to write it a year ago. So far so good. The next thing was to dare to write it, and I'll tell you it took a lot of courage after not having written it for so long. I didn't know how you might take it. But at last I have decided to be brave and here I am actually at it; and before you know it it will be done, for, believe me, it is going to be short. I am off letter writing except to the most favored people and even those are going to have to be satisfied with notes.

You may have noticed that you don't get much thanks or much pay for what you have done for me in the last few years. Well here's where you are going to get both. Eternal gratitude for always reading me aloud everywhere (it keeps coming round to me how much you help my cause) for the bookplates for Pittsfield and for the unrequited letters. Moreover seventy-five dollars (enclosed) for stirring us up to a better bookstore in Amherst. We surely have the better bookstore and it would be my strength and my refuge in teaching literature if I were to continue here. . . .

You know I'm your friend   Robert Frost

248 · To Leonidas W. Payne, Jr.

MORE THAN two years before this letter was written, RF had been entertained hospitably by Professor L. W. Payne, Jr., Chairman of the Department of English at the University of Texas; but he had never gotten around to expressing his thanks for those hospitalities. Hence the tones of embarrassment in this letter and the pleasant attempt to compensate for his remissness, when Payne wrote him asking for permission to reprint seven poems in an anthology. RF compares his slowness with the Kansas-Texas Express.

Dear Mr Payne   4 January 1925   Amherst

You might well doubt the authenticity of any answer from me on time. The great thing about this letter is that it is characteristically late. Let's hope that it isn't too late to get me into your anthology with the seven poems you ask for. But that must be as may be. It cant be too late for proving me a true friend — true to form I mean. For that purpose the later the better.

But to be serious in a serious matter, please accept my apologies for silence. One thing that kept me from writing sooner was my desire to write more at length to you than to the generalty. I have been looking round for someone besides [A. J.] Armstrong at Waco to take it out on for the pleasure I had in Texas. And your letter sort of gave me an opening and made me decide to lavish myself on you. But I had to get around to a real undertaking like that — I had to get around to it. To me six months are pretty much as one day. All I ask in this age of speed is to be allowed to go slow. An oxcart on a soft dirt road, cost what it will, is my idea of a self-indulgent old age. One of the charms of Texas was that the trains I rode on down there were all six hours (just as I am six months almost to a day) behind schedule. Some people wanted to spoil a good story by blaming the retardation on the late war. Absolutely the only sleeper or waker I saw on time was the one

305

you put me onto that night with a gift of fruit outward bound from Austin. It was lovely — I mean of both Texas and you.

And yet speed is a thing I can see the beauty of and intend to write a poem in free verse on if ever I am tempted to write anything in free verse. Let's see how do you write the stuff:

Oh thou that spinnest the wheel
Give speed
Give such speed
That in going from point A
To point B
I may not have had time to forget A
Before I arrive at B
And there may result comparison
And metaphor
From the presence in the mind
Of two images at the same instant practically.

Or again:

Oh thou that spinnest the wheel,
Give heed!
Those long curves of the road to left and right
That I have hitherto experienced with the eye
And the eye only, —
They are too long-drawn for me to feel swayed to
Till my rate of travel shall have risen to a mile a minute.
Swiften me
That I may feel them like a dancer
In the sinews of my back and neck.

But I desist for want of knowing where to cut my lines unhocuspocusly.

You are welcome to the seven poems, should you still want them. I will ask my publishers not to charge you for them, but if they do charge, please let me know the amount and I will at least get it greatly reduced. Remember me particularly to the Katy with which I feel I have much in common.

Sincerely yours   Robert Frost

249 · To FREDERIC G. MELCHER

Dear Melcher: 26 January 1925   Amherst

I won't say I don't like to be made of by the right sort of friends. I am going to let you give me that triumphal dinner on my fiftieth birthday if it is understood beforehand that I don't much deserve it and that I don't necessarily have to look or act exactly the age. Let's see I'm supposed to be getting all this for certain poems. Should you mind telling me offhand which poems? Now wouldn't it be awful if you didn't know any of my poems to name them off hand? You'd be embarrassed.

Don't forget to ask the Untermeyers. Louis has been proposing a little frame-up to console me for my grey hairs. But I told him you were ahead of him in solicitude.

I must always be your good friend   Robert Frost

249-a · ELINOR M. FROST TO AMY LOWELL

                                    27 February [1925]
My dear Amy,-   10 Dana Street   Amherst

I am enclosing the account of your reading in the students' paper the next morning. It seems very agreeable, if not very original. I forgot to tell you that Mr. and Mrs. Olds left word for you that they were very sorry indeed to miss hearing you. They went to Nassau for a month's vacation about three weeks ago, as Mr. Olds needed a rest very badly.

Robert says to tell you that he'll be on hand for your party if there is anything left of him by that time. He has twelve or thirteen reading engagements between now and then (which means a lot of travelling, as you know) besides keeping up his college work, and I just don't know just how he is going to manage it. Then there is his own party on the 26th, which will, of course, be a nervous strain, though a pleasure at the same time. I wonder if anyone will come to *his* party. Please change your mind and come yourself. — I hope you reached home none the worse for the little trip to Amherst. It was a great pleasure to have you here. I wish you could have seen the town in the daytime, and in a clearer atmosphere.

With love to Ada [Russell] and yourself from us both,
                                    Elinor Frost

249-b · Elinor M. Frost to Edith H. Fobes

REFERENCE has been made (letter 125, editor's note) to the many acquaintances the Frosts made with summer visitors in the Franconia region. Among them were Rev. and Mrs. J. Warner Fobes, who owned a relatively large estate about four miles up Ridge Road beyond the Frost farm. The Fobes's winter home was in Peace Dale, Rhode Island, where Mrs. Fobes had many relatives among the socially prominent Hazard and Bacon families, and one of her relatives was the poet Leonard Bacon (see letter 337). The kindness shown to the Frosts by the Fobes family brought about many visits. Among the letters which have survived, written by Mrs. Frost to Mrs. Fobes, the following is the earliest.

Dear Mrs. Fobes,-   1 March [1925]   Amherst

So much has happened since you were here that it seems a very long time and I can hardly believe it is only three weeks. I was glad to get your nice letter. I am glad that you enjoyed being with us a little bit — we certainly enjoyed seeing you, and only wished you could stay longer. Am glad we had that pleasant, sunny day. The weather has been simply awful ever since. We had about a week of fog so thick that we couldn't see the houses on the street above us here. Of course it has been warm, and that has made the winter seem shorter, and has saved coal.

Robert hails a warm spell in winter with such delight that I am always pleased myself. Tonight it is raining torrents, and has been ever since four o'clock this afternoon.

Next Wednesday we start on our travels, and return two weeks from today, after spending a week in Philadelphia and its neighborhood, and three days in Washington. Robert has readings all through March, and about six in April. At the end of April we'll put $2,000 in the bank, which will make $7,000 in the bank against a rainy day. I went up to the farm for three days last week. The baby has begun to gain again, so Lillian won't have to wean him. The doctor changed the schedule . . . [Baby] is extremely bright and attractive, and so cunning with his short dresses. Carol is making grand preparations for his spring work, with two tons of phosphate on hand, and his seed orders all made out. I wish we could be up there through the spring. I just *love* a farm.

James Stevens, the Irish poet, lectured here the night of the 13th and he and his wife stayed overnight with us. They seem to be very likable people. Last Monday Amy Lowell came. She stayed at the Kimball in Springfield, but she was here for supper, and after the lecture I had a little party for her. About thirty people came in for an hour, and as she was in a particularly gracious mood, it went off very well. I had a caterer come in and serve chicken salad, rolls, coffee and ice cream and cake. Some literary people in Boston are getting up a big dinner for her in Boston, just before she sails the first week in April, in honor of the Keats book, and Robert has got to make a ten minute speech in praise of her on that occasion. Robert and I and the Untermeyers are going to stay with her two or three days at that time, and I am sure we'll have a lot of fun. Robert and Louis will be joking about everything and everybody. . . .

    With love and best wishes from us all.

Affectionately yours   Elinor Frost

249-c · Elinor M. Frost to Amy Lowell

AMY LOWELL served as a member of the committee which planned the so-called Fiftieth Birthday Dinner for RF at the Hotel Brevoort in New York City on 26 March 1925. Without aid from RF, friends of Miss Lowell arranged to celebrate the publication of her biographical study, *John Keats*, with a gala dinner at the Hotel Somerset in Boston on 4 April 1925. RF and Louis Untermeyer had agreed to be speakers at this dinner (see letter 249-a). But after illness had forced her to miss the RF birthday celebration, RF and Untermeyer decided not to attend the Lowell dinner in Boston. RF permitted Mrs. Frost to extend his regrets in this letter. Miss Lowell, suffering through late stages of chronic and serious ailments which helped cause her death one month later, had difficulty herself in attending the dinner given for her. Afterward, RF tried to shrug off his characteristic sense of guilt and remorse (see letter 250).

29 March [1925]

My dear Amy,-   420 West 116 Street   New York City

    I am writing to say what we ought to have said decidedly in the first place — that it's simply out of the question for Robert to speak at your dinner. He just isn't able to. He is tired now, and has three lectures ahead of him this week, with much travelling. He is sorry, and we hope very much that it won't greatly disarrange your plans.

    And we hope very much, too, that the occasion will be a happy and satisfactory one for you. I am sure it will be.

        With love to you and Ada

Faithfully yours,   Elinor Frost

249-d · ELINOR M. FROST TO ADA RUSSELL

My dear Ada,-   12 May [1925]   Amherst

Robert and I are terribly shocked and grieved to hear of Amy's death. We have supposed from the newspaper reports of her condition that she was gaining strength rapidly, and was around the home again as usual. We did not dream it was anything serious.

I have intended to write to her every day, but my heart and hands have been occupied with plans for our son's welfare. I went directly to the farm after Robert's birthday dinner in New York, while he went off on a lecturing trip, and I found Carol in what seemed to me a serious condition. He had incipient tuberculosis nine years ago, and it seemed to me that the same condition had returned, after a winter of too many colds and grippe attacks. Since then I have been at the farm most of the time, looking after his food and urging him to rest. He is much better now, and I think it may not have been what I feared, but we are still worrying about him. Robert has been excessively nervous and overtired. I feel dreadfully that we didn't send any message to Amy, of sympathy for her illness and giving up the English trip.

We shall miss her very much. We were fond of her, and were always delighted, when we saw her, with her lovable traits, and her liveliness of mind and spirit. . . .

Affectionately your friend,   Elinor Frost

250 · TO LOUIS UNTERMEYER

Dear Louis   20 June 1925   South Shaftsbury

[. . .] I suspect that what lies at the bottom of your *Schmerz* is your own dereliction in not having gone to her Keats Eats just before Amy died. She got it on us rather by dying just at a moment when we could be made to feel that we had perhaps judged her too hardly. Ever since childhood I have wanted my death to come in as effectively and affectingly. It helps always anyway it comes in a career of art. Whatever bolt you have shot you have still, as long as you are alive, that one in reserve. But, of course, it always does the most good on a world that has been treating you too unkindly.

I didn't rise to verse, but I did write a little compunctious prose to her ashes. And I did go before the assembled college to say in effect that really no one minded her outrageousness because it never thrust home: in life she didn't know where the feelings were to hurt them, any more than in poetry she knew where they were to touch them. I refuse to weaken abjectly.

I dreamed that as I wandered by the way I was assured by you that I needn't worry any more to run hither and thither currying favor with lectures and recitations: my mark was made as much as it was ever going to be made. I could go back like Cincinnatus to my plough. And you don't know what a relief it was. I wept with gratitude toward you. You mean to say, I cried, I am free to putter my days out without even writing any more if I don't want to write? What's the use of trying to beat Two Look at Two, you answered. Will your frosty mantle to Wilbert Snow. And with that you swung your 1917-model Something Apperson car into the Bennington-Brattleboro-Keene road for the Poetry Society at Peterboro. The souvenir pennons and bannerets all over your car were flapping Robinson, Aline Kilmer, Abbie Brown, etc. and you had on one of these new fashioned tail lights that kept winking Stop Stop Stop.

This dream could have been worked out more carefully to make it mean more if I had turned it over in my mind longer before I wrote it out. It will do well enough as it is for a Freudian diagnosis. It combines a good deal.

The first cousin of Waldo Frank and the third or fourth of Loeb the Darrow ward or charge came to me the other day with a tale of just having broken away from his psychoanalyst after a scene in which he had handed the psychoanalyst a letter and made him read it while he waited. He said it was a very bitter letter full of technical terms. I asked him what had the psychoanalyst done, psychoanalyzed him? It seems he had done worse; he had introspectrosized him. At least, I said, he had supplied you with the language to deal with him in. He had and I made him eat it. Have you been — ah — sick, I suggested. My mother is a subnormal society has-been and last month my brother committed suicide. Why did your brother commit that? Because he was tired of the varnish business that belongs to the family and was engaged to be married to an already married woman. Strange that that hadn't occurred to me. The boy is a perfectly unobjectionable last year's graduate except for a poem as I remember it about Gods face being painted on the sunset sky. God's face *painted!* This must be some of this God-the-Mother cult. Unless he meant the Virgin Mary.

Captain Mattison, our postmaster, and a man who has been to France wanted to know of me what they had gone into court out in Tennessee for, to settle it once and for all who we were descended from, monkeys or the Virgin Mary? Speaking of the Virgin Mary.

And so I might sustain the theme indefinitely that you nor I nor nobody knows as much as he doesn't know. And that isn't all: there is nothing anybody knows, however absolutely, that isn't more or less vitiated as a fact by what he doesn't know. But of this more in my next book which I can't make up my mind about, whether to throw it to Holt, Harcourt, MacVeagh, or Knopf.

I recently ran across a biological fact that interested me, as facts go. It establishes exclusiveness much lower down in the scale than you would expect to find it. Exclusiveness in love. Way way down.   Exclusively yours   Robert Frost

251 · To G. R. Elliott

Dear Roy,   June 1925   South Shaftsbury

I'm sorry this had to happen, but we've been riding for it and I can't say it wasn't expected. Elinor had a serious nervous collapse early last week. I saw it wasnt going to do to leave her and I should have wired regrets then, but she hated to be the cause of my failure to keep an engagement and kept me waiting on from day to day to see if she wouldn't be better. I was actually on the point of setting out for Brunswick [Maine] on Wednesday but at the last moment my courage failed me — she looked so sick. The amount of it is, my way of life lately has put too much strain on her. All this campaigning goes against her better nature and so also does some of this fancy teaching, my perpetual at-home charity clinic for incipient poesis, for instance. Time we got back into the quiet from which we came. We've had our warning. I'll tell you more about it when I see you if you make it worth my while by forgiving me first.

Shall we proceed to the consideration of Longfellow?
                                        Ever yours   R. F.

252 · TO SIDNEY COX

Dear Sidney   5 July 1925   South Shaftsbury

If you see any of the aftereffects of physical labor in this letter you may know that it is from hand mowing — my brow is still wet with what Longfellow called honest, and this being Sunday I am just after having broken the Sabbath quite traverse like a puisne tiller. Great to be home farming.

For you to say when you will come down and see us. When Davison was signing up his faculty [for Bread Loaf] our voyage to Europe looked far more probable than it does now though between you and me I can't say it was ever more than probable enough for an excuse to go to a ball game or stay away from a lecture. In other words we have *subsequently* decided not to go to Europe enough so's you'd notice it. Peace is more my style than Europe. Orestes-like I pray for it or like Dante in the not-too-well-known-and-in-danger-of-being-forgotten poem on him by T. W. Parsons the American dentist.

But we'll save me and my needs to talk over when you come and you and your needs too. I confess Davison threw a slight scare into me and right after seeing him I might have been inclined to think that what you needed was — well cautioning. I now know better. I thought maybe you had been inordinately erring on the right side — as in farming for instance. I hold that all farming is erring on the right side. So don't be offended. But as I say I now doubt if you erred at all. On every hand right, left, before and behindhand reports are that you taught 'em dizzy. Sally Cleghorn was the latest. I heard her say unasked that a fellow named Cox with his breezy western energy was worth the price of admission to the rodeo. I saw my chance to shock her by telling her you were from Bates [College]. It shocked her like a bit of or bite off conservative dogma. Her eyes went round and round like the Hermit's boy who then doth crazy go. She couldn't get used to that. Which just shows you.

While I am about it I may as well enquire if you ever found one crumb of the erotic in the four Gospels. You know Plato virtually says himself two thousand years before Freud that the love of the invisible, philosophy is a sublimation of τὰ ἐρότικα, sex love the mans love not only of fair girls but also of fair boys. The metaphor with him is always drawn from sex. Is it ever a single moment with Christ? Great play has been made with the ladies, not all of them sinless, he had around him. Is it anywhere hinted that his business with the most sinful of them was other than to bid them sin no more? Is the erotic note ever struck? — with or without charm? The great test would be the analogies of argument. They're never (are they) sensual or even sensuous. It's reached a point with me where I've got to have it out with myself whether I can think of Christ as but another manifestation of Dionysus, wine in his beard and the love leer in his eye. Is he even a little Pagan? Isn't he pretty nearly all Puritan for better or worse?*

Always yours   Robert Frost

252-a · Elinor M. Frost to Edith H. Fobes

ALTHOUGH the Frosts moved from Franconia, New Hampshire, to South Shaftsbury, Vermont, in 1920, the miseries of hay fever kept driving RF back to the White Mountains for relief whenever possible during parts of August and September. In 1925, Mrs. Fobes offered the Frosts use of a guest cottage on the Fobes estate in Franconia during the hay-fever season. That invitation was gratefully accepted, and for many years thereafter the Frosts spent a few weeks each summer as guests of the Fobes family. References in this letter are to arrangements for the first of these visits (see letter 249-b).

Dear Mrs. Fobes,-   15 July [1925]   South Shaftsbury

I have just lately been told that Carl Sandburg has agreed to come and read to the southern Vermont Poetry Society on the 6th of August, and Robert and I feel that as we have so many times urged him to make us a little visit, we must at least write and ask him to make it at that time. If he thinks he can do so, we will have to stay here until about the 10th, probably. I think he will come, as we saw him at Bowdoin in May, and he seemed to want to. I am sorry to be later coming up than we had planned.

Irma will come with us, and if we can get someone to do the farm work here, Carol and Lillian will drive us up, and stay two or three days. Marjorie will not be able to go for a couple of weeks later. Carol and Lillian can stay at one of the boarding houses if there are not beds enough in the little house. And I

---

* This paragraph nicely illustrates RF's fondness for "rumpling the brains" of his friends with provocations that bordered on insolence. Sidney Cox had to take more of it from RF than any other correspondent (see letter 344).

can buy some cots for Irma and Marjorie, if they are needed. Lesley may drive up to the mountains to sell books from the Knapsack some time while we are there.

I hope very much that you are well this summer . . . Neither Carol or Lillian seem well enough to please me, and I am rather worried and tired. The baby is in splendid health, and so sweet and cunning that it's a great joy to have him.

With love from us all   Affectionately   Elinor Frost

253 · To John W. Haines

Dear Jack,   21 July 1925   South Shaftsbury

Yesterday we were haying in America. We got in about two tons of Timothy not unmixed with clover. We sold to people passing in their cars some five hundred stems of sweet peas at a cent a piece. Lesley called us up on the telephone from her bookstore in Pittsfield Mass. forty miles below us in the same valley to say she was just back from a fairly successful business trip with her book caravan (a converted Ford truck) to the extremity of Cape Cod. Such might be said to be a day with us. It sounds sufficiently I hope as if we made our living as honest farmers, florists and booksellers.

A night is not very different. Last night I was awakened by the cackling of a hen in a brood coop across the road and rising set out just as I was to see what was molesting her reign. It proved to be a skunk a quiet unoffensive little varmint of the New World that operates like a chemical fire extinguisher to subdue ardors. I should have had a gun with me, but I hadn't. I hadn't even a pogamogan. All I had was a dog. There was no moon. On my way I got involved barefooted with a spring toothed harrow and fell heavily. It should have been a lesson to me, but it wasn't for I got involved with it again on my way back. We gave the skunk a good barking at. The skunk is a dignified soldier, who will walk away from anybody but run away from nobody. We should have been able to do him some damage. If there had been more light there would have been a different story. The dog and I got gassed. I had to throw away my night gown before I re-entered the house. The dog won't smell like himself for a month, especially when it rains. Our casualties were four chickens killed before the main body could be brought up. So you see what it is like.

Why I don't buy a ticket and hoist sail for England when

I long to see you as much as I do! We would have to talk and walk in Leddington and Ryton if I came over. I should probably die of internal weeping. We could call on the ladies, Mrs. Badney across from the Gallows who knocked at our door one dark, dark night with the news that the Germans had landed in Portsmouth, and Ledbury was up-side-down. (This was her version of the foolish American Christmas ship bearing gifts to the Germans equally with the Belgian French and English) and Mrs. Farmer next to Little Iddens who was a tree-poisoner as I've heard. She poisoned a whole apple orchard of her own husband's planting to keep it from coming into the possession of her brother when he ousted them from the farm they had rented of him. She had been punished by the Courts. The law was against her, poor lady. I can still hear her making a tremendous noise with a rattle to scare the blackbirds from the cherry trees. She was doing her best to live down her crime. I can't tell you how homesick I am. For the moment I can't seem to content myself with the characters I am in the way of meeting here. A fellow said to me the other day he supposed the trial at Dayton Tennessee would settle it once for all whether we were descended from Monkeys or the Virgin Mary. At least he knew that the same people who doubted the Biblical account of creation found it hard to believe in the immaculate conception.

All sorts of people get educated in this country. I am so deep in the educational problem that I don't write any oftener than I used to. I'm consulted on the way to handle a poem in school so as not to hurt it for the sensitive and natural. You have no idea of the authority I have become. I might do some good if good were a thing that could be done.

> Our love to you all,
> Faithfully thine, Robert Frost

253-a · ELINOR M. FROST TO EDITH H. FOBES

Dear Mrs. Fobes,- 3 August [1925] South Shaftsbury

What you write about the house certainly sounds attractive. I have always been fond of that house, and it seems so strange that we should really be going into it to stay awhile. You have made it extremely comfortable, I can see, and I know we shall enjoy being there and very greatly enjoy being near you at the same time.

Robert says he will prefer the upper corner room for a study. I think it will be quieter.

You may look for us on Tuesday, the 11th. I will wait a day in order to get my laundry done.

Carol is afraid he ought not to take the time to drive us up. The wet weather has delayed the haying, and made extra work in several ways. I should like to have them go with us to have a little change, but I must not urge him against his judgment. If we come by train we will get off at the Sugar Hill station, as I think that is more convenient for you. I will let you know by telegram Monday if we come by train, and the exact time.

If we drive up, we shall probably not arrive until eight or nine o'clock. Looking forward to seeing you.

Affectionately   E. M. F.

P. S.   I will bring blankets and bed linen, and silver — and also some dishes and kitchen utensils if you don't happen to have a few extra things around. The fewer dishes there are, the fewer one has to wash.

I wonder if there is a Morris chair or arm chair that Robert can have to write in — something with arms high enough for a board to lie across comfortably. If there isn't, I can send one by express from here.

I hope our coming isn't proving too much of a care for you. There is no need whatever of the rooms being painted. You know we are used to camping and picnicing, and will enjoy being there, and helping to get things straightened out.

E. F.

253-b · Elinor M. Frost to Wilbur E. Rowell

My dear Mr. Rowell,-   3 September [1925]   Sugar Hill

I am enclosing a letter which Robert received from Jeanie a few days ago. Some of her letters sound very sane, but many of them reveal clearly the conditions of her mind, and I think this one does that, and is also very pathetic. For instance, her saying that when she has the "excited spells" her nose bleeds slightly — and *her hands won't stop bleeding.* In one letter, she said she could see right into, and through, a person's mind, but it was very difficult when there were two heads in a straight line from her, but even then she could do it — with both.

We were in Augusta the first week in May, and she was not able to talk sensibly or coherently for five minutes. Dr. Tyson is a man of ability, culture, and great sympathy. He takes a special interest in Jean, and I think they have tried very hard to cure her, but he does not now expect that she will ever be able to live outside an institution. And he says that on account of the strict sanitary conditions, the average length of life in institutions is longer than outside — so she may go on suffering this way for many years. . . .

We are in the mountains again on account of Robert's hay fever, and shall be here until the 25th, when we go out to Ann Arbor.

Robert enjoyed his stay in Lawrence last spring very much — I was sorry not to be with him, but wasn't well enough. I haven't been at all well the last three or four years, and have to avoid extra travel and excitement.

Robert sends his kindest regards to you and Mrs. Rowell.

Yours very sincerely   Elinor Frost

253-c · JEANIE FLORENCE FROST TO ROBERT FROST

JEANIE'S PREDICAMENT was a continuing anxiety. RF visited her several times each year at the State Hospital for the Insane, where she remained until her death on 7 September 1929 (for earlier references, see particularly letters 193-a, 194, and 195). Some special meaning for RF of the long and very touching letter which follows will become self-evident if it is read carefully.

[c. September 1925]

Dear Rob,-   [State Hospital, Augusta]

I was sorry Elinor could not come to see me. A week with her might do me a very great deal of good.

I am not well, not able and never have been since being here able to be on parole to go out walking on the grounds. I am depressed nearly all the time and when I get a slight relief from that I have the spells of excitement when they dont know what I would do.

I am very peculiar and did not start right. If I ever was well and natural it was before I can remember. I hate to have anyone understand how I feel in a way. To the mind of anyone who could understand the condition of my mind, there could not be any worse horror. This is the way I have been for the past twenty years and before that, only I did not use to understand — I used to lay it to causes that had nothing to do with it. I used to think if I could only get out of Lawrence I would be all right, etc.

People always slight me. That's what I used to mind. It isnt that really now I think. It's just entire boredom, lack of interest in books, everything. My heart is steel, I cannot see, I cannot feel.

> This heart of stone
> Ice-cold, whatever I do
> Small and cold and hard
> Of all hearts the worst of all

When I have been sick here as I have been twice, delirious, so that I couldn't recognize anyone, I imagine myself forever unable to move and without any feeling or interest, or else I pace back and forth feeling forever glum, caring for nothing. It isn't what I see interests me, I wouldn't care if I was blind and couldn't see a thing. It's only what I am that I care about. On the other hand I resist that I *won't* be *ambitious*.

Of course I like the patients in a way and would do things for them if I could. Still I don't care. Mama spoke as if I was childlike, more nearly all right if not perfectly so until I had that sickness when I was three years old and cried every time I was spoken to when they took me to my meals at the hotel so that I had to have my food brought to our rooms and they had a doctor for me who thought I might become subject to spasms. One of the first things I can remember is crying because someone gave me a drink of water, either fed it to me or handed it to me. Probably they thoughtlessly called me a baby when I was slow to learn to dress and I got to worrying about it. I was insulted because I thought I was smart enough to get the water myself. Few people realize how entirely this depression cuts me off from things so that only for occasional moments I might as well be stone deaf and blind.

The ennui I can remember feeling when I was at the Abbotsford [hotel in San Francisco]. I was a little better the summers I was five and six when we got out in the country. I remember waking the morning we left San Francisco to go down to Sausalito to camp out. I thought of it the minute I woke up — I was pleased that I was going. I've hardly ever been pleased at anything else in my life except when I drank coffee or when people praised me.

Then of course there's that contradiction in one that makes me say to "H— with praise or success" and think I'd as soon crack a safe as to be proud of anything I'd done or knew. The summer I was eight when you and I were with "Aunt" Blanche at Mrs. Braggs in Napa my head got into a rather bad condition owing to being separated from mama for such a long time, six weeks. That was the effect it had on me, it affected my mind. I was not homesick, nor would have been especially glad if mama had come.

In fact a relative by marriage of Aunt Blanche asked me if I missed my mother and when I said "No" she said she didn't like little girls who didn't miss their mother. Then I went off and cried. I should have told her I wasn't conscious of missing her. My thoughts became, however, gloomy. The mental trouble is very bad in the patients here who are not homesick and don't mind staying here. At Napa I didn't long to get home. Though when I did get back to San Francisco I rather liked it around home so that I stayed out of school for half a year. Papa was bound up in us and invariably kind to me, too much so, but I suppose he couldn't help it he was so good-hearted that he pitied me. He was sick for three years, had slow consumption and became depressed too for a time. He had a stern manner, but now I like him for it better as it gave him character. At the time I was constrained with him, did not feel at home. At last I took it into my head he didn't like me. The last Christmas I remember his saying to mama "Get Rob a nice present round five dollars," I think he said five or ten. I thought he didn't want me to have anything for Christmas. But of course he spoke that way because you were an older child and would not care for little toys, but would like something really good. I asked the doctor if he didn't think it strange that I didn't like literature Shakespeare, The old Golden Treasury, Meredith, or Conrad. He said "No," it was a part of it, part of the way I have the disease I suppose he meant. He said I was introverted. Well its the most painful thing there could be short of being on the rack and screaming.

A child I went to school with told me her own father didn't like her and I remember thinking that was just my case but I thought I had to pretend he did. So I told her my father thought a lot of me. Then when he bought silk for a dress for me I told her so and that helped strengthen the impression I was making on her of his devotedness.

Papa was an incorrigible tease, and not perhaps especially fond of children but he certainly thought a lot of us. I had a feeling then for him down underneath. And when I've been delirious here I've thought of him. I thought his ghost followed us from San Francisco to Lawrence.

Can't you come over to see me before you go out to Ann Arbor?

The doctor says I put up a defense around myself. Of course I don't consciously. As the doctors say I must fight this off. I think I will make up my mind to have a good time. That's the whole trouble. Want to and can't.

The other night we had a little birthday party out on the violent ward. I enjoyed that and they did. The best patients are on the worst wards, but I suppose they would break glass out here.

Wouldn't you buy me a small graphaphone, the smallest size you can find? It wouldn't cost more than ten or twenty dollars, would it? The patients would like it and could dance by it and we might have some pleasant times. When there's a party now sometimes there's nothing to do for the very insane ones can't play cards.

They have enjoyed the candy you and Elinor have given me for them but now I'd rather give them the music. You see the candy costs $2 or so if you send any amount so that you could buy a graphaphone for what you'd spend on candy if you sent it four or five times. I would want the very smallest size of graphophone that comes.

I have $22.65 in the treasury that I use for fruit and to buy books so you I can save you spending that as I don't like to have you spend too much. You will write for a catalogue won't you, and buy me as tiny a graphophone as they come and send it to me and they can have no end of good times and and my depression is relieved so that sometimes I worry for fear that they will let me alone or treat me well.

The universe seems only a machine to me, flowers, books, and everything, or else long drawn out obsequies. The first is the worst.

If there's a future life of course I'll get well sometime.

The doctor thinks I can get well — doesn't consider my

case incurable. At times I feel almost sure I am incurable — at others afraid. What do you think?

As a baby almost I felt the things people said to me and had that nervous attack. This ennui succeeded it — I got shut in with myself away from everyone. I felt it at the Abbotsford there in San Francisco.

When I get these excited spells I feel quite a little better, my nose bleeds slightly When I put my handkerchief in just once there's blood on it and my hands won't stop bleeding. But when I'm quiet and would seem to one not understanding really well I'm so quiet and rational my blood doesn't flow in such a way as to cause me pleasure. It's my mind, as they say is controlling the circulation of my blood.

It was after "Aunt" Blanche left I had that nervous trouble so I couldn't go to the table so I guess her leaving caused it for she took care of me all time and had me with her at night I guess. Tho if she had come back, it would have done me no good. I need a few things, 3 pair Union Suits (59 cts, a pair) 2 pairs stockings 1 doz. handkerchiefs Pair of bed-room slippers, 98 cts. I like inexpensive handkerchiefs as I am apt to lose them. I like to get as inexpensive things as possible so as to leave more money for books if I should want them.

I like the short stockings Elinor sent me before and they have worn well. And would you send me one paper dollar in a letter?

I read The Cloister and the Hearth but everything almost I read or look at seems to me like eating blueberries slightly sprinkled with salt. This neutrality in me I project into things I read, afterwards, so that I read more hoping it will do me good than because I really want to.

That was a fine lot of magazines you and Elinor sent me. Have you got any more? And if not too much trouble I would like Theatre Classic and Photoplay but I won't ask for these motion picture magazines again as I suppose you have to buy them on purpose. The patients need the magazines.

It is good that Carol is doing so well with his flowers. I should think he might prefer being a florist to anything else, unless he becomes an artist

When one is almost absolutely without resources, doesn't care for travel, books or music, he or she is badly off. Jean

Will be glad if guardianship is appointed so I can pay my board

254 · To John T. Bartlett

[c. 1 January 1926]   The Open Book
Dear John: 124 South Street   Pittsfield, Mass.

[. . .] I can answer a few of your questions. I'm doing at Ann Arbor next to nothing now. I shall have one seminar a week in writing of all kinds but hand next term. You wouldnt say I wrote much. I have done four small books in twenty eight years, one in seven. I think the rate increases a little. I cant be sure. I have got so I answer almost no letters. Do I lecture? I talk as much as I am able to. The platform takes it out of me. One year I hurt myself. Pullman training, dining out and wagging a swallow tail behind a lecturn. This year we are limiting me to less than last year. To give you some idea. I do them by rounds or flights. First round this year: State Teachers' Association, Laconia N. H., public show Philadelphia, Johns Hopkins, Baltimore, State University, College [Chapel] Hill, North Carolina and so home with a cold to bed. I am just about to break loose again. I begin at Bryn Mawr come up to Schenectady and then go to Amherst for two weeks of one thing and another. Oh I forgot I did another set of three, one at Chicago and two at Grand Rapids. Later I go to Iowa State and Illinois State — and Detroit I believe. I try not to have more than three or four on a trip. This we still feel is more than is good for me. My worst year [1922] was forty exposures. Some of the time I have needed the money but mostly I havent. I must have told you I have had tours planned that would have taken me through Colorado. But I didnt feel up to them. I'd like well enough some excuse to visit you. I guess I'll have to visit you without an excuse some time. That's what it will come to.

I am not sure of hanging on long at Ann Arbor though the position is supposed to be for life. It's too far from the children for the stretch of our heart strings. Carol probably wont be budged. And heres Lesley and Marjorie in the book business in Pittsfield. We've just come on to be with Marj for an operation for appendicitis. She's been having bronchial pneumonia. We dont like to be scattered all over the map as long as we dont have to be. Elinor stands being separated from the children worse than I do. What I want is a farm in New England once more.

One advantage of being here is it gives me a chance at all

the brand new books without money and without price. I've just read Lord Grays Twenty-five Years (corker) Charnwood's Gospel of St John (worth a look into if you want to know the latest higher criticism) the Panchatantra (the most ancient book of anecdotes, source of most now going) and Max Eastman's Since Lenin Died (in hopes of getting the truth at last from our fiercest American Communist). Gee they're all good books. Any book I cant let alone is a good book. I go months years without reading a thing. Then I read 'em at the rate of three a day. Willa Cather is our great novelist now. Her Professor[']s House is all right. I wonder what you would say to such an able but sordid book as Sherwood Anderson's Dark Laughter. Probably you wont find that last in your public library.

I'll try to write you a letter of ideas another time. This is all things. My lecture at Bryn Mawr will be on the subject For Poetry to Surpass Prose — if that tells you anything.

Eighteen below here yesterday.

Have a good year   Always yours   R. F.

255 · To SIDNEY COX

Dear Sidney: [c. 1 January 1926]   Pittsfield

[. . .] You're a better teacher than I ever was or will be (now). But I'd like to put it to you while you are still young and developing your procedure if you dont think a lot of things could be found to do in class besides debate and disagree. Clash is all very well for coming lawyers politicians and theologians. But I should think there must be a whole realm or plane above that — all sight and insight, perception, intuition, rapture. Narrative is a fearfully safe place to spend your time. Having ideas that are neither pro nor con is the happy thing. Get up there high enough and the differences that make controversy become only the two legs of a body the weight of which is on one in one period, on the other in the next. Democracy monarchy; puritanism paganism; form content; conservatism radicalism; systole diastole; rustic urbane; literary colloquial; work play. I should think too much of myself to let any teacher fool me into taking sides on any one of those oppositions. May be I'm wrong. But I was always wrong then. Its not just old age with me. I'm not like Maeldune weary of strife from having seen too much of it. (See Tenn) I have wanted to find ways to transcend the strife-method. I have found some. Mind you I'd fight a healthy amount. This is no pacifism. It is not so much anti-conflict as it is something beyond conflict — such as poetry and religion that is not just theological dialectic. I'll bet I could tell of spiritual realizations that for the moment at least would overawe the contentious. That's the sort of thing I mean. Every poem is one. I know I have to guard against insisting on this too much. Blades must be tempered under the hammer. We are a political nation run on a two-party system: which means that we must conflict whether we disagree or not. School must be some sort of preparation for the life before us. Some of our courses must be in rowing. Dont let me oversay my position.

They say time itself is circular and the universe a self-winding clock. Well well just when it reaches the back country that the universe is a mechanism and what reason have we to suppose we are anything but mechanisms ourselves the latest science says it is all off about the universe; it isnt a mechanism at all, whatever we fools may be. It will take fifty years for that to penetrate to the Clarence Darrowsians and Daytonians. The styles start in Paris and go in waves, ten years from crest to crest, to the ends of the earth. Let us put in some of our time merely sawing wood like William II.

Be good   Ever yours   Robert Frost

No I mustnt think of teaching this year. Perhaps another year if you stay on in Montana that long.

256 · To Louis Untermeyer

Dear Louis   11 February 1926   Ann Arbor

We have been East two whole months with a sick Marjorie and are now divided over her, Elinor having stayed on to take care of her and I having come to Ann Arbor to make some show of teaching a little for my year's pay. I'm sad enough about Marj, but I am more busted up than sad. All this sickness and scatteration of the family is our fault and not our misfortune or I wouldn't admit it. It's a result and a judgement on us. We ought to have gone back farming years ago or we ought to have stayed farming when we knew we were well off.

I put my own discombobulation first to lead up unnoticably to yours. I've heard things about you that sound like suffering. And I must see you. I'm no authority on trouble for all the success you ascribe to me in settling Joseph Warren Beach's troubles in the day of them. I'm just your plain friend in favor of the unmelodramatic [marriage] status quo. Not for me to argue anything where I don't know. I just want to hear you talk.

[. . .] J. W. [Beach] really seems to have been serious in that marriage. I made up my mind he should be as serious as lay in me to make him! He rather played it on me the day he used me for a chaperone to sit in his Ford car for respectability while he stole off . . . in whatever takes the place of alders in Minnesota. I could see he thought it was funny to be so romantic at my expense. So to be equally funny and romantic at his I went straight on from that moment, and inside of two days had him sewed up in marriage for the rest of his life. I bought 'em the only champaign I ever blew anyone to either epi or prothalamial. I wanted to know who the laugh was on last. Really I'm glad now if it was on no one. But you mustn't play lascivious tricks on me for a literary man. I help hasten the consequences. One practical joke deserves another. Of course mine was the more serious of the two. I can be rather unthinking. One of my faults is a love of the excitement of putting a thing through — or a person.[. . .]

Ever yours   Robert Frost

257 · To Mr. Skinner

AS RF stated somewhat whimsically in letter 254, he conducted a course in creative writing at the University of Michigan during the spring term of 1926. Mr. Skinner seems to have been one of the students in that course.

Dear Mr. Skinner,   7 April 1926   [Ann Arbor]

My long delay with these stories has given you time to think of some things about them for yourself, alternating between doubt and confidence. It has probably done you good; so I won't apologize.

You know I save myself from perfunctory routine criticism of ordinary college writing on purpose to see if I can't really help now and then someone like you in earnest with the art. Two or three times a year I make a serious attempt to get to the bottom of his work with someone like you. But it's all the good it does. I always come a long way short of getting down into it as far as the writer gets himself. Of course! You ask me if there is enough in the stories to warrant your going on. I wish I knew the answer to that half as well as you probably know it in your heart. Right at this moment you are very likely setting your determination to go on, regardless of anything I say, and provided only you can find within a reasonable time someone to buy and read you. I'd never quarrel with that spirit. I've a sneaking sympathy with it.

My attempt to get to the bottom of a fellow writer's stuff this time put this into my head: All that makes a writer is the ability to write strongly and directly from some unaccountable and almost invincible personal prejudice like Stevenson's in favor of all being as happy as kings no matter if consumptive, or Hardy's against God for the blunder of sex, or Sinclair Lewis' against small American towns or Shakespeare's, mixed, at once against and in favor of life itself. I take it that everybody has the prejudice and spends some time feeling for it to speak and write from. But most people end as they begin by acting out the prejudices of other people.

There are real niceties of observation you've got here and you've done 'em to a shade. "The Laugh" has the largest value. That's the one you show most as caring in. You see I want you to care. I don't want you to be academic about it — a writer of exercises. Of course, not too expressly, overtly caring. You'll have to search yourself here. You know best whether you are haunted with any impatience about what other people see or don't see. That will be you if you are a you. I'm inclined to say you are. But you have the final say. I wish you'd tell me how you come out on thinking it over — if it isn't too much trouble — sometime.

I ought to say you have the touch of art. The work is clean run. You're worth twice anyone else I have seen in prose this year.   Always yours,   Robert Frost

Belief, Belief. You've got to augment my belief in life or people mightily or cross it uglily. I'm awfully sure of this tonight.

258 · To G. R. ELLIOTT

Dear Roy: [c. 10 May 1926]   [Ann Arbor]

We've been converging on each other's neighborhood ever since you wrote the essay on my neighborliness in 1917, till at last it seems we are about to find ourselves on the same faculty in the same town. Our story is rounding out. From now on comes the sequel. Don't you go and spoil it by picking up and coming to one of these big western universities you don't seem to think so badly of from all I can make out. Wouldn't it be a joke if our migrations should cross each other and you should come back west just as I came back east. Stay in Amherst. You are a large part of what I bargained for in returning.

The five thousand is a lot for ten weeks. I'm satisfied with the amount. What I am after is detachment and long times alone rather than money. Nobody knows how much less money I have taken in late years than I could have. Enough is enough. So say I and all my family fortunately agree with me. For at least one or two of them less is enough than for me. There's where my real success lies, if I may be accused of having any, in being so uncursed in my family.

Think of the untold acres I can spade up in the forty weeks of every year I am going to have free for farming. Suppose I live like Landor till ninety. That will give me one thousand six hundred weeks all to myself to put in at any thing I like. I hadnt thought of it before but by that calculation I have more freedom ahead of me than I have behind (and I have a good deal behind). All in all it has been such a lucky and original life that I can't understand my ever being for a moment cross or difficult or dissatisfied or cast down. I came west on an impulse; I go back east on an impulse; and nobody says a word. I am simply indulged in everything regardless of my deserts. Where is there a case parallel? And over and *above* everything I have had the fun of writing a few poems.

Margery begins to lift the load she was off our hearts.

Our love to you all.
Ever yours   Robert

259 · To JOHN T. BARTLETT

Dear John: [26 May 1926]   [Ann Arbor]

Let's see if I can remember what all has happened since the flurry last fall about transporting Carol to Colorado for his health. I was skeptical about prying him loose from his attachments to the South Shaftsbury farm. He's getting more and more dug in there with every tree and bush he makes a hole for. Right now he is adding a hundred Astrachan trees to the dwarf orchard — dwarf so as to get them sooner for the roadside market. He's putting in some sixty of Miss White's (of Whitesbog N. J.) cultivated high-bush blueberries. And a lot of roses. The process is the dragnet process. You try everything and throw away what you dont like. He and Lillian sold a hundred dollars worth of sweet peas last summer with a small hand painted sign. Theres a new girls college just starting at Bennington four miles away on which he builds some hope of a more or less flowery kind of farming. It may come to a hot house in the end. And it may not. He lost one of his great big workhorses a week or so ago. Farming has hard setbacks. In that loss went about all he had earned in teaming in the woods all winter. He's such a worker as I was never suspected of being though I may have been: so don't be too ready to grin you low-minded Rockingham County Mephistophiles. Speaking of the devil as impersonated by yourself in those golden days, do you remember the Comus, Kenneth Miller, whom Mr Bingham trusted with the church communion set for the banqueting scene in Circe's Palace. Well I all but saw him in Grand Rapids. He was looking for me but missed me. He is something in the business end of furniture. Then I ran on to another Pinkertonian in a strange way in one of the trust companies in Wall St — Charles Williams — you may not have known him. He went from Pinkerton to Haverford. He only had his senior year with us.

We're going east again said the pendulum. This was no go this year, or rather it was too much go and what wasnt go was come. Marjories long illness (means more than sickness) kept Elinor with her in Pittsfield Mass and me commuting for months. Every week or so I would run the water out of the pipes and leave the house here to freeze. It wasnt exactly in the contract that I should be away all the time and I wasnt quite all. I'm not going to try to keep it up here with the children back there and such things likely to happen again. And anyway I want a farm. It's all arranged so you neednt exclaim a protest about such whiffling. Amherst, Dartmouth, Bowdoin and Connecticut Wesleyan are going to give me a living next year for a couple of weeks in each of them. The rest of the time I shall be clear away from the academic, feeding pigeons hens dogs or anything you advise for the pleasure or profit in it. The only thing that worries me is that Bennington college coming in on our pastoral serenity. I ran away from two colleges in succession once and they took revenge by flattering me back to teach in college. Now I am running away again and it looks as if they would come after me. I'll probably end with one of the ponderous things in bed with me on my chest like an incubus. Look out or the same fate will overtake you, or so I begin to fear from what you tell me about the friendliness of your University out there. We may both live to be sorry we didnt go through school in the regular course of nature and get it over with.

[. . .] Spring probably is weeks ahead with you of what it is with us. Lilacs are exactly half in bloom. I'm burning wood in the fireplace tonight, May 26-27 (that is to say midnight).

You've got adopted and adapted out there. But me, I'm sort of a Yank from New England. I want to get back, if its just the same to everybody. Nothing's invidious about my preference. I like Michigan people and I like Michigan. Only only.

Best love to you all

Ever yours in everything   Robert Frost

260 · To GEORGE F. WHICHER

Dear George: [c. June 1926]   [South Shaftsbury]

It deserves remark in this connection that I have at last developed a one-legged writing table the materials of which can be found in almost any wood shed and assembled in a minute. The specifications call for one stick two and one half feet long, one piece of wallboard two by one, and two board nails. Once built it can be used in any seat on earth with or without arms. You see the gain. Strange chairs have no longer any terror for me. Formerly what often kept me from moving where I listed was the fear that I mightnt find a chair there that I could be felicitous in. The chair I could write in had to have just the right arms to support a shelf stolen from the closet and not interfere with my elbows. I actually took a Morris chair in a packing case to England to make sure of having just what I wanted. You hope I am properly ashamed of owning to such limitations? I am. But they are a thing of the past. This new invention saves me. At last I am free to wander as much as I would naturally. But dont be disgusted. Naturally may not be as much as you might think from what you know of me. I honestly mean to cleave to Amherst this time till long after the compulsory retiring age. Ninety is the mark I have been setting myself with Roy Elliott. Landor's furthest north — ninety is the Pole isnt it — where a lot of things are true about time and space that are true nowhere else. And so on off into my mysticism where you wouldnt care to follow me. It is an open covenant, then, openly arrived at (awful stuff to fob a nation off with) that ninety shall find me writing my last least lump of lyric at Amherst. . . .

I'm going to permit myself the largest farm house on it that I can buy in south western Vt.* Something so big that if the crime wave went over it and the robbers came in the windows the different members of the family couldn't hear each other getting murdered. Wide hall right through the middle. Four open fireplaces down stairs and four up. Running spring water in the kitchen sink. Tie-ups for twenty cows. Barn in the way of the view.

My Louis [Untermeyer] has a new high school anthology of modern poetry out [*This Singing World for Younger Children*] with exactly two poems in it by his last wife and two by his next. That looks more dispassionate than I'm afraid it is. Our John Erskine has become a great authority with the press on how such things are to be taken by friends and relatives.† Nevertheless I feel put in a hard position. Jean [Starr Untermeyer] has as good as forbidden us to receive Virginia [Moore]. That hangs Louis in Limbo.

Our best to you both.   Ever yours   Robert.

261 · To Edgar Gilbert

STARTING in the summer of 1893, when nineteen years old, RF worked for several months as a light-tender in the Arlington Woolen Mills in Lawrence, Massachusetts. Among his co-workers there his best friend was Edgar Gilbert, eighteen years old. Gilbert later at-

* RF's meaning is half-serious and half-playful: on the strength of his recently completed agreement to return to Amherst College as a permanent member of the faculty, he is tempted to buy another farm. Nearly three years later he did buy a second farm in South Shaftsbury, Vermont (described in letter 272); but it did not measure up to the one he dreams of here.
† RF apparently refers to Erskine's novel, at that time a best seller, *The Private Life of Helen of Troy* (1925).

tended Dartmouth College, was graduated in the Class of 1905, and eventually became successful as a chemist in Morristown, New Jersey. In 1926, Gilbert wrote RF saying that during a recent visit to a daughter studying at Mount Holyoke he had tried and had failed to find RF in Amherst. The following is RF's reply.

Dear Ed: 10 July 1926   South Shaftsbury

I dont suppose we think those days in the mill ever hurt or hindered us a mite. I often speak of them not to say brag of them when I want to set up as an authority on what kind of people work with their hands what they earn or used to earn how they take themselves what they do with their leisure and what becomes of them. There were Hoffman, Brackett, Lang, George, Gilbert, and Frost. You are accounted for and so am I. It seems to me I heard a year or two ago that Billy Golden was still in the Arlington Mills: which would make some people say "Just think of it." I wonder if Horace Hoffman is still courting Billy Golden's sister. The last I knew they had been engaged for some time with no definite marriage intentions.

I remember the Shakespeare and the wrestling and the bulb throwing and the talks over in your quiet dynamo room and John's large family and the carbon dust and the ladders we slid on one leg ahead of us along the well-oiled floors. I learned a lot of things in those days that have been of no particular use to me since but one thing I never learned was to stand over going machinery on the top step of a step-ladder with nothing to hold on to or brace a shin against and unsling an arc lamp from the ceiling for repairs. It always scared me irresponsible. Once after having used a broom to shut the current off at the switch, I carefully but timidly dropped the broom right across all the threads to (or from) a jackspool. I cut every thread. Before I could get down from my high perch I had been danced at gesticulated at and sworn at by a boss and an overseer. Mea culpa!

It wasn't ball, but football between Methuen High and Pinkerton that last time we met. You had a delayed pass or something you beat us with.

Last year I wasn't at Amherst, but I was the year before and shall be next year again — at least for the ten weeks of the winter term (We divide the year in three at Amherst.) So if you're visiting Mount Holyoke do look me up for a good old talk.

It was fine to hear from you.   Always yours   Robert Frost

261-a · ELINOR M. FROST TO EDITH H. FOBES

Dear Mrs. Fobes,   [August 1926]   [South Shaftsbury]

Robert and I have decided to go up to the mountains next Monday the 9th [see letters 252-a and 253-a]. We haven't a time table so I will have to telegraph you the exact time of our arrival at Sugar Hill. It will be the same train we came on last summer.

Irma and Marjorie are going to stay here two weeks longer. Irma can do the house work and they can be company for Lillian during her convalescence. She is getting along splendidly. Robert has become very nervous, and it is necessary for us to be by ourselves, without the children, for a little while, so that he may recover his equanimity. We are looking forward with pleasure to seeing you and Joe again.

With love from us all.   Affectionately yours,

Elinor Frost

I think it would be pleasant to use the corner room down stairs for a bedroom. I am not sure. It depends on how nervous Robert is. We might have the dining table and chairs in there at first and possibly change afterward. The upstairs rooms must be so wonderful with the east windows that the children would enjoy them very much.

262 · TO DOROTHY CANFIELD FISHER

DOROTHY CANFIELD FISHER had apparently sent an early draft of her article about the Frosts' Vermont home, the Peleg Cole House in South Shaftsbury, to RF at Sugar Hill, New Hampshire, while he was making his annual hay-fever retreat. The article, "Robert Frost's Hilltop," was published in *The Bookman* for December 1926 and was illustrated with a woodcut by J. J. Lankes, who had done the "decorations" for *New Hampshire*.

Dear Dorothy   [c. 30 August 1926]   [Sugar Hill]

My children and grandchildren (singular) will believe it when you tell them it is an interesting old historical house they live in. If I told them they might put it down to professional poetry. You go just the right way about fostering their fondness for the place and perhaps planting the family on it forever. There is no time like the present, right on top of this to start making it the ancestral home of the Frosts. Five years isnt much toward making it so, but five years is more than four.

We can surely stand having our house praised over our heads, if you think our new neighbors the cast off countesses can who have been buying in among us. What you say is balm of compensation to us for having been left out of the articles in The [Bennington] Banner on the historical houses they have been recently taking up in the Shaftsburys.

No but seriousness aside you make the old house and the region live for us with strokes of the pen. What you dont know and what you dont remember about men things and happenings in our valley wouldnt take one card in a catalogue. And I suppose we neednt think we have any exclusive place in your memory. You doubtless carry round in your head as much of Kansas Ohio and France as of Vermont. Thats what I am always struck with in your stories — the amount of material you swing. And if I don't always like what you make it come to or seem to prove in the working out, I surely like what you make it come to (you make it prove nothing) this time in Mrs Bascomb [in *Her Son's Wife*]. You pack her figure full. You lump her and leave her for what she is. I wonder where all you got her. It would be fun to hear you deal with her the way you did with the Crazy Quilt [in a talk given] at Ann Arbor and tell what sights and insights she was composited of. I suppose she is just one of your many. I dont know anyone but myself as well as that. I couldnt go as close as you sometimes do there unless by confession.

I meant to tell you I have been telling the editors of The Dearborn Independent that you were the one to help them turn their magazine literary, as is now their ambition since they have exhausted the Jew. They seem fearfully in earnest about doing something for the arts with a slight pardonable emphasis on the American as distinguished from the New York arts. I shall do what I can for them. Wouldnt it be splendid if they could lead off with a set of short stories from you.

Just two or three slightest suggestions about the article. It makes me feel a little unhappy to come off too much better than the artist in it. [Marginal note added by RF: "You do like the wood-cut I hope. We must further Lankes."] Couldnt you say: "All very well as a picture. The woodcut is beautiful admirable masterly. But let the artist take care not to lean for effect to[o] far over on the side of the sombre. This here R. Frost is not etc." And it makes me a little sheepish to get credit for the woodpile and the sweet peas. Wouldnt it be jolly to say, "his son Carol[']s mountainous woodpile," "his daughter Lillian's sweet peas." I'm a hardened case. I accept a lot of praise I dont deserve and then make it right with myself by sacrificing a tithe of it to the Lord. You must connive a little.

I had the tennis court all ready to play John [Fisher] on if you had come. Better come. It's no journey with a car like yours. You could be over and back before you were missed.

Just at this moment (1.30 A. M.) I am interrupted by the bang of an apple on the roof. Another porcupine is up and at it. To arms! Duty and honor call.

With hurried best wishes to you both.

Ever yours   Robert Frost

262-a · Elinor M. Frost to Edith H. Fobes

REFERENCES to RF's second daughter, Irma, in this letter concern her marriage to John Paine Cone on 15 October 1926, in the Fobes guest cottage, Franconia, New Hampshire.

6 December [1926]
Dear Mrs. Fobes,-   South Shaftsbury

We came down from the mountains the 30th of October, and here it is the 6th of December, and I haven't written to you all this time. I was getting somewhat rested after Irma's departure, but the packing and the 11 hour journey down set me back where I was, and then I found the house rather "at sixes and sevens" as the neighbor who agreed to do some cleaning every week had been kept at home by a sick child and Lillian had wisely refrained from doing much of that kind of work, after her operation. Well, I decided to get someone in to paint floors and woodwork and the house is quite fresh and clean now.

We have all been well, fortunately, which is a cheerful state of things. Carol and Lillian and Prescott are really very well, indeed. Marjorie is gaining more obviously than in the summer. . . . The condition of her throat troubles me more than anything now. It is in a rather bad state all the time, and she has to make an effort all the time not to take a real cold.

Irma writes happy and cheerful letters [from the Cone farm in Kansas]. I haven't thanked you myself yet for all you did for her. Your generosity to our children has been so wonderful ever since your invitation to them all to stay with you while Robert and I were in Cambridge in June 1916 that I just haven't words to thank you. But I am very grateful.

Robert is at Wesleyan now — has been there since a week ago yesterday, and I shall join him tomorrow if the weather permits — to stay with him a few days before it's time for him to come home. He is having rather hard things to do there, and I expect he will be nervously exhausted when it is over. Before going there, he went to New York for a few days. He lectured at Barnard, and attended to a lot of business. The writing was going pretty well just before we left Sugar Hill, and he has managed to keep on to some extent here. It's a pity his free time is over. Next spring it will be the same struggle to get started again, and he is getting older every year.

We go to Amherst the 3rd of January. I am going to make an extra effort to give Marjorie a good time while we are there.

Lesley is tremendously busy, with all the work in the store at this season of the year, and with her preparations for the trip [as the manager of a bookstore aboard the SS *Franconia* on a cruise around the world]. The innoculations have upset her somewhat. She has just had a request from the editor of McCalls magazine to write an article on her book caravan experiences, for which she is to get $800 which will just pay her passage. . . .

We all send love and best wishes.

Affectionately yours,   Elinor Frost

AMHERST, COLORADO, CALIFORNIA, TEXAS, AND FLORIDA · 1926-1938

THE POETRY of Robert Frost contains only veiled hints of the ways in which he became deeply "acquainted with the night." The darkest phase of his life probably occurred during the twelve or thirteen years that began in the autumn of 1926 and continued through at least the spring and summer of 1938. His private darkness was, however, strikingly at odds with his public life, for during these years his reputation as a poet became established with great firmness and assurance. He kept his suffering below the surface of his art; indeed he had both the instinct and capacity for keeping the overly curious out of his secret places.

All that the public knew about him during these years were his triumphs. Three new volumes of poetry appeared, and two of them won Pulitzer Prizes: *Collected Poems* (1930) and *A Further Range* (1936). Honorary degrees were showered on him by colleges and universities. He had gone to England with his wife and their daughter Marjorie in 1928 and was warmly received by old friends. Two years later he was elected to membership in the American Academy of Arts and Letters. The next year he crossed the continent for the first time since 1885, gave readings in California, and made a nostalgic visit to his native San Francisco. That same year he was awarded a prize of $1,000 by the National Institute of Arts and Letters, which hailed him as "the poet of the period whom it would most like to crown." He was honored as the Phi Beta Kappa Poet by Columbia University in 1932 which also awarded him an honorary doctorate of letters. He spent the spring term of 1936 at Harvard as the Charles Eliot Norton Professor of Poetry, the first American poet ever to have been so honored.

These were the facts known to the public; what went on

behind the scenes was revealed only to his friends, and, dramatically, through his letters. At first they reflect only a normal variety of petty illnesses, general preoccupations, and family concerns. Then the anguish and tragedy to come are gradually foreshadowed.

262-b · MARJORIE FROST TO EDITH H. FOBES

16 January 1927
Dear Mrs. Fobes —   34 Amity St.   Amherst

I came down with the grippe about a week before Christmas, and have been going through its various stages ever since, or I would have written you long ago. Thank you very, very much for the lovely blanket you gave me. It certainly was an appropriate gift as blankets play a very important part in my life these nights. The rose and brown are lovely together, and I was awfully glad you sent rose as I am planning to have my room in our new home (if we ever have one) decorated in rose.

We had a very nice Christmas together. I was very disappointed not to be able to trim the tree, as I usually do (if I am able), but at the same time I was thankful that I could at least lie on the couch and look at it. Irma writes that she had a very happy Christmas, also.

I wasn't able to come to Amherst with mama and papa, when they came so I made the trip alone about a week ago. Amherst seems the same as ever. We have a very comfortable house this time with one of the oil heaters. Although we hear other people complaining about them, we have found ours very satisfactory so far. There is always good skating here, and I hope I shall be able to take advantage of it.

Carol, Lillian, and Prescott all had colds before mine, and then mama took a very bad one from me. She was very sick. Papa was the only one to escape.

Prescott is awfully cute now that he is beginning to talk. He seems to love to have you read aloud to him, and every time he recognizes a word he repeats it over and over until you come to another one he knows. Irma sent him Peter Rabbit for Christmas. I didn't think he was old enough for it, but I read it to him very loud and with great expression, just for fun, and after that he came to me with the book two or three times a day.

I am going to take music lessons twice a week while I am here. There is a piano here in the house, and I have always wanted a chance to learn. I like my teacher very much and although we aren't going to be here very long I think I might be able to get a good start. There isn't much to do here so I haven't much excuse for not practicing.

Lesley sailed on the 12th at midnight. Papa went down to see her off. She had just had a cold and was pretty worn out getting the books on board. We are hoping she won't be terribly sea sick and that the trip will be something of a rest for her. I hope you are well and thank you again for your gift.

Love and best wishes for a happy new year.

Marjorie

263 · To Sidney Cox

Dear Sidney: [c. 7 February 1927]   [Amherst]

You *would* exaggerate me into the most conspicuous prose writer in your collection [*Prose Preferences;* Frost's "The Poetry of Amy Lowell"] you doting friend and so disqualify me for doing anything to boost the book. I don't care if you don't. A little undeserved praise now and then will only make it up to me in advance or arrears for the undeserved blame I am always getting — or suppose I am always getting — I never look in the reviews to see. . . .

We are still under the cloud of Marjorie's long illness. Our day in the house revolves round her. She reads a little plays the piano a little and plays cards a little: but she has to be kept from doing even such things too much. Sometimes we get fearfully disheartened. More than glimpses of people seem to exhaust her. She cant be left too much by herself. It seems to me it must be something like your sister's case. The doctors now call it nervous prostration. The nervous prostrates I have seen however were set serious. Marj has her ironies and her grins.

Lesley is on one of the winter tours round the world with a branch of her book store. She's past Samoa by now. The last letter from her was from Honolulu. With Irma married into Kansas and Carol away off in Vermont we feel a pretty scattered family. . . .   Always yours   Robert Frost

339

263-a · ELINOR M. FROST TO EDITH H. FOBES

Dear Mrs. Fobes,- 22 February [1927] Amherst

I feel so very badly not to have written all this long time. Part of the time I have been sick, and all the time discouraged and busy. I think Marjorie wrote you that she and I as well as Lillian and Prescott, were quite sick with grippe just before Christmas. I couldn't myself seem to get over it for more than a month. I coughed and felt very weak and miserable, and as for Marjorie she has had one chill after another since then. She is now in the care of the doctor, who had charge of her for several years as a little girl, you know, and he is quite sure it is a case of nervous prostration, and that she probably had it before she had pneumonia last year. He says we must go very easy with her but that it is only a question of time and rest. She is so unhappy now, however, that she cannot rest. She seems to have reached the end of her endurance, and goes for days hardly speaking and she doesn't want to eat. I believe myself that there must be some obscure trouble in her intestines. She really ought to have been in some warmer climate for the winter. . . . She has a very large sunny bedroom, and is as well fixed as anyone could be in this climate.

I have a middle aged colored woman helping me with the house work — a very good cook, and it has been a wonderful help.

Robert has been very well all the winter, and his obligations here are really not tiring him at all. After we finish here, he goes to Ann Arbor for a ten days lecture and conference engagement, and then to Dartmouth, and then to Bowdoin, for the same kind of engagement.

We have had two very enthusiastic letters from Lesley — and Irma writes very happily, though I am afraid she is working too hard. The children at the farm are very well. Prescott is talking a good deal now. Just before we came from S. Shaftsbury, we decided to rent a goodsized house about a mile from the farm, on a quiet side road. We couldn't decide to *buy* anything. We shall have our furniture sent from Ann Arbor the 1st of April and I shall be busy for a while getting settled into another house. I think we shall be very quiet and comfortable there. Robert won't be, of course, much interested in working around out doors, but there is always a lot to do for Carol, who is getting a bit disheartened about farming, poor boy.

If Marjorie gets stronger through the summer, she and Robert and I will go to England the 20th of August, to stay until Christmas. If she doesn't seem able to go, we shall stay on in our new home until November, when I shall take her to New Mexico for the winter. In that case, during the hay fever season, Robert would go up north by himself for two or three weeks — in the worst of it — or I might go with him, leaving Marjorie in Lillian's care. I am hoping, however, that she will improve sufficiently for us to go to England. . . .

Robert, Marjorie and I send love and best wishes and I will write again soon.   Affectionately yours   Elinor Frost

263-b · Elinor M. Frost to Edith H. Fobes

Dear Mrs. Fobes,-   8 May [1927]   South Shaftsbury
How nice it is that you and Joe are going to have a trip abroad this summer! . . . We haven't quite made up our minds even yet about going ourselves, but we have almost given it up. Since coming back to the farm, I have been more frightened than ever about Marjorie. Through the winter she gradually lost all the weight she had gained, and the journey home [from Ann Arbor] seemed to tire her so much that she seemed almost dead for several days, and the cough and bad throat she had had since the grippe at Christmas time, became much worse. For a month she coughed several hours each night. Now she is much better, and has commenced to gain weight again.

The warmer, spring weather, and her interest in the planting have kept her out doors, moving around several hours each day, and that has caused a wonderful improvement. And when she is here with Carol and Lillian and the baby, she stops thinking about the ills of the universe, which is also very good for her. However, even if she should gain a good deal during the summer, I think I should hardly dare to take her across the ocean, traveling tires her so much.

Our furniture came from Ann Arbor about ten days ago, and we have got somewhat straightened out over to the other house, and move over tomorrow. I think Robert will very much appreciate the quiet over there.

We shall not go away for the hay fever before the 18th of

August and shall be gone about a month, perhaps less. If anyone else would use the cottage all summer it seems to me they
ought to have it, but if there is no one else there at the time we
should go, it would be a pleasure to be there again. It is most
kind of you to want us to be there. . . .

We have good news from both Lesley and Irma. It looks
now as if they were going to have a record crop of wheat on
John's farm. I do hope so. It would encourage them so much.

With our very best wishes —

Affectionately yours,   Elinor Frost

263-c · ELINOR M. FROST TO MARGARET MACVEAGH

My dear Margaret —   7 September [1927]   Sugar Hill

Well — we didn't go, after all. We got our passports, and
were on the point of engaging passage by telephone — when
I suddenly had to give up completely and go to bed for several
days. I had been working quite hard, getting ready, and was
worrying so much that I couldn't sleep. Robert decided there
wasn't much chance of our having a very good time, when I
was so tired and worried, and that it was better to postpone going until next spring.

So when I began to feel stronger, we came up here for our
usual fall visit to the White Mts.

Marjorie came with us, of course. She has been doing
more the last two months than at any time since the [appen-
dicitis] operation, and has seemed to stand it very well, so I
am feeling encouraged, though she does not gain weight. She
had such a very nice time with you, and I hope she wasn't too
great a bother. Day before yesterday she climbed Mt. Agassiz,
which is the only climbing she has done for three years. The
mountains and the woods here are as lovely as ever. We arrived just as a new moon was coming on — and have enjoyed
sitting on the piazza for several hours each evening. . . .

With all good wishes —

Affectionately your friend   Elinor Frost

264 · TO MARY E. COOLEY

A STUDENT in a writing course taught by RF at the University of
Michigan in the spring of 1926, Miss Mary E. Cooley was also the

daughter of Dr. Charles Horton Cooley, distinguished Professor of Sociology at the University of Michigan. His book, mentioned in the following letter, was *Life and the Student*.

19 September 1927   Sugar Hill
But South Shaftsbury Vermont
is the place to send the book.

Dear Mary Cooley: We start for there next Monday.

There's nobody I'd rather have a book from than your father. I'm glad it is to be a note book. That sounds like things he has just inevitably thought, let them put together as they will. I'm less and less for systems and system-building in my old age. I'm afraid of too much structure. Some violence is always done to the wisdom you build a philosophy out of. Give us pieces of wisdom like pieces of eight in a buckskin bag. I take my history in letters and diaries, my philosophy in pensees thrown together like the heads of Charles the Bold's army after it was defeated and slain in Switzerland. You may have noticed them this summer.

I've been your father's great admirer ever since the first time I heard him talk. So he will be sending his book to a very gentle reader. He has the gift of truth. . . .

Sincerely yours   Robert Frost

265 · To Wilfred Davison

Dear Davison,   5 October 1927   South Shaftsbury

I want to try to tell you the number of times we changed our minds between going to your pond and not going to your pond [Joe's Pond, West Danville, Vt.]. In the end the day of starting for home caught us determined to go to it; and we went. On the way we were charmed once on the rather terrible detour with a little farm house high up on a banking above the full swift stream of Joe's Brook. Henceforth that will always be one of the spots on earth where we may come to rest from our wanderings. And so might the pond be too if the population around it can be made to fall off a little. For we were charmed with the pond itself. And your cozy house. There's no prettier piece of water in the woods anywhere. I suppose it must be one of the highest-set in New England if not the very highest. We had a beautiful still evening by it and a beautiful morning.

And by way of extravagance to express my feelings I walked on up your road a piece and priced the Ewen farm with all the shore and woods thereunto appertaining. So you can see the lengths I went to. We were all of us sorry not to have longer but it was thought best in solemn assembly assembled to get on while Marj was able. We were late anyway and afraid of the weather's breaking against us. We were all glad we had the night there. We like such things best of all — too well for our poetry, I sometimes fear, which would be more fateful I suppose if it were more about people and less about nature. Elinor is going to ask you down to see us sometime before long.

Thank your mother for her hospitality in absentia. Remember me to your President.   Always yours,   Robert Frost

266 · To Leonidas W. Payne, Jr.

Dear Mr. Payne: 1 November 1927   South Shaftsbury
    I remember somebody away off down there at my furthest South asked the question that I was asked in yesterdays mail by a New Yorker: In my Mending Wall was my intention fulfilled with the characters portrayed and the atmosphere of the place? You might be amused by my answer. I should be sorry if a single one of my poems stopped with either of those things — stopped anywhere in fact. My poems — I should suppose everybody's poems — are all set to trip the reader head foremost into the boundless. Ever since infancy I have had the habit of leaving my blocks carts chairs and such like ordinaries where people would be pretty sure to fall forward over them in the dark. Forward, you understand, *and* in the dark. I may leave my toys in the wrong place and so in vain. It is my intention we are speaking of — my innate mischievousness.
    Isn't that the way to answer them, whether in Texas or New York?
    The book [*Selections from Later American Writers*] pleased me — and your kindness to me in it [see letter 248]. Lets see I have forgotten whether you are of the Graduate School at Chicago. Nearly everyone out of there seems to make anyone later suffer by comparison with Will Moody. I couldnt find that you had expressed yourself anywhere as sorry none of us were as good as he. Very likely we arent. And then again very likely we are. Such comparisons can become unnovel. I

hear — What's his name — that Gilbert Murray of Chicago, has wiped us all off the map with Moody. That ought to be gratifying to my dear friend Mrs Moody. We all come in for some rewards. When one is getting his we can all sit back in a row, the rest of us, and wait for ours. You put the idea into my head of saying something about anthologies next time I go on the tow path.

Some year you and Armstrong must ask me back to the Alamo and San Jacinto. My friend Dwight Morrow has just gone to see if he cant keep us from having another war with Mexico. By the way I suppose you know the chantey that goes

General Taylor won the day
On the plains of Mexico
Santa Anna ran away
On the plains of Mexico.

Well the English sing that the other way round: Santa Anna won the day etc.: which shows that ours is not the only country where history is written with prejudice.

We are having a long warm Indian Summer here that I'm taking advantage of to build or rebuild a causeway through our bog with hardheads, as we call them. . . .

Always yours   Robert Frost

267 · To John T. Bartlett

Dear John: 1 November 1927   South Shaftsbury
[. . .] I wish it was Elinor and I seeing you about now instead of them two irresponsible wastrels our son and daughter [Carol and his wife, Lillian] hell bent for California. I sometimes come within an ace of taking up with invitations out that way. What decides me against it is the family. I can't leave them for more than a day or two. If they ever get so they will consent to follow me across the prairies, the first place I'll lead them them to will be Boulder. Then we will have a good old talk as in the days that were.

Carol is a curious boy. I wonder if this expedition of his is to spy out a new country to live in. He wouldn't say so if it was and it may not be. He'll have told you he is pretty deeply involved here what with his considerable sweet pea business and his MacIntosh apples in prospect.

I've been playing myself out back in the bog in his absence throwing wheelbarrow after wheelbarrows full of stones off the wall into the mud and peat to rebuild the old causeway to the back pasture. We've been having days I doubt if you could beat in Colorado: the air at a standstill, the leaf gold still holding out on the trees, frost just barely some nights, others none. Me for it. But it cant last or I cant — I've got to go down to see a President inaugurated at Amherst day after tomorrow. (I ought not to complain. He is somewhat of my choosing.) I'll have to look up my shoes and see if my clothes have improved any by not having been worn lately. A dip in kerosene coal oil will start the rust. Then I can hollystone it off.

The first report I have had on the biographical sketch speaks chiefly of your contribution to it. I aint agoing to thank you. It was an inspiration of mine to give [Gorham B.] Munson direct access to my past through two or three of my independent friends. I thought it would be fun to take the risk of his hearing something to my discredit. The worst you could [reveal] was my Indian vindictiveness. Really I am awful there. I am worse than you know. I can never seem to forgive people that scare me within an inch of my life. I am going to try to be good and cease from strife.

[. . .] My isnt it a chill to hear how those youngsters of yours are coming up? If they are that old how old must I be? Tell them easy does it. They must be fine children who can be appealed to. You cant so much as grow in this world without affecting somebody to tears. People had better be careful how they grow. There is something invidious about the way the young grow. I'd like to tease them. They look as if they could take care of themselves. I probably couldnt baffle them very much at my crypticest. Never mind I can baffle some people.

It is now 12 P M your time — 3 A M mine. I'm wobbly.

Love to you all   R. F.

268 · To James R. Wells

AN ATTRACTIVE PLAYBOY, with money enough to engage in fine press printing, James R. Wells established the Slide Mountain Press and talked RF into signing a flexible contract. The following letter reveals the various phases of their jockeying for position. In the end RF won; he permitted Wells to print and publish a limited edition of a "One-Act Irish Play" written by RF and called *The Cow's in the Corn*. The text of the play contained a total of seventy-one words, padded with stage directions and amplified with a one-sentence "Introduction" as follows: "This, my sole contribution to the Celtic Drama (no one so unromantic as not to have made at least one) illustrates the latter day tendency of all drama to become smaller and smaller and to be acted in smaller and smaller theatres to smaller and smaller audiences" (see letters 277 and 279).

Dear Mr Wells: 14 July 1928   South Shaftsbury

    I saw the moment I met you you were a real poet's publisher. You would be my friend and helper in whatever you undertook to do with my poetry. You went so far as to say in kindness once that if this contract made me unhappy, I was to tear it up. But your chiefest liberality lay in leaving the book it called for unnamed and undescribed so that I could have it anything I pleased. It simply doesnt seem as if misunderstanding could arise in a relationship like ours, more friendship than business. But certainly a little confusion has arisen that I find very uncomfortable. I wonder if it wouldn't clear the air if I went over some of the plans we have talked about in fulfillment of the contract.

    1) The book could be anything I pleased. When you went away after your first visit, it seemed as if you would be satisfied to have it twenty or thirty old poems with a few new ones to set them off. I got the Holts permission to use the old poems. It still stands I assume.

    2) The next time you came it was with Mrs. [Crosby] Gaige and I could see you were both hoping the poems for the book might be all new. I saw a possibility there if the book needn't be too large. The talk about size was vague, but I gathered forty pages might be enough.

    3) The next I knew we were wondering if the Holts wouldn't let you do the special edition of my next book with them. You never talked about getting my next book away from them entirely. You knew I had tried hard to do that for another publisher [Harcourt] and failed dismally. I made a bad business of it. The wonder was that I had anybody the least friendly left in the firm. The weakness of my position was that I couldnt bear to go to a new publisher and not take my four old books with me. I've got to keep my books together.

    4) There was talk of your taking my future over and making me a Crosby Gaige author at a salary of $4000 a year. I didnt know how serious you were in that. It was a pleasant dream while it lasted.

347

5) Finally you proposed to do a book of new poems to lead off with this year, a book of snow poems, old ones, next year a book of metaphysical poems (old ones), the year after and then a couple of books of plays. You thought you could give me about $5000 in the next five years. You speak of this in a recent letter. The Harbor Press started up your interest in the plays. You mustnt grudge [Roland A.] Wood that small play [*A Way Out*]. It was his play as much as mine. In his acting days he "created" the chief part in it.

Here is or ought to be enough to figure something from. Do you really want to make a definite contract with me for five specific books in the next five years with royalties at 15% when you have to pay the Holts for any rights, 20% when you have nothing to pay them?

Two things are clear. You dont want to go back to the original idea and take a book of new and old poems mixed. The Holts wont let anybody else have a hand in my immediate next book. I have had enough trouble with them about things. You wont ask me to have any more right now.

The book can be anything I please. But of course it must please you too. We are friends in all this. You want it to be new material you are sure? You think it for the best interests of everybody concerned. I rely on your judgement. The question is must it be new verse. What should you say to one of my fairly long short poems that will go to make a book called Talks Walking when I have enough of the same kind? It may be 150 lines long. It is some folk myth in the making. Then I have a poem in the rough on California. How long could I have to polish it off? It is like my New Hampshire. What should you say to a short play in prose ["In an Art-Factory"].* That is about one of my sculptor friends [Araldo Du Chêne].

I take it you don't insist on quantity. George Moore's play is short. There arent fifty pages of it nor twenty lines of speech to the page. Wolfs book is shorter.

Let's get something out of all you have thought of and have it over with. I might even dig you out a few of my poems for the book after next on a pinch. Only it would have to be with the written understanding that they wouldnt be pre-

---

* This "short play in prose," never published, exists in manuscript in the C. Waller Barrett Collection of American Literature, University of Virginia Library.

cluded from the book after next or some other book with the Holts in the end.

You can straighten things out for me. Help!

Ever yours   Robert Frost

Money is nothing to me. Money is nothing to you. You could have the three hundred dollars back at the word. But that isnt what you want. You want to publish something of mine and I very much want you to.   R. F.

269 · To Padraic Colum

EARLY in August 1928, RF sailed for England with his wife and daughter Marjorie. Arrangements had been made, with the help of Dorothy Canfield Fisher, for Marjorie to spend six weeks with a French family in Sèvres, and her parents took her there soon after their arrival in England. After a brief stay in Paris, the Frosts went back to England to visit with old friends. They spent some time in Gloucestershire, staying with Mr. and Mrs. John W. Haines. In London they found F. S. Flint, who took RF to call on Edward Garnett. Harold Monro arranged to have RF give a reading of his poems at the Poetry Bookshop; and on another occasion Monro brought RF and T. S. Eliot together for the first time. Other friends visited included W. W. Gibson, Lascelles Abercrombie, and John Cournos.

Strongly pro-Irish in his sympathies, RF had made plans to visit Ireland. He had become well acquainted with Padraic Colum in New York City and had entertained the poet George Russell (AE) at Amherst. This letter was warmly answered by Colum, so that when RF went to Dublin he was indeed "introduced to Ireland by the right person." While in Dublin he stayed at the home of Colum's friend, the poet Constantine P. Curran.

RF returned to America from England with his wife and daughter late in November 1928.

18 September 1928   The Imperial Hotel
Dear Padraic: Russell Square   London

You may be clear out of Dublin, you may even have gone back to New York; but I am not going to give you up without another trial. (I made one by telegraph a few days ago.) I dont want to miss the chance of being introduced to Ireland by the right person. I may still decide to look into Dublin if you are not there, but it will not be the same thing and I should be sorry if our rendezvous came to nothing. Nobody ever talked Ireland to me as intimately as you did that day lying by the side of a road in Pelham (near Amherst) ten years ago.

Our invasion hasn't gone as planned. We were a long time getting Marjorie settled in France for her French and Elinor has steadily worn down with the effort of travel. Last week we were lying up for her health in Gloucester. She wouldn't be able to come with me to Dublin: I should be alone.

You would have to promise not to let me burden you. I should only stay a day or two. You would tell me a decent hotel to go to.

The address you seem to have given me is The Irish Statesman. My address the rest of this week will be the Imperial Hotel, Russell Square, London, England. God grant that I hear from you.　　　　　　　Yours always　Robert Frost

270 · To SIDNEY COX

11 October 1927 [1928]　London Eng.
now: but I'll be home in S. Shaftsbury
Sidney, Sidney　　　　　early in November. Want to see you.

It won't do. You'll say I've been long enough coming to that brief conclusion. I practically had to wait till I had grown into another person so I could see the problem presented with the eyes of an outsider. Looking in on it from another country and from another time with all the disinterestedness possible I find I'm against the book — at least in my lifetime: when I'm off the scene you can decide for yourself. My greatest objection to the book is that it doesn't put you and me in the right personal relation. I think you would realize that if you took time. Your repeated insistence on the fact that you never came to see me except when summoned has the very opposite effect from what you intend. Instead of making us out equals in friendship as I should have thought we were, it puts you in the position of a convenience used and sent for whenever I had anything for you to set down for posterity. I dont like the picture it makes of either of us. It isnt a true picture either. I cant remember exactly when you asked my permission to keep a record of the best of our talks. But I'm sure it was late in our lives. I invited you to visit me and I wrote to you many times before you could have been so self conscious about it all. I might have to search myself for my reason in singling you out for a conversation a year. I can tell you offhand I never chose you as a Boswell. Maybe I liked your awkwardness, naivete and spirituality. We won't strain for an answer.

Meeting Helen Thomas fresh from her experiment in reminiscences of someone else has probably helped me to my decision. You probably read her "As It Was" between her and Edward Thomas — suppressed in Boston. Its a good piece of work in a way, but it took a good [deal] of squirming on her part to justify it. I wondered if she wasnt in danger of making E. T. look ridiculous in the innocence she credited him with. Mightnt men laugh a manly laugh? E. T. was distinguished at his college at Oxford for the ribald folk songs he could entertain with — not to say smutty. Worse than As it Was are some other chapters in his life she has been undressing to the public since. In one she has him invite to the house a girl he has met and come home full of admiration of. She gives her self away by calling the girl "this paragon of women." But she finds the minute she sees her (how homely she is) that she can conquer her with magnanimity, or conquer her jealousy of her with magnanimity. All women are sisters that the same man loves, she tries to make herself think. Once in the woods listening to a nightengale in the dark E says to the two of them We are knowing, but the nightengale knows all. Then he kisses his wife and to keep the score even his wife makes him kiss the other woman. She pretends to think that is large and lovely but I happen to know it was a dose she was giving him and rubbing in. These things are hard to do sincerely. And unridiculously. In another chapter she has him carry her off to bed on his last leave of absence before going to the front. It reminds me of Schnitzler's Whatsername.

No you'll have to forgive me and be as good friends as if nothing had ever happened, but it wont do. You'll have to reason our relationship on to a better footing than it has apparently been on lately. Let's not be too damned literary.

Really faithfully yours   Robert Frost

271 · To Richard H. Thornton

RICHARD H. THORNTON, a professor of English at the University of North Carolina before he joined the firm of Henry Holt and Company in 1924, was head of the foreign language department. Because RF got along better with him than with members of the trade department, Thornton was frequently drafted to serve as congenial intermediary between Holt and the poet. As Thornton took more responsibility — he served as president of Holt from 1932 to 1938 — his friendship with RF grew.

At Thornton's suggestion, RF began to invest part of his royalties in Holt stock. This letter refers obliquely to Thornton's acknowledgment of RF's "number one" importance to Holt by giving him, at the start of his investment-program, certificates of common and preferred stock numbered one. RF, at the time of his death in 1963, owned approximately $28,000 worth of his publisher's stock.

Dear Thornton   3 January 1929   South Shaftsbury

The certificates came to-day. I did not fail to remark the sentimental and honorary value they had extra in both being numbered one. You may remember what I said last spring about feeling the need of some admixture of friendship in my business relations. You and I and the firm of Henry Holt and Company have come a long way together since then.

We are off for the groves of Academe Monday. Amherst (where we shall be glad to see you at any time) will be our address till April 1st. After that we shall be coming back to a newly boughten farm, 150 acres, 50 woodland, here at South Shaftsbury. (Of course it is much more important that you should visit us there and bring your family with you than that you should visit us at Amherst. There will be all the pastoral details to show you of rough mountain land flowing with springs and an old old cottage full of fireplaces and hell-hinges.) But it will be rather indirectly we come home by way of the University of Virginia, Pittsburg College for Women, some Nashville club and probably Chicago University (William Vaughn Moody Foundation) and maybe one or two more colleges. I must give you a list of dates as soon as I know them definitely. I may go to Dartmouth for one of my stays this year. Lankes tells me he has just been given an exhibition up there in which I figured to a certain extent.

The latest bulletin is that Benchley is running out ahead of me. There's only one thing to be done. You cant speed me up. You have me going now about as fast as it is good for me to go. The one thing to do is to slow up Benchley. A good jockey knows how to "pull" a horse that isnt wanted to win.

The two copies of the Updyke Special [limited edition of *West-running Brook*, designed by D. B. Updike] for my children haven't arrived. I had the bill that seemed to show they were sent all right. I must have a couple.

Sincerely yours   Robert Frost

272 · To Louis Untermeyer

Dear Louis: 6 January 1929 South Shaftsbury

[. . .] I bought a farm for myself for Christmas. One hundred and fifty three acres in all, fifty in woods. The house a poor little cottage of five rooms, two ordinary fireplaces, and one large kitchen fireplace all in one central chimney as it was in the beginning. The central chimney is the best part of it — that and the woods. You mustn't be jealous, though jealousy is a passion I approve of and attribute to angels. May I be guarded and watched over always by the jealousy of a strong nature. It is better than arms around the body. Jealousy alone gives me the sense of being held. My farm probably doesn't compare with yours for view. But it looks away to the north so that you would know you were in the mountains. We have no trout brook, but there is a live spring that I am told should be made into a trout pond. There is a small grove of white paper birches doubling daylight. The woods are a little too far from the house. I must bring them nearer by the power of music like Amphion or Orpheus. It is an old occupation with me. The trees have learned that they have to come where I play them to. I enjoy the power I find I have over them. You must see us together, the trees dancing obedience to the poet (so-called). You'll exclaim.

I ain't going to mention books this time.

Ever yours   Robert Frost

273 · To Frederic G. Melcher

Dear Melcher: 9 February 1929 Amherst

I'm glad Vachel is out of debt, glad you are going to do my bibliography for Colophon, and glad you are coming to pass judgment on our new farm. You remember what the farmers did to the monkeys in Kipling's poetic evolution? Cut off their tails and put them to work. And you remember what the monkeys are in Kipling's symbolism? Henry Ford says he will save the world by putting it to work for him. What's to forbid my saving it by putting it to work for me. My god I hate to have to listen to Cal and Henry laying it down to us spiritual and aesthetic. Some words ought to be copyrighted so that successful duffs shouldn't profane them. But I was going to say: anyone that comes to make fun of my farm this year may have to stay and improve it.

Marj has taken the plunge into the nursing. She may not be able to stand it. We all think it will do her good if she is.

I have a small edition of one copy of an early book of mine [*Twilight*, 1894] that nobody but Elinor and I and the printer ever saw. You'll have to say if it counts in my bibliography.

Ever yours,   Robert Frost

274 · To R. B. HASELDEN

WHEN the letter files of *The Independent* were sold to the Henry E. Huntington Library they contained thirty-eight manuscript poems by — or at least attributed to — RF. The Curator of Manuscripts wrote RF requesting his help in assigning approximate composition dates to the poems and enclosing a list of titles. This is RF's reply.

Dear Mr Haselden: 20 February 1929   Amherst

I recognize just four of your list by the names you give them, the first, second, fourth and ninth. Are you sure I wrote the rest? I wonder if somebody hasn't been imposing on you. Do you know the history of the manuscripts? If they are really mine, they are probably very early and more than probably bad: in which case I don't see why you should want to treasure them against me. I don't know the ethics of these things as well as you must; so do you tell me. Suppose some friend of my youth died (I had only one or two friends it could have been) and some heartless and undiscriminating heir or executor found among his papers the unguarded poems I may have sent him in letters, would they be legitimate merchandise? Would it be all right for the heir to sell them and for you to preserve them without consulting my wishes in the matter? You shall instruct me. I confess that array of forgotten works scares me. Please treat me with consideration. Why, if you are out for a poet's manuscript, don't you come to headquarters and ask for the manuscript of approved poems. Perhaps you got these you have cheap or for nothing — or paid so much for them that you cant afford to throw them away. I have no objection to keeping the four I identify. And I'm glad to help you with them. The Blue Bird to Lesley was written in about 1903, Clear and Colder — Boston Common in about 1891. The Flower Boat in about 1894 or 5, Nature's Neglect in about 1901. Now be fair to me about the others. Let me have copies of them if you will. Then I will tell you if they are mine and which I should be pleased or pained to have you keep. Then you can do by me as you find it in your heart to do.

I am very curious about it all.

Sincerely yours   Robert Frost

274-a · R. B. Haselden to Robert Frost

ANSWERING RF's letter, the Curator of Manuscripts at the Huntington Library added information which evoked further denials from RF. There is one unimportant mistake in the following letter: the authorship of "My Butterfly" should not have been challenged. But the other two manuscripts challenged by Haselden still present an unsolved problem. Each of them is in Elinor Frost's handwriting and in a style of penmanship strikingly similar to that used by her when she signed letter 15, dated 27 December 1896. The first of these two manuscripts contains three quatrains entitled "Sea Dream," and is unsigned. The other contains three quatrains, has no title, and is signed "Robert Lee Frost" — also in the handwriting of Mrs. Frost. RF denied authorship of these two poems in 1929; he repeated those denials in 1932 when he visited the Huntington Library with his wife for the express purpose of examining the two manuscripts. Neither RF nor Mrs. Frost could or at least would make even so much as a guess, in the presence of others, concerning how those manuscript poems became part of the files of The Independent. There is now no immediate way of proving the authorship of the poems; but the possibility of RF's having written them during or before 1896 remains.

1 March 1929   [Huntington Library]
[San Marino, California]

Dear Mr. Frost:

Thank you for your kind letter of February 20th. I am afraid you will have to plead guilty to more than four of the poems on the list I sent you, as they are undoubtedly in your handwriting and also signed; three of them are doubtful as they are in a different hand.

"Sea Dream"

"I went in a great tide under the sea
And my robe streamed on before.
There were leaning towers as I passed by
And shells on the dim sea floor."

The second poem is called "My Butterfly, an elegy"

> "Thine emulous fond flowers are dead too,
>   And the daft sun-assaulter, he
>   That frighted thee so oft, is fled or dead . . ."

The third poem begins:

> "I had a love once,
>   Sweeter than myrrh,
>   You, when you kiss me,
>   Remind me of her!"

It is not within the province of the Curator of Manuscripts to pass judgment on the merits or demerits of poems or literary pieces committed to his care. His duty is to preserve them for posterity and make them available for students and scholars: of course, he can pass judgment on their authenticity and genuineness. Suppose some of these poems of yours are what you call bad; why worry? You thought well enough of them once to put your name to them. I can see no good reason for your wishing to destroy them and I certainly am not at liberty to do any such thing as you suggest.

Imagine me going around destroying the things I did not approve of in the Library. Poor Ruskin would suffer very severely; several of Swinburne's and Byron's effusions would burn to make incense for my nostrils and whole authors would entirely disappear. But I really think it might annoy our trustees if I took home any of the manuscripts to make pipe spills of.

Curators of Manuscripts have no use for ethics or morals; when one lives among manuscripts relating to every conceivable subject from transfer of land by a monastery in the XIth Century to a XVI Century love letter, or from the burning of a fat friar to other documents too unpleasant to mention such things appear trivial, but I will explain the law to you as far as I understand it. If you write a poem and present it to a friend, he is at perfect liberty to sell it, but you still retain the copyright. The poems [of Robert Frost] in our Library were purchased from P. K. Foley [a celebrated Boston bookseller], I believe, who in turn got them from William Hayes Ward. [. . .]   Very truly yours,

                                    [carbon copy, unsigned]

356

274-b · ELINOR M. FROST TO MARGARET MACVEAGH

Dear Margaret   15 May [1929]   South Shaftsbury

Robert and I have been our usual bad selves about letter writing. We both had the grippe in January, and then when that was over, and we had done a considerable amount of seeing friends in Amherst, I was on the point of writing to ask you to visit us, when Lincoln's letter came, saying you were starting abroad. I would have liked you to visit us in the pleasant house we had this winter and last winter. We shall not have it again, for Prof. Tyler has just died, and Mrs. Tyler will either sell the house, or rent it for the whole year. They have enjoyed going to New York for just the three months we wanted to be in Amherst.

Robert has just had a short tour of lecturing. I went to two places with him, but stayed most of the time with Marjorie in Baltimore. Marjorie is training to be a nurse in the hospital where she was a patient last year. She went down the 5th of February — and has been able to stand it all until last week, when she took a bad cold, and consequently had to give up for a few days. She has wanted to do this for two years, and is tremendously interested in the work, and very happy. I hope with all my heart that she will have the strength to go on with it.

Robert and I bought a new farm in December, and are just now overlooking repairs to the house &c. We are not absolutely satisfied with it, but I suppose we couldn't expect to be. We shall stay in the Shingled Cottage, where you came last, until the 1st of August, at least. Won't you & Lincoln & Bunny come again this year? Perhaps the latter part of June. . . .

With affectionate good wishes to you both, from both of us.   Elinor Frost

275 · TO LINCOLN MACVEAGH

Dear Lincoln: [c. 8 June 1929]   [South Shaftsbury]

Welcome back, to modern times. And don't get bitter and sarcastic about having to come back. Occupy your mind with looking for beauty in the New Architecture. I have a book by Frank Lloyd Wright to lend you on the subject in which you will read that the new house will be of glass iron and cement

and flowed into the shape whereas the old of stone and wood
had to be cut into shape. You can see the gain of the new in
suavity and sensuousness. That is to say you can when I can
point you out examples of the new. Here's a house, you can im-
aginate me saying, that was cast. Here's one that was poured.
And here's one that was blown or blowed and you'll be blowed
says you if you likes it. But wait till you have a talk with me
when I am down next week before you do anything about it. I
shall be in town on Monday on my way to Montauk to have another grandchild. But what it will be, boy or girl, no one can
tell beforehand and it doesnt matter because it wont be
named Frost anyway but Francis.

Tell me everything about everything. I must review my
Grecian history. It's got so I hardly know a Pyrr[h]ic victory
from a Parthian shot. Is Tyrtaeus much read in Sparta? The
honey is just in time: the effects of the last you brought have
about worn off. I knew there was something the matter with
me. It seems as if there was with everybody else in the family
too. We are all sick. I hope you are all well.

Ever yours   Robert Frost

276 · To John T. Bartlett

Dear John: [c. 1 September 1929]   [Franconia]
    [. . .] I'd like the engagement at your writers institute as
an excuse to visit you. But I dont know about pulling out at that
time of year and taking Elinor to the altitude of one mile for
any length of time. That would have to be honestly enquired
into. I don't suppose Colorado is specially recommended for the
weak in heart. We're not the strength we were, you have to
remember, and can't do all sorts of things the way we used to.

We had thought of taking you in for a brief visit on a winter tour we were asked to consider by some agent in Denver. It
would be mostly on the coast and it would be through the
mountains and not in them to stay. We hadn't even made up
our minds to the possible hardships of that. The agent's (Theodore Fisher — you may know him) letter — second letter —
has been lying on my table unanswered since early August.

You'd probably prefer us for the summer engagement if
only for the longer visit it would mean. It will have to be
thought about hard.

If we decide I ought to come, I'll do it for anything you say, but if its left to me to say, really for my self respect I should ask for rather more than $600. I say self-respect when I mean the public respect. It is a miserable business being a poet among professors and business men. The only way to make them respect you is to make them pay.

We're off here in Franconia (altitude of house site 1700 feet) for my nose more as a matter of form than necessity for I seem to have lost my nose for hay fever. At least we think I have. Next year we may stay in the lowlands to find out for sure. It would make a great difference in our outlook.

Marj is in hospital in Baltimore where she lay a hopeless invalid two years ago, now training to be a nurse. Lesley is in New York with her husband and her baby. Carol is farming at the stone house where you saw him. Irma is going to college at Mass Agricultural College next year with her husband and her baby. Her husband has been farming near us but is turning to landscape architecture so called. We have three grand children in three different families. One of the grand children starts school this year and so begins again the endless round. The first school I went to at his age was in San Francisco along about fifteen years after the Civil War (We're almost that far from the World War) I cried (wept) myself out of that first school in one day not because the teacher was a negress (which she was) but on general principles. I didnt get back again for two years. I've been jumping school ever since.

Affectionately   R. F.

277 · To James R. Wells

Dear Wells: 7 September 1929   Franconia

For gods' sake dont give up writing to me simply because I dont write to you or anybody else. Probably I am not to blame for not writing letters. Probably it is something in my inheritance diet poverty training and luck; for all of which I should be treated at the root instead of made fun of imprisoned and slighted, or legislated against. Law, I'm pretty sure, will not help in the matter. It has been tried already in a small way to no avail. We made a rule in the family that I should take the first Sunday (if any) after the fourth Monday of every month to write letters and until I wrote them I should not be allowed on that day to attend worship, divine or human. I have suffered cruelly from the ordinance but, as I have said, to no purpose — I have gained no relief in the social pressure that sometimes makes us feel as if we would fly without wing or aeroplane, and the church has gained nothing in attendance, in fact has steadily lost, I learn indirectly, in late years — and none so wise as to know what to do about it. And I leave it to the League of Nations if there is any more lamentable spectacle short of war itself than a man of my sensibility suffering alone in the foreground to no purpose. Do you nothing to add to my contorted suffering with your ironies about my being all abroad, but send the really beautifully written printed and bound books along for me to sign [*The Cow's in the Corn*] and so earn a maximum royalty on the retail published price. I need all the money I can lay hands on without seeming to grab it.

We are away up in the mountains for my hay-fever and shall be for at least two weeks more. Could you send the books here at once? The address is Franconia, New Hampshire.

Ever yours   Robert Frost

278 · To SIDNEY COX

Dear Sidney: [*c.* 19 September 1929] [Franconia]

I may want to write you two or three letters as I think over all you came up here with yesterday — and I may not. One thing I will write about at once that I didnt quite bring myself to talk about face to face. It reaches me from many directions sometimes with the kind of smile I don't care for and sometimes with an out-and-out sneer that I am too much with you in the class room. I am sure you have used me to your own hurt at Dartmouth. I'd just like to see what leaving me entirely out of it for a year or two would do — not severely alone and out of it but just gently and unobtrusively out of it, so that no one would notice the omission till some day toward the end of the two years someone uncommonly observing should wake up and exclaim "Let's see! What's become of Frost in this course?" I doubt if our friends, wives, children, or even ourselves are to be looked on as resources in classroom work. Offhand you might think it was an advantage in teaching contemporary literature to be personally acquainted with me. On the contrary it is a great disadvantage in my way of looking at it. I keep you from talking about me as modestly as you could talk about Mrs William Rose Benet [Elinor Wylie] for instance. Everybody knows something has to be kept back for pressure and to anybody puzzled to know what I should suggest that for a beginning it might as well be his friends, wife, children, and self. That would be the part of *mature* wisdom. Poetry is measured in more senses than one: it is measured feet but more important still it is a measured amount of all we could say an we would. We shall be judged finally by the delicacy of our feeling of where to stop short. The right people know, and we artists should know better than they know. There is no greater fallacy going than that art is expression — an undertaking to tell all to the last scrapings of the brain pan. I neednt qualify as a specialist in botany and astronomy for a license to invoke flowers and stars in my poetry. I needn't have scraped those subjects to the point of exhaustiveness. God forbids that I should have to be an authority on anything even the psyche before I can set up for an artist. A little of anything goes a long way in art. Im never so desperate for material that I have to trench on the confidential for one thing, nor on the private for another nor on the personal, nor in general on the sacred. A little in the fist to manipulate is all I ask. My object is true form — is was and always will be — form true to any chance bit of true life. Almost any bit will do. I dont naturally trust any other object. I fight to be allowed to sit cross-legged on the old flint pile and flake a lump into an artifact. Or if I dont actually fight myself, the soldiers of my tribe do for me to keep the unsympathetic off me and give me elbow room. The best hour I ever had in the class room was good only for the shape it took. I like an encounter to shape up, unify however roughly. There is such a thing as random talk, but it is to be valued as a scouting expedition for coinable gold. I may say this partly to save myself from being misunderstood; I say it partly too to help you what I can toward your next advance in thought if not in office. You'll find yourself most effective in things people find out by accident you might have said but didnt say. Those are the things that make people take a good reestimating look at you. You have to refrain from saying many things to get credit for refraining from a few. There is a discouraging waste there as everywhere else in life. But never mind: there is a sense of strength gained in not caring. You feel so much in in having something to yourself. You have added to the mass of your private in reserve. You are more alluring to your friends and baffling to your foes.

Ever yours you know,   Robert Frost.

279 · To James R. Wells

My dear Wells: 11 October 1929   South Shaftsbury

A thousand thanks for the check or rather six thousand one hundred and forty two thanks — one for every cent in the check. But I dont want any pay for my part in the small book [*The Cow's in the Corn*]. It's only a joke. You keep the money and, if you like, send me ten more copies of the book instead. They'll be something for a visitor now and then to remember his visit by.

I feel awfully afraid in the dark sometimes, especially after too hard a day on the farm, that $4.50 is too big a price for your trifle. You might not think my judgement was worth as much as yours in a matter of business. But let me tell you in all modesty, I am a pretty shrewd old boy for a countryman two hundred miles from New York. My instinct or whatever it is might well be trusted.   Ever yours   Robert Frost

280 · To Lincoln MacVeagh

Dear Lincoln: 15 December 1929   South Shaftsbury

[. . .] I've been East lecturing since I got better and you ought to see the vast book of Catherwood's architectural drawings of ancient Mayapan I picked up at Goodspeeds. The first poem I ever wrote ["La Noche Triste"] was on the Maya-Toltec-Aztec civilization and there is where my heart still is while outwardly I profess an interest more or less perfunctory in New England. Never mind, I'm lucky to be allowed to write poetry on anything at all.

I wish you a merry Christmas sale and the rest of the family just a merry Christmas

I shall see you soon   Always yours   Robert Frost

281 · To Frederic G. Melcher

Dear Fred: [c. 15 December 1929]   [South Shaftsbury]

Stop press! I thought there'd be no harm in letting Good-speed know of my needs lacks and wants and lo a flood of Americana especially a great big portfolio of "Catherwoods Views in Central America Chiapas and Yucatan." — Did you ever see it? Now if I only owned Audubon's Birds, Audubon's Animals and Catlin's Indians wouldn't I be a gentleman? The Catherwood is a defective copy or maybe I couldn't have afforded it. We poor have to put up with the orts. Carol is off at this minute buying three or four pedigreed sheep for a start. He has to be satisfied with bottle-fed orphans and unnatural mothers.

I still want a Stephen's Yucatan if it's in good condition and doesn't cost over five dollars. I'm all supplied with Stephens Central America. . . .

The Pueblo Potter is the thing. Thanks for it. The pictures are wonderful. The text is an amusing professorial attempt to be behavioristic in dealing with art. We live and experience. Best wishes to you all for Christmas.

Ever yours   Robert Frost

282 · To Frederic G. Melcher

Dear Fred: 7 January 1930   Amherst

Isn't it terrible? — from a collector's point of view. I find that I have no first edition of the American North of Boston in blue myself. What do you say we advertise for it? I'll buy if I can afford it. My nearest seems to be a second edition.

The English "A Boy's Will," pebbled cloth, has two fly leaves in front and in the back one blank leaf and one next inside covered with advertising on one side and making acknowledgements for permission to print on the other side. The other A Boy's Will, brick red on white, is exactly the same as to fly leaves. Its page measurements are 7 1/4 x 4 3/4ths. I have sent for the copy of the American edition [North of Boston] done from English sheets. I hope Carol can find the one I mean.

You seem to have most of the articles about me. Garnett, Sergeant, Elliott, Van Doren, Lowell and Untermeyer's.

You might add Sydney Cox's small book (by Henry Holt), Albert Feuillerat's article in Revue des Deux Mondes and Percy Boynton's article in his book "Some Americans." Let's leave Gorham B. Munson's book out of it if only on account of all that nonsense about my noble ancestry. I am more and more taken with Barrett Wendell's idea that the Puritans were all Jews who, having been forced in the early sixteenth century to become Christians, got even with the Church by making schism.

Have that pair of Yucatan books sent to me here will you if they haven't already gone to South Shaftsbury. . . .

Ever yours,   Robert Frost

283 · To Hervey Allen

RF met and became friendly with the poet, novelist, and biographer, Hervey Allen, at one of the early sessions of the Bread Loaf Writers' Conferences in the mid-1920's. The following letter of regret was written in answer to Allen's invitation to a "conclave" of writers, different from the Bread Loaf program in that it would involve no teaching.

Dear Hervey: 7 June 1930   South Shaftsbury

I commend your pains. I can commend your plans too for the most part. (It warms me to the heart to be assured that there will be no manifesto.) Only you couldn't have chosen the time more effectually to leave me out, if you had chosen the first ten days of September on purpose. That's when I'm a fugitive from hay-fever in the higher mountains. I havent been below the ragweed line for anybody or anything between August 20 and September 15th since the year 1905. It wasn't just that the fever was unendurable, but it left me in no condition to face the winter. I'm sorry. But I mustn't think I matter too much. There are one or two on your list who will be no unhappier for not having me of the party. I shall be anxious for the success of the experiment. It is a good idea. (If I remember rightly it was partly mine. At any rate I have long contemplated such an annual conclave on the side hill of my own farm — if I should ever feel executive enough to carry it out. It will amply satisfy me to see some one else carry it out. I shall want to hear all about it.) I wish you could visit me here before you go back to Bermuda this fall and report to me. I like your seriousness in your books and out of them and count some time on more converse with you.

Always yours   Robert Frost

284 · To James R. Wells

Dear Wells   27 June 1930   South Shaftsbury

Fine to see you both. Come along. And bring your forceps. But lets see you or anybody else extract anything from me in my present state of mind.

I ought to warn you if you come here you have to work digging out my fish duck dog and frog pond. You would go round New York sowing suspicion that my farm was the kind where there was no work done. There'll be some done by you all right. Other tools you may as well bring besides forceps are rubber boots and Dutch Cleanser. Also a manicure set and vanity kit. We have a looking glass. — in fact we are a looking glass. As I look out my window this pleasant but torrid morning my eyes rest peacefully on as many as ten bowed autograph hunters, my captives, spading hoeing and weeding in my garden. They came here to pull my leg but I broke their will and put them to work. "Then came the terrible farmer and cut off their beautiful tales — and put them to work etc." (Kipling) You come here to get anything out of me and you're lucky if you get away even. I dont mean to be sinister. Only I'm a great person for utilizing waste power.

Our best to you both
Ever yours   Robert Frost

285 · To Louis Untermeyer

Dear Louis: 14 July 1930   South Shaftsbury

I am left out of the Two Weeks Manuscript Sales Fair [the Bread Loaf Writers' Conference] as I had reason to suppose I would be. I thought perhaps it would be less embarrassing all round if I simply forgot to go to the earlier educational session [School of English] at Bread Loaf. But I have been come after by Pres. [Paul D.] Moody and flatteringly written after by our friend Gay to be present and help them dedicate the Memorial Library to Wilfred Davison on Monday

July 21st. Pres. Moody said frankly that he saw no way but for the second session to go on commercial as it had begun. I judge he thought the two sessions could be kept like the right and left hand each from knowing what the other was doing. He asked me to think of the two as separate. They can't be separate, of course, and in the end belonging to one will mean belonging to both. But I don't care if it does in the end. This year can make no difference in principle, and I hate to put on airs that will hurt either Moody's feelings or Gay's. I agreed to go on the understanding that they would give you your choice of sessions. I knew you said you came a good deal to be there when I was. But of course we are going to see each other here right off anyway, and maybe it would be too ostentatious for you to desert the Farrow [John Farrar] session because I was left out of it. You may be sure I don't mind your being with that gang for a visit if only as a spy and agent provocateur. You can't imagine how cleanly I have forgiven the Johnnie. The explanation is that I am at heart secretly tickled if I offended him unintentionally. I suppose it to have been unintentionally because to this hour I don't know what my offense was. I am too cowardly to offend anybody intentionally and usually too skillfull to do it unintentionally. So I am stuck. I can't hurt anybody no matter how much he deserves it. When I do it is a triumph of the divinity that shapes our ends. It gives me a funny feeling I must say I like. I suppose it's a manly feeling, but I'm such a stranger to it I hardly know. Yes I came off so well with the Johnnie that I shan't care if you do treat him as if nothing had ever happened. I even evened the score between him and Lesley. [. . .]

Ever yours   Robert Frost

286 · To H. L. MENCKEN

My dear Men[c]ken   22 August 1930   South Shaftsbury

The news warms me in my friendship for you. Our Baltimore daughter Marjorie tells us how particularly well you have done and we have other ways of knowing.

I may not be supposed to have heard that your bridal tour is to be through New England and it will be seeing New England for the first time for both of you. But I wonder if you could be persuaded to look in on us for a night in your travels either in our camp near Franconia N. H. before September 15th or at our home here in South Shaftsbury, Vermont after September 21st. See us and you see New England. And we have been married ever since 1905 [1895] We wouldn't talk dialect to you.

Thanks for your kindness to my wood-chopper J. J. Lankes. You remember I said to you once you did more than all the teachers put together to find 'em out and help 'em up. Ruth Suckow sat on our porch the other day and acknowledged her debt to you.   Always yours friendly   Robert Frost

287 · TO FREDERIC G. MELCHER

LETTER 273 contains reference to Melcher's idea of preparing a Robert Frost bibliography for the book-collector's quarterly, *The Colophon*. Previously, Melcher had contributed an article, "Robert Lee Frost: Bibliographical Check List," to *Publishers' Weekly* (1923, Vol. 103, p. 24). Subsequently, he turned the task over to H. S. Boutell, who did "A Bibliography of Robert Frost" for the May 1930 *The Colophon*. This letter begins with a reference to Melcher's part in the compilation.

Dear Fred: 1 September [1930]   Franconia

I got home and found The Colophon. Thanks for that, for the impressive way you treated me in it and for the money that helped me home by way of Baltimore. I enclose my check for $10.50 to show my appreciation. (There was a telegram besides the fare.)

I am going to ask you very privately for a piece of advice. Do you think I would derogate from my dignity or aloofness or anything if I did a series of lectures (so to call them) on poetry this winter at the New School of Social Research. I'm not afraid of the radicals I should be thrown with nor of the Jews. I may be a radical myself and there is a theory that the Scotch were Jews and another that the Yankees were Jews. I am a Scotch Yankee. What I want to know is, do you think I would cheapen myself in some way. I'm half inclined to accept Alvin Johnson's invitation to lecture there if only to save myself from too much humanism.*   Ever yours   Robert Frost

* RF did accept the invitation, and gave four talks at the New School for Social Research on successive Thursday evenings in March 1931.

288 · To RICHARD H. THORNTON

RF's chronic animosities and resentments were stirred anew in late September of 1930 when Richard H. Thornton wrote to tell him that Holt had had a request from Walter J. Coates for permission to reprint some of RF's poems, without charge, in a book of Vermont poetry then being prepared by himself, Professor Tupper of the University of Vermont, and the Committee on Vermont Traditions and Ideals. Some of the factors behind RF's reaction are reflected in this letter.

Dear Mr. Thornton.   [c. 1 October 1930]   [Amherst]

It is good to hear from you again. I have had half a mind to run down to see you. But I am trying to stay in one place as long as possible before the inevitable winter wandering. I shall be in and out with you in January, February and March when I shall be giving Thursday evenings in poetry at The New School of Social Research. I may even set up a tent in Central Park or the Bronx Zoo for part of the job.

It would relieve me of something distasteful if you would deal with this Committee of Vermont Traditions and Ideals (tell it to Men[c]ken!). Have I not put it in plenty good blank verse that the ideals will bear some keeping still about. The Walter J. Coates you mention is no friend of mine. I sat in an audience of twenty-five at Arlington, Vermont, two years ago and heard him read me out of the State and out of the ranks of important poets. Afterward ashamed of himself, he climbed all over me with adulation. I have become an issue in their local literary politics. It makes you laugh. They say I'm a foreigner because I came only ten years ago from New Hampshire. The leaders of this purging movement — I say leaders but should say cathartics — are this Coates, an unfrocked parson from New York State, a Rutland (Vt) editor from Ohio and the reformed-radical Welsh Jew John Spargo. I don't know what their ideals may be, but possibly one of them is to stay black Republican, . . . and elect Taft retroactively as of 1912. Vermont and Utah were the only states Taft carried in that election.

I can barely stand such people. And still I must be careful not to get tarred and feathered and ridden on a rail by them some fine night lest I be suspected of doing it for the advertisement. If you act between us it will be all right probably. Tell them they can have the poems. I'll pretend not to know what's going on. If they send me their Anthology I'll burn it privately only in one of our three open fire places or the kitchen stove. All this sounds more like a mountain feud than it really is. I manage not to seem to notice most of the time.

Let's think of something pleasanter, the book you have made of my Collected. I look forward to seeing it. We both do. Remember us both to Mrs. Thornton.

Sincerely yours   Robert Frost

289 · To Kimball Flaccus

My dear Flaccus: 26 October 1930   Amherst

The book has come and I have read your poems first. They are good. They have loveliness — they surely have that. They are carried high. What you long for is in them. You wish the world better than it is, more poetical. You are that kind of poet. I would rate as the other kind. I wouldn't give a cent to see the world, the United States or even New York made better. I want them left just as they are for me to make poetical on paper. I don't ask anything done to them that I don't do to them myself. I'm a mere selfish artist most of the time. I have no quarrel with the material. The grief will be simply if I can't transmute it into poems. I don't want the world made safer for poetry or easier. To hell with it. That is its own lookout. Let it stew in its own materialism. No, not to Hell with it. Let it hold its position while I do it in art. My whole anxiety is for myself as a performer. Am I any good? That's what I'd like to know and all I need to know. I wonder which kind of poet is more numerous, your kind or my kind. There should have been a question in the census-taking to determine. Not that it should bother us. We can be friends across the difference. You'll have me watching you. We must meet again and have a talk about poetry and nothing but poetry. The great length of this letter is the measure of my thanks for the book.

Always yours friendly,   Robert Frost

290 · To Leonidas W. Payne, Jr.

SEE letters 248 and 266 for evidence of RF's indebtedness to Professor Payne, Chairman of the English Department at the University of Texas. The poet's patience may have been strained, however, when Payne gratuitously sent a list of errors in punctuation, syntax, and choice of words, which he had found, or thought he had found, in the new volume of Frost's *Collected Poems* published on 8 November 1930. This answer reflects the strain; but the friendship between the two men survived the crisis, and they saw much of each other when RF returned to Texas in 1933.

Dear Payne: [c. November 1930]   [South Shaftsbury]

I'm sorry about all those commas and hyphens. But you know I indulge a sort of indifference to punctuation. I dont mean I despise it. I value it. But I seem rather willing to let other people look after it for me. One of my prides is that I can write a fifty word telegram without having to use a single "Stop" for the sense. I'll have those commas and hyphens tended to though, if only for your peace of mind.

I must say you scared me with your formidable-looking list. Fortunately it turned out you were wrong in all your findings of errors except the punctuational. It would have been terrible if I had been off verbally grammatically or metrically. I have to be a pretty exact person when it comes to such a delicate poem as Moon Compasses. Your suggestion there would spoil my meaning. *Was measured* doesnt mean the same thing as *measured*. My passive is perfectly idiomatic. You must remember I am not writing school-girl English.

Codlin should be in your dictionary. It is a form still in use among apple men. Codling is getting the better of it as language goes more and more to school. Codlin is to codling as leggin is to legging, as interval is to intervale. *Codlin'* would look funny in any book of mine. I havent dropped a g that way in a lifetime of writing.

Substituting *but that* for *but* in "Waspish" would show school girl timidity and spoil my metrics. *But* alone will be found all the way down our literature. I noticed it tonight in Robinson Crusoe.

Leaves and bark, leaves and bark
To lean against and hear in the dark

The reversing of the order should remind you of a very ancient figure of speech. Your friends of the Classical Department will tell you about it. I dont want to seem pedantic.

Inserting *its* after *doubt* on page 87 would be school girl English to my ear. I give you credit for being able to supply words plainly understood. Dialogue would be unendurable if all words had to be said outright for complete construction.

No not a word has been dropped out or printed wrong I believe. There was one terrible mistake in the first edition of West-running Brook: roams for romps. One of my friends liked the printers accident better than my intention. Anyway he resented the correction when it was made in the Collected. He was duly embarrassed when he learned how it was. He neednt have been. I didnt mind the criticism implied.

Well here's thinking of you gratefully for all your trouble with proof-reading the book and for reviewing it so finely. I wonder what form of it you lack and would like me to send you. You know Im   Always yours faithfully   Robert Frost

290-a · ELINOR M. FROST TO EDITH H. FOBES

PREVIOUS LETTERS have shown that the poor health of RF and his wife at this time was related to their concern over the physical and mental illnesses of their children. Marjorie's chronic ailments had been especially disturbing to them, and they were greatly encouraged when she was finally well enough to undertake training at the Johns Hopkins Hospital, Baltimore, as a nurse. But within a short period Marjorie became ill again, and this time her trouble was diagnosed as tuberculosis. The Frosts wrote the Bartletts in Boulder, Colorado, and made arrangements to send Marjorie to a tuberculosis sanitarium there.

Matters were further complicated when doctors found that Carol's wife, Lillian, also had tuberculosis; and plans were quickly made for Carol and Lillian to move to California with their son, Prescott. As a result, the senior Frosts traveled to Colorado and California repeatedly. Later, they went as far as Texas and Florida, searching for health.

Dear Mrs. Fobes,-   5 May [1931]   South Shaftsbury
     I am sorry I have delayed answering your letter. Robert and I were in New York nearly five weeks after leaving Amherst. I got very tired there, and Robert had quite a severe attack of grippe, and since coming home there have been a great many things to do, and besides that I have been much disheartened and sad. Not about Marjorie, for just lately the improvement has been marked. Her weight has increased from 110 to 119 lbs and she is now sitting 4 hours a day, and going for a drive twice a week. For quite a while, the gain in her condition was slower than with ordinary tuberculosis patients whose

symptoms are worse than hers were, so they concluded that a partial nervous breakdown was complicating the case. She has felt from the first that it was just the right place for her to get strong in, and lately she is very happy and cheerful, I can see by her letters. I am hoping she will be strong enough to take one or two courses in the Univ. of Colorado next year, but we will not hurry matters. The University is in Boulder, and there is a Writers Conference in the summer school there, and they have asked Robert there to do a week's work, from the 10th to the 15th of August. As it will pay all our expenses out and back, and our board while there, we are going out about the middle of July, to visit Marjorie for three or four weeks. After we return, we shall be happy to go into the Cadarette cottage [the Fobes guest cottage in Franconia] for a while.

The reason I have been almost crushed with discouragement lately is that Lillian, Carol's wife, also has tuberculosis. She hasn't been very well since a year ago this May, and since October she has had a steady cough. . . . The laboratory report was that the presence of tuberculosis bacilli was very evident, and an X-ray shows a spot on one lung. You know Marjorie and Lillian were intimate friends in High School. Isn't it extraordinary that they should both have the same thing at the same time, after being separated most of the time for several years?

Well, Carol and Lillian have decided to sell their farm, and move to a sunnier climate. This doctor didn't advise Lillian to go into a sanatorium, but to take as nearly as possible a bed treatment. They have someone to do the housework, and Carol takes most of the care of Prescott. They are going away as soon as Prescott's school is finished in June, and get settled somewhere before school opens in September. After getting information about a good many places, and considering the matter a long time, they have decided to go to San Bernardino, California. They want lots of sunshine, and a warm winter, and also a place where there is something going on, so Carol can get a job of some kind. You can imagine what a blow it is to me to have them go so far away. I have always wanted to watch Carol a little on account of his lack of vigorous health, and he is very dear to me, while Prescott has become very precious to us. But young people have to work out their own salvation, and their hearts seem to be so set on this that we cannot exert the pressure that would be necessary to change their purpose.

We are fond of Lillian, too, and to have her go so far away, with this serious illness, and Carol to have the responsibility of everything seems too hard. Robert says I am foolish — that it might turn out to be just the right thing for Carol.

. . . in June . . . we shall be at Montauk with Lesley, who expects her confinement the first week in June.

We both send love

Affectionately   Elinor Frost

291 · To John T. Bartlett

Dear John: [c. 7 May 1931]   [South Shaftsbury]

Marjorie wrote in her last letter, Don't say our family never does anything right. In her opinion we did a big thing right when we sent her out where the John T. Bartletts live. I dont know that she says right out, but she seems to imply, that she doesnt think much of your Colorado spring as far as it has got. But that defect sinks into a joke by comparison with all she does think much of. Between you and me (you mustnt tell her for fear of making her self-conscious) you folks and Colorado have changed her tune. You know where to come for thanks if you want any in words.

She wants me to come out there and do the cooking for the sanatorium she intends to establish when she gets well and finishes training for a nurse. She says I am a good meat cook — that's where I would come in. Elinor could do the bread and pastry. Carol could run the dairy and kitchen garden. What dissipates that dream is your altitude. You live too high for us — about 2500 feet too high. Cut your plateau down half and we'll talk with you. Why can't you be reasonable? Twenty five hundred up ought to be enough for anybody who began life on the plains of Raymond, New Hampshire. Come down — I wont say off it — come down with it. Shake down, have an earthquake. I mean it. I'd like to live out there for a few years if it were only possible. We are not wedded to this state. For some funny reason we have never been accepted as Vermonters. We are important enough to have the question raised whether or not we should be accepted. We were that flattered. But the answer has been in the negative. So we can go when and where we please. Well we'll have some farms to sell when we mobilize. Three. Mine of 150 acres a hewn timber house with

373

three open fireplaces on the central chimney and many HL hinges on the doors. Carols of 100 acres and the stone house you remember; very old and historical. John and Irma's of 8 acres and a small old house in a half circle of old spruces. Allow me to sell you a couple. Dont weep for us. I can unload them if I turn my hand to advertising. Give me a year.

We mustn't think so far ahead. It will be something to have a few weeks out there with you this summer. We'll want to be sure of Elinor of course. But if the doctors give her permission, I dont see why we shouldn't all have a gay time together.

[. . .] I'm studying the catalogue of the Summer School so I shall be up on my fellows on the faculty. I ought to have read what they have written when I meet them. Yes and they ought to have read what I have written. But will they have? I ask you. Once in a while I meet someone who has read me. It did him good. I mean it served him right.

This is the time of year that I have been keeping away from my farm things all winter for. Now I am let loose to go the rounds of them all to see how they came through. I didn't winter-kill (though I damn near did in one of those New York hotels). Did they winter kill? A few blew down and a few spruces dried up in the big wind of March 9. But most things stood it and are ready [to] start their new growth. I've got the trellis of a grape-vine to rebuild.

People aren't kind to me about my farming any more. They make jokes like the one I had to listen to today. A friend says to me says he: You look poorly for you. You've had too much city. After you've sat down on your farm for a few months you'll be as good as new. I have to admit that I dont work at anything profitable like milking or pitching down hay. I move trees around the way Amphion did only he did it by music proper and I do it by hand   Our love to you all   RF.

292 · To Louis Untermeyer

Dear Louis   12 June 1931   Montauk Long Island
        . . . today particularly I am in no mood to estimate myself or anything I ever did. Lesley is at the hospital in Southampton (L. I.) in ineffectual [child-birth] pain and has been for three days now. We don't understand what's the matter.

The doctors say nothing's the matter. We'll be convinced of that after everything comes out all right. All our children are an anxiety at once it happens. Marj gains very slowly. Carol's wife (I haven't told you have I?) will have to be taken West for her lungs. Carol must sell his farm just when it is coming into productiveness. The orchards began blooming this year. Irma is on the strain of having a husband at college (John's one of these smart boys that shines in college: so that will probably come out all right). And here is Lesley in trouble too. Elinor just interrupted me to say on the telephone that it is bad but the worst of it is it doesn't get worse.

I hope you three are flourishing. . . .

Ever yours   Robert

293 · To Richard H. Thornton

[c. 12 June 1931]   [Montauk]
(still for a few days
awaiting the event)

Dear Mr Thornton:

I have connections with the Chicago underworld through Carl Sandburg that often make me tremble in the night with fear of being taken for a ride if I show the least sign however unintentional of defection desertion falling away. There is something undeniably sinister in a letter I have just had from Harriet Monroe Editress of Poetry a Magazine of Verse asking me whats this — do I mean to let my publishers stick her up for fifty dollars for four small poems she wants to include in her anthology [*The New Poetry*]. Seeing its she and she lives in Chicago and the times are what they are (morally and financially) suppose we cut that in half if you think we can do it with dignity. I dont want her to think we are *too* scared or the next we know we'll have her dictating my future poems to me subject matter and form. But once you are in with the lawless in verse rum or dope you cant get out and live. I know too many of their secrets about breaking lines where they break them not to be dangerous running at large. I appeal to you to understand the perilous position I am in. Tell her if you can that at my supplication you will let her have the four poems for twenty-five dollars.

Seriously yours   Robert Frost

293-a · ELINOR M. FROST TO EDITH H. FOBES

[Printed heading, crossed out with pen]

MESA VISTA SANATORIUM
2121 NORTH STREET
BOULDER, COLORADO

[c. 18 July 1931] c/o Mr. John T. Bartlett
Dear Mrs. Fobes,-   Boulder, Colorado

Your letter and card came the day before we left home, and I was too rushed to answer. One day on the train was awful — oppressive heat — and I was quite exhausted when we arrived night before last. Yesterday I rested without attempting to do anything, and as I slept well last night I am feeling all right again this morning. It is a fine cool day.

Marjorie looks beautiful — she weighs 120 pounds and her skin is clear and firm. It was a most fortunate decision — to bring her here. The doctors think she has had T. B. for eight or ten years, and only six weeks ago the tuberculin test gave a very positive reaction. She intends to stay in this climate another year, at least, though not in the sanatorium. She will board somewhere, and take one course in the University.

Lillian and Carol expected to start from home today [by automobile]. I hope the weather will not be too hot as they are crossing Ohio and Nebraska. They will reach Boulder in about three weeks, I think. . . . I believe that the climate of southern California will mean a great deal to Lillian, and also to Carol and Prescott.

When Robert bought our tickets he found that he could get round trip tickets to San Francisco, via San Bernardino and Los Angeles, for very little, and so he bought them, thinking he could see the place Carol & Lillian have chosen for their home, and also have a small glimpse of San Francisco, where he was born. He accepted 5 or 6 invitations to lecture here in Colorado, but he has nothing farther west, and he seems to feel that he will enjoy the trip to the coast more for going in this spontaneous manner, without any lectures or readings to think about. But it will mean that we shall not get to Franconia this year. Perhaps we can go down to Peace Dale for a few days in the fall. . . .

We are staying for a few days now with old friends. Robert reads in Denver Monday afternoon, and on Tuesday we shall take Marjorie for two weeks out to a mountain place called Evergreen, where there are furnished cottages to rent. I think we'll have a very good time. I will write again then. Ever so much affection and all good wishes from us both.

Elinor Frost

294 · To Louis Untermeyer

Dear Louis   1 August 1931 Evergreen, Colorado

I am up here 8000 feet high, gasping for oxygen, my walk slow and vague as in a world of unreality. Anything I say feels as if someone else said it. I'm told it's not my heart but the size of my lungs that's to blame. I always was a short distance runner even in my best days. I did one hundred yards in eleven seconds, but hare and hounds was an agony.

We came here to give Marj a vacation from the sanitorium. We're having a fine time all to ourselves in spite of the uneases of altitude. (Marj and I are the sufferers as it turns out, though Elinor was the only one we feared for beforehand.) I clumb some of the nearer dirt hills for the activity I need, leaving the rocky peaks and cliffs till I renew my youth. I'm botanizing all over in an almost entirely different flora. Up one ravine today there were masses of larkspur and monkshood. It's a very flowery country. I'm a little too late for much of it. I've just missed the yellow lady's slipper that seems as common here as the pink slipper at home. Isn't it strange for me to be living away off like this. Three weeks ago I was settled for a month but as if forever in the sand-dunes of extreme Montauk. Such lengths our children drag us to. I'm glad none of the family are foreign missionaries or we should be snatched back and forward very likely from continent to continent instead of as now from state to state. I don't care if God doesn't care.

Who is this Ferris poet [Thomas Hornsby Ferril] in Denver? Is he one of your prospects? He seems a pleasant boy. But I don't like [Theodore] Fisher the entrepreneur. If I have to make a really western tour, someone will have to recommend a better agent than that man. I suppose lecturing for any agent is roughing it. I had a real run in with Fisher. I let him have me interviewed for his publicity twice on arrival, once in the station and once in a newspaper office, a place where in all my years of reading to people I have never gone for anything. On top of that I had to stand a lot of loud anxiety from him about his getting a big enough audience. Damn him. I was against his trying for one in the summer anyway. To hell with him for a bad sport. I can't think he lost much by the size of the crowd I saw in front of me. But I could wish he had. There was nothing handsome about his style. I shouldn't have got into this. I took the Colorado University thing weakly to pay our fare and then one thing led to another. Fisher has been soliciting me for a year or two. I was inclined to let him manage me for a California swing-round. He did himself out of a cool thousand by his inconsiderateness of my age and dignity.

I, we all, go back to Boulder next Wednesday for my talks to the summer school. I may live to be sorry I got into those. Sometimes I do well and then again I get too tired from the strain leading up to a performance. I mustn't complain of how Fisher manages me: I don't manage myself very well. I don't care if God doesn't care.

. . . Sometimes I almost cry I am afraid I am such a bad poet. But tonight I don't care if God doesn't care. . . .

Ever yours   Robert Lee

294-a · ELINOR M. FROST TO EDITH H. FOBES

Dear Mrs. Fobes,-   2 August [1931]   Evergreen

. . . It was frightfully hot in Boulder, but we brought Marjorie up farther into the mountains, thirty miles west of Denver, and the nights have been very cool here. We have a cottage on a hillside, with spruce and pine woods around us. . . . We return to Boulder on Wednesday where Robert has four days lecturing at the University.

We have enjoyed the quiet here, and the beauty of the scenery. . . . Marjorie doesn't seem as well as I had hoped to find her. She must rest in the sanatorium several months longer, I think, before she goes about much or undertakes any mental or physical work. But she seems happy, and I know she will recover, if she cannot be considered already recovered.

With Lillian it is different. I am afraid she may not live, and the great concern I feel for her, and for Carol and Prescott, stretches my endurance almost to the breaking point. Why are we so unfortunate? I have worked so hard for my family all these years, and now everything seems tumbling around me. I do not lament this way to everyone, of course. I am too proud, and with Robert I have to keep cheerful, because I mustn't drag him down, but sometimes it seems to me that I *cannot* go on any longer. Probably I have overworked these last six months, and will feel stronger after we reach home. . . .

Affectionately   Elinor Frost

294-b · ELINOR M. FROST TO EDITH H. FOBES

26 August [1931]   California Hotel

Dear Mrs. Fobes,

San Bernardino, Cal.

Robert and I arrived in San Bernardino yesterday morning at 6:30. Carol, Lillian and Prescott had been here three days. They had already looked at houses here, and had driven up to Lake Arrowhead. We like everything better than we had expected to, in spite of the heat. The air seems pleasant. This hotel is really delightful, next to a park full of palms and pepper trees and is very reasonable in its charges. It seems there are a number of small four room houses with shade trees to be had at $30 a month. Yesterday, however, we drove over to Monrovia, and looked around for several hours. The best house we found was very good indeed. It is in a good locality, close to the mountain, one of the older houses and lacks a coat of paint, but the inside has lately been put in good repair, and there are six good rooms, besides an unusually large and pleasant sleeping porch, and the rent is only $27.50 a month. There is a very large live oak tree in the yard, and several smaller trees, and enough land for Carol to have many flowers and some vegetables. And Monrovia has good T. B. specialists, and a particularly good sanitorium, we are told. . . . We shall probably decide this evening to take the house, and drive over tomorrow morning. . . .

Probably we shall go on toward San Francisco next Monday or Tuesday. . . .   Affectionately   Elinor Frost

295 · To HERSCHEL BRICKELL

RF'S first volume of *Collected Poems* (1930) won him the Pulitzer Prize in 1931. But more than that, at the annual meeting and dinner of the National Institute of Arts and Letters, held in New York City on 11 November 1931, the Institute members voted unanimously to award the Russell Loines Poetry Prize of $1,000 to RF as "the poet of the period whom it would most like to crown." The formal presentation was made by Harrison Morris, Treasurer of the Institute, in Philadelphia on 11 December 1931, at a dinner in the poet's honor given in the home of Robert von Moschzisker, former Chief Justice of the Pennsylvania Supreme Court and friend of RF since Franconia days. Herschel Brickell, to whom this letter is addressed, had succeeded Lincoln MacVeagh as head of the trade department of Henry Holt and Company.

12 December 1931

Dear Mr Brickell   2101 DeLancey Place   Philadelphia

Harrison Morris gave me the enclosed* to help you in telling the world. The emendations are his. He says you can advertise the award as much as you like. He thinks the magnitude of the Prize is important. People should be made to understand that it isn't just one more of the little prizes the country is flooded with. He says the reason no story was made of my getting it was the illness of Mrs. Vanamee, secretary to the president of the Academy. I wish that besides any general publicity you give it you could get it into a straight advertisement like this in a few places:

Robert Frost's Collected Poems
Loines Prize of the National Institute 1931
Pulitzer Prize 1931

Would that be too much to ask?

Sincerely yours   Robert Frost

296 · To Louis Untermeyer

Dear Louis: 23 February 1932   Amherst

Jean [Starr Untermeyer] writes that where e'er you may roam you worry about me. You should. I'll tell you what we'll do: I'll worry about my family; you worry about me; and let Hoover worry about you. Concerning you are all Hoover's expressions of hope and fear — concerning you and the proletariat you represent or used to when you were an editor of the Masses. Me and mine are below the threshold of legislative cognizance. Beyond participation of politicians and beyond re-

* A clipping from the Philadelphia *Ledger* for 12 December 1931, telling of the dinner and the award of the Russell Loines prize.

lief of senates lie our sorrows: if any of the farm block (heads) chance to heave a sigh, they pity us and not our grief. And the chiefest of our sorrows is that the world should go as it does — that thus all moves and that this is the justice that on earth we find. What justice? Do I have to tell you? Why injustice, which we either have to turn on the other fellow with a laugh when it is called comedy or we have to take like a spear-point in both hands to our breast when it is called tragedy. Laugh no more, gentles, laugh no more. For it is almost too hard for anything to succeed in being divine, though Lionel Johnson sware the opposite. But let what will be be. I am so deeply smitten through my helm that I am almost sad to see infants young any more. I expect to look backward and see the last tail light on the last car. But I shall be going the other way on foot.

Yet I refuse to match sorrows with anyone else, because just the moment I start the comparison I see that I have nothing yet as terrible as it might be. A few of our children are sick or their spouses are and one of them [Irma Frost Cone] has a spouse still in college. I and my wife are not well, neither are we young; but we mean to be both better and younger for company's sake. That is to say we mean well, though we aren't well.

I thought I'd just lay it on lugubrious this letter. I saw and heard what you said about me in Springfield, but it didn't cure my evil mood because it threw me into a superstitious fear that you would incur for me the jealousy of gods and men. I shall have to tell you some day just how great I can allow you to say I am — that is if Elinor will allow me to set you a limit. (But she says now if you don't go to extremes for me she will.) The gods I am afraid of are your God of Israel, who admits he is a jealous god, and Edna's [Edna St. Vincent Millay] goddess Venus, who can't deny the love she stands for is a 99 per cent adultery of jealousy. Never mind the names of the men I am afraid of. Now don't for goodness sakes *ever* take me at my word and incontinently give up praising me altogether. I had a letter a while ago from Babette Deuts[c]h asking me to admire her Prometheus in exchange for her respecting my total output. Some cheek. I was chilled to the marrow. I have since suffered cramp. I am all taken down by mere respect. No, admire my work and give me courage for the home stretch.

I admire yours. . . .

I seem slowly to be getting over what I imagined was the matter with me.   Ever yours   Robert

296-a · MARJORIE FROST TO ROBERT AND ELINOR M. FROST

[22 March 1932]

Dear Mama & Papa: Mesa Vista Sanatorium   Boulder

Everything is all settled. Willard [Fraser] and I are engaged to be married, and my only regret is that you are too far away to see how happy I am. I know you will be happy, too, when I tell you that I have found a love and a companionship that I never even dreamed existed for me. It all happened last Saturday night. So of course it is still too new for me to realize all it means. I like him for many, many things, but most of all for his absolute goodness. He is a dear, kind, and considerate man, another real Victorian, papa, with the beautiful ideals that I had feared no longer existed, but I guess always will if you are just lucky enough to find them.

And now to come down to earth. He graduates [from the University of Colorado] this June, but has no money of his own, and will have to make his start in the world with absolutely nothing but his own abilities, which, naturally, I think are considerable. I have no fear whatever that he will ultimately succeed in his chosen field, archaeology, but of course we shan't plan to be married for some little time yet, until he can get on his feet, as we both have hard jobs cut out for us, mine to get a whole lot stronger and really well before undertaking to hold up my end of the partnership and his to find himself, as they say, and at present we would just hinder each other instead of helping.

I am so glad it all came to pass before I planned to leave. That was all that was worrying me when I wrote that disturbing letter. Naturally he won't hear of my leaving now, but it is absolutely the best thing for both of us, for me to go right ahead and carry out my original plans, and though I am almost incapable of being sensible when we are together and he is arguing against me, I am sure I can make him see it my way before Saturday rolls round. The main thing is for me to get well, now, and I am not yet strong enough to be just living here, doing nothing, but continually under an emotional strain.

Margaret, who likes Willard very much, is very much pleased about it all, and she urges that I am doing the right thing in going. At any rate I promised Lillian and Carol I would come. Lillian is sick, and I can make her happy, and where is the use of a new love if you can't be true to your old ties? I may not stay more than three or four weeks, but that part can wait. The whole thing in a nutshell is that I am supremely happy, and I want to keep my self respect so I can continue to be. Honestly this is one of the most perfect things that ever happened in this world, and I want you both to feel just as happy as it is humanly possible to feel for at least a week, if you can't contrive to any longer than that, and if you have ever felt sorry about the way you brought me up, forget it, because what I am and what I am alone has brought me something beautiful that was worth waiting for all these years.

As you see I started this letter yesterday morning. I was interrupted and since then I simply haven't had a chance to get back to it. My days are full to the brim. There are so many things to be done and friends to say good-bye to. Fortunately Mrs. McKeehan came to see me today, and all my other friends are coming here, except Mrs. Romig, whom I promised to visit once more. Margaret is coming up to help me pack on Friday. Willard has induced me to stay until Sunday, so on Easter he will take me to Denver. About his age. I hadn't asked him yet as I never think of it when we are together, but Gertrude said last time she was here that he is older than most of the graduates, 25 or 24 at the very least, so there is really not so much difference in our ages, especially when you consider that no one will believe I am 26, always guessing me to be only 22.

Some more good news. Yesterday I went down for my final examination and Dr. Gilbert seemed to be very much pleased with my progress. Everything looks and sounds fine, and my haemoglobin has gone up to 95.

I got your letter tonight, mama, and I am dreadfully sorry papa isn't so very well. I do hope just taking it easy in California this summer will be good for him. He has just had too much to think about these past years. Well, don't worry about me for a while at least. I shall enjoy my trip out as I shall have so many happy things to think of and I shall have a grand time out there, the change of food and scenes will make me gain rapidly I'm sure. It's not that the San [Sanatorium] has gone bad on me, it's just that I am too well to be here, that's all.

It would surely be great if you were both here so I could tell you everything. Well it won't be so terribly long now till you come out, thank goodness. I hope you will like him almost as well as I do, but I'm sure you will as he has so many, many friends and makes them so easily, though not indiscriminately, like some folks we won't mention. Miss Bigelow thinks he is one of the finest boys here, and she is surely a judge of character if there ever was one. But to think I am sitting here with a fraternity pin over my heart, which is the proper place to wear them, after all I have said on the fraternity subject! We never, never know what we'll come to, so in order to be safe we ought never to say anything against anything, ought we.

Sent off a night letter tonight so you wouldn't worry any more. I am very sorry I ever wrote that letter that upset you folks. I'll try not to do such a thing again. Well I'll be telling you how I like sunny California in my next. Lots of love, Marge

297 · To MARJORIE FROST

Dear Marj: 26 March 1932 Amherst

Just a word from Amherst to welcome you to Monrovia. Your last news from Boulder went to our hearts and imaginations. Willard sounds like a good boy in a sad world. Bless you both. Perhaps on our way out in June we'll see him and on our way back see him and you together.

We are in possession of our Big Home [15 Sunset Avenue] and overwhelmed with the responsibilities of taste it lays upon us. We wish we had all our children here to help us debate the curtains, wall-paper, carpets and paint. We mustn't try too hard to be right.

It must be fun to look on Prescott once more. I'll bet he's quite a Californian, tell him. Tell him I say Texas is bigger than California. So he needn't put on airs. Ask him if he remembers how scared that Californian was of us Vermonters with our Vermont license when we ran him down for speaking rude to us. We easterners are real heroes.

Affectionately Papa

298 · To WILLARD E. FRASER

Dear Willard 18 April 1932 Amherst

That was a fine letter. I know I couldn't have done half as well under the circumstances. What between you and Marj we begin to get quite an idea of you. We ought to reciprocate and describe ourselves to you. But we shall be coming out so soon now where you can see us and save us the necessity. I am particularly glad you are bringing archaeology into the family. Archaeology is one of the four things I wanted most to go into in life, archaeology, astronomy, farming, and teaching Latin. When I saw I wasn't going to be able to go into them all, I began to hope my four children would go into them for me, each taking up one, or, in the case of the girls, marrying into it. Carol is in farming. Marj marries into archaeology. Lesley almost went into Latin. That's rather better than fifty percent of my dream come true to date. Dwight Morrow [Junior] will tell you what a frustrated archaeologist I am. You may have to take me on a small expedition some time for relief. That would be a relief expedition indeed.

We are very happy in Marj's happiness.

Yours henceforth   Robert Frost

299 · To Sidney Cox

Honestly Sidney,   [c. 19 April 1932]   Amherst

You are getting out of hand. I'm afraid you aren't going to let yourself be unduly unfluenced by me any more.

I grow surer I don't want to search the poet's mind too seriously. I might enjoy threatening to for the fun of it just as I might to frisk his person. I have written to keep the over curious out of the secret places of my mind both in my verse and in my letters to such as you. A subject has to be held clear outside of me with struts and as it were set up for an object. A subject must be an object. There's no use in laboring this further years. My objection to your larger book about me was that it came thrusting in where I did not want you. The idea is the thing with me. It would seem soft for instance to look in my life for the sentiments in the Death of the Hired Man. There's nothing to it believe me. I should fool you if you took me so. I'll tell you my notion of the contract you thought you had with me. The objective idea is all I ever cared about. Most of my ideas occur in verse. But I have always had some turning up in talk that I feared I might never use because I was too lazy to write prose. I think they have been mostly educational ideas connected with my teaching, actually lessons. That's where I hoped you would come in. I thought if it didnt take you too much from your own affairs you might be willing to gather them for us both. But I never reckoned with the personalities. I keep to a minimum of such stuff in any poets life and works. Art and wisdom with the body heat out of it. You speak of

Shirley. He is two or three great poems — one very great. He projected, he got, them out of his system and I will not carry them back into his system either at the place they came out of or at some other place. I state this in the extreme. But relatively I mean what I say. To be too subjective with what an artist has managed to make objective is to come on him presumptuously and render ungraceful what he in pain of his life had faith he had made graceful. . . .   Ever yours R F.

300 · To Louis Untermeyer

THE FOLLOWING LETTER was written while RF was working on his poem, "Build Soil — A Political Pastoral," which he first read at Columbia University on 24 May 1932. This letter very largely amounts to a prose draft of that poem.

MOTTO:
Courage he said and pointed toward the *land*.
Alfred Lord Tennyson.

Dear Louis: 13 May 1932   South Shaftsbury
    The land be your strength and refuge. But at the same time I say this so consonant with your own sentiments of the moment, let me utter a word of warning against the land as an affectation. What determines the population of the world is not at all the amount of tillable land it affords: but it is something in the nature of the people themselves that limits the size of the globulate mass they are socially capable of. There is always, there will always be, a lot, many lots of land, left out of the system. I dedicate these lots to the stray souls who from incohesiveness feel rarely the need of the forum for their thoughts of the market for their wares and produce. They raise a crop of rye, we'll say. To them it is green manure. They plow it under. They raise a crop of endives in their cellar. They eat it themselves. That is they turn it under. They have an idea. Instead of rushing into print with it, they turn it under to enrich the soil. Out of that idea they have another idea. Still they turn that under. What they finally venture doubtfully to publication with is an idea of an idea of an idea. The land not taken up gives these stay-outers, these loosely connected people, their chance to live to themselves a larger proportion of the time than with the throng. There is no law divine or human against them when you come to think of it.

The social tyranny admits of squatters, tramps, gypsies because it can't make itself tight if it wants to. It isn't rebellion I am talking. It isn't even literary and intellectual detachment. It is simply easy ties and slow commerce. Refuse to be rushed to market or forum. Don't come as a product till you have turned yourself under many times. We don't have to be afraid we won't be social enough. Hell, haven't I written all that in my first book? But the point is the unconsidered land makes the life I like possible. Praise be to the unconsidered land. That's all. I haven't got through with the farming yet. When I get these sick children rounded up, we are going to make another big attempt at the almost self-contained farm. Almost. No nonsense. Merely much more self-contained than fools would imagine. I'm in favor of a skin and fences and tariff walls. I'm in favor of reserves and withholdings. I'm in favor of individuals with some age on their time apart. Hams cured in one day. Wine matured a week. The trouble with everybody's purse is everybody is caught out in the big market. The trouble with everybody's mind is everybody is caught out in the big forum. Gee you ought to have seen the document Waldo Frank wanted me to sign. He and [Lewis] Mumford and [Edmund] Wilson got it up. He said follow us and you can be a leader of your generation. They propose to use the class-conscious workers for the time being. I have half a mind to tell the class-conscious workers on them. But always ganging up at Geneva or somewhere else. When all you have to do to be saved is to sneak off to one side and see whether you are any good at anything. Can you cook can you make butter can you write can you think can you shoot can you sleep?

I'll leave the rest of this blank for you to fill out.

Ever yours   Robert

300-a · ELINOR M. FROST TO EDITH H. FOBES

[Printed Heading]

ABOARD THE COLUMBINE
FLOWER OF TRAVEL COMFORT

Dear Mrs. Fobes,   June 24 [1932]

I am trying to write a few letters on the train and I am not very good at it. I have owed you a letter since around April 1st but I have been just too busy for words, and have suffered a good deal from insomnia. I would have loved to visit you in April. I have never been to Peace Dale, you know, but there are many engagements in Amherst during the months we are there and I cannot leave for more than a night at a time, and that not many times. Besides, we were overseeing repairs on the house we bought last fall and it proved an absorbing occupation. The repairs are not all done, but the house will be very comfortable for us to go into Nov. 1st. . . .

We will reach Boulder tomorrow, and will stay there five days with Marjorie and the young man she has become engaged to. Yes, it looks as if Marjorie was going to be "swallowed up by a western marriage" as she calls it. She is *very* happy. He is a young archaeologist doing work at the University of Colorado, in Boulder. He has been on 2 or 3 expeditions with the Carnegie Institute people, a companion on them with young Dwight Morrow, whom we know very well at Amherst. He introduced himself to Marjorie because of that acquaintance, when she first went out there, a year and a half ago. We are eager to see him, of course. The Carnegie people are not providing money for an expedition this summer, and he has got a teaching position in Montana (his home state) for next year, and he and Marjorie may be married in September. Well such is life! Marjorie is really well, I guess, but is she strong enough to begin married life way up in the corner of a cold state like Montana? She is going along with us out to Carol's for two months. We have good news about Lillian. Her doctor thinks she will certainly recover, if she has patience to stay in bed long enough, and of course she will have. . . . I suppose Robert and Carol and Marjorie will go to the Olympic Games this summer. I love Colorado much more than California. A glimpse of Long's Peak thrills me. The people are so interesting and cordial too.

We should have come out the middle of May, if it hadn't been for two invitations to take degrees, one at Columbia on June 1st and the other at Williams on June 20th. We have had a hectic month.

We had a good time at Columbia (where Robert read the Phi Beta Kappa poem to an enthusiastic audience) and then we visited Mr. and Mrs. Thomas Lamont at their country home on the Palisades for two days and nights, and afterward visited friends in Scarsdale, Montclair and New Canaan.

At the time of the Williams College degree we were at

South Shaftsbury and President Lewis of the Univ. of New Hampshire and his wife visited us. He also took a degree and also Judge Cardozo, whom we talked with — a remarkably fine and sensitive man.

Lesley's two little daughters are fine. They are all at our new home in Amherst for the summer. Dwight [Dwight Francis, Lesley's husband] has not been well since Christmas but is better now.

Irma and John and Jacky are at South Shaftsbury. Jacky is a darling — almost five years old. John has just graduated from Mass. State College with very high rank — the second or third in his class — and has got a scholarship in the School of Architecture at Yale, so they will live in New Haven, next year. Irma is not at all strong and I am anxious about her. She has had hay fever frightfully last year, and must get away for it somewhere this year. I think they will get a camping outfit and I wondered if you would be willing to have them set up a tent among the trees on the slope beyond your barn, where they would have the view, for three weeks beginning Sept. 14. . . .

Robert saw you a few minutes in Boston. He reported you said, "You can't go out west every year, can you?" No, we cannot. This is the last time. We must both have quiet, and we are going to get it after this journey. . . .

Affectionately   Elinor Frost

301 · To Louis Untermeyer

Dear Louis: 13 December 1932   Amherst

All you say is true — too true — except that about the (my) Phi Beta Kappa poem ["Build Soil"] which I have my doubts about, though it rather stole the occasion for some reason from the great Walter Lippmann. In a way it was a monkey-shine and he needn't have minded poetry's having a little the best of it for once in a political age. But I'm afraid he did mind, whether from wounded vanity or lack of humor; and I'm sorry, for I admire him and should like to count him friend. There is a devil in me that defeats my deliberate intentions. I must show you the poem when and if I get it into closer form. Much of it was almost extemporized.

I larked the same way at a party [St. Botolph Club, Boston] where I met T. S. Eliot a month ago. He offered to read a poem if I would read one. I made him a counter-offer to *write* one while he was reading his. Then I fussed around with place-cards and a borrowed pencil, pretending an inspiration. When my time came I said I hadn't finished on paper but would try to fake the tail part in talk when I got to it. I did nine four-line stanzas on the subject "My Olympic Record Stride." (I might write it out and enclose it for you.)* Several said, "Quite a feat." All were so solemn I hadn't the courage to tell them that I of course was lying! I had composed the piece for my family when torn between Montauk, Long Island, and Long Beach, California, the summer before. So be cautioned. They must never know the truth. I'm much to blame, but I just couldn't be serious when Eliot was taking himself so seriously. There is much to give an old man the fan-tods. [. . .]

Ever yours   R. F.

302 · To Carol Frost

Dear Carol: [c. 18 March 1933]   [Amherst]
    Your Stratton poem is powerful and splendid. You have hammered it close and hard and you have rammed it full of all sorts of things, observations both of nature and human nature — and humor and picturesqueness too. And best of all, as Marge says, it is no sissy poem such as I get from poetic boys generally. It is written with a man's vigor and goes down in to a man's depth. You perhaps don't realize what that means to me. And one thing more: the poem is richly attractive, not repulsive and ugly the way so many think they have to describe life now-a-days to be honest. You are not always quite clear to me but I can put up with some obscurity where there is so much solid truth, such condensation and intense feeling. The clearness must be thought of. But you mustn't sacrifice anything you now have to get clearness. Practice in aiming at the mind of your reader will make you clearer every day. I don't quite know for instance what touch here and there is needed in that remarkably interesting passage about the officers in Stratton. But it is a little too hard just as it is — a little too puzzling. Even I who know more about the subject of more offices than men to fill them have some trouble in working it out. In straightening it out, there would be danger of losing some of the charming twists and turns and kinks. I shouldn't

* With this letter RF enclosed a manuscript copy of the poem.

want to lose those of course. How I like the smooth clarity and high sentiment of

> "The place for me"
>> "And me"

and from there on a way. I think the best of all may be the passage

> "replenished clear
> And cold from mountain streams that ever hear
> Proceeding waters calling from below."

Well you are getting a firmer grip on the art now in every way from rhyming up to packing in the ideas. (I ought to mention the way you vary the length and shape of the sentences in the lines and overlapping the lines to save yourself from monotony also.) It is a question how you can arrange your life to give yourself further opportunities to develop your poetry. You're sure are you, that you want to come east this summer? You've got a lot out of your enforced freedom from heavy farming. Perhaps you've got out all you can for the present. Its worth giving a lot of thought to before you act.

We were impatient to hear about you folks in the earthquake [Long Beach, 10 March 1933]. Prescott's letter came first. Now that you have had an earthquake in California you may feel shaken down into a firmer affection for the state. Marge heard someone say that the whole state was just a shelf over the ocean that would some day fall in and sink. And the expression "on the shelf" for a retired person came from there being so many retired people in California.

Affectionately,   Papa

302-a · ELINOR M. FROST TO MRS. L. W. PAYNE, JR.

THE FOLLOWING gives a glimpse of the visit to Texas made by RF and his wife during April 1933, a visit which included ten public performances by RF in a space of eleven days. He gave most of the talks before academic audiences, including Baylor University in Waco, Southern Methodist University in Dallas, the University of Texas in Austin, Stephen F. Austin State Teachers College in Nacogdoches, Sam Houston State Teachers College in Huntsville, and North Texas State College in Denton.

5 May [1933]

Dear Mrs. Payne,-   15 Sunset Ave.   Amherst

Robert and I reached home Monday noon [May 1], and I expected to write to you before this, but all sorts of things had accumulated to be attended to, and we have been *very* busy.

We had a long but not too tedious ride in the train the day we left you [in Austin, Texas, Wednesday, April 26]. Mrs. [Karle Wilson] Baker and her brother, Ben Wilson, met us at Jacksonville. The drive from there to Nacogdoches was through beautiful scenery, but two thirds of the way the road was under construction, and extremely bumpy and slow. However, we finally reached Nacogdoches. Mrs. Baker's home is very charming. Behind the house it is real woods and fields, with low hills in the distance, and the wood thrush was singing his best.

A reception had been arranged after the reading, so I thought I would take a bath and rest while the reading was going on. Unfortunately I went to sleep before they called for me and was unable to rouse myself sufficiently to dress up and attend. I was sorry.

There was a fine audience there — over a thousand persons — some of them driving 75 miles to hear Robert. The college gave the money for the lecture, so those who came didn't have to pay. I thought it was very touching that people should be interested enough to drive such distances. Mrs. Baker is a charming woman.

The following afternoon, she and her brother drove us to Huntsville. *That* was a wonderful drive, over a fine road, and through pine woods. We liked young Earl Huffor and his wife very much. They had a buffet supper for members of the English department in a room in one of the college buildings.

The next morning Robert and I started for Dallas at 9 o'clock in the bus, and got there at 1:30. After a good meal in the station restaurant I started for Waco in the Interurban. It wasn't as pleasant as the bus, and I was dreadfully tired when I reached Waco at 5:30.

I rested sufficiently in an hour to enjoy a dinner party, and the next forenoon at 10 o'clock, Mrs. Armstrong had a reception for me of the members of some club of women. I think over 70 women came. Then I got on the train homeward at 12:50, Robert joining me at Dallas.

I have told you all these details, thinking you would be interested. When we reached home, we found some friends had had our dog for three days, and that Marjorie had taken refuge with the same friends, on her return Sunday from Baltimore.

Well — I hope you and Mr. Payne were not all worn out when we left you. We certainly appreciated all your kindness. I will send the photograph soon. Do write to me sometime. Robert joins me in sending warmest regards and best wishes.

Most sincerely yours   Elinor Frost

303 · To Wilbert Snow

WILBERT SNOW, a poet of the Maine coast and a professor of English at Wesleyan University, often arranged visits of varying lengths for RF at Wesleyan. During those visits the two poets became affectionate friends, although the Socialist liberalism of Snow's political views and activities offended RF's conservatism. The following letter makes particular reference to certain poems in *Down East*, Snow's third volume of poetry, published in 1932.

Dear Bill   [*c*. 16 May 1933]   [Amherst]

For me especially The Hungry Shark, January Thaw, Wave Music and so on through the lyrics and sonnets. It need not bother you that those against anything or anybody such as an Indian Pioneer, the Ballad of Jonathan Coe, The Evangelist, Heritage and The Flood are less to my taste. Your attitude of political agitator has to be allowed for. You wouldn't be you if you suspected as I suspect that there is really nothing the matter with anybody. We are a sad lot, rather than a bad lot. My mind goes back to how true Turgeneff holds the balance between protagonists and antagonists in the death of Bayarov in Fathers and Sons. He is perfect in his non-partizanship. I never quite like to hear a wife turned on against her husband or vice versa. They know too much about each other and they are not disinterested. They lack, what they should lack, detachment. Maybe it bothers me as a breach of manners. But if manners count so much with me, then why don't I answer people's letters or properly acknowledge their books. I'll tell you in a minute. But first I want to finish with you where we are. The Evangelist reminds me not too painfully of Sinclair Lewis and a song we used to sing fifty years ago:

> "Oh my God I'm feeling blue
> For I'm six months overdue"

Only in this case

> "It was from a grey haired drummer
> Who was round here all last summer."

As George Meredith says we girls are not so much betrayed by evangelists and drummers however; "We are betrayed by what is false within."

But here I go quarreling with your tenets when it wasn't more than a week ago I was saying in public that in verse as in trapeze performance is all. And that's why nothing around college absolutely nothing, is as near poetry and the arts in general as the sports of the stadium. The Greeks agreed with me, or they wouldn't have had drama and games at the same time and place.

And all through the book you satisfy me with your performance. You are a going poet and no mistake. I'm happy to be of your audience and proud to be remembered with a complimentary ticket now and then.

Which brings me back to why I didn't acknowledge your fine book as soon as I got it. Well I got it for last Christmas, didn't I? I thought it would be a good idea if I gave you a letter of thanks for next Christmas. Honestly! And I should have carried out the idea, if I could have stood the strain of being misjudged by you a whole year and liable to one of your narrow condemnations.

Dust to dust and salt of blood back to salt of sea. I may be tempted to steal that some day. But if I do steal it it won't be unknowingly: the source is too deeply stamped in my memory.

Love to you all   R. F.

303-a · ELINOR M. FROST TO RICHARD H. THORNTON

THE BROCHURE mentioned in the following letter eventually became a full-length book, a collection of critical essays on RF, edited by Thornton and published in 1937 under the title *Recognition of Robert Frost*.

Dear Mr. Thornton:-   31 May 1933   [Amherst]

We are still in Amherst. We have everything ready to drive to the farm today, but it is raining, and everything is dark and soaking, so shall postpone the trip until tomorrow.

We have lingered here because of Robert's health. Two

days after he was in New York, he came down with a bad cold. It was a queer cold, with temperature, and has been followed by a prolonged period of temperature and prostration. He has very little appetite, and is intensely nervous. The doctor is watching him, with tuberculosis in mind, and advises absolute quiet for an indefinite period, that is, an avoidance of whatever might be a physical or nervous strain. He stays in bed until dinner time, and then dresses and then wanders around the house, and if it is sunny, sits a little while outdoors. I expect that after we get up to the farm, he will improve, as the air is really better up there, and probably his digestion and appetite will improve. I hope I am mistaken, but my opinion is that he is in for real trouble this time. His cough has settled into something that seems to me to have a permanent quality in it. He has been overdoing too much these last two years.

. . . Some time before Sept. 1st you and Robert must get together on this brochure. We really ought to try to stir up the public libraries in small places. I am taking all the material up to S. S.

About two weeks ago, Robert composed a short biography of about 330 words for the American Academy. Some French enterprise wants one of all the members. It might prove a basis for the one in the brochure.

Don't you think perhaps the Waugh photograph is more striking for the brochure than Fisher's? What do you folks at Holt think about it.

Marjorie is to be married in Billings [Montana] on Saturday. The young man she has been engaged to for a year, has got a job on a weekly newspaper in Helena. He is business manager, and may work in as editor. He seems to be doing nearly everything, and cannot come east for a wedding. As Robert hates ceremonies, it is just as well not to have to have it in our house. It will be a very quiet affair in his father's house in Billings, and then they will drive to Helena.

Marjorie is a lot stronger, and looks fine, but I am rather anxious about the effect of housekeeping on her. . . .

Sincerely,   Elinor M. Frost

303-b · ELINOR M. FROST TO EDITH H. FOBES

Dear Mrs. Fobes,   [6 August 1933]   [South Shaftsbury]

Things haven't happened as I expected them to, at all, this summer. To begin with, I found myself just at the breaking point when we got here June 1st. Robert had been sick a good deal, you know, during the last year. He was in bed most of May. I suppose it was some grippe infection only but he ran a temperature of around 100° in the afternoon all through the month, and was exhausted and weak, so that our doctor warned us of tuberculosis if he didn't take better care of himself than he has the last two years.

Marjorie left home about the 10th of May, and visited Willard's people until the wedding. Robert was too sick for us to think of going out, which was a disappointment to us all, but it was lucky for me that I didn't attempt the trip. As it was I almost had to give up, and go away for a rest. I *did* give up, and rested here. Irma and John and Jacky came the 3rd of June, and Irma and John took charge of the household (with the help of a village girl) until they had to go to camp on the 26th. . . . I have had considerable help with the housework, and am feeling better now, though I have a severe pain in the back of my head too often. Carroll and Prescott came east. Carroll wanted to look after his farm, and do a lot of work in the orchard over there. They are staying with us, but Prescott is no trouble, and Carroll helps with the work in the house, as well as working very hard out doors. . . . Carroll and Prescott will have to leave for California about the 28th. . . .

Affectionately   Elinor Frost

304 · TO CAROL FROST

Dear Carol   9 September 1933   Franconia

It cuts down the size of the United States to have someone in our own family cross it in a small car on the highway in ten or twelve days the way you do. You go sadly out of the dooryard Monday morning and in two days are in the middle of Ohio in four days in the middle of Illinois having seen both Niagara Falls and the Worlds Fair, and before we know it are past the place where we hoped to have a letter in the General Delivery waiting for you. We saw by your rate of travel that we weren't going to catch you at Lawrence with a real letter so we sent you a night letter telegram that should have been handed you at the Lawrence postoffice if you called not earlier than nine oclock in the morning Saturday. If you think of it tell us in your next letter what time of day you did call there. I would like to know who was to blame for your getting no word at all from us. Of course we were most to blame for not waking up to the fact that we would almost have had to send a letter before you started from the Gulley [in South Shaftsbury] to make sure of intercepting you anywhere on your journey. You slept in Gallup your eighth night out; which would mean by my reckoning you may possibly have reached Monrovia by Thursday evening the 7th or at the latest surely Friday. That is unless you delayed somewhere for Indian ruins.

The country must be a pile of transparent pictures in your head that you can look right through without moving them, from palms and pepper trees to birches and maples.

It was melancholy to see you start rolling down the hill, but there is an excitement in all this travel in the family that I can't say it is in my nature to dislike. I am half tempted to want to see California again before you leave it. And I would like to look the Hood River region in Oregon over to see if I don't want to live there.

We got away in our new car for Franconia not two hours after we saw you and Prescott off. I was so sick [with hay fever] I couldn't face another night in the low country. I was really too sick to drive, but I fastened one watery eye on the road and one on the spe[e]dometer and there I kept them for the whole 165 miles up mountains and round curves at the exact average of 25 miles an hour. I had in mind what you said about the art of holding a perfectly even rate and made that my interest and object. All I had to do was vary the pressure of my foot on the gas. I went into second very little and only on the down grade. I hardly used the break. As a matter of fact I hardly knew what I was doing. I suffered a plenty but I should have suffered more if I had lain around at the Gulley all day with nothing to do. I seem to have had a grip cold as well as some hay fever. I was sick several days with a temperature after I got here. We were afraid you two might have developed a germ from me as you journeyed. You haven't have you? That's good. I am getting all right now. We all give Elinor lots of anxiety and she gets awfully tired. I hope life will be easier for her.

Mrs. Nevils gives signs of being about to find the eight thousand for the stone [Peleg Cole] house — or so Kent writes. I shall believe in her when she shows up with the cash. The deed, should we have to make one, will have to go to you for your signature and Lillian's. We can use air mail and it won't take much time.

I forgot to say that I wish I had in one folder the whole set of your poems to look over when inclined. Would it be too much trouble to make me a loose-leaf note book of them some-time this winter? The depth of feeling in them is what I keep thinking of. I have taken great satisfaction in your having found such an expression of your life. I hope as you go on with them, they'll help you have a good winter in the midst of your family.

One thing I noticed in your hand written letter I never noticed before. You don't use a capital I in speaking of your-self. You write i which is awfully wrong. You begin a sentence with a small i too. You mustn't.

Our best to you all three.   Affectionately   Papa

305 · TO WARREN R. BROWN

Dear Brown: 12 September 1933   Franconia

We have had a tragedy. The evening of the day your let-ter came about the new dog, we lost Winnie. She got her face and mouth full of porcupine quills and died under the c[h]loro-form we had to give her for the really terrible operation of getting them out. No dog could ever take her place in our af-fections. No dog will have a chance to. We are all sick and sad. She was the best beast.   Always your friend   Robert Frost

306 · TO JOHN T. BARTLETT

Dear John: 5 December 1933   Amherst

You've got some towns out there in Colorado that I surely like to inhabit mentally when I'm awake at night or out walk-ing: and the names of them are Boulder, Larkspur, Gunnison and Crested Butte. The two best are Boulder and Gunnison. I didnt get enough of either. I believe some time I would inhabit one of them more than mentally if I werent afraid of their altitude for Lowlanders of Elinors and my age — comparative lowlanders. Our mountains leave off at five or six thousand where yours begin and our base stations where we are used to breathe are at eight hundred or a thousand. The doctors seemed to me evasive on the subject of the danger. They probably want to know more than they do about it and would be willing to have us experiment for them. I certainly felt feeble the first time I exerted myself as at Greeley and Denver and I never got over the tendency to gasp once or twice every so often day or night awake or asleep. It really makes me sorry for now that we are all in such an uprooted state of affairs something might easily come of my liking for the Rockies but for the one thing. I think Carol liked parts of Colorado better than anything outside of New England. He has no intention of staying in California. Farming there is too utterly different from what he has grown up to. You have heard, haven't you, that Lillian is pronounced a cured person. After two years or rather a year and a half flat on her back down herself and her lung down the doctor has her on her feet and her lung restored. Its something of a miracle because Dr. Pottinger the big operator and authority out there wouldnt undertake her with her large adhesion. Its only a matter of months now when they will be free to decide for themselves whether they will risk it back in Vermont again on the same old farm. Their hearts seem set on it and particularly on the orchard of a thousand apple trees MacIntosh, Northern Spy, Golden Delicious, Red Delicious and Red Astrachan, just this year in first crop to count. I can understand their feelings but I question their wisdom. There I go again trying to run other peoples' lives. I must question my own wisdom. Too bad I'm not where I can govern the country as a diversion from governing my friends neighbors and relatives. (What a picture I paint of myself. I can rely on you as my partizan from of old to defend me from myself.)

I'm back at Amherst doing very little as yet but picking up the politics of the place. My feller poeticism from the Old South [David Morton] has imperilled his position with us by chivalrously punching the village policeman on the chin for illegally asking a lady what she had done with five dollars entrusted to her as local representative of the Travellers Aid. I dont much take either side. You remember how the mob started to tear Cinna to pieces for conspiracy and when told by him it was a mistake of identity, he wasn't Cinna the conspirator; he was Cinna the poet, they cried Tear him for his verses. I say it as shouldnt say it. My early detaching of myself twice over from colleges when young leaves me with a certain detachment in viewing their troubles now I am old.

I shall soon be out with a ponderous book of one poem [*The Lone Striker*] on how I detached myself from the mills of Man in Lawrence Mass but without prejudice to machinery industry or an industrial age so that there will be no mistake in the record. I'll send you a copy. What are *you* publishing?

You want to be careful what you say to me in reply about this Democratic Nation and the Democratic Policies for the Salvation of the Soul because I have allied myself by marriage with one of the most interesting if extreme young Progressives in the world [Willard E. Fraser] and as always with me it is my family right or wrong. Aint politics a funny thing to be so serious about? I take to such a man as Legge who could be friends with Hoover and Wilson both but loved farming better than men or methods. I believe in blackguarding like Hemmingway if you remember to burst out laughing when you get through. The only nonsense going is this talk about a revolution being on. Revolution with the Supreme Court still sitting undisturbed! You may have heard me say the greatest branch of any government the world ever saw is the Supreme Court of the United States. There it sits. A friend of mine named Landis has recently made a book called The Third American Revolution. I asked him where he got more than one. He thinks the victory of the North in the Civil War was a revolution that brought industry on top and overthrew agriculture. What licked the agriculture of the South was the agriculture of the Middle West under such Middle Westerners as Grant and Sherman. The industry that has swept the world was coming everywhere before the war and wasn't the least hastened by the war. One Revolution is all we have had and you'll wait more years than you[']r[e] allotted for a second. Dont let the Democrats worry you.

[. . .] I wish I were where I could walk a block or two to see you. Those streets from the Boulderado [Hotel] over [to your house] just suited me. I suppose it was their contrast with the mountain roads, which even if I come out there to settle down, I shall always be afraid of.   Ever yours   R.

307 · To Lincoln MacVeagh

Dear Lincoln: 11 December 1933   Amherst

I want to make you an offer. I have been over your Juvenal again by myself. I have consulted no one at all about it; and the conclusion I have arrived at is entirely my own. The translation and the versification are a good job. But they only confirm me in the indifference not to say dislike I have always felt for the subject matter of the original. I believe it gains in harshness said right out in English. You know me: I can stand sorrow better than evil. A little irony is good medicine for the blood; but the out-and-out satire of Men[c]ken Dreiser and Lewis I should hate to join them in — I shouldnt know how to join them in because I am conscious of my resentments as being merely personal and so not to be trusted to build a cause on. I might write a whole book against the administration of Calvin Coolidge and no one would suspect that the inspiration was grudge against him for having dismissed me with a joke when asked by common friends to invite me to the White House. No one else would know it, but I should know it.

Now for my offer. I thought of it before you sailed, and should have spoken of it if I had been able to see you to say goodby. I'll tell you what I should like to write a small preface to: a translation into English of some modern Greek poetry. You say you never heard any race relish their own speech as the modern Greeks do. That must mean lyric poets I should think. Well if the Insull business hasn't made your Greece rancid to you and you are still as felicitously disposed to the country half your own, you find some one sad or glad poet or some group of poets to present to America (by way of making an accounting of your embassy) and I'll join you in a book of them. That would look to me like novel fun. My Greeks the Sarris brothers who keep the College Restaurant in Amherst speak to me now and then of modern Greek poets, though what they seem fuller of than any nationals I ever met is politics. They and all their clerks read my copy of Thornton Wilder's Woman of Andros. One of them said to me "That's my island — Andros." You have all the qualifications for making the translation. I have the one qualification for writing the preface, namely, sympathy with everything Greek or Greecian particularly since having just now after all these years received my Harvard marks in Greek and Greek composition and found they were all A's. Robert Hillyer looked them up on purpose to prove I was not just nobody from the academic point of view. I shall have to brush up on my irregular verbs from self-respect.

We are having fierce weather. We stuck to the farm with nothing but the big open fireplace for heat till the thermometer went to four below zero. How cold are you?

Our best to you all three. This is Christmas greetings if it gets to you in time; if not, New Years.

Ever yours   Robert Frost

308 · To Louis Untermeyer

Dear Louis: 21 December 1933   Amherst

This is silence long enough to show the restraint of a humanist which is what I should like to do once in so often but not too often. Our David Morton has been punching a policeman for asking a lady a question nobody but a lawyer has a right to ask. There is something ungenerous about not calling someone a son of a bitch or punching someone or driving a car drunk or trusting others to keep you from falling off a roof or leaving it to your audience to supply a meaning to what you say. Did you happen to notice the terrible kind of death Hemingway wished the humanist in his "Winner Take Nothing" dedicated to your Archie MacLeish? He hoped he would die without dignity or decorum. I suppose he must have been after Irving Babbitt for getting under his skin for a humanitarian sentimentalist. Just about the time he wished it, Babbitt was dying as if with humanitarian pens stuck into his wax figureativeness, which was good as far as it went, but unfortunately for Hemingway I'm afraid he died with Graeco-Roman euthanatos. Hear me use Greek! I feel that it is my peculiar right, nay duty, since my marks in Greek at Harvard were published by Robert Hillyer the other day.

The mercy of my not writing to you lies chiefly in its saving you a lot of rhyme and meter which it would have been if I had written at all. I think it was your spirited poem set me off on my spree: but it's been for the last month or two so that I could think of nothing except in rhyme and that the same rhyme steadily till it was exhausted. For example I wrote a whole lesson in rhetoric in lines ending in words to rhyme with Flaccus (leaning on Austin Dobson for my rhyming dictionary). The Flaccus I was talking to (not about) was a protegé of mine just out of Dartmouth [see 331], not the Horatius, late of Rome and the Sabine Hills. You ought to have seen it before it was burned. Then again you ought not. You have seen a lot of poetry in your time — a lot of mine. Time you were retired to a pension. I don't mean to imply you act jaded. I heard of you (as well as from you) in Texas. You vivified them down there!

Nobody's with us for Christmas — we're two elders alone with nothing to think about but thoughts and how to keep them out of our poetry so it will be pronounced pure by the authorities on purity self-set up. I am going to give a lecture on What Poetry Thinks presently in prose if I can. I shall begin, Poetry abhors a money-matter. I have carefully phrased it that far so nobody can sing it — can they? I am going to end well, if I knew how I was going to end and get out of the damned thing I shouldn't be as nervous and abstracted in company like a neurasthenic the night before he goes over the top. Why do I get myself in for these things you ask me. So do I ask myself. Principally because you can't be writing poetry all the time or you would produce volumes and volumes till you are self-buried. [. . .]   Ever yours   Robert Frost

309 · To Wilbur L. Cross

Dear Cross: 17 February 1934   Amherst
        I'm glad if I still can please you.* I need all the encouragement you can give me in that kind of poetry to hold me to it. The temptation of the times is to write politics. But I mustn't yield to it, must I? Or if I do, I must burn the results as from me likely to be bad. Leave politics and affairs to Walter Lippmann. Get sent to Congress if I will and can (I have always wanted to), but stick to the kind of writing I am known for.
        I wish I knew when you were likely to be in New Haven. I should like to plan my first visit to Pierson College so as to catch a glimpse of you.   Sincerely yours   Robert Frost

* The reference is apparently to RF's meditative lyric, "Neither Out Far Nor In Deep," which was first published in The Yale Review for March 1934.

310 · To Louis Untermeyer

Dear Louis: 23 February 1934   Amherst

I have been in bed with a bug and a tropical temperature again etiolating and emaciating. Otherwise I should probably have written you sooner about those there two . . . girls' wind-baby that they laid as lightly as a blown bubble on my doorstep so as not to break it with an odor of pewtativeness I suppose.* Probably, but not surely, because I hardly know what to write either to you or to them. If *you* could have got along without two or three of the more physical poems in the book, you can imagine how much more philosophically I could with my less cultivated taste. I suspect a hidden joke between you and them at my expense. There is a fleur-de-mallaisian laughter offstage at the spectacle of my grey hairs being brought down another peg in sorrow to the incontestible verities. It is possible to make too much of the episode — whether joke or clinical experiment. I am well past the age of shock fixation. But if I promise not to make too much of it, will you promise too? You won't take it as an infringement of the liberty of the press if I ask you not to connect me with the book any more than you have to in your reviewing and lecturing. Don't you find the contemplation of their kind of collusion emasculating? I'm chilled to the marrow, as in the actual presence of some foul form of death where none of me can function, not even my habitual interest in versification. This to you. But what can I say to them?   Yours ever   R.

311 · To Willard E. Fraser

Dear Willard: 26 February 1934   Amherst

I haven't known the kind of excitement in the family your politics give us since I was a young democrat campaigning for Grover Cleveland with my father in San Francisco in 1884. We don't get the hang just yet of your Montana affairs, but the Western Progressive is a great help and by the time we get out there for our first visit we'll be qualified to vote in every respect but length of residence. I should judge it to be a pretty

* Sylvia Townsend Warner and Valentine Ackland dedicated to Robert Frost their book of poems, *Whether a Dove or Seagull* (1933).

close state with party ties gone pretty loose. The vote on the impeachment of Gov. Cooley didn't seem to divide on party lines. Are these times extra wild for Montana? There seem to be all sorts of adventures ahead of you.

We were going south for my health. We've decided for the present to stay right where we are and feed the furnace. We are having a winter you have to respect. Many go to Canada for the Canadian winter. They at least can't complain if this year the Canadian winter has come to them. I send you a clipping on our weather from the Bennington (Vermont) Banner. Temperatures there ninety miles away have run a little lower than here in Amherst, but not much.

Dwight Morrow has been in talking about you and very much like a true friend. Life like yours together outdoors makes lasting attachments. I appreciate him better in a talk of this kind. He took very seriously to heart your letter against his settling down to a sheltered life at Amherst. He is moving on for some more education next year. He wants to be a teacher of American history. You and Earl Morris with your facility in manual and practical things scared him out of archaeology, I suspect. He means to be some good to himself and his country. You and Marj must be nice to him in your thoughts. He's your friend.

We or I anyway read your Montana Year Book clean through every little while in further preparation for our visit. You will find us ready to pass examinations in the following subjects:

Montana Politics National and Local (from The Progressive)

Montana Education (from the friend [Sidney Cox] who nearly got strung up for teaching radical ethics or morals at Missoula — and I have no doubt he deserved kicking if not hanging.)

Montana Agriculture and Stock Raising (from the Year Book)

Montana Climate and Scenery (from the Year Book)

Montana Homelikeness (from having you and Marj there)

We shall be along bye and bye. I got out of three lectures I was supposed to give this month or next but to make up for it I shall have to preach the Baccalaureate sermon in June. (If only I had more courage for such things.) After that there won't be anything fixed in our calendar for quite a while.

Affectionately   R.

Has Marj written any more poetry lately? Tell her to send another as good as the last. I like my country written about that way.

312 · To Louis Untermeyer

Dear Louis: 5 March 1934   Amherst

[. . .] Those . . . [two girls] again [see letter 310]. They bother me only a little. From a certain way they had in inquiring about E. T. I am led to wonder if they think all friendships may be like theirs. Maybe I misjudge them. Of course I know they are incapable of doing what they did for the joke of it. It might not be unlike the Warner however to do it for the whimsicality. I saw plainly you were taken aback when I told you the news. It isn't very serious anyway. Don't pretend you haven't heard of more such people than I have and even encountered them in polite society. It isn't your fault. You have merely been out around more than I. I am more prepared for them than I was when I went to England in 1911 [1912]. There I first read of them in The English Review in a series of articles by the heads of the famous public schools — Rugby, Eton, etc. I had just as soon they stayed far from my sphere. It is not my nature to want to slap them in the face. I was tempted to tell them I knew the best poem in the book and would tell them which it was but for the fear of coming between two such with thoughts of rivalry in art.

You are a hero to let anyone down your throat with a knife. It is thought I must be searched for the source of the rheumatism I have more or less always and inflammatorily when I have influenza. I doubt if I dare to go to the table or whiff the nepenthe. I always notice I am most cowardly when writing or just after writing. I mind the cellar at night worst then.   Ever yours   R.

313 · To G. R. Elliott

RF's wife made the long journey from Amherst to Billings to be with Marjorie during her pregnancy. The child, Marjorie Robin Fraser, was born 16 March 1934. Mrs. Frost, anxious because of her husband's illness, which had made her hesitate to make the journey West in the first place, returned to Amherst as soon as she felt that Marjorie was on her way to a normal recovery. Soon after Mrs. Frost's return to Amherst, however, she was informed by telephone that her daughter was suffering from puerperal fever. Both Frosts immediately left for Montana by train. On 26 April 1934 Marjorie was flown to the Mayo Clinic at Rochester, Minnesota, where she died on 2 May 1934.

Dear Roy: 20 April [1934]   Billings

Still the same desperate chance. The doctors tell us the length of time Marjorie has stood the fever is a favorable sign. She has been sick five weeks. She has been out of her mind most of the time and never completely in her mind for more than a week. Fatal as most of the facts of the case sound, we are determined to win the same as we would be when our side was far behind in a game. I don't know what will become of Elinor if we lose. Or Willard either.

Will you do something for me? There is one letter among the disordered jumble on my desk in my study that has turned up in my thoughts to trouble my conscience. Someone named Dillingham was the writer. I think it was Dillingham. Anyway he wrote from a big high school in Brooklyn N. Y. inviting me to be guest of honor with them some time in April or May. Its the kind of thing I like to take notice of — and in fact act on. Could I ask you to write to Dillingham (if that is his name) tell him the seriousness of my predicament and make my excuses? He might be willing to wait for me till next fall. I believe he is an Amherst man, class of '87 or thereabouts. The letter is a long one in type.

I wrote Stanley King [President of Amherst College] how ready I would be for anything and everything if we come out all right, but how utterly against the world and unwilling to face it if fate fails us. He must be the one to decide what to do about my taking part [at commencement] in June. I agree with you I am a pretty bad bet. I seem to find ways of getting out of all obligations this year. I'm grateful to you for filling the bill April 19th.

Help us with your best thoughts.

Always yours   Robert

407

314 · To Louis Untermeyer

29 April 1934

Dear Louis: General Delivery Rochester

We are going through the valley of the shadow with Marjorie we are afraid. She had a baby in Billings, Montana, six weeks ago and most of the time since has hovered on the verge of death. The harm must have been done by her first doctor there of course. The infection was a terrible one. But once it was done her first doctor and the others we have called in have done everything possible for her. Three days ago we put her in a small airplane with a doctor and nurse to fly here. The thousand mile flight seems not to have set her back, and here we can expect the miracles of modern science. Rosenow, the great biologist, finds he has a serum for a close cousin of the organism diffused in her blood-stream. It would be better if it were for the exact organism. But that and blood-transfusions every other day and Marjorie's tenacity and Elinor's devotion and the mercy of God are our hopes. You will probably see us home again alive whatever the outcome, but it will be months hence and changed for the worse for the rest of our days. Always yours Robert Frost

My favorite poem long before I knew what it was going to mean to us was Arnold's "Cadmus and Harmonia."

315 · To Louis Untermeyer

Dear Louis [15 May 1934] [Amherst]

I told you by letter or telegram what was hanging over us. So you know what to expect. Well, the blow has fallen. The noblest of us all is dead and has taken our hearts out of the world with her. It was a terrible seven weeks' fight — too indelibly terrible on the imagination. No death in war could more than match it for suffering and heroic endurance. Why all this talk in favor of peace? Peace has her victories over poor mortals no less merciless than war. Marge always said she would rather die in a gutter than in a hospital. But it was in a hospital she was caught to die after more than a hundred serum injections and blood transfusions. We were torn afresh every day between the temptation of letting her go untortured or cruelly trying to save her. The only consolation we have is the memory

408

of her greatness through all. Never out of delirium for the last four weeks her responses were of course incorrect. She got little or nothing of what we said to her. The only way I could reach her was by putting my hand backward and forward between us as in counting out and saying with over-emphasis *You* — and — *Me.* The last time I did that, the day before she died, she smiled faintly and answered "All the same," frowned slightly and made it "Always the same." Her temperature was then 110, the highest ever known at the Mayo Clinic where as I told you we took her, but too late. The classical theory was not born out in her case that a fine and innocent nature released by madness from the inhibitions of society will give way to all the indecencies. Everything she said, however quaint and awry, was of an almost straining loftiness. It was as if her ruling passion must have been to be wise and good, or it could not have been so strong in death. But curse all doctors who for a moment let down and neglect in childbirth the scientific precautions they have been taught in school. We thought to move heaven and earth — heaven with prayers and earth with money. We moved nothing. And here we are Cadmus and Harmonia not yet placed safely in changed forms.   R.

315-a · Elinor M. Frost to Edith H. Fobes

Dear Mrs. Fobes,   12 June [1934]   Amherst

I believe you would have no way of knowing what Robert and I have been going through, and of our tragedy. I am not strong enough to write much about it — only just that Marjorie's baby was born on the 16th of March, that an infection developed, through some negligence, we suppose, and that she died on the 2nd of May. It was not correctly diagnosed, as child bed fever, for three weeks, when a third doctor was called in. At the end of the fifth week, after hearing of the Elliott heat treatment, we had her taken by plane to the Mayo Clinic in Rochester, Minn. A doctor and nurse accompanied her. We hoped much, but it was too late for them to do anything. They said there that she showed marvelous resistance but that the infection was terrific.

Poor darling child — it seems too heart breaking, that after achieving good health, and finding perfect happiness in life, she had to lose it all so soon. Her baby is a lovely healthy little girl. We have it at present and her husband also is here visiting. He is quite desperate. I hardly know how I go on from day to day. But Robert depends on me, and the other children do to some extent, and I *must* keep up. . . .

Affectionately Elinor Frost

316 · To SIDNEY COX

Dear Sidney: [c. 9 July 1934]   [South Shaftsbury]

I'm proud of you for a book like that [*Prose Preferences*]. Let's see them beat it. It's all front-line stuff and shows how far forward you fight. The little booms are good writing. Where did you find Cooley? He's a real find. I have always admired that book of his, though I doubt if I would ever have had the courage to propose him thus boldly. But then I am not an anthologist-critic and not trained up to the responsibilities of one. I marvel at Louis Untermeyer in his advocacy of such as Merrill Moore. What nerve! I should be much surer in public about Cooley. In private I should be absolutely sure. Two or three of your names are new to me, I'm grateful to say, and many of the pieces. It is all honestly fresh material — so different from some anthologies we know of that merely make themselves out of prior anthologies. The George Moore has always been a favorite memory of mine. I happen at this moment to be reading Paul Elmer More's Socrates in the Shelburne Papers. He's one I've too long postponed. As far as I've got, I admire your representations entirely.

If I had a word of fault to find it might be for Evelyn Scott's ineffably old-south feminine snobbish dirt on Grant. Gee what a painfully great man she makes of Lee. How does she know that Grant looked hard at Lee and Lee averted his eyes? All you have to do is read Grant's Memoirs to prove he was a very modest man to whom the situation of the surrender at Appomattox must have been as embarrassing as to any northern gentleman. I will not venture to speak for the southern gentleman. That's just the way the likes of Evelyn Scott would have tried to work herself up to speak of you or me Sidney. I think it amounts to a betrayal of our class for you to encourage her. Take Grant's coat she makes so much of. It wasn't the ill fitting finery she makes out. It was a common private's coat with two chevrons of three stars each merely pinned on it to show his rank for business purposes — a carelessly assumed uniform I suppose to go to meet the truly great in. I doubt if it was chosen to humiliate anybody. Everything of evidence Grant did to Lee showed the noblest consideration of defeat. American History shouldn't be written by women novelists with English sympathies for the arrogant old slave-holding days. Your people were probably abolitionists. Mine were not: so I would have more excuse than you for letting the south have its way about what kind of people on both sides fought the war and whether or not it was to free the slaves. Some southerners have been saying lately (and allowed to get away with it) that the war was waged by the industrial north to put down agriculture. The fact is it was the agricultural middle west that licked the agricultural south. The civil war wasnt the smallest incident in the world wide industrial revolution of the last century. Lee and Grant ought to be done together some time for the contrast in generalship more than in clothes and graces. Lee was the tragic figure of a fighter who never saw anything beyond winning battles. His vision wasn't large enough for a whole war or even campaign. His dispositions for battle were beautiful. His two great divisions under Longstreet and Jackson were like pistols in his two hands, so perfectly could he handle them. But ask yourself where he could have thought he was going when he set off on the raids that ended at Antietam and Gettysburg. What was he doing when he let Grant come on victory by victory cleaning up the west till the war was lost before ever he had to encounter him for the final show down? He was the great man of the south. He should have taken it upon himself to think and act on the grand strategy of the whole front from Vicksburg to Richmond. Say he didnt have Jefferson Davis with him. He should have had by force and persuasion. Grant had to teach Lincoln Halleck Stanton and the rest of them. The war was one great turning movement grasped as such, first by the mind of Grant and altogether and step by step his in execution. You may not like generals in general, but you have to concede him rank with the greatest our race has had. The World War brought out nobody to match him. I am touched by Lee, so noble in character, so brilliant and punishing a smiter in the field, but so lost in the larger things of statesmanship and strategy. He was not large enough to see the United States. I suspect he was merely romantic beyond a certain point of mentality. I suspect him of a secret resolve never to set foot outside of his native state but to have it out in Virginia win or lose. Otherwise he might well have gone to deal with Grant before he had assumed such proportions. He must have realized however dimly by the time Grant got to Chat-[t]anooga that where Grant was the war was. But he had registered a vow with himself perhaps in consistancy when he gave up all the states for a few of the states that he would really never be devoted to any state but one. He was parochial. He couldnt see largely. I might even represent him in a whole novel, if I wrote history that way, as valuing himself for his loyalty to the First Families of Virginia alone. In which connection, I may add, that my friend J. J. Lankes has been such a success with his woodcuts in Virginia that he has been honored with a chance of being listed in a book of the First Families of Virginia for the sum of five dollars. He was born of German parentage in Gardenville near Buffalo New York and has earned much of his living illustrating tomato cans. I cant see that his Virginia honors have turned his head.

All this merely to amuse you and distract me from our sorrow. I'll tell you a short story for your third book when you get to it. Oh I do think it the most wonderful short story I ever read. It has everything. It is called A. V. Laider. Max Beerbohn wrote it.

Where are you in the near future?   Ever yours   R. F.

316-a · Elinor M. Frost to Edith H. Fobes

Dear Mrs. Fobes,   15 July [1934]   South Shaftsbury
    . . . Thank you for your kind letter about Marjorie. It is true that her two years in training at Baltimore were a great satisfaction to her, and her marriage a great happiness, but somehow the thought of all that does not help me. She wanted to live so badly, and yet she was so brave and noble. The pathos of it was too terrible. I long to die myself and be relieved of the pain that I feel for her sake. Poor precious darling, to have to leave everything in such a cruel and unnecessary way. I cannot bear it, and yet I *must* bear it for the sake of the others here. . . .   Affectionately   Elinor Frost

317 · To G. R. Elliott

17 December 1934   707 Seminole Avenue,
Dear Roy: Key West Florida

You who are about to travel so soon yourself can't say much against my travelling. How really do you discriminate in pronunciation between travel and travail? We admit we have been utterly miserable thus far. But we are always worse abroad at first than later. It is so outrageous to my native pride to have to establish my respectability with land ladies and bankers. Their whole vocabulary comes from having examined applicants for their niceness in clothes, position and pocketbook. I go to a real estate agent for a house and what shall I tell him I am? What in modesty? Here in Key West we have a national rehabilitation project running everything. I am dragged by the house-renting clerk before the Rehabilitator in Chief to see if I will do, that is to say, measure up to his idea of what the new citizenry must look as if it thought, felt and acted on under God and the President at Washington. The Rehabilitator is a rich young man in shorts with hairy legs named Stone. He has recently distinguished himself for something charitable in Buffalo. He is very close to Franklin Roosevelt and Vincent Astor — can bring the President down this winter on Vincent Astor's yacht to give this particular project his personal blessing. The lady assumes to recommend me for a house in town. What can be said for me? What have I said for myself. For one thing hesitatingly that I come from Mass. (I'm not sure that it would be honester to say from Vt.) It sounds as if I were concealing something. I ask myself which would be claiming most to say I was from Mass or Vt. I simply will not boast. The lady wants me to understand Key West is no tooth-pick and suspender colony like Sarasota, Winter Park and St. Petersburg. She can see I am the kind to appreciate that. I remind her of a Mr. Tibbets from Maine, a real gentleman they have just admitted to the payment of house rent. I said yes my name Frost was often mistaken for Tibbets on the telephone. She cried Humor! What the New Deal wants more than anything else especially in Key West is some humor into it. Did I stand accepted then in their sight oh lord? What was my occupation they wondered as we stood there looking sidelong up and down each other. I was certainly old enough to be retired. But from what? From being a farmer, from being a teacher or from being an Arthur. Or wasn't I going to satisfy their curiosity by telling them? The fact was they were turning me into a criminal while they waited to decide my fate. They were turning me into an enemy of everything. Rustics in America and an egg for the Ogpu to deal with. Not that I blame them altogether. I am much to blame for being caught once more where I have to be my own sponsor by out and out declaration or by little indirections with seeming casualness let fall. Let people stay at home where they needn't be forever telling others not to be afraid of them, either socially or financially.

You'll be excited to learn after being kept in all this suspense, did we get a house from the authorities or not. We did, we did! But not on our face value. We never should have got by if it hadn't been for our name. Some clerk, a Jew in the background who had been doing some hard research broke the all-round constraint by doubting, You aint the Frost (I forget his first name) who writes poetry for Michigan University? There are five Frosts writing poetry, I said, two men and three women. I'm not one of the women. I was saved now provided only I would pay my rent for the whole winter in advance. It makes me sick for home.   Ever yours.   R. F.

318 · To Harold G. Rugg

Dear Mr. Rugg: [c. 20 December 1934]   [Key West]

    [. . .] Look where I am. I say it is for Mrs Frost's health and she says it is for mine. Neither of us likes it very much yet. But after all it is part of the earth (a small part, two or three miles long by a mile or so wide, about a dozen times the size of my farm in South Shaftsbury but all cut up into speculators' house lots about the size of family lots in a graveyard). And whatever great thinkers may say against the earth, I notice no one is anxious to leave it for either Heaven or Hell. Heaven may be better than Hell as reported, but it is not as good as the earth. Even as a child I could tell from the way my elders acted about it.

    This town has been nationalized to rescue it from its own speculative excesses. The personal interest of Roosevelt in his second coming has been invoked and both mayor and governor

have abdicated till we can see what absolute authority can do
to restore the prices of the speculators' graveyard plots and
make Key West equal to Miami.   Ever yours   Robert Frost

319 · To FREDERIC G. MELCHER

Dear Fred: 30 December 1934   Key West
    [. . .] This is Kayo Huaso as the Spaniards named it. It
might have been translated into Bone Key. Instead it was cor-
rupted into Key West. It is a very very dead place because it
has died several times. It died as a resort of pirates, then as a
house of smugglers and wreckers, then as a cigar manufactury
(the Cubans moved over here to get inside the tariff wall)
then as a winter resort boomtown. Franklin D. himself has
taken it personally in hand to give it one more life to lose.
FERA is all over the place. It is tropical all right but it is rather
unsanitary and shabby. It has a million dollars worth of con-
crete sidewalks with no houses by them. It has three races not
very well kept apart by race-prejudice, Cubans, Negroes and
Whites. The population once 25,000 has shrunk to 12,000. We
live not twenty feet from the water of very quiet seas. What
with coral shoals and other little keys, the wind has to be a
West Indian hurricane to get up much waves. We are fifty
miles at sea and the lowest temperature ever recorded was
forty degrees above zero. I sleep under one sheet and wear one
thickness of linen. People that know say it is a Honolulu five
thousand miles nearer home. A third of the people at least
speak Spanish but there is not a Spanish book in the poor public library. Neither is there a book with a star map. I went to
make sure if the new big star we had raised was Canopus, Sir-
ius' rival. . . .   Ever yours,   Robert Frost

319-a · ELINOR M. FROST TO EDITH H. FOBES

Dear Mrs. Fobes,-   31 December [1934]   Key West
    . . . We went to Amherst the 15th of October, and I
tried to fulfil some of my obligations there, but I was not at all
well. In November I had a severe attack of angina. So that is
added to the other heart complications, and I am following a
strict routine prescribed by our Amherst doctor.

We are here in the South on Robert's account. He is hoping to avoid one of those grippe and rheumatic infections that he has suffered from the last two winters. . . .

Carol, Lillian, and Prescott are driving down now, to be with us here about three months. Lillian's doctor wanted her to be in a warm place one more winter. She seems extremely well — better than ever before, I think. . . .

Affectionately,   Elinor Frost

320 · To WILLIAM LYON PHELPS

Dear Mr. Phelps: 12 January 1934 [1935]   Key West

I want to report to you in few how it has come out with the son-in-law [John Cone] for whom you got the scholarship at Yale. You probably remember how it happened because you remember everything. Indeed your part in it was a feat of memory. Some of your boys used your name to persuade me to read at Yale for nothing. After the reading you were good enough to thank me in person and offer to do anything you could for me in return. With what I thought great presence of mind, but mostly in irony, I asked you to help my son-in-law to a scholarship in the Yale School of Architecture. The reason for my irony you may never guess: I don't quite like it that whereas the lesser colleges all pay me money for lecturing, the greater colleges seem to expect to pay no one but foreign visitors. I have laughed about it with the foreign visitors. So you can see my irony is not very bad-natured. And by accepting the situation so far as to accept two invitations to Yale, I have condoned anything I had to complain of. Moreover look at how the balance stands now between me and Yale. The first time I went there for nothing I made the lifelong friendship of Stephen Benet and John Farrar (they were the undergraduates I sat nearest at the Elizabethan Club) — if that can be called nothing. The second time I get a very valuable scholarship for one of my family. You brushed aside the irony of my request, if you noticed it, and to my surprise remembered and acted on the substance of it. You must know how I feel about such deeds in a naughty world, which the present world is supposed especially to be. It is that they keep it from being a naughty world. Dean Meeks has been splendid to and for my son and I think would tell you my son has done more than ordinarily well in Architecture. This will be the third and last year.

Don't you think the lady who finds "ornery" so disagreeable in sound should be shown that it is nothing but the word "ordinary" as we no doubt once pronounced it and as the English in England pronounce it to this day? It might teach her that sense is everything in a word.   Sincerely yours   Robert Frost

321 · To Richard H. Thornton

Dear Mr Thornton: 3 March 1935   Key West

I'm sure it will be good advance advertising for the next book [*A Further Range*] to let Henry Canby have Two Tramps.

I was told at Miami they sold all the books you sent them. I had as good a time up there as I could expect to have among a lot of conflicting poets and professors. One of them called me to my face an old fox because he failed to draw me in on his side of the quarrels. Life never ceases to be new.

Thank you for sending the books to Mrs Brown at the Casa Marina on consignment. The favor is to me. I dont know that many of the books will be sold but some trouble had to be taken to keep good will. I play tennis on the Casa Marina court and I have to be careful not to act as if my literary life was none of the rich common people's business.

Best wishes to the firm and the family.

Sincerely yours   Robert Frost

322 · To *The Amherst Student*

THE EDITORS of the Amherst College undergraduate newspaper sent birthday greetings to RF well in advance of his so-called sixtieth birthday. His reply, as follows, was printed in *The Amherst Student* for 25 March 1935.

[*c.* 21 March 1935]   [Key West]

It is very very kind of the *Student* to be showing sympathy with me for my age. But sixty is only a pretty good age. It is not advanced enough. The great thing is to be advanced. Now ninety would be really well along and something to be given credit for.

But speaking of ages, you will often hear it said that the age of the world we live in is particularly bad. I am impatient of such talk. We have no way of knowing that this age is one of the worst in the world's history. Arnold claimed the honor for the age before this. Wordsworth claimed it for the last but one. And so on back through literature. I say they claimed the honor for their ages. They claimed it rather for themselves. It is immodest of a man to think of himself as going down before the worst forces ever mobilized by God.

All ages of the world are bad — a great deal worse anyway than Heaven. If they weren't the world might just as well be Heaven at once and have it over with. One can safely say after from six to thirty thousand years of experience that the evident design is a situation here in which it will always be about equally hard to save your soul. Whatever progress may be taken to mean, it can't mean making the world any easier a place in which to save your soul — or if you dislike hearing your soul mentioned in open meeting, say your decency, your integrity.

Ages may vary a little. One may be a little worse than another. But it is not possible to get outside the age you are in to judge it exactly. Indeed it is as dangerous to try to get outside of anything as large as an age as it would be to engorge a donkey. Witness the many who in the attempt have suffered a dilation from which the tissues and the muscles of the mind have never been able to recover natural shape. They can't pick up anything delicate or small any more. They can't use a pen. They have to use a typewriter. And they gape in agony. They can write huge shapeless novels, huge gobs of raw sincerity bellowing with pain and that's all that they can write.

Fortunately we don't need to know how bad the age is. There is something we can always be doing without reference to how good or how bad the age is. There is at least so much good in the world that it admits of form and the making of form. And not only admits of it, but calls for it. We people are thrust forward out of the suggestions of form in the rolling clouds of nature. In us nature reaches its height of form and through us exceeds itself. When in doubt there is always form for us to go on with. Anyone who has achieved the least form to be sure of it, is lost to the larger excruciations. I think it must stroke faith the right way. The artist, the poet, might be expected to be the most aware of such assurance, but it is really everybody's sanity to feel it and live by it. Fortunately, too, no forms are more engrossing, gratifying, comforting, staying, than those lesser ones we throw off like vortex rings of smoke, all our individual enterprise and needing nobody's cooperation: a basket, a letter, a garden, a room, an idea, a picture, a poem. For these we haven't to get a team together before we can play.

The background is hugeness and confusion shading away from where we stand into black and utter chaos; and against the background any small man-made figure of order and concentration. What pleasanter than that this should be so? Unless we are novelists or economists we don't worry about this confusion; we look out on it with an instrument or tackle it to reduce it. It is partly because we are afraid it might prove too much for us and our blend of democratic-republican-socialist-communist-anarchist party. But it is more because we like it, we were born to it, born used to it and have practical reasons for wanting it there. To me any little form I assert upon it is velvet, as the saying is, and to be considered for how much more it is than nothing. If I were a Platonist I should have to consider it, I suppose, for how much less it is than everything.

322-a · ELINOR M. FROST TO MRS. L. W. PAYNE, JR.

Dear Mrs. Payne,-   24 March [1935]   Key West

Robert and I have been here, way down on the southern tip of Florida, since the middle of December. We return home the end of this week. Our doctor in Amherst insisted on our coming south, on Robert's account, in the hope of avoiding a severe and prolonged attack of grippe, such as Robert has had the last two winters in New England. The climate has been marvelous, and he has benefited greatly. He has walked a lot, and played tennis, and seems very vigorous.

I think the sea level and the steady sunshine have been good for my heart condition, also. I have [been] in a state of nervous exhaustion for seven or eight months, and I have had angina. I am following strict doctor's orders now, and have improved a little.

I cannot write many letters, but I have wanted to write to you about our great loss, as I have felt you would not learn of it in any other way. It happened last spring. You knew our Marjorie, and will be grieved to hear that she died on the second of last May, following the birth of her first baby. It was an infection which must have been caused by negligence at the time of delivery. She lived nearly seven weeks, fighting bravely for her life through ravaging fever and delirium. She was given thirteen blood transfusions — in vain. The agony of those weeks was something that Robert and I will never recover from — but the memory of her nobility of spirit all through her illness, is very precious.

Her child is an exceptionally merry, healthy baby. She was with us in the east for six months, and is now out in Montana with her father and father's family. I shall go out to see her in May, if I am strong enough and shall perhaps bring her back for a long visit.

I hope you and your family are well. . . . Robert joins me in sending kindest regards to you all.

Sincerely your friend   Elinor Frost

323 · To Louis Untermeyer

Dear Louis: 8 July 1935   South Shaftsbury

I wasn't here when your telegram came. No luck. We didn't subside at Amherst till last Saturday — more than two weeks after commencement. I had been wondering the last few years what use I was round the place. Well a use was found for me. I lectured, so to call it, three times, on How a Poem Picks up Thought, New Ways to Be New, and Our Darkest Concern. The last proved the best, though I was scared in it the worst. I burst forth like a Nova in those last days portending war, pestilence, and the end of the present Administration at Washington. I rose for the moment from well below the sixth or visible-to-the-naked-eye magnitude to about the third or second magnitude. Then I sunk back never again to blaze perhaps. The President thought it best to reward me at once before my effect was lost. I'll brag a little more when I see you — not much. I'm a sad old thing now. But tough.

I have several things to talk over with you, your news and mine. I wonder if there isn't some half way-place where we could meet for a night's talk. Elinor is not fit for anything. She is trying to save up energy for a melancholy journey to the terrible scenes in Colorado and Montana. I am doing my best to dissuade her from such a pilgrimage. We can't have a soul in the house for a while. And I don't want to be away from her long at a time.   Ever yours   Robertus Geler

323-a · ELINOR M. FROST TO EMMA MAY LANEY

THESE TWO LETTERS (323-a and 324) mark the beginnings of a unique phenomenon in the bardings of RF. From 1935 to 1962 he made a total of twenty visits to Agnes Scott College in Decatur, Georgia, more visits than he made to any other campus outside New England. The prime mover in the association was Miss Emma May Laney, then Chairman of the Department of English at Agnes Scott. RF's gifts to her of inscribed first editions of his works were presented by Miss Laney to the college library; his later gifts of books and manuscripts, presented directly to the library, were further extended by purchases. As a result the RF collection of books, manuscripts, letters, photographs, and research materials at Agnes Scott has become one of the five largest Frost collections in America. A catalogue, compiled by Mrs. Edna H. Byers, the present librarian, *Robert Frost at Agnes Scott College,* was published in 1963.

My dear Miss Laney,-

24 October 1935   The Webster Hotel
40 W. 45 St.   New York City

My husband and I are in the city for two or three days, and I am taking advantage of a little leisure to answer your letter. Mr. Frost is *too* busy this fall and is rushed with seeing one person and another. I hope you will pardon him for not answering your note sooner.

He is glad you wrote to him about trains. He couldn't get any reliable information in Northampton. He will take the train you suggest, Number 37, on the 6th [of November] and will thus reach Atlanta the next morning at 8.30. He'll be pleased to stay at the Alumnae House on your campus while he is there, and will watch out for someone meeting him at the Peachtree Station to take him to Decatur, but if it isn't convenient for anyone to meet him, he'll go over in a taxi. He would like to sleep some in the forenoon, but if you should wish to have him with you and a small group at lunch and for a drive afterward, he would enjoy it. But after four o'clock he would like to rest again, until the lecture. The reception *after* the lecture is just what he would wish. Then he hopes to take a midnight train for home. There seems to be an opinion in railroad circles that there *is* a midnight train out of Atlanta. In that way, he could reach Amherst (going the last ten miles by motor) about midnight on the 8th. As luck would have it, the meeting of the Alumni Council, about the biggest event in the Amherst faculty year, is on the 8th and 9th. He would like very much to be there for the things that take place on the 9th. Usually, the meeting of the Council is a little later in the month.

I would be very much obliged if you would write us a note confirming this opinion of a midnight train which he could take after the reception is over.

Yours very sincerely   Elinor Frost

We return to Amherst tomorrow.
I will enclose a photograph which you might like to use for publicity purposes.

324 · To Emma May Laney

IN THIS LETTER RF's sense of guilt seems to be the basis for the mockingly playful apologies. Never before had RF been paid $500 for a single reading, the sum he got from Agnes Scott College on 7 November 1935, but never before had he tarried so briefly. Later on, RF would usually remain for several days when he made visits to Agnes Scott.

Dear Miss Laney: 29 November 1935   Amherst

That was all a mistake and, as you perhaps noticed, I felt pretty sheepish about it when I saw what the situation really was. I assumed that Nov. 7th was a particular occasion with you for which you had set aside five hundred dollars. I never would have let you try to get a five hundred dollar audience together for me. When I have all that money, it is for a program of one public lecture, half a dozen to a dozen individual conferences and one or two round tables, so called. The arrangement is my own invention and has grown to be rather my specialty. You didn't know about it or you would have left things more to me. Hand-shaking receptions almost never happen to me. I usually sit somewhere and talk a while to or with any one who will sit on the floor at my feet after the platform is over. We were dealing at cross purposes. I didn't know what you wanted and you didn't know what I could best do. It makes me laugh to think your five hundred dollars was no more than an expression of your notion of how hard I was to get. It came from my badness about answering letters. You figured that a telegram naming money enough was the way to fetch me. The joke is on you as much as on me. You should have tried the telegram alone first. Scientists will tell you never try to prove two things with one experiment. Well I shall make it right with you if you will let me — that is to say if you bear me no ill will for having cheated you unintentionally. We shall be going South just after December 18th. Could we have the 19th and 20th at Agnes Scott? Or would that be too close to the holidays. Perhaps we had better wait till late March or early April. You say.

I have done the sort of thing I describe at three places since I saw you. I am off for round table and public reading at Rockford on Tuesday. Will you address me there? Rockford College, Rockford, Illinois. I told you my daughter was teaching there.

I'm sending you and Frosty Brown books. I thought you might like some of my first editions, my two English and a couple of very small recent American.

Sincerely yours   Robert Frost

325 · To John Livingston Lowes

Dear Mr. Lowes: [January 1936]   [Amherst]

As you may imagine, I should be most happy to be your Charles Eliot Norton Professor next spring; and that not alone for the honor of the appointment. I should value also the compulsion the lectures would put me under to assemble my thinking right and left of the last few years and see what it comes to. I have reached a point where it would do me good.

But let me tell you my situation. Your letter overtakes me on my way to Florida, where, after my last bad influenza I promised the doctor I would spend a couple of winters sunning on the tennis courts. I might as well be in Florida as in bed. (No reflection on Florida intended. Even Florida is no doubt somebody's home. And nothing but good of any of these States ever out of me.) I have already served one of my half terms down there. I am superstitiously afraid I ought to serve the other. If I served it clear out, I could hardly be back before the middle of March. I might risk the first of March. But even that is too late for your purposes. Or is it? I don't suppose I should ask that a Harvard thing so important should be reshaped somewhat to fit a mere person. Nevertheless I am tempted to ask. I am going to be greatly disappointed to see this opportunity pass from me.   Sincerely yours   Robert Frost

I shall be at 3670 Avocado Avenue Coconut Grove Florida by Saturday night — should you have anything further to write.

R. F.

326 · To G. R. Elliott

20 January 1936

Dear Roy: 3670 Avocado Ave.,   Coconut Grove

That sonnet to you on your having been abroad still lacks one half line of completion. So I am asking you to be patient another year. Meanwhile a letter from the tropics — just this side of Hell.

I can tell you about Harvard's having asked me to give the Charles Eliot Norton lectures in poetry this spring because though you are not a Harvard man nor a Unitarian nor even an American by birth you have lived in America a long time, know your way round the Harvard Yard and think any religion is better than none — I'm sure. Let's see — where did I intend to come out with that sentence when I started? I can tell *you*, I mean to say, because you will understand and sympathize. I am going to talk about such things as Vocal Imagination, Does Wisdom Signify (because it does etc) and Poetry as the Renewal of Words. Maybe I won't use the title Vocal Imagination: it seems to me I must have used it before. Instead why not make it Where Form and Content Merge. I shall be in comparison with the British subjects who alone have hitherto given these lectures. Of course I dread it. But you will appreciate the fact that I could hardly refuse the trial. I shan't hope too much of myself. But suppose I merely get by indifferently. There is still the name of having been the first American asked. It seems as if it must strengthen my position. Anyway it excites me a little. The University is one most people have heard of. It was mine after a fashion and my father's more than mine.

We pine for home and friends. This spongey climate is a doubtful good. I drift on toward the publication of my next. How goes the stream of consciousness at your world's far end? I heard Molly Colum defend the method of her friend James Joyce in Ulysses by reading from the Times the last broken sentences of Dutch Schultz. Evidently, says she, there is such a thing as insane maundering. Then why not base literature on it?

With our best to you both,   Ever yours   Robert

327 · To Mrs. Grace D. Vanamee

EDWIN ARLINGTON ROBINSON died in New York City on 6 April 1935, shortly after he had completed reading page proofs of his last book-length narrative poem, *King Jasper*. At the request of Robinson's publisher, RF wrote a "Preface" for the posthumously published work.

A few years earlier, in 1930, Robinson had been one of those who had nominated RF for membership in the American Academy of Arts and Letters. On 5 December 1935, Mrs. Vanamee, as Secretary of the Academy, wrote on behalf of the Committee on Commemorative Tributes, asking RF to write a eulogy to Robinson for inclusion in the Academy *Proceedings*. RF did not answer that letter. Mrs. Vanamee wrote again on 8 January 1936, repeating the request, and this is his answer.

Dear Mrs. Vanamee: 21 January 1936   Coconut Grove

I have been sick in bed most of the time for a month or so, and no secretary to answer my letters for me.

Will you be so kind as to tell Mr. Charles Dana Gibson that I have already said my say about Robinson in my preface to King Jasper. I am not a practiced prose writer and prose costs me a great deal. I went far far out of my way to do honor to Robinson there. What I wrote may not seem enough to his friends, but it was my best and I am sure any attempt on my part to add to it would only take away from it. You must see the beauty of my having learned to let well enough alone. I am told it is one of an artist's most valuable acquirements.

Thank Mr. Gibson for thinking of me and take thanks to yourself for your trouble in all this.

Sincerely yours   Robert Frost

327-a · ELINOR M. FROST TO EDITH H. FOBES

Dear Mrs. Fobes,-   21 January 1936   Coconut Grove

. . . Robert has consented to give the six Charles Eliot Norton lectures at Harvard this spring. He has been asked to give the "Ode" at the 300th anniversary at Harvard in September, and also the Phi Beta Kappa poem there in September, and I think he will undertake to give them, tho he hates to know that he *must* write. It will be a Harvard year for him and I only wish that he was more vigorous at this time. . . .

Affectionately,   Elinor Frost

328 · To L. W. Payne, Jr.

12 March 1936

Dear Payne: 56 Fayerweather St.   Cambridge

Dont be a damned fool. I burned both your checks. You can't buy books from me. And the reason is, not because I hate you, but because I like you. When I forget you let my right hand forget to throw stones. By the way I thought a year ago, a year and a half ago, when I got up from my second bad influenza, I had lost the use of my pitching arm. When I complained to the doctor all the encouragement I got was — Well, I must remember I would never be as young again as I once was. But I fooled him. I have come back. I dont expect ever to pitch in either of the big leagues again. But I feel pretty sure I will have a contract to sign from Terry Hut before the season opens. I am taking a cut in salary of course. Have you signed up yet?

You notice I am coming out with a new book for you to add to your collection. A Further Range is its name. You will have seen a good deal of it in magazines by the time it gets to you. Mercury will have one short poem, The Atlantic one long one, The Virginia Quarterly three half lengths and Poetry a group of Ten Mills and a Dollar in their April issues just a month ahead of the book. The Yale Review too. I forgot that. It will have one of the best — The White-tailed Hornet. This ought to prepare you for the shock of novelty.

I am overdoing here at Harvard. But don't pity me. I come into these things for what I think them worth in friendship and reputation.

Oh I mustnt forget I wanted to correct you in a matter. Somewhere I found you saying lately that my formula of twenty-five years ago — Common in experience and uncommon in writing — meant that the subject should be common in experience but that it should be written up in an uncommon style. I believe that may be Munson's mistake.* You're not to blame for it. The subject should be common in experience and uncommon in books is a better way to put it. It should have happened to everyone but it should have occurred to no one before as material. That's quite different. I was silent as to the need of giving old themes a new setting of words. I am silent

---

* The reference is to a book by Gorham B. Munson: *Robert Frost: A Study in Sensibility and Good Sense* (New York, 1927).

still. My lectures here have these titles The Old Way to Be New, Vocal Imagination the Merger of Form and Content, Does Wisdom Signify, Poetry as Prowess and Feat of Words, Before the Beginning of a Poem, After the End of a Poem.

In giving the second I've just found out what makes a piece of writing good (my latest opinion of anything): it is making the sentences talk to each other as two or more speakers do in drama. The dullness of writing is due to its being, much of it, too much like the too long monologues and soliloquies in drama.

I tell you all this just to be sociable. You know by this time what a bad letter writer I am. That furnishes the background for the surprise of a spontaneous letter like this when you have about given up ever hearing from me again. Be good and set me a good example.   Ever yours   Robert Frost

329 · To Henry Goddard Leach

THIS LETTER rounds out an episode, largely manipulated by RF, involving a controversial poem. On 1 August 1935, he gave a reading at the University of Colorado Writers Conference in Boulder. One of the unpublished poems he read there was "To a Thinker," which RF slyly described as a "suppressed poem." He went on to explain, in a typically mock-serious posture, that it had been written during the early years of the New Deal, that many things said in it had unfortunately come to pass, and that therefore he felt it necessary to suppress its publication. But he sold the poem to the *Saturday Review*, which published it in the issue for 11 January 1936 under the title "To a Thinker in Office." The poem inspired no controversy at the time of publication, but RF was not content to let matters rest there. An article in the Baltimore *Sun* for 26 February 1936, "Latest Poem by Robert Frost Versifies New Deal as Lost," contained these statements:

"Robert Frost has descended from the poetical Parnassus to the political arena. . . . Pausing before catching a train out of Baltimore after a brief visit here the versifier . . . asserted he was anti-Roosevelt. He declared he once had held high hopes for Henry Wallace but had lost them. He bitterly condemned an alleged administration policy regarding farmers as possessors of what he called sub-marginal minds, and with something of a flourish he produced a new poem, 'To a Thinker.' The verse, he indicated, was written about the President. . . ."

Other newspapers picked up the story and the poem. The Springfield *Union* ran an article and the New York *Times* devoted an editorial to it. Apparently as a result of all this publicity, Henry Goddard Leach, editor of *The Forum* magazine, wrote to RF and asked if he could publish the poem. With his answer of 15 March 1936, RF enclosed a page proof of the poem set in the type used for *A Further Range*. In this proof the printed title was "TO A THINKER IN OFFICE," but the words "IN OFFICE" had been deleted by RF with a pen stroke.

Dear Mr Leach   15 March 1936   Cambridge

Here is the offending poem. It is already in book form and about to be published. It first appeared in The Saturday Review. I am sorry you are too late. I should have liked you to have it in The Forum. You will see that it was only by restriction of meaning that it was narrowed down to fit the President. Changing the title from "To a Thinker" to "To a Thinker in Office" helped do the business. As a matter of fact it was written three years ago and was aimed at the heads of our easy despairers of the republic and of parliamentary forms of government. I encounter too many such and my indignation mounts till it overflows in rhyme. I doubt if my native delicacy would have permitted me to use the figure of walking and rocking in connection with a person of the President's personal infirmities. But I am willing to let it go as aimed at him. He must deserve it or people wouldn't be so quick to see him in it.

Sometime soon I'll hope to have something for you — political or unpolitical. Thank you for the kindness of both your letters.   Sincerely yours   Robert Frost

329-a · ELINOR M. FROST TO NINA THORNTON

AFTER THE DEATH of Marjorie, RF and his wife paid tribute to her poetic aspirations by gathering the best of her verse into a small volume, *Franconia*. It was privately printed by Joseph Blumenthal at the Spiral Press in New York City early in 1936.

Dear Nina,-   23 March 1936   Cambridge

We are sending you and Dick a copy of Marjorie's book of poems. She had three brief periods of writing, and while she never offered anything for publication, even to magazines, I know she looked forward to having a book some day. Robert thinks they are very lovely, and all her own. A group was printed in a number of "Poetry" last fall, and one of them "America" was asked for by the Literary Digest anthology of last year's best poems. We have had many letters of praise for that group. Mr. Blumenthal has made a beautiful little book, I think. . . .

It is certainly *grand* about the Book-of-the-Month Club [selection of *A Further Range*]. I rather thought they would take it, because Henry Canby and Dorothy Canfield are always such staunch friends of Robert's work, and Christopher Morley has shown much friendliness the last year.

Perhaps we shall see you soon.

Faithfully yours,   Elinor Frost

330 · To LAWRANCE THOMPSON

RF and the editor of this volume first became acquainted in December 1926 when RF spent two weeks as poet in residence at Wesleyan University where Thompson was then an undergraduate. Nearly ten years later RF gave a reading at Wesleyan. For that occasion, an exhibition of his books and manuscripts and a catalogue (*Robert Frost: A Chronological Survey*) was prepared by Thompson, who was then an English instructor at Wesleyan. While assembling his materials, Thompson was unable to locate a first English edition of *A Boy's Will* and appealed to RF for help. This is the poet's answer.

Dear Mr Thompson: 26 March 1936   Cambridge

Can I do anything to help you? You are so very kind. I'd like to contribute the enclosed remnant of manuscript if I knew who would act as repository. Theres probably no place for such a thing at the University. Anyway you may care to exhibit it. It is a sample of what most of my note books get reduced to in the process of revision. You say you lack the first English edition of A Boys Will. I wonder if Frederic Melcher of The Publishers Weekly wouldnt loan you his copy. Mine is not where I can get hold of it. Dont think I dont appreciate.

Sincerely yours   Robert Frost

331 · To BERNARD DEVOTO

WHEN RF was in Florida in January 1936, he gave three talks at the University of Miami Winter Institute of Literature. There he met Bernard DeVoto, who also participated in the Institute program that year. RF befriended DeVoto, calling on him at his hotel, and a few months later, when RF gave the Charles Eliot Norton lectures at Harvard, DeVoto acted as self-appointed host. RF arranged to have DeVoto lecture at Amherst College in November 1936. This letter was written shortly before the visit, and begins with references to DeVoto's volume of essays and reviews, *Forays and Rebuttals*.

429

Dear Benny: [November 1936]   [Amherst]

Not just the two or three essays I had seen before — I like the whole damned book. I have read most of it more than once and most of it to Elinor aloud as if telling her something out of my head. You and I without collusion have arrived at so nearly the same conclusions about life and America that I cant seem to figure out how we came to vote different tickets at the last election. I suspect what settled it for you was your province's having been plundered by Wall Street. I don't know so much about that of course. And it strikes me that if the West has been exploited on the economic plane by the East in times past it is now being exploited by the East on the plane of sentiment — in the persons of Roosevelt and Farley. I guess the West is a sucker. Don't think I care very much. So far from minding Farley in particular, I find him my chief assurance that the whole outfit isnt Utopian in your worst sense of the word. No communism or even collectivism can result from any election he wins. I am not the least uneasy in the hands of such hands as his and his Pals from New York Groton and Harvard. The Pope would have something to say if Farley helped this country to go People's Front. The nearest Farley comes to being a collectivist is in encouraging stamp-collectors. Lesley says not to grieve: at worst we are in for a benevolent despotism. I should find it harder to bear the benevolence than the despotism. Someone said all my writing was about the poor. Was it because I had no sympathy with them? I am tempted to answer: I never would have written about the poor, if I had thought it would lead to anything's being done about them. Or better: I wrote about the poor as the most permanent subject to hitch onto. I took Christ's word for it that poverty wouldnt be abolished. But now we're asked to join the W. C. T. U. and do away with poverty prostitution drink and death. The great politicians are having their fun with us. Theyve picked up just enough of the New Republic and Nation jargon to seem original to the simple. Something good may come of it. Simon de Montfort couldnt have meant to give us all what he did in the Big Chart. Look at what he turned and did right afterward to the Albigenses. I know what is good, but I'm not sure who is good. Thats why I havent been called to rule. That rules me out.

As a matter of fact I write about the poor because at the receptive and impressionable age I was poor myself and knew none but the poor.

To go back to your essays. I cant get over my not having realized you were on earth. You don't know your power. No one else has your natural sensible and at the same time embracing thoughts about life and America. And the way you lay into the writing with your whole body like an archer rather than a pistolman. Neither perverse precious nor international. I wasn't marked off from the other children as a literary sissy like Yates and Masters. Maybe thats whats the matter with me. Theres consolation in the thought that you werent marked off either.

You've been through worse things than we have lately. But you're younger. And I can stand your miseries better than my own. If I seem to speak lightly of your troubles, dont cry. Your hired girl must seem funny even to you in retrospect. Do you suppose all hired girls are like that. I believe in doing your own housework.

Do as you think best about Holmes' article.* A situation has been created it might take too much delicacy to get out of. My chief fear is that he will make too much of my having been noticed by the English. I'm glad of anybody's approval. But in this case my special pleasure was in any embarrassment the English radicals might be causing the American radicals. I sort of counted on you to get this to a nicety without saying it too flat and outright. I havent seen the four essays the generous boys over there have poured over my poetry. But it will be strange if they dont prove to be a little condescending. You would know how to meet condescention with condescension. I wonder if we couldnt help Holmes article into some other magazine. The Yale Review or the Virginia Quarterly say. But anyway you manage will suit me. Holmes may have done well.

And now comes the hardest of all. I have to admit I havent a thing in verse ready to publish. Too much has happened to me this year. I am stopped in my tracks as if everybody in the opposing eleven had concentrated on me. No, not as bad as that. But I havent dared to look at paper. This is the

* In September 1936 DeVoto became editor of the *Saturday Review*, and the remarks in this paragraph are addressed to him as editor. In November an English edition of *Selected Poems by Robert Frost* was published by Jonathan Cape, with introductory essays by W. H. Auden, C. Day Lewis, Paul Engle (then in England as a Rhodes Scholar), and Edwin Muir. An unsolicited review of that volume was sent to the *Saturday Review* by the poet John Holmes; it was eventually published in the Boston *Transcript*, 13 February 1937, under the title "Robert Frost Conquers the Poetic Realm."

first letter I have written in four months — absolutely the first. I prescribed loafing for myself. I may have been wrong. At any rate herewith I start again (though in bed again) and quit whining and shirking; and it may soon come to my tackling the Harvard talks as I remember them.* You shall have anything you want. But give me time. Look the other way. Look unexpectant. Gee I wish I had a fine long Christmas outbreak in blank verse for you or for myself. What chances I miss. I used to be made unhappy when rejected by editors; now I am unhappy when solicited by editors. What are you going to do about a world like that? I see Yale is pulling a convention to discuss happiness as a human possibility. One thing is sure I never enjoyed happiness till it was over: in which respect it is like pain. I enjoy pain only when it is over.

Well, you're coming to see us. We can talk the rest then. What time of day will you come? Youll stay over night of course. Shall we have a small party. It should be part of my duty here to have my fellows meet the editor of The Review. I'm not a very resourceful host. But I'd honestly like my friends here to get some of the good of you.   Ever yours   Robert

331-a · ELINOR M. FROST TO L. W. PAYNE, JR.

Dear Mr. Payne,-   3 December 1936   Amherst

My oldest daughter, Lesley Frost Francis, is on her way to Taxco, Mexico, with her two children. Robert and I thought we would like to have her meet you and Mrs. Payne, and that perhaps you would like to meet her. She expects to reach Baton Rouge on the 5th or 6th of this month, and will then go on to Texas. She will look you up when she reaches Austin, and perhaps you can find a room for her in your neighborhood.

I have been wanting to get time to send you a small book of Marjorie's poems, which has lately been published, and will do so before we leave for the winter.

Robert hasn't been very well through the summer and fall. He needs to get away for the winter rest very much, and we shall be going soon, but we haven't definitely decided just

---

* RF's contract for the Charles Eliot Norton lectures at Harvard included his agreement to edit for publication a stenographic transcript of the lectures. The transcript was made and sent to him, but he "lost" it and never completed that part of the contract.

where to go. We *may* go to southern Texas, to San Antonio or Corpus Christi, but I greatly doubt that Robert would be well enough to do any lecturing at the University. Of course, however, we should want to see you while we were there. Robert and I would go by train, and our son and his wife and little boy (12 yrs. old) would drive down, so we should have the car there. I feel quite inclined to try a winter in Texas, and Lesley's being in Mexico is a reason why we should go in that direction.

With warmest regards to you and Mrs. Payne, and best wishes for the family.   Sincerely yours,   Elinor Frost

332 · To Harold G. Rugg

Dear Rugg: 4 December 1936   Amherst

After long long consideration (you should say so — and one long more), I have reluctantly come to the conclusion that I dont see how I can ever again promise you or anyone else a poem for an occasion. Look at the way I failed them with not only one poem but two at Harvard.* And look at the sad way Masefield didn't fail them. I'm modest. I often say Who am I that I should hold myself above doing things badly. That's why I rather good-naturedly consent to teach and lecture badly. But poetry isn't teaching and lecturing. I have kept poetry free thus far, and I have been punished for the mere thought of making it a duty or a business. You'll misunderstand. The one or two exceptions to rule have only been seeming exceptions. Three poems I believe I have read for public occasions and very imperfectly fitted them. I made myself wretched and even sick last summer with the dread of what I had let myself in for at Harvard. I now think I was very foolish to try anything at my age so against my lifelong habits. Poetry has been a self indulgence with me and theres no use trying to put a better face on it. I have some times wished I was a ready writer in prose, but never in verse. I have never rhymed for parlor games or for exercises or from a sense of duty to keep the wolf from the door. Aint I useless? Just the same I'm your friend you have to make the best of,   Robert Frost

* See letter 327-a. Illness prevented RF from preparing and delivering either the "Ode" or the Phi Beta Kappa poem at the 300th Anniversary Celebration at Harvard.

333 · To G. R. Elliott

Dear Roy: 1 January 1937 113 Norwood Court

                   San Antonio, Texas

Just exactly when you were making that joke up there about my being Public Something No. 1 I was making it down here to the manager of the Saint Anthony Hotel in San Antonio Texas. He had called me up on our room telephone to tell me in a reeking policy tone of voice how glad he was to have us folks in the house. For a moment I was deceived into thinking he must have heard of us. If he had heard of us it was a striking proof we were famous. I was getting on. It was the second thing within a week to swell my pride. The other was news that the English had started counterfeiting the first edition of my first book. But the manager's voice didn't quite satisfy me. It ran on with a false communality. You bastard, I thought, you say that to everybody you harbor for the night. I won't be treated with any such generalized rotarian hospitality. "Don't be too glad to have us till you look us up in Dunn and Bradstreet's and find out who you have on your hands," I had presence of mind to call back before he had time to hang up in his complacency. "By some I am rated Public Something No. 1." "What do you mean?" he asked with sudden reality. It took me to restore him his naturalness. I dare say he was an honest fellow at bottom. Only calculated and none too disinterested good will on earth had made him as insincere as a bad preacher. I put that "bad" in to hold you objectionless.

Luckily we are out of hotels and settled in common dwellings, or we should begin to ring untrue ourselves. I have a house on the edge of town at 113 Norwood Court, San Antonio Texas. So if you want to write me any news, you have my address. It is noisy tonight with New Years fire crackers reaching their height after a week of it. But ordinarily it will be quiet. Carol's house is a mile and seven tenths away; which insures exercise. Not many have found us out yet. There will be positively no dining out.

You will wonder that our southmost should be San Antonio. Well we wearied of well doing before we explored further. There were too many of us to sustain the expense of long suspense. Willard and Robin got here an hour ahead of us. Lesley, Elinor 2nd and Lee got here the day after us; and Carol, Lillian and Prescott the day after them. Ten of us sat down to Sunday dinner on December 20. Willard went back to Montana today leaving Robin with us. Lesley went along to Mexico with the two girls three days ago. We have heard from her already. She is seeing scenery. There is nothing but good soil to look at here. She was warned to expect bad and even dangerous roads after Monterey in Mexico. Lesley puts so much life into life that I can forgive her her adventurousness.

It isn't quite midnight yet; I will defer dating this till the bells ring and I can date it — January 1 1937 — and wish you a Happy New Year.   Yours since about 1917

(if I am not mistaken in the year you decided I was neighborly)

Robert

334 · To Sidney Cox

Dear Sidney: [1 January 1937]   [San Antonio]

It was not to be Southern Cal after all. We were divided in preference between California and Florida; so we came as nearly as possible to halfway between. We are over across the Gulf from one and over across the deserts from the other in San Antonio Texas — at 113 Norwood Court to be exact for you in case you should want to write me a letter about Dartmouth College or Stearns Morse's party of the vestigial part. I'm sorry not to be where I can see something of you in the wild and unharnessed state. But then I doubt if I should find you very different. You and I are not the kind that can be described as either wild or tame: I always maintain that I would be the same in a society of one as in a society of one hundred and thirty million. My conditioning is all internal. My appetites are checked by each other rather than by anything in my surroundings. Or do I deceive myself? I dont care if I do in this respect. My denial that I am the result of any particular surroundings comes to nothing more than a refusal to think of myself as one who might have been better or worse if I had been thrown with different people in different circumstances. Look out I don't spoof you. About five years ago I resolved to spoil my correspondence with you by throwing it into confusion the way God threw the speech of the builders of the tower of Babel into confusion. My reason is too long to go into tonight (January First, Nineteen Hundred and Thirty-seven. Lucky New Year to you, if you are superstitiously susceptible.) Part of my reason is my dislike of all the printed correspondence I ever saw.

You or anyone else could enjoy a better friendship with

me if I could be sure you were keeping no records of it in the off-hand letters I write. My public talks owe any felicity they may have to the fact that they are gone on the wind. I wrote down not a word for Harvard last year and it would have thrown me off my phrasing to have known of anyone's taking notes on me in my audience. But I am resigned to what I am in for. You have the hint of what would please me: you will use your judgement as a scholar and a critic in dealing with the case.

You've got a novel to write and I have some prose I should be at if I dont feel too averse to it. So perhaps we are as well apart where we cant take it out in talking. Talking is a hydrant in the yard and writing is a faucet upstairs in the house. Opening the first takes all the pressure off the second. My mouth is sealed for the duration of the stay here. I'm not even going to write letters around to explain to collectors my not having had any Christmas card this year. I'm not going to explain anything personal any more. I'm not going to explain my children, except to tell you that Irma has written us how much she likes Alice [Mrs. Cox]. You may not have guessed this. Irma might have difficulty in conveying it to Alice. It would be too bad for you and Alice not to know it. My children are all good but rather offish with the human race. I myself am rather on-ish. I refuse to explain the discrepancy. I refuse to explain my position on a lot of things we brought up and left unsettled in our talk last fall. Why should I press home my conclusions everywhere. Blessed is he that seeketh not his own advantage. I practice such equalitarianism as I please. I wouldn't let a tiger eat me to relieve its starving kittens.   Ever yours,   R. F.

335 · To Bernard DeVoto

Dear Bennyvenuto: [January 1937]   San Antonio

I am going to have you strike that blow for me now if you still want to and if you can assure your wife and conscience you thought of it first and not I. The Benny-faction must be beyond suspicion of procurement on my part or I will have none of it. All depends on the sequence of events; which I leave to your memory. I am not above asking favors, but principle if not delicacy forbids that it should be too soon in a friendship. In a Harvard lecture I based a whole theory of art on my particular-

ity there. In about twenty-five years I may make an important
death bed request of you. Meanwhile give me only the Christmas presents you can get most pleasure out of for yourself.

I have decided to let you make the English Selected Poems
[see letter 331] your occasion rather than the prospective
Harvard essays because I dont want any more depending on
those essays than already depends. I am inhibited badly
enough over them as it is. Damn the essays. Our little grand-
daughter Robin (under three) says her Uncle Bob in Billings
Montana distinguishes between nice damn and terrible damn.
Well I am thinking of terrible damn. I am deep in Texas history on the spot and dont want to be bothered by any but the
ghost of the heroes of Goliad and the Alamo. (And deep in climate too. We have ice on everything for five days.)

Speaking of history on the spot: I had a letter from Ann
Winslow, Secretary, to tell me the College Poetry Society of
America had moved its headquarters from Berk[e]ley Cali-
f[ornia] to Old Fort Laramie on the Oregon Trail. Is this news
for your newspaper? I must have been reading my twelve-year
old grandson the chapter in Parkman about the Fort the night
before. I was comforted with the old fashioned meaning he
makes the word bourgeois ring with.

And speaking of history, what are we going to do about
these Southerners who however amiably will insist on the Civil
War's being between the business interests of the north and
the agriculture of the south? Let them have it as they please
forever out of consideration for their wounded pride? Speak
after sentence — yea, until the end of time. My what a thing
defeat is even unto the third and fourth generation of them
that get it. But honestly and truly, I wonder if something isn't
due the victors in a war. Have you happened to see Women of
the Confederacy? It was written south of the line. Was it by
Southerners? Is it a sly book?

Some more history. (You are right: history is certainly
better than literature in terms of the departmental in college.)
If I had been a person of forensic command, you would have
seen me at Dayton Tenn defending the farmers from the
city guys. The country has as much right to its guiding metaphor as to any other of its mores. For seventy years the educated that is to say the uninnocent world has been growingly
disposed in the name of evolution to respect God the Fight-
promoter rather than to love God the Father. But if the country

jakes cling to the figure of God the Father whose universal parentage makes us all brothers under obligation not to hurt each other a l'outrance, all they had to do was hang on: help was coming from the Jews again in an addition to the Bible by no less a humanitarian than Carl Marx. It may very well be the New Jerewsalem this time that shall not pass away. Like it or not! With which paragraph I feel as if I might be started on my Harvard essays. So goodbye for the present.

Ever yours   Robert

336 · To ALFRED HARCOURT

Dear Alfred: 22 January 1937   San Antonio

Louis [Untermeyer] has told me you were sick, but he wasn't impressive enough. You have apparently looked over a brink I have never had sight of except through the eyes of others. But we wont talk about that. In your place I should have been thinking How too bad for such a good publisher to leave off publishing so young. How old would I have to be to be satisfied? It is rather a delicate matter to bring into the open, but since you ask me, pretty old. Not that I couldn't work up an interest in the hereafter — getting a job with the Government (I suppose all jobs will be with the Government in heaven, just as they are getting to be here as we grow more and more heavenly) and choosing a mansion in "my Fathers house" (sounds like a Soviet appartment house). The way things are going in politics I'm afraid heaven will come to me before I go to it and then how will I like life with all the gamble taken out of my game. We can joke, can't we, about what you are safely out of?

No Florida for us this year. Maybe we'll be near you again next year if you stick to your Pompano. We had to investigate our third citrous (sp) region before we decided on a home. This is the least sophisticated of the three, most like farming as we were brought up to it. We are bent on some farming of the winter kind. One of the things we are looking into is tung nuts to sell to Messrs Sloan Ford and C[h]rysler.

Stay well. Remember us both to Ellen [Mrs. Harcourt].

Ever yours   Robert

337 · To Leonard Bacon

RF and the poet Leonard Bacon had become acquainted through
the Fobes family in Franconia (see editor's note to letter 249-b).
Bacon's dedication of his volume, *Rhyme and Punishment,* to RF
inspired this letter.

Dear Leonard Bacon: 24 January 1937   San Antonio
    I don't know whether you are in this world or in the Old
But I wanted to tell you before what is between us gets too cold
How much moral satisfaction not to say pleasure I took in
              your punishing rhymes.
I can see you feel pretty much as I do about these provocative
              times.
Neither of us would be driven to drink by them nor to suicide
But that we find them rather too diverting from our preferred
              pursuits cannot be denied.
Still we wouldn't have missed them, would we, by any of the
              close calls we have ever had?
For my part I have got more out of the last four years perhaps
              than out of any previous Olympiad.
The only exception to our almost absolute unanimity
Is the way you ride the Methodists to an extremity.
As a good Congregationalist out of Peace Dale, I take it you are
              willing to interpose the Episcopalian
Between our Puritan institutions and the none too sympathetic
              Catholic alien.
But after using the Episcopalian in their way you have him
              on your hands unless you are foxy
Enough to bring in Methodism to render him harmless to our
              Orthodoxy.
Set an Anglican to catch a Roman and a Chapel-goer to catch
              an Anglican
And I don't see how the good old world can ever again be stolen
              from the honest man.
I'd say we called a meeting and organized a party to promote
              our politics
But I know myself too well; I have had that idea before and it
              never sticks.
There may be a show-down coming, but if there is, we'll just
              have to wait for the day

Before we go to Abercrombie and Fitch's outfit for the fray.
I rely on the large number of our kind there must be in a coun-
  try like this that don't easily get worked up and excited.
They can stand no end of being left out of account and slighted
They even enjoy looking unimpressive
To the truculent and aggressive.
But there's a concentrated something in them away at the core
That I'd advise anybody to look out for if it ever comes to a
  war.
No there's nothing that we can do for the present except write
  poems and farm
And meet in some quiet place like Franconia for a talk next
  summer—that couldn't do any harm.
Don't think I got this trick of rhyme without much obvious
  metre from Ogden Nash, dod rot it.
No I got it from the Sweet Singer of Michigan where he is hon-
  est enough to acknowledge he got it.

Ever yours   Robert Frost

338 · To Bernard DeVoto

Dear Bennyvenuto: 16 February 1937   San Antonio

On third thought and after reading what you did to Edmund Wilson [*Saturday Review*, 13 February 1937] I have
decided to have you leave me out of it a while yet, so that my
enjoyment of your editorship may be unmixed with self-
interest. You go ahead and let me applaud under no obligation.
Dont think I dont realize what I am foregoing

I believe you came into the world to save me from trying to write social moral and aesthetic criticism by making me
feel a failure at it before I got started. You can see the temptation I have been trembling on the verge of in my old age. I
have caught myself in time. I draw back. You write the criticism who can really write it.

I ought to send you a scrap of a poem I once wrote on
sleep's having been given us to keep our logic from concatenat-
ing too far. The best minds are those good at premises. "A soldier's a man." Right. "A life's but a span." Right. But except in a
song it would be perilous to go further by putting the two to-

440

gether and reaching a conclusion. May I live to the end in premises and rest in processes. This is anent.   Ever yours R F

I've just read Webb's book about the plains and I must now get into this Rhodeses book.

339 · To Bernard DeVoto

Dear Benny: [26 March 1937]   San Antonio
All right, let's hear how good a poet I am. Perhaps it was to tell me and the world your flu spared you. The article as you block it out is too much for me to deny myself, especially the block for the head of [Horace] Gregory. I have never read a word of that ganglion's regrets about me in prose, but I suspect they are to be explained by his not unwarrantable if intuitive suspicion that I hate his obscratulations of the muse in verse. There is no baser form of hypocrasy than a false air of disinterestedness.

I am all packed (as by the time you read this the Supreme Court will be) and ready to return to the vital places (as they fondly seem to suppose themselves to be). I am only going to stay in the vital places long enough however to give the People's Front a good stab in the Back. Then I am going to retire to a safe place of observation near the Canadian border where I can eat vegetables till I have the bucolic. Some very seductive real estate agents have failed to sell me a sheep ranch down here among the rather sheepish Democrats who would undoubtedly stop voting the Democratic ticket if there was anything else but the Republican ticket to vote. I doubt if I could learn to answer the name of Rancher. I'm a farmer and a one-horn one at that. My mind turns on an acre place at Concord Corners Vt. I'll have you look at it next summer. Time I was thinking where I mean to end my days. I cant hope to live later than 1975 at best. I mean in this world. I wish I could find some place under the American flag where there is no income tax. We pay too much for our advantages. I still cling to the American flag, though I suppose I wouldn't be saying so if I clung as blindly as of old. They can do things, I warn them, that will turn me against not only my own country but Russia Germany Italy France Spain and even England. I'll go without a country god dam it. The same as I'll stop patronizing the mails if Farley repeats his "There will be no reprisals" after next election. I wonder why I mind that so much.

We are parting with our grandaughter at St Louis on Sunday. Her father meets us there and regathers her to Montana and his Democratic politics. It comes hard on us to lose her. It amuses me to think of the heresies she is bound to grow up to. I hope she learns to shoot and ride like you.

I'll be seeing you in a week.   Ever yours   Robert

My birthday being ten minutes old

339-a · ELINOR M. FROST TO EARLE J. BERNHEIMER

THIS LETTER represents an early stage of a friendship which was to pass through several peculiar phases before it became embarrassing to both parties. Bernheimer was a rabid collector of Frost books and manuscripts, and RF encouraged him by autographing first editions which Bernheimer bought from various dealers. At times, RF went so far as to make attractive but misleading presentation inscriptions in these first editions. A unique phase of the relationship began when Bernheimer wrote asking if RF would consider selling the only existing copy of *Twilight*. RF replied (letter 376) that he "might not be able to refuse serious money" for it. As letter 376-a indicates, Bernheimer finally paid $4,000 for *Twilight*, the price asked by RF. About eighteen months later RF made the next business move (see letter 383) by offering to sell two manuscripts to Bernheimer for a total of $2,000. Rejecting that specific offer, the collector made several counter-proposals, one of which RF accepted: that Bernheimer would send RF a monthly check for $150, just so long as RF continued to send him whatever manuscripts, or poetry, the poet was willing to release. These monthly payments continued for several years — the cancelled checks have been preserved — and Bernheimer also sent large checks as Christmas gifts. Eventually, the total amount of money paid came to approximately $9,000. In addition, RF accepted lavish entertainments, hospitalities, and personal gifts from Bernheimer.

When the number of manuscripts sent by RF dwindled without satisfactory explanation, Bernheimer stopped his regular monthly payments. Apparently troubled by guilt for having failed to fulfill his obligations to Bernheimer, RF did his best to make amends, and the friendship continued precariously. Some of RF's manuscript letters to Bernheimer suggest obliquely that he was trying to pay off a portion of his debt in this way. Even after relations became strained, Bernheimer occasionally sent a big check as a Christmas present, and RF always accepted it — see letter 407, for example. But in letter 411, dated 16 October 1947, RF wrote, "You speak of a present for this Christmas that Santa Claus can't get down the chimney. That's like you in form and content. But don't send the present please. I want a chance to catch up with you. . . . Now remember: you, your friendship and kindness but no more presents."

But the friendship entered another phase. It became even more strained when Bernheimer got into financial difficulties which he felt might force him to sell a good deal of property, including his collection of Frost books and manuscripts. RF was unsuccessful in his attempts to stop Bernheimer from selling or, barring that, to steer the big collection into the library of a college or university. An auction sale was scheduled for 11-12 December 1950, and the auction catalogue was published early that fall. A maliciously unjust attack on Bernheimer in the form of an unsigned letter implying that the collector was betraying RF by selling books and manuscripts that had been genuinely presented as outright gifts appeared in *The Antiquarian Bookman* for November 1950. RF knew of this false accusation, but he never chose to correct it, either publicly or privately.

My dear Mr. Bernheimer, —   19 April 1937   Amherst

We *are* at home again, after our winter in San Antonio, Texas. Mr. Frost is better than he was last fall, but we didn't get as much sunshine as we hoped for, and he isn't completely recovered from the nervous exhaustion of last year. However, he is resuming his activities and with the summer ahead of us, I am sure he will be all right. He will be pretty busy for around two weeks but after that, he will be perfectly willing to autograph the books for you. I shall let you know when the package arrives.   Sincerely yours,   Elinor Frost

340 · To Bernard DeVoto

Dear Benny: [May 1937]   [Amherst]

We've seen plenty you've done for the Review, you and the people you've brought into it. We hope to hear others have been noticing it too. You have a problem to make the public realize anything in particular has happened. It isn't as if you were just out with a brand new publication breathing fire and policy. It must be harder to get a thousand new subscribers for an old magazine than the first ten or fifteen thousand for a new magazine. Rivals could help a lot by battling up with you. Bunny Wilson may well have meant well in his accusations of unprincipled criticism and uncharted freedom of thought. Anything for a row. At any rate he gave you as good a chance

as I could ask for to show in all your freshness and reality. (Not
to mention depth.) Dont let them jockey you into the position
of having to apologize for any least generalization you may
need for your clarification. You are as good at generalization
as the best of them. Only you are not fool enough to judge
one work by the generalizations underlying another work,
much less to judge all work by the generalization underlying
your own work. These are little old men you are dealing with.
I'll tell you how I know. It is a mark of age to go on the assumption that what we have been trying for all our lives in art
must be more or less what everybody is trying for. We failed of
it but there is some satisfaction in the fact that the others
failed of it, albeit they failed for the simple reason that they
were trying for something else. All criticism must be ad hoc
as you insist. But it can be all the way ad hoc, I mean clear to
the principles in the thing. What I suspect we hate is canons:
which are no better than my guidances insisted on as your
guidances. You cant sail by the North Star at the South Pole.
I dont know what they sail by down there. There should be
something. Even the compass needs all sorts of corrections. If
Hazen in running the line between Mass. and New Hampshire
hadnt been given the wrong corrections by Gov. Andros (?),
Williams College would have been in the State of Vermont
and what more would we have needed for self-containment in
case of secession?

You're going to take a degree somewhere — you don't
say where. That sounds as if your thrusts had gone home with
some one. People are bound to be impressed with your great
pen. You say I dont know how good I am. You dont know how
good you are. We are two modest men. I'm getting the [Har-
vard] degree I missed in the conclave of unification last year.
Thought by some to be my reward for not having done the two
poems I was down for.

There's a lot to talk about. I hope I haven't made you too
unhappy by having thrown my weight into your decision to
leave teaching. Nothing is momentous. Nothing is final. You
can always go back if back is where you can best strike from.
Some like a spear some like a dirk. The dirk is the close-in
weapon of city streets. Anybody can take his choice of weapons
for all of me. I suspect you're an all round handiman of the
armory. I had no idea of sacrificing you to the job down there
— or letting you sacrifice yourself. You're there to lick em for

us. To Hell with their thinking. That's all I say. I wish I were any good. I'd go up to the front with you. As it is — as I am — I must be content to sick you on. Results is all I ask.

Fine to have you in Vermont. I'll be there just ahead of you. (You say you wont be there till the 15th.) I have one lecture to give. Its at Oberlin for commencement. Heaven is My Destination. My self assigned subject: What Became of New England? Then for some much needed self-indulgence. For a person who set out to have his own way in the world I am ending up a horrible example of duteous unselfishness. Dont tell anybody in that article — which by the way I really ought not to see till it's in print if I dont want to feel guilty of having written it myself.

Till the 15th then — unless by chance I look in on you in New York before then. I may be down about my head. I promised Aroldo Du Chene a sitting or two to finish off what he started almost twenty years ago.　　　Ever yours　Robert

341 · To Richard H. Thornton

RF took part in the dedication ceremonies, held on Sunday, 15 August 1937, in Bennington, Vermont, at the restored Old First Church of Bennington, making it a "colonial shrine" for the state of Vermont. The restoration had been achieved primarily through the zeal and enterprise of the minister of the church, Dr. Vincent Ravi-Booth. Less than four years after the dedication RF bought a plot in the burial ground there, since he could not make satisfactory arrangements for scattering Mrs. Frost's ashes in Derry, as she had requested (see letter 359), and since his son, Carol, had died, on 9 October 1940. Gravestones were ordered and recesses prepared in the ground for the cremation ashes of both Carol and Mrs. Frost. In September of 1941, without ceremony, the urns containing these ashes were committed to the prepared places by RF and his grandson, William Prescott Frost, the only other person in attendance being Lillian Frost.

In June of 1963, and with private ceremony, the urn containing the ashes of RF was committed there by his daughter Lesley.

17 [16] August 1937
South Shaftsbury

Dear Mr. Thornton:

I'm sorry we're so good for nothing these days. We both wanted to see you for a day or so, but neither of us is really up to it. The damned nonsense of yesterday took the tuck all out of me. I never before got mixed up in such a pretentiousness.

445

It was the oldest church in Vermont being rededicated (to I dont know what) after being restored rather beautifully in the image of Mr Rockerfeller, Williamsburg Virginia. It was brag brag brag. I was tricked into it by the wily minister of Scotch-Italian parentage who got up the show and also got up the idea of the Bennington College for Women and Sarah Lawrence. He's been outwitted by the presidents of those colleges and lived to see them teach the radicalism (Muscovite) that he as a Tory hated. But he was smart enough to outwit me. I cant get over it.

Here are Elinors plans for the first part of the book, and my list of the essays to follow. We thought "Recognition of Robert Frost" might be a fairly good name for the book — unless you think of a better.

We are off for Concord Corners Vermont for my hayfever. That will be my address for a few weeks.

Ever yours   Robert Frost

342 · To John Holmes

DURING the late summer of 1936, after making the usual hay-fever retreat to the Fobes Cottage in Franconia, RF decided that he wanted to buy an inexpensive house in the region primarily for use during the hay-fever season. He found and bought two small houses not far over the New Hampshire boundary line at Concord Corners, Vermont. He later sold one of those houses to his friend, the poet John Holmes. RF had been instrumental in arranging to have his own publisher, Holt, bring out Holmes's first volume of poems, *Address to the Living* (1937). The jacket of the book quoted RF in praise of Holmes: "Here are poems again, and it is gratifying to find that they hold their own, even gain, thus assembled from the magazines. They certainly put together into a new and attractive poet."

Mentioned in the following letter is a mutual friend of the two poets: Robert S. Newdick, a Professor of English at Ohio State University, who had recently begun to gather materials for a Frost biography with the consent and assistance of RF.

19 August 1937
Dear John: [Concord Corners, Vermont]
    [. . .] I'm glad the book [*Address to the Living*] has won the extensity of life you speak of. The great thing is it got such good reviewing. I just noticed what a good word it got from Louis Untermeyer in the last of the brevities in the American

446

Mercury. I for my part consider 500 [copies] a fine six months' sale for a first book of poetry. Now for the next step. Always remember the pursuit of poetry is more important than the pursuit of poetic fame. All we need is just enough fame for licence to go ahead.

And speaking of fame, I seriously doubt if I want mine promoted by resort to any such book of garlands from the living as Newdick proposes. Newdick is all right and I like him in most ways — and apparently he likes me in most ways, too. But his zeal for me seems excessive. You can help me there if you will, by abating him if only a little. It would pain me to have even my best friends called on to say my praises. Bromides! My being solicited for Robinson some years ago [on the publication of *Tristram*] went near to destroying our friendship. I got one letter asking me in on a symposium. He knew how much I thought of him. I had put it into a personal letter. I threw the demand (it was from someone named Marsh) into the waste basket. Then I got a second: "Surely you won't fail to be in on this extraordinarily spontaneous outburst of admiration for E. A. Robinson." I stayed out and looked ungenerous. It took Robinson some years to forgive me for behaving so Cordelierly. I might behave more politically now — and I might not. I trust I don't grow too much worn as I grow older. Newdick might manage my apotheosis with discretion. But you and I know how a delicate matter like that is apt to go wrong. I should hate it and suffer over it. And what's more — let me ask you a question. Does it seem egotistical and conceited of me to wonder if I need the advertising? You and he can get in better licks for me out of your own affection in the years to come. Promise not to let the world forget me when my address is some graveyard in Lawrence, Franconia, Amherst, South Shaftsbury, Florida, Texas or California. If the last, the stone could quote Kipling, "Ending as he began." Did you ever hear of the Feather River region in California. It is said to be better for oranges than down where the movies coarsen. "Look for me old fellow of mine" "in a cavern in a canyon" where the ground is getting its second time over for what is second only in my estimation to fame. I got the suggestion for the way to finish from an old man in wet clothes I saw out there washing pay dirt down a long strip of old Brussels carpet he was under obligation to it for. There is no escapism on my part. It is sim-

447

ply an instinct for a place like a nest where lays can be laid. I turn to you for sympathy and understanding.

Ever yours   Robert Frost

343 · To Richard H. Thornton

Dear Mr Thornton: 7 September 1937   Concord Corners

For me to do my best for you [Book Fair, Boston, 9 November 1937] (and I should want a chance to do no less) arrangements ought to give me the evening and at least the half hour you speak of. Those two things are important. The date I leave to you. I am practically free all that part of November. Try to get the most strategic time. Could Fred Melcher advise you whether I had better be early or late in the show?

That puts me in mind: I may as well supply you now with my schedule as so-far made out:

October	13	Clark University Worcester
"	15	Mt Holyoke College
"	20	Hartford (Conn.) Poetry Society
"	25	Haverford College
"	26	Princeton University
November	17	Church Mission of Help, Albany N. Y.

I have had a good two day talk with Newdick and he goes to you loaded to the muzzle with my latest ideas [on *Recognition of Robert Frost*]. The only thing we forgot in making out our list was Christopher Morley. I think he ought to be in among the briefer pieces. Newdick seems willing to help you a lot. And theres a lot to do particularly in the reduction of the things coming under the head of The Idea. And a lot of discretion to be used as to quantity and emphasis. Maybe one or two or three will need to be taken whole. A large part of the book will necessarily come under the head of The Idea. It's the part of the book I am most uneasy about. I think we've got all the earlier sections rather good and amusing. I especially like having Amy Lowell's opinion of my humor on record. It may save me from being thought flippant in my old age. Her article in The New Republic comes in just right under First American Notice. Newdick will discuss with you the possibility of having Ezra Pound in. Ezra probably wouldnt give his consent. Very likely Poetry a Mag of Verse wouldnt give its. Could we quote anyhow?

We had a pleasant picnic with the Newdicks on Willoughby Lake. I hope his thoroughness with the surface of me will wear him through into the depths of me (such as they are). I could well afford to have him find me a little deeper than I am. I wish he would keep on getting delayed by new discoveries below the surface till I am dead and out of hearing. I want to be perpetuated: I want the world told about me. But I dont want to be told about myself.

Ever yours   Robert Frost

344 · To Harold G. Rugg

RF's interest in the forlorn and nearly abandoned village of Concord Corners, Vermont, was heightened by his discovery that Samuel Read Hall had established a training school for teachers there in 1823, that he had written his famous *Lectures on School-Keeping* (1829) there. Knowing of RF's interests, Harold G. Rugg wrote from Hanover that he would like to present a first edition of the *Lectures* to RF. This is the poet's reply.

Dear Rugg: 8 September 1937   Concord Corners

I thought something was said about your looking in on us this summer, domum ferens. Would you like to come up here and present the book ceremoniously on the spot where it was written or, as I understand it, delivered as lectures to the first Normal School in the country, if not the world? That would be fun to remember. You could see our properties, overlooking Samuel Read Hall's Pond and facing the big mountains of New Hampshire. The place to admire New Hampshire from is certainly Vermont. I may write another poem on New Hampshire if I sit up here long enough — and give you the manuscript. I haven't forgotten my promise and good reason: it will mean more to me than to you to have a good piece of manuscript lodged with you [in the Dartmouth College Library] for as long as the bad paper I usually write on can be expected to last. I am very gradually improving my paper, and I've thought perhaps you would prefer to wait till I had something on all-rag. It's a scandal the stuff I've written on. I never thought a thing about it till lately. It is hard for me to feel at home in anything but a five-cent copy book.

449

This is a strange place for me to have landed by luck. It looks as if fate wanted to reconcile me with pedagogy. It will be the last surrender. I have been a long time making my peace with the academic, but I can't be said not to have made it in full.   Sincerely yours   Robert Frost

345 · To Louis Untermeyer

[4 October 1937]

Dear Louis: Hotel Stonehaven   Springfield, Mass.

I tried two or three times yesterday to tell you that Elinor had just been operated on for a growth in her breast. I doubt if she fully realizes her peril. So be careful how you speak in your letters. You can see what a difference this must make in any future we have. She has been the unspoken half of everything I ever wrote, and both halves of many a thing from My November Guest down to the last stanzas of Two Tramps in Mud Time — as you may have divined. I don't say it is quite up with us. We shall make the most of such hope as there is in such cases. She has come through the operation well, though there was delay over her for a day or so at the Hospital for fear her heart wouldn't stand the ether. Her unrealization is what makes it hard for me to keep from speaking to somebody for sympathy. I have had almost too much of her suffering in this world.   Ever yours   R.

346 · To Richard H. Thornton

9 December 1937   The Brown Cottage,

Dear Mr Thornton: Hotel Thomas, Gainesville

Here we are where we meant to be. The climate is at least no colder than it has been in Amherst Mass for the last month. We are north of oranges and right in the middle of the tung nuts. We are looking into the tung nuts with the suspicion acquired in years of general and particular farming. Don't worry about us. I should have to see Franklin D. for personal reassurances before I invested in tung nuts or anything else. All our grandchildren but one are with us to give us a sense of responsibility to the future. . . .

Elinor was very sick after that one day in New York. I suppose I might have kept her out of things by a little lying. But I hate not to have her in things with me. If she is going to have to stay out I must stay out more and more myself. She took a medicated rest in Baltimore before we took the train south. It was a lively train on its track. We felt afterward as if we had come the whole thousand miles on horseback. Now for peace (locally).

Our best to you both and all.   Ever yours   Robert Frost

347 · TO RIDGELY TORRENCE

28 December 1937

Dear Ridgley: 734 Bay St North   Gainesville

Let's play you are poetry editor of the New Republic as of old when the world was happier (because we were young) and these are submitted in fear and trembling. I hope to God you like them, but this is still an unlimited republic, I am not the head of it and you are still free to think anything you please of anything. Not that I hold any brief for not having the licentious mob taught by torture if need be that the mind and heart too for that matter can be regulated to abject obedience to the state. I delight in boys on whom it has dawned that a little brotherhood is worth a lot of bloodshed. They seem uplifted by a new and fresh cant. They become unafraid to be dangerous and it gives them a sense of superiority to those they may have to kill without prejudice. The world is theirs, and the future thereof. They can have it when they get it. But until they do get it, I intend to be just as naughtily an uncollective and un-collected child as the truant officer, the police officer and the post officer permit. And I want you to be — as my friend. Think anything you please. Like anything you please. Always within the law as it used to be and damn the laws ahead which are too hard for our minds anyway.

I had a long talk with Alvin Johnson in the evening after the show [RF's reading at the New School for Social Research, 30 Nov. 1937]. He said I was a Utopian and I said he was a soft-soapian. It came to a point in the discussion of me where he said a man must be a hypocrite if he boasted he had never been caught wanting anything he couldn't have. Now we are

451

getting down to China. There's a very shrewd eft sits at the center of passion even to choose reasonably. Force for fools. For the wise it needn't come to force.

What a New Years letter to one I care for so much and whose I am ever.   R.F.

348 · To Bernard DeVoto

RF's general conservatism, coupled with his outspoken attacks on the New Deal, evoked a variety of leftist attacks against him as poet and man. The appearance of *A Further Range* in June 1936 had been met with a barrage of criticism which included Horace Gregory's review in the *New Republic* for 24 June 1936, Richard Blackmur's in *The Nation* for 24 June 1936, and Newton Arvin's in the *Partisan Review* for June. A poetic defense of RF, made by Robert Hillyer and entitled "A Letter to Robert Frost," appeared in the *Atlantic Monthly* for August 1936; it was answered with an unpublished mocking poetic parody by Granville Hicks entitled "A Letter to Robert Hillyer." But when Hicks submitted it to the *Saturday Review* for publication, Bernard DeVoto, the editor, simply rejected it. DeVoto was eager to get into the fight but was restrained by RF for various reasons until 26 March 1937, when he wrote: "All right, let's hear how good a poet I am" (see letter 339). The article thus authorized was delayed. It finally appeared in the *Saturday Review* for 1 January 1938 under the title, "The Critics and Robert Frost," and was a typically unrestrained piece of savagery. RF received an early copy and acknowledged it as follows.

Dear Benny: 29 December 1937   Gainesville

I sat and let Elinor pour it over me. I took the whole thing. I thought it couldnt do me any harm to listen unabashed to my full praise for once in a way. I said to Sidney Cox years ago that I was non-elatable. While I wasn't actually fishing I suppose I hoped he might see I wanted to be contradicted. All I got out of him was "That's a serious thing for a poet to confess." He was plainly by his tone crediting me with courage of self-betrayal. After hearing all you said in my favor today, I tried it at the wistfullest I could command on Elinor. "What a lie," she answered. "You can't talk in public or private without getting elated. You never write but from elation." Well I trust I am at least heavy-hearted enough to keep my feet on the ground no matter how personally successful I may seem to myself as for instance at this moment. I should like to think I had consideration and considerateness enough to hold myself down and didn't need to be held down by someone else like the triumphant balloon giants in a Macy's Halloween parade up Broadway. Elinor gave me permission to be as depressed as I pleased in emergencies. This is a hard world and it becomes us to pay our respects to its hardness some of the time. But some of the time I was free to bask self-consciously in being generously understood. You may recall the poem I wrote in those stormy March days at Harvard [1936]. I named it "Happiness makes up in height for what it lacks in length."

Yours ever   Robert

Cant you come down for a few days?

348-a · Elinor M. Frost to Nina Thornton

30 December 1937

Dear Nina,-   North Bay St., Gainesville

. . . We are very lucky this year, in coming to Gainesville. The first five days we were here were cold, below the freezing point, but the sun shone steadily all through those days, making things rather cheerful, anyway. And since then, the weather has been so warm we haven't needed any heat in the house, except sometimes in the evening. The sun has shone every day but two since we came. It is wonderful. Moreover, we have more adequate heating than we have had other winters, in case the weather does get cold. We have oil heaters and fireplaces in all three houses. The fireplaces are for soft coal, which burns slowly like what we had in England. It makes a pretty fire, and has the virtue of not going out for hours after it looks quite dead. It can be stirred up and started again. Very likely this kind of coal is what you use in North Carolina.

Carroll, Lillian, Prescott and little Robin are in a house by themselves about a block away — with very large grounds where the children can play. Robert and I are upstairs in a new house, just finished, and Lesley, with her two children, are downstairs. The rents are very reasonable.

We had our tree and our Christmas dinner altogether, over at Carroll's, and everything went smoothly. The children played all day without quarrelling. We have all been very well so far. I rest a great deal of course. The nights here are cool, almost cold, even after warm days, and one needs two or three cotton blankets for covering, which helps me to sleep well. I had trouble sleeping in southern Florida, where the nights were hot and damp.

I hope the next three months will be as good as December, but of course they very likely won't be. . . .

Affectionately,   Elinor Frost

349 · To the Editor of *New Hampshire: A Guide*

REPRESENTING one part of a successful New Deal effort to provide work for the unemployed during the Depression, *New Hampshire: A Guide to the Granite State* (1938) was compiled and written by the "Workers of the Federal Writers' Project of the Works Progress Administration for the State of New Hampshire." The anonymous editor-author of the "General Background" essay on "Literature" apparently asked RF for information about his New Hampshire connections, and the following part of his answer was quoted on page 103 of the *Guide*. It provides a good example of RF's capacity to "turn it on," imaginatively, for an occasion. In his rhetorical reach for hyperbole, he often gave slightly fictitious information. For example, his first teaching position was actually in Methuen, Massachusetts, and the poem entitled "A Servant to Servants" in *North of Boston* is a dramatic portrait of a Vermonter who lived on the northern shore of Willoughby Lake.

[c. January 1938]   [Gainesville]

. . . Not a poem, I believe, in all my six books, from "A Boy's Will" to "A Further Range," but has something in it of New Hampshire. Nearly half my poems must actually have been written in New Hampshire. Every single person in my "North of Boston" was friend or acquaintance of mine in New Hampshire. I lived, somewhat brokenly to be sure, in Salem, Derry, Plymouth, and Franconia, New Hampshire, from my tenth [eleventh] to forty-fifth [forty-sixth] year. Most of my time out of it I lived in Lawrence, Massachusetts, on the edge of New Hampshire, where my walks and vacations could be in New Hampshire. My first teaching was in a district school in the southern part of Salem, New Hampshire. My father was born in Kingston, New Hampshire. My wife's mother was born in New Hampshire. So you see it has been New Hampshire, New Hampshire with me all the way. You will find my poems show it, I think. . . .

350 · To BERNARD DeVOTO

Dear Benny   20 January 1938   Gainesville

Let's see you suppress her [Mary Colum] then. What she's doing seems in biddy bad taste. I got all out of sorts with her public ways once before, when she was around bragging that she destroyed Irving Babbitt's reputation as a scholar. I dont know anything about her own scholarship but I distrust it because she seems to have to establish her authority with diplomas and certificates like a graduate from a business college. Why wouldnt she know more than any American about anything when she has degrees from Dublin University and two or three other Catholic Universities I dont know enough to remember the names of? It is a very presumptuous air of condecension she has been allowed to get away with in our literary world. I wonder if she repeated in her book [*From These Roots*] (which I haven't read) the scorn with which she dismisses William James as an American census-taker who owed everything he ever thought of to Charcot and other Europeans. The thesis seems to be nothing in form or substance can originate here. I asked Perry (what's his first name? Phil Perry it should be) if he could tell me where she got the crack about the census-taker. His indignation was roused. Possibly it was her figure for a sure statistician. I got mad at her on Babbits account. She and Carl Van Doren that platitudinous Latitudinarian made a Roman holiday out of doing Babbitt in on some platform in New York. She liked to tell how she made up to Babbitt afterward out of pity but as soon as he learned her name he drew off and went out alone into the rainy night. There had been some sort of public debate and he had been licked in popular estimation and knew it. As you know I was never humanist, but something cheap about all this got my goat at the time. I got over it and met Molly on friendly terms at Miami. But now I am mad at her manners again. Nothing will do her any good but a thorough showing up where she lives, namely, in scholarship. She is no thinker. That deserves mention. There wasnt an idea in a carload of what she said in Miami. I listened carefully. There was simply an almost girlish airing of the kind of stuff we learn in college Protestant or Catholic and learn to leave out of polite conversation. She took it with a naive seriousness that made me wonder how far back into the eighties and the provinces I had been transported. It seems as if Jonesey [Howard Mumford Jones] himself would want to give you a helping hand with her after a sufficient lapse of time for appearance sake. She not only needs laying as an alien but she needs punishing for our having let her scare us. What's she doing in our country trying to take it down? Does she aim to magnify Europe or only herself? Or is it that we simply give her a pain. She once invaded Lincoln MacVeagh's office with her invective of the fish market. Thats what drove him from publishing clear into diplomacy. When I was mad at her the other time I wrote her up for Gorham B. [Munson] in a letter he may not have forgotten. But I'm not in the business of laming blue stocking shrews. After what Carl Van Doren said for her in Books [New York *Herald-Tribune*] it needs to be said that she contributes not one thing to thought, and doesn't exist in the realm of thought. But the important thing is a little proof that she hasn't even any unusual knowledge. That'll topple her. Supply the proof and save your country.

Ridgley Torrence wrote he didn't see how those three you dealt with for me [in "The Critics and Robert Frost"] would ever get up from the slaughter house floor. I'll send you a poem in memory of one of the three. I hadnt noticed him lately or I might have written it sooner. You recalled my attention to him.

Gee we're sorry you have so much real sickness. Perhaps its a mistake after all to have only one child. Perhaps God sends so much sickness to a family and where the family is large each child has to do with less to make it go round. That just occurred to us. We've sometimes had our doubts about the advantage of having large families. Just in this one particular of sickness. Don't misunderstand me.

What do you suppose we keep our curiosity packed in that we havent asked you in so many words what the changes are you speak of so mysteriously?   Ever yours   R. F.

351 · To Lawrance Thompson

RF gave a talk, "The Poet's Next of Kin in a College," and a reading of his poems at Princeton University on 26 October 1937. A record of the talk was made at the request of Thompson, who asked permission to publish it in *Biblia,* a periodical issued by the Friends of the Princeton Library. RF answered by telegram, "YES, IF YOU WILL

UNDERTAKE TO MAKE IT READ LIKE SOMETHING. CUTTING MIGHT HELP." Before it was published (February 1938), RF wrote this letter.

Dear Lawrence: [c. 21] January 1938   Gainesville

I'm not anxious to hear that you printed my speech on The Poet[']s Next of Kin but I am to hear that if you printed it or tried to print it it didnt get you into trouble with the athletic authorities. I assume you got my telegram of permission. You know my feeling about these speeches. I am getting less and less reluctant to have them published. Thats because my scattered thoughts of a lifetime are beginning to group up into natural shapes. You can always have the forced shapes the department teaches. Give me Doors for a subject and I can elaborate it by plan till it is as big as an essay without a real sentence having been written or a happy thought having been had. I was asked the other day by an otherwise good teacher if I laid out such a thing as The Death of the Hired Man. My way of writing seemed inconceivable to him. My prose if I ever produce any will have to be written like my verse. — Not very important to us, but I confess to an uneasiness as to how bad a stir my brutal heresies left behind me at Princeton.

Ever yours   Robert Frost

351-a · ELINOR M. FROST TO WILLARD E. FRASER

Dear Willard,   26 January [1938]   [Gainesville]

I hope your warmish weather continued a long time. You are certainly building under difficulties, having to guard the premises by night. What an extraordinary state of affairs! But have you read of the awful state the labor situation is in, on U. S. merchant ships? And it is entirely due to Roosevelt's encouragement of the C. I. O. Many people have realized from the first that some of his advisors wished to ruin business, so the government could take it over and turn us into a state socialism. I think that event isn't far off.

I wish Wheeler wouldn't support the anti-lynching bill. It's just another blow to state's rights. Lynching is diminishing in the south. Women all around down here have formed societies against it. It is just to court the northern negro vote.

Well — I am not bothering much about politics now. I am

really not strong enough. I am rather weak, to tell the truth, and don't imagine I shall ever feel much more vigorous. But there is no sign of any growth starting any where, and that is something to be thankful for. All the folks here are well. Lesley is *very much* better. Robin is fine, and lively. She is going to a very superior nursery school, and enjoys it — immensely.

We have had lovely warm weather for a while — one day it was 84° in the afternoon. Today is cold again. It must be almost down to freezing, I think — and the wind is blowing, which is unusual here except in the fall. Write again soon.

Affectionately Elinor

351-b · G. R. ELLIOTT TO ROBERT FROST

15 February 1938

Dear Robt: 23 Orchard St.   Amherst

Just now I received a letter . . . in reminiscent and appreciative vein. I am too old a bird to be moved much; this is my thirtieth year of teaching; and I have received stacks of letters to the same general effect. But as I read this letter, I began to recall vaguely that someone, not long ago, accused me of intimidating my students — or infuriating them — no, no, that was not the word; it was "indoctrinating." That was it. And it was YOU, R. Lee Frost (Arlee Frost), that said that word to me, right in this room. So you'd better read the following extract . . .

"I now know that when I was your student you did not so much give me ideas, you made my own natural ideas articulate. What you did give me, and what stays in my mind as my real debt to you, lasting and without price, is a real feeling for literature. . . . Harry H. Clark, here, said to me one day: 'Elliott is a humanist: how does he do it in class?' I replied that you didn't; I meant, doctrines are very subordinate with you. . . ."

Brown also says that though he was much obsessed with Babbitt's humanism while here, it was not I that caused that: the cause was his own New-England nature, appealed to by Babbitt. And I recall, now, how young Brown used to bore me with Babbitt-talk. That happens with one or two of my students every year or so. Babbitt and More are of course references in my work, when I am treating poets upon whom they wrote; but the boys know that I am always critical of their attitude to poetry.

Now, I wonder who it was that told you that I inosculate — no, indoctrinate — my students? Probably it was one of my least sensible boys. But do not tell me who it was. But the next time you see him, tell him I said he is a pussy-cat, a blinking, winking, slinking, stinking, padding, puffing, purring, scratching, poisonous pie-faced Poosy-Cat!!!

[. . .] . . . indoctrinating them? I cannot stop that because I do not do it. . . .

Are you going to publish your next book through Holts? Don't.

> Holts?
> They're dolts
> In need of jolts.

Having sloughed off shingles (the virus disease), I feel that Amherst is a great college. We have an excellent president, a thoughtful faculty, and, above all, a superb student-body. . . . I am now chairman of this department and I am working hard to get discipline, loyalty, cooperation, *secrecy,* etc. into this department. I am very autocratic. So watch out, Arlee! Toe the mark, or me and [President] Stanley [King] —????? Yours for more and more efficiency,

G. R. Elliott,   Chairman

352 · To G. R. Elliott

Dear Roy   [c. 21 February 1938]   [Gainesville]

That's the way I like to hear you talk back to your critic. I get a vicarious satisfaction out of seeing anybody's critic laid low. You can say things as a teacher that I simply cant as a writer. A good Anglican calls me in print, "the last sweepings of the Puritan latrines." There is nothing for me in my position but to suffer him in silence and try to sleep him off. I will tell the young man what you call him, since it is your wish. He will never get up from the slaughter-house floor. Not though you canvas every boy you ever taught will you find out who he is. He will be too scared to own up. But I'll make him sorry. Leave him to me. Let me say this for him however: I doubt if he meant as much as you get out of it. I didn't take it that he was complaining of humanism and your connection with

Babbitt and More. My assumption was that you had been wracking the devil in him with your Christianity. He is a sadly sinful young man such as for the sake of whom I could conceive of your saying to a class, as you said to me once, one can no more be religious, outside of the church than one can be patriotic without belonging to a country. (You should have said, without belonging to the army.) I don't believe it is even in bad taste for you to talk in that missionary way. The righteous are licensed "to teach babes in brace their grammar." I didn't say what I said as heavily as you seem to take it. I just wanted to be sure if you were going to use poetry for the salvation of souls you had counted the cost to poetry. But you deny in your letter that you ever had used poetry for the salvation of souls. Really it would be all right with me if you had. Use poetry or friendship or anything else you please to corner me for my soul's salvation. We are all each other's keepers. Look at Japan in China, England in India. — I'd like to know what my publishers have to do with all this. Does their book advertising me [*Recognition of Robert Frost*] offend you? I think myself it was hardly a book to sell. It started out not to be. But it got bigger than they thought they could afford to give away and they decided to make it big enough to sell. I couldn't blame them much in the very hard times I know they are having. They saw a chance to get some clean profit without paying me royalties. Perhaps having gone so far in the direction of the omnibus they should have gone the rest of the way and included a fair proportion of the out-and-out hostile in my criticism. Much that they did include is in effect adverse. Many parts of it cancel other parts I can see without reading it. — Or have the Holts been rejecting some book of yours for some very bad silly reason? I'll tell you this about them: their literary department is pretty nearly on the rocks. I have my doubts of their future. This in confidence.

Jesus Christ! let's be Christians. The place seemed to go screaming wild with fear of DeVoto. All is calm now or can be calm I hope. I don't fail to note you underline secrecy in your letter. Is that for my benefit too? Well well Roy, be patient with me but a little longer. Maybe when my slight connection with the department [of English at Amherst College] is severed I'll be more than   ever yours   R. F.

353 · To R. P. T. Coffin

AT THE annual dinner of the Poetry Society of America in New York City on 1 April 1937, RF had been the guest of honor. He had talked on "Crudities" and then had combined those remarks with others on "Opposites." Coffin, having heard the talk, wrote to ask if RF could send him notes on it; Coffin wished to use them in preparing lectures he was to give at Johns Hopkins University in Baltimore. This is RF's first answer, but further encouragement from Coffin elicited a second answer (see letter 356).

Dear Coffin,   24 February 1938   Gainesville

It is my bad luck I am away off down here where I can't help you help me. I suppose you have nothing to call you even part way in this direction till you come to Baltimore for your lectures. I would venture some way into the cold but I mustn't come so far as to seem inconsistent to those with whom I have used the cold as an excuse to stay away from their platforms and dinner tables. A lot would come out in talk once you got me started with what you happened to remember of that Poetry Society affair. I'm terrible about my lectures. In my anxiety to keep them as long as possible from becoming part of my literary life, I leave them rolling round in my head like clouds rolling round in the sky. Watch them long enough and you'll see one near-form change into another near-form. Though I am sure they are hardly permissable on the platform, I continue to bring them there with no more apology than to a parlor or class room. Their chief value to me is for what I pick up from them when I cut across them with a poem under emotion. They have been my inner world of raw material and my instinct has been to keep them raw. That can't long retain their state however. The day approaches when they will lose their fluidity and in spite of my stirring spoon become crystal. Then one kind of fun will be over and I shall have to find another to take its place (tennis most likely or hoeing). I thought I was about ready to let them set when I accepted the Harvard invitation to deliver them in writing after delivering them by word of mouth. Something in me still fights off the written prose. The nearest I ever came to getting myself down in prose was in the preface to Robinson's *King Jasper*. That is so much me that you might suspect the application to him of being forced. It was really no such thing. We two were close akin up to a certain point of thinking. He would have trusted me to

461

go a good way in speaking for him particularly on the art of poetry. We only parted company over the badness of the world. He was cast in the mold of sadness. I am neither optimist nor pessimist. I never voted either ticket. If there is a universal unfitness and unconformity as of a buttoning so started that every button on the vest is in the wrong button hole and the one empty button hole at the top and the one naked button at the bottom so far apart they have no hope of getting together, I don't care to decide whether God did this for the fun of it or for the devil of it. (The two expressions come to practically the same thing anyway.) Then again I am not the Platonist Robinson was. By Platonist I mean one who believes what we have here is an imperfect copy of what is in heaven. The woman you have is an imperfect copy of some woman in heaven or in someone else's bed. Many of the world's greatest — maybe all of them — have been ranged on that romantic side. I am philosophically opposed to having one Iseult for my vocation and another for my avocation; as you may have inferred from a poem called Two Tramps in Mud Time. You see where that lands me on the subject of Dante's Beatrice. Mea culpa. Let me not sound the least bit smug. I define a difference with proper humility. A truly gallant Plantonist will remain a bachelor as Robinson did from unwillingness to reduce any woman to the condition of being used without being idealized.

But you didn't ask me to distinguish between myself and Robinson. I fell accidentally into a footnote to the *King Jasper* preface in self defence. What you asked for is any recollection I have of my recent talks. I may be able to bring some of them back in detail — give me time. What in the world did I say in New York. Was my subject "Neither or Both." Do you want to show me the notes you made? Is there time? I'm going to hurry this off tonight for a beginning and then if you say so try to tell you a little more. One of my subjects at Harvard was Does Wisdom Matter. I mean in art. Does it matter for instance that I am so temperamentally wrong about Beatrice. You can hear more if it is worth your while. Another subject was The Renewal of Words. Molly Colum had been saying the world was old, people were jaded and the languages worn out. My whole lecture was an answer to her defeatism, though I took good care not to name her — and don't you name her. Poetry is the renewal of words forever and ever. Poetry is that by which we live forever and ever unjaded. Poetry is that by which the world is never old. Even the poetry of trade names gives the

462

lie to the unoriginal who would drag us down in their own powerlessness to originate. Heavy they are but not so heavy that we can't rise under them and throw them off.

Well well well ――――――

Sincerely yours   Robert Frost

354 · To RIDGELY TORRENCE

Dear Ridgely: 24 February 1938   Gainesville

Somehow I got it into the back of my head from your letter that you were sending me some poetry of your own. A vague expectancy has been hanging about me so that every once in so often I will ask myself Let's see what was I expecting? But on looking back at your letter I find that what you said was you weren't sending some poetry. All right then I'll never send you any more. How am I going to know who I am dealing with unless I see what you are writing in these last days of the world? You speak lightly of our personal age. How am I to judge your mental age without any samples of your verse? How am I to tell whether you care whether the world goes to Hell or not? I certainly don't. I've got another world. You may say (but you don't) Tenderness forbids that I talk in this heartless way about a world so populous. That brings up the question of how tender we have to be now-a-days or else get shot. Well let them make a law establishing a standard of tenderness. Some bootcher in Congress could draw it up. I'm perfectly willing to be legal tender.

Ever yours anyway   Robert Frost

355 · To BERNARD DEVOTO

Dear Benny: 6 March 1938   Gainesville

Those who can write, will ― "save by an evil chance." Writing is like anything else: it is a possession with some people. They cant let it alone and they forsake all else for it. My how justly you can say a thing right from where you live. It's a comfort to think those unbalanced bastards neednt cease to tremble simply because you have relieved them of your editorship of the Saturday Review. First they put on a false air (hair) of being the movers and shakers of the world forever it seems. They know a damsite better, but that pose does something for them for a few decades that it seems they cant get along without. Now theyre abnegating — all going down in droves of self-disgust. They don't mean it either way. They are just so made that they cant help taking up solemnly with the idea some original like Shaw says for fun. Aren't they really terrible? I ask you, because I'm getting too old to trust myself in judging infantilism any more. I suppose poets have about as much influence on the course of events as business men. Anyway they have as much as is good for themselves or the world. I really hate to think of my verse as of great or little influence. There will be pretty work in the Saturday Review in days to come no doubt; it will have a hard time being as pretty as your last editorial (and several besides).

Ill be home soon now. I want to hear more of your plans for the future. You'd better go up into Vermont and write for a while. I have more than half a mind to do that very thing myself. Wait till I tell you all that has been happening at Amherst to make me sick of the smallness of academic ways. I dont blame the professors too much for their hostility to the writers out in the world. They have their own positions to magnify and defend. I have to remember the college is the whole of their life whereas it is only a very small part of mine. But my English department werent very good to me about the incursion of Louis [Untermeyer]. George Whicher attended all four lectures; none of the others, even for my sake, would show the least interest. It was all right, but deliver them from my friends. It is not enough consolation that Louis had a triumph with the house-full that came. I say Love me love what's mine. And I am in a position to enforce that rule. What puts me in that position and keeps me there is my recklessness of consequence.

Well well well any resentment I have against anybody I can leave to you to take out on Edmund Wilson. (Look at what, in that long article in the Saturday Review, Lyons praises him for saying.) Let's agree on him as your favorite scapegoat.

Till I see you then — R.

356 · To R. P. T. Coffin

Dear Coffin: [c. 7 March 1938]   [Gainesville]
    Your letter [see the editor's note preceding letter 353] brings back my animus of that April 1st. I was gunning for the

kind of Americans who fancied themselves as the only Americans incapable of crudity. I started off with some crudity I knew they could join me in laughing at and I ended up with some they might not be so incapable of themselves. But I protested all the way along my love of crudity. I thank the Lord for crudity which is rawness, which is raw material, which is the part of life not yet worked up into form, or at least not worked all the way up. Meet with the fallacy of the foolish: having had a glimpse of finished art, they forever after pine for a life that shall be nothing but finished art. Why not a world safe for art as well as democracy. A real artist delights in roughness for what he can do to it. He's the brute who can knock the corners off the marble block and drag the unbedded beauty out of bed. The statesman (politician) is no different except that he works in a protean mass of material that hardly holds the shape he gives it long enough for him to point it out and get credit for it. His material is the rolling mob. The poet's material is words that for all we may say and feel against them are more manageable than men. Get a few words alone in a study and with plenty of time on your hands you can make them say any thing you please.

You remember the story of the neighbor who asked me how much I got apiece for my books. Then there was the man who after telling me for hours about his big bold business adventures asked me toward morning what I did with myself. I staved off the confession. I likened myself to him in adventurousness. I was a long-shot man too. I liked not to know beforehand what the day might bring forth. And so till he lost patience with me and cried "Shoot!" Well I write poetry. "Hell," he said unhappily "my wife writes that stuff." And it turned out she did. I came on a book of her verse at the house of the President of Sophie Newcomb in New Orleans where she lived and her husband visited. I must tell you the latest. A forty year old telegraph operatress had drawn her own inference from my telegrams. "You write," she said to me one day. "Yes." — "Poetry?" "Yes." "Just the person I'm looking for then. I lost my father a year or so ago and I'd like to get a poem written about him. I'll tell you what I want said." She took paper and pencil. — But how much better or worse was she than the man [Hermann Hagedorn] out of Harvard, New York, real society and literature who came a long way to ask me to write something American to save America? He was sure I could write something really American if I tried. But I must remember to like crudity even in high places and I must be willing to be crude myself for other people's purposes.

In my book of 1923 [*New Hampshire*] I dealt with the crude importunacy of those who would have you a prude or a puke (mewling and puking in the public arms). Choose you this day to be a puke or be disowned by the intelligensia. Fifteen years have gone by and the almost equally disgusting alternatives offered are collectivist or rugged individualist. (Can you bear it?) Here I have to recall myself as a workman to my duty of liking crudity in however amused a way. In this connection I probably told the story of my getting called a counter-revolutionary for not writing my poetry "tendential." By tendential in politics they mean what is sure to happen. After making sure it is going to happen, they don't trust it to happen of itself: they take hold and make it happen. Just so the horsey bets on a sure thing and then does all that in him lies with dope and counter dope, sponges in the nose, bribery and threat to make the sure thing surer. There is a horrid crudity of morals in our idealistic tendential friends. But I must stick to it that I like crudity.

Hegel saw two people marry and produce a third person. That was enough for Hegel — and Marx too it seems. They jumped at the conclusion that so all truth was born. Out of two truths in collision today sprang the one truth to live by tomorrow. A time succession was the fallacy. Marriage, reproduction and the family with a big F have much to answer for in misleading the analogists. Fire flashes from the flint and steel of metaphor and if caught in lint it may be spread, but that is no reason why it should spread to burn the world. That is monomania or monometaphor.

Take Justice and Mercy (you got my pairs of opposing goods exactly). A mind where there was a mind wouldn't think of them as breeding a third thing to live on after they are dead and gone. Justice and Mercy stand each other off and the present stands up between them. Divine Right and Consent do the same with the same result. They are like the two hands that, by first tightening and then loosening the double string between them, make the tin buzzer buzz like a little buzz saw. You must have played with a tin buzzer on the Kennebeck.

Mind where there was a mind would be ashamed to have been radical when young only to be conservative when old.

Life sways perilously at the confluence of opposing forces. Poetry in general plays perilously in the same wild place. In
particular it plays perilously between truth and make-believe.
It might be extravagant poetry to call it true make believe —
or making believe what is so.

Of course use anything you can or will. It's a good idea to
leave out people's names.

I thought my Education by Poetry [a talk by RF, published in *Amherst Graduates' Quarterly*, February 1931]
might help. It was taken down without my knowledge.

Ever yours R. F.

357 · To Louis Untermeyer

Dear Louis: [10 March 1938]   [Gainesville]
Your book [*Play in Poetry*] is more than a keen interest:
it's an out-and-out pleasure. And how well it shaped up as you
cut it for the Saturday Review. As your extra essay rounded
off the book I thought Benny DeVoto's editorial capped your
article. This accidental team work suggests what you and he
and I could do to these times if we wanted to stage a deliberate putch. But we are reserved for better things than steam-
rolling over our enemies. Only I confess my imagination is possessed with the magnificence of the forces let loose in action all
round us and I am tempted to wish I was one of them instead
of what I am. Two years ago I half wanted to be a Senator
(none knows how.) Now I'm caught thinking I'd like to gang
up with a few friends and run a magazine a few numbers for
the rectification of public thought. Luckily this plethoric energy didnt manifest itself when I was younger or you might
have seen me a ward politician working for Tammany.

Thanks for the discretion of your Phi Beta Kappa review
of my recognition [see note to 303-a]. Gee I have had some
queer feelings about that book. We have to remember it is
chiefly an advertisement. It can't help making me wonder what
I am though. The best of your criticism of me all these years is
that you have never treated me as welfare-minded or of social
significance. Its an accident that the welfare-minded have made
a path to my door. I don't consider myself to blame for their
mistake. Ferner Nuhn (Henry Wallace's ghost writer) is still
at me for having led him on with North of Boston to expect
better of me than A Further Range. Its his damned party poli-

tics. I tried to tell him and his like in the Need of Being Versed in Country Things that my subject was not the sadness of the poor. He puts his finger on The Lockless Door with uncanny shrewdness, but not enough to quite bring him through. He says the rich in their top hats knocked at my cottage door and though having provided no way to keep them out I retired through a back window and left the place to them, it was only to join them mischievously by circling round behind and taking their view of the house I had built. Funny but except for one person Robert Von Mos[c]hzisker all the rich who ever came to my door were the conde[s]cending welfare minded and they came under the mistaken impression that what I had built was a house of the poor. I was flattered by their attention and I decided to let them have the house any way they would. I wanted to be honest with them in all gentleness: and I satisfied my conscience with hints at the truth, as in the last part of the poem New Hampshire and in The Need of Being Versed in Country Things. But lately I have been getting cross with their fatuosity. My house may be only a one-room shack but it is not the Poor House: it is the Palace of Art. North of Boston is merely a book of people, not of poor people. They happen to be people of simplicity or simple truth miscalled simplicity. Before I get through I'm going to drive these social servitors back to the social settlements or to concentration camps where I can starve their sympathies to death. [. . .]

R. F.

358 · To Willard E. Fraser

21 MARCH 1938   GAINESVILLE

ANOTHER SORROW. ELINOR DIED TODAY OF HEART ATTACK.

ROBERT FROST

358-a · Hervey Allen to John Farrar and Stanley Rinehart

22 March 1938

Dear John and Stan: The Glades, Coconut Grove

[. . .] Am running up for a day or two to Gainesville, Florida — about a day's run — because of the serious condition in which Robert Frost is. You know his wife died. She has

been sent to Jacksonville to be cremated and there will be a funeral at Amherst later. I talked to the University of Florida people this morning, where Frost has been lecturing, and they say he is in a state of complete collapse. They seemed to have the jitters themselves and almost fell on the telephone when I mentioned I might come up. I don't know just what I can do, but I may be able to help and as Frost is really so great a person and we all have an enormous feeling of gratitude and affection for him I am taking a little time off just on the chance of being helpful. Probably by the time you get this I shall be back at "The Glades" again. Anyway I shall keep in touch. With best wishes to you both.
Faithfully, Hervey

359 · To Carol Frost

Dear Carol: [c. 5 April 1938] [Gainesville]
Well, you're hard at work up there and that must be some comfort. I hope you have an interesting summer. You'll be getting new trees and baby chicks and I suppose putting on the dormant spray. There was nothing Elinor wanted more than to have you take satisfaction out of that home and farm. I wish you would remember it every day of your life.

We plan to have the funeral either on Friday April 15th or on Monday or Tuesday of the week following. Something will depend on when the minister can come. I am going to ask Sidney Snow of Chicago to read some poem or two that she liked and some not too religious verses from the Bible. Stanley King says we can use either the College Church or the Chapel. In the College Church there is a side room where the family could sit out of sight. I don't believe there is any privacy to be had in the Chapel. But the Chapel means more to me. It is a beautiful room and the pulpit has been one of my chief speaking places. I don't know if she ever heard me there, but she was always waiting anxiously at home to hear how my talk came out. The Chapel has had so much to do with our position at Amherst that my sentiment is for it. Maybe Otto [Manthey-Zorn] will know of a place to keep out of sight there. We'll see.

Lesley is getting Rosa down from New York to take care of the children while she comes north with me for the funeral. After the funeral we can all drive over to Derry and scatter the ashes out in the alders on the Derry farm if the present owner will let us.* By all I mean just the family and perhaps one or two of our closest friends.

I shall be working hard myself at lecturing in May.

Affectionately   Papa

360 · To Hervey Allen

Dear Hervey: 12 April 1938   Gainesville

> And I the last go forth companionless
> And the days darken round me.

But it is written also by the same hand,

> Let darkness keep her raven gloss.

I shall never forget your coming to me with such sympathy.

Ever yours   Robert

361 · To Bernard DeVoto

Dear Bennyvenuto: 12 April 1938   Gainesville

I expect to have to go depths below depths in thinking before I catch myself and can say what I want to be while I last. I shall be all right in public, but I can't tell you how I am going to behave when I am alone. She could always be present to govern my loneliness without making me feel less alone. It is now running into more than a week longer than I was ever away from her since June 1895. You can see how I might have doubts of myself. I am going to work very hard in May and be on the go with people so as not to try myself solitary too soon.

I suppose love must always deceive. I'm afraid I deceived her a little in pretending for the sake of argument that I didn't think the world as bad a place as she did. My excuse was that I wanted to keep her a little happy for my own selfish pleasure. It is as if for the sake of argument she had sacrificed her life to give me this terrible answer and really bring me down in sor-

---

* The ashes of Mrs. Frost were not scattered. RF made a preliminary visit to the farm in Derry, talked with the owner about the possibility, and felt enough misgivings about the attitude of the owner to cause him to abandon his plan. The urn containing the ashes was eventually buried in Old Bennington. See editor's note to letter 341.

row. She needn't have. I knew I never had a leg to stand on, and I should think I had said so in print.

All the same I believe a lot of mitigating things, and anything I say against the universe must be taken with that qualification. I always shrank from hearing evil of poor little Edgar Allen Poe and my reason was when I come to search it out of my heart, that he wrote a prose poem out of those lovely old lines

> Stay for me there I will not fail
> To meet thee in the hollow vale.

What is more he used a cadence caught from the Exequy to make the whole of his poem The Sleeper. Never mind that he couldn't be tender without being ghoulish. You have to remember he was little Edgar Allen Poe.

We are to have a funeral over the ashes I bring home at Johnson Chapel Amherst College at three oclock in the afternoon of Friday April 22. Perhaps I wish a little that my friends who can easily will come. I dont know how you feel about such things. I am uncertain. Of course there is no question of her honor. You and I and others will take care of that in more important ways wont we?   Ever yours   Robert

362 · To Mr. and Mrs. G. R. Elliott

Dear Roy and Alma: [13 April 1938]   [Gainesville]

I am coming back to Amherst on Tuesday or Wednesday for some more of the finalities I haven't yet learned to accept with the flesh. Otto and Ethel [Manthey-Zorn] have asked me to their house since I don't seem to want to see the inside of my own. It will be good of you if you will do as you said about John, Irma and Jack. I *wish* the whole family could be together, but we can be later. I shall probably wander round among them for a while till I can decide who I am now, and what I have to go on with. Some of the old ambitious resolutions may come back to me in some form. The danger will be that they may too openly concern her. Pretty nearly every one of my poems will be found to be about her if rightly read. But I must try to remember they were as much about her as she liked and permitted them to be. Without ever saying a word

471

she set limits I must continue to observe. One remark like this and then no more forever.   Faithfully yours   Robert

363 · To WILLARD E. FRASER

Dear Willard: 28 July 1938   South Shaftsbury

We're glad to hear of your progress in politics. Now the Legislature and next Congress. Be a Senator when you get round to it. I looked in on them at work down there when I came by in May. I liked the Senate best. But that will wait till you are forty if FDR doesn't purge it so drastically it dies of colera morbus. Don't think I would care personally. I like our institutions, but I would be willing to sacrifice any one of them for social excitement. Every time I meet anyone whose income is under two thousand five hundred I get so sad I would be willing to sacrifice not only the Supreme Court but Magna Charta itself. Wouldn't you?

This is just a word leading up to the subject. Wouldn't it be a good idea just to leave Robin with us in the east this year as long as the summer is so far along and the time so near when we could give her another winter in the south. I thought you were planning to take the asthma cure with us this fall. You could satisfy your fatherly [love] for her then. For her own good I don't suppose she ought to be kicking back and forth between us after she gets much older. You'll probably have to have her out there, though if you get to Congress soon enough you might like to make your headquarters with us and let us help you bring her up. Lesley has become assistant director of the King-Smith Studio School in Washington; which will mean her having a home there where I shall spend some of my time.

About my visit to Laramie in November. It is going to be a very hurried one between engagements in New York and Boston, so I can't promise to branch out sideways very far. I should like to get to Boulder and Billings. I shall know more about possibilities when I have the details about Laramie. They're going to do me some honor at the [Wyoming] State University. I can't scant them on time.   Affectionately   R. F.

You may have heard of my having given up Amherst. There were all sorts of things in it. But it was a step I had thought of for several years. It leaves me with greatly reduced income

but with more freedom to do any writing I may have left to do and relieved of an obscure anxiety to please people that I imperfectly understood.
R. F.

364 · To CHARLES DAVID ABBOTT

Dear Mr. Abbott: 14 August 1938   South Shaftsbury
Of course I should enjoy seeing you and Buffalo again. There is additional inducement in the news you will have to give me of the old friends in England with whom I should be exchanging letters but amn't. What should you say to my coming on my way back from Iowa in the second week in November — early in the week? I shall be a seasoned veteran of the season by then. Columbia, Ohio State and Iowa will be behind me.
Yours ever   Robert Frost

365 · To JOHN S. VAN E. KOHN

A POET in his own right and a collector of first editions before he became a New York dealer in rare books, John Kohn specialized in finding and selling Frostiana. In this capacity he had become acquainted with RF. The following letter begins with RF's acknowledgment of an unusual gift from Kohn: a local history of Coös County in New Hampshire, containing an anecdote which had originally inspired RF's poem "The Witch of Coös."

Dear Mr. Kohn: [c. 24 August 1938]   [Bread Loaf]
Your Coos County History received, read with great interest and elevated to a place on my shelves. You have done so much for me and my books that I hesitate to ask you to do more. The nature of my request is a peculiar one. I want my two first books, first printing in first binding, and I want to pay the market price of the moment. Can you supply me with either or both? I have a very special sentimental use for them.
I liked your horrible fear of where I might come out with my Young Wretch [in the poem "To a Young Wretch"]. That's the way I want to be watched by my friends and may I perish when I fail to keep them thinking what I will do next.
Ever yours   Robert Frost

Notice my address till September 1   Bread Loaf   Vt
After that it will be Concord Corners for a week or two.

473

366 · To John S. Van E. Kohn

Dear Mr Kohn: 2 September 1938   Concord Corners

    I am in a mood to accept any sacrifice from anyone man or woman. And I think it would be unromantic of me not to accept ruthlessly your romantic offer of my two firsts though one of them has to come out of your personal collection. But you are not to be allowed the only price-fixing. I propose to do some of it myself. I enclose my check for two hundred and fifty dollars, that is to say, one hundred for A Boy's Will and one hundred and fifty for North of Boston. The destination of the books is such and my obligation for favors so great there, that the more I pay for the books the more my gratification. It is a case where there is no pleasure in discounts. And there must be this understanding that when you find another copy of A Boy's Will you will charge me with anything it costs you above a hundred dollars. All this appeals to my imagination and you must indulge me cheerfully and without compunction. You shall be my witness that on this day I bought for two hundred and fifty dollars books of my own that twenty five years before I could have bought for exactly four shillings or one dollar. The transaction flatters me I suppose. The sooner I have the books the happier I shall be.   Yours ever   Robert Frost

VIII

BOSTON, HARVARD, MIAMI, AND RIPTON · 1938-1943

ONE LIFE CLOSED for Robert Frost when his wife died, and for some time it seemed impossible that he would want to make another life. Soon after the memorial service at Amherst College, on 20 April 1938, Frost resigned from his academic duties there, sold his home, and went to stay with Carol in South Shaftsbury. Apparently at loose ends, he seemed indifferent as to where he would live or what he would do.

But some of his Harvard friends wanted to draw him back to the world. One of them was David McCord, a poet in his own right and executive secretary of the Harvard Fund Council. So swiftly did these friends work that in June of 1938 Frost was elected to the Board of Overseers at Harvard College. Even earlier, a plan had been set afoot to make him a lecturer at Harvard.

Closely associated with McCord in these schemes was Theodore Morrison, also a poet, who supervised the English A course at Harvard. He and his wife, Kathleen, had entertained the Frosts in Cambridge during the spring of 1936. Morrison was also the Director of the Bread Loaf Writers' Conference, which Frost had indirectly helped to found. During the summer of 1938, Morrison invited Frost to extend his stay at Bread Loaf, and the invitation was accepted. It was in this way that the Morrisons began to assist Frost when he desperately needed the attention and affection of friends.

That summer at Bread Loaf, Kathleen Morrison helped the poet to handle his mail and make his arrangements for the fall schedule of readings. After McCord had assured him that plans were well under way to bring him back to Harvard as "Ralph Waldo Emerson Fellow in Poetry," Frost took up residence in Boston. In the autumn of 1938, Kathleen Morrison continued as his secretary and schedule planner.

475

Almost desperately Frost threw himself into a strenuous schedule of talks and readings during the next few months. On 10 May 1939, McCord's promise was kept when a public announcement was made that Frost had been appointed Ralph Waldo Emerson Fellow in Poetry at Harvard. The next summer Frost returned to Bread Loaf, purchased the Homer Noble Farm nearby, shared it with the Morrisons, and converted a guest-house cabin on the farm into a private retreat. His friends had helped him to avoid a complete collapse, and he felt that he owed his new life or what was left of his old life to the Morrisons; he frequently said so. In the spring of 1941 he purchased a house near the Morrisons, at 35 Brewster Street in Cambridge and moved into it.

Doctors had repeatedly warned Frost that his susceptibility to bronchial ailments, particularly to pneumonia, made it advisable for him to avoid the coldest months of the year. During the winter of 1940, while staying briefly in Coconut Grove, Florida, as a guest of Hervey and Ann Allen, he looked for a small winter home in that neighborhood. The Allens helped him find and buy five acres of undeveloped property nearby, and within the next few years Frost erected two small prefabricated houses on the property. The entry of the United States into the Second World War delayed the construction, but as soon as the first house was built, the poet established a pattern of annual migration — Massachusetts, Florida, Vermont — which continued for the rest of his life.

Early in January each year he would leave Cambridge and go by train to "Pencil Pines" on Davis Road in South Miami, usually remaining there until late in March. On his way down or back he would stop off regularly to give readings at several colleges: most often at Agnes Scott in Decatur, Georgia, frequently at the University of Georgia in Athens, occasionally at the University of North Carolina in Chapel Hill, less frequently at Duke University in nearby Durham; once in a while at the University of Virginia in Charlottesville. By the end of March he would usually be back at 35 Brewster Street. But before the end of May he would be taken by the Morrisons to the Homer Noble Farm in Ripton, where he would often stay alone for a few weeks, with neighbors enough to look after his needs. As soon as vacation time started at Harvard, the Morrisons would drive up to the farm with their two children, and would remain until fall. In the summer months Frost would regularly take part in the two separate programs at Bread Loaf; in the fall he would return to Cambridge with the Morrisons. During Christmas vacation he would enjoy a brief taste of Vermont winter with the Morrisons, when they were able to take him there, but he usually started for Florida early in January. And so the pattern repeated itself year after year.

It was not greatly changed when he accepted the invitation in 1943 of his first alma mater, Dartmouth, to spend a limited amount of time there each semester as the "George Ticknor Fellow in the Humanities." He liked to say that he merely commuted to Dartmouth from Cambridge. The house at 35 Brewster Street remained his fall and spring home until his death.

367 · To Carol Frost

AFTER SPENDING the summer of 1938 in Vermont, RF had gone to Amherst to arrange a move to Boston. The hurricane which swept New England on 21 September 1938 overtook him on his way by train from Springfield to Boston, as explained in this letter.

Dear Carol: [26 September 1938]   [Boston]

I was glad to hear you had suffered no serious loss from wind or water at the farm. I should have supposed the Northern Spies would all fall off and some of the larger trees be broken.

I set out from Springfield to go to Boston at a little after noon. Already the water was too high for the direct route. So my train was sent to New Haven to aim for Boston by the Long Island shore tracks. It never got further than New Haven and it was twelve hours getting there. I waited in it for half the next day and then went up to Pierson College at Yale for the next night. I had a pleasant time with friends. But I was restless to get to where I could be located by Lesley should she be in trouble. So I hired a taxi for thirty dollars and came from New Haven by the Post Road one hundred and fifty miles to the St. Botolph Club 4 Newberry St. Boston Mass which will remain my address for some time to come. I saw a lot of ruin the whole way, but we had no trouble in getting through and were in no danger. The wildest time was in the train during the hurricane. The train stood still and let it blow the trees down all around. The train shook and the passengers joked. Luckily the train was a sleeper from St Louis with not many left in the sleeping cars. That gave everybody in the chair cars a chance to hire beds for the night.

Lesley got a telephone call through to me soon after I reached here. She had been in real danger with the children. She will probably be telling you about it all in a letter.

I hear from the Morrison's that upper Vermont was probably worse damaged than in the flood of 1926.

You'll be writing to tell me just what did happen to your farm and to mine.   Affectionately,   Papa

368 · To CHARLES DAVID ABBOTT

30 September 1938
Dear Mr. Abbott: St. Botolph Club   Boston

All right then, Wednesday, November 9th. I shall hope to be in shape for a little more than the mere lecture engagement. I want to see you in your country home. I am not entering on the winter in very good health for some reason. I am resting and training to improve myself. Let me introduce my secretary. She is more friend than secretary. She is going to try to help me be more polite about my letters. You have her name, Mrs. Kathleen Morrison. My letters will be expected to come to Apartment 30 at 88 Mt. Vernon St., Boston Mass from now on. I can be reached through this club also.

Sincerely yours   Robert Frost

368-a · KATHLEEN MORRISON TO VINCIL C. COULTER

PROFESSOR VINCIL C. COULTER, Chairman of the Department of English at the University of Wyoming, began in the spring of 1938 to develop a plan for building a Frost Poetry Library of books and manuscripts at Laramie. The poet was informed of the plan, and made an initial gift of nineteen inscribed books and pamphlets to serve as a nucleus for the collection. Arrangements were made for dedicatory exercises to be held at Laramie whenever RF could conveniently visit the University of Wyoming as guest of honor. Professor Coulter offered to arrange several speaking engagements in the Rocky Mountain area and the offer was accepted. All of these plans were temporarily postponed when RF developed a bronchial illness and was hospitalized early in October 1938. Letters 370 and 374-a represent further steps in the planning.

13 October 1938

Dear Professor Coulter: 88 Mt. Vernon St.   Boston

Now that Mr. Frost is out of the hospital and safely established at 88 Mt. Vernon Street plans for the winter can be
rushed ahead. He would like to come to Laramie on the seven-
teenth of April and talk on the eighteenth. He expects to be
with Professor Norman Foerster at Iowa on April 12 and stay
there about three days.

Will you be good enough to act as a clearing house for
two engagements in your part of the country? I am wrong,
three engagements. Miss Elizabeth McCoy, at New Mexico
State College, Professor [President] George Norlin at [the
University of Colorado] Boulder, and Professor J. M. Adam-
son, at the University of Utah, have all asked to be included
in the Western trip. I am ignorant of train service and mileage
and afraid that letters may cross and confusion result. I have
written all three people and explained that Mr. Frost is to be
with you and that all other engagements must conform to your
plans. Do you mind very much?

Thank you very much for all the trouble this letter may
cause you.   Sincerely yours
                    Kathleen Johnston Morrison
                    (Mrs. Theodore Morrison)
                    Secretary to Mr. Frost

369 · To Mary Goodwillie

Dear Mary: 13 October 1938   Boston
You look for me in vain in my old haunts and you look
for letters from me in vain. A bad correspondent seems to have
become a worse. I have been running pretty wild and irresponsible the last few months. The fixtest mentionable thing
about me in this appartment number 30 at 88 Mt Vernon St
where I have put some books on shelves to be waiting for me
when I come back worn out from my lectures. I have given up
Amherst and given up the idea of settling down with any of the
children. Luckily things are fine for at least two of them and if
none too happily for the third surely beyond my personal powers to make any happier. I am filling my immediate future full
of lectures for distraction and propose to go it till I almost drop.
I shall welcome the chance to speak or read to your Friends of
the Library. Please do pay me my usual fee (two hundred) if
only to maintain my self respect. I shall need money very pos-

sibly before I get through my turn on earth. See my poem Provide, Provide in A Further Range. Money is much, particularly if it is extorted from my well-wishers; but visits with friends are more. We will have a good sit by the fire and I will tell you a lot more by intimation than I can be expected to tell outright. If you have measured me at all you know my chief virtue is that I never look behind me before I leap. My idea would be to fit the lecture in with a couple of others I will probably do at Washington in the first two weeks in December. I am telling Lesley to talk business with you. She is at the King Smith Studio School in Washington.   Ever yours   Robert

370 · To George Norlin

Dear Mr Norlin: 15 October 1938   Boston

I am slower to respond in writing than in spirit. I have been intending with all my heart to visit you again ever since I got your invitation. There had been talk of my going to Laramie for some honors this fall, but it would have had to be late in the fall when the mountain weather might have been adverse. It is now decided that I am to wait till late April. Could you have me at about the same time? And would some one with you take it up with Professor V. C. Coulter at the University of Wyoming as to exact dates in order? It will be good to see you again as in the days at Columbia and in your prickly garden in the Rockies. Your book about Meleager and Isocrates is right in front of me on new shelves in my new apartment in Boston. I think of your mind as more darkly tinctured than mine. Things have happened to make me give in, but I dont think I know enough to be sure the world or the times are bad. They may very well be.   Ever yours   Robert Frost

371 · To John S. Van E. Kohn

AFTER PURCHASING from Kohn a copy each of the first edition of A Boy's Will and North of Boston (see letters 365 and 366), RF wrote again on 10 September 1938 acknowledging receipt of the books and adding, "You offer to do more for me. Let me tell you what you can start doing for me at once — finding me another first of A Boy[']s Will and another first of North of Boston. They will go to some one I care for only less than the person I am giving the first pair to." That request was modified in the following letter. Mention is made here of two prominent book collectors, Paul M. Lemperley of Cleveland Heights, Ohio, and H. Bacon Collamore of Hartford, Connecticut. RF had met and become well acquainted with Collamore, whose Frost books and manuscripts had been the basis for the Wesleyan exhibition mentioned in the introductory note to letter 330.

Dear John Kohn [c. 18 October 1938] [Boston]

I might have made the attempt on Lemperley you suggested but Collamore had already spoken to him for me and got no better than a conceited old collectors surly answer. Never mind. It isnt as important that I get the books this time as it was the first. You are goodness itself to have worked so hard on the case. Buying my own books at such an advance on the original cost was a real adventure in romantic friendship. I mus[t]nt expect to recapture that fine careless rapture. My gratitude toward one person has been satisfied as I doubt if it will ever need to be again in this world. The requirements in the second gift will be amply met I think with A Boy[']s Will alone. I guess I had as well cancel the order for North of Boston. Come to think of it I wouldnt want the second gift quite to equal the first gift in value. There would be poetic injustice involved. I enclose the check for 143* fully realizing I am getting the book cheap from you by favor. I don't want to plaster you with thanks, but thanks just the same. You can send the book to my new address 88 Mt Vernon St Boston Mass. Ever yours Robert Frost

* Lets make it a round $150

372 · To Bernard DeVoto

THE FRIENDSHIP between RF and DeVoto was placed under peculiar strain while the two men were serving on the staff of the Bread Loaf Writers' Conference in the summer of 1938. As they took leave of each other, DeVoto shook hands with RF and said reproachfully, "You're a good poet, Robert, but you're a bad man." That epithet rankled in RF's thoughts and helped to inspire this answer several weeks later.

Dear Benny:
[c. 20 October 1938]
[Columbus, Ohio]

Being out here with my faithful biographer [Robert S. Newdick] inevitably puts me on the defense of my native badness. If just because I once said:

They would not find me changed from him they knew
Only more sure of all I thought was true

they needn't work up a theory that my philosophy is altogether static. Any decent philosophy and all philosophy has to [be] largely static. Else what would there be to distinguish it from science? It is the same with religion: it must be the same yesterday today and forever. The only part of Genesis that has changed in three thousand years and become ridiculous is the science in it. The religion stands. My philosophy, non-Platonic but none-the-less a tenable one, I hold more or less unbroken from youth to age. But it wouldn't be fair to my flesh and temper to say that I am always tiresomely the same frost I was when winter came on last year. You must have marked changes coming over me this summer. Who cares whether they were for the worse or not? You may as a serious student of my works. But Avis [Mrs. DeVoto] and I don't give a sigh. One of the greatest changes my nature has undergone is of record in To Earthward and indeed elsewhere for the discerning. In my school days I simply could not go on and do the best I could with a copy book I had once blotted. I began life wanting perfection and determined to have it. I got so I ceased to expect it and could do without it. Now I find I actually crave the flaws of human handwork. I gloat over imperfection. Look out for me. You as critic and psychoanalyst will know how to do that. Nevertheless Im telling you something in a self conscious moment that may throw light on every page of my writing for what it is worth. I mean I am a bad bad man

But yours   R. F.

373 · To John S. Van E. Kohn

RF is jesting when he imagines, incorrectly, that Kohn "would naturally prefer my sexiest poem The Bearer of Evil Tidings . . ." But with this letter, by way of thanks to Kohn for assistance rendered (see letters 365, 366, and 371), RF enclosed the manuscript of an unpublished poem, which is indeed one of his "sexiest": "Pride of Ancestry." It belongs to a category illustrated in The Letters of Robert Frost to Louis Untermeyer (page 374), a category brought under discussion by RF's offer to make some contributions of his own to a second edition of Untermeyer's Treasury of Ribaldry.

Dear John Kohn: [c. 7 November 1938]   [Boston]

Anyone who would drag in Freud to explain my having failed to autograph a solitary check would naturally prefer my sexiest poem The Bearer of Evil Tidings to anything else of mine he ever saw. But if he liked that one best I think I can show him one he will like better. I wrote it once a year or two ago in impatience with the family of nobodies it celebrates. Here's where you get my autograph a couple of times more:

Ever yours   Robert Frost   and on the poem

374 · To Louis Untermeyer

Dear Louis: 28 November 1938   Boston

The above [city address] indicates what it has come to with me. Be moderately sorry for a poor old man of iron will. Nothing I do or say is as yet due to anything but a strong determination to have my own way. I may show as sick, but it is for practical purposes. I dont know what I deserve for a nature like mine. I was boasting to David [McCord] this very day that I was clever enough to beat my nature. Did he suppose I wasn't?

Well among the things I don't deserve but hope to get is what I am about to propose from and for you. If you consent to do it you will be doing more than one thing to make my immediate future a joy forever. Not to beat about the bush a page longer it is: Come to Bread Loaf and team up with me in poetry criticism four or five days a week for the two weeks of the Conference. You could go home over the week end and I could go with you. We would make the poetry consultations and clinics a joint stunt to the nation. I got up this idea and Ted Morrison took to it like live bait. I needn't go into my mixture of motives except to say that they are all honorable by now. I am growing more and more honorable every time the moon comes safely through an eclipse. (Subject for a poem.) I am really a person of good aspirations and you know I am or you wouldn't stay my indulgent friend through all my errancies the way you do. There is nothing to report on my present state of mind but that though it is better, it can still be alleviated by any kindness you will do me. I sometimes take it pretty hard to be left in a city apartment alone with the night. Dont think I haven't myself well in hand, though, and beyond the need of psychoanalysis. As I have said, I cut up no ructions but with design to gain my ends even as aforetime when I was a child in San Francisco I played sick to get out of going to school. There's a vigorous devil in me that raises me above or drops me below the level of pity. Nevertheless I sometimes weep internally with sorrow (but not as often as externally at the eyes

483

with cold weather). Grant me my request, oh friend of many many years!

This year I have worked hard in the open, and I think it has done me good. My secretary has soothed my spirit like music in her attendance on me and my affairs. She has written my letters and sent me off on my travels. It is an unusual friendship. I have come to value my poetry almost less than the friendships it has brought me. I say it who wouldnt have believed I would ever live to say it. And I say it with a copy of The Independant containing my first published poem on the desk before me. I was thrust out into the desolateness of wondering about my past whether it had not been too cruel to those I had dragged with me and almost to cry out to heaven for a word of reassurance that was not given me in time. Then came this girl stepping innocently into my days to give me something to think of besides dark regrets. My half humorous noisy contrition of the last few months has begun to die down. You have heard a lot of it and you are hearing it still a little here. I doubt if it has been quite dignified. I am told I am spoken of as her "charge." It is enough to be. Lets have some peace. You can figure it out for yourself how my status with a girl like her might be the perfect thing for me at my age in my position. I wish in some indirect way she could come to know how I feel toward her. Ever yours Robert

374-a · KATHLEEN MORRISON TO VINCIL C. COULTER

Dear Mr. Coulter: 6 December 1938 Boston

I have been slow in answering your letter about Mr. Frost's Western trip but he has been tired from the Ohio three weeks and was not ready to sit down and make plans for another trip until now. I have a poor idea of distances and may have made some silly mistakes in the outline I am enclosing but you will be kind and arrange things as they should be, I am sure.

Have we ever discussed fees? I have been assuming the usual fee of two hundred dollars and suddenly realized that there may have been no discussion before I came into the picture. You mention Fort Collins and Greel[e]y as places near. Do they expect to pay the usual fee? Will you be good enough to let me know? I believe Mr. Frost feels that Utah should pay two hundred and fifty dollars to offset the railway fare. It seems silly to have to discuss this matter of fees and I know that Mr. Frost would rather leave the whole question to the people themselves if he did not have to plan more carefully now that he has given up his regular appointment at Amherst.

This is a general outline of what Mr. Frost would like to do. He would prefer to take on what lectures you see fit for him to do without too much exertion but prefers to avoid large crowds at dinners and teas. He easily becomes exhausted by talking informally to large numbers of people. He loves to sit down for hours with half a dozen or more for talk. He can lecture and read without tiring but cannot travel each day and talk each night. He plans to be at Iowa on the twelfth of April and will be free to leave there the sixteenth.

April 12-16	Iowa — in care of Norman Foerster
April 17	Laramie
April ?	Utah
April 24-29	Colorado University, Boulder
	Side trips to Fort Collins and Greel[e]y
April (on return trip)	Kansas
April-May?	Ball State Teachers College, Muncie
May 2-3?	Michigan.

Will you revise this as you wish and send me the final program.

With many thanks for your help,

Kathleen J. Morrison
(Mrs. Theodore Morrison)
Secretary to Mr. Frost

375·To Lawrance Thompson

PREVIOUS letters contain references to Robert S. Newdick, Professor of English at Ohio State University, who was gathering material for a biography of RF with the poet's permission. Newdick's work was still in an early stage when he suddenly died. Some weeks before his death, Thompson had asked RF for permission to write an interpretive study, which was later published as *Fire and Ice: The Art and Thought of Robert Frost* (1942). The following letter, in answer to that request, makes particular reference to problems created by Newdick's death. To deal with those problems a visit was arranged, and during their meeting RF invited Thompson to become his official biographer. According to RF, this would provide him with a stock answer for many who, like Newdick, approached him with plans for books on Frost and his work. Thompson agreed to the proposal on 29 July 1939, accepting RF's proviso that the official biography would not be published during the lifetime of the poet.

Dear Lawrence: 17 July 1939   Ripton

. . . We have a lot to talk over. The book you now propose [*Fire and Ice*] can give me nothing but pleasure. That's settled before we talk. But there's all the sad problem of Newdick's literary remains to consider. I need your advice. You knew him pretty well and how completely he had thrown his life into writing mine. I am told his mind ran on me in his last delirium. What is a miserable hero to say to a worship like his? I naturally want to deal tenderly with his memory. You be thinking my predicament over and come along when you can. A weekend (Saturday and Sunday) soon would be the best time for me. My devoted secretary Mrs Kathleen Morrison suggests that you might like to wait and look in on the Bread Loaf Conference over which her husband presides. The date of that would be from about the 15th to the 30th of August. Suit yourself and you will suit me. But there is the reason for an early visit that Mrs Newdick is coming for a visit some time in the summer and I should like to have seen you when I see her.

Ever yours   Robert Frost

376 · To Earle J. Bernheimer

THE CONTEXT of this letter is given in the introductory note to letter 339-a. RF's despondency following the death of his wife had brought about some wild acts which he later regretted, but the sale of *Twilight* to Bernheimer was partly influenced by an even earlier despondency. Almost from the time it was printed, the booklet had been steeped in unpleasant associations. Prompted to destroy his own copy, RF had nevertheless preserved the only other one, which he had originally given to Elinor. Her death reawakened all the old resentment and bitterness connected with *Twilight,* and made RF willing to part with it.

Dear Mr. Bernheimer: 18 November 1939   Boston

I might not be able to refuse serious money for the unique Twilight, but it would have to be really serious money that would mean something to my family. You say what you think could be done. There may be merit in your suggestion that you could buy or lease the book with an agreement to leave it in the end to some person or institution by me designated.

Sincerely yours   Robert Frost

376-a · George K. Baum to Robert Frost

8 January 1940
Dear Mr. Frost: [Kansas City, Missouri]

At the request of my partner, Mr. E. J. Bernheimer, who called us by long distance telephone this morning and requested that we send you $4,000.00, we are enclosing herewith draft of the First National Bank, Kansas City, Missouri, dated January 8, 1940, Number 4954, in the amount of $4,000.00, drawn on the Second National Bank, Boston, Mass.

We trust this is entirely in accordance with arrangements made between you and Mr. Bernheimer.

Yours very truly, George K. Baum
BAUM, BERNHEIMER COMPANY

377 · To Sidney Cox

Dear Sidney   [12 March 1940]   [New York]

[. . .] I have been very sick largely we now think from some very drastic medicine that doctors tried on me for cystitis. I went crazy with it one night alone and broke chairs ad lib till a friend [Merrill Moore] happened in to save me. I have had a strange two years — not all as bad as it might have been and perhaps should have been. I was in one bed or another pretty much all of December and January — and in one pain or another. Kathleen Morrison took me south pretty much on my back all the way. I got going again in Key West and so on to two or three or even four miles a day of walking. I only furnish you with these data to use on any of my well wishers who may be *living* in hopes of my dying. . . .

You can see from this paper where I have guiltily been.*
I got out Sunday.   R. F.

* This letter is written on stationery bearing the printed letterhead "2000 El Bravo Way, Palm Beach, Florida," but the postmark is "New York, N. Y., March 12, 1940." Also see letter 378.

378 · To HERVEY ALLEN

Dear Hervey: 31 March 1940   Boston

I'd be a bad man as well as a bad author if I couldn't squeeze a report for you out of my pen on how I came out after I left you. Dr. Waterman at Palm Beach thought he didn't think me too bad yet didnt think me quite good enough to face the lectures in North Carolina and Virginia. So I made a long hop for here and the source of the letters I was always waiting for at the Glades. Soothing converse and time have brought me along till I begin to believe I may yet live to resemble my old self. But never mind if I dont. You and I won't care will we, please? All I need is a very few friends to set their hearts right on me just as I am without one plea. I refuse to be taken as promising. I have been all through that and I have had enough of it. It makes me sick in the nerves to be counted on for anything. Cheers for my moral improvement would start me down hill on the road to ruin. This time with you I began to be sure you understood. And I was encouraged to advance a step toward buying the Page acres [land near the Allen property]. I don't see how we could hurt each other by being contermi-nous. Your neighborhood would give me pleasure. My devoted secretary to whom my problems are an open book likes the things I have told her you say to me. They abet me and I might have acted on the realization last year. If I hesitated to buy land near you it was from fear that you would take me as a serious responsibility. I was foolish. You are not the kind to take me and I am not the kind to be taken too seriously. Pleas-ure decides for us. Which being the case I don't see why I should be squeamish about asking you to press the business a little further with Page. I'd probably listen to an offer of five acres for twenty five hundred, five hundred to be refunded me when I built a house. Would it be too much trouble for you to get the other man's terms across the road from you — for comparison? A graceful way to get out of all this lies open to you if I seem unwise. All you have to do is ignore my inquiry and broach a new subject next time you write, or let the matter rest till the child forgets his whim.

Always yours in any case   Robert

378-a · HERVEY ALLEN TO ROBERT FROST

8 April 1940   "The Glades"
Dear Robert,   Coconut Grove

Thank you for your fine, frank letter. It is a great relief to know that you are feeling better. I am glad the Doctor at Palm Beach advised you not to take those lectures in on the way north. I was really anxious about that because, while it seemed to me that you were coming along while you were with us, frankly I was a-scared that you would overdo it on the way north and undo your time in Florida.

I don't feel we really have to do much explaining of ourselves to each other. I have no moral program for other people and I really don't go through life giving folks good and bad marks for the emotional events which overtake them. To do so would imply two things, either that I was possessed of some peculiarly superior type of holiness, or that I regarded myself as the recipient of some authority of wisdom that conferred upon me the capacity to arrange my friends and acquaintances in a moral hierarchy. Well, I just don't. The truth is, I feel, that what we all need is a hell of a lot of loving kindness both in deed and attitude — a constant attitude of warm sympathy. I do not mean something soft and glowing, but a sympathy that is hard and durable. It is only fatigue that occasionally makes me shy off, or break out in irritation, both in the family and to my friends. On certain days I like to complain. In the final analysis it is the quality of being of a person that I care or do not care about, and, to a great extent, I feel that is entirely above, or rather beyond any code of action or manners. . . .

Now as to the land down here. Having you as a neighbor would be delightfully full of that pleasure which, as you say, is the only thing upon which people can get along. I will therefore see Paige again and try to persuade him on the basis of your suggestion. . . .   Affectionately yours   [Hervey]

379 · TO HERVEY ALLEN

Dear Hervey: [23 May 1940]   Boston

Well it seems well settled that we are to be settled down near each other for some months a year for the duration. As you are a cross between a Maryland farmer and a Florida farmer, I am now a cross between a Vermont farmer and a Florida farmer. Some figures ought to [be] derivable from us of value to future agronomy. I mean we ought to be able to find out what sets a poet back most: farming in Maryland Vermont or Florida. My check for the binder is enclosed. This is just a word of thanks to you and Ann [Mrs. Allen] for choosing the plot . . .

In haste as I hurry off to start the first row of peas at the farm at Ripton Vermont with my secretary-farm-manager.

Ever yours   Robert

380 · To William M. Sloane III

WILLIAM M. SLOANE III became head of the trade department at Holt in 1938, and continued there until he established William Sloane Associates in 1946. The volume of prose mentioned in this letter was a selection of RF's previously published prefaces, talks, and essays; but it never materialized. The volume of poetry was *A Witness Tree*, which was published on 23 April 1942. The concluding poem in that volume is "The Literate Farmer and the Planet Venus."

Dear Bill: 17 October 1940   Boston

I hereby promise in the presence of Kathleen, my secretary, that I will give you both the books you want, prose and verse, at approximately the times you name. Tell me right back in your next letter what's the latest you can wait for the prose book. I, of course, want to do all I can to celebrate your (I was going to say our) seventy fifth anniversary [of the founding of Holt]. You know me well enough to know that I wouldn't make these undertakings if I hadn't the books practically written already. I could hope the poetry book would get a little fatter before next June. I am sure it will if I am kept happy enough by you and my secretary and such outlying friends as Bill Snow.

We are sending in this letter — but hold on a minute, maybe we're not sending the one I was going to name. It has just occurred to us that we might offer you something longer than usual [for the annual Christmas poem]. What should you say to a rather amusing skit in blank verse of one hundred and fifty lines. It is called THE LITERATE FARMER AND THE PLANET VENUS, A DATED POPULAR SCIENCE MEDLEY ON A MYSTERIOUS LIGHT RECENTLY OBSERVED IN THE WESTERN SKY AT

EVENING (from TALKS WALKING). If length isn't fatal let us know and we'll send it down. Otherwise we'll find you the shorter one. Don't worry about not seeing them both! You will in the end. And don't worry about me too much. But thanks for caring.   Yours always   Robert

381 · To Louis Untermeyer

RF's particular concern for his only living son has been reflected in several previous letters. From boyhood, Carol had shown an increasing variety of nervous and psychic aberrations. One expression of them was his repeated threat to commit suicide. Early in October 1940, just after his wife, Lillian, had undergone surgery and while she was just beginning to recover, he behaved in an alarming fashion. RF went from Cambridge to South Shaftsbury, spent several days with him and his sixteen-year-old son, Prescott, and returned to Cambridge, hoping the visit had been helpful. Less than a week later, on 9 October 1940, Carol carried out his often-repeated threat. He killed himself with a deer-hunting rifle in his own home. It was characteristic of RF that his deep anguish and grief over this third death in his family during a period of less than eight years became intensified by a conscience-stricken sense of his own failure as a father.

Dear Louis: 26 October 1940   [Boston]
    I took the wrong way with him. I tried many ways and every single one of them was wrong. Some thing in me is still asking for the chance to try one more. There's where the greatest pain is located. I am cut off too abruptly in my plans and efforts for his peace of mind. You'll say it ought not to have come about that I should have to think for him. He really did most of his thinking for himself. He thought too much. I doubt if he rested from thinking day or night in the last few years. Mine was just an added touch to his mind to see if I couldn't make him ease up on himself and take life and farming off-hand. I got humbled. Three weeks ago I was down at Merrills [Merrill Moore] telling Lee [Simonson] how to live. Two weeks ago I was up at South Shaftsbury telling Carol how to live. Yesterday I was telling seven hundred Harvard freshmen how to live with books in college. Apparently nothing can stop us once we get going. I talk less and less however as if I knew what I was talking about. My manner will be intended to indicate henceforth that I acknowledge myself disqualified from giving counsel. Kay says I am not to give myself up. Well then I'll be brave

about this failure as I have meant to be about my other failures before. But you'll know and Kay will know in what sense I say things now. . . .

It was the thought of a real friend [for you] to ask Prescott to Elizabethtown for the winter. That would have been a fine life for him. But his immediate future had already been arranged for with some friends of his and Lillians in the neighborhood. He ought to keep on with his school another year where he is — another year anyway. He had been up all night alone with Carol talking. He heard the rifle go off downstairs. He didn't flee the house. He called the police. He called me. He stood by till the police came. He called his friends the Hollidays and went home with them to wait for me and Lesley. Lillian has lain close to death in the Pittsfield (Mass) hospital for several weeks. She had to be told. She couldnt be persuaded at first that Prescott hadnt been killed too.

I failed to trick Carol or argue him into believing he was the least successful. Thats what it came down to. He failed in farming and he failed in poetry (you may not have known). He was splendid with animals and little children. If only the emphasis could have been put on those. He should have lived with horses.   This is a letterful

Yours   Robert

382 · To Sidney Cox

Dear Sidney: 11 January 1941   Boston

I dont know what you are talking about in your letter. I dont assume that I need to know. It sounds as if somebody had been telling you what somebody else — what he thought somebody else had been telling me he thought you had been saying about my literature. Never touched me. Never came within a mile of me. I'm resting comfortably and I trust you are. Lets hear no more about it. Explanations only tend to confuse the issues and bring on wars.

You went to the last war like a good boy. I dont know what you think of this war. I peek at the papers just enough to have about one idea of my own a week about it. For instance, last week I was just beginning to resent the word appeasement in the mouth of a party whose boast had been all along that it had appeased the proletariat and saved the country from a revolution. If I may be permitted to speak for the proletariat we refuse to be appeased. Todays news makes me wonder if perhaps George B. MacClellan wasnt right in his letters to his wife about the countrys need of a dictator and Lincoln wasnt wrong in muddling along democratically through the crisis of Sixty-one-to-four. Little Mac may have been the most smeared man of his generation. Sandburg hasnt remarked this. He has gone right on with the self-righteous work of smearing the already smeared. Roosevelt is too self-conscious a second-come Lincoln to notice discrepancies, however glaring. A time like this doesnt seem *very* much harder to understand than any other time. Living alone I am made aware of how regularly I am supposed to make up my bed fresh every day. Just so my mind. . . .   Ever yours   Robert

383 · To Earle J. Bernheimer

1 June 1941
Dear Mr Bernheimer: 35 Brewster Street   Cambridge
    I am rather in need of about two thousand dollars right now and would like to sell you two of my most valuable manuscripts at one thousand dollars apiece. One would be the original manuscript of my only full length play to date ["The Guardeen"] with all its emendations crude upon it. The other would be the Robinson preface [to *King Jasper*]. I thought perhaps your interest in collecting me would go to this length. You already have so much more than anyone else except perhaps the Jones Library at Amherst. I dont want to make you feel bothered. I value your friendship too much and appreciate what you are doing for my perpetuation.
                        Sincerely yours   Robert Frost

384 · To Willard E. Fraser

Dear Willard: 2 November 1941   Cambridge
    I must seem an entirely unsatisfactory grandfather to your daughter. By luck I found her picture deep in a copy of Natural History. It gives me a good idea of how old she is getting to be. I ought to send her a picture of myself to show her (and you) how old I am getting to be. I suppose she thinks, poor child, that she is still a Democrat. You used to be a New Deal Democrat. I suspect you have gradually been changing for personal reasons. I must be careful what I accuse you of. I

don't want to get you taken out and shot by Stalin's new friends of the New Deal. You must be careful not to compromise me with the secret service by quoting me indiscreetly. I am I must confess far less of a New Dealer than Mist-the-Presidency Wilkie. I guess I'm just waiting round for the party to spring up that I could belong to. I'm sorry for your Senator Wheeler. I believe he's misunderstood and has himself much to blame for so being. He ought not to talk as if we were afraid to fight or unable to fight when what he means is we don't want to fight anybody's battles but our own. Our seaboard sentimentalists think of nothing but saving England. Some of them would go so far as to sacrifice America to save England. They are the Anglophiles with an English accent. One of the seven colleges of Harvard is presided over by such a patriot. Only one. But there are more who act and talk from a fear that to save America we must save England. I brush all this aside. We are able to fight and we are not afraid to fight. My only doubt is whether we need to join in England's fight. I should like it better if we had it all to ourselves so the issue would be something I could understand and if we won we would get the loot the glory and the self-realization. That last is the great thing. I don't want to see a lot of bloody trouble unless we are going to bring America out a nation more distinct from all other nations than she is already. But as I am in the hands of my government in business so am I in war. I rather hope from certain signs he has given that the President would let the British merge us in their empire. I mean he will take care to get something out of this war for us. He made a good beginning in the swap of destroyers for island bases. You see I am not much worked up over politics. There are some people round I can't bear to listen to — that's all that ails me. I heard two commencement addresses the argument of which was that this was a war to make the world safe for Shakespeare. The Athenians might have made the rhetorical claim that the object of their war with Sparta was to make the world safe for Thucidides and Sophocles. They lost to Sparta, but the great dramatists were still the great dramatists over and above the conflicts of politics and nations. There's where the only peaceful brotherhood of man will ever be, above opinion and parliaments in the realm of music poetry science and philosophy. Religion ought to be included in my list and might be if it would only behave religiously and cease to try to pray God on one side or the other. Men should be able to kill each other in settling differences of opinion, but at the same time recite and sing to each other the same poems and songs of international greatness. Well, well, well —

I come no where near you in my travels this year. The northwest knows me not or at any rate never sends for me.

I am getting a new book of verse ready for Henry Holt and Company.

Tell Robin I have a black dog with white nose tip, white tail tip, white shirt and white stockings. It is a branch sheep dog the kind that takes part in sheep driving trials but is never exhibited in pens at dog shows. His name is Gillie. The first gillies in history were the camp servants of the Scotch who accidentally won the battle of Bannocburn by rushing onto the field prematurely and being mistaken by the English for reenforcements. He's very intelligent and watches everything I do in hope that it will mean food or play or a walk for him. He's no fighter though. He's a pacifist. His virtues are all gentle. Remember me to everyone. My love to you and Robin.

Affectionately, R. F.

P.S. I don't know whether I made it clear in all the foregoing that my international politics were in no way hostile to England. I admire England beyond any great power since Rome. Benny DeVoto goes round saying he wishes the war was over so we could go back to hating England. He means twisting the Lion's tail. I have never been a Lion's-tail-twister. I am for the moment impatient with the mighty nation that it should be crying baby to us to come and save it again. I wish it would try to keep my admiration by winning its own war: or else get clear off the field and out of our way so we could win the war not for England but for ourselves.

385 · To EARLE J. BERNHEIMER

Dear Earle: 16 December 1941   Cambridge

We have now two versions of the play ["The Guardeen"] ready for you in two volumes. The second is better because more compact. There may yet be a third. If so, you shall have it. From your point of view I know the more versions the merrier. I never have versions of a poem or hardly ever; so I will try to have as many versions of this play as I possibly can. We would like to get the two we have off our hands and into your safekeeping where the Japanese bombs are falling and the earthquake shaking your house down but we hesitate to consign them to the Railway Express when clogged with Christmas presents. But if you say the word by return air mail they will come along. [. . .]   Robert

386 · To James Barstow

Dear Mr. Barstow: 5 January 1942   Cambridge

I seem to want to return for a moment to the subject of your Tilbury Town.* Hagedorn puzzles you. I have known him a little for many years. He has come after me three times, once to get any Robinson letters he could out of me, once to tell me that some real American poetry was needed in the present emergency and he thought I could write it if I only would, and once to bring me to Buchmanism. The present emergency was not the war but the presence of the wrong Roosevelt family in the presidency. Hagedorn is a gentle creature and doubtless means well toward all. His utter misunderstanding of an American small town such as you describe so well (though not fully enough) arises from his being a city person and even worse than that a European in mind and heart. I was surprised that he should have been called in or let in on the Robinson biography. The slight stab I suffered at his hands is nothing. He did wrong in saying that Robinson and I were not friends. I admired Robinson most of my contemporaries and he knew it. I had it from him in speech and writing that he admired me. It would be too bad if it were in the power of Hagedorn to set going any story to the contrary. But I have forgotten the personal hurt in a larger resentment against the outsider who will persist in repeating the same old literary lies about the democratic naturalness of our American small town and the classless society you and I grew up in and base our hopes of the future of the Union on.

When your letter of two years ago came I was in no state of mind to answer anything. I believe my friend Mrs. Morrison made you some acknowledgment at the time. I shouldn't be satisfied to leave it at that. I want to take sides with you over my own signature of   Yours sincerely   Robert Frost

* Barstow's attack on Hermann Hagedorn's biography of Edwin Arlington Robinson was published in a pamphlet, *My Tilbury Town.*

387 · To Louis Untermeyer

FOR THE THIRD TIME in RF's letters to Untermeyer, the poem, quoted in this letter, appears; for earlier versions see letter 214 and footnote. This variant of the poem is no longer, but the letter endows it with additional meaning, if not with an entirely different meaning. In its first version the poem served to represent abasement and self-mortification caused by a guilty feeling of extreme egotism. In the second version the poem was made to illuminate the poet's guilt at showing cowardice in the face of death. The setting of this third version makes the poem reflect some kind of failure and a consequent mood which prompts consideration of death by suicide.

Repeatedly, throughout his life, RF indulged in a spoiled-child attitude toward any major crisis that thwarted his own wishes; he seemed to feel, at least temporarily, that such a crisis denigrated him to a point at which he was justified in throwing his life away as "an unconsoled and utter loss." See the introduction to "Part II: Salem and Lawrence" for reference to an early example of this tendency, which led him to (but through) the Dismal Swamp in Virginia in 1894.

In the immediate crisis, the details of which are not given, RF goes so far as to permit the poem by extension to imply an analogy between his own predicament and that of one crucified. Given his apparent emotional state, the sentimental fusion of suicide and crucifixion is not a paradox. But notice the self-conscious ambivalence established by the line, "Oh, if religion's not to be my fate," and his comment in the letter, "I believe I am safely secular till the last go down." Fear of death seemed to keep RF from ever being "safely secular."

To listeners whose sympathetic insights he trusted, he was outspoken concerning his own religious beliefs and affirmations; increasingly so, as he approached "the last go down." To others, he self-protectively masked his religious beliefs behind postures of profane and seemingly blasphemous secularity.

[15 January 1942]   [Cambridge]

To prayer I think I go,
I go to prayer —
Along a darkened corridor of woe
And down a stair
In every step of which I am abased.
I wear a halter-rope about the waist.
I bear a candle end put out with haste.
For such as I there is reserved a crypt
That from its stony arches having dripped
Has stony pavement in a slime of mould.
There I will throw me down an unconsoled
And utter loss,

497

And spread out in the figure of a cross.
Oh, if religion's not to be my fate
I must be spoken to and told
Before too late!   R. F.

Dear Louis: You had the first of this from me long ago and I recently had a copy of it back from you. You never saw the end
of it. You never saw how it came out. There was no end to it
till now that I could write that I *had* been spoken to and told
— you know by whom. This is merely the letter I always owe
you and it's all my news for the moment — if it can be called
news. It's not such as to get me into the newspapers. I believe
I am safely secular till the last go down — that's all. I decided
to keep the matter private and out of my new book [*A Witness Tree*]. It could easily be made too much of. I can't myself
say how serious the crisis was and how near I came to giving
in. — It [death] would have been good advertising. R. F.

388 · To Lawrance Thompson

NEARLY seven years after RF had told Thompson that the first book
he "remembered the looks of" was a handsomely printed gift edition of Robert Herrick's *Poems*, Thompson accidentally saw listed
in a bookseller's catalogue what seemed to be a "mint" copy of that
edition. When the book was mailed to him, RF guessed the source,
but he erred in describing the circumstances of the find, as is made
clear in this letter.

Dear Larry   [*c.* 21 March 1942]   [Cambridge]
        Youd be just as suspicious as I about childhood memories
especially when romantic and like me you would like to see
them tested. I said at sixty or so the first book I remembered
the looks of was a book of verse by Robert Herrick that must
have come into our house for my mother to review in my fathers newspaper when I was seven or eight years old in San
Francisco. Without prejudice to my honesty, you check back to
see if any such book was advertised by the publishers of that
date. You find it listed, you send out tracers for it and you find
a copy as fresh as the day it came into our house. It was a real
research. You deserve credit. But so do I for not making fiction
of my past. After this you will have to believe almost everything I tell you. The remarkable thing is that I who was treated
as not up to books of any kind till I was fourteen should have
been impressed with the name (if nothing else) of a poet like

Herrick when I was seven and reading not at all. It gives me a feeling. It is the very book. Damn you for a detective. The last possible look I could have had at the book was in 1883 or 4 — sixty years ago.

I didnt get you down to Florida. Kathleen came along and shut up my squalling. She calls herself the Damned Belle Sans Merci, but she knows she isnt.

I wish you could come up here to see us before you go to the wars. I have a new outcome for them all thought out.

Kathleen says I am challenged to single combat by Carl Sandburg in an article in the Atlantic for March. His works prove you can play tennis more imaginatively with the net down, or so he maintains. He suspects me of having meant him in my witticism: and merely incidentally to his patriotic campaign to help Archie [MacLeish] save the country he rushes to the defense of himself as an American poet. Sauve qui peut (sp.) It is something if he saves one poet in the general wreck. Kathleen says he says many a teacher says her average pupil often says he never liked poetry till Sandburg came and his own failed to receive him not. (sic-k). Did I never tell you how his daughter once caught a magnate reading my NoB [*North of Boston*] early one morning before he thought anyone was up. Why father she stinted, I thought you never read poetry. This isn't poetry he said crossly throwing it in the open fire. The great object of great art is to fool the average man in his first or second childhood into thinking it *isnt* art.

Why dont they have me speak at Princeton. I have a new piece on that I have called Three Dread Words: Civilization Freedom and Democracy. I started it before the PEN people badly from fright. It now is something. Perhaps Id better be left at home to write it out. Kay thinks so. The doubt is will I write it out.   Yours ever   R. F.

389 · To William M. Sloane III

Dear Bill: 26 March 1942   Cambridge

I'm sending you separately some poems I have had on my mind on my conscience and on the shelf for too long a time. I didn't write them. But I like them rather well though not nearly as well as I like the fellow who did write them. He is the interesting Iowa farmer I may have spoken to you about. Many of us are his admiring friends including the Iowan Vice president of the United States [Henry Wallace]. His name is James Hearst and it is already known for one volume of verse (Prairie Press publishers) that went through an edition. The story that goes with him helps sell the verse. He is partly paralized from a diving accident and only holds up his end with his brother farming a big Iowa farm by virtue of what he can do with the big machinery once he is lifted into his seat by someone else. His brother has devoted himself to giving him a share in the farm life and has stayed unmarried, I suspect at a sacrifice. They are a noted pair. Their farm is one of the best in Iowa. I tell you all this for obvious reasons. And I might add that I have wondered if Henry Wallace mightnt be induced to go on the jacket of his book with the idea of bringing Hearst out of his regional existence into a national. Now you've got all the elements, you can be left to judge for yourself. Only please deliver judgement quickly — Hearst mustnt be kept waiting cruelly long. Mind you I am not pressing. Some of the poems I like very well. Maybe the book would gain by the elimination of the poems that echo Spoon River.   Ever yours   Robert

His address is Cedar Falls Iowa.

390 · To Whit Burnett

AMONG the many anthologies which contain representative selections from the works of RF, one of the most unusual is *This Is My Best* (1942) edited by Whit Burnett. Each contributor was invited to select a group of favorites from his own work and to explain his choices in a letter. RF selected sixteen poems, starting with "The Need of Being Versed in Country Things"; his letter of explanation is reprinted here from *This Is My Best*, pages 277-278.

26 July 1942   Ripton

It would be hard to gather biography from poems of mine except as they were all written by the same person, out of the same general region north of Boston, and out of the same books, a few Greek and Latin, practically no others in any other tongue than our own. This was as it happened. To show that there was no rule about place laid down, I may point to two or three poems reminiscent of my ten years as a child in San Francisco ["At Woodward's Gardens," "A Peck of Gold," and "Once by the Pacific"] and a few others actually written in California at the time of the Olympic games ["Neither Out Far Nor In Deep" and "A Record Stride," 1932]. More than a few were written in Beaconsfield and in Ryton, England, where I farmed, or rather gardened in a very small way from 1912 to 1915. My first two books were published in England by the Scotch and English, to whom I am under obligations for life for my start in life. This too was as it happened. I had on hand when I visited England the material of those two books and more than half of another. I had had poems in American magazines, but not many, and my relative unsuccess with magazines had kept the idea of a book from ever entering my head. It was perhaps the boldness of my adventure among entire strangers that stirred me up to try appealing from the editors of magazines to the publishers of books.

I have made this selection much as I made the one from my first book, *A Boy's Will*, and my second book, *North of Boston*, looking backward over the accumulation of years to see how many poems I could find towards some one meaning it might seem absurd to have had in advance, but it would be all right to accept from fate after the fact. The interest, the pastime, was to learn if there had been any divinity shaping my ends and I had been building better than I knew. In other words could anything of larger design, even the roughest, any broken or dottet continuity, or any fragment of a figure be discerned among the apparently random lesser designs of the several poems? I had given up convictions when young from despair of learning how they were had. Nevertheless I might not have been without them. They might be turned up out of the heap by assortment. And if not convictions, then perhaps native prejudices and inclinations. I took thirty poems for *A Boy's Will* to plot a curved line of flight away from people and so back to people. For *North of Boston* I took group enough to show the people and to show that I had forgiven them for being people. The group here given brings out my inclination to country occupations. It began with a farm in the back yard in San Francisco. This is no prejudice against the city. I am fond of several great cities. It is merely an inclination to country things. My favorite implements (after the pen) are the axe and the scythe, both of which besides being tools of peace have also been weapons of war. The Hungarian peasantry under Kossuth carried the scythe into battle in their attempt at independence from Austria, and the axle of an ancient war chariot was prolonged into a scythe at either end. In three of the poems I celebrate the axe, in one the scythe.

Robert Frost

391 · To SIDNEY COX

Dear Sidney   8 August 1942   Ripton

You needn't worry about having written and consigned to the mails (beyond recall) a letter somewhat too intemperate. It was all right as long as it was to me. I know exactly how to take you in most of your manifestations. God bless you, you shall have your copy of my book [*A Witness Tree*] and from the heart as you have had the rest of the set. I haven't forgotten you for new companions. Nothing is as for the moment you seem to imagine. You should have had the book sooner; but I had used up all the promulgation there was in me publishing and had none left for distributing. I am restored and ready to go to work doing up parcels. I had better be. You can't be the only friend who has been laying it up against me for my seeming neglect.

And you may be wise in not reading Larry Thompson's book about me [*Fire and Ice*] till you have written your own. You have your own ideas of me that you dont want to get all mixed up with his. I hear Larry has done me well. I have come to make it a rule not to read anything about myself till it is in print, and not necessarily then. I shall read how Larry understands me. He has been close to me in my latter days and come closer still in going out to be the only soldier I can call my own at the front. He is on sea duty and as I think on a merchant vessel gunning for submarines. I seem to want to win the war not for the Russians, nor yet for the British (much as I admire the Russians for sticking at nothing to accomplish nothing and much as I owe the British for my start in life) I want to win it for the U.S.A. in general and for Larry Thompson in particular.

I am expecting you to write a book on and for me some day — and a deep one. You may not have noticed anything, but I have been taking measures steadily to put off the day till you should assume the toga of a man and my equal. You made a bad start with the note of inferiority you struck in your first chapter, long ago. You were afraid people would think you had sought my society rather than I yours. I was ashamed for you. I probably did seek your society. I administer this with benevolent malice. I remember seeking you in Plymouth at least once for the pleasure of teasing the young fellow I had found so easy to tease on our first meeting at that dance at the Normal

School. What added to the wicked pleasure was revenge for your having asked Silver or someone if drink was the explanation of my not having got anywhere at my age. After I came to like you, I can't tell how it was, whether you sought me or I you. I naturally live above or below such considerations with my friends. I am almost morbid in my avoidance of the subtler forms of rivalry and strife. Take this matter of biography between us for instance. Why should you be writing mine and not I yours. You are just as much of a character as I am. Why has it never occurred to me before? I know a lot of good stories about you. I am not going to have it said of me that I let people write biographies of me without returning the compliment.   Ever yours   Robert

392 · To LAWRANCE THOMPSON

Dear Larry   20 August 1942   Ripton

    I have read enough of the book [*Fire and Ice*] to see I am going to be proud of it. I take now and then a dip into a chapter, gingerly. I don't want to find out too much about myself too suddenly. You gave me an anxious moment about my "golden mean." I should hate to get stuck in the golden mean. You make it all right in the end. You leave me plenty of play between the tugs and the holdbacks. The friendship that could give so many years to my art and thought is one of the great things of my life.

    You are my one soldier at the front in this war, and my clearest reason for wanting to win. The British are all right as allies. You have to take comfort from any animal heat you can snuggle up to in a cold storm. And we must never forget how much I owe the British for my start in life. You mustnt and Kay mustnt and I mustnt. The Russians I admire for having stuck at nothing to accomplish nothing. It is a privilege to have been let look on at their spectacle of ruthlessness for its own sake (as it turns out). I accept but dont rejoice in them as allies. But until I had you right in the fight I seemed to suffer from the sinfulness of the accidia I once lectured on at the Grolier Club. I didnt seem to stir up. I went back to old wars for my fabulae. The professional emotionalists filled me with Cordelian shame that I could not rise to the occasion. I judge from what you had to say for me on the jacket that you may have been worried just a tiny little bit about how I might look to Carl [Van Doren] and Archie [MacLeish]. Dorothy Thompson has just summoned me to sing out for her Land Army. If I remember rightly it was Mrs Roosevelt herself that asked me a month ago to set something about the future to rhyme and meter. I dont want to write poetry. I want to lick somebody. And since I can't do it myself, I want you to do it for me. My satisfaction depends entirely on you.

"Just at the self same beat of times wide wing" when you were peering through the fence meshes of our Lost Paradise of Casa Marina, I was picking up a charred billet of wood out of the grass by the garden to remind me of the night you and I failed in our attempt to save the vegetables from frost — year before last. Thus do our travels tie places together. We three must celebrate the victory the first thing we do when you win it, by going back for a few days to Key West to walk its streets and alleys together.*

I must send you a new poem but in another envelope so as to swell your mail. Always yours   Robert

393 · To WILLARD E. FRASER

26 September 1942
Dear Willard: Homer Noble Farm, Ripton

I've heard from you directly several times as well as indirectly through your sister and sisters-in-law. So it's about time you heard from me in reply to any question you may have asked. One question was: How is our war going in upstate Vermont? We think we are beginning to win it. At any rate I think we are as of September 26 1942 and may as well put it in writing. The only time I have said as much before was last year when the Russians made me think they were breaking the Germans winter line and were coming right through to the English Channel, bringing their typhus with them. I wish I knew better how the Vermonters were taking the war. Our few young men of Ripton are dutifully but very quietly winding up their affairs and disappearing for the camps. They say little.

---

* In January 1940, Mrs. Morrison had served as nurse while taking RF to Key West from Boston, following a serious operation; in February 1940, Thompson relieved her of her duties there and stayed with RF at the Casa Marina Hotel in Key West until RF returned to Cambridge.

They have none of the encouraging bravado you can get any hour of the day or night over the radio — I mean the gay songs and big talk about our celebrating Christmas in Berlin and next Fourth of July in Tokio or vice versa. I should probably feel more excitement if I were in the city. I am told that in New York and Washington you are no longer free not to proclaim this a Holy War. I am told that real mobs gather there to demand an immediate second front for the relief of the Russians. The tendency of people in crowds is to hold each other up to their ideals. One suspects another of not pressing his tin cans and asking a third if he ought not to be reported. We live so scattered that we have to get along without the help of crowd psychology. Not that we make no effort to understand the war. Mrs. Homer Noble the older lady than I am who sold me this farm recently read me out of a local paper that our able Governor had been saying it was a Christian war we and the Russians were waging. He made out a perfect case to her mind. I had to confess that if it was a Holy War what made it so for me was what seemed to make it so for Henry Wallace, namely, its promise for the common man all over the world including India, Egypt, Mexico, Abyssinia, Java, Korea, the Phillipines, Ashantes, Liberia, the Gold Coast, Porto Rico, Devil's Island, Tristan da Cuna and the Andamans. Don't doubt I am aware of the sentimentality this verges on. It is nearer Carl Sandburg than me in philosophy. To get right down to my way of thinking, the most I count on from the war is an improvement of our National position with friend and foe. We are a great democracy now. I trust the President's leadership to make us a greater. I should regard it as too bad if we hoped the war would leave us without a foe in the world. Everything has its opposite to furnish it with opposition. There are those in favor of democracy like you and me and there must always be the contrary minded. With us the emphasis is on the answerability of the ruler to those he rules; with our opponents the emphasis is on the answerability of the ruler to the highest in himself and to God. The conflict is a matter of emphasis. Each side has something of both principles in it. It flatters my patriotism to believe our system has both in the happiest proportion. But no victory however complete must make us forget that enmity to our faith is deeply grounded in human nature and will always be there ready to take arms against us.

It is wintry here already, but I hang on for a few days

longer. I shall be at 35 Brewster Street in Cambridge Massachusetts by October 1st. I have a book to send you when I get over being so lazy.   Affectionately, my boy,   R. F.

394 · To G. R. ELLIOTT

Dear Roy   9 October 1942   Cambridge
    I have decided to break the ice by setting foot in Amherst before all hearts are completely frozen over against me. I may be making a mistake. But no matter: it wouldn't be the first time. Don't let me sound as if it had been a hard decision to make. It comes about as the naturalest thing in a careless life. Harriet Whicher asks me to lecture at Mt. Holyoke and then spend the night with them at Amherst. Rand asks me to read at Massachusetts State and spend the night with him. This Thursday and Friday the fifteenth and sixteenth are accounted for. And I am wondering if you mightn't be induced to seize the occasion to have me Saturday night. You could get Otto over to your house alone perhaps and obtain merit in the next world after the world war by presiding over our reconciliation. I am somewhat alarmed at myself for the ease with which I relinquish my Christian disapprovals. It must mean my native fibre is weakening. After all these years of estrangement, I made up with Alec Meiklejohn at St. Johns under the auspices of your St. Thomas Aquinas and the presidence of Scot Buchanan last spring. It ought not to make me feel better, but it does. I may as well go ahead and forgive everybody while the enthusiasm for peace is on me. Everybody, mind you. Of course I shall want to see the Bairds, the McKeons, the Browns and the Craigs too. Not that I love my friends less but enemies more. You know how mixed up it is possible to get with mercy and justice. If you don't know it is because you are inexperienced in abstract thinking and need to read my play on the Forty-third Chapter of Job [*A Masque of Reason*]. If my application for an invitation in these terms appeals to you please let me know by telegram in care of Bill Snow at Wesleyan where I shall be reading Tuesday or if it takes you longer to give in to my importunities, in care of Mrs. Russell Johnson 314 North Quaker Lane, West Hartford Connecticut for whom I shall be reading Wednesday. Believe me none of this is said lightly with the easy assurance you will like it and fall in with it.   Always yours   Robert

395 · To John T. Bartlett

Dear John: 20 January 1943   Cambridge

This is just to tell you and Margaret there's another Frost in trouble in your region. I hope the trouble isnt going to prove very serious. Prescott, just past eighteen, enlisted a month or so ago in the Signal Corps and was sent to Camp Carson for his basic training. All well and good so far. But now comes word that he has gone down with pneumonia and partly recovered — all in one message. Probably he has been given some of the new medicine I won't attempt to spell. There is nothing you can do. But I thought if he was invalided out temporarily and not sent clear home he might find time on his hands and you might help him spend it by asking him for a night's visit at Boulder. I reminded him in my only letter so far that he had you or the thought of you for moral support not too far off. I don't know what such a sickness means to the army doctors and how it will affect Prescott's career as a soldier. I wait for further news with some anxiety. The further news has just this minute come in through the slot in the front door. The pneumonia was the bad kind and he was probably only saved by the drug I can't spell the name of. That changes nothing I have said above. Prescott may write to you some time along. He may sign his name Prescott as of old, but it is to be noticed that the army has decided to know him as Private William P. Frost. His great grandfather, my father, was always called William Frost though he had the same Prescott for a middle name.

I wish I could see you. There is some chance of my going by and dropping in on my way to engagements in California next fall if the war doesnt cancel them. I thought I would be out entirely but I am still hired now and then by people who can bear to hear something talked about besides the war. I can talk about the war upon occasion, but what unfits me for most platforms is that most people believe in this war only whereas I believe in any and all wars. I mean I sympathize with all the brave people who go out to die for causes. They are the great boys, beside whom I am nothing.

It was nice to hear from Margaret the First [Mrs. Bartlett] and to see Margaret the Second [the Bartletts' daughter, then attending Wellesley].   Ever yours   Rob

395-a · WILLIAM M. SLOANE III TO ROBERT FROST

11 May 1943   [Henry Holt and Company]

Dear Robert: [New York]

This is the first opportunity I have had to write you a real note about the Pulitzer Prize.* You can imagine how happy we all feel about it here and how glad for you we are. It seems to me that the outcome could not have been happier; you and we did nothing to try to win the prize, but retired (so to speak) from the active lists. However, the book was so infinitely the best of the year that even the Pulitzer Prize judges could find no competitor — and that is that. Four times in a single lifetime is a tremendous honor, it seems to me. I have talked to Louis about it, and I think we both owe him a great debt of gratitude for the tact and friendly judgment with which he handled the whole situation.

All best, and I hope I shall see you before the summer comes.   Bill

395-b · BERNARD DeVOTO TO ROBERT FROST

Dear Robert,   7 June 1943   [no place given]

Various remarks you made about me in Bloomington [Indiana] have been faithfully reported to me. I find myself not liking one of them, one which you have been making for a number of years in various parts of the country. It is reported to me from Bloomington by one of the eight faculty men at the dinner where you made it in words which he says are exactly or substantially yours, as follows:

"DeVoto, you know, has been under the care of a psychiatrist, who has told him that I am not good for him, that if he is ever to succeed, he must not cultivate my company: I am too strong for him and have a bad effect on him . . ."

* See Untermeyer's comment on p. 333 of *The Letters of Robert Frost to Louis Untermeyer*. He explains that in 1943 the Advisory Committee on the Pulitzer Prize for Poetry consisted of Bliss Perry, Wilbur L. Cross, and himself; that Perry and Cross had recommended to the judges that the prize be given to *Have Come, Am Here* by José Garcia Villa, that he held out for *A Witness Tree*, that the divided opinion with his minority report was sent to the judges at Columbia University "whose decision established a precedent when it announced that *A Witness Tree* was the final choice and that Frost was the only author ever to win the Pulitzer Prize four times." The earlier awards had been made for *New Hampshire* (1923), *Collected Poems* (1930), and *A Further Range* (1936).

Another guest at that dinner separately reports you in almost exactly the same words. Over a period of some years various friends and acquaintances of mine have reported your saying the same thing, or variants of it, in a good many places.

The statement is altogether false. No part of it is true. I think you know that. What satisfaction you get from circulating a false and damaging statement about me I don't know or care, but I have made no earlier protest out of respect to years of friendship with you. I have decided, however, that I no longer care to submit to it. I do not want to hear of your making that statement again in public or in private. Please see to it that I do not have to act any farther in the matter than thus calling it to your attention.   Yours,   Benny

396 · To Bernard DeVoto

THIS LETTER is transcribed from an unsigned and revised first draft. RF mailed a recopied version of it.

Benny Benny!   [c. 10 June 1943]   [Cambridge]
The first thing Kay did when she got here was to give me what you in your unconventional Western way would call Hell for talking about you too much in company. (She did not say in public.) And now comes your letter to give me more Hell for the same thing. I feel injured and misunderstood. You bring up an evening at Bloomington when the conversation not unnaturally got round more than once to your lectures there and to your latest book [*The Year of Decision: 1846*]. In any "faithful" report of that evening I should have ranked as second to none in praise of the lectures and of the book. When never mind who said the book might be something better than history but it wasnt history I asked if he meant in the sense that Herodotus Plutarch and Tacitus weren't history or had he in mind the sense in which Frude [James Anthony Froude] didnt seem history to the partizans of [Edward Augustus] Freeman. When somebody else said he had stayed away from your lectures because you hadnt found anything nice to say about life on the Mississippi I answered neither had Mark Twain himself. I said I had to laugh at your being shunned as a disparager of anything American: my admiration for you had begun in an article you wrote in admiration of life on submarginal Vermont farms where the cash income was something

509

like three hundred dollars a year. What was more your lectures had been one hammering denunciation of disparagers in general. I never speak of you but to praise. I have been mentioning you for membership in the Academy. I have predicted that you would have to be called back to Harvard. But I am nobody's propagandist. You know my danger. I am prone to think more things are funny than you would. I suppose it may have been in self defence, but the disappointed novelist pent up in me started to play with the idea the minute I heard that your doctor had advised you not to associate with me. You say the story isn't true and I take your word for it but I had it on the best authority and your attitude toward me for the last two years has tended to make it seem plausible. I dont see why you want to spoil it. By changing your name to John August you can write a twenty thousand dollar novel for Colliers any time you please. An Italian Catholic English Morman blend in birth you are neither a Catholic nor a Mormon in religion but Freudian in philosophy. I dont think these facts take away from your greatness as a writer. They do add to your interest as a character. Just so with the story you so much object to. I wouldnt have thought it hurt either of us and it makes us both more amusing. Get it straight from me though. For you I played up the absurdity of your letting any extraneous doctors come between us to tell you I was too strong for you — a gentle versifier like me too strong for a powerful prose man like you. Rats. But true or not true I wouldnt for the world go on repeating the story if it bothers you or anybody else. You want to be friends I can tell by your manner in Bloomington. I want to be friends as you can tell by my manner in this letter. Now lets forget differences and get to writing again.

IX

CAMBRIDGE, DARTMOUTH, MIAMI, AND RIPTON · 1943-1949

SEVERAL IMPORTANT EVENTS marked the six years that Robert Frost spent as George Ticknor Fellow in the Humanities at Dartmouth College. The first of these tested his growing physical strength; he seemed to be getting tougher as he approached seventy. But he had a cavalier habit of overtaxing his energies. The doctors' warnings about cold weather were vividly recalled when a bronchial condition, which he had ignored, kept bothering him through the late autumn of 1943 and finally brought him down with pneumonia. There was considerable doubt that he would survive this illness, and he was forced to spend a long Christmas vacation in the Dartmouth College Infirmary. But by the end of January he was recuperating at "Pencil Pines" in Florida, and by March he was writing from there to one of his friends: "The pneumonia didn't hurt my wind that I can see. I felled a pine tree today and swung a big pick ax half an hour enlarging pot holes."

Recovering with remarkable stamina, Frost seemed to draw on deep reservoirs of strength so that he could write. In this relatively brief six-year period, he published three small volumes and one large one: *A Masque of Reason* (1945), *Steeple Bush* (spring 1947), *A Masque of Mercy* (autumn 1947), and *Complete Poems 1949* (he had made the date a part of the title itself). He also found energy enough to cross the continent for the sixth — but not the last — time, in order to give readings in California and receive an honorary Doctor of Laws degree from the University of California.

In those years, as he began to write and publish poetry at an increased rate, he wrote fewer letters. A glance at the "Table of Letters" will show a decided change in the habits and interests of his correspondence after the death of his wife. Even before that, he had frequently complained that he had grown

511

tired of letter-writing; and it must have been with great relief that he allowed Kathleen Morrison, as his secretary, to write his letters for him. Starting in the autumn of 1938, he carried on very little private correspondence, at least until unexpected and phenomenal events involved him in trips to Washington, D. C., then to England, Ireland, Israel, Greece, and Soviet Russia. There is particular significance that in the eighteen-year period, starting with 1939 and going through 1956, the average number of letters in this volume is fewer than four a year. Although other letters will come to light in due time, they can not markedly upset the evidence of a decided falling-off in Frost's letter-writing activities during this period.

397 · To Earle J. Bernheimer

Dear Earle: 15 July 1943   Ripton

It's a long time since you had any news from me direct. There should be a lot to tell if I can assemble it. I hadnt realized and apparently neither had you that Jonathan Cape had brought out *A Witness Tree* in a pretty little war economy format in England. The first notice I had of it was a copy sent to me for autographing. If the publishers sent me any the Germans must have sunk them in the ocean. What have your dealers been doing that they haven't found any for you? We must get some. You try and I'll try. There is a letter from Bill Sloane today about a contract Jonathan Cape wants him to sign to permit publication of *Come In* in England when the war is over. I'm touched by such interest in me at such a time. I must never forget my obligations to the English — the British (so as to include my mother's people and Kathleen's too, the Scotch). I never have failed for a moment to appreciate their greatness, their imperial greatness. Not once in the present emergency have I joined in the easy talk of our liberals disposing of their possessions in the break up of the Empire so fondly predicted. Only as they are not Americans and show their enmity toward America do I show my enmity toward them. That is a stand-off. I want enough keeping of our distances apart for assurance we nations wont all run and smash together into Wil[l]kie's One World. We wont. I dont worry. There are traits and interests vaster than the Atlantic to separate us. I used to count wholly on the Atlantic to make the New World new.

I was disappointed there and have had to shift my ground to the spiritual chasms between us to recover confidence in our staying different.

We are farming more than usual but with no sense of heroic effort in the cause. My nearest to feeling the war personally was in Prescott's enlistment in the Signal Corps and that it seems can't come to anything. Last winter he had pneumonia twice and today word comes that an Xray examination has found him out as having a deflated bronchial tube that may never bother him in private life and wouldn't in the army in summer, but spoils him for being a soldier in winter. So he comes home. I'm sad. I couldnt be glad. But I'm relieved a little for the time being. He has his life to pick up again where he left off a year ago to get ready to fight. I hope he will be able to look back on his army training, what he got of it, as beneficial.

Me, I am in transition from one college to another. My position at Harvard was entirely honorary this year. There was no pay at all. I had to take it out in satisfaction of being the first honorary member of the Harvard faculty ever elected by the Board of Overseers. Harvard has been planning something more profitable for me. But I didnt know it and have let Dartmouth join me to the faculty up there. I shall remain in Cambridge where Kathleen can take care of me and go up to Hanover for week ends part of the year. I may keep some connection with Harvard. That is being talked about.

I have published nothing since *Come In,* either in a book or in a magazine. I have written little but a masque of four hundred lines. I may send you a copy by and by. I call it A Masque of Reason.

I will write to Louis Mertins. I mean to tackle his book [*The Intervals of Robert Frost*] when I have a whole day free.

Ever yours   Robert

398 · To A. J. ARMSTRONG

Dear Mr. Armstrong: 1 September 1943 Ripton

You can't help wondering what prompted me to write about Petra, sight unseen, when I was but sixteen and had never been outside of the United States.* I can't help wondering myself. If I look into the matter I shall expect to find it

---

* "Petra and Its Surroundings," a prose essay by RF, appeared in the *High School Bulletin* (Lawrence, Massachusetts), December 1891.

was my love of desolation. I should have been an archaeologist. The evidence is written large in my books all down the years. You could flatter me by setting one of your graduates to work on that neglected side of my nature. In one poem I came near mentioning Petra in that part of Asia that "wedges Africa from Europe." I should like to hear you talk about Petra, its sculptured rimrocks and oleandered arroyos. You have been pretty much everywhere. The last I knew you were flying in the Andes. The war may keep you at home for the moment, but as I take it, that letterhead is maintained as brave notice to Hitler that you don't mean to be kept out of Europe much longer.

Always yours faithfully   Robert Frost

399 · To EARLE J. BERNHEIMER

AS A Christmas remembrance for his friends, Bernheimer had requested RF's permission to use a facsimile reproduction of a page from RF's unpublished prose play, "The Guardeen." RF finally gave his permission, but in this letter he makes an alternate suggestion.

Dear Earle: 12 September 1943   Ripton

How would it be to use a leaf out of the *Masque of Reason* manuscript (which as you know is yours) instead of *The Guardeen*? The Masque has the advantage of being more concise and in verse. I assume you will be willing the Masque should stay here for the exhibition at Dartmouth beginning October first. They are making big plans up there but won't really succeed without your help. (You have me so nearly cornered, Kathleen says) We have led them to hope that you and your wife are to be there sometime in the month. It will be for you to decide whether you will bring your loan with you when you come or send it ahead by express. Of course the earlier they can enter your things the better they will like it. They are making more of my advent up there than anyone ever has before. I seem to be either the one lost sheep or the prodigal returned.

[. . .] By the time you receive this letter I shall be thinking of closing up for the winter and going back to Cambridge. After September eighteenth 35 Brewster Street will reach me.

Always yours   Robert

400 · To Harold G. Rugg

THE REFERENCE in this letter to some document revealing what RF refers to as "the animosity I once showed poor old Ezra" would seem to refer to RF's unmailed declaration of independence from Pound (see letter 57). But Dartmouth records indicate that the manuscript was presented to Dartmouth by RF in 1952. One possibility is that Rugg received it for the Library in 1943 or earlier, but that RF, torn by the temptation mentioned in this letter, may have requested and achieved the return of the manuscript.

Dear Rugg: 12 September 1943   Ripton

Now less than ever should I feel like making public the animosity I once showed poor old Ezra. He is down and there are enough people on top of him without adding my weight to the pile. I disapproved of him when he was flourishing. It seems to me the people who approved of him then ought logically to stand by him in his disastrous end. But let's not worry about him. He may find asylum in the Argentine or somewhere else where he can pipe up with the rest of his scolding cantos. I may be tempted sometime to ask you to destroy what I said of him if his fate is too terrible. . . .   Always yours   Frost

401 · To Lawrance Thompson

                           4 March 1944   RFD #2
Dear Larry: Coconut Grove

My chronic deserter has just deserted me in Florida again and there seems nothing I can ask you to do about it this time since you wont cant and shouldnt desert the Navy. She went north on a passenger train as long as a freight and rudely crowded full of Hialeah race track sports who as it comes out in today's Sunday paper have been paying a hundred dollars apiece extra for their berths. The F. B. I. has arrested thirty railroad ticket office employees and hotel clerks for having taken the money. I don't hope my deserter had a rough ride and in fact I have already heard with a pleasure unaccountable in a person of my temperament that Henry Wallace's common people treated her very well and she got to Lesley in Washington without indignity. It's as yet uncertain how I am going to find a berth to follow her. I am threatening from the public platform next Monday night that I will hitchhike and see if I can't make Henry Wallace's common people ashamed of themselves for not taking care of such an old man of twenty (honorary) degrees above zero. My best bet is the respect I am still held in in certain quarters in spite of everything. Someone on some high place who has read my book may save me. The General Passenger Agent of the Pennsylvania for instance (he is in New York) has interceded with the Atlantic Coast Line for me. My engagements to read to the boys of the Army and Navy at Dartmouth and Harvard can be pled as quasiwareffort deserving priority — or quasi priority. My ostensible however is not my real reason for wanting to get north. Lets be honest.

Our two small houses are being put to year-round use now for Prescott's education at the University of Miami. . . . We bought a few more trees to plant and keep me busy over when left alone. We now have ten citrus trees, orange grape-fruit lemon and calomondon. Our increase was a few oranges and calomondons this year. We should do better next year.

I am intending to talk on some such subject as this Monday night: Is Pacifism an Idealism?

What are *you* thinking about?   yrs e'er   Robert

402 · To EARLE J. BERNHEIMER

Dear Earle   7 March 1944   South Miami

Florida has been a terribly hard place to get into and out of, this year. I am not safely out of it yet. I should get away on March 14th but here it is the 7th and no reservation on the trains has been found for me. I lecture at the University of Miami on the night of the 13th on some such subject as Where is the Place of Ideals and Who is Their Keeper. If I don't use it then I will a month later either at Chicago University, Rockford College, Miami University (at Oxford Ohio) University of Cincinnati, Kenyon College, Dartmouth, or Harvard. There you have my schedule for the spring. . . . I havent written much. I seem pretty well. The pneumonia didnt hurt my wind that I can see. I felled a pine tree today and swung the big pick ax half an hour enlarging pot holes. You never saw such land as this for farming. It's all coral rock under or partly under the sand and but for the said pot holes would be hopeless. They are scattered irregularly four or five or six feet apart (you have to feel them out), are as large as large flower pots (but deeper) and can be widened by chopping or blasting. It amuses me because it is so different from any farming I ever did before.

We were disappointed not to see you and your wife. There is still a chance that I may come out to [the University of] California for the big degree. I should think much must depend on whether I can get train reservations or not. Travel as well as other things may get worse for a while yet. The war moves slow if it moves at all. I keep changing my expectations about it. At first I thought it would be long; then I thought it would be short, now it begins to look long again. Im not worried about it. Neither am I troubled about the future in general. Things are coming out our way. I feel more and more sure.

Our kind of people are beginning to speak up for our kind of world. Take Louis Bromfield for instance. And more particularly because more philosophically the John Chamberlain who regularly reviews books for Harpers Magazine. I'm glad there is such a fellow as that writing. I've just begun to watch him there and in the N. Y. Times. I was coming to think there was no use in my contending in my unaggressive way against the Predominant Nonsense: I was so much alone in my instinctive prejudices. I was resolved not to lose my temper and get going. But I decided to give the immediate future up as lost to the bad thinkers crusted from the social settlements and leap forward to set my heart on vindication from the more distant future when I shant be here to triumph. I sold out too easily. There are more of us than me and you. [. . .]

Ever yours   Robert.

403 · To Lillian and Prescott Frost

FOR SEVERAL YEARS after Carol's death RF assumed considerable financial responsibility for his son's widow, Lillian LaBatt Frost, and son, William Prescott Frost. After Prescott was given a medical discharge from the Army because of a bronchial ailment (see letter 397), he completed a course of study at the University of Miami in Florida and lived with his mother in RF's modest prefabricated winter home in South Miami. They rented rooms nearby when RF made his annual winter pilgrimages to Florida.

22 March 1944
Dear Lillian and Prescott: Cambridge

Not a patch or a flake of snow anywhere all the way from Miami to my door at 35 Brewster St. where I arrived Sunday night at eight oclock. By Monday morning there was half a foot, by Tuesday morning nearly a foot and winter had begun all over again.

Gillie the dog was from Wednesday morning till Friday morning in the crate. He looked out of sorts and sick when I went forward to visit him in the baggage car Wednesday night. He wouldn't eat. But he is as good as ever now. He accepts his changing of habitat without a sign of caring.

I grow to like it down there in the Tropics. I have the pleasantest time with you. The place is one of our homes. We must have another building on it pretty soon.

You'll be out boating again. And you will be seeing people we like. You don't know about how much satisfaction I take in thinking of you both so well fixed in the life of the town and college.

Two small things to attend to for me:

(1) I left a blue scarf somewhere. At least I feel sure I must have. Will you send it to me.

(2) Better hold the coconuts a week or so and then send them to Lee and Elinor at Putney. The girls will be arriving here in Cambridge tomorrow evening.

I saw a lot of Lesley's friends Justices etc. It was like Spring in Washington. I saw Elmer Davis' wife, Justices Stone, Black and Douglas and a friend Shafroth who ought to be on the Supreme Court.

My publisher is back from China, Bill Sloane. I told him about the Joseph Rock from Yeman we met at the Fairchilds. I thought he might get a book out of Rock on plant hunting in the Himalayas.

About April 10th I set forth for Chicago University, Rockford College, Miami University (at Oxford Ohio), Cincinnati University, Vanderbilt (at Nashville) and Kenyon (at Gambier O.) I may go to Athens Georgia too. In that case I would be almost back to South Miami Florida. No distances seem very great any more.

Lesley's idea would be to spend a few months with you maybe just resting maybe doing some work at the airport. You could all have a fine summer together. There would be a boat full what with all the Frosts, Hjorts and Francises.

I must send you a book to deliver to David Fairchild. I should send one to Tharp — yes and one to Margery Douglas perhaps.

Keep us informed about college and the fruit trees.

Affectionately   Father

404 · To Earle J. Bernheimer

[Printed letterhead]

DARTMOUTH COLLEGE · HANOVER · NEW HAMPSHIRE
The George Ticknor Fellowship in the Humanities

At present I am living in Vermont

Dear Earle: 20 July 1944   (Ripton)

This is the very first sheet of this paper with the above heading supplied by Dartmouth to correct the mistaken idea anyone may still entertain that I am connected with Michigan University or with Amherst College or with Harvard University. I have still a lecture or two to give the V-12 students at Harvard but it is as a visitor from Dartmouth. I am the George Ticknor Fellow in the Humanities at Dartmouth College, Hanover, New Hampshire. I finished at Michigan twenty years ago at Amherst six years ago and at Harvard last year as can be proved by reference to Who's Who. So if you expect to be noticed when you shout to me across the street or across a crowded drawing room or night club you want to be sure you give me my title in full. The "Humanities" of it means I am in favor of Latin and Greek and opposed to Homer and Virgil in translation. I gave a talk to graduating students at Burr and Burton Seminary [Manchester, Vermont] the other day. That was an unusual and an uncomfortable not to say cruel thing for me to be doing. But the point is what I told them. I didn't ask them what they had learned in school — I told them. I told them that they had learned to read and that's all anybody ever learned or ought to be expected to learn in school. It was the first fruit of my thinking in my new capacity. That is just the beginning. Theres no telling what may come of my new job. Every new fix I get into makes me think of something new.

519

I'm not keeping the [manuscript of the] Masque [of Mercy] back to tease your interest. It is yours and so marked. I simply want it for some possible alteration I may make in it in the next week or two. I'll let you know when I consign it to the mail or express   Ever yours   Robert

405 · To EARLE J. BERNHEIMER

Dear Earle: 8 August 1945   Ripton

This is just to ask you your news and to tell you ours. Our principle one is that I have at last had the idea I needed for the final touch to A Masque of Mercy and after reading it next week here at the Writer's Conference and after hearing from you about where you are and how you want it sent I am going to add it [the manuscript] to your collection. As Kathleen told you we think you may very well have decided that you have made me presents enough. That will make no difference in my feeling of obligation to your friendship and your interest [in] my works as items in the greatest collection of me in existance. I always take your side in any rivalry there may be between you and another collector. Kathleen sent you the only belly band off a book presented at my party with Henry Holt and Company that could possibly have got out.* I wish you could have been there. But we had nothing to do with the invitations which were very few. The affair was supposed to be more or less of a surprise to me. The great surprise was the Holt gift to me of the Araldo Du Chene bust I so long wanted someone who could afford it to buy in out of neglect. I had never expected to own it myself. There was one party on top of another in our few days in New York, all of them surprising. They damned near surprised me to death. I wasnt too sure I liked being made so conscious of my age. It was as if people thought they could afford to be nice to anyone so nearly gone by. I came home somewhat sick from my mixed emotions and had to have the

---

* The publication date of A Masque of Reason had been fixed at RF's request to coincide with his so-called seventieth birthday. On that day a small luncheon party was given for the poet and a few intimate friends by his publisher in New York City. For the occasion, unusual place cards had been prepared. At each place around the luncheon table lay a copy of the limited edition of A Masque of Reason, with a heavy paper band bearing the printed name of the guest. RF inscribed his copy "To Earle from Robert / March 26, 1945 / Anno poetae editi LXX" and and laid into it the band bearing his printed name.

doctors orders to break several important engagements to perform on the platform.

There is still talk of my coming to Berk[e]ley (Calif) but I am stalling about it.* I dont want to qualify my pleasure in such a visit to my native state with the difficulty of travel in wartime. These will grow worse before they get better. Even for a while after this war the trains must be needed for getting the army home from Asia. Maybe I am too much influenced by what I read in the papers. But my own experience getting south last winter was pretty bad. I am writing President Sproul an apologetic letter. I mean I am on the point of writing him and have been for months — months I am afraid it is. If it weren't for Kathleen I wouldn't communicate with anyone by mail. The only writing that interests me is on the second Masque or on a poem now or then. I plan prose and promise prose but with no very sincere belief I will do it at any particular time. There are two or three essays I might write and almost incline to write before we go to press with my somewhat advertised book of essays and speeches.†

You speak of coming East with things for me to subscribe to. Tell us more about it.   Ever yours   Robert Frost

406 · To Earle J. Bernheimer

Dear Earle: 19 October 1946   Cambridge

Louis Cohn has just telephoned me from bed in New York that he is better and wants to come up and see me soon with some books to sign for you. That's fine with me. I'll look forward to seeing him and signing your books. But why be so offish? Why don't you send the books directly to me as of old? I have been accused of losing books for other people but I don't think I have ever lost anything of yours.

K. has accumulated a few small items for you and will be sending them along. I have two basics, the new Masque and the new manuscript volume of short poems [Steeple Bush] Holt will bring out next spring, which she will send you when I

---

* President Robert Gordon Sproul of the University of California had been trying for some time to lure RF to Berkeley to receive an honorary degree. The honorary Doctor of Laws was finally awarded on 22 March 1947 — some two years after the first invitation was extended.
† The "somewhat advertised book of essays and speeches" was never completed. See earlier reference in letter 380.

have got through touching them up. These will be really something for your collection, though I don't ask you to consider them as evening things up between us. I owe you a great deal.

It looks now as if I might be taking up with your invitation to visit you in Beverley Hills next March. I have an engagement at the University of California, in Berkley for March 23 although this should not be mentioned outside of your house. My idea would be to swing south from there and take the Chief home perhaps by way of Denver for a possible lecture in Boulder.

That's all for now. K. will be writing you next week when she sends the things. I am off to Dartmouth for three weeks.

Ever yours　Robert

407 · To Earle J. Bernheimer

RF's so-called gifts of manuscripts and books inscribed to Bernheimer had dwindled so disappointingly during the early months of 1945 that the check dated 1 May 1945 was Bernheimer's last monthly payment to RF. In letter 405 the poet had tried to explain the uniqueness of his most recent gift, and had promised to send Bernheimer the manuscript of *A Masque of Mercy*. RF made the same promise approximately two months later (see letter 406), and in addition promised to send the manuscript of his unpublished book of poems, *Steeple Bush*. In the same letter he said, "These will be really something for your collection, though I don't ask you to consider them as evening things up between us. I owe you a great deal." Months passed and the promises remained unfulfilled. But RF did send some less important items, and Bernheimer responded by mailing the poet a check for $250 as a Christmas present in 1946. Oblique reference is made to that gift in the first sentence of this letter.

Dear Earle:　　　　　　　14 January 1947　Cambridge

That was a startlingly pleasant remembrance. It seems like old times again. I'm headed your way and shall be seeing you in your home pretty soon now. I can tell you more exactly when after I see my arrangements a little more clearly in mind. I've been kept off the subject by distresses in the family I wont go into except to say they had to do with the divorce of my daughter [Irma] and getting her settled in a house of her own where she can rest from her unhappy wanderings of the last six months. She has a son in the army in Germany and a younger son, six years old, who we are specially anxious for. Kay and I have scanned pages and pages of newspaper advertisements and driven miles and miles looking at small town small houses near enough Cambridge. But some things go all right if some others dont. I cant say I dont get some amusement out of house-hunting. I'm an inveterate house hunter. My first or rather second book (my first in this country not counting your Twilight) took its name from an expression I had seen used over and over again in the real estate a[d]vertisements in one of my earlier goes at house hunting in New England. I had been nurtured in house hunting in San Francisco. We lived at nearly ten different addresses in my first ten years out there.

I shall be having a good look at the streets I ran as a youngster: Le[a]venworth, Washington, Broadway, Polk, Larkin, Clay, California, Van Ness, Steiner, Sutter, Bush, Farrell, Kearney, Valejo, DuPont — but I of course had nothing to do with DuPont except to cross it at right angles in fear and wonder. I wish they hadnt put Alcatraz to such terrible use. I shant want to look in that direction. Why couldnt they have hid their Devils Island somewhere out of sight? — instead [of] spoiling the best bay in the world with it?

I now have the packets of all the imprints of my Christmas card ["A Young Birch"]. I'll pack you one off before I go south. Ill try to tend to the valise full Captain Cohn brought. But if I dont get time for them you wont mind. Theyre in a safe place, unscattered, and where no rival can steal them. You're going to get the MS of the other Masque when Kay and I get through with it. We have signed up to deliver it to Henry Holt & Co by March for publication in the fall. I'm coming out at a great rate lately. There was the Pocket [Book] edition* and the Modern Library [edition] last year. The new lyrics called Steeplebush come this spring. The Atlantic will publish the entire Masque simultaneously with the book. I shall be so all over the place it will be hard for the sun to set on me.

Kay is fixing it for me to go. Her best wishes herewith along with mine   Robert

---

* *A Pocket Book of Robert Frost's Poems* (1946) was an enlargement of *Come In and Other Poems* (1943). Each contained a biographical introduction and commentary by Louis Untermeyer and illustrations by John O'Hara Cosgrave II, but the *Pocket Book* edition contained thirty additional poems and additional commentary.

408 · To Earle J. Bernheimer

Dear Earle: 20 January 1947 Cambridge

There seems to be a movement on foot to celebrate my birthday in the city of my birth. I don't make out too clearly who is behind this, but it is partly Mr. Sproul's representative at the University [of California] and somewhat our friend, Mr. [Louis] Mertins, of Redlands. Now, I won't be satisfied, in fact I'll be very dissatisfied, if you are not one of the sponsors of the affair too. I want you there in name and in person as my friend and chief collector on earth. Please make it pleasant for me by getting into communication with Mertins about particulars. My proposal will be that we can have the party in San Francisco the night of March 24th. Then we could slip away and go quietly down to your house. Family troubles I can tell you about later are using up most of my time this winter so that I have to go short on everything else. They have to do with getting a daughter settled after a distressful divorce. I'll look forward to a quiet pleasure time with you and your wife.

K. joins me in best wishes. She has shared this problem with me — and it has been a problem.   Ever yours   R. F.

409 · To Earle J. Bernheimer

Dear Earle: 20 February 1947 South Miami

Apparently the date for the party at the Bohemian Club has been changed to Sunday March 23. Mertins will confirm this to you. I should think it a good idea for me to leave for your place some time on March 24. How would a night train do — starting late and not getting there too early in the morning? You know my habits but travellers must not be too particular. I am prepared to rough it a little. I am afraid I have got myself into a tighter place than I had intended. I never allow myself enough time or enough money for an expedition. We thus provide for my lecturing once on the twenty fifth or twenty sixth at one of the universities you mention. You'll have to choose the one. I don't think I ought to use myself up with too many lectures. My usual fee is three hundred and fifty but I want to make it the same as I am getting from Mertins at Redlands which is two hundred and fifty, I think. I am lecturing for Mertins on the twenty eighth and leaving those parts on a train due in Denver at 7:45 A. M. — an unholy hour. The ticket from there is being got for me by my agent in Boston. I have no ticket from San Francisco to Los Angeles. Good of you to think of my accommodations in San Francisco but I suppose the University will be taking care of me.

We must find a little time for quiet and rest for me at your house. It will be fine to see you and your family out there on your side of the nation.

K. is writing this for me and sends her regards to both of you.   Ever yours   Robert

[Postscript in ink:] Leaving here for Cambridge this week. The enterprise of going back where I started from seventy odd years ago is almost too much for my brains.

410 · To G. R. ELLIOTT

THE APPROXIMATE DATE for this is given in a note written by Elliott: "Postmark Hanover N. H. April 22, 1947. In reply to my invitation to him to spend a week or so with me after his lecture at Amherst."

Now Look, Roy   [c. 22 April 1947]   Hanover
Your dream of getting me where you want me long enough to do me any good is not destined to be fulfilled yet a while. My motto for today is Keep Moving. I am a nomad in my own house. I have slept in every one of its rooms but the kitchen. My motto for yesterday was Dont let being mixed make you feel confused. It makes [Arthur] Koestler feel confused because he is blended of flesh and spirit, comfort and peace, like Mocha and Java. Keep moving. Keep changing your motto. I'm touching in Amherst only for four nights this time — I have decreed it and it cannot be otherwise. I can remember the time when I would have made the cowardly excuse that someone else wouldnt let me stay longer. Two world wars and a few private catastrophes have made a man of me who doesn't mind blame. Neither for my sins of omission nor commission am I afraid of being punished. All that is past like a vision of Dante or Gustave Doré. My fear of God has settled down into a deep inward fear that my best offering may not prove acceptable in his sight. I'll tell you most about it in another world. My approach to the New Testament is rather

through Jerewsalem than through Rome and Canterbury. Old friend forgive me. I want to see a lot of you and Alma. But it had best be in excursion from the Presidents house. This time. I want to scatter myself somewhat. There is Otto to see. I'm not quite up to living in his house yet. Old pains come back to my mind.

I get to Amherst Thursday afternoon.

Ever yours   Robert

411 · To Earle J. Bernheimer

Dear Earle: 16 October 1947   Cambridge

I want to tell you something I have never said to anybody before and throw myself on your generosity and understanding. Don't think I haven't appreciated your generosity from the very first display of it in connection with the smallest book [*Twilight*]. At the time I was in the mood to take that as a rich man's joke between us. You were willing to be a little absurd for a poor poet's benefit. Now I hear you set a value of ten thousand dollars on the smallest book. Another pleasantry for the encouragement of the arts. Till you came along I had no notion my by-products were worth considering. And I hope you will give me credit for having tried to requite your favors. I take some satisfaction in believing that when I send you the original of the Masque of Mercy and another of my copybooks, I shall have put your collection beyond rivalry. You speak of a present for this Christmas that Santa Claus can't get down the chimney. That's like you in form and content. But don't send the present please. I want a chance to catch up with you. We've played an amusing game. I'm no collector and I can't say I have taken collecting too seriously. But I've attained to an experience of it that begins to tell on my nerves. There is a strain of responsibility for my waste paper and my disowned poems in print that I shall have to have a rest from. Someone in Chicago asks to republish a poem I left behind in the Saturday Review and as it might be assumed intentionally. I have been lucky in not having been admitted to the magazines with much I would now consider bad or negligable. The gods take care of fools and drunkards. You pose a hard question when you ask to use a poem from *Twilight* for Christmas. The only poem I cared for enough to keep in *Twilight* was "My Butterfly" and I only brought that into my collection for the eight lines or so beginning "The gray grass is scarce dappled with snow" which was when I first struck the note that was to be mine. I shouldn't object very hard to your using "The Waterfall" ["The Falls"] if it would help you wile away the time as your law troubles draw to a climax. You have all my sympathy in your emergency as I hope I have yours in mine. Kay may have told you about what I have been through and am still going through in the separation of my daughter from her husband by divorce and putting her away in a hospital for the insane — probably a hopeless case — A terrible end to see a child come to. But if in pleasing yourself you want to please me too you won't make too emphatic a thing of the little poem (The Falls), and to prevent jealousy, you'll let me have twenty or twenty five copies for friends. I don't dislike "The Falls." "Twilight" itself would never do. It represents everything I had to cleanse myself of.

I have been sunk in apathy toward poetry and pretty much everything else or I should have tended to your manuscripts before this. I have yet to mail a single copy of "Steeple Bush." I must brace up — or permit myself to be braced up.

Now remember: you, your friendship and kindness but no more presents.

May I be further confidential. I confess to long having entertained the hope that you would deposit your collection some day where it would link our names in public for the years to come. What you said when I was out there rather was calculated to kill that hope — wasn't it? It's your collection to do what you like with. I have no more to say. I've had a lot of fun helping you to build it. Ever yours   Robert

412 · To Margaret Bartlett

AFTER John and Margaret Bartlett had made a financial success of journalism, they began to think about a book based on their friendship with RF, but they needed his permission to use his letters to them. After Bartlett died, on 23 January 1947, without ever broaching the subject to RF, his widow wrote saying she would like to carry out this plan. RF answered as follows.

Dear Margaret: 26 December 1947   Cambridge
    You would have several advantages over anyone else that might attempt my biography. I mean anyone else outside of my own family. Only Lesley's memories would go back further

and go in deeper than yours. That ought to make me afraid of you. But its not from fear that I must ask you to spare me another ordeal of the kind in my lifetime. It is from something I find it hard to explain or even talk about. I am sick at heart from having had my picture taken and my portrait painted. Having my life written up is as bad. I am having it right now by one and threatened by several others. Much more and I will stop being an active man and sit back in a pose merely self-conscious. Let me tell you what I wish you would do: write anything you please about me, but put off publishing it till I am dead and gone. You ought to be able to outlive me. If you find you aren't, you can pass the documents you create on to your most trustworthy heir. Then for both of us the glory will be posthumous. This is permission for you to tell anything you please on me, but to posterity. Now let's pretend you haven't spoken to me in the matter and I will try not to think about what you may be busy with. Do I seem to make too much of myself in all this talk of avoiding self-consciousness? I know it is not important whether my life is written up or not. All the same if you want to please me you will take it off my mind that I may have to face another version of my fortunes and misfortunes. The latter pile up as the years run. You may not have heard the sad ending to Irma's story. She is at once too insane to be out of an institution and too sane to be in one. So she suffers the sense of imprisonment where she is, in one. But I didn't start this letter to let you further into my dismalities. I have things to be thankful for. I have friends for instance. I have had you and John.   Sincerely yours   Robert

413 · To LAWRANCE THOMPSON

THIS LETTER illustrates typically Frostian ways of using words to confuse issues in order "to keep the over curious out of the secret places . . ." Starting in the summer of 1946 and for six summers thereafter, Thompson and his family rented a Ripton farmhouse, known as the Euber place, which was owned by RF. In June of 1948, when the Thompsons got to Ripton, this letter was found conspicuously propped against a sugar bowl on the dining table. In conversation the next day RF asked if he had satisfactorily answered the question concerning his religious belief. It was a tight place. In his fear of voicing comments that might sound like complaints, Thompson replied that while the letter hewed consistently to a solid line of argument, some of the chips that flew seemed more interesting than the line itself. RF accepted that, nodded as he winked one eye, and said quite sympathetically, "Don't let me throw any dust in your eyes." Then he changed the subject.

Dear Larry   12 June 1948   Ripton

You might be thinking it would be a pretty mean fellow who wouldnt write so much as an annual letter to a friend when anything the fellow wrote would bring serious money on the market at auction. And I was going to say you wouldnt be far wrong. But as a matter of fact you would be very far wrong. Because a letter a year to say two or three special friends would in a life time mount into enough to be too plentiful for rarity and so break the market and destroy its own value.

I will put it in writing however that I recently came across you in a curious and romantic way when I was getting out my old clothes here at the cabin for summer wear. One of them a shirt puzzled me by its material and the size of its collar. It was of wool which I never wear in a shirt summer or winter and the collar must have been size thirteen if I wasnt mistaking a cuff for a collar. I can remember when I wore thirteen. (Never quote yourself. At least never accurately. I haven't time to verify the passage.) In my perplexity and without stopping to consider that I might be invading another mans privacy I dove into one of the pockets for any thing identifying and what I turned up was a set of questions in your typewriting that you had evidently resolved to corner me with that day if the rain hadn't intervened to save me from telling you lies.

The questions are fine and searching. You may not believe it, but I like best those about the art of meaning because they take me out of myself where I like to spend most of my time. But the one I propose to deal with here is the one that touches my religion. You seem to reason that because my mother was religious, I must have been religious too at any rate to start with. You might just as well reason that because my father was irreligious I must have been irreligious too. Theology fascinated me from very young, but perhaps no more than other children. I couldn't have been more than four or five when I relished hearing a boy somewhat older ask if in hitting a nail on the head with the hammer in his hand he was hitting God on the head. "I must be hitting him somewhere since he is everywhere." A little later (ten years later when I had learned to read) I was tickled hilarious by Shelley's note on his dictum

529

that there is no God. I was bored by Queen Mab and the Revolt of Islaam and all such truck. But I thought Shelley and Godwin as much fun to contemplate as Mark Twain's Mrs McWilliams and the Lightening or his Editing a Newspaper in Arkansaw. Those were the days when Carl Burrell and I in my Uncles house in Lawrence laughed loud and long at Phoenix Shillaber Mrs Partington Artemas Ward Mark Twain and the other jokesmiths indescriminately. I still think what makes Mark best of them all is the best thing he ever wrote himself The Jumping Frog. We could make all the noise we wanted as late at night as we pleased. My Uncle (Colcord) was away south all winter and Carl was caretaker in his empty house. Carl's rather big library was a collection of American humor and on the serious side of the British scientists Clodd, Grant Allen, Huxley and Darwin. It would be found that Grant Allen wrote a book on the Evolution of the Idea of God. I grinned inside at the time. One of my teachers warned my mother that Carl was too old for me. He may have been twenty eight to my seventeen. He had been a real convert from religion of the kind you're looking for. I doubt if I was ever religious in your sense of the word. I never prayed except formally and politely with the Lord's prayer in public. I used to try to get up plausible theories about prayer like Emerson. My latest is that it might be an expression of the hope I have that my offering of verse on the altar may be acceptable in His sight Whoever He is. [See letter 430] Tell them I Am, Jehovah said. And as you know I have taken that as a command to iamb and not write free verse. It would be terribly dangerous to make too much of all this. I looked on at my mothers devoutness and thought it was beautiful. She had purity of spirit. I looked on at her socialism and thought that was nice too. We have come a long way and still we havent got to the point where I make my stand. You think something came over me in my twenties. Are you on the track of an idea there. Take swearing for instance. I have done a little of it — not much. My Grandfather was rather irreligious I always thought. But he never said worse than Goudemn it or dem it and he put a window in memory of his wife into the Universalist Church in Lawrence. I grow curious about my soul out of sympathy for you in your quest for it. As you pronounce lastly on it of so much place in in Heaven I expect my reward. I'm afraid I stay a semi detached villain. But only semi. My passion for theology must mean something. It's the frosting on the cake for me to discover Thomas Acquinas' explanation of the Holy Ghost. You know my mild prejudice against Ghost Writers. But I am sublimated out of my shoes by the religious thought that in Heaven we will all be Ghost Writers if we write at all. Maybe we won't write any more than we marry there. Everything will be done out of wedlock and said off the record. You see where that lands you in logic? Stop press a moment till I get in something I omitted to say about my Grandfather. I think he may have respected God as a property man: he owned so many churches. My spirituality rises above that anyway. But I can leave it to you to give me a soul if you can. I know you will do your best for me. Louis [Untermeyer] qualifies I suppose as a man of faith. He believes in woman or he wouldnt be marrying again as advertised. He believes in Stalin or he wouldnt be boosting Wallace's latest book as advertised. He believes in Peace or he wouldnt be leading in Wallace's campaign. He believes in War or he wouldn't show so much pride in his legitimate son's arrest for gun running to the Israelites. Faith faith! What a thing it is. The last pop of poppycock was for Santaanna [Santayana] to say, "true illusion and false illusion that is all there is to choose between." True illusion would be the falsity then and false illusion the truth. Did it ever strike you that we owe it entirely to two or three Greeks that we arent all orphic (alias Christian) mystic fools crossing ourselves up with word tricks. Such as that the truth will set you free. My truth will bind you slave to me.

You can do some very objective figuring about man and the universe by taking God's name not altogether in vain. But you have to look out or you will end up using Jesus to rationalize the sixth marriage of Henry the Eighth or our Louis the First and Only.

Speaking of any change that may have come over me at any time reminds me of a funny episode of my visit to lecture at Gainesville Fla this winter. A boy of GI age came to interview me for the college paper.

"You're a changed man from what you were when you were here two years ago," he charged me rather rudely. "Oh yes you are. Dont you try to bully me out of my opinion. You're a changed man. That's what I'm going to say in tomorrows paper."

"Hold on," I said. "I'm not contradicting you. Tell me about it. I have a friend — two friends who could use this."

I was afraid of insults but I took the risk. "In what respect have I changed?"

"You came on that stage like a cowboy."

"Oh thats the difference: my tread is manlier."

"Dont you try to laugh me off. You're a changed man if I ever saw one."

"All right I'm changed then and shall so report to the two people most concerned. I shall be interested to see what they will do about it. One thing more before you leave. Don't hurry off." He seemed to want to get out the door before he was changed himself. "Granted I am a different man. How do you account for the change?"

"You've been associating with better people." I would have given anything to know what he meant by better people — freer stronger simpler finer richer poorer stricter. Was there party implied?

I am aware of having been uncramped once in my life. Just in case you are looking for a fact to build on.

My garden is all planted. But you neednt be jealous. It is probably rotting with rain. R.F.

414 · To Earle J. Bernheimer

Dear Earle   10 September 1948   Ripton

What a nice letter of concern for me. I am all right but it is as you so sympathetically surmise my distractions (amounting to troubles) keep me from writing letters any more. Kay will perhaps tell you what I have been through with my daughter's divorce and insanity. I have to keep going to earn a living as you know for more than just myself. But my mood would be rather against the fooling of that scrap about my uncle's rheumatism.* If you wanted to please me you would look for some serious paragraph from the unpublished play you have. You would hate to have your collecting interests make me too uncomfortable. You go ahead and find some passage in the Guardeen to propose and then there's another favor I may ask of your friendship. Why dont you come east for a visit? I'd rather talk than write to you or anybody else. You could bring along your items for my signature. I dont set

* "Old Age," a casual free-verse "scrap" twenty-six lines long, which is quoted in The Letters of Robert Frost to Louis Untermeyer, pp. 30-31.

much store by what you have to buy for me to sign. I dont see why *you* do when you have so many things of mine genuinely inscribed to you. I have a couple to send you right now that I can truthfully call gifts from me to you. It will mean something when I write on them to Earle   from Robert

415 · To WILLARD E. FRASER

Dear Willard: [September 1948]   Ripton

Just a word to encourage you in your campaign. I find that anyone I take sides with usually wins. I got Wilbur [Wilbert] Snow elected Lieut Gov of Conn by coming out privately in his favor and I failed to get him elected Gov the following year by neglecting him that time. It's in the lines in the palm of my hand the Psalmist tells me. I had a seance in August to be brought up to date. The three leading candidates each a little less leading than the one ahead of him till you get down to Wallace and Thomas have been sniffing around my door sill for my blood. You know the old song, Scots who hay wee Wallace bled. But I refuse to commit myself except with a secret ballot. I'm a Democrat to be sure, but not New Deal. New Deck I guess. Anyway somewhat Southern with a middle name like mine. In local elections I permit myself great lassitude. I would naturally be your partizan from the minute you were nominated. Though I fear you won't find the climate of Washington D. C. just what you are after for your health. You'll have to take it in dives the way the regular divers do for pearls. One good thing: it will mean seeing you oftener if you come east to live a spell a year. And you'll have Robin with you. And think of all the letters *that* will save my writing. We could have a good talk now and then. Robin was fine to see. How she can play the piano. How intelligent she is about politics and Montana. I'm very proud of her and the way you have brought her up. You and your mother. There are the matters that seriously count. It's fun to win in politics but the game becomes more or less of a joke with me as I get less and less childish. I never could make you realize how tragic it was for our family away back there beyond you in California in 1884 the year my father was defeated for tax collector of San Francisco and in six months died. He didn't come home for days afterwards. He took it too hard. He was wrong about it. I can say that to you.

You and I have been through a lot together. Forgive my preliminary nonsense.   Affectionately   R. F.

416 · TO JOHN SLOAN DICKEY

WARM FRIENDSHIPS developed between RF and two presidents of Dartmouth College: Ernest Martin Hopkins, who retired in 1945, and John Sloan Dickey, who succeeded him. Because of this it was particularly difficult for RF to break his ties with Dartmouth and to announce his return to Amherst, as he did in the following letter.

Dear Mr Dickey: 14 February 1949   South Miami

You have some thing to listen to that I hope will give you a little pain if only because it gives me a good deal of pain. I am being asked back to the college of my first and longest employment and on terms so extravagantly generous that I couldnt expect anyone else to match them. My recent five years back at the college of my first attendance has meant much to me under both you and Mr. Hopkins and my admiration for you both in your different ways will always come out in my talk wherever I go. I particularly admire the political stir you have given Dartmouth with the new ["Great Issues"] course. I shall be proud if you will let me see you once in a while as a friend to learn of anything new — like that — you may be projecting. But I must beg you to let me leave you now with your blessing. Please understand that what takes me away is not just more money, though that has to be considered even by the improvident. It is largely the appeal of being provided for at one stroke for the rest of my time in and out of education. The men I owe this promise of ease (haecotia) to were some of them boys I preached my heresies to from twenty to thirty years ago at Amherst. For it is Amherst calling and with a warmth I don't think you would think should be denied. There is sentiment in the situation and even something of rapprochement. I was nineteen years connected with Amherst and nineteen more should see me a nonegenarian. I will tell you the rest when we meet in April. I speak now merely to prepare you to receive me with forgiveness.   Sincerely yours   Robert Frost

417 · TO ALFRED C. EDWARDS

IN RF's continuous relationship with one publisher, Henry Holt and Company, he dealt primarily with the man in charge of Holt's trade department. As changes occurred in that department, new friendships developed. Earlier letters have indicated that from 1915 to 1919, Alfred Harcourt served as the Holt liaison with RF; from 1919 to 1924 the intermediary was Lincoln MacVeagh; from 1924 to 1932, Herschel Brickell; from 1932 to 1938, Richard H. Thornton; from 1938 to 1946, William Sloane III. But of all these friendships, the longest and the most intimate was with Alfred C. Edwards. When this letter was written (primarily concerning the publication of *Complete Poems of Robert Frost 1949*) Edwards was serving not only as Holt's representative with RF but also as Holt's executive vice-president. In 1951, before Edwards became president of Holt, RF named him in his will to serve as sole executor and sole trustee of his estate.

Dear Alfred   5 June 1949   Ripton

It was great having that long pre-publication ride with you toward our better and better acquaintance. I was afraid we should have had some of that twenty-dollar shark-skin soup on the bill-of-fare at the Chinese restaurant to build up our strength for what we had to face. Just reading about it seems to have been enough. Look at the power we are showing. Dont think I would claim more than my share of the credit for it either. Friends are bobbing up in every mail and calling up from hundreds of miles off on the telephone to compliment me on the sendoff I have had from my publishers. Nothing will satisfy the demands of friendship, I fear, but quite a number of autographed, nay inscribed copies of the important book in question. Perhaps I had better ask you right now if you will set aside for me some of both the ordinary and the special edition. I have seen neither as yet, but I have had nothing but praise for the form of both and the reviews we are getting. Kay is as happy as I am about it all.   Ever yours   Robert

X

CAMBRIDGE, AMHERST, WASHINGTON, MIAMI, AND RIPTON · 1949-1963

HIS HARVARD FRIENDS came to Frost's rescue after his resignation from Amherst; Dartmouth friends did the same when Harvard resigned from Frost. Those of his friends at Amherst, however, wanted very much to bring him back into their midst, and a way was provided primarily by Charles Woolsey Cole, Amherst Class of '27 — who became President of Amherst College in 1946 — when he made an offer that the poet could not resist. Frost was promised very light duties at Amherst, together with a generous retirement annuity whenever he might give up his duties. In the fall of 1949, then, Frost began to spend a few weeks at Amherst, and he continued those visits until his death.

But his activities during the last fourteen years of his life were by no means restricted to Amherst. Most of the time he was kept busy harvesting a new crop of honors at home and abroad. Invitations took him from one end of his country to the other, and on to South America, England, Ireland, Israel, Greece, and Russia. Most of his honors came after he delightedly assumed the posture of poet-politics in Washington, D. C.

The Department of State had a hand in arranging his last four trips out of the country. Asked to undertake "good will missions" abroad, with expenses underwritten by the State Department, so that he might help offset international misunderstandings, he began playfully but half-seriously to boast that he might become one of the "unacknowledged legislators of the world."

In 1954 he made his first official trip, going to Brazil as a delegate to the World Congress of Writers. A few years later he was pleased with preliminary and tentative proposals to send him to England under the auspices of the State Department, but he made it clear in many quarters that he would not agree to go until he was "sure of the demand" for him. With the intercession of influential friends, who picked up the hints, he received invitations to accept honorary degrees at Oxford and Cambridge within two days of each other, and a third came soon afterward from the National University in Ireland. The 1957 visit to Great Britain and Ireland gave him the great pleasure of closing the circle of events that had begun with his 1912 voyage to England as a stranger.

The Department of State did not initiate Frost's visit to Israel and Greece in 1961. He was asked by the Hebrew University of Jerusalem to be the first "Samuel Paley Foundation Lecturer," and then Washington requested once more that he serve as "ambassador of good will" in Israel and Greece. He performed brilliantly in Jerusalem and Tel Aviv; and on his way home he stopped off in Athens, stayed with the American Ambassador to Greece, Ellis O. Briggs, and spoke twice to appreciative audiences in Athens. Then he continued homeward by way of London, where he was given a birthday luncheon by the American Ambassador to Great Britain, David K. E. Bruce. After that strenuous expedition he vowed, he would never go abroad again.

But in 1962, at the age of eighty-eight, he very eagerly accepted the State Department's suggestion that he visit the Soviet Union on an "exchange of poets" mission. He was warmly received by the Russian people in Moscow and Leningrad, and praised by Premier Khrushchev in a private interview on the shore of the Black Sea.

These were spectacular honors, acknowledging Frost's reputation abroad; and the poet relished them. But he saw as even more precious some of the tributes made to him at home. One of the greatest events, he felt, was his participation in President John F. Kennedy's inauguration on 20 January 1961. Almost as important to him was the presentation, on his eighty-eighth birthday, of a Congressional Medal, in a ceremony at the White House. On the same day, 26 March 1962, his last book of poems, *In the Clearing,* was published; and that evening a gala dinner was given, with four hundred distinguished guests honoring him, at the Pan American building in Washington, D. C. Arrangements for that birthday celebration had been made by Secretary of the Interior Stewart L. Udall and Alfred C. Edwards, President of Holt, Rinehart and Winston.

Throughout his last years Frost was plagued with illnesses which he tried to ignore. Repeatedly warned that he needed prostate surgery, he kept postponing the operation. His remarkable stamina enabled him to keep up a frenzied pace — almost as though he hoped to put off death by staying in action — but he was finally persuaded to enter Boston's Peter Bent Brigham Hospital for a thorough checkup on 3 December 1962. A brief glance at his public appearances during the two previous months may serve to show the intensity of his final commitments:

After his return from Russia, Frost spent the early part of October in Ripton before returning to Cambridge; but in mid-October he went to Washington, D. C., to participate in the National Poetry Festival.

He went to New York City from Cambridge on 8 November to receive the Edward MacDowell Medal and to give a reading.

He received an honorary degree at the University of Detroit on 13 November, and read before an audience of 8,500 at the University on the following day. On the 15th he went on to Chicago by train to give a reading to aid *Poetry* magazine, and then returned to Cambridge.

He gave a public reading at the Young Women's Christian Association in Greenwich, Connecticut, on 23 November.

At the opening on 27 November of the luxurious Hopkins Center for the Performing Arts at Dartmouth in Hanover, New Hampshire, he gave a public lecture in defense of "Extravagance."

He went from Cambridge to New York City on 29 November to take part in a closed-circuit television show, *An American Pageant of the Arts*, which was originated by President Kennedy for the benefit of the National Cultural Center in Washington.

Having agreed, reluctantly, to enter the hospital for his checkup on 3 December, he nevertheless insisted on keeping one more appointment: on the evening of 2 December he read his poems before an overflow audience in Jordan Hall, Boston.

Frost refused to quit, even after he had undergone an operation far more serious than the doctors had foreseen. Death held absolutely no attraction for him and he met the last fifty-six days of his life with a spirit of stubborn tenacity. For a time he seemed to be making a slow but determined recovery. But on 23 December he suffered a heart attack so severe that immediate members of his family (represented by his daughter Lesley) and close friends were called to his bedside. On the same day the hospital issued its first bulletin about him, acknowledging that he was there, reviewing his very satisfactory response to surgery, but making no mention of the heart attack; the statement merely admitted that "more recently his condition has been less satisfactory."

In regular bulletins issued by the hospital for several days thereafter his condition was described as serious. But again he recovered strength, and he improved so much that guests were permitted to visit him daily. Then on New Year's Day of 1963 he suffered a first pulmonary embolism; on 7 January he suffered a second. The next day minor surgery was performed to try to avoid a third and predictably fatal embolism. As he revived in strength and spirit — remarkably — his doctors even made tentative arrangements for him to leave the hospital in a week or ten days. Domestic services were hired and sent to 35 Brewster Street to make ready for his homecoming. On 12 January he said in a dictated letter: "It is no time yet to defer a little to others in my future affairs." In another letter, dictated the same day, he said, "If only I get well . . . I'll go deeper into my life with you than I ever have before."

He suffered the third embolism on 29 January 1963, and so Robert Frost died, still going deeper into life.

418 · To Margaret Bartlett

SEE LETTER 412, in which RF parried Margaret Bartlett's request for permission to write the story of the Frost-Bartlett friendship. Nearly two years later Mrs. Bartlett informed RF that she was dying of cancer but that she still had time to edit and publish RF's letters to John Bartlett, if she could have permission. This is RF's answer.

Dear Margaret: [c. 22 November 1949] [Cambridge]

All the more in an emergency like this I seem disinclined to let you make a publisher's venture of the letters I wrote you and John in the simplicity of the heart back there when none of us was anybody. I take it your main idea is to put the record of our friendship beyond danger of being lost. Let me suggest one way you could do that without sacrilege. You could deposit the letters as a lot with one of the three or four collections of me I consider most important, the Jones Library of the town of Amherst (which is A No 1). The Amherst College Library (because I have spent half my time at Amherst College in the last thirty five years), the Middlebury College Library (because John went to Middlebury a little) or the Dartmouth College Library (because I went to Dartmouth a little). The Jones Library's collection is going to be the one most visited by investigators into my past if I remain at all interesting to posterity. But any one of the four libraries would be sure to treasure anything you gave it. Nor need you give complete possession of the letters. You could keep for your heirs the right to publish them in a book whenever they should get my heirs' permission. Your heirs would probably be your daughter Margaret; mine would be Kathleen Morrison and my daughter Lesley. I'm not forgetting the property value in the letters that may be greater now than it will be later. But you are not dying indigent, you are not thinking of money. You have more serious thoughts to think of than money.

Your fortitude in the face of approaching death makes it hard not to grant you the permission you ask as a last favor. I am in deep mourning for you. But even so I remain enough myself to shrink from wearing my heart on my sleeve. I say to myself if you can be so sensible about leaving this world it cant be too cruelly much for me to ask you to be sensible about a small matter like these letters. They are even trivial at a time like this. I wonder at your coolness — like Bennen's on the avalanche in Sills fine poem. If I seem to speak with the least coolness, I have caught the tone from your courage.

Affectionately   Rob

419 · To Earle J. Bernheimer

My dear Earle   19 March 1950   Cambridge

Please please! I had begun to infer from your silence that something must be going wrong. You make it sound like some bad domestic dinner you took satisfaction in making a scene of by suddenly avalanching all the dishes off the table with one sweep of one arm or one strong pull of the table cloth and then bursting out of the dining room (wildly) to go hunting wild game in Africa. I have felt that way myself. I can see how something tragic might make you want to clear your life of everything in it. You cant be too sweeping of property for my understanding and you cant be expected to stay dispassionate all the time. Throw collecting out of your life if you must and throw away your collections. But hold on a minute. You've been my friend and I've been yours. We've exchanged favors in the largest way. How many friends have you ever had who could speak to you as I am speaking now? I make no secret of it that I have had a romantic pleasure in your being my one and only Maecenas. If anybody else had bestowed on me with your generosity I might now be rich enough to take up with your offer of your Frost collection for sale. Surely our friendship has gone too far for you to want to chuck it along with the collection. Dont treat me like the women who have bedevilled you. Let's keep our kindness to each other in mind as the central fact in all this. You can see how you would hurt my sensibilities a little in seeming to assume that I would be willing to act for profit as a middleman between you and any purchaser of the books I have inscribed for you. You are in a petulant mood and not saying what you really mean. Of course I'll try to find you a purchaser in a creditable quarter if that is your insistance. But what I would very much rather do is what I have wanted to do all along — persuade you to end as you began ma[g]nificently by sending me that tailor made coat to replace the old one I used to stuff your bag with in returning you your books signed. How do I mean magnificently? I mean becoming a man of your means and intelligence. I mean by giving the whole big rubbish heap to some one library to be preserved in your name and mine as the Bernheimer Frost Collection. Our names are inextricably woven together in it. It will never explain itself except with your name made prominent on its treasure chest, showcase or room. Come, some sentiment in the grand manner for my birthday. Why not take a plane east on the momentous errand of arranging with me which will be the institution we bless with our riches. You could afford to let me share in the gift — take part of the credit. It would lift you out of yourself and out of all those miseries of litigation and resentment. I shall be delivering a lecture at the American Academy on May 26. Come there and be my guest with Kay and my daughter Lesley. And lets snatch a little fun for ourselves. Lets go to a theatre. And then maybe we could go to Amherst together with the Jones Library in mind or to Middlebury College with the Abernethy Library in mind or to Dartmouth with the Dartmouth Library in mind. I must leave out the Amherst College Library. Im inclined to think Dartmouth would give us a room all to ourselves — the room I used to teach in while there. (I belong to Amherst now.) Anyway there are four places likely to give us the prominence required. The Library [of Congress] is another possibility. The Librarian [Luther B.] Evans is a friend and would welcome us to Washington. Only there I should be afraid of being lost in the throng. It would be novel and exciting business. We have much to talk over. Once the collection was placed you could forget or not as you pleased. I would continue to add to it in your name as I went on making. I[n]deed I would add a few items to it right now.

This is in haste by air on the only paper I find in the house after my two months south.　　　　　　Ever yours　Robert

419-a · EARLE J. BERNHEIMER TO ROBERT FROST

My dear Robert:-　　　　[c. 27 March 1950]　[Beverly Hills]

Your long and friendly letter was most welcome, indeed, and I have read it over most carefully.

At the outset I want to assure you that the idea of delivering the Frost collection to a reputable and deserving institution, such as you named, was uppermost in my mind all along. But financial conditions and other important reasons have precluded the possibility of my doing this. The money that my books will bring is of great importance to me now. I must get all that I can, in every way I can. True, the Frost volumes have been inscribed for and to me — but so have all my Tarkington volumes and Steve Benet's. I must be coldly indifferent to these memories of great friendships, it seems. I cannot deposit these collections in Libraries that might treasure them. Believe me, such was, as you know because we talked of it, my treasured idea. It has to be abandoned in favor of a way that will benefit me most considerably. I thought a long time about it before I decided to write you about selling the assemblage I took greatest pride in — my Robert Frost's. I also thought about the reaction you would have. I want you to believe anything but that I want to "chuck" the collection and forget all about it. The associations with you will be, like the Birthday you celebrated yesterday, a diamond Jubilee in my wealth of memories of the past years.

I am not depressed by something that another might call tragic. I never was happier nor more content, ever. My son not being under my roof is the only thing I miss at all. That does not affect my wanting to dispose of my home and library and most of the furnishings. There were many times in my life, when I felt this same way. Felt that valuable possessions were confining — too much so. A tramp, I sometimes believe, is to be envied. He carries his holdings on the end of a stick wherever he goes.

I must emulate the tramp, slightly. Anyhow, I must shape a pattern to fit my piece of cloth. Meaning by that that I must live in a much less pretentious manner. What the general alleged friends think makes little difference to me. What a man like you thinks of me makes all the difference. I surely don't want to offend you. But I must sell ALL the things that demand so much space as an extensive library. Other things, too, that will allow me to maintain a small apartment or very small house. Financial outlays must be curtailed and I can't help who knows it. I have no reason now and want to assume no false stratum of living, in future — ever again.

So, as I wrote you without very much explanation, it is necessary that I forgo what was a cherished dream of giving several of my collections to institutions. In fact, I seem to think that it was I who mentioned to you, years ago, that such a gesture was uppermost in my mind.* Certainly, I never intended to make you feel like a middle man peddling something for a small profit. I really felt that such considerations as you have shown me deserved more tangible evidence of thanks than I have been able to bestow upon you. Long ago, and but now I admit it, I quit sending you monthly evidence of my gratefulness and genuine affection. I believe that you are entitled to make something for efforts you can make in placing my Frost collection. Your weighty word, in the right place, would benefit me greatly, indeed, and you should be compensated.

Very confidentially, I am negotiating with a New York auction gallery to dispose of my collections — other than the Frost assemblage and a couple of others. I would much rather have them kept intact and carefully preserved for posterity.

* Support for that statement is contained in letter 376.

More than any others, your volumes deserve preservation as a whole. It is a true regret that I am at a loss as to how this should be done. You are so able to assist me, I know. It is either as a whole or by piecemeal auction, unfortunately.

In the Fall, they say, will be as soon as a sale [can be arranged]. In the near future they want me to send my library East so the cataloguing may be done over the Summer.

Will you let me know, without too much delay, what you are able to advise or to accomplish?

My kindliest good wishes, always.

Most cordially yours
Earle Bernheimer

420 · To Earle J. Bernheimer

THIS LETTER ended the correspondence between RF and Bernheimer. A public auction was held on 11-12 December 1950 at the Parke-Bernet Galleries in New York City. The auction catalogue, *The Earle J. Bernheimer Collection of First Editions of American Authors Including His Remarkable Collection of the Writings of Robert Frost*, listed the Frost items in 240 lots. They brought a total of $14,695 in a bearish market which was depressed by those misunderstandings mentioned in the editor's note to letter 339-a.

The unique *Twilight*, for which Bernheimer had paid RF's price of $4,000, was bought by House of Books (Mr. and Mrs. Louis Henry Cohn) for $3,500, "reportedly the highest price ever paid for a single work by a contemporary American author" (Arthur Dempsey, "About Books," New York *Times Book Review*, 24 Dec. 1950, p. 12). Sometime later, House of Books purchased from Bernheimer some RF letters and documents which had been withheld from the auction room. Sending them the original 1940 cancelled check or draft of $4,000, Bernheimer wrote to Mrs. Marguerite Cohn on 13 November 1953, "I would like this to be placed somewhere so that, in future, talk about my selling things he 'gave' me might be stopped forever . . . No one else might give a hoot, but I would like it positively known that *Twilight* was purchased as well as most other IMPORTANT items." (This letter, the check, and the unique copy of *Twilight* are now in the Clifton Waller Barrett Collection of the Library of the University of Virginia.)

The next time RF chose to offer any of his autographed books and manuscripts for sale, he turned to Louis and Marguerite Cohn (see letters 423 and 424).

Dear Earle: 15 April 1950   Cambridge

All I can do then is spread the word among the benefactors of my colleges and see if I can find you a purchaser. I can tell by their looks that $18,000 is a lot of money for them to spend on collecting me. I am afraid the auction room is what it will come to. And probably you will feel better satisfied to have had the trial by market that I had told you in verse ["Build Soil"] everything must come to.

There should be nothing more to say. Nevertheless I am going to indulge in one last word of protest. I still think it would be a real triumph of sentiment if you made yourself the final benefactor by conferring the collection in your name on one of the colleges I spoke of. That would be fine for us both. I wish I could get at you personally for a good old persuasive talk. Please go slow in taking your decision. Mind you, the sale of the collection will give me no offence. I merely speak to save you from what you might come yourself to look on as a mistake. Of course you'll tell me if there's any chance of your being East.

Do you think I could help you better if I had a fairly complete list of what you have to dispose of?

Ever yours   Robert

421 · To Louis Henry and Marguerite Cohn

THE COHNS had sold Bernheimer most of the books in his Frost collection and had arranged to have RF autograph many of them for Bernheimer. A warm friendship had developed between RF and the Cohns. Quite naturally they were consulted by Parke-Bernet while the Bernheimer catalogue was being compiled, and they bought the largest part of the collection when the auction took place. Over the years, and in return for all his services to them, RF received many gifts from the Cohns.

Dear Louis and Margie: 14 September 1950   Ripton

Your last thought on leaving was boxes for us; your first thought on arriving is Bury [J. B. Bury, *History of Greece*] for me. Thanks should overtake you in Paris, Kay says, if I use air mail. It crossed my mind that you have probably backslid into a Frenchman by now and my English will be thrown away on you — you cant read a word of it. Thanks is an idiomatic use of the verb thanks as a plural noun to express gratitude and then some.

The format of Bury turns out to be not so much better than the one I have (Modern Library), but it has the advantage of some fine folded maps. It's my favorite recent history.

You two are natural born travellers and can be wished in all sincerity a splendid time. I enjoy thinking of travellers more than I do sharing their vicissitudes. You travel for me (I mean as my plenipotentiaries) and I stay at home for myself. It's a rainy day here among the Vermountains (Vermont is almost a French word) and Kay and I are shut in up in the log cabin, she making a fair copy of my latest long poem and I am making this. I find such pleasure in writing friends that I wonder why I dont write oftener. Her talk about you set me going. We were saying how glad we were to hear you had been called in on the Bernheimer collection sale. You'll tell us more about it when you get back.

If I were visiting France a principal interest would be in looking up a certain farmer named La Fargue whose family have their title to their farm from Charlemagne and have lived on it all these thousand years since. I saw their thrifty figures in smocks pictured in a farm magazine once and read the citation they got from the French government with a medal for having stayed so long in one place. Relatives of mine have just given up a farm near Kittery Maine that they had held for three hundred years. But what is three hundred compared with a thousand? If you see the La Fargues in society remember me to them. Tell them I too am landed and could wish myself a French peasant with a long long pedigree.

I believe I never sent you a poem. You may not want one. But I believe I will send you one herewith if only to break the rule.*

Our best to your both.   Ever yours   Robert

422 · To Edward Connery Lathem

WHILE he was an undergraduate at Dartmouth College in the Class of '51, Lathem began collecting first printings of RF's poems in magazines. He later presented the collection to the Baker Library at Dartmouth. After he had trained for library work, Lathem became Director of Special Collections in the Baker Library and then Associate Librarian of the College. His intensive and successful efforts helped to make the RF collection of books, manuscripts, and letters at Dartmouth one of the major Frost collections.

This letter marks the beginning of an important friendship;

* The enclosure was a manuscript of "Doomed to Bloom," used by RF as his Christmas poem for 1950.

it was written just before Lathem began his senior year at Dartmouth.

Dear Lathem: 15 September 1950   Ripton

Research-boy, chronicler, historian all are worth being in an ascending scale. You are certainly off to a good start for the first and even second — yes and even third. It seems to me for you to decide how far you want to go. I sometimes wish there were more strict chroniclers for me to read. Though historians are my favorites they can disturb me with a tendency to be novelists. They can overindulge the dramatic and narrative faculties till I lose my confidence that there is any such thing as a fact. Maybe there isnt any such thing. For every fact of history I have had faith in a low-down has turned up to the effect that it's a lie. But examine a first class history like Bury's Greece for the irreducible reality and theres really a considerable share of it to rest on. Where there are dubeities they are frankly marked. For instance we might like to think but do not know that Asia was beaten by Europe at Himera in Sicily and away off beyond communication at Salamis on the same day exactly. It shapes up fine that way. But is that enough to let it go at that? I am not satisfied to call it history when it leaves me as insecure as that. Fiction has one kind of thing it has to be true to and history another. I like the two kinds kept as separate as possible. I have been told they inevitably mingle. I may as well give in and enjoy them both for being true to ideas or to human nature or something else they may aim at. (No, I disagree. I wont give in.)

You'll be amused to have the enclosed magazine [*The Forge* containing "Locked Out"] for your Dartmouth collection. Do I understand you are helping build me up in the Baker Library? I'm not telling you what to do with the gift. Do what you please with it. It's a rarity I think. One of the editors sent it me lately.   Ever yours   Robert Frost

423 · To Louis Henry Cohn

WHEN RF had offered to sell Bernheimer two manuscripts for $1,000 apiece in 1941 (see letter 383), and Bernheimer had made a counteroffer to which RF had not immediately replied, Bernheimer wrote to Cohn on 2 July 1941 to ask if he had offended the poet. Cohn answered: "I cannot see how you could possibly have offended Frost by offering to advance him a thousand dollars. He may be slightly annoyed that you did not fall for his little game of getting two thousand out of you for a couple of manuscripts not worth half that sum. He may have thought that you were more naive than you are."

Ten years later, when RF offered to sell Cohn the first-draft manuscript of his Modern Library preface, "The Constant Symbol," and a manuscript of his unpublished one-act play, "In an Art Factory," for $1,200 apiece, RF may have merely been horse-trading or simply underestimating Cohn's grasp of market prices. Cohn discussed these prices with the collector RF had in mind as a possible buyer, and after amicable negotiation Cohn paid $1,000 to RF for the unpublished play and $500 to Mrs. Morrison for the preface. For RF's reaction and acceptance of the terms, see letter 424.

Dear Louis   [18 July 1951] [Ripton]

The manuscripts are before you. Don't you think that being what they are — the preface an actual first draft and the play the only existing draft of by all odds the best I have written — K. ought to have twelve hundred for the first which is hers and I ought to have twelve hundred for the second which is mine? I gave her the first when she typed the copy of it for the Modern Library edition. The late auction has influenced us in fixing the prices but if you think them too high I wish you would tell us frankly how much you would reduce them. It would be a fine thing if they could go to swell the important collection of Mr. Barrett. The money, at least part of it, would be a fine thing to swell my investment in this farm. My ambition has lately run to farming.

You gave us a good time with your visit and we were glad to hear you got safely home like Joseph and Mary by another way.   Ever yours Robert

424 · To Louis Henry Cohn

Dear Louis: 27 July 1951 Ripton

If you are satisfied that's all we ought to have and if it is to be by count of pages, why all right, go ahead. Remember that the play belongs to me and the essay to K. It must be hard for you to be the intermediary in a matter like this but cheer up, you'll soon be in the happy hunting grounds across the Atlantic where French is spoken with a French accent.

Best wishes to you both and thanks
      Ever yours Robert

425 · To Louis Henry Cohn

Dear Louis: 12 September 1951   [Ripton]

This purports to be the spurious collector's item I promised you over the telephone. The only thing to authenticate it will be the signature at the end which is a new one I have just adopted in acknowledgement of what the sculptors did to me at the Hanover Hospital. General Ridgeway in Asia would call it Operation Save Face, and that's all right with me, if it turns out that my face is saved — more or less. Anyway that is a great hospital over there as I can testify from its having saved me not only my face but now for the second time my life.

We ought not put on humanistic airs to make fun of science because though it can postpone death, it can't do away with death. I for one, I am willing to be under obligation to it for postponing death. I count every year beyond the time I had pneumonia in 1906 as velvet. I had hardly accomplished a thing then that I had in my heart if not in my mind to do.

No we mustnt forget to give science its due. It is much though not everything that it prolongs my individual life and yours. It is much though far from everything that it maintains the human race on the planet beyond all expectation. And now you may have noticed its mouthpiece Prexy [James B.] Conant has undertaken for it to make the planet less uncomfortably crowded with a new kind of manna (manna from Hell not Heaven, a religious friend Al Edwards calls it), a contraceptive to be taken at the mouth so we can stop breeding without having to stop futution. I made a five line poem on the event entitled Pares Continuas Fututiones (Catullus XXXII). You may object to the word "futution" as pedantic and rare even in classic Latin. But remember I have never been either a soldier or sailor like you and you must allow for the limitations of my vocabulary. I know what you are thinking. You wish I would shut up and deliver the goods. Well then — if you want the poem, here it is

Pares Continuas Fututiones

Says our Harvard Neo Malthushian
"We cant keep the poor from futution;
But by up to date feeding
We can keep them from breeding."
Which seems a licentious conclusion!

There I guess that's the way I want that to stand.

I begin to wonder if I am furnishing you with any internal evidence that I am the author of this letter. Let's see what more I can say to convince you that it is I that speaketh. My predicament is like the ghost's on the Ouiga Board. I wish I could mention something nobody but you and I could possibly know the answer to: such as for instance that leaning old silo in the Elysian Fields we used to suck fermentation out of with a straw in the interval between our last two existences but one. Some philosophy warned us against it as habit forming. It proved to be worse than that. It killed us — killed us out of heaven back into life. Remember?

Take care of yourself. My best to Margie.   Scarface

426 · To Louis Henry and Marguerite Cohn

Dear Louis and Margie   17 January 1952   Cambridge

Your Christmas present this time beat all that went before. It must mean religion and wine have some necessary connection. I'm no wine-bibber as you know. But I'll say this for wine: it doesnt cloy. Candy cloys, cheese cloys, fish cloys. We have tried them all and I can report on them. The worst that wine does on top of a good meal and after a good meal has almost put you to sleep is put you to sleep entirely. I should say the best it does. And that I've figured it out at last was what it was sent into the world for by way of the grape. I've been awfully slow in my realizations. It just dawned on me late in life putting away those pint sauternes one a day at noon in the best company that wine was intended to promote carelessness. I always thought I didn't care enough but after this week's experience I don't care if I don't. We have you to thank for my edification. From now on I expect to be an easier man to live with. It is out of sheer newly acquired good nature that I am sending you as a gift to treasure or sell for yourself off the counter what I take to be the first edition of a book [Edna St. Vincent Millay, *A Few Figs from Thistles*] that expresses what I take to be the gospel of carelessness. All I have left to care for in this world is a few friends. You're two of them.   Robert

427 · To Robert Chase

My dear Robert Chase: 4 March 1952   South Miami

You have the family name of my chief friend on the board of trustees of Pinkerton when I was a teacher there: John Chase, owner of the small factory in Derry Village where he made wooden tree labels and wooden tongue depressers for doctors. I ought to find you something you could use in memory of him. He was a thirty-third degree Mason and an important man in the world. He had me out to walk with him botanizing now and then and his notice gave me any security I may have had in my position teaching without any college degree. His notice and the Rev Charles Merriam's, pastor of the Congregational Church on the hill there in the village — also a trustee. I mustn't forget either of them. Mr. Merriam really got me into the Academy after I was introduced to him by the Rev Mr Wolcott of Lawrence as a young writer whose poetry he had read in the New York Independent. Mr. Merriam said if I would read a poem to his Men's League Banquet it might prove all that was needed to win me a place on the Pinkerton faculty. I told him I would never dare to read in public, but I would give him a poem for him to read and sit beside him when he stood up to read it. The poem was A Tuft of Flowers, that sounds as if it might have been composed on purpose for such a fraternal occasion. It wasnt, but it happened to fit. It was a success and started me off on my more serious teacher's life.

Poetry has got me indirectly or directly practically all the living I have had. It got me my job in Pinkerton then and got me into Amherst College later when I came home from England. It brings me to visit many colleges nowadays. I worked many hours a week at Pinkerton; I should hardly dare to tell you how many. But many of them were as good hours as I ever had. I became great friends with some of the students such as John and Margaret Bartlett and Harold Abbott. The fellow teacher I cared most for was Miss Sylvia Clark. I believe Robert Lincoln O'Brien, the famous old Pinkertonian, was the chief speaker the night my poem was read on trial. Miss Clark was there. She will probably tell you more about my Pinkerton days than I can myself.

For two years I was only a part-time-teacher. Then for three I taught a little more than anybody else, I think the records would show. But I never took my turn leading chapel. I was so obviously too scared they let me off — both the heads I came under, Mr. Bingham and Mr. Silver. I taught English chiefly, but also history Latin and geometry.

You might be interested to know that during my ten years in Derry the first five of them farming altogether and the last five mostly teaching but still farming a little, I wrote more than half of my first book much more than half of my second and even quite a little of my third, though they were not published till later.

I might say the core of all my writing was probably the five free years I had there on the farm down the road a mile or two from Derry Village toward Lawrence. The only thing we had plenty of was time and seclusion. I couldnt have figured on it in advance. I hadnt that kind of foresight. But it turned out as right as a doctor's prescription.

For the rest you must consult Louis Untermeyer's prefaces. I don't feel sure anybody but Miss Clark will remember my Derry past. My near neighbors names were Miltmore, Berry, Lowe and Webster. By this time they have probably gone their ways or passed on. You are free to look them up in your investigation of me. But to be a good article about me your story should rise above gossip to make discoveries of your own in my poetry. Make some identifications on your own insight. For the sake of the old obligations I have done more for you than I have for anyone else I remember.

Sincerely yours   Robert Frost

428 · To Lawrance Thompson

Dear Larry: [c. 1 May 1952]   [Amherst]

While you were waiting patiently for my report on herman's quarrel with god, you doubtless had plenty to occupy your mind in the reports you got on it from your rival melvillians. As you know I take in no reviews and learn what reviewers think only by hearsay. They seem to have been favorable to you, though not quite able to go the whole length with you in your belief that herman hated god. One look at your book and I should be sure that if they disagreed with you materially they were wrong. I have encountered in the flesh both before and as it has happened after you came out two or three of the party of "acceptance" in the explanation of Billy Budd. They have sounded to me sadistically foolish in their enjoyment of the inexorable they never experienced except in literature. Of course Melville hated God every step of the way in doing Billy in. You did a great chapter there. Melville hated evil for the rather personal reason that Emerson's God included evil as just some more good and Melville couldn't stomach Emerson.

I got real satisfaction out of your conclusion too. As I jump to the last chapter of a love story to see if "she got him" for all the course of true love didnt run smooth, so I began with your summary to see if you got Melville. Having made sure of that I can take my time with the rest of your exposition. I've already talked about it in a class George Whicher lent me, and brought it up with sundry at Yale, Bowdoin and Smith. Newton Arvin praised you, though I gathered he was in print on the acceptance theory of Billy Budd.

That's an awful story really. I think it the worst outrage ever written. The purpose couldnt be anything but to discredit God. But I am glad you take the position that Melville's wrongness, unsoundness or whatever we call it matters next to nothing at all in our judgement of him as a great story teller, one of America's splendors in art. Does wisdom matter, I once asked in public. My answer was then and is now and as yours is, not at all or at least hardly at all. I must confess you do take away from Melville's stature a little in making him bother to believe in a God he hates. How could he have failed to see he had got round by a series of insensible cog-slips to where he should have changed God's name to Devil. He seems rather weak on the brain side. But as you say never mind. We may admire him more wrong than almost anybody but Hawthorne right. It should be a lesson to undergraduates not to pay too much attention to the disproportionately long hours their lecturers spend on a good poet's good or bad philosophy so called. What an inducement to endless discourses a poet offers who begins as a bad thinker and ends up another kind of thinker. In his last state he may be too easily mistaken for a good thinker. He's a godsend to the critics just the same. Graham Greene's formula for an entertaining salvation is to have sinned deeply and repented greatly. Always lots of nonsense abroad. He must be thinking of St. Augustine more than St. Thomas Acquinas. Thomas was a good boy from first to last. I believe he weighed too much, but the Church will have it his weight was glandular.

Did it ever occur to you there was a certain air of nouveau richeness to Herman's style as if he wasnt quite a Bostonian but it couldnt be helped. He had (or may be suspected of having) the embarrassment of a parvenu with his hands and feet (metrical feet) in Mass society. I began to notice it years ago when I read Typee aloud at home. He tried to be elegant without having first got sophisticated. In another way Marquand has suffered more than necessary from the ineffability of Boston. The editor of the Boston Globe said to me once if he and I weren't perturbed in our Harvard days by the Porcillian Club it was because we didn't know of its existance.

It is one or two o'clock true or false in the morning and I must be giving Gillie his bed time half hour on the Amherst streets. Ever yours   Robert

429 · To Louis Henry Cohn

ONE OF the fanciest pieces of bibliopolic horse-trading between RF and Cohn is only touched on in this letter. After a public reading in New York City, RF showed Cohn the copy of *Complete Poems* which the poet had used on the platform that night, a copy into which RF had written some unpublished poems. It made an interesting "association copy," and in a moment of weakness Cohn offered $500 for it. The offer was immediately accepted and the exchange was completed. Some time later Cohn sent the "association copy" back to RF requesting that RF enrich it a bit more with some additional manuscripts and notes useful for future readings. RF complied. It is now in the Barrett Collection at the University of Virginia Library.

Dear Louis   4 August 1953   Ripton
The book you sent back for more signs and marks of usage, having now been through another campaign, looks to me in as ideal a condition for your purposes as you could expect me to make it. You dont want me to go on with it till you and I and it fall to pieces. A lot has got crowded into it on flyleaves and elsewhere because as I tell my audiences the very name of the book forbids my having any more poems outside its covers. That's a poetic fiction I play with till I can get around to having another book in the spirit of The Gift Outright, For Columbus Day, and The Cabin in the Clearing.

I had my conscience tweeked by a nice letter from Freddy Adams about you and some items you let him have . . . Otherwise you might not be getting your property so suddenly. I shall mail it today.   Yours devotedly   Robert

430 · To Victor E. Reichert

THE FRIENDSHIP between RF and Rabbi Victor E. Reichert of Cincinnati, Ohio, developed over many years. At RF's urging, Reichert purchased in 1944 a renovated schoolhouse-summer home not far from RF's Homer Noble Farm in Ripton. At that time the Bible was a favorite topic for their discussions, particularly the Book of Job; Reichert had previously published a scholarly study of Job, and RF was currently working on *A Masque of Reason* and *A Masque of Mercy*.

While visiting the Reicherts in Cincinnati on 10 October 1946, RF accepted the Rabbi's invitation to give a brief talk that day in the Rockdale Avenue Temple as part of the service celebrating the First Day of the Feast of Tabernacles. The talk was subsequently printed in pamphlet form, with RF's permission, as *Sermon by Robert Frost*. Some of RF's remarks in that Sermon echoed and extended the prayerful utterance in Psalm 19, verse 14. RF later told Reichert that the service had helped him find precisely the ending he wanted for *A Masque of Mercy*:

> We have to stay afraid deep in our souls
> Our sacrifice, the best we have to offer,
> And not our worst nor second best, our best,
> Our very best, our lives laid down like Jonah's,
> Our lives laid down in war and peace, may not
> Be found acceptable in Heaven's sight.
> And that they may be is the only prayer
> Worth praying. May my sacrifice
> Be found acceptable in Heaven's sight. . . .

This letter, written six years after the publication of *A Masque of Mercy*, indicates that RF had forgotten and wanted to be reminded of the precise biblical passage that had provided inspiration for the climactic speech.

Dear Victor: [5 November 1953] Amherst

Do you want to tell me where in the Bible if at all the idea occurs as a prayer that our sacrifice whether of ourselves or our property may be acceptable in His sight? Have I been making this up out of nothing? You know how I am about chapter and verse — somewhat irresponsible some would say. I went wielding the phrase *culpa felix* to my own purposes for a long time before I pinned myself down to what it may originally have meant in Church history.

Someone may be getting after me in the matter of this prayer I have gone about so cheerfully quoting as the heart and center of all religion. It is kindred in spirit to

Nevertheless not my will but Thy will.

But that isn't enough. I feel sure it occurs more than once.

As from one mountaineer to another Robert

430-a · VICTOR E. REICHERT TO ROBERT FROST

Dear Robert: [c. 8 November 1953]   [Cincinnati]

[. . .] You most assuredly have not been making this up out of nothing. On the morning, memorable for us of the Rockdale Avenue Temple, the First Day of the Feast of Tabernacles, Thursday, October 10, 1946, you read these words of prayer out of our Union Prayer Book:

"Look with favor, O Lord, upon us, and may our service ever be acceptable unto Thee. Praised be Thou, O God, whom alone we serve in reverence."

In our morning service for the Sabbath, there is also a prayer that begins:

"Our God and God of our fathers, grant that our worship on this Sabbath be acceptable to Thee."

Turning now to the Bible, the prize passage that completely supports your view . . . the key passage is Psalm 19, verse 14:-

"Let the words of my mouth, and the meditation of my heart be acceptable before Thee, O Lord, my Rock, and my Redeemer."

[. . .] In affectionate regard to you, Robert, who keep teaching me how to climb that mountain,   Ever,   Victor E.

431 · TO LAWRANCE THOMPSON

IN DECEMBER of 1954, RF was asked to participate in a television program *The Enjoyment of Poetry*, which was to be produced the following January by the National Broadcasting Company. His interlocutor was to be Thompson, who suggested that the discussion might be built around a dramatized version of "The Witch of Coös" so as to bring out similarities and differences between what appealed most to the author and what might appeal most to the general reader in that poem. RF seemed to accept these suggestions. As this letter makes clear, however, and as the actual broadcast eventually proved, RF was determined to use his time on the program as a means of attacking what he considered to be the misuses of poetry exemplified by the analytical procedures of the "new critics" and college professors. He got what he wanted. The program was entirely ad lib, except for a fine dramatization of "The Witch of Coös" with Mildred Dunnock in the leading role. As soon as he was "on camera" RF forgot all his promises to let himself be led in discussion. Each tendentious point made by Thompson was pounced on, growled over, and torn to shreds by the poet. All the "enjoyment" was his.

Dear Larry: 29 December 1954   Ripton

What you mean is to steer the conversation where you and I will have a chance to say some bright things about the way poetry might be supposed to be taken by the writer of it, the teacher of it, and the natural reader of it. I don't want to make a show of conflicting with you and it is easy to avoid this by according you the position of the natural reader — and claiming it for myself. I don't mind operators on poetry any more than I mind operators on the human body (divine) but I hate to have everybody that goes to college treated as if he was going to be an operator on either poetry or the human body (divine). I am sure you agree with me. The object of college should be to get as many educated as possible without spoiling them as natural readers.

The right virtue of the natural reader is the nice ability to tell always when a poem is being figurative and when it is not being figurative; just as it is the indispensible [virtue] of a member of society to know how to judge correctly whether his friends and relatives are hinting or not hinting.

Besides the danger of seeing figures and symbols where none are intended is the dangerous presumption on the part of the critics that they can go the poet one better by telling him what he is up to. He may think he knows what he means but it takes a modern critic to catch him at what he is up to. Shelley for instance thought he meant the desire of the moth for the star when he was merely up to seduction. A little of the low-down on motivation goes a long way. None of this is meant to memorize for the occasion. I'm going to leave it to you to lead the talk where you please in this or any other direction. Hope your courage is good. Write me anything you think will help. Happy New Year to all the Thompsons.

Ever yours   Robert

432 · To HOWARD G. SCHMITT

RF once made the casual and humorous suggestion that a good patchwork quilt might be made out of the silk hoods he had received with honorary degrees from a great many colleges and universities. The suggestion was made in November 1954, in the presence of Howard G. Schmitt, a book-collecting friend of many years, who immediately said that three of his aunts, veteran patch-quilters, would be delighted to carry out RF's thought. The project was undertaken and completed very beautifully during the next six months by Miss Ida and Miss Louise Schmitt and Mrs. Anna

Schmitt Braunlich in Hamburg, New York. Two complete quilts and a small throw were made from the hoods. Stitched into each quilt was a chronological list, printed in India ink, of the institutions represented, the degrees, and the dates awarded.

Because the quilts were presented to RF in Hanover on the day when Dartmouth College awarded him still another hood, RF immediately requested that Schmitt take the quilts back to his aunts to have the new hood incorporated somehow. This was done by sewing triangle-shaped patches of green on all four corners of each quilt.

Dear Howard: 17 June 1955   Ripton

You were a good boy: you turned up at President Dickey's just at one of the highest moments of my academic career to blanket it with such a distinguished work of quilting as never was before on land or sea. Somehow it had occurred to me that somewhere in your background might lurk just the right artist to synthesize the hoods I had been getting by degrees, but I confess my surprise to learn you had three such artists as your aunts right in your family. Your gift was a many-colored surprise to all of us, I, me and the assembled commencement company at the President's house. You capped the climax of a great day. And we mustnt forget such things have their importance though of course they are only incidental to what my life is all about.   Ever yours   Robert

433 · TO SHERMAN ADAMS

WHILE Sherman Adams was Governor of New Hampshire (1949-1953) he and RF met under pleasant circumstances. On a visit to Boston, Adams was taken to the St. Botolph Club to hear RF give a reading of his poems, and at the end of the evening the Governor was called on for remarks. Much to the poet's surprise, the Governor quoted from memory several appropriate lines of RF's poem "New Hampshire." Their friendship continued to develop.

Later on Adams, then Assistant to President Dwight D. Eisenhower, conceived the idea of sending RF to England as an ambassador of good will under the auspices of the Department of State. As a preparatory move he wrote to RF on 15 May 1956 suggesting that they have a reunion in Washington; he wrote again on 7 June 1956, and was also instrumental in having the Department of State send a representative to Ripton for an exploratory talk. This letter makes reference to the sequence of events.

Dear Sherman: 21 June 1956   Ripton

Great to be named after a general so great. He and Grant were a pair. Such are the things I could wish you leisure to talk with me about sometime. Meanwhile we *should* meet if only for a hasty moment to talk over whatever it is you mean you have so close at heart for me to do. I could hardly more than guess what it is from the pleasant man that came up to see me from the State Department. I should like to think I was willing to be serviceable but I shrink from being official and using my pen on purpose to popularize my country. Your messenger told me we were loved by nobody in the world. If in their small way the poems I write don't make us friends (in their small way) they at least represent the best I can think of writing. Surely I am better at verse than at prose. May I suggest that possibly the best thing *you* could do for the cause would be to keep on magnifying me the way you have been ever since you descended in state on us that night at the St. Botolph Club: for which I shall be   Always gratefully yours   Robert

433-a · SHERMAN ADAMS TO ROBERT FROST

[Printed letterhead]

THE WHITE HOUSE
WASHINGTON

THE ASSISTANT TO THE PRESIDENT

Dear Robert: July 3, 1956

I went to Ripton once on skis — about ten years before anybody knew how to ski. Maybe someone has told you about where the Pleiad Lake Lodge stands. We shoveled two feet of snow off the bunks, and that was our second mistake. The first was trying to ski the long trail, a foolhardy undertaking at best. This I think was in 1917.

Some of us think Eisenhower should continue to be President, and most of us are confident he will be able to. We thought you might like to lend your moral strength to a group which we will call Committee of Artists and Scientists for Eisenhower, which you will see spelled CASE. You would not have to do any more than give it a blessing.

It has been altogether too long since we have seen you. If

you are in Ripton all summer, perhaps we could drive by and pick a few blackberries. These are my favorite, especially when they go into a three-decker shortcake.

Sincerely,   Sherm Adams

433-b · HAROLD E. HOWLAND TO ROBERT FROST

[Printed letterhead]

DEPARTMENT OF STATE

December 10, 1956

Dear Mr. Frost,   WASHINGTON, D. C.

Our Embassy at London has informed us that it is planning an exhibit concerning your life and work some time this winter or the spring of 1957. The Embassy has further stated that a personal visit by you would enhance immeasurably the effect of this exhibit on the English public.

The Department of State, recalling your splendid cooperation in visiting Latin America several years ago, wholeheartedly endorses the Embassy's suggestion. A visit to Great Britain by you at this time would render tremendous assistance to the task of emphasizing the common Anglo-American heritage. The Department of State therefore takes this opportunity to extend to you an invitation to visit Great Britain at your convenience some time between February and June 1957. The Department would, of course, defray your expenses.

Please be assured of our best wishes.

Sincerely yours, Harold E. Howland
Leaders-Specialists Division
International Education Exchange Service

434 · TO HAROLD E. HOWLAND

Dear Mr. Howland   1 January 1957   Ripton

The State Department honors me. What you propose is very interesting. I should like to hear more about it. You realize going to England on a mission so to speak would be a considerable undertaking at my age. To be sure I am kicked around at home a good deal, but that is among the home folks. You exaggerate the importance of what I did in South America. As

I told Mr. Dulles when I came back a little Spanish and Portuguese would have given me better entree down there. I was none too satisfied with my results. But Brazil and Peru are not England. . . . For confidence I must be made sure of the demand for me. And I must see things planned pretty well ahead. . . .   Sincerely yours   Robert Frost

435 · To Eustace Seligman

Dear Eustace   2 January 1957   Ripton

You may remember the boy you gave the gold cuff links to on his eightieth birthday and had the almost public altercation with before the Amherst Trustees on the value of permanent peace. Well, he's in trouble now you may gather from the enclosed letters [433-b and 434] we have copied out for you. I might want to go to England on the errand they are talking about if the terms were right and the behest were on a high enough level. I thought it would be a good chance for you to make it up between us by interceding in my favor a little as you and I know you could away up where it would do some real good. You can tell by the tone of voice that I do and I don't care for the prospect. I surely don't want to bestir myself for anything but big stakes for anybody less than yourself, your partner Mr. Dulles, Mr. Whitney, and Sherm Adams, not to mention the President. You know all about me. What with my barding round the colleges and the poems I publish in print and by word of mouth and the build-up I get nowadays on television my ambition is pretty well sated. Still if there is any further step upward in this you think I ought to take and can take, please tell me. I can throw myself on you at least for advice. Don't go any further than advice unless so inclined. I fear I am getting so self-complacent that I am only cross at temptations to new effort. I trust this isn't presuming too much on the importance you said I had for you as the only modern poet you keep on reading since you gave up Housman. . . .

Ever yours   Robert Frost

435-a · JOHN FOSTER DULLES TO ROBERT FROST

[Printed letterhead]

DEPARTMENT OF STATE

February 12, 1957

Dear Mr. Frost: WASHINGTON, D. C.

I have recently learned that you have been invited by the International Education Exchange Service to undertake a "good-will" mission to Great Britain this coming spring. I well recall the success of your previous mission of this kind to Latin America. In our discussions shortly thereafter we mutually agreed on the importance of such visits by prominent literary figures.

I sincerely hope that you will be able to accept this new call upon your services as a distinguished representative of the American cultural scene. I can assure you that the Department of State and the American Embassy in London will wish to render all possible assistance in the event that you undertake this mission. . . .   Sincerely yours,

John Foster Dulles
Secretary of State

436 · TO JOHN FOSTER DULLES

Dear Mr. Dulles: 26 February 1957   Cambridge

Your letter helps me to a decision. I feel better with your assurance that the State Department and our Embassy will take care of me to see that I am kept reasonably busy. I wouldn't want to be shot off as an unguided missile. I have personal friends in England and Scotland, though not so many as once upon a time when I lived with them a while before the great wars. My books are over there with Jonathan Cape and I must have some readers. But I wouldn't want it to look as if I had just come over to laze around amiably on vacation. I wish you could tell Mr. Howland that it is not overwork that I fear. I want my time planned for. At home as Mr. Howland probably knows my specialty is talking ideas and reading my own poetry. For instance I shall be talking at Michigan right away on the "Adventure Into Materiality" and at Chapel Hill on "Maturity No Object." I have long been holding back one "In Praise of the West India Company, Clive and Warren Hastings." And Burke! I might risk it on the British. I detain you thus only to warn you again the kind of liberal you are turning loose to disport himself currying favor with our cousins. Some day I may be thanking you for this opportunity if it works out.

Most respectfully yours,   Robert Frost

436-a · HERBERT BROWNELL, JR., TO ROBERT FROST

AMONG the many artists, writers, and statesmen who worked for Ezra Pound's release from imprisonment-without-trial, the most self-effacingly active and successful was the lawyer-poet-dramatist-liberal, Archibald MacLeish. He was the man who brought RF reluctantly into "The Pound Case," and he conducted his backstage manipulations of RF with exceptional tact. Eventually and mistakenly, RF assumed he had played a truly decisive part in securing Pound's freedom.

The full story of MacLeish's elaborate campaign on behalf of Pound cannot be told here, but this letter brings him in obliquely. In it, Attorney General Brownell thanks RF for a letter MacLeish had written: an appeal on behalf of Pound signed by three literary figures whose reputations were calculated to have a good deal of weight with the Republican Party members of the Eisenhower regime. The final draft of the appeal had been typed on the letterhead of The American Academy of Arts and Letters at the request of MacLeish, member and former president of the Academy. He had then collected signatures from Ernest Hemingway in Cuba, T. S. Eliot in England, and Frost in New England.

[Printed letterhead]

OFFICE OF THE ATTORNEY GENERAL

February 28, 1957
WASHINGTON, D. C.

Mr. Robert Frost
The American Academy of Arts and Letters
633 West 155 Street
New York, New York

Dear Mr. Frost:

This will acknowledge receipt of your recent letter, also signed by Ernest Hemingway and T. S. Eliot, regarding Ezra Pound who is confined in St. Elizabeths Hospital in Washington at the present time. I have asked that a review of the matter be made, and when it is completed I will communicate further with you.

Very truly yours,
Herbert Brownell, Jr.
Attorney General

436-b · SIR DOUGLAS VEALE TO ROBERT FROST

[Printed letterhead]

UNIVERSITY REGISTRY

OXFORD

Dear Mr. Frost,   9 March 1957

I have much pleasure in informing you that the Hebdo-
madal Council has resolved to propose to the Convocation of
the University that the Degree of Doctor of Letters, honoris
causa, be conferred upon you.

I understand that you will be visiting this country in
April or May, and if you are willing that the proposal for the
honorary degree should go forward I should be glad if you
could let me know the exact dates of your visit so that arrangements could be made for the conferment of the degree. . . .

436-c · SIR BRIAN DOWNS TO ROBERT FROST

[Printed letterhead]

THE VICE-CHANCELLOR OF THE UNIVERSITY

THE MASTER'S LODGE

CHRIST'S COLLEGE, CAMBRIDGE

My dear Sir,   March 11, 1957

The Council of the Senate of the University of Cambridge
desire to propose your name to the University as a recipient
of the Degree of Doctor of Letters honoris causa.

At the direction of the Council, with which I have the
greatest pleasure in complying, I beg leave hereby to enquire
whether you are willing to accept the Council's invitation to be
presented for this Degree.

The Congregation of the Senate for the conferment of
Honorary Degrees has been fixed for Thursday morning, June
13, 1957; candidates for Honorary Degrees are required to
present themselves in person. . . .

437 · TO SIR DOUGLAS VEALE

Dear Mr. Veale: 26 March 1957   Cambridge

Few things could give me the pleasure of such an honor
from the country ("half my own") that published my very first

book. That was nearly fifty years ago when I was living and writing not fifty miles down the line from you in Beaconsfield. I shall look at it as a rounding out that we seldom get except in story books and none too often there. Third acts and last chapters are notoriously hard to write. So much for the degree; then there is the matter of the invitation from your Assistant to read and talk to your faculty; which I shall leave to my friend, Mrs. Morrison, to tend to when she has deciphered the signature. I very much like the idea of meeting the Faculty of the University as a troubador that way. It's as a sort of troubador I've been to so many of our American colleges. She'll be writing tomorrow. I am in a very happy frame of mind over this visit to England.   Sincerely yours   Robert Frost

438 · To Lawrance Thompson

Dear Larry: 16 April 1957   Cambridge

I wasnt going to come clear out into open company with it like something important enough to be much made of, but I did want to tell you the other night the pleasant news of what I am really sailing (by plane) for to England on May 19. I am after degrees at both Cambridge and Oxford. The one at Cambridge they have already publicly announced in The Times (London) so we are free to talk about that if we like. We shall be free to mention the other after April 25. I shall probably be taking a third at Dublin too if a date can be arranged. (I shall be sorry if it cant: you know how I have always felt about Ireland.)

Al [Edwards] and Kay know all about it all. I know you will be one of the chiefest concerned. You will start thinking with me from scratch about its meaning in the story. It will sort of round off things I initiated with Mrs David [Mrs. Alfred] Nutt in a small office in Bloomsbury among total strangers forty five years ago already almost too old to bet on. There is that in it anyway. It will also sort of round off my rather great academic career in general. I have had about everything I can have in my own country. Now for the mother country. We are not talking of deserts. No triumphs for me. But satisfactions I dont see why I shouldnt be permitted.

The expenses are to be taken care of by our Dept of State, for whom I shall have certain duties as I understand it to perform. There was word from Dublin, none from any higher up. I can't help thinking how different that might have been if Robert Taft had been President. His son was to have entertained me in Dublin. He has just given up being Ambassador in the Old Nick of Time.

If I ever have the least danger of feeling successful it is from the growing evidence that America has accepted me as one of her poets. What the British are doing is in foreign recognition of this fact. Kay seems even gladder of it than I am as yet. She had both father and mother from over there. Also she was partly educated over there. I had only a mother. And I never so much as set foot in Oxford or Cambridge before.

Many many thoughts! I wanted you to share them.

Ever yours   Robert

439 · To Lawrance Thompson

RF was eighty-three years old when he made plans to visit England and Ireland; he wanted and needed a traveling companion. But so many volunteers stepped forward that he felt forced into a slight subterfuge in making a choice. He flew to London without a companion on 19 May 1957 and Thompson joined him there the next day. The subterfuge and the backstage arrangements are hinted in this letter.

Dear Larry: 24 April 1957   Cambridge

It has been brought to my attention that you are to be in England when I am there this spring. What a happy coincidence! We should find all sorts of ways of getting together. For good collusion perhaps we should get together here in advance. I am disinclined to create literature by writing it all out in letters. Is there any chance you could come up to Amherst for a little talk on the quiet on Monday, May 6, Tuesday May 7, or Wednesday May 8 when I shall be there saying some goodbys? These are strenuous excitements.   Ever yours   Robert

440 · To T. S. Eliot

Dear Eliot: 2 May 1957   Cambridge

It would be a great disappointment if my more or less official return to England didn't mean furthering our acquaintance; and I should be less a respector of persons than I am if I didn't hope to give you before I get through with this here world the highest sign of my regard. You and I shot off at different tangents from almost the same pin wheel. We had America in common and we had Ezra in common though you had much more of him than I. If I was ever cross with you it was for leaving America behind too far and Ezra not far enough. But such things look less and less important as we age on. You have been a great poet in my reading. Evaluation hasn't been any part of my livelihood and judging my contemporaries only bothers my sincerity. But I was always sure of Robinson. It was on Robinson that Ezra and I got together in 1913. And I can tell how sure I have been of you by the regret I feel that your delicacy kept you out of Auden's anthology of American poetry. Jonathan Cape will help me find you, I suppose. He talks of a party on May 29. I shall hope there can be more to it than just that.

By right vested in me as your senior by many years. There's Harvard in it, too.   Ever yours,   Frost

440-a · T. S. Eliot to Robert Frost

[Printed letterhead]

FABER AND FABER LTD
PUBLISHERS

24 Russell Square London WC1

Dear Frost: 7 May 1957

I was very happy to get your letter of May 2nd. Of course, I had already heard some time ago from private sources that you were coming over to take a Cambridge degree, and I have since heard that you are collecting several others: my warmest congratulations, though I feel that these honors are long overdue.

My wife and I have been invited to a party at Jonathan Cape's to meet you on May 29th, and we are hoping to hear you lecture at London University on May 21st, but I hope there will be more to it than that. Indeed I hope that you will have time, amongst your numerous engagements, to have a meal with my wife and myself. I shall communicate with you at the Connaught Hotel, on, or after, the 20th. . . . We are all looking forward most eagerly to greeting you.

Yours ever   T. S. Eliot

440-b · A. MacLeish to Kathleen Morrison

THIS LETTER represents additional moves by MacLeish to involve RF on behalf of Ezra Pound. (See letter 436-a, in which Attorney General Brownell states that he will write to RF after a review of Pound's case is completed.) The promised communication, dated 10 April 1957, came from William P. Rogers, then acting as Deputy Attorney General and soon to become Attorney General in place of Brownell. Rogers stated he would be willing to meet with the three signers of the original letter to discuss Pound's case. RF didn't respond immediately, for he was busy at the time making arrangements for his trip to England. But in May 1957, while RF was staying at the Hotel Connaught in London, he met MacLeish, who was also staying there. MacLeish was on his way back to America from Europe, where he had called on Pound's friends and relatives. The London conversations resulted in RF's promise to go to Washington with MacLeish as soon as possible to talk with the Attorney General or his Deputy about a way to free Pound. Before he left England, RF also discussed the Pound case with T. S. Eliot.

17 June 1957   Uphill Farm
Conway, Massachusetts

Dear Kay:

I am writing you because I don't know how to reach Robert who must, I suppose, be back by now. Please forgive the trouble.

Robert told me in London he would be willing to talk to the Assistant Attorney General who wrote him about the Pound case. I said I would go down with him if he went. It's a lot to ask of him in the heat of summer. However, if we let this chance go by it may go by for good.

I should like to suggest two things:

First, that Robert should reply to the Assistant Attorney General — actually Deputy Attorney General — whose name is William P. Rogers — if he has not already done so. In his letter of April 10 Mr. Rogers said the Attorney General would like to meet with Frost, Eliot and Hemingway and that he, Rogers, would be writing again soon to arrange a conference. Probably Robert has already replied but if he hasn't it might be helpful to write now suggesting a time when Robert could come. Hemingway MIGHT be willing to come up too. I've written him. Eliot is, of course, in England.

Second, I'd be grateful if you or Robert would let me know whether he feels he can go and if so when so that I can make my plans since I have to do a bit of running around this summer for lectures. I'm bankrupt what with Europe and all.

Love to you both   Archie

441 · To Archibald MacLeish

THE FOLLOWING version of this letter is transcribed from a first draft, typewritten, revised in ink, and unsigned.

Dear Archie   24 June 1957   Ripton

My purpose holds to help you get Ezra let loose though I won't say my misgivings in the whole matter haven't been increased by my talks with Eliot lately, who knows more about Ezra than anybody else and what we can hope to do for his salvation. I should hate to see Ezra die ignominiously in that wretched place where he is for a crime which if proven couldn't have kept him all these years in prison. So you go ahead and make an appointment with the Department of Justice. I suppose we might be prepared to answer for Ezra's relative sanity and ability to get himself taken care of out in the world. Neither you nor I would want to take him into our family or even into our neighborhood. I shall be acting largely on your judgment. I can't bear that anyone's fate should hang too much on mine.

I am tied up here for the moment. I could be in Washington for any time on Wednesday July 17 or Friday the 19th after three o'clock or Saturday. But I should have thought that this time of year wouldn't find people in Washington and the affair might better wait until the Fall.

So much for business — bad business. We mustn't forget the good relations we have promised to have with each other this summer.

Ever yours — on either side of the Atlantic

441-a · Archibald MacLeish to Robert Frost

Dear Robert: 28 June 1957   Conway

Bless you. I won't forget the promise and I know you won't. I don't suppose we could tease you down here? Would you come if I drove up and got you?

About Ezra — I agree. And I don't feel too sure of my judgment but I can't bear to have him rot. That's about all I am wholly sure of.

I have asked Miss Geffen at the Academy to write the Deputy Attorney General asking whether July 19 (late in the PM) or the 20th would do. Of course I would go along if you want me. I have also written Ernest asking him to send you a full statement of his views and I shall ask Tom to do the same so that you will go fully armed. Maybe it would be easier if their letters came to me so that I could turn the whole file over to you.

More when I know more. It was GOOD to see you in in London.   yours aye   Archie

441-b · ARCHIBALD MACLEISH TO EZRA POUND

Dear Ezra: 22 July 1957   Conway

Robert Frost and I went to see the boys at the Department of Justice last Friday. Hot as it was, Robert came all the way down from Ripton, Vermont.

We had with us letters from Tom Eliot and Ernest.

What the conversation boiled down to was about what we expected: though maybe a little more hopeful than we feared.

For the immediate future and so long as the [John] Kasper mess is boiling and stewing the Department will not move. I have never understood — and neither, incidentally, has your daughter Mary — how you got mixed up with that character.

Beyond that, though there are no commitments, the Department does not close the door provided somebody can come forward with a sensible plan for your future. The impression we got was that that future would have to be in the United States.

Robert has some ideas about a sensible plan which he would be glad to explore if you approve and which seem promising to me: a sound professional arrangement with your publishers which might work for you as it has for him over many years.

All this, you understand, is hypothetical as Hell. No commitments or near commitments were made. But the door wasn't closed and we were left with the impression that once the Kasper stink has blown over they would be willing to consider proposals.

We ran into one thing you ought to know about. Somebody has spread the rumor at the Department of Justice (I heard it also in Italy) that you and your wife would really prefer to stay on at St. Elizabeths. If it is false, as I assume, your wife ought to make that clear to the Department. But if she does, ask her please not to quote me.

Did you ever get my note about our visit with that lovely Mary?   Yours faithfully   Archie

442 · To William P. Rogers

RF made his second visit to the Department of Justice on behalf of Ezra Pound on 23 October 1957, and was encouraged to hope that the matter might soon be settled; but this did not happen until 18 April 1958.

Dear Mr. Rogers: 19 November 1957   Cambridge
    Please tell your daughter how proud I am to have had my small plea listened to by the Attorney General about-to-be. Won't you ask her if she doesn't think it would be nice for us to go from this start and do a little more if only socially to satisfy your curiosity about how it goes with poets in a great nation like ours.

    I assume people are less busy the higher up they get and the bigger the questions get or I would apologize for taking your time for the rest of this Pound business. The money seems assured for the private institution and Archie MacLeish tells me this morning that he has Dr. Overholser's consent for Pound's transfer the minute he himself is released from holding Pound as a prisoner. I may have to call you on the telephone next. I grow impatient. The amnesty would be a good Christmas present.   Sincerely yours,   Robert Frost

443 · To Sherman Adams

ON 16 January 1958 the Poetry Society of America held its annual banquet and presented to RF its Gold Medal for Distinguished Service. During the ceremonies a telegram of greeting from President Eisenhower to the Poetry Society of America was read aloud, including this passage: "It is fortunate that our Nation is blessed with citizens like Robert Frost who can express our innermost feelings and speak so clearly to us of our land and life. It is a pleasure to join in tribute to the great gifts of Robert Frost."

Dear Sherman Adams: 12 February 1958   South Miami
    That was a splendid telegram both for me and the cause I had from you and the President. Of course I saw your hand

in it. You have a great influence up there. Few in your position have ever thought of the arts at all. Some day it seems as
if you might want to have me meet the President to thank him
in person at a meal or something, so that it needn't go down in
history that the great statesman and soldier never dined socially with any but big shots, and these preferably statesmen,
warriors, and Holly woodsmen. I read in today's paper that
you are sending Bob Hope and Bing Crosby to represent us in
the arts at the World's Fair in Brussels. And when I say this
half seriously it is not just for myself that I am speaking.

  You are a tried and true friend and I am

Ever yours Robert Frost

443-a · Sherman Adams to Robert Frost

[Printed letterhead]

THE WHITE HOUSE
WASHINGTON

THE ASSISTANT TO THE PRESIDENT

Dear Mr. Poet Laureate: February 15, 1958

  I understand that through some circuitous means you
have been invited to come and spend the evening with the
President on the twenty-seventh. I hope you may be able to do
so. If you find it convenient I should hope to see you at the
same time, although I shall probably not be going to the dinner.

  Of course, what we really need is a person who thinks
about the arts. Most of us keep our minds on more mundane
problems. We miss many opportunities to promote a growing
appreciation of cultural activities. Perhaps we need you on the
White House staff. What think you?

  Warm regards.   Sincerely, Sherm Adams

443-b · Dwight D. Eisenhower to Robert Frost

ROBERT FROST   1958 FEB 16 PM 6 41
5240 DAVIS ROAD SOUTH MIAMI FLO

I WONDER IF IT WOULD BE CONVENIENT FOR YOU TO COME TO
AN INFORMAL STAG DINNER AT THE WHITE HOUSE IN WASH-
INGTON ON THE EVENING OF THURSDAY, FEBRUARY TWENTY-

SEVENTH. I HOPE TO GATHER TOGETHER A SMALL GROUP, AND I SHOULD LIKE VERY MUCH FOR YOU TO ATTEND IF IT IS POSSIBLE FOR YOU TO DO SO.

BECAUSE OF THE INFORMALITY OF THE OCCASION, I SUGGEST THAT WE MEET AT THE WHITE HOUSE ABOUT 7:30, HAVE A REASONABLY EARLY DINNER, AND DEVOTE THE EVENING TO A GENERAL CHAT. WHILE I AM HOPEFUL THAT YOU CAN ATTEND I REALIZE THAT YOU ALREADY MAY HAVE ENGAGEMENTS WHICH WOULD INTERFERE. IF SO, I ASSURE YOU OF MY COMPLETE UNDERSTANDING.

I SHALL PROBABLY WEAR A BLACK TIE, BUT A BUSINESS SUIT WILL BE ENTIRELY APPROPRIATE.

AS A PERSONAL FAVOR TO ME, WOULD YOU KEEP THIS INVITATION REASONABLY CONFIDENTIAL UNTIL AFTER THE EVENT. DWIGHT D. EISENHOWER

444 · To Sherman Adams

THE HONORABLE SHERMAN ADAMS
THE WHITE HOUSE [1958 FEB 16]
WASHINGTON [SOUTH MIAMI]

BE IT UPON YOUR HEAD BUT I AM ACCEPTING THE PRESIDENT'S INVITATION BLACK TIE AND ALL. TRUST I DON'T HAVE TO PROVE MYSELF WORTHY OF THE HONOR. WHAT'S ON MY MIND WOULD BE MORE APT TO BE BROUGHT OUT IN TALKS WITH YOU SEPARATELY. SUFFICIENT UNTO THE MOMENT THE GREAT PLEASURE OF MEETING THE PRESIDENT OF MY COUNTRY. I AM A CASTAWAY OUT OF COMMUNICATION ON A DESERT ISLAND [Captiva] TILL SATURDAY. MY ADDRESS THEN WILL BE 5240 SW 80TH STREET SOUTH MIAMI — TELEPHONE MOHAWK 7-9663. CAN YOU GET ME A SEAT ON SOME MID-AFTERNOON PLANE FROM MIAMI ON WEDNESDAY FEBRUARY 26 AND ANOTHER ON A MORNING PLANE FROM WASHINGTON TO MIAMI ON FRIDAY THE 28TH. THESE MAY PROVE TOO HARD FOR ME TO GET MYSELF. MUST BE BACK HERE FOR APPOINTMENT FRIDAY NIGHT. UNTOLD APPRECIATION. ROBERT FROST

445 · To Dwight D. Eisenhower

THE PRESIDENT
THE WHITE HOUSE   [1958 FEB 16]
WASHINGTON   [SOUTH MIAMI]

YOUR INVITATION ACCEPTED WITH GREAT PLEASURE. ONLY TOO
SENSIBLE OF THE HONOR. THURSDAY EVENING THEN THE 27TH
AT HALF PAST SEVEN.   ROBERT FROST

446 · To Raymond Holden

JUST AS Raymond Holden was finishing his volume, *The Merri-mack*, for the "Rivers of America" series, he wrote asking RF to do a preface for it. Holden argued that the Merrimack River had been so closely associated with RF's life that such an addition would be particularly appropriate. This is RF's answer.

Dear Raymond: 20 February 1958   South Miami

The longer thought of, the less plausible it seems to connect me with the Merrimack River. To be sure Lawrence is on it and I went to the Lawrence High School. I did tend the fish way at the Lawrence Dam one season. I did boat on it for the devil of it one day in a hurricane (real one that blew all the New England apples off). I did dig clams at the mouth of it one day and I worked in some of the mills the river used to turn; but I never swam in it, skated on it, or fished in it. It would be stretching it a good deal to make it literarily mine. And then it goes against my nature to connect myself with it in a preface. I'm awful about prefaces. All I have written in forty years could be counted on the fingers of one hand. And I have stayed out of them much more than I have been left out of them. I did the one for Sidney Cox [in *Swinger of Birches*] under all sorts of pressure. His wife was his widow when she asked me to do it. I did it wholesale in one stroke for all those boys coming up. That was for once in a way in an excess of generosity. All my books in their pristine editions have come out naked so to speak.

But O dear, you are too much my friend for me to have to plead my way out of trouble with you. I will say more if necessary when I see you next. I can trust you not to look at this as an obligation I am artfully avoiding. You know I am

Ever yours   Robert

446-a · Sherman Adams to Robert Frost

IN AN earlier communication (see letter 443-a) Adams had said
that although he probably wouldn't be at the White House dinner on
27 February 1958, he did hope to see RF. In accepting the invitation to lunch in the staff dining room of the White House, RF asked
Adams to invite William P. Rogers, who had by then succeeded
Brownell as Attorney General. Rogers was Adams' only other guest.
Before the lunch, Adams learned that Rogers was already favor-
ably disposed to the release of Ezra Pound.

ROBERT FROST

UNIVERSITY CLUB   WASHINGTON

WASHINGTON D C   26 FEBRUARY 1958

WILL YOU COME TO LUNCH WITH ME THURSDAY, FEBRUARY
TWENTY-SEVENTH, TWELVE THIRTY, WHITE HOUSE MESS,
WEST WING. NO LIABILITIES.   SHERMAN ADAMS

447 · To Thurman Arnold

THURMAN ARNOLD acted for Ezra Pound in the Federal District
Court in Washington, D. C., on 18 April 1958, the day the Court
dropped charges against Pound. Next morning a front-page story
in the New York *Times* concluded: "The person most responsible
for today's announcement was not in court. He is Robert Frost, the
poet, who has waged a persistent public and private campaign
during the last two years for Mr. Pound's release. Among other
things Mr. Frost had called on Attorney General William P. Rogers."
     That evening at the Poetry Center in New York City, where RF
gave a reading, he acknowledged prolonged applause by referring
for the first time to the news of the day. "This morning's paper said
I took two years to get Ezra Pound out of jail," he stated, "but the
truth is I did it all in just one week."
     Truth of the matter was that a great many prominent figures
had been bringing pressure on the Department of Justice to obtain
Pound's release, and the chances are that he would have been freed
around the middle of April even if RF had played no part at all in
the struggle. A liberal like Archibald MacLeish was aware of the
influence a conservative "poet of the people" like Frost might wield
in such a fight, but the strong impetus came from other sources, as
a brief review of the final stages will show.
     No progress in the Pound case had been made by RF and
MacLeish when they met with Attorney General Rogers on 19 July
1957. But on 21 August, Usher L. Burdick, Representative of North
Dakota, introduced House Resolution 403 — which was passed —
demanding a full-scale investigation of the Pound matter. As a first
move the Legislative Reference Service of the Library of Congress

was directed to compile a full report on the case. While that report was being put together, Dag Hammerskjöld appealed directly to the Department of State and Under Secretary of State Christian Herter wrote to Dr. Winfred Overholser, Superintendent of St. Elizabeths Hospital, asking him to "drop in some day" to discuss "this difficult individual, Ezra Pound."

The day after the Legislative Reference Service completed its report, Attorney General Rogers held a press conference and sent up a trial balloon. The next day, 2 April 1958, the New York *Times* said: "Attorney General William P. Rogers disclosed . . . that Ezra Pound may escape trial and be allowed to go to Italy . . . He said Pound's fate depended upon new diagnoses by doctors at Saint Elizabeths Hospital here, where the writer is confined as insane . . . . 'Is there any point in keeping him in there if he never can be tried?'"

The public responded very satisfactorily to the test, and now all that was needed was a prominent figure to cut through the red tape. Again, with MacLeish's prodding, RF went to Washington, called on Rogers, and said, "I've dropped in to see what your mood is in regard to Ezra Pound." Rogers replied, "Our mood is your mood, Mr. Frost." He then suggested that RF consult William Shaffroth, the official governmental "expediter" in legal matters. Shaffroth recommended Thurman Arnold as lawyer for the defense and immediately arranged an appointment by phone.

Arnold took the case and asked RF to draw up an informal statement in support of Pound's release, which the poet did that night before leaving Washington. On 14 April 1958, Arnold submitted RF's statement and his own formal request to dismiss the indictment against Pound to Judge Bolitha Laws of the District Court. Laws had presided in the same court when Pound was committed to St. Elizabeths twelve years before.

RF was not able to be in court on 18 April 1958, but his presence was felt when Arnold read the informal statement into the record for him:

"I am here to register my admiration for a government that can rouse in conscience to a case like this. Relief seems in sight for many of us besides the Ezra Pound in question and his faithful wife. He has countless admirers the world over who will rejoice in the news that he has hopes of freedom. I append a page or so of what they have been saying lately about him and his predicament. I myself speak as much in the general interest as in his. And I feel authorized to speak very specially for my friends, Archibald Mac-Leish, Ernest Hemingway and T. S. Eliot. None of us can bear the disgrace of our letting Ezra Pound come to his end where he is. It would leave too woeful a story in American literature. He went very wrongheaded in his egotism, but he insists it was from patriotism — love of America. He has never admitted that he went over to the enemy any more than the writers at home who have despaired of the Republic. I hate such nonsense and can only listen to it as an evidence of mental disorder. But mental disorder is what we are considering. I rest the case on Dr. Overholser's pronouncement that Ezra Pound is not too dangerous to go free in his wife's care, and too insane ever to be tried — a very nice discrimination.

"Mr. Thurman Arnold admirably put this problem of a sick man being held too long in prison to see if he won't get well enough to be tried for a prison offense. There is probably legal procedure to help toward a solution of the problem. But I should think it would have to be reached more by magnanimity than by logic and it is chiefly on magnanimity I am counting. I can see how the Department of Justice would hesitate in the matter from fear of looking more just to a great poet than it would be to a mere nobody. The bigger the Department the longer it might have to take thinking things through."

Arnold secured the dismissal of the indictment against Pound that day, without difficulty, and refused to take a fee for his part in the fight. By contrast, RF seemed to feel he had done more than any other toward the liberation of Ezra Pound. "I did it," he kept saying to reporters.

This letter is RF's note of appreciation to Arnold for his participation in the Pound case.

Dear Thurman Arnold: [c. 28 April 1958]   [Cambridge]

Friendship and not just thanks is what I want you to accept in payment for all you did to make simple and easy for me my first raid on the Capital City. I hope to see more of you and your pardners as we call them in Laramie [Arnold's birthplace]. But I must wait till next season to express myself more fully. Things are shaping up to turn me into something Washingtonian right now. I shall have more to tell you about it later. We shared in an unusual campaign. We must not neglect to celebrate it once in so often. It would be fun if we could do it once with Ezra before he retreats into mediaevality. I may urge him to prove the love of America he professes by villaging here a while anyway. I think Hemingway and Lockland [James Laughlin, Pound's publisher] would set him up to a cottage.   Ever yours   Robert Frost

448 · To Sherman Adams

Dear Sherman Adams: 29 April 1958   Cambridge

This is no more belated than might be expected from such a staggering experience. Since it is all your doing from the start I naturally ask you to see it through the rest of the way. My obligation is first to you and by way of you to the ruler of the greatest nation in the world. I wish you would take a look of indulgence at my words to him to make sure they will do.

I shall hope to see you before too long.
The Pound affair came off with dignity.

Affectionately,   Robert Frost

449 · To Dwight D. Eisenhower

Dear Mr. President: 29 April 1958   Cambridge

To be stood up for and toasted alone in such august company by the ruler of the greatest nation in the world was almost more to me than being stood up for in acclaim by whole audiences of his people and mine. At any rate it left me with less to say for myself on the thrill of the moment and was so like the outcome of a life story, it leaves me with nothing to go on with but possibly some more of the same kind of very quiet poetry that seems to have started all this unquietness. I hope you will accept a book of it from me to take to your farm some day. I am a great advocate of some library in the farm house to mix with the life of the farm. Not that I would underestimate its value in the capitol to mix with the life of the Capitol. Books and paintings and music tend to temper the harshness of politics. I shall treasure the memory of the aside you took me on to appraise the portrait of William Howard Taft by Anders Zorn. I still see the Taft and I still see your vivid portrait of the fine young All-there-and-ready-to-take-on-the-world, your grandson.   Sincerely yours,   Robert Frost

449-a · L. Quincy Mumford to Robert Frost

SHERMAN ADAMS' proposal that RF might one day serve as a White House adviser on cultural activities (see letter 443-a) never came to pass. But Adams also suggested RF's appointment as Consultant in Poetry to the Library of Congress. This letter from the Librarian completed the arrangements.

[Printed letterhead]

THE LIBRARIAN OF CONGRESS
WASHINGTON 25, D. C.

Dear Mr. Frost: May 2, 1958

It gives me great pleasure to offer to engage you as Consultant in Poetry in the Library of Congress from October, 1958, through May, 1959.

The enclosed contract . . .

It is our understanding that you will make definite plans to be at the Library of Congress next October 13-18, December 8-12, March 30-April 3, and May 18-22, and that on the evenings of December 8 and March 30 you will give a talk, with such readings as you may choose, in the Library's Coolidge Auditorium to an invited audience. . . .

On May 21, the date of the proposed release, the Library of Congress would like very much to have you be present during the afternoon to meet members of the press, and to visit with a few members of the Library staff. . . .

Sincerely yours,   L. Quincy Mumford

450 · To HENRY RAGO

THE ISSUE of *Poetry* magazine for July 1958 was a special number devoted to "Contemporary Israeli Verse." It was edited in consultation with Simon Halkin, poet, novelist, and Professor of Modern Hebrew Literature at the Hebrew University of Jerusalem. The unusual quality of that issue inspired RF to write this letter some two years in advance of the day when he was invited to visit Israel as the first lecturer in the Samuel Paley Foundation series at the Hebrew University.

Dear Henry Rago: 16 July 1958   Ripton

Your July number has what I mean. I shall keep it like one of my books. It illustrates the conflict set forth in the last paragraph of Simon Halkin's fine essay. It achieves a dominant idea without excogitation. All those young poets intent on themselves come out with an effect on me almost dramatically not to say tragically national. It is very striking. It is very moving. I wish you more numbers like it. It is hard for us in a country two hundred years old to strike the same note at once individual and national that these young poets get in a young country. Being in on the ground floor of an enterprise heightens their double consciousness.

Sincerely yours   Robert Frost

451 · To SHERMAN ADAMS

SHERMAN ADAMS attended the reception given in RF's honor at the Library of Congress on 21 May 1958. Not long after, pressures were brought on Adams to resign his position as Assistant to the

President because he had accepted favors from the New England industrialist, Bernard Goldfine. This letter was written soon after Adams' resignation.

Dear Sherman   8 October 1958 Cambridge

    The news of your resignation came just in time to keep me from mailing the letter I had ready to forbid your resignation. I had hoped you would stand on your integrity and stick it out. I didn't see why you should sacrifice yourself to save the Fall elections. The elections were probably lost anyway by reason of the probably general misunderstanding of Mr Dulles foreign policy.

    But lets talk no more of this horrid business. I shall be in Washington all next week and look forward to finding you at worst in a state of philosophy. I'm camping out in luxury and defiance of captious criticism at the Hay-Adams [hotel].

Ever yours   Robert

451-a · JOHN F. KENNEDY TO ROBERT FROST

INTERVIEWING RF on his eighty-fifth birthday, newspaper reporters asked him if he thought New England had lost its vitality. RF rose vigorously to the defense of New England and reminded his interviewers that many parents sent their sons and daughters to New England preparatory schools, colleges, and universities from all parts of the United States. He also made two prophecies which later came to pass: that the next Secretary of State would be a New Englander (Christian A. Herter) and that the next President of the United States would be a New Englander. Many newspapers carried the statement as RF's flat prediction that Senator John F. Kennedy of Massachusetts would be our next President. Kennedy wrote the following letter, and later met and became a friend of the poet. This paved the way for Kennedy's invitation to RF to participate in his inauguration on 20 January 1961.

[Printed letterhead]

UNITED STATES SENATE

WASHINGTON, D. C.

Dear Mr. Frost: April 11, 1959

    I just want to send you a note to let you know how gratifying it was to be remembered by you on the occasion of your 85th birthday. I only regret that the intrusion of my name, probably in ways which you did not entirely intend, took away some of the attention from the man who really deserved it —

Robert Frost. I want to send you my own very warmest greetings on which is for all of your admirers a milestone, but for you is only another day in the life of a young man.

I do, however, share entirely your view that the New England heritage is not a fading page but that it has continuing vitality and a distinguished future. I was more impressed than ever by this during the past fall when for the first time in six years I had an opportunity to move intensively across the state from town to town and to see again first-hand the very special qualities of the New England mind and New England heritage.

With best thanks and all good wishes to you,

Sincerely,   John F. Kennedy

451-b · Dwight D. Eisenhower to Robert Frost

[Printed letterhead]

THE WHITE HOUSE
WASHINGTON

Dear Mr. Frost: May 22, 1959

I understand you are completing your tour of duty this week as Consultant in Poetry to the Library of Congress.

Much as I should have liked personally to thank you for your service in a post to which you have brought great distinction, I am flying to Annapolis within the hour and will be away all weekend. I therefore take this occasion to wish you Godspeed, and to thank you, on behalf of all of us, for contributing so freely of your great talents.

With best wishes and warm personal regards

Sincerely,   Dwight D. Eisenhower

452 · To Winston L. Prouty

JUST BEFORE RF's eighty-fifth birthday the U.S. Senate unanimously passed a resolution, introduced by Republican Senator Winston L. Prouty of Vermont, that "the Senate of the United States extend to Robert Frost its good wishes on the occasion of his anniversary and salute him as a citizen, as a man, as a poet, and as a representative of our Nations' art and culture."

On 18 June 1959 Republican Senator Francis Case of South

Dakota introduced "A Bill to Provide for a National Academy of Culture." RF was aware that this bill was being introduced, and implied as much in this letter to Prouty in which he also refers to the Senate birthday resolution.

Dear Senator Prouty: 18 June 1959   Ripton

The only thing that could mean more to me than recognition by the Senate would be a seat in the Senate which I may say I have given up all hope of with two such Senators from Vermont [Prouty and George D. Aiken] already in situ. But thank the Senators for this second great honor [the first, felicitations on RF's seventy-fifth birthday] they have crowned my days with. If it is a small matter to them in the midst of their world affairs, it is a very large one to me personally and I like to think no very negligible one to the arts in general. It is thoughts and designs for the arts that have delayed me with this letter. I have been getting up the presumption to suggest seeing you some time in Washington or at home in Vermont for a talk about some more permanent connection than mine between them and the government. It would have to be some office, appointment to which would be by some such higher-ups as say, a committee of the Chairman of the House, the Chairman of the Senate, one member of the Supreme Court (chosen by the other members), and two editors or authors called in by my first three. All this for protection from the spoilsmen and the literary gangsters. The term of office might well be from forty on for twenty-five years. I should want the government to impress itself with what it was doing for the arts by making this a well rewarded honor. Wouldn't it be a great thing for a latter day senator from Vermont to obtain merit in history by doing the same kind of thing to bring art and state together that an earlier senator from Vermont [Justin Smith Morrill] did to bring education and state together by his Land Grant Colleges.

Again my thanks to the Senate. The government has gone a long way towards making this my culminating year. You perhaps know the President and his White House have come into it.   Sincerely yours   Robert Frost

453 · To Lionel Trilling

RF's publisher held an eighty-fifth birthday banquet for the poet in New York City on 26 March 1959. The major speaker of the evening was Lionel Trilling, whose carefully considered remarks in praise of certain "terrifying" elements in the poetry of RF unintentionally created a teapot tempest, primarily stirred up by J. Donald Adams in the New York *Times Book Review*. Trilling responded in the *Partisan Review* for June 1959 and sent a copy to RF expressing the hope that the after-dinner speech and the subsequent hubbub had not distressed him.

Dear Trilling: 18 June 1959   Ripton

Not distressed at all. Just a little taken aback or thrown back on myself by being so closely examined so close by. It took me more than a few minutes to change from thoughts of myself to thoughts of the difficulty you had had with me. You made my birthday party a surprise party. I should like nothing better than to do a thing like that myself — to depart from the Rotarian norm in a Rotarian situation. You weren't there to sing "Happy Birthday, dear Robert," and I don't mind being made controversial. No sweeter music can come to my ears than the clash of arms over my dead body when I am down. We should see something more of each other. I wish the Holts hadn't let your trade book get away from them.

Sincerely yours   Frost

454 · To L. Quincy Mumford

ON 26 June 1959, the Librarian of Congress formally prolonged RF's relations with the Library. Mumford wrote: "It is a privilege to appoint you Honorary Consultant in the Humanities of the Library of Congress for a term of three years. During your term as Poetry Consultant, you frequently expressed the idea that you welcomed consultation in the broad realm of the humanities. It is for this reason, and because we desire your continued association with the Library of Congress, that we offer the humanities to you for your honorary consultantship." RF's acceptance follows.

Dear Quincy: 10 July 1959   Ripton

. . . I am honored by the summons of your appointing me consultant in the humanities which I more or less arbitrarily take to mean practically everything human that has been brought to book and can be treated in poetry — philosophy, politics, religion, history, and science. Everything, everything.   Yours ever   Robert

455 · To Lawrance Thompson

Dear Larry: 11 July 1959   Ripton

It won't be long before you see me again to assert your right to get me right or wrong in our long continuum. It's odd. We've managed each other so well in a situation that has its perils. It does us both credit. (Listen to me taking my share of the credit.) I've meant to give you all the advantages, supply you with all the facts, and keep nothing back, save nothing out for my own use even in case I ever should write my own story. And I have left entirely to your judgment the summing up and the significance. You've had a long time to turn me over in your mind looking for some special phrase or poem to get me by. By now you may think you have plucked the heart out of my secret and I don't care if you have. All is easy between us. We have sized each other up without disillusionment. I state the case thus for the purpose only of making it conclusive that any disturbance you felt from Elsie's [Elizabeth Shepley Sergeant] getting ahead of you in time was foolish. You are ahead of her in plenty of other ways. Carlos [Baker] has just been here talking to me about your book about me in some series [Minnesota pamphlets]. He was quite specific in his praise. I look forward to having K. read it to me. I trust my philosophy still bothers you a little. It bothers me. You should have heard me talking the other night about the Uriel your class in American Literature wouldn't let you talk to them about. One or other of us will fathom me sooner or later. Did Trilling have something the other night? I was a little bothered by him but chiefly because I didn't hear very well. We are to have another chance at his speech; it is appearing presently in "The Partisan Review." At least he seemed to see that I am as strong on badness as I am on goodness. Emerson's defect was that he was of the great tradition of Monists. He could see the "good of evil born" but he couldn't bring himself to say the evil of good born. He was an Abominable Snowman of the top-lofty peaks. But what a poet he was in prose and verse. Such phrases. Arnold thought him a voice oracular. ("A voice oracular has pealed today.") I couldn't go as far as that because I am a Dualist and I don't see how Mathew Arnold could because he was a Dualist too. He was probably carried away by the great poetry. Wisdom doesn't matter too much.

Stafford Dragon tells us that a flock of my descendants

alighted at your place in migration the other day and were entreated kindly. So long — (long enough)   Ever yours   R. F.

456 · To John F. Kennedy

RF did not vote in the 1960 presidential election: he was giving a series of readings in California at the time. But on the night after the election he spoke in Los Angeles and characterized the Democratic victory as "a triumph of Protestantism over itself."

On his way home from California, RF visited for two days in Tucson with his Mormon friend, Stewart L. Udall, then Congressman from Arizona. The two men had become well acquainted in Washington during the previous two years. Shortly after his return to Cambridge, RF learned that President-elect Kennedy had appointed Udall as Secretary of the Interior in his new Cabinet. This telegram was inspired by the news.

PRESIDENT ELECT JOHN F. KENNEDY   [*c.* I DECEMBER 1960]
WASHINGTON, D. C.   [CAMBRIDGE]

GREAT DAYS FOR BOSTON, DEMOCRACY, THE PURITANS AND THE IRISH. YOUR APPOINTMENT OF STEWART UDALL OF AN OLD VERMONT RELIGION RECONCILES ME ONCE FOR ALL TO THE PARTY I WAS BORN INTO.   ROBERT FROST

456-a · John F. Kennedy to Robert Frost

AFTER his Cabinet appointment, Udall suggested to President-elect Kennedy that he should try to persuade RF to participate in the inauguration program. Since RF was a poet of the people, the honor would pay tribute to all American literary artists. Udall was immediately authorized to approach RF with the proposal; after RF had informally accepted, Kennedy sent this telegram.

ROBERT FROST   13 DECEMBER 1960
23 [35] BREWSTER ST   WASHINGTON
CAMBRIDGE MASS

I WOULD BE DELIGHTED IF YOU WOULD PARTICIPATE IN THE INAUGURAL CEREMONIES JANUARY TWENTIETH. I KNOW THAT IT WOULD GIVE THE AMERICAN PUBLIC AS MUCH PLEASURE AS IT WOULD MY FAMILY AND ME. THE JOINT CONGRESSIONAL INAUGURAL COMMITTEE WILL SEND YOU A FORMAL INVITATION IN THE NEAR FUTURE. WITH BEST PERSONAL WISHES,
                                             JOHN F. KENNEDY.

457 · To John F. Kennedy

PRESIDENT ELECT JOHN F. KENNEDY   14 DECEMBER 1960
WASHINGTON   DC   CAMBRIDGE

IF YOU CAN BEAR AT YOUR AGE THE HONOR OF BEING MADE
PRESIDENT OF THE UNITED STATES, I OUGHT TO BE ABLE AT MY
AGE TO BEAR THE HONOR OF TAKING SOME PART IN YOUR INAU-
GURATION. I MAY NOT BE EQUAL TO IT BUT I CAN ACCEPT IT FOR
MY CAUSE — THE ARTS, POETRY, NOW FOR THE FIRST TIME
TAKEN INTO THE AFFAIRS OF STATESMEN. I AM GLAD THE IN-
VITATION PLEASES YOUR FAMILY. IT WILL PLEASE MY FAMILY
TO THE FOURTH GENERATION AND MY FAMILY OF FRIENDS AND
WERE THEY LIVING IT WOULD HAVE PLEASED INORDINATELY
THE KIND OF GROVER CLEVELAND DEMOCRATS I HAD FOR PAR-
ENTS.   ROBERT FROST

458 · To Stewart L. Udall

SECRETARY OF THE INTERIOR Stewart L. Udall continued to play an
active part in arranging public and private occasions in honor of
RF in Washington. His suggestions lay behind an invitation sent
out prior to the writing of this letter, an invitation which read
"Under the Honorary Chairmanship of Mrs. Kennedy, The Members of the President's Cabinet request the honor of your presence
at 'An Evening With Robert Frost' on Monday the first of May at
eight-thirty o'clock, State Department Auditorium."

Dear Stewart: 5 April 1961   Cambridge

    How brotherly it all seems. By the accident of our falling
in friendship with you and Lee [Mrs. Udall] we have been
brought out on top of a new pinnacle of view that makes me
for one feel dangerously like a monarch of all fifty states I
survey. I could have been willing to leave it to anyone if I
wasn't pretty American but I seem different. That dedication
poem goes on being added to in my mind till it threatens to become a history of the United States to rival the one Harry Tru-
man says he is writing. You know one of my missions is to get
a secretary of the arts into the President's cabinet but I am as
good as in there now with you to talk to. I have been reaching
the President through you for some time. Somebody's been
telling him our economy is manic. I'd like to tell him that a big
vigorous economy like ours can't keep itself from overstocking
and so having to have a clearance sale once in so often. That's

the kind of figure of speech I'm good at. The beauty of my position is I'm only listened to for amusement. But seriously you have made my life a real party for the last go-down. K. and I are looking forward to the visit to Washington and what it sounds as if you had in store for us. Roy Basler from the Library has just been talking to K. about it. You know I am consultant in the humanities. By humanities I mean parks and all that. The President wants a park made of his region on the Cape. I might want a park made of our place in Vermont.* Watch out! I hear all sorts of things you are writing about fish and game and such. You like to write. So do I or I wouldn't do it. People everywhere have been talking about your piece ['Frost's Unique 'Gift Outright' "] in "The New York Times" [26 March 1961].   Ever yours   Robert

459 · To SYLVIA CLARK

IN 1906, when RF began teaching at Pinkerton Academy in Derry, New Hampshire, Miss Sylvia Clark was already a member of the faculty there. Her father was a prominent physician in Derry. Miss Clark had attended Wellesley College for one year, in the 1890's, on a scholarship won in a literary prize contest conducted by the Boston *Herald*. RF had accidentally seen her prize-winning essay when it was published.

In January 1961, when a grammar school in Lawrence, Massachusetts, was to be dedicated and named after RF, Miss Clark was invited to the ceremonies. She wrote expressing her regret that she would be unable to attend. This is RF's answer to her.

Dear Sylvia: 18 January 1962   Cambridge

We are about old enough to call each other by our first names. You and your family — your father, your mother, and your sister — are among my earliest and best recollections of Derry; you for your paper on the Pyncheon hens in the Boston Herald, your venerable father for the stormy night he came to our farm house to see one of our children and had to dry his mitts on our wood stove, your mother, your sister, and you again very particularly for the wit and humor with which you entertained Silver, Potter, and me at your house. I am sorry I shan't see you in Lawrence. Perhaps something can be ar-

---

* RF did want to have the Homer Noble Farm in Ripton, Vermont, taken over by the Department of Interior and made into a memorial park. He and Secretary Udall made several steps toward that goal before serious complications developed, and then they abandoned the plan.

ranged for later at Hanover where a room is to be opened for me in the College Library.   Ever yours,*

460 · To WILLIAM A. JACKSON

ON 12 September 1960, President Dwight D. Eisenhower signed a bill previously passed by Congress awarding a $2,500 Congressional Gold Medal to RF. Originally the bill had been introduced by Senator Leverett Saltonstall of Massachusetts, and it authorized the President to present a suitably inscribed medal to RF on behalf of Congress "in recognition of his poetry which has enriched the culture of the United States and the philosophy of the world." Delays in the making of the medal occurred so that it was finally presented to RF at the White House by President John F. Kennedy on 26 March 1960 — RF's eighty-sixth birthday. That evening a gala birthday dinner was given at the Pan American building in Washington in honor of the poet. Four hundred guests attended. Arrangements for the dinner had been made by Secretary of the Interior Stewart L. Udall and Alfred C. Edwards, President of Holt, Rinehart and Winston, RF's publishers.

Mr. William Jackson,   Houghton Library,   Harvard University

Dear Bill: 30 March 1962   Cambridge

    I am consigning to you the medal I have just had from the Congress and the President. May I ask you to take care of it with the understanding you may use it as you see fit and may expect to come into permanent possession of it for Harvard University at no very distant date at the discretion of Kathleen Morrison. It should be regarded as in memory of my father William Prescott Frost's days as a student at Harvard and my own days later as a student and a teacher there.

    It should be of record that the idea originated with Senators Saltonstall and Aiken and that President Eisenhower had a part in it and Mr Sherman Adams with him. Our David Mc-Cord had a good part in it too. I received it in a blaze of honor from the hand of President Kennedy. Secretary Udall was seeing to it all along that the interest never flagged in my getting what he thought I deserved. He has become a devoted friend.   Ever yours   Robert

* The letter is unsigned, but has this explanatory note: "Dear Miss Clark: Robert has been so bothered by his publishers and the public that I couldn't get his signature before he left for the South. It seems better to forward this letter unsigned with what I know are his best wishes. Sincerely yours, Kathleen (Mrs. Theodore) Morrison."

461 · To JOHN F. KENNEDY

WHILE RF was visiting in Washington during May 1962, Secretary Udall arranged a meeting between RF and Anatoly Dobrynin, the Soviet Ambassador to the United States. The conversation went so well that Udall asked the Ambassador to approve a "cultural exchange" — a visit to Russia by RF in exchange for a visit to the United States by a Russian poet. After the Department of State had successfully completed preliminary arrangements President Kennedy sent a formal invitation to RF. This is his reply.

Dear Mr. President: 24 July 1962   Ripton

How grand for you to think of me this way and how like you to take the chance of sending anyone like me over there affinitizing with the Russians. You must know a lot about me besides my rank from my poems but think how the professors interpret the poems! I am almost as full of politics and history as you are. I like to tell the story of the mere sailor boy from upstate New York who by favor of his captain and the American consul at St. Petersburg got to see the Czar in St. Petersburg with the gift in his hand of an acorn that fell from a tree that stood by the house of George Washington. That was in the 1830's when proud young Americans were equal to anything. He said to the Czar, "Washington was a great ruler and you're a great ruler and I thought you might like to plant the acorn with me by your palace." And so he did. I have been having a lot of historical parallels lately: a big one between Caesar's imperial democracy that made so many millions equal under arbitrary power and the Russian democracy. Ours is a more Senatorial democracy like the Republic of Rome. I have thought I saw the Russian and the American democracies drawing together, theirs easing down from a kind of abstract severity to taking less and less care of the masses: ours creeping up to taking more and more care of the masses as they grow innumerable. I see us becoming the two great powers of the modern world in noble rivalry while a third power of United Germany, France, and Italy, the common market, looks on as an expanded polyglot Switzerland.

I shall be reading poems chiefly, over there, but I shall be talking some where I read and you may be sure I won't be talking just literature. I'm the kind of Democrat that *will* reason. You know my admiration for your "Profiles." I am frightened by this big undertaking but I was more frightened at your Inauguration. I am glad Stewart will be along to take care of me. He has been a good influence in my life. And Fred Adams [Librarian] of the Morgan Library [in New York City]. I had a very good talk with Anatoly Dobrynin in Washington last May. You probably know that my Adams House at Harvard has an oil portrait of one of our boys, Jack Reed, which nobody has succeeded in making us take down.

Forgive the long letter. I don't write letters but you have stirred my imagination and I have been interested in Russia as a power ever since Rurik came to Novgorod; and these are my credentials. I could go on with them like this to make the picture complete: about the English-speaking world of England, Ireland, Canada, and Australia, New Zealand and Us versus the Russian-speaking world for the next century or so, mostly a stand-off but now and then a showdown to test our mettle. The rest of the world would be Asia and Africa, more or less negligible for the time being though it needn't be too openly declared. Much of this would be the better for not being declared openly but kept always in the back of our minds in all our diplomatic and other relations. I am describing not so much what ought to be but what is and will be — reporting and prophesying. This is the way we are one world, as you put it, of independent nations interdependent — the separateness of the parts as important as the connection of the parts.

Great times to be alive, aren't they?

Sincerely yours   Robert Frost

462 · To LAWRANCE THOMPSON

Larry, Larry: 15 August 1962   Ripton

Who's told you that I was afraid that I had hurt you by not bringing you with me to Russia. Could it have been someone with awkward good intentions? I easily assumed that you would understand. A first thought is that I want a variety in the followers on my trail and I want some of them to be not too critically intent on who and what I am. I can take Freddy Adams to keep me from falling out of the plane. I didn't want to be made too self conscious in this momentous expedition. I got into it by the accident of an almost too genial evening with the Russian Ambassador to this country. The President and Stewart Udall are in it too and I am committed. I must lean pretty heavily on reading my poems to people who don't understand English. I am given a faint hope that I may meet and talk with some important people but to avoid disappointment I must stay in a mood to take it all off-handed. You would have seen nothing in me that you haven't seen many times before. I shall read them "The Lost Follower." Bill Meredith [poet and professor at Connecticut College] doesn't believe anyone ever gave up writing poetry for sociology to make a better world. The two I speak of [in "The Lost Follower"], Jean Flexner and Carter Goodrich, may have been rare cases but some of the poems in the Russian anthology I have been reading seem to be saying in verse they were making the same sacrifice. My two before they gave up wrote better poems than many who kept on. I have never been without sympathy for the equalitarians who pray or act for the Kingdom of Heaven on earth. What makes the angels something special is that they have no physical wants-appetites. The issue before Russia and us is which comes nearer — their democracy or ours — placating everybody. I may tell them what the issue is but won't claim it is nothing to fight about. Let's be great about it, not petty with petty twits. We both have a mighty history. I hope we can show ourselves mighty without being ugly. I get round once in so often to the word magnanimity, don't I? I shall be prophesying not just predicting from statistics — talking of the next hundred years ahead. I may tell them theirs is an imperial democracy like Caesar's Rome, ours a senatorial like the Roman republic. I have been having all sorts of ideas but as I say for dignity I shall depend on the poems few will understand. I guess you pretty well know my attitude. I shall praise them for art and science and athletics. I may speak of the severity they've been easing down from towards socialism and our liberality we've been straining up from to the same socialism. And then again I may not. I go as an opportunist on the loose. I'd like a chance to ask the great Kruschev to grant me one request and then ask him a hard one. There. K. says this letter is getting to be a book.   Ever yours   Robert

462-a · CHARLES H. LYTTLE TO ROBERT FROST

AFTER SPENDING ten days in Russia, RF returned to the United States by plane on 9 September 1962. Reporters who interviewed him at the International Airport, Idlewild, soon after he landed, were particularly interested in his conversation with Khrushchev.

An article in the New York *Times* for 10 September 1962 began as follows: "Robert Frost returned from the Soviet Union yesterday and said Premier Khrushchev had told him he thought the United States would not fight. 'Khrushchev said he feared for us modern liberals,' the 88-year-old poet said. 'He said we were too liberal to fight. I suppose he thought we'd stand there for the next hundred years saying, "On the one hand — but on the other hand." ' "

In the same interview RF was quoted as saying, "Yes, I have a message from Khrushchev for the President. I don't 'plan' to see him. I wait for the President."

He waited in vain. The President did not send for him and did not ever again convey any word to him during the five remaining months of RF's life. "The story is that Mr. Kennedy . . . was displeased with a quotation attributed to the poet after his visit to Russia," wrote Washington correspondent Walter Trohan in the Chicago *Tribune* for 23 February 1963. Be that as it may, there were others who suspected that RF might have put the phrase "too liberal to fight" into Khrushchev's mouth to unburden RF's own conservative and familiar obsession for equating "liberal" with "cowardly."

Two public figures who challenged him directly and asked him to explain his (or Khrushchev's) statement were Dr. Charles H. Lyttle, Pastor of the First Unitarian Society of Geneva, Illinois, and Norman Thomas, former Socialist candidate for President. RF's answers to both men, which follow this letter, tend to confirm the suspicion that RF did largely attribute to Khrushchev his own unflattering definition of a liberal. In the letter to Thomas, however, RF coyly hedges by saying he admires Thomas' own brand of liberalism.

13 September 1962
5729 Dorchester Avenue
Chicago 37, Illinois

Dear Mr. Frost,

Owing to the very high regard in which you are held in our church circle several of our members have felt a bit distressed over certain aspects of the enclosed newspaper account of a purported interview with you on your arrival in New York from your visit to Russia.

Your remarks concerning your attitude toward socialism did not puzzle or disturb us — some of us feel as you do on that subject — but your (alleged) report that "Premier Khrushchev believes the United States will not fight to protect its rights . . . he thought that we are too liberal to fight," is the cause of our dismay.

For the John Birchers in our community this is most welcome grist for their mill!

For those of us who are striving to prevent war, the report is confusing and distressing — if the press item is accurate.

We would be greatly obliged if you would, with the most convenient yet positive brevity, inform us of the accuracy or inaccuracy of the press notice. Some of us suspect that the press deliberately misrepresented you, on this point at least.

Your courtesy in clearing this matter up for us will be greatly appreciated.

Respectfully and cordially yours   Charles H. Lyttle

463 · To Charles H. Lyttle

Dear Mr. Lyttle: 20 September 1962   Ripton

The Sun gets me right. Surely you can have no objection to my getting Kruschev exactly right. He is power personified ruling over four hundred million people seemingly of one accord. My stay was too brief for penetrating into any dissidence, if such exists. The Russian nation expects to try us out in one way or another. The stage or arena is set (by you-know-Whom) for a rivalry between us for the next hundred years in athletics, art, science, business, and in democracy, our kind of democracy versus their kind of democracy (so to call it by courtesy). Mr. Kruschev agreed to all this magnificently. We are confronted with a gordian knot in the problem of whether it is as important for them to achieve great things as for us to achieve them. Liberals would rather fuss with that gordian knot than cut it. They're wasting time in an emergency. That's the way Mr. Kruschev sees it as a nationalist. He and I didn't talk about peace or love or coexistence. We talked about surpassing excellence and the survival of the fittest. His amusing and slight contempt was for people who enjoy wanting something they haven't the force to get. Sidney Snow used to have me out your way to talk about these things to his young Unitarian ministers. One of my subjects that I remember was "The Greed to Win" — nobly, of course. You can't do nothing with nobody that doesn't want to win, Nobly, of course. Sidney's friendship is one of my greatest memories.

Sincerely yours,   Robert Frost

464 · To Norman Thomas

ON 21 September 1962, Norman Thomas wrote to RF in part: "There are a lot of us who would be enormously grateful to you if you could now give your own interpretation of Khrushchev's re-

mark about Americans, 'too liberal to fight.' It does make considerable difference, doesn't it? One interpretation may quite directly
contribute to war sentiment. The other might somewhat check it.
I honestly think you will add something more to the enormous service you have rendered to our country."

RF dictated an answer, but did not mail it; he kept it for
revisions which he never completed. The following transcript is
made from the first draft as dictated to and written down in long-
hand by Mrs. Morrison.

Dear Norman Thomas: [c. 28 September 1962]   [Ripton]
Everyone seems to want to start joking with me about the
word "liberal" but as you say it's no joking matter. It was almost
that with Khrushchev. Shall I try to tell you the affable way
he used it with me in Gagra. He was just being good-natured
and literary when he expressed concern for American liberality. He was quoting either Gorky to Tolstoi or Tolstoi to Gorky,
I forget which, when he said there was such a thing possibly
as a nation's getting like the bald-headed row at a leg show so
it enjoyed wanting to do what it could no longer do. I was interested to find the great old powerhouse so bookish. People
have asked me if he was literary like Kennedy and you and me.
I think I broke down his figure by answering we were too
young a nation for that worry.

There are all sorts of liberals and I have amused himself
with defining them. Khrushchev's was a good crack. My own
latest is that they are people who have had the liberal education that I fled and have come back to assert my difference
within their own stronghold, the colleges. If Matthew Arnold
is their gospel, I come pretty near being a liberal myself. I
have teasingly described them as people who can't take their
own side in a quarrel and would rather fuss with a Gordian
knot than cut it and as "Dover Beach-combers" and as Matthew
Arnold's wisest "who take dejectedly their seat upon the intellectual throne." They are never arbitrary enough "to bid their
will avouch it" like a real leader. But all that aside after it has
entertained you enough. I yield to no one in my admiration for
the kind of liberal you have been, you and Henry Wallace. One
of the great moments of my life was when we three foregath-
ered at Larry Spivak's party and I stood between you and Henry
for a chance photographer to take our picture. My son-in-
law [Joseph Ballantine] had been rebuking Henry for going to
China when Hull had warned him not to go. Henry had al-

ready admitted he shouldn't have gone. My son-in-law had dispersed in the crowd and I had put my hand on Henry's shoulder in affectionate sympathy. Then you came along and there we three stood in a row against the world. I treasure the picture — and if you want these sentiments signed I'll come and have a talk with you whenever you're inclined. I can't see how Khrushchev's talk got turned into what you quote that we weren't men enough to fight. I came nearer than he to threatening: with my native geniality I assured him that we were no more afraid of him than he was of us. We seemed in perfect agreement that we shouldn't come to blows till we were sure there was a big issue remaining between us, of his kind of democracy versus our kind of democracy, approximating each other as they are, his by easing downward towards socialism from the severity of its original ideals, ours by straining upward towards socialism through various phases of welfare state-ism. I said the stage or arena is set between us for a rivalry of perhaps a hundred years. Let's hope we can take it out in sports, science, art, business, and politics before ever we have to take it out in the bloody politics of war. It was all magnanimity — Aristotle's great word. I should have expected you to approve. Liberal in a good sense of the word. Browning tells of a post-office bulletin notice in Italy, "two liberal thieves were shot." If only a word would stay put in basic English.

[unsigned]

465 · To LESLEY FROST BALLANTINE

WHEN RF suffered a heart attack in the Peter Bent Brigham Hospital on 23 December 1962, his daughter Lesley hurried to his bedside not expecting that he would recover. But after he was out of immediate danger she wrote to him and praised his "lionhearted" courage. In a hopeful frame of mind he dictated this answer.

Dear Lesley: 12 January 1963   [Boston]

You're something of a Lesley de Lion yourself. I am not hard to touch but I'd rather be taken for brave than anything else. A little hard and stern in judgment, perhaps, but always touched by the heroic. You have passed muster. So has Prescott. You have both found a way to make shift. You can't know how much I have counted on you in family matters. It is no time yet to defer a little to others in my future affairs but I have deferred not a little in my thoughts to the strength I find in you and Prescott and Lee and very, very affectionately to K Morrison and [her daughter] Anne Morrison Gentry, who are with me taking this dictation in the hospital, and to Al Edwards in all his powerful friendship. I trust my word can bind you together as my party in friendship as long as my name as a poet lasts.

I am too emotional for my state. Life has been a long trial yet I mean to see more of it. We all liked your poems. It must add to your confidence that you have found a way with the young.   [unsigned]

466 · To G. R. and Alma Elliott

Oh Roy and Alma: [12 January 1963]   [Boston]

How the years have come between us. You were one of the first that gave me any stature, as they call it nowadays, and remember I went to see you at Bowdoin on purpose for your kind of recognition. Things have come out fine for you. I'm sorry you don't go to Florida any more but that's a small matter. We read each other's books and we know what we're thinking about. Metaphor is it and the freshness thereof.

I'm mighty glad you like this poem for Christmas ["The Prophets Really Prophesy as Mystics . . ."]. Why will the quidnuncs always be hoping for a salvation man will never have from anyone but God? I was just saying today how Christ posed Himself the whole problem and died for it. How can we be just in a world that needs mercy and merciful in a world that needs justice. We study and study the four biographies of Him and are left still somewhat puzzled in our daily lives. Marking students in a kind of mockery and laughing it off. It seems as if I never wrote these plunges into the depths to anyone but you. I remember our first walk to Harpswell together.

This is being dictated to Anne Morrison Gentry who writes shorthand and her mother Kathleen Morrison who devises all my future. They are helping me through these hard days in a grand and very powerful hospital. If only I get well, with their help, I'll go deeper into my life with you than I ever have before.   Affectionately,   [unsigned]

APPENDIXES

GENEALOGY

❧❧❧

THE SELECTIVE genealogy here given is designed primarily to clarify certain oblique references in the letters.

Of the six children born to RF and his wife, two died in infancy; four grew to maturity and married, presenting to their parents a total of six grandchildren. RF lived to boast that he had thirteen great-grandchildren and that one of them was named Robert Lee Frost.

So many discrepancies occur in various genealogical tables of the Frost family that these facts must be taken provisionally. Information has been compared and compiled from various sources including four works cited below in chronological order of publication:

Everett S. Stackpole, *Old Kittery and Her Families*. Lewiston, Maine, 1903.

Norman Seaver Frost, *Frost Genealogy in Five Families*. West Newton, Massachusetts, Frost Family Association of America, 1926.

Gorham B. Munson, *Robert Frost: A Study in Sensibility and Good Sense*. New York, Doran, 1927.

John Eldridge Frost, *The Nicholas Frost Family*. Milford, New Hampshire, The Cabinet Press, 1943.

1 NICHOLAS FROST
> born: c. 1595 in Devonshire, England.
> married: January, 1630, to Bertha Cadwalla of Tavistock, Devonshire.
> died: 1663 in Kittery, Maine.
> eldest son: Charles[2]
> Until he sailed with his family for America from Plymouth, Devonshire, in June, 1634, Nicholas Frost lived in Tiverton, Devonshire. He landed at Little Harbor (now Rye), New Hampshire, and lived there for a short while before moving to Sturgeon Creek (now a part of Eliot), Maine. His occupation was farming, but he served for some years as a Select Man in Kittery.

2 CHARLES FROST

born: 1631 in Tiverton, Devonshire.
married: before 1665, to Mary Bolles
died: 4 July 1697, in Wells, Maine.
second son: John[3]

As a young man Charles Frost became a soldier, and served with local forces who tried to protect the frontier from Indian raids. He became well known in New England as an Indian fighter, and attained the rank of major. The Indians, who had ample reasons for hating him as a ruthless killer, finally avenged themselves by murdering him in ambush. Immediately after his burial they dug up his body, carried it to the top of "Great Hill" (now known as "Frost's Hill") in Wells, Maine, and hanged it from a stake. An obituary poem, "Hero of Great Hill," written by Dr. William Hale of Gloucester, Massachusetts, honored Charles Frost as

> "The last of that grand triumvirate,
> Unflinching martyrs of a common fate,
> Waldron and Plaisted and Frost, these three,
> The flower of New England chivalry."

For another poem about Charles Frost in a different vein, by his descendent RF, see end of this appendix.

3 JOHN FROST

born: 1 March 1681.
married: 4 September 1702, to Mary Pepperrell of Kittery, Maine.
died: 25 February 1732, in New Castle, New Hampshire.
eldest son: William[4]

John Frost served for a time in the Royal Navy along the New England coast, commanding at one time the man of war HMS *Edward*. He later became a merchant in New Castle, and served as a member of the Governor's Council. His wife was sister to Sir William Pepperrell.

4 WILLIAM FROST

born: 20 August 1705, in New Castle, New Hampshire.
married: 24 November 1750, to Elizabeth Prescott of Salem, Massachusetts.
died: 1778, in New Castle, New Hampshire.
second son: William[5]

William Frost[4] succeeded his father in a mercantile business at New Castle. His wife was sister to the famous William Prescott (1726-1795), who is fabled as having said at Bunker Hill, "Don't fire until you see the white of their eyes." Several Frosts were named after him.

600

5 WILLIAM FROST

born: 15 November 1754, in New Castle, New Hampshire.
married: 2 December 1777, to Sarah Holt of Danvers, Massachusetts.
died: 28 September 1836, in Andover, Massachusetts.
only son: Samuel Abbott[6]

William Frost[5] served as a lieutenant in the Continental Army during the American Revolutionary War; it was through direct descent from him that RF became a member of the Society of the Cincinnati.

6 SAMUEL ABBOTT FROST

born: 11 June 1795, in Andover, Massachusetts.
married: 18 October 1821, to Mary Bount of Portsmouth, New Hampshire.
died: 11 January 1848, in Brentwood, New Hampshire.
eldest son: William Prescott[7]

Samuel Abbott Frost served in the War of 1812, and later became a farmer.

7 WILLIAM PRESCOTT FROST

born: 11 July 1823, in Eden, Maine.
married: 27 September 1846, to Judith Colcord of Kingston, New Hampshire.
died: 10 July 1901, in Lawrence, Massachusetts.
only son: William Prescott, Jr.[8]

William Prescott Frost, paternal grandfather of RF, tried various occupations and moved about a great deal before settling in Lawrence, Massachusetts, where he became an overseer in the Pacific Mills.

8 WILLIAM PRESCOTT FROST, JR.

born: 27 December 1850, in Kingston, New Hampshire.
married: 18 March 1873, to Isabelle Moodie, of Scotland, in Lewistown, Pennsylvania.
died: 5 May 1885, in San Francisco, California.
children:
  Robert Lee[9]
  Jeanie Florence
    born: 25 June 1876, in Lawrence, Massachusetts.
    died: 7 September 1929, in Augusta, Maine.

William Prescott Frost, Jr., wrote an account of his early life and ancestry as part of the record of his Harvard College Class of 1872, an account which exists in two autograph manuscript forms: Harvard Archives, Class of 1872, Harvard College Library; the Clifton Waller Barrett Library of the Univesity of Virginia Library. Each version of the account includes this passage: "I resided at Kingston, N. H., from Dec., 1850 to Aug. 1852; at Milton, N. H., from Aug. 1852 to Oct. 1853; at Manchester, N. H., from Oct. 1853 to Jan. 1855; at Nashua, N. H., from Jan. 1855 to Nov. 1855; at Lawrence, Mass., from Nov. 1855 to Nov. 1858; at Southbridge, Mass., from Nov. 1858 to Oct. 1860; and at Lawrence, Mass., from Oct. 1860 to June 1872. During my former residence at Lawrence I attended primary, intermediate, and grammar schools, from Mar. 1856 to Nov. 1858. While residing at Southbridge I attended a grammar school from the spring of 1859 to the autumn of 1860. I attended the 'Oliver Grammar School,' at Lawrence, of which George A. Walton was the principal, from the spring of 1861 to May 1864, at which latter date I was graduated. I attended the 'Lawrence High School' from May 1864 to June 1868. . . . I had no intention of entering college. I have been engaged in no occupation or business other than studying, except that I have reported for the Boston 'Saturday Evening Gazette' since 1 July, 1871. I was led first seriously to think of going to college, in May 1868, by my failure to obtain an appointment to West Point, for which I had made considerable effort, and in which I was thwarted by political influence. I entered [Harvard College] in July 1868, at the age of 17 yrs., 6 months, with two and a half conditions. I received a detur in my Sophomore year, and a first 'Bowdoin' prize in my Junior year for an essay on 'The Hohenstaufens.' I am a member of the Phi Beta Kappa society. . . . I have a considerable fondness for the study of history — especially political history, — and take much interest in Political Economy. My plans in life are as yet unshaped, though I shall probably go into either journalism or law. At present I am quite undecided as to which of the two to choose." [Dated, "24 June, 1872."]

9   ROBERT LEE FROST

born: 26 March 1874, in San Francisco, California.

married: 19 December 1895, to Elinor Miriam White of Lawrence, Massachusetts.

died: 29 January 1963, in Boston, Massachusetts.

children:

  Elliott

    born: 25 September 1896, in Lawrence, Massachusetts.

    died: 8 July 1900, in Methuen, Massachusetts.

  Lesley

    born: 28 April 1899, in Lawrence, Massachusetts.

    married: 10 June 1928, to James Dwight Francis.

    divorced: 1932.

    remarried: 23 August 1952, to Joseph W. Ballantine.

    children:

      Elinor Frost

        born: 11 May 1929.

        married: 14 July 1947.

        children:

          Marcia Heath, born 16 March 1948.

          Katherine Gowen, born 18 April 1950.

      Douglas MacNiel, born 19 May 1951.
      Prescott Frost, born 27 February 1958.
   Lesley Lee
      born: 20 June 1931.
      married: 13 June 1961, to Stanislav Zimic.
      daughter:
         Deborah Lee, born 13 April 1962.
Carol
   born: 27 May 1902, in Derry, New Hampshire.
   married: 3 November 1923, to Lillian LaBatt.
   died: 9 October 1940, South Shaftsbury, Vermont.
   only son:
      William Prescott
         born: 15 October 1924
         married: 12 June 1947, to Phyllis M. Gordon.
         children:
            Carol Marie, born 23 June 1949.
            Elinor Gordon, born 23 March 1951.
            Robert Lee, born 25 October 1952.
Irma
   born: 26 June 1903, in Derry, New Hampshire.
   married: 15 October 1926, to John Paine Cone.
   divorced: 1947.
   children:
      John Paine, Jr., born 29 September 1927.
      Harold, born 6 October 1940.
Marjorie
   born: 29 March 1905.
   married: 3 June 1933, to Willard Edward Fraser.
   died: 2 May 1934, in Rochester, Minnesota.
   daughter:
      Marjorie Robin
         born: 16 March 1934.
         married: 12 April 1958, to David Beecher Hudnut.
         children:
            David Beecher, Jr., born 20 February 1959.
            Marjorie Elizabeth, born 13 December 1961.
Elinor Bettina
   born: 20 June 1907, in Derry, New Hampshire.
   died: 22 June 1907.

POEM: "GENEALOGICAL"

❦

RF's interest in his ancestry was first aroused when Miss Sarah Couch, postmistress of West Derry, New Hampshire, showed him genealogical clippings about the Frost families in and around Eliot, Maine. Early in 1908 the poet wrote to Susan Hayes Ward, in letter 29, "I must send you sometime some Whitmanism of mine on my bad ancestor the Indian killer [Charles Frost] who sleeps under a bowlder in Eliot Me." It is probable that a clipping provided by Miss Sarah Couch inspired the "Whitmanism," which RF eventually sent to Miss Ward with letter 30, dated 19 December 1911. The manuscript of that poem was preserved in the files of the New York *Independent,* and is now in the Huntington Library; the following version is from that manuscript.

Genealogical

It was my grandfather's grandfather's grandfather's
Great-great-grandfather or thereabouts I think —
One cannot be too precise in a matter like this.
He was hanged the story goes. Yet not for grief
Have I vowed a pilgrimage to the place where he lies
Under a notable bowlder in Eliot, Maine,
But for pride if for aught at this distance of time.
Yearly a chosen few of his many descendants
At solemn dinner assembled tell over the story
Of how in his greatness of heart he aspired
To wipe out the whole of an Indian tribe to order,
As in those extravagant days they wasted the woods
With fire to clear the land for tillage.
It seems he was rather pointedly *not* instructed
To proceed in the matter with any particular
Regard to the laws of civilized warfare.
He wasted no precious time in casting about
For means he could call his own. He simply seized

604

Upon any unprotected idea that came to hand.
I will not set up the claim for my progenitor
That he was an artist in murder or anything else,
Or that any of his descendants would have been
Without the infusion of warmer blood from somewhere.
Were it imperative to distinguish between statesman and artist
I should say that the first believes that the end justifies the
    means
The second that the means justify the end.
The Major (for such was his title) *virumque cano*
Was one of your thoroughgoing jobbers
Who held that the end and means justify each other.
He knew that the Indians were usually in a state of not having
Eaten for several days and hungry accordingly.
So he invited them to a barbecue (if that isn't an anac[h]ro-
    nism)
And all that he didn't slay he bound and sold
Into slavery where Philip the Chief's son went.
And then well satisfied with the day's work
He doubtless called the place something and claimed the vic-
    tory.
All that detracted from the glory of his achievement
Was the escape of a few of the devoted tribesmen
Either by running away or staying away
An awkward remnant that would have lain, methinks,
Even upon my somewhat sophisticated conscience
Given to the sympathetic fallacy of attributing to savages
The feelings of human beings,
More heavily than those who were slain.
He good sleeper and eater serenely forgot them.
But here again he just missed greatness as a captain.
For these waylaid him one Sunday on his way home
From the proper church completely edified
And slew him in turn with great barbarity
And left him outspread for filial burial.
His sons with dignity dug him a decent grave
And duly laid him to rest.
But the Redskins, not quite sure they had done enough
To satisfy the eternal vengeances,
Returned and had him out of the ground and hanged him up.
And so he was hanged!
The indefatigable sons cut him down and buried him again,

"GENEALOGICAL"

And this time to secure him against further disturbance,
With the help of their neighbors at a sort of burying bee
They rolled a stone upon him that once it was sunk in place
Not strong men enough could come at together to lift it.
And there he lies in glory the ancestor of a good many of us.
And I think he explains my lifelong liking for Indians.

INDEX

INDEX

❧❧❧

IN THIS SELECTIVE INDEX, letter-entry numbers are given within parentheses and are always followed by page numbers, without parentheses. Whenever page numbers are not accompanied by letter-entry numbers, they refer to elements in supplementary matter, such as the Introduction, the Chronology, the Appendix.

The forty-three topical subheads under the main entry, FROST, ROBERT LEE, are grouped below with page numbers. The quotations cited are representative, and are those which the editor considers of special interest.

A

Dulles, John Foster (*con't.*)
  562; letter from RF to, (436)
  562–563

E

Eastern Poultryman, The,
  RF publishes one prose narrative in, lii; (18-hn) 33
Eaton, Walter Prichard,
  letters from RF to, (125) 182–
  183, (135) 191–192
Edwards, Alfred C.,
  President of Holt, Rinehart,
  Winston, Inc., reference to, as
  sole executor and sole trustee of
  estate of RF, (417-hn) 535; letter from RF to, (417) 535
Eisenhower, Dwight D.,
  telegram from President to
  Poetry Society of America, (433-
  hn) 571; telegram from, to RF,
  (433-b) 572–573; telegram from
  RF to, (445) 574; letter from
  RF to, (449) 578; letter to RF
  from, (451-b), 581; signs Congressional bill awarding Gold
  Medal to RF, (460-hn) 588
Elliott, George Roy,
  letters from RF to, (192)
  243–244, (196) 248–249, (201)
  255–257, (204) 259–260, (217)
  274, (251) 312, (258) 328,
  (313) 407, (317) 413–414,
  (326) 424, (333) 434–435,
  (352) 459–460, (352, analyzed),
  xvii–xviii, (394) 506; letters
  from RF to, and to wife Alma,
  (362) 471–472, (466) 596; letter to RF from, (351-b) 458–
  459, (351-b, analyzed), xvii
Emerson, Ralph Waldo,
  RF praises "Monadnoc,"
  "Uriel," and "Give All to Love,"
  by, (176) 228; RF quotes "Out
  of the good of evil born," from
  "Uriel," (217) 274; RF mentions "Uriel," (223) 281; RF on
  the style of, (244) 299; RF appointed Ralph Waldo Emerson
  Fellow in Poetry, 1939, at Harvard, lix, 476; RF awarded
  Emerson-Thoreau Medal, American Academy of Arts and Sciences, 1958, lxiii

England,
  RF's first visit to, account of,
  50–51; letters written by RF
  from, during first visit, (38–101)
  52–152; RF's second visit, 1928,
  (269-hn) 349; RF's third visit,
  1957, 536–537; (439-hn) 566;
  letters concerning third visit,
  (433–440-b) 558–568; RF's
  fourth visit, 1961, 537
Epstein, Jacob,
  RF's brief acquaintance with,
  (78) 121
Erskine, John,
  mentioned, (260) 331

F

Fairchild, David G.,
  oblique hint of friendship between RF and, in Florida, (403)
  519
*Farm–Poultryman Semi–Monthly,
  The,*
  RF's contributions to, (18-
  hn), 34; letters from RF to,
  (18) 33–34, (19) 34–35; RF's
  retrospective references to, (45)
  67, (68) 103
Farrar, John Chipman,
  first Director, Bread Loaf
  Writers' Conference, 1926–1928;
  RF recalls that his "lifelong
  friendship" with, began at Elizabethan Club, Yale, (320) 416;
  RF expresses his enmity toward,
  (285) 365–366
Ferril, Thomas Hornsby,
  RF meets, in Denver, Colorado, (294) 377
*Fire and Ice: The Art and Thought
  of Robert Frost,* by Lawrance
  Thompson, (375) 485–486,
  (391) 502, (392) 503–504
Fisher, Dorothy Canfield,
  letter from RF to, (262) 333–
  335; mentioned, (188) 239,
  (201) 256, (269-hn) 349,
  (329-a) 429
Fisher, Theodore,
  RF's one and only lecture
  agent, (276) 358, (294) 377–
  378
Fletcher, John Gould,
  RF's tirade against, (244) 300
Flint, F. S.,
  RF's indebtedness to, 50; (57-

Frost, Lillian LaBatt (*con't.*)
388, return to Vermont, 1934, (306) 399

goes to Key West with RF and EMF, winter, 1934–1935, (319-a) 416; goes to Texas with RF and EMF, winter 1936–1937, (333) 434; is slowly recovering from major surgery at time of husband's death, 1940, (381-hn) 491

moves to Florida with son, "Prescott," after his medical discharge from Signal Corps, (395) 507, (401) 516, (403-hn) 517

FROST, ROBERT LEE [26 Mar. 1874–29 Jan. 1963]

ACCOUNTS, BIOGRAPHICAL

Chronology, xlvii–lxiv; Genealogy, 602–603; Introduction, vii–xviii; Prefaces: [I] 3–4, [II] 15–17, [III] 31–32, [IV] 50–51, [V] 153–155, [VI] 253–254, [VII] 337–338, [VIII] 475–477, [IX] 511–512, [X] 536–539

AMBITION

"But this inflexible ambition trains us best," (5) 19, ". . . even in my failures I find all the promise I require to justify the astonishing magnitude of my ambition." (6) 20; "If it is seriously I must speak, I undertake a future." (11) 26; "But don't think to laugh with impunity at my boast," (30) 43; "I . . . hate and abhor giving up what I have once really set my heart on." (31) 44; "the work I have set my hand to." (35) 47; ambitiously, RF promotes his own work, 50; "scorn of the scorn that leaves me still unnoticed," (38) 52; "I expect to do something to the present state of literature in America." (58) 88; "My dream would be to get the thing started in London and then do the rest of it from a farm in New England where I could live cheap and get Yankier and Yankier." (68) 103; retrospectively: "I didn't mind looking unambitious," (172) 223

BADNESS

"You're a good poet, Robert, but you're a bad man." (372-hn) 481; "I have been bad and a bad artist," (214-fn) 271; "I belong to the unendurably bad." (195) 247; "I'm going to try to be good if it isn't too late." (214) 271; "I'm a mere selfish artist most of the time." (289) 369; "Sometimes I almost cry I am afraid I am such a bad poet." (294) 378; "I am a pretty bad bet." (313) 417; "It came from my badness about answering letters." (324) 422; "I'm afraid I deceived her a little in pretending for the sake of argument that I didn't think the world as bad a place as she did." (361) 470; "I'd be a bad man as well as a bad author if . . ." (378) 488; "I am a bad bad man." (372) 482

BOOKS OF POETRY

Twilight (1894), titles of poems in, 1; circumstances of private printing, 16; RF to Melcher on, in 1929, (273) 354; RF sells, (339-a-hn) 442, (376) 486, (376-a) 487; RF's comment on quality of poems in, (411) 526-527; in Barrett Collection, (420-hn) 544

A Boy's Will (1913), ms of, accepted, (38-b) 54–55; (39) 55–56; RF signs contract for, (41) 59; RF tells friends, (41) 59, (43) 62, (46) 69–70, publication of, in London, liv; RF sends copies home, (48) 72, (49) 73, (51) 74; RF on reviews of, (52) 75–77, (55) 84, (58) 88, (59) 89

North of Boston (1914), "Some of the manuscript has been passed around," (64) 98; titles considered for: "New England Eclogues," (59) 89, "Farm Servants and Other People," "New Englanders," "New England Hill Folk," (63) 96; first reference to title used, (66) 99; early reviews of, listed, (80-hn) 125; RF's comments on, (81) 127, (82) 128, (83) 129, (86) 132; first

BOTANIZING

RF's interest in, start of, (14) 28;
quest for rare ferns and orchids
Lake Willoughby region, summer
1909, liii; (112) 167; recalls "pursuit of the Cypripedium" or Lady's
Slipper, (47) 71; "Perhaps you
will lead me to some flowers I
havent met before," (118) 175;
reminds Haines that "we met you
first . . . with your canister for
tall flowers," (149) 205; related
passage, (126) 183; also reminds
Haines of "the fern we groped on
the little cliff for by the light of a
match," (149) 205; in Colorado:
"I'm botanizing all over in an
almost entirely different flora."
(294) 377; oblique hint of actual
friendship with botanist David G.
Fairchild, Florida, (403) 519

COWARDICE

"I am too cowardly to offend anybody intentionally," (285) 366;
"Humor is the most engaging cowardice." (244) 300; "I always notice I am most cowardly when
writing or just after writing. I
mind the cellar at night worst
then." (312) 406; see also Fears

DEATH

"I don't think I have any right to
like it [World War I] when I am
not called on to die in it." (97)
147; "That is my last, my ultimate
vileness, that I cannot make up
my mind to go now where I must
go sooner or later." (214-fn) 271;
poem on death, (214) 270–271,
(387) 497–498; "There's some
hope that I may die again." (68)
103; "I am willing to be under
obligation to it [science] for postponing death." (425) 549; "Your
fortitude in the face of approaching death makes it hard not to

ILLNESSES

INJUSTICE

INSANITY

FROST, ROBERT LEE (*con't.*)
son Carol, (381) 491–492; on putting his daughter Irma "in a hospital for the insane," (411) 527; "I went crazy with it one night alone and broke chairs ad lib till a friend happened in to save me." (377) 487; "And I suppose I am a brute in that my nature refuses to carry sympathy to the point of going crazy just because someone else goes crazy . . ." (195) 248

KNOWLEDGE

". . . neither knowledge nor thought is an end and neither is nearer an end than the other. The end they both serve, perhaps equally, is deeds . . ." (213) 270
RF on the distinction between knowledge and thought at Amherst, 1923–1924, (246) 302
". . . there is nothing anybody knows, however absolutely, that isn't more or less vitiated as a fact by what he doesn't know." (250) 312
"I'm less and less for systems and system-building, (264) 343
RF, after suicide of Carol: "I talk less and less however as if I knew what I was talking about." (381) 491

LETTER-WRITING

"A letter once in a while can do no harm to him that sends or him that receives, though damn letters as a rule." (148) 204
"I'd write you a letter but that I've soured on letter writing for good and all." (160) 214
"Anything to save letter writing." (219) 277
"I am off letter writing except to the most favored people," (247) 304
"I have got so I answer almost no letters." (254) 323
"For gods' sake dont give up writing to me simply because I dont write to you or anybody else." (277) 359
"Look out I don't spoof you. About five years ago I resolved to spoil my correspondence with you

by throwing it into confusion the way God threw the speech of the builders of the tower of Babel. . . . Part of my reason is my dislike of all the printed correspondence I ever saw." (334) 435
"I find such pleasure in writing friends that I wonder why I dont write oftener." (421) 546

LETTERS ABOUT

The selection includes a total of 55 letters about RF from 13 correspondents; *see* Table of Letters, xxi-xxxviii

LETTERS FROM

The selection includes a total of 466 letters from RF to 123 correspondents; *see* Table of Letters, xxi-xxxviii

LETTERS TO

The selection includes a total of 40 letters to RF from 34 correspondents; *see* Table of Letters, xxi-xxxviii

MASKS AND MASKING

RF's dramatic maskings, vii, xiv
"It is only a matter of time now when I shall throw off the mask and declare for literateur mean it poverty or riches." (8) 23
"I have about decided to throw off the light mask I wear in public when Amy is the theme of conversation." (197) 249
"I have written to keep the curious out of the secret places of my mind both in my verse and in my letters to such as you." (299) 385
"I probably couldnt baffle them at my crypticest. Never mind I can baffle some people. (267) 346
"I trust my meaning is not too hidden in any of these places." (133) 189
"I am not undesigning." (55) 84

MISCHIEVOUSNESS

"It is my intention we are speaking of—my innate mischievousness." (266) 344
"Ever since infancy I have had the habit of leaving my blocks carts chairs and such like ordi-

POETIC PRACTICE

". . . it voices the complaint of everyone who writes anything, viz., that nothing he writes quite represents his thought or his feeling." (42) 61

"What counts is the amount of the original intention that isn't turned back in execution." (42) 61

"A poem . . . begins as a lump in the throat, a sense of wrong, a homesickness, a lovesickness. . . . It finds the thought and the thought finds the words." (143) 199

"My object is true form—is was and always will be—form true to any chance bit of true life." (278) 361

"I fight to be allowed to sit crosslegged on the old flint pile and flake a lump into an artifact." (278) 361

"My whole anxiety is for myself as a performer." (289) 369

"Poetry is the renewal of words forever and ever." (353) 462

POETIC THEMES

RF repeatedly stresses the artistic gains derived from being able to impose forms on the raw materials provided by any chaos, xii

"When in doubt there is always form for us to go on with. Anyone who has achieved the least form to be sure of it, is lost to the larger excruciations. I think it must stroke faith the right way." (322) 418

"The artist, the poet, might be expected to be the most aware of such assurance [derived from form-giving], but it is really everybody's sanity to feel it and live by it. (322) 418

"I thank the Lord for crudity which is rawness, which is raw material, which is the part of life not yet worked up into form," (356) 465

"You wish the world better than it is, more poetical. You are that kind of poet. I would rate as the other kind. I wouldn't give a cent to see the world . . . made better." (289) 369

"I'm in favor of a skin and fences and tariff walls." (300) 387

POETIC THEORY

"I am possibly the only person going who works on any but a worn out theory (principle I had better say) of versification." (53) 79

". . . the few rules I know in this art are my own afterthoughts . . ." (5) 19

RF's principle for choosing the subject matter: "The subject should be common in experience and uncommon in books . . . It should have happened to everyone but it should have occurred to no one before as material." (328) 426

RF urges that "what makes a piece of writing good" is "making the sentences talk to each other as two or more speakers do in drama." (328) 427

See also Sentence Sound, Sound of Sense

PROFANITY

(Some examples of RF's favorite expletives, used when under stress.) "I haven't read Braithwaite's g. d. book," (143) 198; "I won't do one single thing in verse or out of it or with it till I God damn please for the rest of my natural life." (246) 403; "For gods' sake dont give up writing to me simply because I dont write to you or anybody else." (277) 359; "I'll go without a country god dam it." (339) 441; "Jesus Christ! let's be Christians." (352) 460

PROSE

(RF's prose pieces—essays, plays, prefaces—mentioned in the letters and notes.)

PUNISHMENTS

"All this sickness and scatteration of the family is our fault and not our misfortune or I wouldn't admit it. It's a result and a judgement on us." (256) 325

"I have kept poetry free thus far, and I have been punished for the mere thought of making it a duty or a business." (322) 433

"I've been punished often enough in the past for pretending not to see what was wrong with the poor." (223) 281

See also Fear, Death, Religious Belief

PURPOSE, DIVINE

"Some purpose I doubt not, if we could but have made it out." (33) 46

". . . the evident design is a situation here in which it will always be about equally hard to save your soul. . . . or if you dislike hearing your soul mentioned in open meeting, say your decency, your integrity." (322) 418

"The conviction closes in on me that I was cast for gloom as the sparks fly upward." (170) 221

". . . a Job in our time." xi

RELIGIOUS BELIEF

Formative influence of RF's intensely devout mother's, xi; (V) 13–14

Fluctuations in RF's unorthodox, heretical, and puzzling, xi-xiii, (193-hn) 244

"If there were no God—but there is one . . ." (143) 200

RF retrospectively summarizes his various church affiliations, actually his mother's: "Presbyterian, Unitarian, Swedenborgian, Nothing." (174) 226

"I discovered that do or say my dambdest I can't be other than orthodox in politics love and religion: I can't escape salvation." (170) 221

"I shouldn't wonder if my last end would be religious," (214) 271

"I'll bet I could tell of spiritual realizations that for the moment at least would overawe the contentious." (255) 325

RF generalizes obliquely on the role of the serpent in the Eden story: "Something hates us and likes to spoil our fair beginnings." (240) 296; "There is a devil in me that defeats my deliberate intentions." (301) 389

". . . all you have to do to be saved is to sneak off to one side and see whether you are any good at anything." (300) 387

"Whatever progress may be taken to mean, it can't mean making the world any easier a place in which to save your soul . . ." (322) 418

"Marjorie's tenacity and Elinor's devotion and the mercy of God are our hopes." (314) 408; "We thought to move heaven and earth—heaven with prayers and earth with money. We moved nothing." (315) 409

"When in doubt there is always form for us to go on with. . . . I think it must stroke faith the right way." (322) 418

"If there is a universal unfitness and unconformity as of a buttoning so started that every button on the vest is in the wrong button hole and the one empty button hole at the top and the one naked button at the bottom so far apart they have no hope of getting together, I don't care to decide

FROST, ROBERT LEE (*con't.*)
whether God did this for the fun
of it or for the devil of it. (353)
462

RF's recurrent gloss on the
meaning of the parable of the
talents: ". . . answerability of the
ruler to the highest in himself and
to God." (393) 505

Immediately following the death
of EMF, RF hints of his belief in
an after-life, (361) 471

"I cant hope to live later than
1975 at best. I mean in this world."
(339) 441

"I was thrust out into the desolateness of wondering about my
past whether it had not been too
cruel to those I had dragged with
me and almost to cry out to heaven
for a word of reassurance that was
not given me in time." (374)
484

In his *Sermon* (1946) RF echoes
and extends the prayer in Psalm
19, verse 14: "Let the words of my
mouth and the meditations of my
heart be acceptable before Thee, O
Lord . . ." (430-hn) 555

"My fear of God has settled
down into a deep inward fear that
my best offering may not prove
acceptable in his sight." (410) 525

"My latest [theory about prayer]
is that it might be an expression
of the hope I have that my offering of verse on the altar may be
acceptable in His sight . . ." (413)
530

RF, in "A Masque of Mercy," re-
states thus: "We have to stay
afraid deep in our souls [that] our
sacrifice . . . may not be found
acceptable in Heaven's sight."
(430-hn) 555

"Do you want to tell me where
in the Bible if at all the idea occurs as a prayer that our sacrifice
whether of ourselves or our property may be acceptable in His
sight?" (430) 555

RF's final utterance on the subject: "Why will the quidnuncs
always be hoping for a salvation
man will never have from anyone
but God?" (466) 596

See also Death, Fear, Punishment

RESENTMENTS

"These Gardiners are the kind that
hunt lions and they picked me up
cheap as a sort of bargain," (60)
90

"I ought not to give way to
thoughts of revenge in the first
place." (64) 97

"Christ forgive me the sin of
vengefulness: from this hour forth
I will have no more of it." (67)
100–101

"I'm really more modest than I
look sometimes when resenting
imaginary affronts to my dignity."
(74) 114

"His is the kind of egotism another man's egotism can't put up
with." (79) 123

RF relishes the First World War
and hopes all the pacifist leaders
may be killed by it, (88) 134

". . . sometimes I harden my
heart against nearly everything."
(143) 200

RF's resentments against Untermeyer's liberalism, xv–xvi, (178)
229–230; against Sandburg, (220)
277; against his Ann Arbor land-
lady, (223) 281; against Burton
Rascoe, (234) 289–292; against
J. W. Beach, for being "so romantic
at my expense," (256) 326; resentfully warns Untermeyer not
to "play lascivious tricks" on RF
unless braced for consequences,
(256) 326

"I get to railing and I can rail
myself into damning my best
friends to Hell." (153) 207

"Well well well any resentment
I have against anybody I can leave
to you [DeVoto] to take out on Edmund Wilson." (355) 464

RUNNING AWAY

"Cut and run away from every
care: that is the rule." (158) 213

"I would work at almost anything rather well for a while, but
every once in so often I had to run
off . . . (172) 223

"I ran away from two colleges

L

LaBatt, Lillian, *see* Frost, Lillian

Landor, Walter Savage,
RF quotes from "Finis" by, (223) 281; RF mentions, (260) 331

Laney, Emma May,
letter from EMF to, (323-a) 421–422; letter from RF to, (324) 422–423

Lankes, J. J.,
RF on woodcut "decorations" of, for *New Hampshire*, (239) 295; mentioned, as doing a "sombre" woodcut of RF's home, (262) 333, 334; RF mentions an exhibition of, (271) 352; RF thanks Mencken for kindness to, (286) 367

Lanier, Sidney,
"I have never read Lanier's poetry," (6) 21; RF thanks Miss Ward for poems of, (7) 22

Lathem, Edward Connery,
letter from RF to, (422) 546–547; author of *Robert Frost: His "American Send-off"—1915*, (38-b) 54; co-editor of *Robert Frost: Farm-Poultryman*, (18-hn) 33

Lawrence, D. H.,
RF praises a poem of, (122) 179

Lawrence, Massachusetts,
boyhood home of RF's father, 3, birthplace of RF's sister Jeanie, in 1876, xlix, 4; burial place of RF's father, xlix, 4, and mother, lii, 16, and sister, lvii, (253-c-hn) 318, and of his first child, Elliott, li; RF attends high school in, moves near to, and then lives in, 15–17; marriage of RF and EMF in, 16; RF visits in, after return from England, 154; 1925, RF gives a reading at, (253-b) 318; 1962, RF attends dedication ceremonies of a school named after him, (459-hn) 587

Leach, Henry Goddard,
letter from RF to, (329) 427–428

Lectures on School-Keeping, by Samuel Read Hall, (344-hn) 449

Lewis, Edward Morgan,
President, University of New Hampshire, oblique hint of friendship between RF and, (300-a) 389

Letters of Robert Frost to Louis Untermeyer, vii, xix; (106-hn) 160, (214-fn) 271, (373-hn) 482, (395-a-fn) 508, (414) 532

Longfellow, Henry Wadsworth,
RF's poem entitled "The Later Minstrel" used at Pinkerton commemoration, liii; RF participates in a Bowdoin commemoration, lvi

Lynch, John,
Irish farmer in Bethlehem, New Hampshire, with whom RF and family stayed, mention of, lii; (27) 40, (28) 41; letter from EMF to wife of, (38-a) 52–54; Frosts go to live with, in 1915, 153; (102-hn) 155, (111) 166

Lyttle, Rev. Charles Harold,
letter from, to RF, (462-a) 591–593; letter from RF to, (463) 593

M

MacDowell Colony,
mentioned, (168) 219; RF awarded Edward MacDowell Medal, lxiv, 538

MacKaye, Percy,
instrumental in securing Michigan appointment for RF, (212-a-hn) 267–268; letter from RF to, (215) 271–272

MacLeish, Archibald,
account of RF's association with, on behalf of Ezra Pound, (436-a-hn) 563, (440-b-hn) 568, (447-hn) 575–577; letters from, to Kathleen Morrison, (440-b) 568; to RF, (441-a) 569–570; to Ezra Pound, (441-b) 570–571; letter from RF to, (441) 569

MacVeagh, Lincoln,
letters from RF to, (227) 285, (230) 287, (231) 287–288, (235) 292, (238) 294–295, (239) 295, (240) 295–296, (245) 301, (275) 357–358, (280) 362, (307) 401–402; letter from EMF to wife of, (263-c) 342

N

O

P

S